A WILD KIND

The

Edited by

Foreword by

WILLIAM B. EERDMANS PUBLISHING COMPANY
CHICAGO HISTORICAL SOCIETY

A WILD KIND OF BOLDNESS

The Chicago History Reader

OF BOLDNESS

Chicago History Reader

Rosemary K. Adams

Studs Terkel

GRAND RAPIDS, MICHIGAN / CAMBRIDGE, U.K.

CHICAGO

Published jointly 1998 by
Wm. B. Eerdmans Publishing Co.
255 Jefferson Ave. S.E., Grand Rapids, Michigan 49503 /
P.O. Box 163, Cambridge CB3 9PU U.K.
and by
Chicago Historical Society
1601 N. Clark Street
Chicago, Illinois 60614

Printed in the United States of America

02 01 00 99 98 7 6 5 4 3 2 1

Library of Congress Cataloging-in-Publication Data

A wild kind of boldness : Chicago history reader /
edited by Rosemary K. Adams : foreword by Studs Terkel.
p. cm.
Includes index.
ISBN 0-8028-3019-6 (cloth : alk. paper)
1. Chicago (Ill.) — History. I. Adams, Rosemary K.
F548.3.W73 1998
977.3'11 — dc21 98-6687
CIP

Contents

PART II. INDUSTRIALIZATION AND IMMIGRATION

PART III. THE PROGRESSIVE ERA

CONTENTS

Foreword

This is Chicago! An audacious city that set herself up in a swamp: but the swamp long ago was obliterated and only the audacity remains.

Robert Shackleton,
The Book of Chicago (1920)

It was a wild kind of boldness, of a hunger for new beginnings, that sprang a way station, a town out of mud, out of fire, out of strife into the archetypal American city. Broad-shouldered, Sandburg called it, so long, long ago. It has tasted triumphs, taken beatings, and is still around and about, like a punch-drunk fighter who will not fall down and bawls: Here I am.

Louis Sullivan, who envisioned the skyscraper, a tallness, belonged here. He, who, like Walt Whitman, envisioned democratic vistas, set his bucket down in Chicago and said: Here I am.

Jane Addams, who envisioned a community of rainbow colors and many cultures, chose Chicago and said: Here I am.

Nelson Algren said it his way: "Once you become part of this particular patch, you'll never love another. Like loving a woman with a broken nose, you may well find lovelier lovelies. But never a lovely so real." He set his itching feet down in Chicago and announced: Here I am.

At a time when so much of our past has been erased or diminished by thirty-second sound bites, a one-volume portrait of our city, *A Wild Kind of Boldness,* provides a vivid retelling of Chicago's past. An anthology of articles that have appeared through the decades in *Chicago History,* CHS's award-winning magazine, the book consists of a flowing narrative as engaging to the general reader as it is scholarly to the student. It ranges from the city's early days as an outpost, to the epochs as an industrial capital, through the days of protest from the 1880s to the 1960s. Here are the thoughts, the dreams, the trials, and the hopes and the contributions of those immigrants of all colors, of the men and women of little renown, as well as of the celebrated and powerful. This is Chicago that says: Here I am.

Studs Terkel

Preface

The Chicago Historical Society (CHS) does not lack for institutional ego. With a collection numbering close to 20 million items, a wonderful exhibition and storage facility, and a peerless staff, this institution has much reason to be proud of its past and confident of its future. Yet no aspect of what CHS does inspires more praise than its magazine, *Chicago History.* Members, visitors, scholars, and Chicagoans of all stripes marvel at the beauty and quality of *Chicago History,* which sits comfortably between being identified as a scholarly journal of record and magazine of popular history.

This volume, which includes a selection of some of the best articles from the magazine in the last two decades, is ample evidence of why *Chicago History* is held in such high esteem by professional and amateur historians alike. All the magazine's virtues are here in abundance: sprightly prose, careful editing, beautiful graphics, and, most important, authoritative discussions and interpretations of the history of our great city. Readers will find this a rewarding volume, whether they read it from cover to cover or merely dip into subjects of particular interest. The book is one that any aficionado of Chicago's history will want to keep close by, right next to his or her membership card in the Chicago Historical Society.

No book of this quality comes to the press without careful stewardship. In this case, Rosemary Adams, director of publications at the Chicago Historical Society and editor of *Chicago History,* provides that stewardship. In addition to Rosemary, the other editors of *Chicago History* in the last quarter century, Russell Lewis, Timothy Jacobsen, the late Fannia Weingartner, and Isabel Grossner, supplied the editorial skill and high standards upon which this volume rests. Speaking for myself and for the Board of Trustees of the Chicago Historical Society, I express my gratitude to them and to each of the authors whose work appears here.

Douglas Greenberg
President and Director
Chicago Historical Society
February 1998

Introduction

Chicago History magazine began publication in 1945, under the editorship of the Chicago Historical Society's (CHS) then-director Paul Angle. Over the intervening fifty-three years, it has evolved from a pamphlet dedicated to the CHS's collection and activities to one of the nation's most respected history journals. Today, the editorial philosophy is simple: make the most recent historical scholarship accessible and available to a broad audience. The backgrounds and interests of the contributing authors have changed dramatically over the last two decades to include professional academics and independent scholars from the fields of history, American studies, political science, women's studies, ethnic studies, and urban planning, among others. Their work illuminates the people and events of Chicago's past and gives them meaning in the present.

A Wild Kind of Boldness: The Chicago History Reader comprises thirty-five articles that appeared in *Chicago History* magazine between 1974 and 1996; together, these articles provide a one-volume history of the city. The book is divided into five parts, each corresponding to a major period in the city's metamorphosis from a frontier outpost to a great metropolis: "The Rise of a Commercial City," "Industrialization and Immigration," "The Progressive Era," "The Chicago Cultural Renaissance," and "Chicago in Modern Times." These sections strike a balance between the process of city building and the making of city people; each section highlights the contributions of all Chicagoans to the social, political, economic, and cultural life of the city and the nation.

As with all projects at the Chicago Historical Society, the entire staff contributed to this book's publication. In particular, I'd like to thank Douglas Greenberg, president and director of the Chicago Historical Society, for his continued enthusiastic support for *Chicago History* magazine and for this anthology. Russell Lewis, CHS's deputy director for research and collections and former editor of *Chicago History* magazine, first shaped this project and provided intellectual support through its publication. Phyllis Rabineau, deputy director for interpretation and education, provided ongoing encouragement and good counsel. Lesley Martin coordinated the manuscript reproduction and the photo research with her usual thoroughness, patience, and good humor. Cynthia Mathews diligently tracked down photographs. Photographers John Alderson and Jay Crawford brought digital expertise to the publication and meticulously scanned photographs. Publications interns Skye Perkins and Kelly Gospadarek retyped and proofread manuscripts.

Over the years, many editors, designers, researchers, and photographers — more than I can name here — brought the highest professional standards to the magazine, and I am very proud to keep that tradition alive. Finally, I am indebted to the many authors whose work has appeared in *Chicago History* for their curiosity, scholarship, and enthusiasm for sharing their work with a broad audience.

Rosemary K. Adams
Director of Publications
and Editor, *Chicago History*
Chicago Historical Society
February 1998

PART I

THE RISE OF A COMMERCIAL CITY

The Launching of Chicago: The Situation and the Site

Harold M. Mayer

In due time we reached the Des Plaines River where, for the first time, I caught a view of Lake Michigan. Away in the distance I espied a little dot on the horizon, which proved to be the flag that floated over Fort Dearborn.

James M. Bucklin, Chief Engineer, Illinois and Michigan Canal, on Chicago in 1830

The filing, by James Thompson, on August 4, 1830, of a plat for a 267-acre portion of Section 9 of Township 39 North, Range 14 East of the third principal meridian, may be considered as marking the beginning of Chicago. The platted area was small, amounting to considerably less than a half square mile, but it was — and is — one of the most significant and strategic areas on the North American continent. The act of filing that plat established the foundation for legal titles to the nucleus of Chicago.

The site was not promising as the locus of an urban settlement: it centered upon the junction of the north and south branches of the Chicago River, the waters of which flowed a mile eastward toward Lake Michigan. Thus the platted area consisted of three parts, separated by the waterways. The low-lying land, barely above the river and lake level, was subject to flooding each spring. At the time that the area was platted, it was part of a treeless plain, unbroken landward to the horizon without interruption to the monotonous uniformity of the landscape. Eastward the river flowed slowly turning south to avoid a sandbar built up and maintained by the southward-flowing currents of the lake. A dozen log cabins were visible in the river fork vicinity, while to the east was the palisaded Fort Dearborn with a small military contingent. The residents of the area, in addition to the military, numbered scarcely forty or fifty, and the small cluster of cabins southeast of the fork were connected to the fort by a primitive road. The cabins north and west of the fork were accessible only by primitive ferry.

To understand the significance of the location, it is necessary to look both backward and forward in time. In contrast to the unpromising character of the particular site, the situation of the land for which Thompson filed the plat was and is little short of ideal for the development of a metropolis of continental and world significance. Geographers of an earlier generation would have predicted that a great city was destined to develop near the mouth of the Chicago River, at the southwesternmost penetration of the Great Lakes into the heart of the continent. Modern geographers hold a somewhat different point of view, believing that nature offers opportunities and imposes constraints, but that people, individually and collectively as societies, determine the extent to which opportunities will be utilized and constraints overcome, within very elastic limits. Choices are made among many alternatives, and are subject to the changing social, economic, political, and technological conditions of the society. In the 150 years since the platting of Chicago's nucleus, the metropolis has developed as the result of many choices made by the generations that followed. It turned out that the choice of location in 1830 was, indeed, a good one, in spite of the immediate disadvantages of the site.

Nature had set the stage. The succession of continental glaciers which covered much of northern North America, including the site of Chicago, scoured out a series of basins which became the Great Lakes. About twelve thousand years ago, during the most recent — or Wisconsin — glaciation, a basin somewhat larger than the present Lake Michigan was filled with meltwaters as the northeastward recession of the great glacier took place. The preglacial drainage toward the northeast, through the St. Lawrence valley, was consequently blocked. As the glacial front slowly receded, with some interruptions lasting hundreds of years, the ponded waters eventually sought an alternative outlet. These waters formed a lake, called Lake Chicago, between the glacier's front and the moraine — the ridge of deposited material brought down by the glacier — which was parallel to and some miles to the west, southwest, and south of the present lake shore.

The generally level and poorly drained plain which was the bottom of glacial Lake Chicago is now occupied by the city and some of its suburbs. The low-lying land of that plain is drained by the Chicago and Calumet rivers and their branches, the outer limit of which is in the form of a low, almost imperceptible divide that separates the Great Lakes drainage basin from that of the Mississippi River system. Nowhere in North America is this subcontinental divide closer to any of the Great Lakes shores than in the vicinity of Chicago and northward toward Milwaukee. Thus, the two great waterways of North America — the Great Lakes–St. Lawrence toward the northeast and the Mississippi system to the southwest — almost meet in the vicinity of Chicago. These two routes formed the principal axis of settlement of the trans-Appalachian west in the years preceding and following the American Revolution.

The early explorers found several places where the waterways on the two sides of the low subcontinental divide were sufficiently close to make a short portage possible. In 1673, Pere Marquette and Louis Jolliet, searching for the Mississippi, journeyed from a mission station at De Pere on Wisconsin's Fox River, up that river and across the portage to the Wisconsin River, thence down the Wisconsin and Mississippi to what is now Arkansas. The crossing of the subcontinental divide was where the city of Portage, Wisconsin, now stands. On their return, Marquette and Jolliet voyaged up the Illinois and Des Plaines rivers, portaged to the South Branch of the Chicago River near the present southwest boundary of the City of Chicago, thence down the South Branch and main stem of the Chicago River to Lake Michigan. Thus, they

The Chicago Portage route linking the Great Lakes and the Mississippi River is clearly marked on this French edition of John Mitchell's "Map of the British and French Dominions in North America." First published in London in 1755, this edition appeared in 1777.
(CHS, ICHi-14168)

were probably the first persons of European origin to visit the site of Chicago. A year later Marquette returned south; illness and the onset of winter forced him to make camp from December 1674 to March 1675 near the Chicago Portage, approximately where Damen Avenue now crosses the South Branch of the Chicago River.

There are two other routes within the Chicago region which Marquette and Jolliet could have used to cross the drainage divide. One is the Calumet Sag, between the Calumet River and the Des Plaines; the other is in nearby northwestern Indiana, between the Calumet and the Kankakee rivers (the Kankakee joins the Des Plaines southwest of Chicago to form the Illinois River).

The strategic location of Chicago at the place where the two great inland waterways of the continent are separated only by a low portage, later breached by a canal, has been a major factor in its development as the most important transportation node and first-ranking city of inland North America. Before the industrial revolution of the mid-nineteenth century, the waterways furnished the easiest transportation route: overland travel was slow, dangerous, and expensive. The early railroads were essentially feeders to the waterways. Once established, the settlements which were oriented to the waterway routes, and especially the nodes and transfer points on these routes, could easily compete with later settlements not so favored.

The colonies along the Atlantic and Gulf coasts were more easily in contact with their respective mother countries across the Atlantic Ocean than they were with each other. The Atlantic colonies of Britain, and later the original states, developed coastal shipping, in part stimulated by the existence of protected sounds, bays, and lagoons. The French settlements were strung out along the St. Lawrence–Great Lakes–Mississippi waterway, thus hemming in the westward advance of the British beyond the Appalachians. The present landscape of the continental interior, characterized by long, narrow fields, is the land subdivision pattern characteristic of the French occupance in regions as far apart as the lower St. Lawrence, the lower Wabash valley of southern Indiana and Illinois, and the lower Mississippi delta of Louisiana.

Although the treaty ending the American Revolution was signed in 1783, it was not until 1796 that the British abandoned the forts controlling Lake Michigan at the Straits of Mackinac, thus opening up large-scale fur trading in the territory west of the lake. And fur trading was the original lure that brought the first settlers — French and French Canadian — to the area around Chicago which had for many centuries been occupied by American Indians.

The year 1803 was a momentous one for Chicago in several respects. The Louisiana Purchase transferred to the United States the vast territory west of the Mississippi. Lewis and Clark were sent to explore the newly acquired territory, which doubled the nation's area. And Fort Dearborn was established at the mouth of the Chicago River, marking the point of access between the Great Lakes and the region to the west and southwest.

While the prospect of permanent settlement was anathema to the French and French-Canadian fur traders, it was not long after the Great Lakes and Mississippi regions passed into the possession of the United States that it became evident that more profits were to be gained from land speculation than furs. But the Indians still had possession of the land around Chicago at the time, and the outlook for land speculation and subsequent permanent settlement would remain clouded until they could be satisfactorily accommodated.

Meanwhile, the resumption of hostilities between Great Britain and the United States in 1812 led to the evacuation of Fort Dearborn by the American garrison and the subsequent massacre of the early Chicagoans by British-inspired Indians. In 1816 a second Fort Dearborn was established and a trickle of settlers followed. However, until 1830, the residents of Chicago, few in number and living under primitive pioneer conditions, were squatters. Legal ownership, consequent upon sale of the land which was in the public domain, had to await survey and platting.

Two circumstances, among others, were relevant to the platting of Chicago's nucleus in 1830: the situation, which gave rise to the prospect of a canal across the drainage divide linking the two great inland waterway routes in the vicinity; and the federal land survey system, which controlled the nature of the original and subsequent plats as settlement of Chicago and its hinterland proceeded.

The canal across the portage from the South Branch of the Chicago River to the head of navigation on the Illinois was not a new idea: Marquette had suggested the possibility in his journal on the journey in 1674-75. The importance of the route was underscored by the Treaty of Greenville in 1795, by which the Indians ceded to the United States "one piece of land six miles square at the mouth of the Chicago river emptying into the southwest end of Lake Michigan, where a fort formerly stood."

The portage route, as well as the North

Branch of the Chicago River and its tributaries, furnished access to the hinterland where the furs could be obtained. In 1805 a government fur trading post — competing with private fur traders — was established near the mouth of the river. The private traders, however, competed effectively with the government trading system because they offered credit, and because they followed the Indians to the hunting grounds. Moreover, to promote access to the hunting areas, they offered the Indians liquor, which the government agents were not permitted to do. Decline in the government trading operation finally forced its termination in 1822. The leading private trader was John Jacob Astor's American Fur Company, a giant organization in its day.

The advantages of a canal leading into the hinterland of Lake Michigan appeared so great that when Illinois was admitted as a state in 1818, the boundary with Wisconsin was shifted northward from the latitude of the southern end of Lake Michigan to include the site of Chicago as well as the ten present counties of northern Illinois. Thus, Illinois was given not only a Lake Michigan shoreline, but also the entire prospective canal route.

The new state was to finance the canal by sale of alternate square-mile sections of land five miles on each side of the proposed route. This land was granted to the state by the federal government on March 2, 1827. A commission was appointed and a survey of the prospective canal route was made by its chief engineer, James M. Bucklin. Town lots were to be surveyed at the two terminals of the canal in Chicago and in Ottawa, where the canal was to join the Illinois River. It was this survey of Chicago, conducted by James Thompson, which constituted the original plat — the nucleus — of the future city of Chicago.

Another canal furnished much of the impetus for the advocates of the Illinois and Michigan Canal project. That was the Erie Canal — commenced by New York State in 1817 and completed in 1825 — between the Hudson River and Lake Erie, connecting the Atlantic coastal settlements with the Great Lakes. The Hudson-Mohawk lowland furnished a natural route across the Appalachian barrier, between the Catskill Mountains on the south and the Adirondacks on the north, which was much more favorable than the trans-Appalachian routes of the competitor seaports of New York City. Philadelphia was planning a system of canals utilizing the Juniata River watergaps through the folded Appalachians, while Baltimore and Washington were developing the Chesapeake and Ohio Canal to reach the Ohio River. Both were designed to connect the Atlantic seaboard with the Ohio River, which had long been the principal avenue of settlement in the trans-Appalachian area. At a time when Chicago consisted of a few log huts, sophisticated urban communities were growing along the Ohio: Pittsburgh, Wheeling, Marietta, Cincinnati, and Louisville among others; while inland settlements, not favored by river transportation such as Lexington and Frankfort, Kentucky, grew much less rapidly. The Ohio had earlier been an axis of French settlement, from Fort Duquesne — which became Pittsburgh — to settlements on the major Ohio River tributaries, such as Terre Haute and Vincennes, Indiana, on the lower Wabash, to Cape Girardeau, Ste. Genevieve, and St. Louis on the Mississippi above the junction of the Ohio. To connect the latter settlements with the Great Lakes through Illinois was one of the objectives of the proposed Illinois and Michigan Canal.

The Erie Canal had stimulated growth of settlements along the south shore and in the hinterland of Lake Erie. The Connecticut Western Reserve in northeastern Ohio, for

"Entrée de la Rivere de Chicago," based on a sketch by Francis de Castelnau who visited Chicago in the late 1830s. From *Vues et Souvenirs de L'Amerique du Nord,* Paris, 1842.
(CHS, ICHi-14175)

example, owes much of its early growth to the all-water transportation made possible by the Erie Canal. The cost of transporting produce to Eastern cities was reduced to about ten percent of its former level. Cleveland, founded in 1797, was a small settlement, not unlike the Chicago of three decades later, until the opening of the Erie Canal. The state of Ohio authorized a system of several canals connecting Lake Erie with the Ohio River, in order to open up the interior of the state; Akron, for example, was connected to Cleveland in 1827, when its development began.

The Erie Canal was the original and principal instrument by which the main axis of pioneer settlement, and along with it the early urban development, shifted from the Ohio valley axis to the Great Lakes region. In the mid-1820s the canal era was at its height. Chicago's Illinois and Michigan Canal was one of the last of the era; when it was finally opened in 1848, the first stretch of railroad had already been built westward from Chicago, and four years later two Eastern railroads reached the city around the southern end of Lake Michigan. By 1854 the Mississippi was reached by rail, at Rock Island, and by 1856 Chicago had already become the greatest railroad center of the continent, if not of the world. Passenger packets operated on the canal for only four years, between its opening in 1848 and the opening of the Chicago and Rock Island Railroad to Ottawa in 1852; but the canal continued to carry bulk freight for many years, reaching a peak of just more than one million tons in 1882. (Completion of the Chicago Sanitary and Ship Canal in 1900 finally ended commercial navigation on the Illinois and Michigan Canal, by then hopelessly outmoded.)

The Illinois and Michigan Canal boats connected the Great Lakes route with the head of steamboat navigation on the Illinois

River, and thus with the Mississippi. In addition to freight barges, the canal was a major route for settlers and other passengers during its first four years. The American Railway Guide and Pocket Companion of 1851 indicated that the 100-mile stretch between Chicago and La Salle was served by three daily packet boats in each direction on regular schedule. Two of the boats were "expressly for passengers" at a fare of $4.00 for the total distance, leaving each terminal at 8 A.M. and 5 P.M. and "through in about 22 hours." A third, Express Freight Packet, was scheduled "for the conveyance of emigrants and movers with their furniture etc., and other light freights. Fare, including board, $3.00, and in proportion for less distances." These packets were advertised "to connect at La Salle with one or more daily lines of Steam Packets for St. Louis and intermediate places on the Illinois River." The through fare was $9.00, and the time "from 60 to 72 hours."

The situation of Lake Michigan astride the main east-west transportation corridor of the continent forced the Eastern railroads to converge around the south end of the lake in order to reach Chicago. Thus, the city at the junction of the lake system with the inland waterway system — opened up originally by the Illinois and Michigan Canal — became the transcontinental gateway between the agricultural Midwest and the urban-industrial East: the greatest inland port and at the same time the dominant railroad gateway, both of which positions it has retained since the mid-nineteenth century. At the same time, Chicago's central position relative to the major transportation routes stimulated many of the agriculturally based industries that would dominate the metropolitan region's economy during most of the nineteenth and early twentieth centuries. These included meatpacking, other food processing, the manufacture of agricultural machinery, and the furnishing of the many supplies required in the burgeoning settlements of the Midwest and the western hinterland. As a result, Chicago developed as the leading trading center for agricultural produce, as exemplified by the growth of the Chicago Board of Trade and several major commodity markets.

Geographers often differentiate the *situation* of a location (its external relationships) from the *site* conditions (the internal, within the site). The site conditions of the original plat of Chicago — the internal spatial pattern of the plat — were governed by the federal Land Ordinance pattern of 1785 and the Northwest Ordinance of 1787, which applied the pattern of the federal land survey specifically to the Midwest trans-Appalachian region. Together, these ordinances outlined the spatial pattern of land subdivision which largely continues to control the layout and landscape of Chicago and the Midwest in general.

Along the Eastern seaboard, boundaries of properties were generally established by "metes and bounds" surveys, which proceeded from point to point and produced very irregular parcels. The "prior survey," in which a system of boundaries was to be established and surveyed in advance of land sales, was a new concept when introduced to the Midwest. The newly established national government had determined upon a policy of not recognizing titles to land west of the Appalachians until a systematic survey was made, and of then transferring title in accordance with boundaries related to the survey. Thus, James Thompson's platting of the original nucleus of Chicago, along with subsequent platting, resulted in a rectangular set of blocks and lots which constitute the physical framework for settlement and development of the Chicago region.

The Land Ordinance of 1785 provided for the land to be divided by rectangular coordinates, bounded by parallels and meridians.

The parallels were to be sun eyed relative to the equator, and were designated as township lines (not to be confused with the "townships" which were areas forming the basis of governmental units). These parallels, or township lines, were to be designated as north or south of certain base parallels, and located six miles apart. They would be intersected by north-south meridians, also six miles apart crossing the parallels at right angles. Such meridians were designated as "range" lines, east or west of certain "principal meridians."

In accordance with this procedure, Thompson's plat was designated as Township 39 North, Range 14 East of the third principal meridian. Because meridians converge at the north and south poles, in order to obtain relatively constant distances between the meridians, certain baselines and correction lines were established along the parallels, where the meridians were offset. Within the parallels and meridians, areas of 36 square miles — six miles along the township lines and six miles along the range line — were to be designated as "townships." These townships were, of course, not all exactly equal in area because of convergence of the meridians and inevitable surveying errors. They were to constitute "survey townships," and as settlement took place, local governments were established by "civil" townships. Counties, consisting of several townships, were in turn generally bounded by the parallels and meridians. Within each township, "sections" were to be surveyed, bounded by "section lines" spaced one mile apart north-south and east-west, and numbered consecutively, beginning in the northeast corner of each township. Thus, the Thompson survey was of a portion of Section 9. Within each section, rectangular boundaries were to be established for each lot and parcel offered for sale.

This system of land survey was applied to the trans-Appalachian area northwest of the Ohio River, by the Northwest Ordinance of 1787, thus determining the settlement pattern. The ordinance also provided for the system of government to be applied to the territory, which was to constitute five states when sufficiently populated: Ohio, Indiana, Illinois, Michigan, and Wisconsin. Subsequently, the survey pattern was extended to other areas, and eventually furnished the model for surveys in many other parts of the world settled during the nineteenth century.

A significant feature of the survey was that a strip of land 33 feet wide was to be reserved around the periphery of each section for use as public road. Since the strips bordering adjacent sections are contiguous, the rights-of-way for roads throughout the Midwest are 66 feet wide, the length of an English surveying "chain." Thus was the basic framework for both rural and urban settlement throughout the Midwest established. In rural areas, this pattern resulted in scattered farmsteads, each along a section line road, in contrast to the nuclear village pattern of rural occupance in most of the world. In turn, this led to excess roads, which today constitute major drains upon the finances of many township and county governments, in contrast to the traditional irregular metes and bounds patterns of roads and rural occupance in the older areas of the country along the Eastern seaboard.

The blocks of the original Thompson plat were rectangular within the limits of the platted area. This was bounded by what is now Kinzie Street on the north, State Street on the east, Madison Street on the south, and Desplaines Street on the west. The first sales of lots within this area took place on September 4, 1830, and the highest price — for an 80-by-180-foot lot fronting on the river — was only $100.

For the first two years after the initial land sales, Chicago did not grow. There were twelve houses in 1830, and there were still

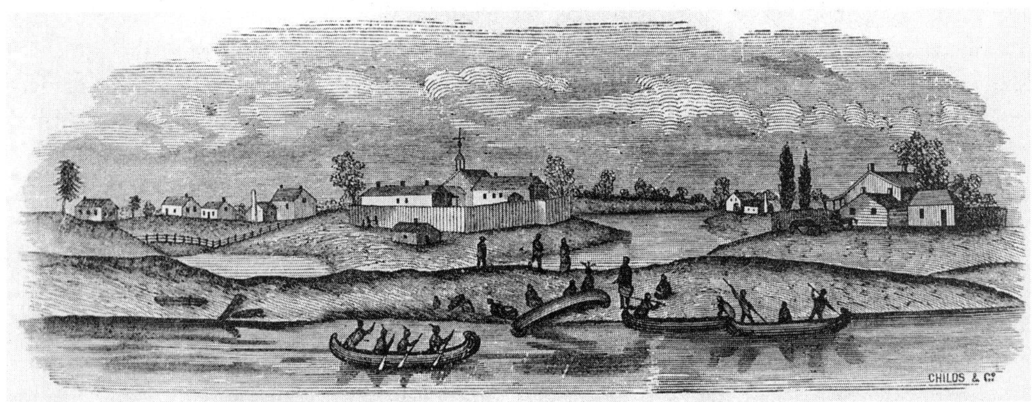

Engraving based on a drawing by explorer Henry Schoolcraft, who passed through Chicago in 1820. It was said to include "every house in the village." From *Chicago Magazine,* May 1857.
(CHS, ICHi-05626)

only twelve houses near the end of 1832. By the end of that year, however, there were thirty buildings and several hundred settlers. Log bridges connected the three portions of the settlement; one bridge crossed the South Branch near Randolph Street and another crossed the North Branch at Kinzie Street. In the following year about 150 buildings were erected, including commercial structures along the south bank of the river's main stem (South Water Street, now Wacker Drive) and on the north side, small industries serving local needs. These included a tannery, a meatpacking plant, a soap factory, and a brickyard. Settlers and supplies came in by lake vessel. Seven such vessels arrived in 1831, 45 in 1832, and 120 in 1833. At first they anchored in the lake offshore, but the first harbor improvement, with $25,000 appropriated by the federal government, began in the latter year, permitting vessels to enter the river. The little settlement, with a population of about 350, was incorporated as a town on August 12, 1833.

With the resolution of the Indian occupance after 1833, the beginning of local government, and definite prospects for a start on the construction of the Illinois and Michigan Canal, land speculation on a large scale became prevalent and accompanied the subsequent rapid growth of the settlement. Its population grew from about 2,000 in 1834 to 3,264 in 1835, 3,820 in 1836, and 4,179 in 1837, at which time Chicago was incorporated as a city. The lots in the Thompson tract were soon sold, and before long adjacent areas were platted, and speculation drove up the prices very rapidly. By mid-1836, the area within the Thompson plat was estimated to be worth $2,650,000, a thousandfold increase since 1830. North of the river, Kinzie's Addition east of State Street was platted in 1833, and Wolcott's and Bushnell's additions, in 1835.

Especially noteworthy was the School Section — the square mile southwest of the original plat, bounded by Madison Street on the north, State Street on the east, Twelfth Street (now Roosevelt Road) on the south, and Halsted Street on the west. The Northwest Ordinance had reserved Section 16 of each survey township for educational purposes, and the School Section was one of them. On October 4, 1833, the 142 blocks in this section were sold at an average price of $60 per acre, as contrasted with their value of $1.25 per acre three years earlier. This School Section includes most of the present Loop area, containing some of the most valuable land in the nation, if not the world, but education in Chicago received inconsequential benefit from it because of its hasty sale in 1833.

Chicago's situation as the southwesternmost terminal of the St. Lawrence–Great Lakes route, significant since the earliest fur-trading days, continued to play an important role in the city's development during subsequent years. The advantage of the city's location was reinforced with the opening of the enlarged St. Lawrence Seaway in 1959. The present seaway is not a new route, but is rather the most recent improvement of a centuries-old one. Following the War of 1812, the British developed the first of a consecutive series of canals to circumvent the rapids of the St. Lawrence River and Niagara Falls. Through these canals Chicago exported its first full cargoes of produce directly, without transshipment, in the 1850s.

Small ocean-going vessels reached Chicago from time to time in subsequent years, and in 1933 the first regularly scheduled small cargo liners connected the city with overseas ports. The opening of the present seaway permitted medium-sized ocean-going cargo vessels, carrying both general cargoes and bulk commodities, to operate to and from Chicago. General cargo peaked in the early 1970s, then declined rapidly, but late in the decade there were indications of a revival of scheduled liner services, although changes in both water and land transportation technology indicate that the general cargo movement, on regularly scheduled vessels, will probably never again reach the peak of a decade ago. By contrast, bulk cargoes — especially export grain — carried in "tramp" or unscheduled vessels, still constitute a major cargo. Some grain is carried in "lakers" for transshipment in the lower St. Lawrence to ocean-going ships, but a substantial portion of such cargo is moved directly from Chicago in salt-water vessels.

Waterborne traffic in Chicago Harbor and the adjacent river has been declining for many years. Since 1906 Calumet Harbor and River have handled more than Chicago Harbor and River. This reflects the shift from the

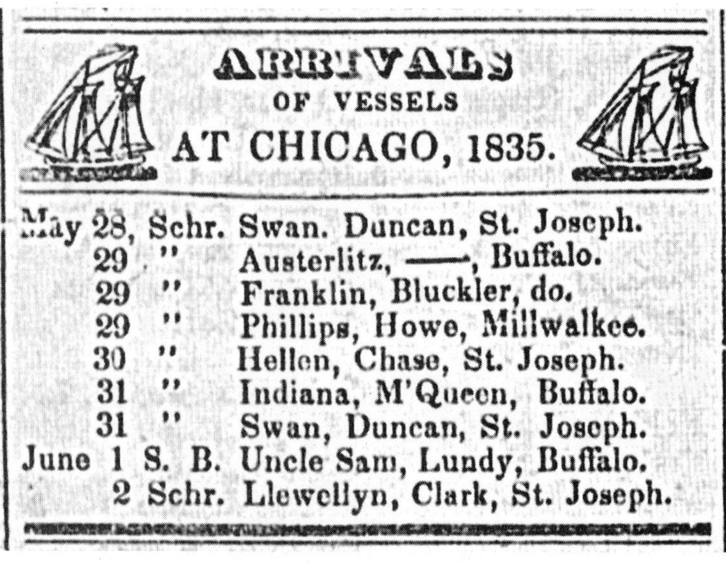

ARRIVALS
OF VESSELS
AT CHICAGO, 1835.

May 28, Schr. Swan. Duncan, St. Joseph.
29 " Austerlitz, ——, Buffalo.
29 " Franklin, Bluckler, do.
29 " Phillips, Howe, Millwalkee.
30 " Hellen, Chase, St. Joseph.
31 " Indiana, M'Queen, Buffalo.
31 " Swan, Duncan, St. Joseph.
June 1 S. B. Uncle Sam, Lundy, Buffalo.
2 Schr. Llewellyn, Clark, St. Joseph.

Chicago became an important shipping center early in its history, as this listing from the *Chicago Democrat* of June 3, 1835, shows.
(CHS, ICHi-14182)

passenger and package freight vessels of an earlier period, to the ever-larger bulk commodity movements associated with industrialization of the Calumet district of South Chicago and northwestern Indiana. Before the St. Lawrence Seaway opened, the Chicago Regional Port District developed a terminal complex in Lake Calumet to handle both lake and ocean traffic on the one hand, and the anticipated increase in barge traffic with enlargement of the Calumet Sag route on the other. After a quarter-century of attempts to secure a more satisfactory location for a general cargo terminal than Lake Calumet (which is six miles inland from Lake Michigan), the Port District has this year completed development of a modern container terminal, Iroquois Landing, at the Calumet River entrance on the Lake Michigan shore.

The ports of metropolitan Chicago handle about 80 million tons of waterborne traffic each year, divided approximately equally between the Illinois and Indiana portions of the metropolitan complex. Most of it is internal Great Lakes bulk traffic, but in recent years about two million tons of overseas cargo — bulk commodities and general cargo — have moved through the metropolitan harbors annually.

Within the metropolitan region, the Chicago–northwestern Indiana port complex includes six lakefront harbors — Chicago Harbor, Calumet Harbor, Indiana Harbor, two private harbors (Buffington and Gary, Indiana), and the more recently completed Burns Waterway Harbor east of Gary. It also includes the Calumet River, navigable for six miles into Lake Calumet for ocean and lake vessels, and the two inland waterway connections: the Chicago River–Chicago Sanitary and Ship Canal route, and the Calumet Sag route.

Chicago's role as the most important inland port of North America in large measure springs from the decision to construct the canal connecting Lake Michigan with the Illinois River. The more immediate outcome of that decision was the platting of the area at the junction of the branches of the Chicago River in 1830 to make possible the sale of lots to finance the canal. Having developed as the major port in the Midwest, the settlement then attracted other transportation modes: the railroads in the last half of the nineteenth century, the highways in the twentieth, and, finally, the air carriers, culminating in the development of Chicago O'Hare International Airport, which last year handled more passengers than all three of the major airports of the New York region.

Thus, two interrelated developments — the first platting of land for sale in Chicago, and the Illinois and Michigan Canal, which was to receive the proceeds of that land sale — were major elements in the determination of the physical and economic development of what was to become the foremost city and major focus of the interior of North America.

To Be the Central City: Chicago, 1848-57

William J. Cronon

If any single year can be said to mark the end of Chicago's existence as an outpost of the frontier, that year is 1848. To set such a date does not mean that the place suddenly became "urban" in that year, since with 20,000 inhabitants it was already the largest town in Illinois, having displaced Galena from that position around 1842. It was the major port of Lake Michigan, and served as home for several major manufacturers. The distribution of wealth within the town was so skewed — with the top one percent of the population owning over half the city's wealth — that it surpassed much older cities such as New York for inequality. Yet Chicago was far from having left all of its frontier trappings behind: most of the streets were still unpaved, filled during wet months with famously unplumbable mud. Even where planking had been laid down, it could scarcely conceal the pools of standing water which at times covered nearly three-fourths of the city's area. Drainage was virtually nonexistent, so that sewers which emptied directly into the streets joined refuse and horse manure to create the city's summer stench, its fever, and its cholera. The rawness of the frontier and the haphazard expansion of settlement in these early decades would stay with Chicago for many years.

But 1848 nevertheless marks a boundary. It was a year of failed revolutions in Europe, a year followed by decades which, in the words of historian E. J. Hobsbawm, consolidated "the global triumph of capitalism" and opened much of the Western world to industrial expansion and agricultural transformation. Chicago was integrally a part of — indeed, it was created by — these changes. Revolution in Germany would send to Chicago crowds of "Forty-Eighters" and others who nearly doubled its German population in the decade ahead and contributed to the growth of ethnic neighborhoods, beer gardens, and foreign-language newspapers, as well as to a new vision of radical politics. By 1850 over half the city's population would be nonnative to the United States. Continuing famine in Ireland brought a similar influx from that country and added to a rising European demand for breadstuffs (initially unleashed by the repeal of the English Corn Laws) which was critically important to Chicago. The events of that year, and the possibilities they represented, gained their importance from the way in which they served to make Chicago the chief link between the developing region of the upper Mississippi valley and the metropolitan economy centered on New York, Liverpool, and London. 1848 saw the frontier pass beyond Chicago for the same reasons that the frontier came increasingly to center upon it.

We can itemize the key events of 1848 in one of those lists of Chicago's "firsts" so popular with the city's early historians. On January 15, the first telegram was received in Chicago — from Milwaukee — and on April 6 a telegraph message was relayed via Detroit from New York itself, taking less than a day to arrive. On March 1, the Galena & Chicago Union Railroad Company let a construction contract for its first 32 miles of line; by November, the road was completed as far as the Des Plaines River, 10 miles west of Chicago. On October 10, the railroad's first locomotive, the *Pioneer* (now housed at the Chicago Historical Society), arrived by sailing ship and was put into service. On March 15, the Chicago Board of Trade was established by the grain dealers and commission merchants of the city, meeting in a set of rooms above Gage and Haines's flour store on South Water Street. On April 16, the Illinois and Michigan Canal, the construction of which had begun twelve years earlier, was officially opened, enabling boats to travel from Chicago to LaSalle and on down the Illinois River to St. Louis. In May, the construction of the Southwestern Plank Road, the first such road in Illinois, was started. It would eventually reach the area of Naperville in 1851, allowing teams and wagons to cross the wet prairies and marshes surrounding Chicago without battling the mud. On June 27, in a moment more symbolic of future than of present possibilities, the first ocean-going steamship, the *Ireland,* arrived from Montreal, putting Chicago, at least in a single instance, in direct communication with the Atlantic economy. The year 1848 also saw two important new structures added to Chicago's built environment: the city's first stockyard, "Bull's Head," located near Ashland Avenue and West Madison Street; and Captain R. C. Bristol's steam-powered grain elevator, the first in Chicago, completed in September with an unheard-of capacity of 80,000 bushels.

Canal, railroad, stockyard, elevator, telegraph, Board of Trade: it is too easy in the midst of such lists to lose track of the changes they represented. Contemporary promoters of Chicago had no such problem. For them, these things were linked together in a vision of inevitable empire. As transportation routes made their way out into a waiting countryside, a wealth of rural productions would descend upon the city destined to receive them. In his report for the Chicago River and Harbor Convention in 1847, Jesse Thomas wrote that the canal and railroads would "at once, and by magic, change the condition and prospects of our city; increase its population; introduce capital to operate in our staples, produce provisions, lumber &c; enlarge every avenue of commerce, and promote the growth of manufactures." History and the tributary countryside would conspire to make Chicago an imperial city.

Real estate speculators in every city in the West engaged in promotion of this sort, and the more determined by nature a city's future could be made to appear, the more likely would it be that Eastern capital would invest in that city's manufactures, markets, and real estate. It was a vision of economic growth with which Chicago boosters were particularly taken. So insistent were they in predicting Chicago's destiny as "the great Central City of the Continent" that the *Detroit Free Press* felt compelled to report that the Chicago Common Council would soon vote "to extend the limits of that city, so as to take in all east of the Rocky Mountains; all south of

I. T. Palmatary's bird's-eye view of Chicago in 1857 encompassed what was already being hailed as the "great Central City of the Continent." *(CHS, ICHi-05665)*

fifty-four degrees of latitude and all north of Patagonia." The *Chicago Tribune* had tongue only halfway in cheek when it replied that Detroit had better be on good behavior if it hoped to become a suburb.

Wisconsin, Iowa, and downstate Illinois were never to become suburbs of Chicago, but they were to be more or less bound to it by economic relationships which were most visible in the transportation network. During the canal's first season of operation, corn shipments from Chicago multiplied eight-fold. Clearly, shipments *to* Chicago had increased as well, and the canal would become the city's chief source of this grain until after the Civil War. Lumber receipts at Chicago from the forests of Michigan and Wisconsin nearly doubled, and one-fourth of this lumber continued on down the canal to be used for houses, fences, and farm buildings. Perhaps most interestingly, receipts of hogs at Chicago actually declined in 1848, despite all expectations that the canal would instantly augment this portion of the city's trade. Ironically, the reason for the decline lay in Chicago's salt market, for the city shipped 32,000 barrels of salt down the canal in 1848 to towns which promptly used it to increase their own packing operations at Chicago's expense.

What the canal accomplished was a significant reorientation, toward Chicago, of downstate communities which had previously found their chief market in St. Louis. Until the opening of the canal, the only way farm produce could arrive in the city was by horse teams, and those who had access to water transport — downriver to the Mississippi towns — generally used it. But Chicago's stock of manufactured goods and its superior prices, made possible by its access to New York via the lakes and the Erie Canal, lured farmers from remarkable distances. It was not unusual for one to three hundred wagons to arrive daily in the city, bearing wheat and corn which would be traded for dry goods, groceries, hardware, and salt. In peak season, the opening of a bridge on the Chicago River could create quarter-mile-long traffic jams of these wagons. Farmers making such a journey often took two weeks to do so, and they could not make it often. The canal gave at least some of them cheaper and more rapid access to the city, and convinced many to abandon St. Louis as their chief shipping destination.

But it was the railroads which cast Chicago's net across the entire Midwest and encouraged many farmers to stop using water transit altogether. The 10 miles of railroad entering Chicago in 1848 had expanded to more than 3,600 miles by 1856. By that year, the railroads had reached the Mississippi River at no fewer than eight points, and had bridged it at one, Rock Island. Each such intersection drained additional trade from St. Louis, which could only seek to prevent bridgings of the river wherever possible. In the decade following 1848, Chicago gained rail access to virtually all areas in Illinois, southern Wisconsin, and eastern Iowa, with enormous consequences for both city and country.

Even in 1852, with only 125 miles of line completed, the Galena & Chicago Union was already bringing more wheat to Chicago than the canal and the farmers' wagons put together. In the course of the decade, the railroads surpassed the canal in virtually all commodity receipts but corn, and increasingly became the primary carriers for Chicago's manufactured goods as well. In 1850, the chief markets for Cyrus H. McCormick's famed reapers were concentrated southwest of Chicago, along the canal, the Illinois River, and the Mississippi River. Ten years later, those markets had veered north and were now located due west of Chicago, along the railroads leading into Iowa. What was more, reapers were being sold to points all the way across Iowa and Minnesota, whereas in 1850 they had been limited to counties bordering the Mississippi and Missouri rivers. In the interim, Chicago's hinterland had grown by hundreds of miles.

The railroads did not simply extend the *range* of Chicago's hinterland; they transformed its whole way of doing business. Previous to their arrival, merchants located in, say, a town on the Iowa bank of the Mississippi did most of their business directly with St. Louis, Philadelphia, and New York. They often sold a full range of retail goods — hardware, shoes, clothing, groceries, agricultural implements — and, in turn, bought grain, hogs, and other produce from farmers. Many deals were carried out by barter, and merchants extended long-term credit to customers as an unavoidable expense of doing business. When the Mississippi froze between November and April, business virtually ground to a halt. A merchant had to spend a substantial amount of money just to store the fall harvest until spring, and there was no telling what would happen to prices in the meantime. On occasion only the backing of a friendly capitalist in the East or in St. Louis saw a dealer through hard times. It took a person with a sizable amount of capital, shrewd business sense, and personal connections stretching halfway across the continent to survive for long under such circumstances. As a result, a handful of merchants usually dominated the business of any given place.

The coming of the railroads changed all of this. In the words of J. M. D. Burrows, a merchant in Davenport, Iowa, they "revolutionized the mode of doing business" and "rather bewildered" merchants who had been accustomed to older methods. Now, someone possessing as little as $250 could set up in business as a commission merchant by engaging a railroad car one morning, buying enough grain to fill it, and shipping it off to Chicago by mid-afternoon. This not only did away with the costs of hiring workers, maintaining a store and warehouse, and offering credit, but allowed a small amount of money to turn over much more rapidly than it had in the past. Older merchants with large fixed investments in buildings and stock had trouble competing with such operators, and either had to specialize, change their scale of business, or go out of business. Transportation services no longer ceased during the winter months, so that marketing was spread out over the entire year, giving merchants continuing access to the cities where they bought their goods.

This railroad transformation of country merchandising had an equally significant impact on Chicago. The more rapid movement of grain at harvest time and the relative decline in the importance of country warehouses helped increase the storage facilities of the city warehouses. By 1857, the grain elevators of Chicago had a total storage capacity of four million bushels, and each of the three biggest elevators was nearly ten times larger than the one erected by Captain Bristol in 1848. Comparable increases had taken place in the produce and lumber storage capacity of the city. At a place where so much was stored, wholesaling (as well as manufacturing) was bound to become a key economic activity. By 1854, the city's editors were labeling Chicago "The Greatest Primary Grain Port in the World."

The centering of a dozen railroads on Chicago by 1856 not only brought in great quantities of goods; it made the city the central point of exchange between Western and Eastern railroads. Moreover, competition with lake transport kept Chicago's rail rates lower than those at other points. Midwestern

Panorama photographed by Alexander Hesler from Sturges, Buckingham & Co. grain elevator in 1858. The Illinois Central Railroad complex dominated the lakefront at Randolph Street.

(CHS, ICHi-13888)

rates were established to Chicago and from Chicago, so that shippers came to regard that city as the destination of first resort. Concentration bred more concentration. In few other Midwestern cities could a merchant do as much business in as many different lines of commerce as in Chicago. In the past, buying trips to New York or Philadelphia could be undertaken by country merchants only once or twice a year, each trip taking from six to eight weeks. Now dealers could travel by rail to Chicago once or twice a month. This allowed them to reduce their total stock and respond more quickly to their customers' demands. Little wonder that I. D. Guyer, one of the city's early booster-historians, could write that "Railroads are talismanic wands. They have a charming power. They do wonders — they work miracles. They are better than laws; they are essentially, politically and religiously — the pioneer, and vanguard of civilization."

What could a person find in Chicago on a buying trip in 1856? To answer this question is to define the city's hinterland and its role as frontier entrepôt. Corn from the Illinois valley and Iowa, and wheat from southern Wisconsin and northern Illinois, sat in the city's elevators and freight yards awaiting the ships in its port. Lumber in the yards along the South Branch of the Chicago River came from as far away as Saginaw, Michigan, but principally from mills at Muskegon, Michigan, and Green Bay, Wisconsin, many of which were already dominated by Chicago capitalists. Livestock raised in Illinois, Missouri, and Iowa and fattened in the feedlots of northeastern Illinois could be purchased at John B. Sherman's new thirty-acre stockyards on the lake shore between 25th and 31st streets, which could house as many as 5,000 cattle and 30,000 hogs. At the city's wholesaling houses, country retailers could find an endless range of dry goods, furniture, books, canned goods, and other wares, some of which were imported from the East, some manufactured right in Chicago. Perhaps most important, anyone needing workers, whether to harvest the year's crops, to cut the forests of Michigan and Wisconsin, or to run the ships of the Great Lakes, came to Chicago as the chief labor market of the region. On the docks of Chicago, men looking for work, and men looking to hire, found each other and struck their contracts.

What was being created at Chicago in the 1850s was a new kind of market. The concentration at one point by a new technology of so many commodities from so large an area meant that purchases and sales at Chicago tended to set prices for the entire region. At no other place in the country, other than perhaps in New York, was so much information on the conditions of agricultural supply available. The telegraph, which had arrived in 1848, had preceded the railroad in penetrating the countryside, and now it brought constant news of crops in the West and markets in the East. "It seemed," wrote the Reverend J. P. Thompson of the telegraph network he saw while traveling in Iowa, "like the nervous system of the nation, conveying, quick as thought, the least sensation from extremity to head, the least volition from head to extremity." Drought in Iowa and war in the Crimea deserved equally rapt attention. If on those wires, as Thompson thought, one "could hear the sharp quick beating of the great heart of New York," it was also true that none listened harder to that heart than Chicago.

It was here that still another creation of 1848 had come to play a major role by 1857. The Chicago Board of Trade was a slow starter. Practically moribund by 1851, its daily meetings were occasionally held with no one at all present, grain sales being conducted entirely in the streets of the city. The increasing amount of grain brought by the railroads, however, and the handling of its bulk in elevators, necessitated that some agency take control and supervise Chicago's markets. The Board of Trade did this in 1857 when it adopted standardized inspection and grading procedures for the city's grain. Although the revolutionary effects of this grading system — the futures markets with their attendant speculative possibilities — would not be fully apparent until after the Civil War, the concentration of information flows was immediate. More and more, Chicago's trading — and hence a goodly share of the trading for the entire region — was done on the floor of the 'Change, as it was known.

A city so completely focused on its markets was bound to bear their mark. The more or less invisible transformations of economic institutions were matched by changes in the visible world of Chicago as well. If one takes the lofty perspective of artist I. T. Palmatary's bird's-eye view of Chicago in 1857 — a vista no human being in that year could see in real life, akin to the imperial visions of the city's boosters — one can begin to picture the place. By 1857, the population of the city had risen to more than 93,000, a more than fourfold increase since 1848. Their habitations and places of work, slowly being lifted from the mud in an endless process of grade-changing, stretched beyond Fullerton to the north, Western to the west, and the bend of the South Branch to the south. On the hazy line roughly defined as the city's edge, prosperous farmers did market gardening, cut hay, and grew orchards, as much a part of Chicago's world as the downtown. By 1860, Cook County accounted for 13 percent of Illinois's total market gardening — twice as much as any other county — all to supply Chicago's food.

Where country lanes turned into the grid of city streets, rapidly erected balloon-frame buildings housed the city's workers, already defining themselves into areas of concentrated working-class and ethnic residence. To the north, alongside the cemetery which would one day become Lincoln Park, was the largest concentration of Germans. To the south, along the far side of the river and lining the canal they had helped build, lived the Irish, in an area already regarded by the "better classes" as one of the roughest in the city.

But it was when one crossed the river, amidst a forest of ships' masts which were visible even from the prairie that one found the Chicago which seemed so different from the world of the farmers and small-town merchants who traded there. At the center of all was the river, cluttered with bridges and ships and canal boats. Its mouth was marked on the north by a breakwater to stop the southward march of the too sandy shoreline, and on the south by the great looming shape of Sturges and Buckingham's 700,000-bushel grain elevator. Fanning to meet the elevator and its own impressive station, the Illinois Central Railroad occupied much of the land between the south bank of the river and the shore of the lake, land it had gained after a vehement struggle in the Council in 1851-52. The railroad entered the City on a trestle in the lake paralleling Michigan Avenue, which still marked the water's edge. Trees and prominent residences lined that street, one of the most elegant in the city, as they did the well-to-do neighborhoods on the Near North Side.

Walking west from the Illinois Central station, one found oneself amidst the frenzy of South Water Street, center of Chicago's wholesaling activities. With the buildings on its north side fronting the docks of the river, the street formed a key break-in-bulk point for merchandise arriving from the East. One block south, on Lake Street, was the principal retailing district. But business overflowed these streets and filled much of the downtown, creating traffic which rivaled that of any street in New York but Broadway's. If there were now fewer farmers' wagons bring-

The Chicago River was crucial to the city's commercial life, and the destruction of bridges and shipping in the 1849 flood was a great calamity. Engraving based on a daguerreotype.
(CHS, ICHi-02060)

ing produce directly from the country to help clog the streets, their absence was more than made up for by the carts and wagons of the city's teamsters, shuttling goods between warehouses, railroad terminals, and the river. The motions of business and exchange were everywhere.

What did such a city mean? Local boosters returned perpetually to Chicago's markets, the volume of goods passing its docks and railroad stations, the crowds on the streets and bridges, and above all its possibilities for future growth. But its very newness made it seem somehow temporary, a creation of the moment which lacked the refinements of an older, more Eastern, civilization. A writer in *Putnam's Monthly* described it as one of Emerson's "representative towns," but made his reader unsure of just how much of a compliment this was. "It is the type of that class of American towns," he wrote, "which have made themselves conspicuous, and almost ridiculous, by their rapid growth." *Almost ridiculous.* The phrase bespoke a certain Eastern contempt. A town with its eyes so much on the main chance, said *Putnam's* writer, was bound to experience "a lack of those healthful restraints which exist in an older community," something which had "undoubtedly combined to weaken and lower the moral sense of the people, in regard to business transactions." Chicago's unrestrained market, as this New Yorker saw it, threatened to destroy the city's moral universe.

By 1857, Chicago's leaders were beginning to resent such demeaning comparisons, and to feel the tug of their own high cultural possibilities. The same confidence which allowed boosters to promote the city as an

View looking northeast from the dome of the Chicago Court House, photographed by Alexander Hesler in 1858. The main business district (near the river on Lake and Water Streets) appears in the distance. *(CHS, ICHi-05740)*

economic rival of New York led professionals and men of wealth to ponder whether Chicago ought not to acquire a few of New York's cultural appurtenances as well: monumental buildings, learned societies, even a history commensurate with future greatness. Perhaps this was one reason why Chicago elites began to look to their own past in the 1850s. For those who reflected upon how much had been accomplished by the generation then living, comparisons with Chicago's own past helped mute invidious cultural contrasts with cities like New York and Boston.

When, in 1857, Zebina Eastman launched his *Chicago Magazine: The West As it Is,* he sought to make it an oracle which would serve as "a go-between, carrying to the men of the East, a true picture of the West." A chief means for accomplishing this end was to preserve the unwritten history of places like Chicago, "before the men now living, in whose memory it is treasured, shall die, and the record perish." Although the *Magazine* lasted barely half a year, every issue contained a chapter on the history of Chicago, telling of Marquette and Jolliet, the Fort Dearborn massacre, and the first visions of the canal, in the loving detail of the historian who was also myth-maker. The story had barely reached 1830 when publication of the magazine ceased.

But the men who treasured Chicago's

memory as their own were not content to let their story die with them. That was why, on April 24, 1856, a small group of doctors, lawyers, and businessmen gathered in the law offices of Scammon & McCagg at Lake and LaSalle streets to found a historical society. Among them were men who had lived in the city during fur-trading days, who had helped direct construction of the canal, directed the first railroad, led the assault on Chicago's inadequate drainage and water supply, and held key offices in city government. They were men who had grown wealthy or at least prospered as the city grew, and through whose offices, in February 1857, the Chicago Historical Society was incorporated to honor their city and state, "to collect and preserve the memories of its founders and benefactors, as well as the historical evidences of its progress in settlement and population, and in the arts, improvements and institutions which distinguish a civilized community."

It was no doubt a particular version of the past which these men sought to preserve, one which saw Chicago's early growth in terms of heroic achievement and great men. Though Chicago's real transformation had occurred in scarcely ten or fifteen years, carrying the city of 1856 worlds away even from that of 1848, they tended to look farther back for their "historical evidences," to the 1820s and 1830s, when the place that would be Chicago was little more than a speculation in real estate. Theirs was a history of first things. When they thought of the canal, they remembered not the anonymous thousands who had dug it or the many more whose lives had been permanently altered by it, but the few who had first thought of it in 1816 or 1826 — presumably because they found in those earlier thoughts a vision which paralleled their own. Discovering the earliest origins of a canal or a railroad or a line of business, and identifying the first authors of each, thus served to explain and legitimate the city accused of having no past.

The filiopietism inherent in this use of history was something which the prominent men of Chicago shared with many of their nineteenth-century contemporaries, and it inevitably constrained their sense of the past. The revolution in social and economic organization which had conspired to change Chicago in the short time between 1848 and 1856 was perhaps too recent, too authorless, and too collective a creation to be recognized as genuine history by such men. For them, it too was heroic, and they were its most likely heroes. Little in the past of the 1820s or 1830s could have predicted the growth of Chicago in the 1850s, however inevitable the boosters might try to make that growth appear, and no one man or group of men could claim responsibility for the city's transformation. Yet that transformation had made the city. The historical society these men founded, in outliving their memory, came to be the chief witness of a place changed beyond recall by a history they did not see.

Goodbye, Madore Beaubien: The Americanization of Early Chicago Society

Jacqueline Peterson

About midnight on November 13, 1833, blazing meteors fell from the winter sky illuminating the eastern half of North America. In the Midwest, the astral showers were accompanied by a remarkable atmospheric change. Warm winds throughout November and December prevented Lakes Michigan and Huron from freezing as far north as Mackinac Island, and Indians thereabouts were said to be making maple sugar (a spring occupation) in December.

Sky gazers interpreted these marvelous occurrences variously, but Indians viewed "the falling of the stars" with alarm, believing it a dreadful omen, a sign of doom. The preceding summer, the last Indian resistance movement in the Great Lakes had been quelled, Black Hawk defeated, his people cut down on the mudflats of the Mississippi or at the hands of enemy Sioux. Only two months earlier, in September 1833, the United Band of Potawatomi, Ottawa, and Chippewa had ceded 5,000,000 acres of remaining lands in Illinois and Wisconsin for a thinly disguised exile in the West. Now, settlers, land speculators, hopefuls, and hangers-on of every stripe were beginning to swarm into northern Illinois.

At Chicago, the community of fur traders slumbered in the shadow of Fort Dearborn. If the meteoric display were a portent, few, if any, of the town's old settlers recognized this at the time. Despite the momentous happenings of the preceding two years and a widening trickle of Eastern migrants, Chicago appeared little changed from the unprepossessing village Thompson surveyed in 1830. The population had tripled, perhaps, growing from about 100 to 300 persons. But aside from the single commercial thoroughfare — muddy South Water Street with its hastily thrown-up storefronts and shanties — Chicago sprawled in seeming disorder. The low-slung, white-washed log and bark-covered cabins of its early residents followed the meanderings of the river's branches, rather than sitting smartly in neat platted rows.

According to Thompson's survey, which laid down the square imprint of a grid upon this curving and unfettered landscape, Mark Beaubien's tavern, the Sauganash, sat smack in the middle of a newly created road. But Mark Beaubien, like other early settlers, "didn't expect no town." Nor did they want one, at least not the sort of place that Easterners envisioned. In the early 1830s, Chicago was still remarkably free of the institutional trappings associated with American town life: it possessed no village square, no grassy mall, church steeple, sundial, schoolhouse, or jail. Roads hewed to the contours of the land, rather than crossing at right angles, and titles to house and fenced cornfields were, for the most part, unwritten.

Yet this was no random sprawl. Lifeways at Chicago were waterways. Households occupied the high dry ridges of the Chicago River's triumvirate arms, gardens and outbuildings straggling into the thin stands of scrub oak, poplar, and hemlock behind. Moreover, even for so small and dispersed a community, family and clan units had carved out territorial divisions. On the north side, the two branches of John Kinzie's descendants reigned. The Anglophile fur-trading branch from Detroit — the primary Kinzie line — controlled portions of what would later be known as the Magnificent Mile and the Gold Coast, although in the 1830s most of "Kinzie's Addition" was swamp and sand dune. The other branch — Kinzie's children by an early "country" wife, Margaret Mackenzie, and their Virginia relatives — settled further west, their farms, distilleries, and stockyards stretching up the north arm of the Chicago River.

On the south side, the log dwellings of the Beaubien brothers — fur trader Jean Baptiste and the younger Mark — and their burgeoning families, flanked Fort Dearborn. Both homesites had been shrewdly located. In acquiring the former Dean house, a jerry-built five-room structure at the foot of Madison Street where the Chicago River took its last sluggish turn into Lake Michigan, Jean Baptiste Beaubien positioned himself so as to intercept the *bateaux* brimming with trade goods when they first arrived from Mackinac Island via Lake Michigan. Similarly, Mark Beaubien's tavern, situated at the juncture of the river's branches and opposite Wolf Point, caught the eye of land and water traffic from three directions.

A few miles up the south branch, at the entrance to Mud Lake and the portage, a fluctuating population of traders and voyageurs and their families clustered at Hardscrabble (now Bridgeport). The names usually associated with this location included Robinson, Chevalier, Bourassa, LaFramboise, and sometimes Ouilmette, although the latter's permanent home and trading station was to be found on a ridge above Lake Michigan at Grosse Pointe (now Wilmette) on the road to Waukegan and Milwaukee. Here, by the early 1830s, Antoine Ouilmette's children were also settling with their spouses, as had a few newcomers like Stephen J. Scott. The closest Indian settlements were located on the Des Plaines near Laughton's tavern (Riverside) and near Alexander Robinson's and Billy Caldwell's encampments in the environs of present Sauganash. However, when the intense July heat dried the wetlands about Chicago, many Potawatomi families moved closer in to trade, bringing their belled ponies to feed untethered on the luxuriant grasses and pitching their cool summer lodges on the prairie just west of Wolf Point, where the arms of the river joined.

The dispersed nature of early Chicago often caused outsiders to denigrate its significance if not to miss the settlement altogether. Yet this *was* a community, similar in design, human composition, and culture to dozens of other settlements established in the Great Lakes region prior to the 1830s. While there was no grid, old settlers at Chicago instinctively chose to congregate at the center, making Wolf Point a social and economic core. Here, fair weather trading stores proliferated, the Wolf and Green Tree taverns rose to accommodate Chicago's early travelers, and the town's first tannery and meeting house were erected.

The Point functioned as a kind of free zone where clan rivalries, social classes, and master-servant relationships momentarily dissolved as diverse races and ethnicities commingled. The Anglo-American Kinzies, French-Canadian Beaubiens, the Potawatomi, and others all gathered here, swapping tales, bartering produce and peltry for trade goods, gambling, racing horses and carioles, and occasionally attending the exhortations of an itinerant minister. Whatever their private animosities and prejudices, a common dependence upon the Indian trade and a liberal use of the universal solvent — whiskey — brought these folk into community. If tensions flared, they were soothed by the lighthearted strains of Mark Beaubien's fiddle, for with the opening of the pretentious two-story, blue-shuttered Sauganash in 1826, frolicking and jigging became, next to drinking, Chicago's favorite preoccupations.

There was something else which set these insouciant folk apart from their American counterparts to the east in the early 1830s: a naive and ultimately devastating disregard for "progress." The members of Chicago's early fur trade community shared in common a belief system, or a way of looking at the world, which valued harmony and unanimity over competition; leisure over excess productivity; family and clan over economic interest and class; hospitality over exclusivity; generosity over saving; and today over tomorrow. It made no sense to attempt to bottle time or alter the natural bent of things. Life was a circle. Such ideas and values lent a suspiciously Indian cast to Chicago's old settlers, and for good reason. The vast majority of these folk were of mixed Indian and white ancestry, the product of two cultures. They had either married into or grew to maturity within households sharing at least two languages, two sets of kin, and a material culture which innovatively combined elements valued by both Indian and Euro-American societies.

Such a community was unprepared for the events set in motion by Thompson's coming in 1830. Although the more astute English-speaking Kinzies privately entered their claim to 102 north side acres in 1831, the platting of the town and downstate interest in building the Illinois and Michigan Canal failed to inspire a public-spirited drive or entrepreneurial schemes. For a time, bidding for town lots appeared more as novelty than shrewd business investment, and the lots themselves as possessions to be swapped, given away, or to put up at horse races rather than hoarded. But then momentum from elsewhere began to build. In 1833, Robert Allen Kinzie returned from a buying trip back East with the astonishing news that New York speculator Arthur Bronson had paid $20,000 for Kinzie family lands on the north side. By early August, coached through the unfamiliar legal procedures by experienced Yankee newcomers, 28 Chicagoans gathered at Mark Beaubien's tavern to incorporate their settlement as a town, and to elect a president and board of trustees.

In bowing to downstate pressures and by organizing a town government with powers to heap regulations upon their lives, Chicago's old settlers unwittingly provided a formal mechanism for their own undoing. Within a few short years, the harmonious multiracial trading community straddling the Chicago River's arms was metamorphosed into a strait-laced, institution-ridden, class-conscious urban metropolis which could have been anywhere. Momentarily, however, the original inhabitants held

John Harris Kinzie (1803-65), son of trader John Kinzie, was first an Indian subagent, then a Chicago businessman.
(CHS, ICHi-10967)

onto the reins, as the elections of 1833 and 1834 demonstrated.

Madore Benjamin Beaubien (1809-83), elected to the first board of town trustees in 1833, and John Harris Kinzie (1803-65), second town president from 1834 to 1835, were second-generation scions of Chicago's two most important early lineages. Their fathers, Jean Baptiste Beaubien and John Kinzie, had been fur trade associates and intimates. The sons, under normal circumstances, would have been expected to assume the mantle of their fathers' social and economic position. But Chicago was not a normal or stable place to be in the 1830s. Instead the destinies of these young Chicago men abruptly separated, just as the new town split and spun away from the old. This was no coincidence. To a remarkable degree, the life histories of these two figures — Madore Beaubien, of French-Indian and Catholic heritage, and John Harris, Anglo-Saxon and Protestant — were to mirror the contradictions and strains underlying the growth and transformation of early Chicago into a modern city. But in order to understand how that remarkable change came about, we will have to go back to the beginning of Chicago's history.

The place called Chicago — a windswept glacial plain marked by patches of scrub oak and poplar, sandhills, and low-lying marshes

Madore Beaubien (1809-83), part Ottawa Indian, was known as the "handsomest man in Chicago." He later settled on the Potawatomi reserve in Kansas.
(CHS, ICHi-14153)

— had been, from the 1690s forward, the habitation of a small, shifting population of fur traders and adventurers. Such antiquity should not mask the secondary "backwater" characteristics of the spot, however. In the larger eighteenth- and early nineteenth-century world — a fur trade universe stretching from the counting houses of London, New York, and Montreal to the warehouses of Mackinac Island and Detroit, and to the vast fur fields beyond — Chicago was only one of dozens of subsidiary trading hamlets dotting the waterways of the Great Lakes and Mississippi River drainage systems.

Prior to the American Revolution, Chicago functioned as one of the northernmost trading outposts of French- and later Spanish-controlled Louisiana. Traders like Chicago's first settler, the well-heeled Santo Domingan mulatto, Jean Baptiste Point du Sable, who occupied a commodious French-style house with numerous outbuildings at the mouth of the Chicago River until 1800, were drawn northward from the Illinois country and Peoria to the vicinity of the Chicago portage. By the 1790s, however, the locus of influence had shifted toward British Canada and the newly created United States. The Montreal pedlars of the British North West Company rarely penetrated as far south as Chicago; however, most independent traders who exploited Chicago as a "jack-knife" or subsidiary wintering post after 1800 were supplied by British merchants at Detroit and Montreal. While the French-Canadian employees, or engagés, of such traders built trading huts along the river's branches, it was not until Fort Dearborn rose at the site in 1803 that men of higher rank and of Anglo-Saxon heritage migrated permanently to Chicago.

John Harris Kinzie's father, old John Kinzie, was not the founder of Chicago, but he does own the distinction of being its first English-speaking resident. Kinzie Sr. was born in Quebec in 1763 of British parents, but after his father's early death, his mother married a Scots-Irishman, Thomas Forsyth, who kept a tavern and a farm in the Grosse Pointe district of Detroit. Thus, John was raised within the old French-Canadian fur trading community along the straits connecting Lakes Ontario and Huron, a community where British influence and intrigue persisted well beyond the American Revolution.

Aged forty in 1803, the year of Fort Dearborn's founding, John Kinzie had already acquired a considerable reputation as a trader among the Potawatomi on the St. Joseph River in southwestern Michigan, as well as in the Sandusky and Fort Wayne environs. Indians knew and respected him primarily for his silverworking abilities, but Detroit merchants recognized his keen business sense. In company with his half-brother, Thomas Forsyth, Kinzie and a coterie of frontier entrepreneurs nearly wangled an illegal Indian cession of lands in Michigan and Indiana before General Anthony Wayne could complete the Treaty of Greenville in 1795.

Sometime during his late teens or early twenties, Kinzie and a fellow trader, Alexander Clark, set up housekeeping near Sandusky with two Giles County, Virginia, girls — Margaret and Elizabeth Mackenzie. These were no ordinary wives. During Lord Dunmore's War in the early 1770s, Margaret and Elizabeth had been captured by the Shawnee and raised among them. Years later, when given to or purchased by Kinzie and Clark, they served as able Indian interpreters and intermediaries for their novice trader husbands. By the end of the American Revolution, Kinzie and Margaret had three children: James, William, and Elizabeth. Clark named his only son by Elizabeth, John Kinzie, after his associate and friend.

Kinzie's marriage terminated abruptly when the elder Mackenzie arrived at Detroit to retrieve his stolen daughters. The reasons for Margaret's rejection of Kinzie are obscure, but the sisters packed up their children and fled to Virginia, where they promptly found new husbands in Jonas Clybourne and Benjamin Hall, Giles County men. This "southern" Kinzie line would eventually come back to haunt John Kinzie at Chicago, but in 1803 he had embarked upon a second marital adventure, marrying Elizabeth McKillip, the Detroit widow of a British officer. Their first child, a son named John Harris Kinzie, was born in July.

Significantly, in Elizabeth McKillip, Kinzie acquired another "white captive" familiar with Indian custom, language, and values and thus a useful helpmate to an ambitious Indian trader. While Kinzie and his wife would later be regarded as the first "white" family at Chicago, Kinzie had twice spurned traditionally reared and protected American or English women in favor of ladies with Indian affinities or attributes. This was not unusual. Prior to 1816, every successful trader operating in southwestern Michigan, Chicago, and Milwaukee had hewed to the custom country within fur trade society. That is, they took to wife, often informally, a woman of Indian descent, thus forging an alliance with her male kin. Even Kinzie's half-brother Thomas Forsyth temporarily married a Chippewa woman early in his career. By 1803, John Kinzie had won the trust of his Indian clients, but marriage to Elizabeth McKillip was a fair compromise.

In partnership with his half-brothers, Thomas and Robert Forsyth, Kinzie now schemed to get the jump on less astute competitors. The harvest around Chicago of valuable winter peltries such as beaver and marten had notoriously yielded a poorer return than other trading sites. However, in Kinzie's view, the posting of soldiers at Fort Dearborn promised a tidy traffic in sundries and necessities. Hoping to combine this with a monopoly on the Potawatomi trade in northern Illinois, Kinzie and entourage traveled overland, skirting the sandhills which lined the lower bowl of Lake Michigan to the tiny hamlet of Chicago. John Harris was carried in a *Tipinagan* — a Chippewa child's house or cradleboard — on the back of an Indian servant who probably was also his wetnurse. Shouldering aside French-speaking Canadians and French-Indians like the interpreter Jean Lalime, Kinzie set himself up in Du Sable's establishment near the lakeshore on the north bank of the Chicago River. Soon constructing a trading house on the opposite bank, near the fort, Kinzie quickly emerged as the undisputed "big man" of Chicago.

First in partnership with the Forsyths and later as an independent agent for the Southwest Company, the volatile redbeard cast a long shadow. Prior to the outbreak of the War of 1812, nearly everyone at Chicago was either in Kinzie's debt or his employ. Yet he did contribute to the village's growth by importing employees like Billy Caldwell and Alexander Robinson from the St. Joseph region, and by persuading Milwaukee traders Mirandeau and LaFramboise to apprentice their part-Potawatomi children to him as household servants. Even the fort felt Kinzie's presence. Not only did he render laughable the U.S. Factory, established by the government to undersell independent traders like himself and thereby end their insidious influence among the Indians, but he wangled his way into becoming supplier to the fort — a very lucrative office indeed. Available cash at Chicago flowed in Kinzie's direction. When the garrison's pay failed to arrive on schedule, the shrewd trader was able to advance the soldiers' wages, knowing full well that the specie would soon return to his till.

Kinzie's four children — John Harris, Ellen Marion, Maria Indiana, and Robert Allen — all born between 1803 and 1810, basked in their father's light. Indisputably, they were

Mackinac Island, headquarters of the American Fur Company. From *Vues et Souvenirs de L'Amerique du Nord,* Paris, 1842. *(CHS, ICHi-14177)*

members of Chicago's wealthiest and most powerful family. Moreover, they were white, a fact of no weighty moment in the first decade of the nineteenth century, but one which gained them social entrance to the officers' quarters at Fort Dearborn and the attention of American officials. The War of 1812, which called British sympathizers into question, caught the Kinzie family off guard, however. By 1813, in the wake of the Fort Dearborn Massacre, old John Kinzie languished in a Quebec jail, his finances in shambles, and his wife and children dependent upon relatives at Detroit. During the war years, the Kinzie estate fell into ruin. Only the Ouilmettes and Alexander Robinson remained at Chicago, earning a meager livelihood by cultivating the cornfields and gardens of the former garrison.

In 1816, with the rebuilding of Fort Dearborn, the repatriated John Kinzie and his family returned to a village seemingly untouched except for the macabre reminders of the massacre lying among the sandhills south of the fort. Yet, the final defeat of British efforts to hang on to the Great Lakes fur traffic set in motion devastating social repercussions. Increasingly, Chicago was to become a town of impoverished middlemen directed from the American Fur Company's big house on Mackinac Island, as its formerly independent trade employees were drawn into the ravenous maw of John Jacob Astor's fur trade monopoly.

Kinzie, who had worked for Astor's pre-1812 Southwest Company, never regained his former economic status or influence. When he proved unable to best John Crafts, an independent trader irritatingly lodged at Hardscrabble after 1816, Astor's managers at Mackinac Island transferred a young French-Canadian trader — Jean Baptiste Beaubien — then working at Milwaukee, to Chicago. In 1817, Chicago's second founder (and father of Madore Beaubien) moved into the old government warehouse beneath the pickets of Fort Dearborn.

Jean Baptiste Beaubien was born in 1787, a full generation after Kinzie, into the same Grosse Point district of Detroit. Yet unlike the newcomer Forsyths, Beaubien hailed from a prolific and highly respected French-Canadian creole family, whose roots at Detroit went back three generations. His aunt, Angélique Cuillerier Beaubien, was the heroine of Pontiac's Rebellion, revealing the Indian plot to the British at Detroit and thus thwarting an intended massacre. Clannish, devout pillars of the Catholic Church, small farmers and orchard tenders, the Beaubiens were among the more distinguished families in post-American Revolutionary Detroit, years when American and British enterprise worked to reduce the string of tiny riverfront farms to a French-speaking ghetto.

Jean Baptiste was something of a prodigy. His entry into the fur trade coincided with the tightening of the upper ranks of the occupation against French Canadians, but it is doubtful that he was aware of this. Nor did his early career reflect the growing ethnic prejudice which made of the voyageur and engagé ranks virtually a French-Canadian and French-Indian caste. Prior to 1800, while barely a teenager, he had served as an apprentice clerk to Joseph Bailly at St. Joseph and Grand rivers. By 1804, his trading sphere had enlarged to include Milwaukee, Chicago, and Mackinac. In that year he turned seventeen.

Beaubien followed the usual diplomatic protocol in establishing a commercial relationship with a tribe or hunting band. In marrying Mahnobunoqua, a Grand River Ottawa woman, Beaubien not only won the favor of her extended kin, but also a trading relationship and lifelong friendship with Shabbona, head of a band in the Chicago area. Their first child, Marie, was born at Chicago in 1805, followed two years later by Charles Henry. The third, Madore, was born at the mouth of Thorn Creek in Michigan during July of 1809, probably in a small birthing hut erected behind his father's trading house. The clan name bestowed upon this boychild by his mother's relatives has not survived; however, his father memorialized a brother or uncle by naming him Medard. Chicago residents later made a double entendre of the name, calling this gracefully featured half-Ottawa boy Madore, meaning "love me!"

Madore's first recollections of Chicago conjured up the charred remains of Fort Dearborn and the scattered bones of the massacre victims. He later claimed that this visit occurred when he was four, in 1813, but his recollection that old John Kinzie guided the Beaubien family through the ruins was surely mistaken. More likely the visit occurred in 1811. By 1813, Madore's mother, Mahnobunoqua, had been dead for at least two years, and harnessed with three small children, two of which probably had not yet been weaned, Jean Baptiste sought an immediate replacement. He made a fortunate choice in Josette LaFramboise, a Kinzie house servant and part-Potawatomi daughter of Milwaukee trader François LaFramboise. This happy partnership, which produced fourteen children and endured until Josette's death in 1854, solidified Beaubien's standing with the Potawatomi and Ottawa on both sides of Lake Michigan and linked him to a sizeable fur trading family whose members resided on Grand River and Mackinac Island in Michigan as well as at Milwaukee and later Chicago.

Although he was a French Canadian and Kinzie's junior, Beaubien's prior success as a trader and his influential kin connections won him appointment as the American Fur Company's number one man at Chicago in 1817. But even though Beaubien's credibility was bolstered by the simultaneous migration of the LaFramboise clan from Milwaukee, he ultimately proved no more adept at curtailing the trade of the company's independent rival, John Crafts, than old John Kinzie. Finally, Astor, in a well-calculated move, bought out Crafts, turned the Chicago trade over to him, and demoted Beaubien to a secondary slot. The successful Easterner's ascendancy embarrassed both Beaubien and

Kinzie. Upon Crafts's untimely death in 1825, Kinzie and Beaubien jointly represented the company on shares (Beaubien holding the lesser one-third), but by this time the dwindling wildlife about Chicago was hardly worth the effort. Kinzie began to look to government appointment through the recommendations of his Indian agent son-in-law, Yankee Alexander Wolcott. Mercifully, perhaps, old John Kinzie died in 1828, the same year that Astor sold the American Fur Company's Illinois interests to Gurdon S. Hubbard, company trader on the Wabash. These events signaled the waning importance of the fur trade at Chicago — the chief activity that had brought the community into being, organized its social relations, and provided the only livelihood most old settlers knew well how to pursue or to pass on to their sons.

Old John Kinzie spent his final months in the household and care of Jean Baptiste Beaubien and his wife Josette. This was as close to equality as the two traders from Detroit ever came, and there is at least slight evidence that although of differing ethnic and religious background, these men respected one another. The physical proximity of the two families might have presented an opportunity for the development of similar

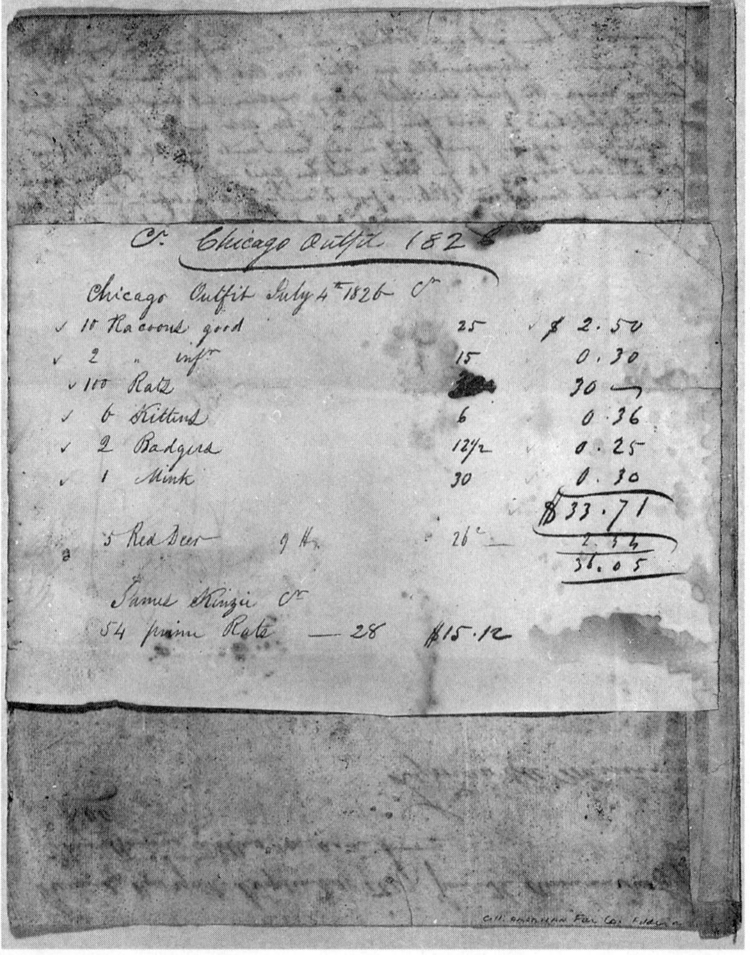

Cr. Chicago Outfit 182[illegible]

Chicago Outfit July 4th 1826 Cr

✓ 10 Racoons good	25	$ 2.50
✓ 2 " infr	15	0.30
✓ 110 Rats	[illegible]	30
✓ 6 Kittens	6	0.36
✓ 2 Badgers	12½	0.25
✓ 1 Mink	30	0.30
		$33.71
5 Red Deer 9 lb	26c	2.34
		36.05

James Kinzie Cr

54 prime Rats — 28 $15.12

Receipt for furs delivered to the American Fur Company in Chicago, 1826. By this time, dwindling wildlife had all but ended the fur trade in the area.
(CHS, Archives and Manuscripts)

ties between the leading males of the second generation, but in 1828 neither John Harris Kinzie nor Madore Beaubien resided in Chicago. Actually, the life courses of these scions were perpetually unsynchronized. Between 1816 and 1834, they spent only two years — 1816 and 1817 — in Chicago simultaneously. And in those years, Madore's childish prattle most likely annoyed rather than engaged John Harris, six years his senior.

We may surmise, however, that a certain unspoken social relationship had grown up between the two young men. Madore's stepmother, Josette, had lived among the Kinzies as a servant and possibly as a nursemaid at a time when Kinzie wealth and prestige were at their zenith. John Harris's later attitude toward this part-Indian (or Métis) woman, whom he could have viewed alternatively as surrogate mother or Indian servant, probably determined his feelings about the part-Ottawa child Madore.

Kinzie and Beaubien both received the usual advantages available to sons of traders of middling rank; but in their earliest educational and occupational experiences one can see discrepancies subtly reflective of their separate cultures and racial identities. First schooling occurred informally, and at home. In Kinzie's case, a spelling book shipped in a tea chest was all that his tutor-cousin Bob Forsyth had to work with. Beaubien probably learned to read and cipher from a family member; his older brother Charles later ran a school for the children of J. B. and Josette Beaubien. Yet, unlike Kinzie, whose Indian education was gleaned primarily from the guarded and often dissembling lips of Métis servants, Beaubien was enveloped in a rich cultural and linguistic tradition openly transmitted to him by his maternal kin.

During the wartime exile of the Kinzie family, John Harris received several years of formal instruction at Detroit. His younger brother and sisters were likewise educated at Detroit or Middletown, Connecticut. When Madore's time came, however, his father rejected a French Catholic training at Detroit for the new Protestant missionary establishment at Niles, Michigan, run by Isaac McCoy. This school, ostensibly begun for the benefit of Potawatomi and Ottawa children, primarily attracted their Métis relatives. Madore was a bright pupil; he spent only two years, 1823-24, at the mission. Yet the experience was to fix his identity as an "Indian boy."

Ironically, of the two young men, it was Madore who was to receive the college education and Eastern connections most likely to win attention in the rapidly urbanizing milieu at Chicago after 1833. Between 1825 and 1828 he attended Hamilton College in upstate New York. His brother Charles was enrolled at Princeton. The fact seems to have been lost on Madore, however, that it was as "Indian boys" in a philanthropic experiment that McCoy's promising students were shipped to Eastern schools. He arrived back in Chicago in 1829 with aspirations to be a merchant, not an Indian trader like his father.

John Harris Kinzie, meanwhile, was learning the mysteries of the Indian trade. The elder John Kinzie's reputation had been sufficient to secure his son an apprenticeship at the big house on Mackinac Island, the inner sanctum of the American Fur Company. Between 1818 and 1823, under the direction of Astor's stern, Presbyterian agent, Kinzie sorted, weighed, and priced skins. He also cut and carted wood, balanced accounts, made up trade assortments, mastered various Algonkian languages and the violin, and learned to manage Indian clients and Canadian employees. All this knowledge came too late, however, and Kinzie could see how the world was turning. Following his long apprenticeship, he spent only three years in the company's employ as clerk and then trader at Prairie du Chien.

In 1826, Kinzie hitched himself to the rising political fortunes of Lewis Cass, governor of Michigan Territory and regional superintendent of Indian affairs. For the next three years, while part-Indian Madore affected Eastern airs, Anglo John Harris served as one of Cass's "Indian experts." He accompanied delegations to Washington, assisted at treaty negotiations, collected historical and cultural information for the superintendency, and compiled grammars and dictionaries. He gained particular familiarity with the Winnebago, and in 1829, after Cass became secretary of war, Kinzie was appointed Indian subagent at Fort Winnebago. John Harris's commitment to Indian society was of a different order from that of his father, however. In 1830 he married Juliette Magill of Middleton, Connecticut, the niece of his brother-in-law, Alexander Wolcott. Three years later, and with some regret on the part of the romance-struck Juliette who had come to regard the Winnebago as her "children," Kinzie resigned his Wisconsin post and struck out for civilization and Chicago.

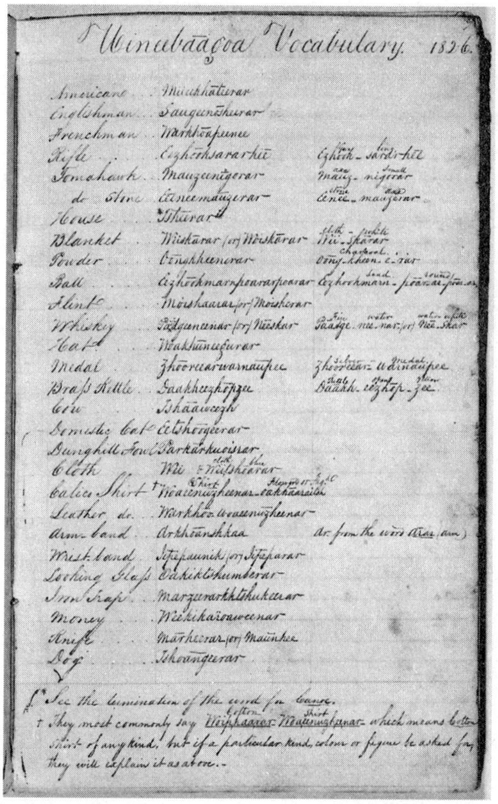
Winnebagoa Vocabulary. 1826.
American
Englishman
Frenchman
Rifle
Tomahawk
do Stone
House
Blanket
Powder
Ball
Flint
Whiskey
Hat
Medal
Brass Kettle
Cow
Domestic Cat
Dunghill Fowl
Cloth
Calico Shirt
Leather do.
Arm band
Wrist band
Looking Glass
Iron Trap
Money
Knife
Dog

The first page of the Winnebago grammar prepared by John H. Kinzie while serving as Indian subagent in Wisconsin, 1826.
(CHS, ICHi-14166)

When John Harris Kinzie returned in 1833 to lay out lots in the Kinzie Addition in anticipation of a real estate boom, the city was already experiencing birth pangs. The several years following incorporation were frivolous, heady, almost frantic. In this unsteady state, the paths of John Harris and Madore finally converged as the two temporarily functioned as culture brokers, interpreters between the old residents and the human deluge pouring in from the East. They were links to the past, thin pegs around which a giddy society whirled. But they were also trying out new roles and wrote permutations on old ones. Beaubien — at one moment the respectable citizen — invested in town lots, built a store on South Water Street, and acquired an American business partner from Pennsylvania, Valentine Boyer. In addition to sitting on the town's board of trustees for a year, he and his father and uncle organized Chicago's first Catholic church. And, in 1835, he married an Eastern seminary girl, his partner's impressionable eighteen-year-old old sister, Mary Boyer.

Beaubien also exploited his Indian savvy. In feathered headgear, whooping and hollering across the prairie after a pack of startled wolves, Madore captured the imagination of greenhorn Yankees. He was no doubt responsible for dubbing the dances that Chicago's respectable young men sponsored, "Grand Wabanos," after an all-night Potawatomi fire-handling display. Whether in feathers or black cravat, Madore Beaubien was, by all accounts, the "handsomest man in Chicago." And a devilish charmer.

Kinzie lacked Madore's studied elegance and youthful panache. But his name, political connections, and seriousness won him respect. Elected town president upon his arrival in Chicago, he established a forwarding and commissioning business with his brother-in-law, David Hunter; organized an Episcopal church, for which he generously donated the property (as the Beaubiens had done for the Catholic church); and set to developing the Kinzie property on the north side. He had a lighter side as well, and a shrewd understanding of the "at arms length" fashion in which Easterners liked to experience their Indian culture. An accomplished native dancer and mimic, Kinzie billed himself the star in the all-white Indian show which he and a group of Chicago lobbyists for the Canal Bill took to the state capital in 1835.

In that same year, a wedding took place in Chicago which newcomers of 1833-35 delighted in recalling years later. It united Therese LaFramboise, Métis cousin by marriage to Madore (and daughter of Joseph LaFramboise) with Thomas Watkins, the popular postal clerk and early schoolteacher. Watkins began by running off a few invitations, but the demand was so great that he finally invited the whole town. The affair drew together the disparate elements of the community and found Easterners painted, dressed and dancing like Indians, and reserved Métis women in black stroud and beaded leggings jigging with Irish laborers. It was the last gathering of its kind.

Thereafter, the fluid, frontier characteristics of Chicago began to dissipate as the population swelled into the thousands. By 1837, cleavages in the social fabric were apparent. "No trespassing" signs had been posted at Hardscrabble, and calling cards and private dances were beginning to replace the community-wide, come-one-come-all revelries of earlier years. On the north side, increasingly a Yankee preserve, the pretentious brick Lake House, the premiere first-class hotel in Chicago, rose in 1835, followed in 1837-38 by St. James Episcopal Cathedral. The Methodists, most of whom were unlettered Southerners, were "encouraged" to move their church building to the south side, alongside the Catholics. French-Indian families watched their Potawatomi relatives begin the sad trek to the western reservation and began to deliberate among themselves.

The speculative insanity which had kept Chicagoans and their hopes aloft for four years collapsed in 1837. The crash shook out the thousands of hapless investors and left a widening chasm between rich and poor at Chicago. It also confirmed the growing separation between old settlers and new. John Harris Kinzie survived the panic, but much diminished. He was perhaps the natural choice for mayor in the year of Chicago's incorporation as a city, but the election of 1837 went to a financial heavyweight, New Yorker William B. Ogden, a recent arrival in town. Thereafter, Kinzie relied upon a series of patronage appointments from the Democracy such as Collector of Tolls (from the year of the Canal's completion to 1861) and Receiver of Public Monies (1849-65). A mild and gentle man, whose name has been successfully bolstered by his wife's rosy portrait of the Kinzie family in her romantic history, *Wau-bun,* John Harris enjoyed a small local renown until his death in 1865. He helped to establish the Chicago Horticultural and the Chicago Historical societies and continued to entertain both visiting Indians and Eastern friends with his recollections. One gets the sense, however, that Chicago's new leaders trotted him out as their "old settler" and Indian expert more for amusement than enlightenment.

Madore Beaubien was one of those people who, as the Indians said, was thrown away. By 1838, he was financially embarrassed and deeply in debt to John K. Boyer, the father of his one-time business partner. Another Boyer, his wife, abandoned him shortly thereafter, vanishing from the historical record with their two babies, George and Susan. These events evidently pained Madore deeply. By 1840 he had made a decision. In that year, he cast his fate with the United Band of Potawatomi, Ottawa, and Chippewa, settling at Council Bluffs and accepting employment as an interpreter. Most of the mixed-blood families at Chicago eventually took this route. Subsequently, Madore removed with the Potawatomi to their reserve in Kansas, and in 1854 he married his cousin, the handsome widow Hardin, née Therese LaFramboise.

By the 1860s, after the Citizen Band of Potawatomi had elected to take up lands and citizenship, Madore founded a townsite at an oxbow in the Kansas River west of Topeka, on the road to California. Numerous other old settlers from Chicago and Milwaukee, long forgotten in the towns of their birth, came to reside in the township surrounding this ford, euphemistically called "Silver Lake," and Madore was given the honor of election as the town's first mayor. Beaubien's letters and interviews given during a last visit to Chicago for an old settlers' meeting in 1882 hint at a guarded resentment against the city and civilization whose race prejudice discarded him, but he must have taken some small satisfaction in the knowledge that he had been a "big man" somewhere. It was perhaps more than John Harris, surrounded and overwhelmed by the progressive enterprise of white society which claimed him, could say.

Epilogue: A magical change had taken place at Chicago during the 1830s. Few mourned the disappearance of the town's old settlers or the destruction of the fur trade community. Quite to the contrary. By 1840 Joseph Balestier, spokesman for the Eastern newcomers and the author of *The Annals of Chicago,* could proudly proclaim:

> Capacious warehouses and commodious dwellings have taken the place of the "log and bark houses, low filthy, and disgusting" — "The miserable race of men" have been superceded by a population distinguished for its intelligence and enterprise: and all the comforts of our Eastern homes are gathered around us.

Early Days on the Illinois & Michigan Canal

John M. Lamb

The long-awaited celebration of the opening of the Illinois & Michigan Canal occurred on April 16, 1848, when the *General Fry* arrived in Chicago. The boat, a large passenger packet weighing 150 tons and measuring 99 feet long and 18 feet wide, had been launched earlier at Lockport, Illinois. It made the twenty-nine-mile voyage to Bridgeport at a speed of five miles an hour, and the next day the Chicago *Weekly Journal* reported its arrival as follows:

> Yesterday was an eventful period in the history of our city, of the State and of the West. — It was the wedding of the Father of Rivers to our inland seas — a union of the Mississippi with Lake Michigan; . . . The first boat borne on the Illinois Canal passed safely through from Lockport to our city yesterday.
>
> At an early hour yesterday afternoon the whole city was in motion. Carriages, wagons and pedestrians were all on the move to Bridgeport, to welcome the first boat from below, while the propeller [driven] "Rossetter," with the Mayor and the committee of reception, accompanied by a large number of citizens, proceeded by the way of the river.
>
> By three o'clock it seemed as if the whole city had been emptied down at "Lock No. 1." The splendid machinery for pumping water into the canal was in operation, and was examined with great satisfaction by all present, working as it did, with such clock-like regularity. About half past four the "GENL. FRY" hove in sight upon the ribbon like sheet of water which was stretching far away to the south-west, and a volunteer escort dashed off, carriages, ladies on horseback, and horsemen, to meet her as she came on, crowded to her utmost, with ladies and gentlemen from the interior.
>
> At a little after five she reached the lock, where "three times three" were given for the boat and delegation, and the bands striking up enlivening airs, she passed easily in the river, The FIRST BOAT THROUGH. . . .
>
> Upon the conclusion of the address of welcome by the Mayor, GENL. FRY of Lockport introduced to the crowd G. D. A. PARKS, Esq. of Lockport, who spoke. . . .

The first boat to arrive from La Salle, Illinois, the western terminus of the Canal, came in on April 24th. This was the *General*

Thornton (named, like its sister ship, for a canal commissioner), and it was loaded with produce from New Orleans. The *General Thornton* was built and owned by Isaac Hardy, a contractor who built the first lock, at Lockport. Hardy, a brother-in-law of William Gooding, chief canal engineer, also ran a packet boat line on the Canal a little later. His ship made history doubly, for the produce it carried was reloaded onto a steamer bound for Buffalo, New York — where it arrived two weeks before the Erie Canal was opened to navigation. Knowing full well that construction of the Erie Canal had begun in 1817, almost twenty years before the construction of their own Canal started, Illinoisans cheered the news, and a proud Abraham Lincoln brought it to the attention of the nation in a speech before the House of Representatives.

In its early days, the Illinois & Michigan Canal contained two "extra" locks designed to raise boats from the Chicago River to the "summit" of the Canal. One was right at the River, the other some miles away. A pumping station brought water from the Chicago River into the Canal, and additional water between Chicago and Lockport (where the first "regular" lock was located) was channeled into the Canal from the Calumet River.

The pumping station, or hydraulic works, at Chicago was considered the engineering marvel of the day. Designed by Alfred Guthrie (although some claim that honor for John M. Van Osdell, Chicago's first architect), it pumped seven thousand cubic feet of water a minute. The Canal Board of Trustees described it in a circular:

> The building in which the engines are placed is of brick, resting upon a foundation of stone. It is 166 feet long by 55 feet wide, with foundations on the water fronts laid with great care 6 feet below the ordinary stage of the river, or 14 feet below the surface of the water in the Canal.
>
> The machinery for raising the water from the river into the Canal, consists of two large steam engines, one of which drives four cast iron cylinder pumps, of 54 inches diameter and 7 feet long each. And the other gives motion to a wheel of 32 feet diameter, the water being lifted by sixteen float boards or buckets 7 feet long, working in a trough nearly water tight, and delivered into a flume which communicates with a basin, and this again with the main canal.
>
> Each engine is furnished with six cylinder boilers 26 feet long and 42 inches diameter, each with two flues of 16 inches diameter. The furnaces being arranged for burning either wood or coal.

Naturally, it was one of the sights to which Mayor "Long John" Wentworth escorted the Prince of Wales when his highness visited the city in 1860.

The passenger packet boat was at first an important part of the commerce of the Canal. In 1848, soon after the Canal was opened, the Chicago *Daily Journal* ran an advertisement for the Illinois & Michigan Canal Packet Boat Co., informing the public of "a daily line of Packets between Chicago, LaSalle and Peru, which are furnished in the most comfortable style possible, and nothing will be wanting on the part of the Captains and Company's Agents to make this mode of conveyance attractive and agreeable." The boats left Chicago at 8 A.M. from the foot of Washington Street, the price of a ticket was $4, and the trip took over twenty hours.

While undoubtedly more comfortable than the stagecoach, the packet boat does not appear to have been "attractive and agreeable," as advertised. Sir Arthur Cunynghame, an English army officer who traveled in the United States in 1850, took a Canal trip from Chicago to La Salle that fall. In his book *A Glimpse of the Great Western Republic,* he described the trip:

TOLLS,

ESTABLISHED UPON THE

ILLINOIS AND MICHIGAN CANAL,

FOR THE YEAR 1857.

On Freight Boats, per mile, - - - - - - - - - 2½ cents.
On Passenger Boats, per mile, - - - - - - - - - - 3 do.
On each Passenger 8 years old and upwards, (60 lbs. baggage allowed free of toll,) per mile. 2 mills.
On the following articles, per 1,000 lbs. per mile, and in the same proportion for greater or lesser weight, the rates are as follows:

	Mills.		Mills.		Mills.		Mills.
Ale,	5	Coke,	2	Lime, common,	3	Rye,	3
Agricultural Implements,	6	Clay,	1	Lime, hydraulic,	3	Salt, in sacks or bbls.,	3
Animals, (domestic,)	3	Eggs,	5	Lead, pipes, sheet, and roll,	4	Seeds,	4
Beef,	3	Flour,	4	Lead, pigs and bars,	1	Saleratus,	5
Beans,	3	Fruit, home,	5	Merchandise, including—		Soap,	5
Beer,	5	Fruit, foreign,	6	dry goods, groceries, hardware,		Sumach,	5
Bones, (rough,)	2	Fish,	4	cutlery, crockery, and glassware,		Scales,	6
Butter,	5	Furniture, Household,	8	and all articles not specified,	5	Sugar,	5
Baggage,	5	Feathers,	8	Malt,	4	Stoves and hollow ware,	6
Beeswax,	6	Furs & Peltries, Buffalo		Molasses, in hhds. or bbls.,	5	Sleds and Sleighs,	5
Bacon,	3	and Deer skins,	6	Meal,	4	Shorts and screenings,	3
Brooms,	5	Grease,	4	Marble, wrought,	8	Ship stuff,	3
Broom Handles,	5	Glue,	5	Marble, unwrought.	5	Spikes,	4
Broom Corn,	3	Grindstones,	4	Mill Stones,	5	Starch,	5
Buhr Blocks,	6	Gypsum,	4	Machinery,	5	Shot,	3
Barley,	3	Glass and Glass ware,	5	Mechanics' tools,	5	Steel,	5
Buckwheat,	3	Hemp,	4	Nuts,	5	Spirits, except whisky,	6
Blooms,	5	Hides, dry,	6	Nails,	4	Staves,	3
Bran,	3	Hides, green.	5	Oats,	3	Sand and other earth,	1
Bark, Tanner's,	3	Horns and Tips,	5	Oil Cake,	3	Stone, cut and sawed,	3
Barrels, empty,	5	Hair,	5	Oil, Linseed and Corn,	5	Tallow,	5
Coffee,	5	Hops,	5	Oil, Lard,	5	Tar,	4
Cheese,	5	Hams,	4	Peas,	3	Tombstones, not marble,	6
Crackers,	5	Household furniture, ac-		Provisions, salt and fresh,	3	Trees, shrubs, and plants,	4
Cordage,	5	companied by and be-		Pork,	3	Tobacco, not manufactured,	5
Cotton, raw, in bales	3	longing to emigrants,	8	Pot and Pearl ashes,	5	Tobacco, manufactured,	6
Cotton yarn and batting,	5	Hay and Fodder,	3	Porter,	5	Tin plate,	5
Coopers' ware,	5	Heading,	3	Pumps,	5	Turpentine,	5
Carpenter & Joiners' work,	5	Hoops and materials for,	3	Potters' ware,	5	Varnish,	5
Carriages,	5	Hubs, boat knees, and bolts,	2	Pitch,	4	Vinegar,	5
Candles,	5	Iron, pig and scrap,	4	Potatoes & other vegetables,	3	Whisky and high wines,	3
Corn,	3	Iron, Railroad,	4	Paper,	5	Wool,	5
Cider,	5	Iron, wrought or cast,	5	Powder,	8	Wooden ware,	5
Clocks,	8	Ice,	1	Rags,	5	Wagons and other vehicles,	6
Charcoal,	2	Leather,	5	Rice,	5	White Lead and paints,	5
Coal,	1	Lard,	5	Rosin,	4	Wheat,	3

On the following articles, toll per mile will be computed by number or measure:

On each 1000 feet of Lumber, per mile, - - - 1¼ cent.
" " 1000 " Siding, " " - - 6 mills.
" " 1000 Lath or Shingles, " " - - - 2 "
" " 1000 Brick, " " - - 1 cent.
" " 100 cubic feet of Timber, hewed or round, if transported in boats, per mile, - - 1 "

On each 100 cubic feet same, in rafts, per mile, - - 2 cts.
" " 100 split Posts or fence Rails, " - 1 "
" " cord of Wood for fuel, (from Lockport,) per mile, 1 "
" " cubic yd., (27 cub ft.) dress'd or dimension Stone, 6 mills
" " " " " " undressed or rubble " 8 "

The weight of box, bag, crate, vessel, or thing in which any article may be contained, shall be added to the weight of the article itself, and toll computed accordingly.

By order of the Board of Trustees,

Canal Office, Lockport, 1857.

WILLIAM GOODING, Sec'y.

☞ Wood transported from any point on the Canal below Lockport, will be subject to no additional charge, that is to say, the rates per cord will be 80 cents from all points below Lockport to Bridgeport, or vice versa.

Tolls on the Illinois & Michigan Canal in 1857, as published by William Gooding.
(CHS, ICHi-05834)

On Saturday evening, the 12th of October, about 5 P.M., I embarked on board the canal boat, the "Queen of the Prairies," bound for La Salle, a town situated south-west of Chicago, about 100 miles distant, and at the head of the navigable portion of the Illinois River. The cabin of this canal boat was about 50 feet in length, 9 feet wide, and 7 feet high. We numbered about 90 passengers within this confined space, in which we were to sleep, eat, and live; the nominal duration of our passage was twenty hours, but it eventually proved to be twenty five; our baggage was secured on the roof of the boat, and covered with canvass, to screen it from the effects of the weather. A sort of divan surrounded the cabin, the portion appropriated to the ladies screened off during the night by a curtain.

For the first few miles we, in company with three more canal boats, were towed by a small steamer, but having passed the locks, not very distant from Chicago, three horses were attached, which towed us smoothly along at the rate of five miles an hour.

Other inconveniences with which Cunynghame had to contend included poor meals and sleeping berths stacked like library shelves into which the passengers were tightly packed. The windows were nailed shut for fear that malaria would creep in from the surrounding lowlands, and the lack of ventilation trapped "nauseous vapors" which caused the author to awake with a terrible headache. Things were much better after the boat reached La Salle and Cunynghame was able to check into Isaac Hardy's "fine" new hotel. But the author had sad news to report about that enterprising contractor: Hardy had overextended himself financially, had become bankrupt, and was about to lose his fine new hotel.

Cunynghame, good reporter that he was, appears to have embarked at Chicago on a quiet day, for he recounts no difficulties with the tender of Lock No. 1, P. Fox. There were seventeen regular locks on the Canal (not counting the extra two at Chicago), and each of the locks had a tender, most of whom lived in a house by the lock. Mr. Fox, like the others, had to open the gates to let ships enter, and close them after the entry was completed. He was paid $300 a year, had to be continuously available (even in winter, when the Canal was closed), and was not allowed to sell liquor.

Like the other lock tenders, Fox soon discovered that his job was not simply a matter of opening and closing the gates. At his, the first lock, three or four boats would arrive simultaneously, towed up the Chicago River by a towboat. Locking a boat in took about fifteen minutes, and each boat had a captain who wasn't likely to yield place to any other captain on the scene. It is hard to believe that, in an era when full speed was five miles an hour, a delay of fifteen minutes or so would create the difficulties it did, but here is Fox's own report of some of his troubles. On September 22, 1851, he wrote to the canal superintendent to ask for help:

> I rush to have some instrucktions from you Concerning the Locking of Boats Towed up the river[.] my rule has ben to Lock the Boats in the same order that they Hitch to the Tow Boats[.] the reason why I call on you for is this 2 Boats the St. Lawrence and the Walter Smith Towed up to the Lock to gether a bout ten Days ago[.] the Smith made Fast the Tow Boat first[.] after Casting off from the Tow Boat the St. Lawrence being heavey loaded held her headway and Entered the Lock about half her Lenght when the Smith weged fast in besyolen her[.] Now Both Cald on me for the first Lockage. according to my former rule in this Case l made the St. Lawrence Hawl out and Locked the Smith up first
>
> Mr. Notingham [of the *St. Lawrence*] tell me this morning that he stated the Case to Mr Wm Gooding and to Mr Singer [canal officials at Lockport] [.] he says that they tell him that I was wrong that I had no wright to interfear with Boats Below the Lock[.] Now if I am wrong I want to have som Directions in the matter that I may be right hereafter[.] it Frequently happens we have 6 or 8 Boats Formed in below the Lock all want to be Locked first[.] if left to Boatman to Decide who should first take the Lock I think weol have some gloureous Fights every Day

The same year, the lock tender at Marseilles (Lock No. 11) sent a not-very-different report:

> Sir on the evening of the 11 [of April] the Boat Montsuma came upt to the Lock with out Light or even given any Signal at all and Run into the lock and the first that we heard was the wickett stanchion [used to open and close the sluice gate at the bottom of the lock gate] and then the gate[.] we than told them not to tuch the Lock gate and forbid him but he forst his way through in spite of all we

could say or do[.] he having a lot of pasangers and they and the captain abused us in all posible way they could[.]

A dispute over waterpower between the towns of Joliet and Lockport caused headaches even earlier for the keeper at Joliet (Lock No. 5).

The promise of waterpower was one of the most important assets of the Canal to towns and town sites along its course. Theoretically, Lockport would have had the most waterpower, because it was here that the Canal made its sharpest drop, about sixty feet in five miles. The possibility that this circumstance would be fully exploited caused a great deal of consternation in Joliet, Lockport's older neighbor. Joliet had achieved a degree of importance because of the waterpower it obtained from the Des Plaines River, but the plan was for the Canal to divert that water. Jolietans (actually at the time Joliet was called Juliet) believed that the Canal officials were overly solicitous of Lockport's interests, for most of them lived there. A letter to the Joliet *Signal* on March 8, 1847, complained that the amount of waterpower being planned at Lockport would mean insufficient water for navigation on the rest of the Canal:

> These statements of the Chief Engineer [William Gooding] which he sends forth with his annual report, seem tinged with too much partiality to the place of *his residence.* I have no objection to the creation of all the water power in Lockport . . . that can reasonably be had, but it appears to me rather extravagant that the waste waster of a canal 60 by 6 feet prism, will be sufficient with 20 feet head to carry 30 run of stone without seriously obstructing navigation.

This argument, over the water level in Joliet and the supposed machinations of the Lockport Canal officials, reached something of a climax in 1849. The Joliet *Signal,* on July 10, took exception to the Lockport *Telegraph*'s report on the number of cholera deaths in Joliet. The editor of the *Signal* admitted that deaths had occurred, but he attributed them to the decisions of the Canal officials:

> Taking this, in connection with the conduct of the Canal Superintendent [Edward Talcott] in having the basin in this place drained, there certainly is displayed a most unwarrantable policy on the part of a few at Lockport to injure a neighboring town. — The reports of the Board of Health show to what extent cholera has raged here, and beyond question assigned the principal cause of its prevalence. Upon the shoulders of the individual who ordered the basin drawn off, rests the charge of a great portion of the sickness and deaths which have occurred in this place.

That inflammatory statement produced results — the tender of Lock No. 5 was assaulted by an angry mob which prevented him from opening the lock gate and then proceeded to throw him into the Canal. On July 14, the canal superintendent reported on this and related incidents to canal trustee Joseph B. Wells:

> Sometime since a committee of the citizens [of Joliet] called upon Mr. Gooding in relation to this matter and he assured them that the pool between the two dams should be kept as near full as practicable without wasting water over the lower dam.
>
> From my interview yesterday I am satisfied that malicious persons have opened the gates at night to cause difficulty, and that in the present stage of feeling with a few (I do not believe it to be universal) there is a manifest disposition to exaggerate and magnify every thing pertaining to the matter.

> Several of the citizens, have interfered to prevent the Lockkeeper from a proper discharge of his duty, by closing the gates — and recently by throwing him into the Canal when he was in the act of opening the gates — In short they have so intimidated him that he says he dare not discharge his duty from fear of personal violence.

Canal Superintendent Talcott threatened legal action, among other things, and further violence was avoided. Positions did not alter much, however, and on July 24, the *Signal* stated that Joliet would stand firm against Lockport and the Canal officials:

> We reiterate again that we are every day more strongly convinced that the act of drawing the water off was premeditated and intended for the injury of our town. That the people of Lockport approve of such conduct, we can not persuade ourselves to believe. In conclusion, we assure the *Telegraph* that we feel not the slightest jealousy towards Lockport, neither do the people of this place, but at the same time, we will not submit in silence to be trodden upon by a few canal officials who hold property in that village.

By 1878, George Woodruff, a Will County historian, was able to view the Joliet-Lockport rivalry with a certain humor. The old quarrels had been laid to rest, Joliet had become much larger and much more important than Lockport, and Woodruff was, after all, on the winning side. Discussing the internal conflicts of Joliet, he added:

> But we had a common enemy — Lockport — and, like Jews during the siege of Jerusalem, we used, temporarily, to forget our domestic quarrels and combine to fight the common foe. The [Joliet] *Signal* and the [Joliet] *True Democrat* let each other alone occasionally, and both pitched into the Lockport *Telegraph*. The Canal authorities seemed, at least to our jaundiced eyes, to throw all their influence to favor and build up a rival city. We issued to dilate largely against Archer road and the Canal basin and the Canal office, etc., etc. One thing which specially galled us was a map, which was reported to be drawn and exhibited to speculators and persons seeking a location, displaying the Canal route from Chicago to Ottawa, on which all the villages were noted, with one exception. There were Romeo and Athens, Kepotaw and Scotchtown, Lockport and Channahon, etc., etc.; but the only thing to indicate the whereabouts of Juliet was a spot marked McKee's Dam. That was a good joke; and if we did not meet it with something equally foolish, it was not for want of disposition.

Some of the problems on the Canal were not due to human fractiousness or municipal competition. Some were economic. In 1850, for example, 22,614 passengers took the Canal from Chicago to La Salle, and about 17,000 traveled from La Salle to Chicago. Three years later, the Rock Island Railroad was completed. The new railroad line paralleled the Canal and offered faster transportation. The Canal's passenger business rapidly faded.

But what of freight? Big ships, laden with freight, could compete successfully with any railroad. Alas, the Canal had not been built for them. During extremely dry summers, the Illinois River became so shallow that large steamboats could not reach La Salle, where the Canal terminated.

By the 1860s, there was already considerable agitation for large-scale improvements. In 1862, Rep. Francis P. Blair introduced a bill in Congress to enlarge the Illinois & Michigan Canal and to improve the Illinois River channel. Great efforts were made to support this bill. On February 12, 1862, the Chicago Board of Trade petitioned:

> . . . for the enlargement of the Illinois and Michigan Canal, so as freely to pass vessels of war, gunboats, and schooners between Lake Michigan and the Mississippi River. In favor of early passage of the bill, your memorialists beg leave to urge as sufficient and controlling reason, that when, a few months ago, circumstances threatened the sundering of our peaceful relations with Great Britain, a long list of English gunboats was published, showing that an immense fleet might, as soon as the ice was out of the St. Lawrence Canals, be thrown upon the lakes, by which our commerce, more than equaling in value the entire foreign commerce of the nation, could be destroyed, and our lake cities become an easy prey to a conquering enemy.

While the Board of Trade might couch its plea in terms of war and the threat of enemy attack, cities down the Canal from Chicago had more pressing reasons for wanting more water in the Canal. The Joliet *True Democrat* took note on June 7, 1862, of the tremendous stench coming from the Canal, "enough to make a horse sick." This, it reported, was caused by pumping out the Chicago River. The Joliet paper prayed that the pumps at Bridgeport would keep working so that not only would the Chicago River be cleaned, but downstream as well, and that "water in this section become settled before warm weather and the season for juveniles to go in swimming." The fact was that the Chicago River was becoming an open sewer — the only way to alleviate this condition was to send the water down to the Gulf of Mexico, for the United States would not allow the River's sewage to be dumped into Lake Michigan.

In June 1863, a National-Ship Canal Convention was held in Chicago to support Blair's bill. Some five thousand delegates met in a tent in Lake Park (now Grant Park) and called for the enlargement of the Illinois & Michigan Canal, the Erie Canal, and the New York canals. William Gooding proposed to dam the Illinois River and enlarge the Canal so that the largest steamboat on the Mississippi could travel to Chicago. And still the bill did not pass.

Some five thousand delegates met in this "monster" tent for the National-Ship Canal Convention in 1863. The assembled were warned by the sign at the left to "look out for pickpockets."
(CHS, ICHi-05833)

The festivities at the long-awaited opening of the "deep cut" channel of the Illinois & Michigan Canal in 1871.
(CHS, ICHi-05836)

In 1866, General James Wilson surveyed the Illinois River for the United States secretary of war and recommended the enlargement of the Illinois & Michigan Canal to a width of 160 feet and a minimum depth of 7 feet. His plan also called for a channel of similar depth from Lockport on, created by building a series of locks and dams on the Des Plaines and Illinois rivers. Congress again refused to act.

Meanwhile, the Chicago River continued to ferment, and the canal superintendent was urged to pump more fiercely at the Bridgeport works. In June 1867, the Chicago Board of Public Works requested that the pumps be run at full capacity, and that the Canal's banks be raised to hold the higher water.

The problem was finally solved, or so it was thought, in 1871, by eliminating the first two extra locks and digging a deeper channel on the summit level of the Canal. This deepening of the channel — known as the "deep cut" — had actually been proposed very early, in the 1830s, when plans for the Canal's construction were being formulated. Governor Joseph Duncan had planned, in 1834, to build the Canal large enough to accommodate steamboats coming from Lake Michigan. William Gooding had envisioned a canal sixty feet wide and six feet deep that would be cut deep enough through the rock of the Valparaiso moraine to allow direct passage from the Chicago River to the Canal. Benjamin Wright, the chief engineer of the Erie Canal, had also concurred in the practicality of the "deep cut" after studying the project in 1837. However, the state of Illinois had not been able to raise the capital necessary to finance the "deep cut" and finally settled for the extra locks and the marvelous hydraulic works at Chicago.

The "deep cut" project cost $3,000,000. The pumping station was no longer needed, since the Chicago River now flowed directly into the Canal. With no more locks to tend, the lockkeepers were eliminated. As *Frank Leslie's Illustrated Newspaper* put it:

> The magic by which this foul ditch has been sluiced, and its current directed toward the Gulf of Mexico resembles in principle the method taken by Hercules to cleanse the Augean Stables.

If the Chicago River was the Augean Stables, Hercules' labors were not yet over. In 1881, the city would be required to build another pumping station and, finally later in that decade, to begin constructing the Chicago Sanitary Canal. But in 1871, it appeared that Chicago had cleansed its river by reversing its flow and, in the process, had sent such a flood of water downstream as to provide all the promises made for the Canal in the 1830s and 1840s, both in waterpower and better navigation. And the festivities were, if anything, more prolonged in 1871 than they had been in 1848.

A Furor of Benevolence

Beverly Gordon

While most Chicagoans are aware of the significant symbolic and real impact of the 1893 World's Columbian Exposition held in their city, many do not know that Chicago sponsored two other major fairs of similar cultural importance much earlier in the century. To raise funds for the United States Sanitary Commission — the government agency that provided Union soldiers with medical and nonmilitary supplies during the Civil War — women's aid groups throughout the North held a series of regional fund-raising events called sanitary fairs between 1863 and 1865. Chicago was the site of both the first and last large-scale sanitary fairs; in the words of Ann Hosmer, an active participant in both, the city represented the "alpha and omega of the Sanitary Fair phenomenon."

Fund-raising fairs were not new. Women who wished to support a common cause had been holding "ladies' fairs" in England and the United States since the 1830s. They prepared refreshments and small items such as pincushions, mats, and caps and offered their food and fancywork for sale in a town hall or other public space. Visitors, lured by the promise of conviviality, good food, and entertainment, came to buy. Most early fairs were set up to assist charitable causes such as a missionary society or a group of destitute widows and were organized and patronized by women of particular church organizations. There were also larger urban fairs with more political purpose, however, such as the Anti-Slavery Fair held annually in Boston from 1842 through the 1850s. Abolitionist sympathizers from all over New England contributed to these fairs, and novel attractions such as an illuminated Christmas tree hung with presents which sold for a few cents drew in large crowds of curious townspeople. Boston-area women determined to raise funds to complete the Bunker Hill Monument also held a regional "Monument Fair" in Charlestown, Massachusetts, in 1840.

The largest fund-raising fair of the antebellum era, which was also political, was English. The Anti-Corn-Law League, a group devoted to repealing legislation which disproportionately taxed the poor, drew 100,000 people to a bazaar in London's Covent Garden in 1845. As at American fairs, women of various towns were asked to contribute their work, and communities from around the country had their own displays. Mechanics and farmers, asked to donate foods for the bazaar, did so in great numbers.

Inspired by the fund-raising fairs of her youth in New England, Mary Livermore, an associate manager of the Chicago branch of the U.S. Sanitary Commission, proposed a fair to benefit the Union soldiers. The success of this first sanitary fair in 1863 inspired other cities to launch their own events.
(CHS, ICHi-22144)

When the Civil War broke out in 1861, women of the North quickly formed local aid societies. Most of their energy went into sewing, knitting, and cooking for the soldiers, but they also staged several fund-raising fairs in the early years of the war. Some fairs were held to earn money for materials to make soldiers' shirts and bedding or to purchase reading matter or other amenities. The proceeds of other fairs were donated directly to the Sanitary Commission. There was a citywide fair of this type in Lowell, Massachusetts, early in 1863, and Boston was astir with plans for a soldier's fair shortly after. In the summer of 1863 a number of impromptu children's fairs in support of the soldiers were held on private lawns in Chicago, presided over by young people ages nine to sixteen. Children's fairs, like their adult counterparts, featured cushions, toilet mats, bookmarks, dolls, and candy.

So, in 1863, when Mary Livermore and Jane Hoge, the "lady managers" of the Chicago branch of the U.S. Sanitary Commission, proposed a grand-scale fund-raising fair for the Northwest, it was not without precedent. Mary Livermore had grown up in Boston and attended schools in Charlestown, site of the Monument Fair. She was probably well aware of the mechanics and efficacy of the regional fair. In her reminiscences of the war, Livermore claimed that the men of the commission were skeptical about the fair, but she and her twenty-six fellow organizers were confident that it would replenish the treasury. In their circular announcing the fair, they confidently projected a possible profit of $25,000.

The women called on every aid society, prohibition group, and religious congregation in the northwestern states (Illinois, Wisconsin, Michigan, Minnesota, Indiana, Iowa) to solicit donations from their members, much as the Anti-Slavery Society and Bunker Hill Monument Fair committees had called on their constituencies in the past. Like their predecessors, they staged the event in an available public space (Bryan Hall, on Clark Street between Randolph and Washington streets) and saw that decorations transformed it into a festive environment. The lower part of the hall featured a large, well-outfitted restaurant serving full-course dinners. As many as 1,500 gentlemen who ordinarily dined in downtown eating establishments were expected to eat at the hall on any one night. According to the circular announcing the fair, such a restaurant was also "an inevitable accessory to all Fairs held in Chicago."

The fair's profit far exceeded even the most optimistic expectations — approximately $80,000 was the final net figure earned. The profit reflects the enthusiasm and excitement with which the fair was greeted, and it is a good measure of the importance of the event for the people of the Northwest and the nation at large. Contemporary sources, including newspapers and the writings of Mary Livermore, speak of the patriotic zeal and "fair mania" that gripped the city and its environs. "Such a furor of benevolence had never been known!" exclaimed Livermore in *My Story of the War.* "Men [they caught the spirit and joined in once the fair became a reality], women and children, corporations and business firms, religious societies, and political organizations all vied with one another enthusiastically as to who should do the most for the Fair." The German community worked particularly hard; their displays alone raised $6,000.

Even allowing for nineteenth-century hyperbole and romanticization, one cannot help being impressed by the accounts of the fair and the sense of how deeply the cause touched the lives of everyone, even in the most remote communities. States around the Northwest were "ransacked" for contributions — machinery that could be inspected by fairgoers and sometimes raffled off (manufacturers contributed goods such as stoves, plows, wagons, and pianos); produce that could be sold or used in the restaurant (farmers contributed barrels of crops such as potatoes, sorghum, or wheat); bizarre or unique items to be displayed in the Curiosity Shop; paintings, statues, and engravings that could be displayed in the Art Gallery; and any imaginable object that could be offered for sale. The very personal response to the cause is seen in the lists of donations to the fair. Selections from the list of donations from the Ladies Aid Society of Madison, Wisconsin, for example, indicate the intimate involvement of individuals:

Miss Nancy H. Smith	1 shell hanging basket
Mrs. James Morrison	2 infant's shirts
Miss Edith Billings	1 bead collar
Mrs. J. H. Carpenter	1 complete needlebook
Mrs. A. Morse	1 breakfast shawl
Mrs. N. H. Watson	1 pr. Infant's embroidered shoes
	3 prs. gents' socks
	1 sacque
Miss Florence Hastings	1 doll's cape, 1 pr. cushions
Mrs. Professor Sterling	1 infant's skirt
Mrs. J. C. Prichard	1 watch case, 1 transparency
Mrs. E. S. Oakley	1 basket wax blackberries
Miss Bertha Pratt	1 oil painting
Mrs. William Wyman	3 cans peaches, 5 bowls jelly
Mrs. E. D. Illsley	1 doz. plated forks
Mrs. Hoyt	1 doz. photographs of a famous guerilla

Several young Madison boys also donated what they could. Master Willie Sherwin gave two bookmarks, and Sidney Cole and Fred Prithcard donated beaded mats. Girls often worked together to prepare contributions. The School Girls Soldier's Aid Society of the Fourth Ward of Milwaukee, for example, was comprised of twelve girls under the age of thirteen who did all their work on Saturday afternoons. In addition to cushions, watch cases, and penwipers, the girls donated such unexplained items as a "French fender holder" and a "gentleman's horror." People

Donations to sanitary fairs ranged from the grandiose — such as the original copy of the Emancipation Proclamation given by Abraham Lincoln — to simple items like this potholder. Its political message recalls the antislavery fairs held in Boston during the 1840s and 1850s. *(CHS, 1969.1737)*

also contributed items they had previously purchased, such as Polish boots, china ornaments, and Chinese vases.

Clearly, this was a "people's" fair — everyone, no matter how young or geographically distant, could become involved and feel he or she had made a difference in some small way. This was satisfying on many levels. One felt gratified in doing something to affect the lot of the soldiers, who were fighting the war or trying to recover from wounds under truly appalling conditions. The satisfaction of being part of the most talked-about event of the year, an event that was giving the frontier areas of the "Great Northwest" a sense of identity and importance in the eyes of the rest of the nation, was important, too. Finally, the fair was a happy, even uplifting event in a time of difficulty and sorrow, and it caught the imagination of the people and gave them something to work for. To work for the fair was to counteract the demoralization of the war.

The people of the Northwest were not disappointed when they came to the "Great Fair." If they had arrived on the opening day they could have participated in a major holiday parade to Bryan Hall. The usual affairs of the city were suspended — post offices, courts, schools, factories, and stores were all closed — and the enormous procession included marching bands, farmers with wagonloads of vegetables, decorated horses, and waving banners. If they had arrived on a later day, perhaps on one of the special excursion trains provided by the railroads, they still would have been subjected to "densely packed" crowds. Daily attendance averaged about 6,000, and they might have waited a few hours to get into the hall. Once inside, they were continually elbowed by fellow fairgoers as anxious to see everything as they were.

The decor of the main hall, according to contemporary sources, was pleasing and festive. The "leading architect of the city" (his name was not given) was responsible for the overall interior design, and further decoration was entrusted to a committee of German artists. The hall was arranged with two semicircles of double booths and featured a two-story octagonal pagoda as its centerpiece. A band played on the upper floor of this structure. Red, white, and blue flags and bunting were suspended and festooned from the ceiling and arches and wrapped around supporting columns. The adjacent hall, which was used for entertainment, was similarly draped and also included sculpted busts and patriotic mottoes tacked to the walls. Evergreen boughs and wreaths were arranged around the halls, adding a pungent aroma to the sensory onslaught of the thousands of things to see (sales tables were continually replenished and never looked depleted) and the press and din of the crowds.

The Curiosity Shop section of the fair was visually overwhelming. In the true nineteenth-century style, it was a hodgepodge of "natural and artificial curiosities" displayed in temporary quarters in the rooms of the nearby courthouse. Battle-torn flags, both Union and Rebel, were displayed with other war mementos such as pistols, shells, camp stools, slave shackles, pieces of cloth made by secessionist families, and specimens of moss or cactus from different battlefields of the South. Non-war curiosities included lichens, algae, and the like, and Indian specimens donated by a missionary to the Menominee. The biggest "trophy" of all, the original copy of the Emancipation Proclamation donated by President Abraham Lincoln, was featured in its own separate display. Auctioned to the highest bidder, it commanded $3,000.

The Art Gallery was housed in yet another nearby hall. The space was subdivided into small alcoves, their walls covered with art. Most of the works were loaned for the occasion (some came from as far away as Pittsburgh), but several Chicago artists donated their work to the cause. This gallery was a major feature of the fair, and about 25,000 people visited it. Public interest was so great that it was kept open two weeks longer than the fair itself, and 7,000 catalogues were sold. Chicago was an industrial frontier city, and the age of the public museum had not yet arrived. A gallery of this type, therefore, was a major cultural achievement. Several of the "most attractive and cultivated ladies of the Northwest" were on hand in the gallery to interpret the art to the "uninitiated," and a visit to the gallery must have given patrons a sense of another kind of social refinement as well.

Understandably, this first fair left Chicago and the Northwest with a sense of accomplishment and solidarity, even euphoria. Other cities, impressed with the results, caught the fair mania and followed with their own fairs in rapid succession. After the Boston fair in December, Americans patterned a rash of fairs on the Chicago model, trying to outdo it and all that followed. In addition to fairs in small cities (such as Yonkers and Warwick, New York; South Adams, Massachusetts; and Wheeling, West Virginia), large events appeared in Rochester, New York, and Cincinnati, Ohio, by Christmas of 1863. The Brooklyn and Long Island Fair and the Albany Relief Bazaar both opened in February 1864, followed shortly by the Northern Ohio Sanitary Fair (Cleveland), the Poughkeepsie, New York, fair, the Metropolitan Fair (New York City), the Mississippi Valley Fair (St. Louis), and in June, simultaneous events in Pittsburgh, Philadelphia, and Dubuque, Iowa.

The succeeding major fairs were larger, more elaborate, and more financially rewarding than the Northwestern Fair; Cincinnati netted more than $275,000, Brooklyn, $403,000, and New York and Philadelphia, each more than $1,000,000. Organizers realized that the larger the fair, the larger the profits would be. Almost immediately following Chicago's first event, the Cincinnati fair committee decided not to rely solely on existing structures, but to erect large buildings especially for the fair. This practice became standard. The Philadelphia committee sited its new buildings on a coordinated 200,000-square-foot fairground.

Simple displays of goods and festooned flags and evergreen boughs were not elaborate enough for these larger fairs. Halls were transformed into "fairylands"; individual booths were no longer mere tables heaped with goods but were outfitted as gypsy tents or as tableaux representative of exotic places. In the Turkish Booth in Rochester, for example, a "Grand Turk" sat smoking in his oriental trappings. Roman and Calabrian peasants in holiday attire sold statuettes next door in "Italy." Costumes and stage sets were augmented by dramatic activities. Several fairs had Dutch or New England kitchens — thematic restaurants where apple paring, quilting parties, and similar activities were ritualistically carried out. In Brooklyn a married couple reenacted their nuptial ceremony in colonial costume for visitors who had purchased tickets to their "New England Wedding." Environments were also transformed through the use of plants, flowers, and fountains. The Horticultural Departments in Philadelphia, Pittsburgh, and Cleveland were actual "natural" environments with mazes of paths, lakes, waterfalls, hillsides, and exotic palm and banana trees.

The second Northwestern Fair was predicated on these intervening events. Chicago was anxious to show that it would not be outdone. Jane Hoge and Mary Livermore once again acted as coordinators, reluctantly at first because of the amount of work involved. The fair, originally planned for late February of 1865, was postponed: after the assassination of the president and the formal end of the war in April, it was almost cancelled altogether. It finally opened on May 30 to honor Union generals and to raise money to pay off Sanitary Commission debts and construct a Chicago Soldiers' Home.

This fair, like the first, depended on donations from Illinois and surrounding states, and the same kinds of personal contributions were sent in by individuals of all ages. Although the organization of this fair was similar to the first, the men of the commission cooperated more and supported the effort from the outset. The standard attractions — food, entertainment, a bazaar of commercial and handmade fancy goods, and exhibits of machinery, curiosities, trophies, and artworks — were featured. This last fair expressed a different quality, however, one that reflected both the recent dramatic events and the coming-of-age of the sanitary fair. It was a more sophisticated and "professionalized" event, less fresh and spontaneous.

The enormous number of people drawn to the fair found a calculated, planned piece of theater rather than a spontaneous emotional outpouring of charity, patriotism, and regional loyalty. Participants in the first Northwestern Fair experienced a novel event. Although fairs were not new to Americans, fairs that large and festive were. After two years had passed, however, the Great Fair was anything but novel; people would not be attracted merely by the presence of appealing goods and a worthy cause. Evermore novel attractions had to be provided, almost in inverse proportion to the familiarity of the event itself. The selling environment changed, and fair organizers viewed their patrons less as contributors than as consumers.

The fair opened on a different note as well. Once the war ended, much of the public viewed the Sanitary Commission as a part of the past. The Soldiers' Home, furthermore, was more of a local than a regional concern. (Wisconsinites devoted their energies to a Home Fair in Milwaukee for their own soldiers and did not participate fully in the second Chicago event.) The mood of the people was also more subdued, as general fatigue and a sense of mourning tempered the relief and gladness that the war had ended. The organizers could not ride the wave of patriotic zeal as they had before and were forced to devote some of their initial energy to showing that the fair was still necessary.

The second fair must, however, be considered a success. Attendance figures were

Volunteers sell badges at this booth at the second Northwestern Sanitary Fair.
(CHS, ICHi-15123)

actually higher than they had been in 1863; more than 10,000 people attended on a single afternoon. Net proceeds after three weeks were about $300,000, nearly four times the profits of the first fair. Ample donations still poured in; volunteers and excitement were plentiful.

Bryan Hall was put to use once again. This time it was occupied solely by the Arms and Trophies department (the equivalent of the Curiosity Shop), only one of the many attractions on the fairgrounds. All of Dearborn Park was used for this fair, and Michigan Avenue was enclosed for the entire length of the park. One of the centerpieces of the fair, the by then expected Horticultural Hall (sometimes called Floral Hall), measuring 60 feet wide, 400 feet long, and 40 feet tall, was worked into this enclosure. Light came in through stained glass and other filtering devices, transforming the space into an "epitomized and intensified Central Park," according to a description in the special fair newspaper, *The Voice of the Fair.* Its periphery ringed with cedars, this hall was landscaped into meadows, ponds, and graveled walks. "Point Lookout," named after one of the sites of Union victory, was a miniature mountain at one end of which visitors could climb by a picturesque winding staircase. Waterfalls splashed down from the peak and flowed into streams that crisscrossed meadows below. Rustic-style bridges crossed the streams, which were filled with fish; fawns, eagles, swans, and a crane wandered freely about. A more formal garden featuring statues representing the four seasons and structured beds of flowers was situated at the other end of the hall. Horticultural Hall also featured "Jacob's Well," an arbor roofed in evergreen, complete with a costumed Jacob and Rebecca serving lemonade and other beverages to thirsty passersby; a "Greenland of Fancy," where ice cream could be purchased; a bower where young ladies constructed and sold wreaths and bouquets; and a grotto and summer house where horticultural implements and books were offered for sale. "Nobody who visits Horticultural Hall goes away without investing greenbacks," remarked *The Voice of the Fair.*

Instead of the single flag-bedecked dining hall of the first fair, a number of smaller, more picturesque eating establishments catered to visitors at the 1865 fair. Several of these restaurants were professionally run. John Wright, a Clark Street confectioner, oversaw a "Floral Restaurant" set on a platform overlooking the formal garden in Horticultural Hall. His regular staff of "colored helps" was assisted by young volunteers. Visitors could choose to have a complete meal at "The New England Farm House," which was couched in a theatrical setting similar to eating establishments at previous fairs. Even the menu was thematic: it featured fish chowder, bean porridge, Indian pudding, and similar foods. On June 17 the Farm House featured a wedding much like the one that had taken place in Brooklyn. Only costumed patrons were admitted, and tickets cost $1. After the ceremony and meal, the seventy guests played games such as Blind Man's Bluff and Thread the Needle. Costumes were *de rigueur* everywhere at the fair — even a coffee stand run by ladies of the Baptist church featured identically costumed hostesses.

At the first Northwestern Fair the "ladies were somewhat unprepared" for the animals that area farmers donated. In anticipation of animal donations in 1865, organizers integrated them into the spectacle. Livestock auctions were routine, and when a large elephant was brought in on loan, room was found for it. The fair also featured two mascots: a huge ox dubbed "General Grant" who had been raffled off at the Metropolitan Fair in New York and at a Sailor's Fair in Boston, only to be donated again in Chicago; and the

"Fort Sumter Kitten," an animal "born under the Rebel flag." There was also a special stall for a stuffed eagle carried throughout the war by the Eighth Wisconsin Division which became an emotional symbol of the Union cause. Chicago sculptor John Volk later made a model of the eagle, and the bird was presumably cast in a more permanent medium.

Children had sold pictures of this stuffed eagle throughout the North prior to the fair. Alfred Sewell had organized the "Army of the American Eagle," in which boys and girls who sold pictures could become "officers." The sale of 10 pictures earned a child the rank of corporal; 30 pictures earned a sergeant's badge, 100 a captain's, 300 a major's, and so on. Fifteen thousand dollars came into the sanitary fund from the sale of these pictures before the fair opened. Through this "army," even children's participation in the fair had been coordinated and formalized; it was a far cry from the spontaneous front-lawn juvenile fairs of two years earlier.

"General Grant" was not the only attraction recycled from previous sanitary fairs. A piece of black bread that had been purchased at Gettysburg for five cents was sold at the Philadelphia fair for $100, redonated, and sold again for $290. It appeared in Chicago in the "Temple of Relics" in the Arms and trophies department. Flags and other trophies were displayed again and again. A letter to the Northwestern Fair Committee from the quartermaster's office in Madison, Wisconsin, requested that the Wisconsin flags be returned so they could be sent to the upcoming Soldiers' Home Fair in Milwaukee.

Notable personalities were asked to make contributions to one fair after another. Painter Frederick Remington Church was so beleaguered by these requests that he declined to donate any of his work to the second Chicago fair, claiming, "You cannot have the slightest conception of how much Artists have been taxed to contribute to hundreds of fairs . . . held all over the Union. If I had acceded to all the demands I would have done nothing else for two years."

Despite Church's refusal to participate, the Art Gallery at the 1865 fair was a major attraction. A number of Jacob Bierstadt paintings were on display, and a sculpture by Annie Hosmer, an American living in Rome, caused a great stir. (The sculpture had previously been seen in New York and Boston, and was much discussed in the newspapers of the respective cities.) One visitor to the Art Gallery described its rather rarified atmosphere. "The turmoil and hurry of the crowd at the great building, the feverish hunger and . . . clatter of plates at the New England Kitchen and the barking of dogs of war at the [miniature exhibition of the ship] Monitor [were] all absent" at the Gallery, he claimed. A "dim religious light from above," combined with the black drapery suitable for a period of national mourning, set the artworks off in a dramatic fashion.

Most sanitary fairs raffled off large, expensive objects, although the practice was a controversial one, and the managers of each fair had to determine their own policy about it. Raffling took place at both Chicago events. The second Northwestern Fair also featured a related fund-raising scheme, which consisted of awarding a predetermined prize to the person who received the greatest number of paid "votes." Contests of this sort were begun at sanitary fairs in 1864. At the second Northwestern Fair the races were hotly contested, and running totals of the contests were reported each day in both city and sanitary fair newspapers. Contests included elections for the most popular general, who was awarded a set of prize pistols, and for the prettiest girl in Chicago, who was awarded an English dressing case valued at $1,000. The latter contest stirred up great feeling among the young people in the city. "The

This illustration by Thomas Nast depicts the Sanitary Commission members as "heroines of the war."
(CHS, ICHi-22101)

young beaux are extremely anxious" about the outcome of the vote, reported the *Voice of the Fair,* "and the girls are all in a flutter." Anna Wilson won the contest, but barely so; 1,073 votes had been cast for her, 1,068 for runner-up Mattie Hill, and 1,022 for Amelia Carley. A description of "Sanitary Voting" of this sort noted that each vote cost $1, and people took "especial pleasure in neutralizing their predecessor's vote." There was no limit on the number of votes an individual could cast, either altogether or at a single time.

Although the second Northwestern Fair was the last of the nation's sanitary fairs, many of the traditions they established continued. Men became much more involved in fund-raising fairs for charity, and "ladies' fairs" gained credibility and prestige. Other sorts of expositions and agricultural fairs also proliferated. All of these events were influenced by the development of the sanitary fairs. "Voting" was one of the most prevalent features of the fund-raising fairs of the 1870s and 1880s, for example, and elaborate costumes and theatrical environments remained important at such fairs until well into the twentieth century. The type of "uplifting" natural environment provided in Horticultural Hall at the second Northwestern Fair was echoed in the conservatory (also called Horticultural Hall) of the Centennial Exposition in Philadelphia in 1876, and again in a more formal manner in the 1893 World's Columbian Exposition. The whole mix of activities that became associated with the "world's" fairs — industrial and cultural displays, art exhibits, handwork, and entertainment — was present at the sanitary fair. Capturing the attention of the consumer by presenting goods in an appealing and imaginative setting — a concern that had increased so quickly in two short years in this Civil War period — was soon intensified in the growing importance of the department store and the public museum.

The evolution of the sanitary fair from an "innocent," predominantly spontaneous event to a "sophisticated" one with a more programmed format is clearly illustrated by the contrast between the two Northwestern Fairs. They represent indeed the "alpha and omega" of the Civil War fairs, and presaged other types of fairs and a growing consumerism.

PART II

INDUSTRIALIZATION AND IMMIGRATION

Smoldering City

Karen Sawislak

The Great Chicago Fire began on the evening of October 8, 1871. Because the entire upper Midwest was in the throes of a nearly two-year-long drought, fires were no rarity in the city. One immigrant peddler later recalled that he felt no particular sense of alarm upon first hearing that part of the city was in flames; secure in the knowledge that "there was a fire every Monday and Tuesday in Chicago," he reacted to the first report of the Great Fire by yawning and going to bed. But this fire, driven by a gale-force southwest wind, rapidly grew far out of control. From its origins in a southern residential quarter, the fire swept north through the business district. The blaze made short work of the central city's mostly wooden buildings. Stone structures fared little better; the intense heat pulverized limestone and marble. The fire next leapt the natural barrier of the Chicago River and destroyed thousands of North Side working-class homes.

As the night went on, and the magnitude of the fire became increasingly apparent, Chicagoans frantically worked to save themselves and some of their possessions. The sleeping peddler woke up to a nightmare: the flames cast an eerie illumination upon the spectacle of the masses struggling through stifling clouds of dust, smoke, and cinders to the relative safety of the lake shore or the western prairie. More than twenty-four hours later, when the fire was finally extinguished by a fortuitous rainstorm, people began to take stock of the damage. One witness made a poignant assessment of the fire's impact: "The seeds of permanent or temporary disease sown, the bodily suffering and mental anguish endured can never have statistical computation or adequate description." Still, a few important numbers do indicate the scope of the disaster. Almost 300 people had died, and among the survivors, more than 100,000 of the city's approximately 300,000 residents were left homeless. In addition, the blaze leveled more than 18,000 buildings. The number of jobs lost is impossible to estimate; thousands of citizens became unemployed because their places of work were destroyed. In the immediate aftermath of the fire, Chicagoans faced terrible human and economic emergencies. The *New York Tribune* observed, "Since yesterday Chicago has gained another title to prominence. Unequalled before in enterprise and good fortune, she is now unapproachable in calamity."

The stage was thus set for what would

later be termed the "Great Rebuilding." Though observers of the reconstruction often mythologized the process as a magical transformation from "a wilderness of piled-up bricks, stone, iron, and rubbish" into "the forms of symmetrical walls, sound pillars, imposing fronts, and massive roofs," this period was hardly devoid of gritty physical and ideological struggle. The Great Chicago Fire brought a time of enormous hardship and turbulent transition to the city — and no group felt these effects more than the working class. After the fire, Chicago's working-class residents were forced to confront major threats to their work, their homes, and their family life. In the first days and months after the disaster, most workers and their families — along with now-destitute Chicagoans from other classes — faced stringent standards for obtaining aid. Once reconstructing the city was well under way, laborers became embroiled in conflicts relating to wages and hours. These disputes tested the strength and efficacy of their trade unions. In addition, the city's enormous and largely working-class immigrant community mobilized to contest laws it perceived as direct attacks upon both ethnic culture and the rights of American citizens. To protect their traditions and their Constitutional freedoms, Chicago's immigrants turned to popular political action. During the first months and years of the postfire city, Chicago's working class engaged in two distinct types of activism. And as institutional expressions of the working class, trade unions and immigrant politics would certainly meet with two distinct types of experiences.

In the first days after the fire, any thoughts of rebuilding came second to the immediate concerns of housing, feeding, and clothing the city's population. Because the fire received international news coverage, donations of money and goods began to flow into the city from all over the world. Mayor Roswell B. Mason decided — prodded by civic leaders who did not want the incoming funds controlled by the notoriously corrupt official city government — to turn over the administration of relief efforts to an established, independent charitable organization. The Chicago Relief and Aid Society, a bastion of the city's upper- and middle-class reformers, had, since 1857, aided those among the "worthy and industrious poor" who found themselves, "through sickness or other misfortune," in need of "temporary assistance."

Before the fire, when the Society was aiding approximately 7,000 people every year, an extensive bureaucracy attempted to ascertain whether an applicant was indeed truly deserving of assistance. This system and ideology seemed destined to change in the aftermath of the fire, which expanded the Society's caseload to 157,000 people in the course of a single day. But though the Society's board of directors now confronted practically an entire city of apparently worthy poor, there was no new largess in the distribution of aid. Even in the face of such massive disaster, the Relief and Aid Society — ever fearful of creating or perpetuating a permanently dependent clientele — maintained strict standards regarding those who received aid. The compassion evoked by the extent of destruction and personal loss never overwhelmed prefire charitable ideologies and practices. In the year and a half that the Society performed fire relief, only the worthy poor — as defined and closely monitored by Society staff — were considered appropriate recipients of short-term aid.

Amid the shock and confusion of the first few days after the fire, the Relief Society decreed only one practicable rule: the hungry should be fed. Sheltering the homeless, due to the rapid onset of harsh late autumn and winter conditions, also became a top priority. Since all remaining houses, schools, and churches were immediately filled to overflowing, the Society constructed barracks at five locations in the burned district. Once these life-threatening situations were brought under control, however, the Society concentrated on implementing a system designed to force unworthy recipients off the dole.

The Relief Society was soon transformed from a relief entity into an employment agency, opening on October 16 in temporary quarters in the heart of the burned-out

When word of the fire victims' plight reached towns and cities throughout the country and around the world, donations of food, clothing, and other supplies poured into Chicago. Painting by Jules Emile Saintin, 1872.
(CHS)

downtown. Those traditionally considered neediest — women who headed families, the aged, and the infirm — could still expect aid. But getting Chicago workers back on the job would become the task of utmost importance; such efforts served to rebuild both the city's physical structure and the prefire social order. Relief administrators quickly created a hierarchy of authority and bureaucracy to insure that the Society never did its job too well; leaving families with a certain amount of discomfort guaranteed that able-bodied men and women, in the words of a *New York Times* reporter, would not be "so demoralized . . . by a few days of idleness and gratuitous living that they stand aloof, and take no part in the pressing emergency now at hand." According to the Society's records, more than 85 percent of those who lost their homes resided in the working-class, heavily German, Irish, and Scandinavian northern wards of the city — precisely the people who were, in the eyes of the Society's directors, most prone to falling into dangerous habits of idleness. Though Society officials and newspaper reports later admitted that people who refused to go to work were rare exceptions, in the first days after the fire the press frequently portrayed the entire working class as a recalcitrant, shiftless group. The *New York Tribune*, for example, claimed that due to "the evils of careless benefaction . . . out of the immense numbers of houseless and unemployed not a tenth part of the needed force can be obtained."

Because of the supposed positive moral effect of a household, the Society rushed to give families the materials to erect one-room wooden shanties of their own. According to the *Tribune*, this facet of relief work allowed people to once again "be surrounded by the sacred and conservative elements of family, of independence, of respectability, and of individual responsibility which are so immense a moral force in the community, and without which a community has in it the seeds of anarchy and dissension." If an applicant did not have the skill to erect a home or the means to hire a carpenter, the shelter committee ordered further aid. But in fact, more than 90 percent of the 30,000 people who received material either built the house themselves or earned enough to pay someone else to do it for them, a development that must have pleased Society officials. Construction proceeded quickly: 3,000 shanties went up by the end of October.

The relief strategy of transportation — providing a one-way ticket out of town — exemplifies the Society's ability to invest its role in the aftermath of the disaster with its own time-honored attitudes toward charity. Railroads had generously responded to the plight of Chicagoans by offering them free rides out of the city. More than 6,000 people took advantage of this opportunity during the two weeks immediately after the fire. But once again, Society officials cut off those they considered "undeserving persons," who had no good reason to leave the city, and were thus guilty of "imposing upon the generosity and good nature of the Railroad companies." As the *New York Times* noted in a report filed exactly one week after the flames died, "These passes are now carefully restricted to the aged, sick, and feeble, to women and children, and to large families, it being justly held that there is employment enough in Chicago for all able-bodied men who are willing to work." As far as the Society was concerned, if a man could work, he should stay in town to reconstruct his own life and contribute to the resurrection of his city.

The Relief and Aid Society practiced what it preached. Two divisions of the organization were specifically devoted to getting Chicagoans back to their labors: the Employment Bureau and the Committee on Special Relief. Every able-bodied man or boy who applied for aid at a subdistrict office was given a ticket and sent over to the Employment Bureau. When the Bureau placed a man, he surrendered his ticket, which was then returned to the superintendent of the district where it was issued. But if the ticket never made it back to the district superintendent, it was taken, according to Society records, as "presumptive evidence that the bearer preferred to eat the bread of idleness rather than work for his own subsistence." If such a man ever again dared to appear at Society offices, his claim was immediately rejected. Ironically, in the short run, his virtuous counterpart, who had dutifully sought and secured employment, often found himself and his family in similar dire straits. For as a letter to the editor of the *Chicago Tribune* noted, "the moment a man obtains work his rations are cut off." But because "no laboring man can draw daily his pay for labor," many Chicagoans endured a period of one or two weeks during which they had jobs but no income — and no access to relief. "It is not an uncommon thing," the writer went on to state, "to see children crying and begging for bread merely because their fathers have found work." The Relief and Aid Society clearly did not feel the need to help anyone once they were seemingly equipped to help themselves.

The Committee on Special Relief, a second employment division, disbursed aid in a different manner; rather than arrange a job, it provided the items necessary for self-sufficiency. This committee funded various projects, among them outfitting the offices of dentists and doctors, stocking grocery or dry-goods stores, and paying a fledgling establishment's rent for the first month. Though the Committee primarily served middle-class merchants and professionals, it also supplied tools to skilled workers such as carpenters and bricklayers. Almost one-quarter of the Committee's funds went toward obtaining new sewing machines for women who had lost their sole means of support in the fire.

Working women, along with the middle class, were indeed of special concern to the Society. The Society established its own clothing factory to turn out garments to replace those lost in the fire; more than one hundred women were thus supplied with immediate employment. Additionally, the Committee provided many women with the furniture and the funds required to open boarding houses. This type of business was exceptionally lucrative and important during the year after the fire as first the homeless, and then transient workers, patronized such establishments.

Hard work, the officials of the Relief Society believed, would save Chicago and the moral character of its citizens. For the first few months after the fire, every worker could not help but be highly virtuous, since the initial steps toward rebuilding the city involved an enormous amount of effort. For as the *Lakeside Monthly,* a local magazine, observed: "A fire does not simply destroy what is valuable; it leaves behind, and to be cleared away, much that is worthless." As soon as the ashes cooled — which, due to the intense heat of the fire, took as long as a week — thousands of men and boys moved in to knock down crumbling walls, reclaim usable bricks and scrap iron, and daily dump 5,000 wagonloads of useless material into the lake. This process eventually created approximately five acres of what is now Chicago's prime downtown lakefront real estate. Preliminary clearing continued under difficult conditions. Along with smoke, fog, rain, and cold, laborers battled an oppressive dust, which, according to the *New York Tribune,* "powdered all until as white as millers." Because of the late autumn's short days, men remained on the job until long after dark. But in spite of these hardships — or perhaps because they served as constant reminders of the winter conditions soon to follow — work went forth with extreme speed. One reporter marveled that the mass of "busy men, boys, and teams" was "working as energetically as if the whole burnt district was to be restored before Christmas." Once the people demonstrated their willingness to work rather than collect charity, newspapers changed their tune, and yesterday's lazy bums became today's heroic sons of toil. Twenty days after the fire, the *Tribune* offered the following tribute: "All honor to the brave men who have met misfortune by resolutely beginning the work of reconstruction . . . preferring to earn the bread and shelter they enjoy. . . . Labor and skill . . . in combination with energy and enterprise" would resurrect Chicago. By spring, the paper predicted, "the desolate places will be desolate no longer, and from the ashes will have arisen monuments of industry and faith."

In their eagerness to rebuild, however, Chicagoans did not wait for the arrival of spring. Although the winter of 1871-72 was quite severe, outdoor manual labor did not cease. Special difficulties accompanied such out-of-season work. Bricks, for example, had to be kept dry, and mortar kept warm. If the mortar froze before the bricks set, the wall would not stand solid. This problem prompted *The Workingman's Advocate,* a nationally circulated labor newspaper published in Chicago, to note that "the rapidity with which Chicago is coming up after the fire is as astonishing as the rapidity with which she tumbles down again." Several newly constructed four- and five-story brick buildings apparently failed to withstand a late December day's "gentle zephyrs," and, as a reporter wryly observed, "lie as flat in their cellars today as their predecessors did on the morning of the memorable October 9." In addition, winter conditions doubtless extracted a heavy physical toll from all workers. According to the metaphor-laden prose of the *Lakeside Monthly,* "Hannibal crossing the Alps, and Napoleon retreating from Moscow were mere skirmishes in comparison with the battle waged all winter long by Chicago builders." But due to the short working days, the limited number of workers, and high demand by employers, this winter work was, during its first one or two months, exceptionally lucrative.

The rebuilding of Chicago at first presented an unprecedented opportunity to both skilled and unskilled construction workers. But by electing to heed the *Chicago Tribune*'s frequent "no extortion" pleas — aimed at all city workers and businesses — the building tradesmen refrained from exploiting the situation. (The city's lumber and brick dealers, in contrast, asked so much for their stocks that builders generally found it cheaper to purchase and transport materials from merchants in Milwaukee and eastern cities.) The bricklayers, for example, pledged "to work at ordinary wages" while reconstructing the city. While altruism and community spirit certainly influenced this decision, Andrew Cameron, the prominent union activist who edited the *Advocate,* also saw it as good strategy. Cameron believed that since many employers had also been "just as sorely stricken by the great calamity," they should not be immediately subjected to more pressures. If labor kept still until the spring, Cameron reasoned, the commercial climate would be so healthy that the increasing demand for skilled labor would cause wages to rise. Recognizing the probable consequences of a premature push for higher wages, Cameron warned that "any false move at this juncture will only have the effect of flooding the city with foreign labor; and lessening instead of increasing the rate of wages."

Despite Cameron's caution, out-of-town labor — lured by hopes of steady jobs and

William Bross, former lieutenant governor of Illinois and part owner of the Chicago Tribune, traveled east after the fire and urged workers to "Go to Chicago now!" *(Photograph by John Carbutt CHS, ICHi-09607)*

high pay — did stream into Chicago. This migration of between 30,000 and 40,000 people within a year of the fire so clogged the labor market that no one collected particularly high wages. The city needed thousands of workers to attend to the massive job of rebuilding, and the local, national, and international press publicized the city's need. The *Tribune* of October 28 addressed the desperate unemployed of New York and other cities in calling for 500 stone masons, 2,000 carpenters, and any number of plumbers, gas-fitters, and iron-workers willing to work through Chicago's winter at $4 to $5 per day. The article promised twice as many jobs in March. Further afield, the *New York Times* noted that "there is work for an army." As the construction industry in almost every other American city shut down for the winter, Chicago's rebuilding was just beginning. In the face of seasonal unemployment, moving to Chicago seemed highly favorable.

Some enterprising individuals actively recruited labor and skills for Chicago. William Bross, former lieutenant governor of Illinois and part owner of the *Tribune,* rushed from Chicago the day after the fire to speak in several eastern cities. In his lectures, Bross asserted that the fire's leveling of the city had also leveled all class differences. He claimed that "all can now start even in the race for fame and fortune." At the climax of his performances, Bross delivered this impassioned invitation: "Go to Chicago now! Young men, hurry there! Old men, send your sons! Women, send your husbands! You will never again have such a chance to make money!" Bross's self-appointment as a sort of pied piper of Chicago was no doubt motivated by his wish to rebuild his beloved city. But a more cynical theory also should be noted. Bross, whose anti-unionism made him a special target of labor organizations in his campaigns for statewide office, may have deliberately attempted to flood Chicago's labor market and thereby depress wages.

Workers rushed to Chicago quickly and in large numbers. The first people to arrive in search of fortune came from nearby cities; as the *Tribune* noted one month after the fire, "men are currently coming in from all adjacent towns." Later, in November, an Ohio newspaper plaintively reported that "another delegation of carpenters left Sycamore on Monday for Chicago, and there are not enough left now to keep Sycamore in repair." The next arrivals came from the East, California, Canada, and England. But unless a worker was one of the very first to reach postfire Chicago, he could not expect to find employment.

Along with job shortages, housing was extremely limited, and rents were often astronomical. The Relief and Aid Society maintained a boarding house directory in connection with its employment bureau. But many out-of-town laborers had to settle for accommodations located far outside of the burned district, and as the *Advocate* noted on November 11, "it is not very agreeable for men to travel, in mid-winter, seven and eight miles to and from their work." As early as November, the *Tribune* reported that "More carpenters are applying than there is a demand for," and in late January, the Relief and Aid Society, fearful for "a city already overburdened with the destitute," issued a nationally circulated warning against traveling to Chicago.

Regardless of the warnings of the Relief and Aid Society, false testimonials extolling Chicago's boundless opportunities added further illusory appeal. Shipping lines and passenger agencies drummed up business by advertising the city's high salaries and plentiful jobs. Despite — or more probably because of — this artifice, such campaigns were apparently quite successful. In March of 1872, under the headline "EMIGRATION BY WHOLESALE," the *Advocate* reported that 400 bricklayers, direct from England, had arrived in the city. By April, "arrivals of batches of 25 or 30 unknown bricklayers, carpenters, and plasterers, especially from Old England," were "of daily occurrence." But when English tradesmen began to arrive in late winter, any misconceptions "that a committee with a blue rose'tte would meet them at the depot and escort them to the job," as the *Advocate* sarcastically put it, were rapidly and brutally dispelled.

The task of rebuilding revived trade union activism in the city. Trade unions had operated in Chicago with varying degrees of success since 1852, when city printers had formed National Typographic Union Local No. 16. According to Illinois Bureau of Labor Statistics reports, iron moulders, tailors, stonecutters, shoemakers, carpenters, and cigarmakers followed the printers' lead, organizing during the 1850s and 1860s. In 1864 — following the examples of Boston, New York, St. Louis, and Rochester unions — a General Trades Assembly was created to coordinate the activities of the 8,500 workers belonging to the city's 24 union lodges. But in spite of these impressive numbers, almost all Chicago unions of this period shared the same weakness; though their organizers harbored hopes of complete solidarity, they never managed to enroll every practitioner of their trade. Because of the aggressive leadership of Andrew Cameron, the city's trade unions did wield some political clout during the mid-1860s. In what initially appeared to be a major triumph of worker concerns, for example, the Illinois legislature passed the nation's first eight-hour law on March 5, 1867. This act, however, was somewhat toothless; it made the eight-hour day operational only when no agreement existed to the contrary. A spectacular May 1 demonstration and week-long series of strikes and riots that paralyzed much of the city's industry did not persuade Chicago employers to adopt the eight-hour standard; as the *Chicago Tribune* commented, "the strenuous efforts were not anywhere attended with success." Perhaps in part because of this discouraging chain of events, by 1870 the General Trades Assembly had "died a natural death." But individual unions did remain in-

Entrance to the Insurance Exchange on LaSalle Street. Positions for workers — plentiful at first, as shown by this "laborers wanted" sign — filled quickly as carpenters, bricklayers, and plasterers rushed to Chicago from American cities, Canada, and England. *(CHS, ICHi-20845)*

tact; the city directory for the same year listed twenty-six labor organizations, seven of which were building trades associations.

The job of rebuilding after the fire greatly expanded the city's building trades unions. Cameron and other labor leaders spurred enrollment by ceaselessly preaching the benefits of solidarity. "There never was a better opportunity presented to the mechanics of any city than is now present to the workingmen of Chicago," the *Advocate* declared, "to practically illustrate the advantage and practicability of co-operation." Thousands of men joined the unions throughout the winter. Every weekly meeting of building trades organizations brought substantial numbers of new members onto the rolls. The Carpenter's and Joiner's Union, for example, added six new locals (nos. 2-7) in three months to accommodate a membership that soared from 500 to close to 5,000. And in March 1872, the unions resuscitated the moribund General Trades Assembly.

In a curious way, though far more people belonged to the trade unions than ever before, these organizations did not act aggressively to secure benefits for workers. On the contrary, most organization was a product of the sense that unionization was necessary to protect skilled labor from capitalistic threats. Surveying the situation in March 1872, Cameron concluded that "there never was a time in the history of labor unions in our city when greater dangers threatened their inaction — inaction which unscrupulous employers are sure to avail themselves of, to their advantage and your injury, than at present." The enormous influx of workers and consequent oversupply of labor, union leaders feared, would send wages plummeting. Many men never joined the unions; trades expanded so quickly that it was impossible to prevent workers from arranging private contracts that invariably undercut the unions' standard wage. In addition, substantial numbers of men with no construction experience chose to work temporarily at a building trade. In a letter to the *Chicago Tribune*, a builder castigated the "large number of incompetent contractors and property owners who are employing their own workers — tailors, shoemakers, laborers, etc., in bricklaying, who cannot tell the difference between them and good workmen." Such bastardization of the trade went against all professional standards and took jobs away from the many legitimate artisans. Throughout the entire period of rebuilding, then, the explosive increase in the number of workers in Chicago forced trade unions to approach all activism from a defensive posture. Quickly realizing the futility of any early postfire dreams of extra-high pay or improved working conditions, the unions dug in to safeguard their members' "power to secure an honest day's wage for an honest day's work."

During the winter, while the trade unions prepared for the challenge of the coming construction season, popular political protest — the second form of working-class activism — made its first postfire appearance in response to a proposed municipal ordinance. In the November mayoral election held less than a month after the fire, Joseph Medill, *Chicago Tribune* publisher and long-time failed Republican candidate, finally swept to a landslide victory as the standard bearer for the "Fireproof" ticket. Once in office, Medill took steps to fulfill his campaign pledge to reconstruct a flame-resistant city and pushed for the adoption of "fire-limits." Inside these boundaries, the erection or repair of wooden buildings was to be prohibited. Arguments within the Common Council over the exact placement of the fire limits stalled formal action for approximately three months, during which time opportunistic builders rushed to erect wooden edifices in areas that would soon be legally

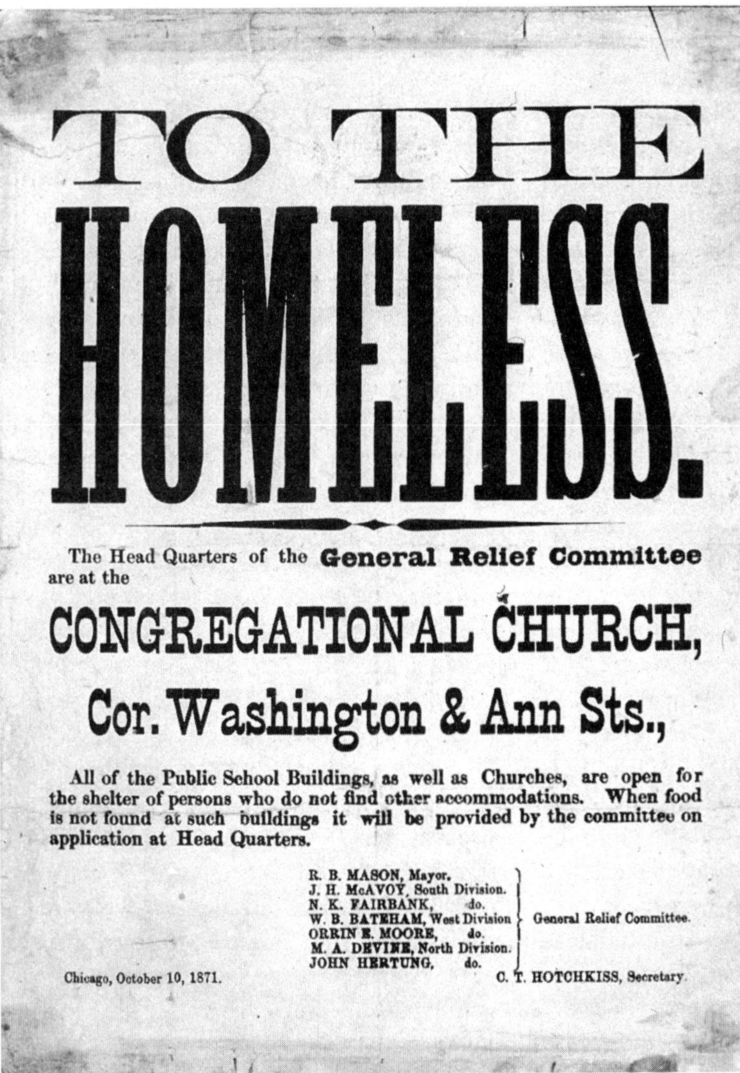

TO THE HOMELESS.

The Head Quarters of the **General Relief Committee** are at the

CONGREGATIONAL CHURCH,

Cor. Washington & Ann Sts.,

All of the Public School Buildings, as well as Churches, are open for the shelter of persons who do not find other accommodations. When food is not found at such buildings it will be provided by the committee on application at Head Quarters.

R. B. MASON, Mayor.
J. H. McAVOY, South Division.
N. K. FAIRBANK, do.
W. B. BATEHAM, West Division
ORRIN E. MOORE, do.
M. A. DEVINE, North Division.
JOHN HERTUNG, do.
General Relief Committee.

Chicago, October 10, 1871.

C. T. HOTCHKISS, Secretary.

More than one-third of the city's 300,000 residents — primarily of the working class — lost their homes in the Great Fire.

(CHS, ICHi-06194)

off limits. In late November the *Tribune* — in loyal support of Medill, now officially on indefinite leave of absence from his responsibilities at the paper — observed that "unless the ordinance becomes a law within a very short time Chicago will be in as good a condition as ever for a conflagration which will astonish the world." In mid-January 1872 such warnings were finally heeded, and newspapers reported that the Common Council verged on approving an ordinance that set fire limits encompassing the burned-out downtown and the entire North Side.

On the North Side, where most of Chicago's immigrant working-class population lived, the proposed ordinance set off a furor. On the evening of January 15, between 2,000 and 3,000 people participated in a torchlight parade from the North Side to the temporary downtown city hall, where a Common Council meeting was in progress. Although this rally essentially addressed working-class concerns, leadership also came from the ranks of the more prosperous, and far less numerous, immigrant middle class. Headed by Frank Conlan, a former alderman, and Anton Hesing, the influential publisher of the German-language daily *Illinois Staats-Zeitung,* marchers carried American and German flags and posters bearing such sentiments as "No fire limits after this calamite [*sic*]" and "Leave a home for the Laborer." With this protest, immigrants sought to protect their right to reestablish their prefire traditional neighborhoods. Hesing explained matters to the *Tribune.* "North Siders own only their little lots, and they don't want stores, but simply houses." "Fancy dwellings of brick" were fine, Frank Conlan asserted, for those who wanted them, "but let the fire limits on the North Side be where the people want them." The January protest march thus defended an element of ethnic culture and further signaled the immigrants' refusal to relinquish what they viewed as their democratic right to self-determination. As Hesing stated succinctly, "these people cannot afford to build of brick, and they will not stand any law that compells [*sic*] them to."

This popular action proved quite effective. Though the *Tribune* sniffed that "the majority of the 'procession' was composed of men who never owned a foot of ground, and never will, if they do not spend less money for beer and whiskey," flooding the meeting with hundreds of angry North Siders impressed Chicago's elected officials. After a temporary recess to clear the council chambers — during which time "The Municipal Fathers" were, according to a *Tribune* headline, "Forced to Seek Shelter in the Cloak Room" — the aldermen approved a revised plan that permitted the erection of wooden buildings under sixteen feet in height throughout much of the North Side.

In one sense, this protest was unnecessary because the fire limits were, for the most part, not enforced. The *Tribune,* on May 5, decried "the flagrant disregard of the fire ordinance in all parts of the city," claiming that "Policemen walk by the illegal works, chat with the workmen, and never think of interfering to prevent violations." When a reporter asked the city employee in charge of issuing building permits how people could procure a permit to build a frame house within the fire limits, the clerk simply shook his head and replied: "You ought to know how things work."

Early in the process of reconstruction, immigrant leaders learned that popular pressure, if applied through the right political channels, could safeguard working-class traditions against reform. This form of worker activism, doubtless empowered by its initial success, was a force during the season of reconstruction, and even came to dominate the city's political scene during the next municipal election.

With the arrival of the spring building season, memories of the winter fire ordinance protest faded, and trade unionists were doing their best to expunge any lingering impressions of an unruly and moblike working class. (Vague rumors had circulated throughout the city that in mid-May the unions would mastermind a general strike.) On May 15, 1872, the building trades associations staged an event designed to recast middle- and upper-class perceptions of the working people. In the course of a massive parade and rally, Cameron and other union leaders tried to show Chicago that labor was a force of order, not discord, and asked only for fair wages. The parade and rally were absolutely peaceful. Nearly 6,000 men decked out in traditional union regalia (slightly makeshift, since most banners and costumes had not survived the fire) marched through downtown. The marchers then settled with thousands of other workers on a West Side lot to hear addresses by Mayor Medill and

Cameron. About 30,000 building trades workmen skipped work to attend the Wednesday rally, suspending construction in the city. The demonstration, Cameron later claimed, proved "a disappointment only to those who had predicted or desired a riot."

It is difficult to see how any sort of riot could have been expected. On May 6 Cameron had gone to a board of police meeting to request an escort of forty mounted policeman (approved) and to ask for a police commissioner's participation (denied). In keeping with the trade unions' policy of defensive strategies, the labor assembly sent a message of conciliation and reason. Mayor Medill, for example, drew enthusiastic cheers at the end of a speech offering an analysis of economic relations. "Capital and Labor," he asserted, "are naturally partners; the one is the complement of the other. Labor without the aid of Capital, is naked, and starves. Capital without the help of Labor, cannot increase, but decays." Strikes and lockouts, Medill believed, could never benefit either side, but a refusal to work was a particularly irrational undertaking for wage earners. He argued that in any "attempt to force Capital to surrender by the method of starvation . . . it is labor that starves first." To promote a harmonious process of "rebuilding the city with the utmost vigor and rapidity," Medill urged cooperation and arbitration. His address finished with a climactic plea for worker adherence to the prevailing American middle-class moral standards.

> Work steadily at the best wages offered: practice economy in personal expenditure; drink water instead of whiskey; keep out of debt; put your surplus earnings at interest, until you have enough to make a payment on a lot, build a cottage on it at the earliest day possible, and thus be independent of landlord; go with your wife to church on Sunday, and send your children to school. If you have no wife, court some worthy girl and marry her.

If laborers "pushed forward hopefully and perseveringly," Medill concluded, they could rise above their working-class origins and "become independent long before old age."

Following the mayor's speech, the assembly adopted a series of resolutions that mirrored most of Medill's sentiments. The trade workers called for written contracts between unions and employers and for the creation of a board of arbitration, "half of which shall be selected by the employers, the other by the employees," to render binding decisions "in such future disputes as may arise." The demonstrators disavowed all violent coercion and expressed a belief that "moral suasion is more potent to secure the cooperation of our nonunion workmen than threats or intimidation." The resolves ended with a ringing defense of the honorable character of unions and workingmen. Inviting all nonunion men to ally themselves with their respective trade organizations, the assemblage assured the city that "in union there is strength, their object being to ask nothing but what is right — to submit to nothing that is wrong."

While workers did not respond overwhelmingly to Medill's plug for middle-class moralism, Chicago trade union leaders constantly sought to gain the approval of the city's more prosperous citizens. The demonstration's highly ordered procession and the extra care taken to include visible symbols of authority, such as the mayor and the police commissioners, reflect this concern. According to Cameron, Chicago's welfare depended upon the industry of its workers. But though laboring men and women were "as much interested in the city's prosperity as any other class," all they ever received for their trouble was "indiscriminate slander" at the hands of the upper classes. If the working class collectively displayed the virtues held near and dear by their social betters, however, "the most violent of their revilers" would be "compelled to pay homage to the dignity of labor." In pursuit of this goal, Cameron could sound very much like Medill. In a March 1872 issue of the *Advocate,* for example, he set forth the following instruction for a worthy way of life: "Give the saloon as wide a berth as possible; establish a library and lecture room; talk co-operation, whenever you have a chance; act as though the success of the movement depended upon your own exertion, and depend upon it, you will become better men, better husbands, and better citizens." Cameron's notions about self-betterment, not surprisingly, were suffused with the tenets of collectivism, a sentiment not at all apparent in Medill's preachings. But even though Cameron's standards of moral conduct differed from the middle-class version, union members did not necessarily find his advice, let alone that of Medill and the middle class, to be particularly palatable.

For many immigrant Chicago workers, acceptance by the upper classes seemed less important than maintenance of their own ethnic traditions. City unions were in great part composed of foreign-born workers; some trades, such as the stonecutters, were almost exclusively German. Chicago's trade unions, though heavily immigrant, ironically followed the leadership of men who badly wanted organized labor to be accepted by the city's mostly native-born middle and upper classes. The most prominent labor leaders therefore were not completely in tune with the aims and attitudes of much of the unions' immigrant rank-and-file. Germans, Irish, and other European-born workmen might well have welcomed calls for the primacy of religion, thrift, family, and responsibility, since all of these were valued within their own ethnic communities. But these same immigrants would never agree to temperance. And as the season of reconstruction continued, this issue — the workers' right to drink whenever they pleased — caused immigrant tradesmen to turn away from union-led activity in favor of popular political activism. Political activity aggressively confronted middle-class reformers. Trade unionism, in contrast, was tactically guided by leaders who did not seem to recognize that attempting to appease the middle-class might not be the best way to win concessions for workers.

For the entire spring and summer, workers and employers apparently heeded the message sent forth by the May 15 rally. The *Advocate* reported in July, "everything seems to work harmoniously." The *Chicago Tribune* estimated that between 25,000 and 30,000 building tradesmen, aided by 20,000 to 25,000 common laborers, toiled at work sites for ten to twelve hours per day, six days per week.

In the course of such rapid rebuilding, Chicago became a showplace for all the latest labor-saving machinery. According to the *Tribune,* "every appliance which the ingenuity of man has devised has been brought into service." Horse- and steam-driven elevators, for example, meant that a crew of fourteen could do the work formerly done by a hundred laborers. "Hod-carrying," the report proclaimed, "is now a lost art." Derricks were invaluable to builders. The same article noted that even while "they occasionally fall and kill some hapless workmen or passerby, their immense utility to the general public counterbalances the damage to individuals, fatal though it be."

Construction always involved danger, but one trade-off for the unparalleled speed and new technological methods of the rebuilding process was the loss of many workers' lives. Even "with forests of derricks, with the streets choked up with teams, with huge stones and masses of iron dangling in the air all summer over the heads of pedestrians," the *Tribune* claimed that "scarcely more accidents have happened than occur in an ordinary season, and certainly no greater loss of life." But the *Advocate* presented a very different picture, asserting that "the number of deaths by accident among our workmen has been frightful — some days as much as a dozen being killed or maimed for life."

While reconstruction proceeded without interruption throughout the summer months, this did not mean that workers were entirely content. To the contrary, the postfire turmoil had created much bitterness within Chicago's working class. The question of housing and rent was a particularly sensitive issue. Landlords, taking advantage of the intense demand and short supply, charged an average of 30 to 40 percent above prefire rates. That property owners did not hesitate to gain personal profit from the same misfortune that tradesmen had pledged not to exploit outraged many workers. "A Mechanic" angrily asserted in a letter to the *Chicago Tribune:*

> Has not this very fire been a pretext used by the moneyed elite to extort and almost rob the mechanics and laborers of the little they may possess or gain? Are not they who own

State Street between Monroe and Adams. In the wake of the Great Fire came opportunity for the thousands of workers required to rebuild Chicago.

(CHS, ICHi-02813)

> cottages and prate about losses by the fire grinding the very life's blood out of the class they most need to build them up by compelling them to pay out in rents more than double former rates, and yet have not doubled the wages of those they employ?

The Bricklayers' Union attempted to alleviate this problem by organizing a worker-owned construction business to purchase land and erect affordable housing. Though the *Advocate* ran a prominent advertisement for this "Mechanics' Building Company" from July through December, the venture — perhaps due to the hefty \$3 per week demanded from each of the cooperative's investors — never attracted enough members to buy or build anything. Formal working-class protest may have remained submerged for much of the season of reconstruction, but a city with a housing market operating under conditions "of oppressive injustice," in the *Advocate*'s words, could hardly be termed free of inter-class tensions.

The uneasy peace between builders and workers finally began to disintegrate in the early fall of 1872, when first the carpenters, and then the bricklayers, went on strike. The carpenters' union, though numerically strong, had been handicapped throughout the construction season by intratrade squabbles over apprenticeship requirements and association leadership. "Their very bickering," the *Advocate* reported, "made them an easy prey to their enemies." Bricklayers, stonecutters, and plasterers maintained stronger unions and received \$5 per day; carpenters, only \$2.50 or \$3 for the same amount of labor. Carpenters viewed this inequity as unfair; their craft required longer apprenticeships than any other building trade, as well as a more substantial and expensive array of tools. And carpenters went to work on a structure only after construction was fairly advanced. They hoped to capitalize on their specific skills being in far greater demand late in the building season than they had been during the spring and summer months. At a mass meeting on the evening of September 16, the union resolved to request from all employers wages of \$4 per day and threatened to call a strike if this demand was not met in a week's time.

But even though the carpenters had delayed any action until, as the *Chicago Tribune* noted, "the lateness of the season and the large number of buildings now in carpenters' hands will enforce the demand," the high number of unemployed and non-union carpenters in the city virtually guaranteed failure. The city's contractors, meeting the day before the strike was to begin, remained singularly unmoved by the union's threat. They were confident that the strikers could be easily and quickly replaced. The carpenters' association was weak and troubled, and many union members ignored the "order" of the strike and negotiated individual contracts with their employers. Other union men accepted conditional terms specifying that if they returned to work immediately, their employer must raise their wages should workers who continued to strike gain concessions. This sort of agreement undermined both trade solidarity and the very tactic of the strike. Only a few hundred of the more than 5,000 union carpenters who worked at sites where the owners were anxious to avoid even a temporary delay gained a boost in wages — and this by only fifty cents per day. But all other union strike activity ended in defeat within forty-eight hours. For the carpenters, then, the union offered no effective protection against Chicago's glutted postfire labor market.

The bricklayers' strike, by contrast, was much more successful. Unlike the carpenters, who were striking to increase their wages, the bricklayers left their jobs to protest a pay cut. Claiming that the price of brick had substantially increased, on October 2 contractors reduced bricklayers' wages from $5 for ten hours of work to $4.50. The contractors immediately rejected the union's counteroffer of $4 for eight hours. Workers reacted to this pay reduction — clearly intended, they believed, to increase the builders' profits at their expense — with extreme anger. As a result, on October 4 all union bricklayers stopped working. One bricklayer, writing in the *Advocate*, commented on what he saw as the hypocrisy of the situation: "Now mark their conduct in October with ours in May, and it is a poor rule that don't work both ways. 'Don't take advantage of Chicago's misfortune,' was their watchword then. 'Don't take advantage of Chicago's misfortune,' is now our response to their demands."

In contrast to the carpenters' beleaguered organization, the bricklayers' union — earlier termed "extraordinarily earnest and aggressive" by the *Chicago Tribune* — stood together against the contracts. With this strike, the union finally dropped the defensive posture of the past spring and summer and energetically confronted employers and nonunion workers. Pledges against violent intimidation were forgotten as gangs of strikers roamed the city to scare replacement workers off the job. On October 10 the police moved in to disperse a rowdy mob of 125 union bricklayers who had assembled to protest nonunion work at the site of the new McCormick reaper factory. The next day, city builders took steps to protect their replacement employees, serving notice that "if any man at work should be assaulted or intimidated, at work or elsewhere, on account of being at work," they would "employ private detectives to arrest the guilty parties, and have them prosecuted to the utmost extent of the law." But the union bricklayers had already managed to send a clear message; the *New York Times* noted that outside nonunion workers were afraid to step in as strikebreakers. The cooperative spirit preached by Medill and Cameron back on May 15 clearly seemed impracticable to this trade union.

The successful disruption of work, however, did not automatically signal victory for the bricklayers. While the employers of approximately one-third of the union bricklayers acceded to the union conditions during the first two weeks of the strike, many other employers vowed to resist the demand for the eight-hour day "to the finish." Perhaps fearing that any concession might rekindle the kind of activism surrounding the passage of the eight-hour law in 1867, the contractors "after lengthy debate . . . decided that it is better to stop all building operations until next year, rather than submit to the dictation of the strikers." Only in mid-November, at the very end of the building season, did nearly all contractors agree to the eight-hour standard. By this time, the days were so short that workmen were unable to stay on the job for more than eight hours. But this strike, especially when compared with the carpenters' disastrous strike attempt the previous month, largely succeeded. The union essentially beat back the attempted pay cuts and secured a proportionally equal wage for fewer hours. It is important to remember, however, that the bricklayers never asked for any new benefits; their struggle revolved strictly around an effort to defend the summer's standard wage against what was perceived as the contractors' avarice.

The bricklayers' strike was both the first and last notable display of union strength and solidarity in the immediate aftermath of the fire. As the 1872 construction season drew to a close, masses of men were thrown out of work, and the city's building trades organizations began to fall apart. "In our city," the *Advocate* reported in January of 1873, "there are thousands of workmen idle at the present time; not idle from choice, but from necessity. 'No work to do,' is what you hear from morning 'til night." In the face of such terrible unemployment, survival took precedence over trade business, and most unions dwindled to a few faithful members. A January 10 convocation of the General Trades Assembly, for example, drew only four men, leading the financial secretary — the only officer who had bothered to appear — to suggest rather lamely that no more meetings be scheduled until the "thaw." Many among the army of workers who had streamed into Chicago now moved on to search for employment elsewhere. In mid-December an *Advocate* correspondent visiting city train depots "noticed many of our workingmen, especially stone-masons, bricklayers, and carpenters, taking their departure for states north, south, and east of us. . . . This general stampede indicates a large suspension of work on various buildings in course of erection, and the general disinclination of builders to commence on new contracts." The early spring migration into Chicago was partially balanced by the early winter exodus. Still, thousands of building tradesmen had made a permanent move and now faced a jobless winter.

Even as trade unions dissolved and employment prospects became grim, many of Chicago's laboring people began to organize once again. This time class conflict over an attempt to infringe upon immigrant traditions — and by extension, democratic rights — took place on a far grander scale. In the course of the battle, the two sides fought for control of the city government. The temperance issue — the one plank in the reformist platform that the immigrant working class would not accept — triggered these events.

The initial catalyst for reviving ethnic political activism was, ironically, a unified city movement against crime. Toward the end of the great rebuilding, many Chicagoans became quite concerned about a crime wave sweeping the city. In the immediate aftermath of the Great Fire, Chicago experienced a substantial rise in the numbers of homicides and robberies. (This phenomenon can probably be attributed to the transient nature of many who had been drawn to the city by its disaster.) On September 10, 1872, Henry Greenebaum, a banker and civic leader of German descent, spoke to the *Chicago Tribune* about his plans for a massive anticrime rally:

> The people of all classes are thoroughly aroused and in earnest. The feeling goes well beyond party, nationality and religion, and is shared alike by all good citizens. The Germans are particularly up in arms, and I would not be surprised to see 10,000 of that nationality alone at our meeting. The Irish are also with us, and will come in masses to the meeting.

The meeting, held at the newly rebuilt Board of Trade, attracted a mixed crowd. The assemblage unanimously agreed to demand swift capital punishment for convicted murderers and to create the Citizens' Committee of 25 "whose duty it shall be to aid the authorities in the prompt arrest, speedy trial, and sure punishment of criminals." But the proceedings hit a snag when someone raised the issue of Chicago's Sunday liquor law — a heretofore totally ignored 1845 ordinance that forbade any sale of alcoholic beverages on the Christian Sabbath day. Some believed the law should be enforced, and a rather loud argument ensued. Approbation mixed with condemnation as "Some hissed and some applauded."

Though antitemperance men succeeded in tabling the motion at the Board of Trade rally, the issue immediately leapt to the forefront at the first meeting of the Committee of 25 on September 30. In his testimony before the Committee, Mancel Talcott, the president of the board of police commissioners, attributed the great majority of illegal conduct to alcohol. He boldly asserted that "nine-tenths of the crime is brought about by drunkenness. . . . If you enforce your existing law against keeping open your saloons late on Saturday night and Sunday . . . your rowdyism and shooting affrays would in a great measure cease." Henry Greenebaum, the chairman of the Committee, discounted Talcott's statements and instead attributed the crime problem to out-of-towners who had no intention of remaining in the city permanently. He went on to warn, according to the *Tribune,* that "plenty of hard-working Germans went out with their families on Sunday, and they would consider it a great hardship to be deprived of harmless amusement." But Greenebaum's defense of the immigrants' right to drink fell upon unsympathetic ears, and zealous religious leaders and moral reformers seized control of the Committee. Within three weeks, the anticrime movement turned against the same immigrant workers who had rallied to its support.

The Committee of 25 — reduced to twenty-three when Greenebaum and Anton Hesing handed in their resignations — pressured Mayor Medill to enforce the Sunday closing ordinance. Medill, trapped in a dilemma, stalled for time. While personally sympathetic to the working-class concerns, he knew that it would be politically fatal not to appease the highly vocal reformers, who presented themselves as the agents of God, morality, and law and order. Hoping to defuse the issue, Medill noted that New York, Boston, and Brooklyn did not enforce their Sunday prohibition laws, and that the police force would be overburdened by any effort to monitor Sabbath day drinking. He further asserted that the all-talk, no-action reformers offered no concrete assistance in this area. Medill complained to the *Tribune,* "I am unable to procure any promise of efficient aid, whether moral, legal, religious, or physical; their business seems to be to censure, but not to encourage and support the authorities." But these attempts to evade a decision did not put off the reformers. The Committee of 25, due to intense public interest, expanded into the Committee of 70, and women's civic and religious organizations added their voices to the general clamor. By mid-October Medill could no longer resist the temperance lobby, and he gave the order for police enforcement of Sunday prohibition. October 20 took on a special significance for the city — it was to be the first dry day.

Chicago's immigrants reacted to Sunday prohibition with disbelief and hostility. Anton Hesing, in the *Staats-Zeitung,* angrily asserted that "A saloon has the same right as a church, so long as it is quietly and decently carried on." A *Chicago Tribune* article describing the day of a typical German-American, "Mr. Schmidt," provided a satirical but telling account of the threat of Sunday prohibition to immigrant culture. "Mr. Schmidt," finished with morning church services, wandered over to his neighborhood saloon, only to find that the door was locked and no business was being conducted. He refuses to believe it. It is incredible. It is against religion. It strikes at the very foundation of belief. . . . He asks himself whether the result of a long civil war, of the loss of 100,000 lives, has been that he, an American freeman, is deprived of the inestimable blessing of drinking beer on Sunday. Has free government come to this? Had he left a despotism abroad, where drinking was allowed, to come to a republic where it was not permitted?

In a somewhat impromptu and rowdy protest, North Siders marched behind a wagon loaded with kegs and freely dispensed beer. This spectacle, which flaunted the law by taking advantage of the technicality that beer had to be sold to be illegal, must have horrified the reformers; for all their attempted good work, potential drunks guilty of disorderly conduct now brazenly paraded through the city's streets. But since brewers and saloon owners could not afford to give their stocks away, simple economics precluded any repeat of this sort of carnivalesque event. German and other immigrant workers soon concluded, with Hesing, that "there is only one thing to be done: determined resistance and firm union."

After the enforcement of prohibition, immigrant protest began to take a popular political form. On October 23 the *Staats-Zeitung* urged all of its readers to discount any other issues and vote only for those candidates who pledged to repeal the temperance ordinance in the upcoming aldermanic elections. On October 24 the city's German leaders assembled to discuss strategy. Two days later a delegation of representatives from that meeting called on Mayor Medill, who managed to send them away "satisfied with his position." But just as the Germans began their political mobilization among the working class, the temperance reformers took a temporary hiatus. During the winter, the Committee of 70 went into dormancy. Medill, for the moment relieved of reformist demands, suspended enforcement of the Sunday prohibition ordinance.

In the spring the Committee of 70 emerged from its hibernation, and the temperance dispute heated up quickly. On April 28, 1873, the general superintendent of police, with Medill's apparent blessing, issued an order requiring all policemen to "enter frequently on Sunday all places or rooms on their respective beats where they have good reason to suspect that intoxicating drinks are sold." In response to this dictate — which, due to internal dissension within the police board, did not go into effect for a few weeks — German leaders held a mass meeting at the North Side Aurora Turner Hall on May 21. The rally resolved to address the immigrant working-class grievances at the November municipal election. Speaking first, Hesing swore that through his vote he would "teach the Puritanical element that Sunday afternoon could be pleasantly and orderly spent." Other orators chose to transcend the specific issue of temperance in their appeals. Rudolph Thieme, a grocer, proclaimed: "Here we are a hundred thousand German Americans like one man, under the banner of freedom and order, determined not to secure beer on Sunday — but to overthrow the venal Strumpet which has occupied the throne of the Goddess of Freedom, and dishonored the Republic." Still other speeches compared the temperance movement to the nativist "Know-Nothing" movement, which had frequently victimized German and Irish immigrants. After the Saloon-Keepers' Union ceremoniously changed its name to the Union of Liberal-Minded Citizens, the meeting concluded with Hesing pronouncing the birth of the People's party.

Starting with eight mass meetings organized on the evening of May 29, the People's party quickly gained momentum and supporters. This party, rooted in immigrant working-class activism, had the potential to muster enough votes to take control of the mayor's office and the Common Council. Many seasoned politicians — mostly Democrats thrown out of power with the ascension of the Republican-backed "Fireproof" ticket — began to ally themselves with the upstart political force. The most important figure to jump on the People's party bandwagon was Daniel O'Hara. This controversial but very popular political boss, who already held the office of clerk of the criminal court, brought much Irish support to the party.

As the party began to organize itself into campaign committees, the grocers, teamsters, stonecutters, and carpenters who had stood in the initial ranks of leadership began to be replaced by insurance brokers, lawyers, bankers, and merchants. Saloonkeepers, liquor merchants, and brewers — not surprisingly — maintained an especially constant and active role in party affairs. As in many populist movements, the leaders of the People's party eventually lost touch with those who had originally sparked the effort. The People's party, through the influence of the veteran politicians, began to take positions on municipal issues of little or no concern to most immigrant workers. But opposing temperance always remained the campaign's central goal. Municipal politics thus became a moral battleground.

Medill — probably because of the abuse he endured over the Sunday liquor law — decided not to seek re-election. When the "Fireproof" administration left the scene, a coalition organized under the slogan "Anything to beat the Hesing-O'Hara combination!" The "Law and Order" ticket — described by a contemporary commentator as "one of the strangest fusions . . . that has ever been recorded" — united nativist Americans from all classes, Democratic and Republican party politicians shut out of the People's party, and, of course, the temperance men.

But the "Law and Order" ticket by this time could do little to stop the People's party juggernaut. As election day neared, immigrants even began to appropriate traditional American institutions in order to gain political clout. Daniel O'Hara, the People's candidate for city treasurer, used his position with the criminal court to set up what the *Tribune* termed a "naturalization mill." Processing more than 500 immigrants daily — all of whom swore that their "first papers" had been destroyed in the fire — O'Hara manufactured thousands of votes for his party. The People's party so effectively countered the reformers' attack on worker traditions that many perceived a total reversal of the cultural conflict that had triggered this political activity. The claim now arose that the immigrants were oppressing native-born Americans. In a reaction to the *Staats-Zeitung*'s publication of "appeals to the foreign-born population to come out and vote down Puritanical Yankees" in nine different languages, the *Chicago Tribune* accused the People's party of "German Know-Nothingism."

On election day, the People's party ticket, headed by Harvey Colvin, swept to an easy victory. Colvin was an American-born compromise candidate picked after Hesing's mayoral ambitions were dashed by a disclosure that he had arranged for the passage of an 1865 city ordinance that netted his *Staats-Zeitung* more than $86,000 in public funds. Voter turnout more than doubled that of the 1871 election, indicating the extent of working-class politicization. The day after the victory, the *Chicago Tribune* predicted a grim future for Chicago, lamenting that "the election proves that the ignorant and vicious classes, added to the entire German vote . . . have the power to govern." But the *Staats-Zeitung*, in a joyous celebration, countered with a far different view of the electoral triumph. For the immigrants, the victory of the People's party was not a "subjugation of the Americans by a horde of foreigners," but a pure and simple "victory of honorable and true American citizens over a smaller number of American citizens."

The People's party had won — but the working people did not control Chicago. Once in office, the new administration immediately suspended enforcement of Sunday prohibition. Still, though the People's party had secured the working class's right to drink, it could not insure its right to work. By December of 1873, the postfire working-class experience had come full-circle as the Relief and Aid Society once again assumed a prominent role in city affairs. By this time, a nationwide economic collapse had brought Chicago's commerce to a near-halt, and tens of thousands were out of work. Near Christmas, unemployed workers took to the streets to demand that $600,000 of fire relief funds still held by the Relief and Aid Society be turned over to the Common Council and used for public works projects that could "employ the idle men who were wanting work." But funds were not released; the Society's general superintendent told the *Tribune* that he "remained convinced that a great many of the able-bodied men who are loafing about the streets could get something to do if they were not too lazy to look for it." Of course, economic circumstances differed completely from the booming postfire job market. This time the work did not exist. The financial slump triggered by the Panic of 1873 lasted until nearly 1880 in Chicago, causing most of the city's workers to endure six years of acute financial hardship. Neither trade unions nor immigrant politics would do much to lessen the severity of this lengthy depression.

In evaluating the experience of the working class during Chicago's Great Rebuilding, it is easy to conclude that the trade unions collapsed while immigrant politics succeeded. But the story is surely more complicated. For while the immigrant political leaders certainly delivered on their promise to beat back temperance, they failed to secure for their working-class constituents anything more than the right to drink on Sunday. This victory, though important, can hardly be termed a triumph for the city's workers. Many questions about what could be done to alleviate the difficult conditions of working-class life remained unanswered; these issues remained far outside the sphere of immigrant politics. A defense of ethnic tradition was possible, but any defense of the right to work for a fair wage was quite unrealistic. After the fire, Chicago's working class fell prey to the simple economic facts of the labor market. What had at first seemed to be a golden opportunity soon turned into a constant fight for survival due to an oversupply of workers. All working-class activism must be viewed in light of these extremely pressing economic circumstances. Instead of an assessment of achievement or failure, the Chicago working class's gradual shift of its postfire struggle from the labor marketplace to the world of immigrant culture is best seen as a move into the realm of the possible.

Chicago's Great Upheaval of 1877

Richard Schneirov

For three July days during the nationwide railroad strike of 1877, Chicago's streets were filled with tens of thousands of workingmen forcibly closing factories, driving off strikebreakers, and conducting a general strike. At the height of the conflict, thousands of men, women, and teenagers fought with police and state militia units in the fiercest class warfare the city had ever known.

Historians of the labor rebellion of 1877 have tended to view those who took part in it in roughly three ways. The first chroniclers, including eminent Chicago historian Bessie Louise Pierce, followed contemporary press reports in depicting participants as members of an irrational mob. This ignored the beliefs, aims, and aspirations of the rioters. Later historians perceived the Great Upheaval as little more than a series of unorganized strikes over higher wages and shorter hours.

More recently, another group of historians has begun to seriously study popular activity, as distinguished from the statements of organized leadership or the perceptions of those in power at the time. The latest work, *The Great Labor Uprising of 1877* by Philip S. Foner, reflects this advance in scholarship but treats Chicago chiefly within a national framework. As yet, nobody has offered a comprehensive description and analysis of the Chicago crowd of 1877, nor examined that crowd in the context of the development of the city's labor movement.

In 1877, the city's economy was changing from a merchant-dominated commercial-transportation economy supplemented by small-scale craft industry to a modern corporate industrial economy oriented primarily toward mass production of consumer and capital goods. Until the 1870s the city had been mainly a center for the transshipment of Western primary products eastward to the nation's manufacturing areas. By the 1880s, however, Chicago's strategic location near iron ore, coal, and lumber sources, the maturation of the national economy, and the steady westward movement of population which generated a wide regional market for manufactured goods combined to make Chicago the nation's third largest manufacturing center. Meatpacking, printing, and the manufacture of iron and steel, garments, foundry and machine shop products, furniture, and agricultural implements led the fast-growing industrial development. Nevertheless, the transport of primary products remained vital to the city's economy. It was here and in the extraction and use of building materials that the men engaged in unskilled outdoor labor — lumbershovers, coalheavers, railroad freighthands, sailors, and brickyard laborers — were concentrated.

Men engaged in unskilled, heavy outdoor labor were distinguished in a number of important ways from other categories of workers. They contrasted most sharply with the more educated, organized, and politicized skilled workers in the machine and print shops, foundries, and fast-disappearing crafts, who often supervised and regulated production and hired their own helpers and apprentices. Outdoor laborers were distinguished as well from factory workers in general by their highly seasonal employment. Because most worked only half a year, outdoor laborers were forced to maximize their income during the busy summer months by striking for higher wages; during the winter and early spring they searched for odd jobs in competition with the unemployed, took up work in the packinghouses (another seasonal industry), or remained idle. Outdoor laborers were most like unskilled factory workers, with whom they shared a common social status and lack of job stability due to business cycles and competition from Chicago's large pool of unskilled, immigrant labor.

What all outdoor laborers had in common was their method of strike. Because of their lack of skills and because effective organization was only beginning among these workers, their strikes tended to be unorganized, explosive affairs conducted by large crowds marching from business to business driving off strikebreakers. Furthermore, the outdoor nature of these strikes often transformed what began as private disputes into public confrontations as police clashed with large bands of workers — often physically robust, hard-drinking, and combative men. In the course of such encounters, a strike could easily turn into a community riot as family members, neighborhood residents, and other outdoor laborers were drawn into the street.

Among Chicago's workingmen, ethnicity generally overlapped and reinforced class standing. About two-thirds of those employed in manufacturing and mechanical pursuits were foreign born, and most of the rest had foreign-born parents. Among unskilled workers the percentage was probably higher. Many of the foreign born — particularly German and Irish — were in cultural conflict with the evangelical Protestant middle class over the latter's attempts to reform the drinking habits of the city's workingmen. Longstanding opposition to this reform by the city's immigrant workers would intensify class antagonisms during the 1877 upheaval.

Most workers of foreign parentage lived in the eight wards that straddled the river, where most industry was located. On the North Side, the Fourteenth through Seventeenth wards, where the rolling mills, brickyards, and tanneries around Goose Island were located, were predominantly German, with some Irish and Scandinavians living there. On the South Side, the Fifth Ward housed the principal Irish community of Bridgeport south of the river near the stockyards, brickyards, and rolling mills. The Bohemians were concentrated on the north side of the South Branch of the river in the Sixth Ward by the lumberyards. The Seventh and Eighth wards on the Near West Side were largely German and Irish and supplied workers to the iron and wood manufacturers along Canal, Clinton, and Jefferson streets. These eight wards were the prime sites of crowd activity in 1877.

The beginning of the 1873-79 depression marked a turning point for Chicago workers as wage cuts and mass unemployment began to weigh heavily on outdoor laborers and unskilled workers generally. The effects of the

 **WORKINGMEN OF CHICAGO!** 

HAVE YOU NO RIGHTS?—NO AMBITION?—NO MANHOOD?

Will you still remain disunited while your masters rob you of all your rights as well as all the fruits of your labor? A movement is now inaugurated by the Money Lords of America to allow only property-holders to vote! This is the first step to Monarchy! Was it in vain that our forefathers fought and died for LIBERTY?

They have now passed a law authorizing the arrest, as a vagabond, of any workingman out of employment who may wander in search of work,—no warrant being necessary.

They have passed a law making it a criminal offense for workingmen to combine for an advance of their wages—an offense punishable by imprisonment and fine! The right of employers to combine in reducing our wages and bringing starvation and misery to our homes is protected by all the police and soldiers in the country! These aristocrats refuse to pay their taxes but demand all the improvements!

HOW LONG WILL YOU BE MADE FOOLS OF?

Every day—every hour, that we remain disunited, only helps our oppressors to bind more firmly the chains around us. Throughout the entire Land our brothers are calling upon us to rise and protect our Labor. For the sake of our wives and children, and our own self-respect, LET US WAIT NO LONGER! ORGANIZE AT ONCE!!

MASS MEETING on Market St., near Madison, TO NIGHT!

Let us act while there is yet time!

THE COMMITTEE, Workingmen's Party of the United States.

Although the immediate cause of the strike was a wage cut, the political emphasis of this socialist handbill prefigured the insurrectionary direction taken by the strike.

(CHS, ICHi-14001)

depression were also felt in a decline in unionization, which had proliferated after the Civil War. Some unions, notably the Knights of St. Crispin, comprising factory-employed shoemakers, ceased to exist. The unions that did survive — mostly composed of skilled craftsmen — were severely weakened by loss of membership. This lack of effective organization during the depression is a partial explanation of why so many workers resorted to crowd actions to oppose wage cuts.

Just as important in prefiguring the shape of events in 1877 was a change in the nature of the labor movement and the response to this by Chicago's business leaders. The upsurge in unionization between 1866 and 1873 had been accompanied by the emergence of a labor reform movement. Reformers called for a legislated eight-hour day and inflation of the economy through currency and banking measures in order to increase wages, reverse the concentration of wealth, and make credit available to producer cooperatives.

With the onset of the depression immigrant socialists began to challenge these labor reformers for leadership of the labor movement. Marches of unemployed workers during the winter of 1873-74 gave birth to the Workingmen's Party of Illinois, which two years later became the Workingmen's Party of the United States (WPUS). At the same time, fear of immigrant mobs led Chicago's wealthy businessmen to establish and equip the First Regiment of the Illinois National Guard with a membership drawn largely from the city's established families and middle-class clerks.

The pattern of labor activity which culminated in the Great Upheaval of 1877 was further elaborated on June 15, when South Side coalheavers struck in response to a wage cut instituted by merchants on the Coal Exchange. Brandishing clubs, hundreds of coalheavers went from yard to yard ejecting men who remained on the job. One week later the brickyard men and lumbershovers also struck. At the height of the conflict thousands of strikers gathered in the Fifth Ward's Bohemian Hall to listen to socialist speakers call for a workers' militia. Soon afterward German socialist workers formed their own armed unit, the *Lehr und Wehr Verien,* while socialist-leaning Bohemian workers organized the Bohemian Rifles as a company of the Illinois National Guard.

Though 1875 had passed without any violent encounters, in May 1876 a much larger strike of lumbershovers, marching in large crowds from yard to yard, led to clashes with police and mass arrests. One group of 1,500 men was dispersed only by police firing in the air, and a striker was killed by a lumberyard clerk. Meanwhile, the socialists again held mass meetings exhorting their Bohemian and Polish listeners to take a stand. A week later large crowds of West Side brickmakers skirmished with police in the course of their strike. So began the pattern of strikes and confrontations that would dominate the summer of 1877.

The Great Railroad Strike of 1877 began July 16th in Martensburgh, West Virginia, as a response to a wage-cut, and spread rapidly west along the rail arteries through the growing industrial centers. In Baltimore, Maryland, and Reading and Pittsburgh, Pennsylvania, bloody encounters between railroaders and police and militia raised fears in the press of an American version of the Paris Commune of 1871. Chicago press headlines talked of Civil War. It seemed only a matter of time before the strike would hit the railroad center of the Midwest. Indeed, when the strike finally did reach Chicago on Tuesday, July 24th, the *Tribune* only had to headline "It is Here."

Monday, July 23

> *We fought for the Negro and brought him up to the level of the white man. Now why not do something for the workingman?*
>
> Union Army veteran speaking before a Socialist Rally

Over the weekend all eyes had been on Chicago's railroad workers. A small group of switchmen from various railroads had met Sunday night to discuss the strike. Albert Parsons, the charismatic socialist leader, addressed the group and urged the men to "strike while the anvil is hot." Discussions continued early on Monday evening when the long-awaited strike call went out.

Railroad officials and City Hall had also been busy. Worried over the possibility of violence and seeking to contain the strike, many railroads canceled their freight runs. The North Western restored the paycut of its engineers, the only unionized group of railroad workers, who in return vowed to stay on the job. At the same time Mayor Monroe Heath ruled out the boarding of trains and the escorting of strikebreakers by police and militia. In not attempting to break the railroad strike the railroads and city officials avoided the property damage that had marked the Pittsburgh strike. The avoidance of confrontation also denied to railroad strikers the central role they had played in the East, and allowed the strike pattern of 1875-76 to reassert itself. Although the railroaders were to play an important part in

Tuesday's events, their participation thereafter steadily receded.

Meanwhile, socialists in the WPUS had issued a circular Monday calling for a downtown rally. Its theme was one popular for the time, the corruption of the American Republic by concentrated wealth, meaning the transformation of the pre–Civil War republic of small property holders and artisans into an oligarchy of monopolists. Echoing a widespread fear, particularly among those of European parentage who recalled aristocratic rule in the old country, the circular claimed that the "Moneylords of America" were planning to restrict suffrage to property holders as the first step back to monarchy. As evidence the circular cited the fact that workingmen suffered under unequal and humiliating laws: the law against combinations made it practically illegal to strike, and the city's so-called Tramp ordinance allowed unemployed men on the streets to be arrested without warrant. The circular closed with an urgent appeal to action: "For the sake of our wives and children and our own self-respect . . . let us act while there is still time."

That night one of the largest gatherings the city had ever known — between 10,000 and 30,000 — crowded into the intersection of Market and Madison streets. The audience was in an excited and militant mood as Albert Parsons began his address. Parsons, formerly an ardent Republican, delivered a speech that was similar in tone and theme to Lincoln's Gettysburg Address. As Lincoln had done with the Civil War, Parsons attempted to interpret the meaning of the great events of 1877 within the American republican tradition. In a pointed allusion to the Grand Army of the Republic he began as follows:

> We are assembled as the grand army of starvation. Fellow workers, let us recollect that in this great republic that has been handed down to us by our forefathers from 1776, while we have the Republic we still have hope. A mighty spirit is animating the hearts of the American people today. When I say the American people I mean the backbone of the country — the men who till the soil, guide the machine, who weave the material and cover the backs of civilized men. We are a portion of that people. Our brothers . . . have demanded of those in possession of the means of production . . . that they be permitted to live and that those men do not appropriate the life to themselves, and that they be not allowed to turn us upon the earth as vagrants and tramps. . . . We have come together this evening, if it is possible, to find the means by which the great gloom that now hangs over our Republic can be lifted and once more the rays of happiness can be shed on the face of this broad land. [*Inter-Ocean*, July 25, 1877]

As the throng swelled beyond the point where any single speaker could be heard, additional rostrums were improvised at various locations, and speakers emerged from the crowd to air their views. Among them was an Irish Union Army veteran who had fought at Shiloh. His speech looked back to the war and expressed his subsequent disappointment.

> The Black man has been fought for; and we have given him the ballot; the people have shown an interest in him, and have done all they can to bring him up to the point where he could compete with the white man. Now why not do something for the workingman? . . . I was through the war. I fought for the big bugs — the capitalists — and many of you have done the same. And what is our reward now? What have the capitalists done for us? [*Tribune*, July 24, 1877]

The words of Parsons and the Shiloh veteran — expressing a sense of disillusion and disinheritance and resentment at being denied equal rights as free citizens — would be reflected in the actions of strikers in the days to come.

The rally ended with a presentation of the Workingmen's Party of the United States program by chairman Phillip van Patten. It called for an eight-hour day; a twenty percent wage increase; and government takeover of the railroads and telegraphs.

Tuesday, July 24

We are working for the rights of all.

John Hanlon, railroad worker

No man ought to work for less'n a dollar'n half.

Boy in crowd

The strike, inaugurated formally on Monday by the railroaders, was prosecuted in earnest on Tuesday. The actual manner of strike belied the typical press characterization of the strikers as "hordes of ragamuffins, vagrants, saloon bummers and generally speaking the dregs of the population." As the *Inter-Ocean* admitted Thursday, the crowds were really "roaming committees of strikers." Most crowds appeared to have informal leadership, and the purposeful action of many crowds, notably the railroaders, presupposed some rudimentary organization and planning.

The initiators of the strike action were a small group of Michigan Central switchmen who were soon joined by freighthands and a large group of teenagers. The leader was a discharged railroad hand named John Hanlon, "a dark complexioned man with chinwhiskers and a pipe in his mouth." Carrying pine sticks, the men marched along the railroad tracks by the lakefront, stopping at various freightyards. At each stop Hanlon, attempting to persuade rather than intimidate, led a small delegation inside the shop. Not all men suspended work voluntarily, but railroad officials, instructed to avoid property damage at all costs, generally told all hands to go home when confronted with the crowd. At one yard some men didn't want to quit, saying their paycut had been restored. Hanlon asked if the restoration applied to all employees on the line. When told that it didn't, he responded that "they were working for the rights of all" and that work must cease until wages had been restored to all employees.

During this time Bohemian lumbershovers, joined by a crowd of teenagers and some women, commenced a strike for the third year in a row. But it was the first time that the strike had spread beyond the railroads. The crowd roamed throughout the lumber district ejecting the few men remaining on the job and then moved on to close the brickyards and stoveworks. By 2 P.M. a portion of the same crowd returned to the area led by an old man carrying a banner reading "Down with the wages of slavery: We want labor and justice."

By late afternoon the railroad strike was no longer merely a railroad strike. Not only had the lumbershovers joined spontaneously, but the strike had spread to the heavily industrialized area just west of the river. Bands of workers and teenagers roamed up and down Canal, Clinton, and Jefferson streets shutting factories. One group led by a tall, brawny man named Flinn attempted to convince workers to strike of their own volition. Many did, but in other cases, as the crowd approached, proprietors closed their shops and factories and sent employees home before they could call a strike. At least one group of employees, the German and Bohemian furniture workers, many of whom were socialists, joined the crowd.

As yet there had been no opposition from police, and the mood of the crowd was exuberant — almost like being "out on a holiday," a disapproving reporter noted. Every instance of shutdown was lustily cheered and buoyed the group's enthusiasm. Occasionally there were shouts of "Vive la Liberté" and "Down with the Thieving Monopolies." One Bohemian, with the assent of his Irish companion, attempted to start up the *Marseilles,* the anthem of the French Revolution now sung as well by socialists and free thinkers.

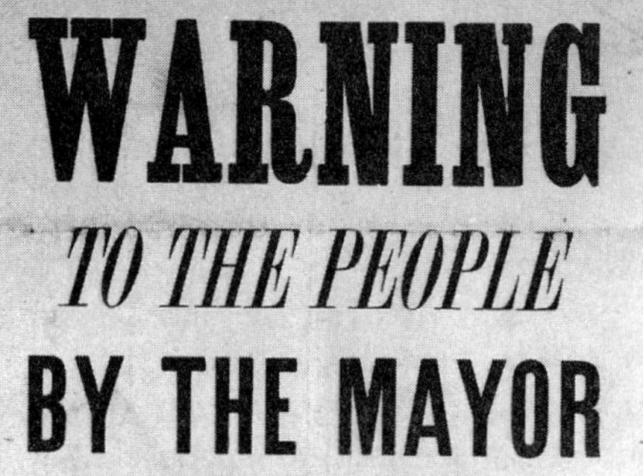

Mayor Heath was caught between the mass actions of the crowd and the reaction of the frightened business community. In this broadside he warns "idlers and curious people" to stay off the streets.

(CHS, ICHi-14000)

Later that day Tom Littleton, a discharged railroad hand, led one section of the West Side crowd to his former place of employment, where they shut down the freight depot. Another portion stopped at Fortunes Brewery for free beer dispensed by an anxious owner. At Monroe and Franklin 200 shoemakers closed two factories.

At least half of most crowds were young men between the ages of twelve and twenty. "It seems strange," remarked the *Tribune,* "that full grown men should at the bidding of half-grown men and boys quit their work, but so it was." In fact, the phenomenon was not at all strange. Half-grown men and boys were simply parts of America's growing industrial workforce. Until effective compulsory education in the late 1880s, teenagers worked at low wages in sweatshops or as apprentices and helpers of skilled workmen or scrounged up odd jobs. Many simply roamed the streets collecting odds and ends to help their families survive.

At City Hall Mayor Heath, still hoping to avoid the violence of the Pittsburgh strike, ordered police to interfere with crowds only when property was threatened and to employ blanks if weapons were to be used. Apparently police restraint was not intended to apply to the WPUS. The socialists were the only group agitating for a general strike, and the authorities and the press were already accusing them of inciting the initial strike.

While publicly denying responsibility for starting the strike, the socialists did attempt to direct it. The WPUS issued a circular Tuesday calling on workers to appoint delegates to a provisional strike committee; in the meantime workers were urged to "Keep quiet!" until an orderly strike could be planned. The committee did meet once again to issue a call for a general turnout in favor of a twenty percent pay increase and an eight-hour day, but it was to have little influence on subsequent events.

In spite of the WPUS circular three thousand workers, including a contingent of railroaders, gathered Tuesday night at the spot of the previous night's rally. The socialists were absent, but the police were not. A phalanx of bluecoats charged the peaceable gathering, clubbing indiscriminately and firing over the heads of the panic-stricken crowd. The police ignored a rival meeting of labor reform leaders and twenty trade union delegates which endorsed the railroad strike but withheld support from the general strike, recommending currency reform as the solution to the depression.

The police attack on the WPUS meeting was the first during the strike in which widespread clubbing and shooting had been employed to disperse a peaceful crowd. This set a precedent for a pattern of police violence which intimidated the socialists and prevented them from organizing an orderly and effective general strike. That such a strike was possible is evident from the St. Louis general strike the same week, in which authorities refrained for three days from attacking socialist gatherings, allowing them to organize and direct the strike. Tuesday's police attack and those to follow the next day also indicated to workers that any presumed rights to organize and strike would not be respected. The subsequent elevation of the strike to a battle with the police and militia owed much to this realization.

Wednesday, July 25

Let us kill those damned aristocrats.

From the crowd

On Wednesday the strike's center of gravity shifted from the railroads to the main industrial areas of the city. The composition of the crowds also changed: most of Tuesday's crowds were teenagers; Wednesday's crowds were largely made up of adult workingmen.

Now that the strike had spread beyond the railroads, the policy of the local authorities toward the crowd changed. Mayor Heath responded to pressure from the business community by mobilizing the militia, calling on cities to arm themselves to preserve order, and enrolling special police. It became clear that the police would be given free rein. The *Times* editorialized that the great mistake of the police had been to let the mob "run unmolested Tuesday." A few days later the *Tribune* summarized the results of the new policy: "The police are gradually beginning to shoot with lead in front of their powder and shoot lower; it would have been much better if the Mayor had allowed this to be done Tuesday — it was a day lost."

The action resumed early as between 600 and 800 Bohemian and some Polish lumbershovers gathered in the lumber district again. Armed with clubs taken from scrap, they scattered the few lumbershovers remaining at work, closed the Union Rolling Stock Company, and advanced on McCormick's Reaper Plant. The crowd, now grown to 1,500, was confronted by a squad of fifty bluecoats; the McCormick Reaper Plant was a prize they would protect at all costs. The police commander ordered the workers to disperse, but his words were met with jeers and curses. The lumbershovers were the most combative group of workers in the city, and the Bohemians among them were known to the police as strong socialists. It was not surprising, therefore, that when the police attempted to arrest their leaders, the lumbershovers replied with a shower of stones. The police, who had begun to feel acutely their lack of numbers, fired into the crowd, wounding two and causing a wild retreat.

Part of the crowd reassembled on the

prairie west of the city and held an informal political meeting. According to a reporter who joined them, the men seemed united on the socialist strike demands. But all were embittered, and none more so than the Bohemians, several of whom were apparently officers in the Bohemian Rifles and talked of calling this unit out to protect their strike. This would have meant a confrontation between the police and an Illinois National Guard unit. News of such a possibility must have reached the authorities, for that same day General Torrence, commander of the National Guard, signed an order disarming the Bohemian Rifles.

By early afternoon the entire city was in ferment. A group of South Siders had carried the strike to the North Side by shutting the Chicago Rolling Mills and precipitating a strike of the unskilled tanners along Goose Island. On the West Side crowds patrolled Canal Street to ensure that all factories remained shut. Occasionally groups traveled west to join the lumbershovers. On the South Side, a large contingent of Bridgeport youths and Canal Street "toughs" closed the South Side Street Railway Company. At the Union Stock Yard in the Town of Lake, south of the city, a more organized group of packinghouse workers ejected a crowd of boys — they wanted to appear respectable and distinguish themselves from the city mob — and made their own tour of the various packinghouses, forcing the proprietors to sign agreements which raised wages to two dollars a day.

With so many discontented people lining the streets, any small group of workers with purpose and a target could get up a crowd. Conversely, a large crowd often would melt away just as quickly as it had formed. The police were forced to march back and forth dispersing crowds that seemed to rise up, disappear, and reappear at random. That many suffered from bloody feet by the end of the day was a measure of the widespread nature of crowd activity.

The incidence of small crowds was so great that most were not reported. A notable one was a small group of unemployed dockworkers and laborers gathered near the lake. Finding nearly everything shut down, the group stopped by an abandoned flatcar, whereupon its leader, an Irish boathand, jumped up to make a speech.

Pointing out that if they had nothing to do in the summer they would have nothing to eat in the winter, he spoke with considerable vehemence.

> "Look at me," he continued, casting ferocious glances; "do I look like a loafer or a laboring man?" The crowd yelled and cheered and assured him that he was one of them. "Of course I am," he said; "I am as honest a workingman as ever worked in a shop. Look at my hands. . . . These hands show what I am. We know what we're fighting for and what we're doing. We're fighting those God d — d capitalists. This is what we're doing. Ain't we?" The crowd hurrahed and yelled and a number of them shouted, "Let us kill those damned aristocrats." He had been a railroad worker himself once, he said, and knew what he was talking about. They had the thing started and they were going to keep it going until those big bugs had been put down. . . . He was ready to die for the workingmen and so were they all. [*Tribune*, July 26]

During the day the city was preparing itself for a full-scale insurrection. Two regiments of the U.S. Army had arrived from the Dakotas, where they had done battle with the Sioux Indians. Their arrival was a relief to fearful businessmen and clerks who felt more secure behind the bronzed and grizzled veterans. But as the soldiers marched west on Madison to the Exposition

Building, they were followed by a jeering crowd from Canal Street.

Meanwhile, in response to the mayor's call, the city's middle classes began to arm themselves. One alderman organized a makeshift cavalry, and 300 Civil War veterans organized in the heavily Republican Fourth Ward. Citizen patrols were formed in the Third, Ninth, Eleventh, Twelfth, and Eighteenth wards. Reports of patrols were noticeably absent in the strikers' wards. At 5 P.M. a late afternoon shower seemingly cooled the disturbance, but not for long. For two days workers had endured clubbing and occasional shooting without retaliation. Now they were to claim their revenge.

After dinner a crowd of about 1,500 gathered at the Burlington yards. Upon satisfying themselves that the yards were not being worked, they were about to disperse when a squad of sixteen policemen under Lt. Callahan pulled up. The "peelers"* were met with shouts of defiance and a volley of stones. The police responded by firing at the crowd with their revolvers. Amazingly, the crowd did not flee. A *Times* reporter wrote in language reminiscent of the late great conflict, "They faltered not in the least but stood up under fire like war-scarred veterans or men resolved to perish for their cause rather than abandon it." Some workers replied to the police fusillade with stones and sporadic fire from their own weapons. Shots were exchanged for fully two minutes until the police ran out of ammunition. Having no time to reload, they turned south on Union and ran for their lives. The workers followed in close pursuit. The roles of the past two days had been reversed, and for the first time the crowd had taken the offensive.

*The use of this term for police was imported from Great Britain. It derived from the name of Robert Peel, founder of the Irish and English constabulary.

During the battle WPUS members were attempting to hold another meeting, but before it could begin the police attacked from the rear and sent participants into wild flight. Though the socialists continued their attempt to organize a series of orderly strikes, by Wednesday crowd actions by the unskilled and unorganized workers had gone beyond a strike and approached insurrection.

Thursday, July 26

If there was a coward in the battle he could not be detected.

Tribune

The strike, which had turned into an armed confrontation Wednesday night, continued along these lines Thursday morning. Now the scene of activity shifted to the residential areas. By 9 A.M. a crowd of 3,000 men, women, and teenagers from surrounding neighborhoods had gathered along Halsted Street between 12th Street and the viaduct at 16th Street. This area of Halsted was narrow, skirted by frame buildings, and could easily be blockaded.

Soon a squad of police arrived on the scene and attempted to break up the crowd by chasing it south on Halsted. At 16th Street, confronted by an angry crowd of 5,000, the police emptied their revolvers into the crowd. "Although men were seen to drop away at every minute the mob dragged or carried them away at the instant. . . ." When they had almost expended their last round of ammunition the police turned into headlong retreat north over the viaduct. They were closely followed by the crowd, which pelted them with stones. One officer later admitted, "I was never in such close quarters in my life before." One block later the police picked up a squad of reinforcements and again turned on the crowd, firing and clubbing mercilessly. One of the crowd who had been shooting at police fell mortally wounded; this had a "sobering effect," and the tide turned again. But after the officers had chased the rioters across the river, a "gang of roughs" raised the bridge and isolated a small band of police on the south side. The police might have been annihilated had not a small boy turned a lever to lower the bridge and allow a squad of volunteer cavalry to ride to the rescue of the beleaguered peelers.

The "battle of Halsted Street" reached its climax in the early afternoon. At the Union Stock Yard a contingent of 500 stockyard workers from Bridgeport set out along Archer Avenue to join the lumbershovers on Halsted. Many of them were butchers, still wearing their aprons and carrying butcher knives and gambrels for clubs. At the front of the procession two boys carried a banner bearing the words "workingmen's rights." The crowd, now swollen to 1,500, was a "determined one," conceded the *Tribune,* composed of "men in every sense of the word . . . brave and daring in the extreme. . . . When the police called on them to disperse they vowed they would rather die than return." A desperate battle for possession of the Halsted Street bridge ensued, lasting nearly an hour. "Every inch gained was warmly contested by both sides. If there was a coward in the battle he could not be detected." Only the arrival of a squad of police reinforcements shooting into the crowd decided the contest, and the stockyard workers retreated to Bridgeport.

Mayor Heath had given in by this time to pressure from the business community to call out the National Guard. By the late afternoon, the Second Regiment took up its position at the Halsted Street viaduct, backed up by the First Regiment, stationed at 12th

FRANK LESLIE'S ILLUSTRATED NEWSPAPER

NEW YORK, AUGUST 11, 1877.

A probably fanciful depiction of the July 26 fighting on Halsted Street. In fact, the U.S. army played no part in this action. From *Frank Leslie's Illustrated Newspaper,* August 11, 1877.

(CHS, ICHi-04892)

Street and the river. There were now 3,000 militia and regulars in Chicago, more men than had been employed against Chief Sitting Bull.

The crowd that continued to throng on Halsted Street was neither beaten nor overawed. An astute *Tribune* reporter noted, "A mob cannot retreat. A charge is death to it. It must stand or disperse. 'Fire and fall back' is impossible. The work of the morning had demonstrated the impracticability of combined action in force. Consequently a guerilla warfare was resorted to."

By now 10,000 people packed Halsted, mainly on the sidewalks and alleyways. Most, probably, were onlookers, but seemingly all were sympathetic to the strike and outraged at the police. When police or cavalry approached, the crowd would part and then close behind them, many chucking stones and pieces of wood. The police might turn on their tormentors, but the crowd would melt away into the alleys.

When the crowd actions shifted to the neighborhoods, women became more actively involved. According to the *Times,* they constituted at least one-fifth of any gathering. Mostly they were there to encourage the men, but in a few instances they engaged in combat with the police. On 22nd Street between Fisk and May, hundreds of Bohemian women gathered in the afternoon at a door and sash manufactory. The newspaper reporters' descriptions of the ensuing affray reflected their dismay at such seemingly unfeminine behavior: "Dresses were tucked up around the waists," and "brawny sunburnt arms brandished clubs" torn from the fence surrounding the factory. When the police arrived to protect the factory from what the *Inter-Ocean* styled an "Outbreak of Bohemian Amazons," the women remained firm and stoned the hated bluecoats till they dispersed.

Back on Halsted Street the Bohemian women brought stones in their aprons to the men, encouraging them to "clean out and kill the soldiers." Police detectives roaming the crowd sought out women wearing one stocking on the assumption that they had used the other to carry stones for use as weapons.

Outdoor laborers, followed by teenagers and factory hands, had played a precipitating and continuing dynamic role in the events of the week. In contrast, the trade unions of Chicago's skilled workmen had generally stayed aloof from the spontaneous strike and crowd actions. Thursday, a number of trades began to hold meetings and discuss possible strikes. The men soon found that the authorities were making no distinctions between the proverbial "honest workingman" and the rioters. The coopers, cigarmakers, stonecutters, and tailors all had their meetings proscribed or attacked by police.

The most blatant abridgement of the right to free assembly occurred at the South Side Turner Hall, where 300 journeymen cabinetmakers were meeting with their employers to discuss their demands for an eight-hour day and other trade issues. With no provocation a band of police rushed into the hall, clubbing and shooting indiscriminately. At least one carpenter — Carl Tessman — was killed and dozens wounded. Two years later the Harmonia Joiners Society won a suit against the policemen involved, the judge terming their action a "criminal riot." But for years to come the city's labor movement would bitterly recall the Turner Hall incident.

As evening approached, the battle on Halsted Street subsided. Here and there police exchanged fire with snipers and occasionally cleared out homes, but the high tide of the upheaval had passed. The city was now virtually an armed camp, and mobile crowd actions were impossible without instant opposition.

But as the crowd actions receded, hitherto sporadic attempts by workers to hold meetings, organize themselves, and call strikes over longstanding grievances began to bear fruit. The West Division Street railway stockmen, stonecutters, West Side gas workers, South Side glass workers, and lime-kiln workers all went on strike. Most railroads, as well as the city's rolling mills, lumber, and stockyards remained shut into the next week. By then a significant minority of those involved, notably the railroad workers, had won restoration of recent wagecuts.

Throughout the city's West and South sides Irish, Bohemian, German, and Polish families mourned their dead relatives and neighbors, mended the wounded, or attempted to raise bond for the almost 200 men who had been arrested. Approximately thirty workingmen had been killed and another 200 wounded. By contrast, no police had been killed and eighteen had been wounded, none seriously.

Analysis of casualty lists published by the newspapers tends to bear out conclusions drawn from various accounts of the riot. Of 88 reported victims 45% were boys, 19 or under. Of those whose addresses were listed, most were from Sixth and Seventh Ward neighborhoods where Thursday's fighting took place. Teenagers were just as likely to have been killed as men, but if that category is broken down into ethnic groups, we find that teenagers with Irish-sounding names were two and a half times as likely to have been killed as German and Bohemian teenagers.

A slight majority of all victims had Irish names; almost all the rest were German, Bohemian, or Polish. Virtually all the riot victims whose residences were identified came from the Fifth, Sixth, and Seventh wards. The single largest percentage, 42%, hailed from the Sixth Ward. Of the total identifiable by residence, 22% lived in the Sixth Ward's largely Bohemian precinct near the lumberyards.

In the perspective of post–Civil War Chicago history the 1877 Great Upheaval had an important impact on the development of the city's labor movement. For the first time since the eight-hour day strike and riot of 1867 the city's unskilled and unorganized workingmen had united to oppose Chicago's business class and the powerful national railroads. But with the following difference. The 1867 strike had been initiated by skilled craftsmen with some middle class support as a means of enforcing eight-hour-day legislation. The 1877 upheaval was initiated by unskilled laborers in opposition to the entire business establishment, and their demands were more general and open-ended.

A crisis of the magnitude of the 1877 upheaval provides an important opportunity to discover the views and values of unskilled and unorganized workers, since it was one of the few occasions when their words and actions were documented. Contemporary accounts suggest that at the most basic level Chicago's industrial working class was acutely conscious of itself as a group set apart from the rest of society, "looked down upon and despised," as one young man put it. This feeling powerfully underpinned the workers' sense of unity as demonstrated by the eventual participation in the strike of most occupational groups, the joining of different ethnic groups in the crowd marches, and the unusual degree of involvement of women and teenagers.

The corollary of this was an always implicit, sometimes explicit, social and political standpoint. Workers viewed the concentrated wealth and political power of the kind represented by the railroads as ill-befitting an egalitarian republic and, therefore, illegitimate. Using names which had long served as terms of opprobium, they referred to the powerful industrialists as "aristocrats" and "monopolists." But rather than holding a more sophisticated political position of the kind represented by the radical labor reformers or socialists, most crowd members would have agreed with the worker who demanded in sweeping terms, "Bring the big bugs down to our level." This desire to level the capitalists in the same way that the Southern slaveholders had recently been leveled, together with the workers' affirmation of their "manhood," explains the mass violence of 1877 more than any motive of mere revenge against the police.

Despite the socialists' inability to significantly shape the events of 1877, the WPUS was the most immediate beneficiary and representative of the surge in class feeling and thinking among workers. As socialist leader George Schilling later wrote, "Our influence as a party both in Chicago and elsewhere was very limited until the 'Great Railroad Strike of 1877.'"

In the fall of 1877 the first socialist candidates were elected to office in Chicago, drawing their support from the Germans and Bohemians living in the eight key wards of the 1877 strike. The Irish, on the other hand, stayed with the Democratic Party. In the rest of the country the reform-oriented Greenback-Labor Party benefitted most from 1877 strikes, receiving more than one million votes in the 1878 national elections. In Chicago, however, the Greenbackers received far fewer votes than the socialists; indeed, by 1879 Chicago had become the most important site for socialist activity in the nation.

The participation of all varieties of workers in the Great Upheaval and their tendency — fully evident by Thursday — toward spontaneous self-organization, imparted impetus to a revival of unionism where it had existed before the depression, and also to the organization of new unions among the unskilled. In the 1880s this helped shift the center of gravity of the labor movement away from skilled craft workers. The Knights of Labor, an organization preaching labor unity, sprang up in Chicago immediately after the Great Upheaval, founded by a former member of the Knights of St. Crispin. By 1886 the Knights were drawing much of their support from the South and West Side factory workers who had been so active in 1877.

Among leaders on both sides of the struggle the intense class conflict of 1877 consolidated the change in outlook and policy that had its origins in the unemployment marches at the onset of the depression. Openly abandoning the traditional belief that European-style class conflict was impossible in America, those in power built armories in the city, strengthened the state militia, increased the size of the police force, and passed a state law prohibiting private military companies from drilling in public. In another approach to working-class insurgency, evangelical church groups and social reformers, attributing the poverty, misery, and violent behavior of workers to drink, organized urban missions and a renewed temperance campaign.

Albert Parsons, reflecting the polarization engendered by the conflict of 1877, drew a different conclusion. Defending the fast-growing and by then much-publicized workers' militia movement, he said, in an April 1878 interview, "The Social Revolution began last July. The issue is made and sooner or later it must be settled one way or another." Indeed, the uprising of 1877 was followed by several smaller-scale confrontations during strikes between 1879 and 1885. To many socialists these confrontations offered support for the belief that a small band of armed, professional revolutionaries could spark an insurrection during a mass strike. In part, this assumption underlay the tactics of the short-lived anarchist movement in Chicago, which rejected electoral politics and by 1880 opted for an armed mass strike.

But the anarchists misread the meaning of 1877. The upheaval was as much a transitional mode of struggle as it was a harbinger of things to come. The lumbershovers so prominent in the 1875-77 strikes sharply declined in numbers as much of the lumber business began to move out of the city in 1881. Moreover, by the early 1880s they and many other outdoor laborers had joined the Knights of Labor and other unions, and so had adopted a more disciplined and effective form of collective bargaining. Indeed, by the late 1880s, the lumbershovers had one of the most powerful unions in the city.

In general, with the opening of the era of labor organization, industrial workers increasingly eschewed crowd actions in an attempt to win public acceptance for their organizations. Moreover, the growing strength and effectiveness of the police and militia severely discouraged any enthusiasm for insurrection except among radicals. Though riotous clashes between police and strikers would continue to plague the city, never again would there be a wholesale, spontaneous uprising like the Great Upheaval of 1877.

Cataclysm and Cultural Consciousness: Chicago and the Haymarket Trial

Carl S. Smith

Catastrophes and major disruptions like Haymarket have an imaginative as well as a tangible history. In an important sense, this imaginative history — the way things work themselves out in the individual and collective consciousness, as opposed to physical damage done and action taken — defines the social meaning of an event. What distinguishes Haymarket from most other disorders, both natural and manmade, is its imaginative range and richness. Haymarket was the most notorious and widely resonating social upheaval of its time, and the one whose continuing presence as fact and symbol has been the strongest and widest. The homemade bomb that immediately killed Officer Mathias Degan and led shortly after to the deaths of six other Chicago policemen (one more died several years later from his wounds) undoubtedly had more far-reaching effects than even its unknown maker ever anticipated, for it set off a fundamental reconsideration of the nature of urban community and modern life.

Cataclysmic moments test the adequacy of a society's shared ideas about itself, as individuals and groups attempt to explain what has happened, or demand that someone explain it for them. The first response is self-defense, as people try to make troubling events fit into established patterns of belief, expression, and action. Next follow any necessary adjustments of these patterns. At such points of heightened stress, cultural values and the conventional forms in which they are communicated and shared become most visible, as they are defended and attacked, reaffirmed and altered. Those developments that are most troubling are the ones that require the most adjustment. What slowly emerges is what people believe about the nature of experience, or at least what they want to believe. What they believe shapes the reality in which they live.

Almost from the moment the bomb exploded, Haymarket has been intensely discussed, analyzed. and debated. The bombing, the trial, the appeals, the executions, and the pardons were widely reported and commented on in daily newspapers and the periodical press, as well as in countless speeches, sermons, and pamphlets. Several histories of the case, all highly partisan, soon appeared. A few of these were written by central participants, including Captain Michael Schaack, commander of the Chicago Avenue police station and one of the leaders of the original investigation; and Dyer Lum, the anarchist editor and spokesman who is believed to have smuggled into Cook County Jail the explosives with which Louis Lingg killed himself rather than submit to the hangman.

Haymarket soon figured in fiction, from dime novels (even before the verdict was in, the New York Detective Library issued *The Red Flag; or The Anarchists of Chicago*) to Frank Harris's melodramatic and inaccurate treatment in *The Bomb* (1908). As a result of Haymarket the more general topics of radicalism and unrest also became more prevalent in stories and novels, most notably in *A Hazard of New Fortunes* (1890), by William Dean Howells, who was a lonely if outspoken member of the American literary community in defense of the accused. In addition, Haymarket contributed importantly to what has been called "the cataclysmic consciousness" in American thought, which generated scores of both reasoned and crackpot books and articles about the grim future of civilization and dozens of utopian and dystopian novels and treatises which centrally discussed urban chaos and class conflict.

Haymarket quickly entered the folk culture of labor, radical, and immigrant groups who mythologized the accused as martyrs in pageant, song, and story. To this day, it is re-

Haymarket Square, May 4, 1886. Illustration from *Harper's Weekly,* May 15, 1886.

(CHS)

called when labor strife or other conflicts with civil authority flare up. Pilgrims commune with the monument to the hanged men at Waldheim Cemetery west of the city, at whose base radical activists yet yearn to be buried. Haymarket has hardly been the sole property of outsiders and dissenters, for it has also served as a reminder of the sacrifices made to preserve the sanctity of law and order. When in 1969 someone evidently protesting the Vietnam War blew up the monument to the dead policemen that had been dedicated eighty years earlier in Haymarket Square, an outraged Mayor Richard J. Daley led the emotional public outcry. The statue was repaired, but a year later it was bombed once more, leading to extraordinary security measures and its eventual removal to presumably safe refuge in the Chicago Police Academy. Advocates of political ideas of every conceivable stripe still invoke Haymarket to legitimize and substantiate their own causes. Outside the Chicago Historical Society on the day its Haymarket centennial exhibition opened, an anarchist group claimed that the Society had distorted the truth about Haymarket. Another leafleteer urged that the commemoration be dedicated to attacking "the Zionist connection to apartheid, Naziism, Central America and the atomic bomb."

But it is important to go back and sort through the discussions of Haymarket in its more immediate context if we are to understand its significance in its own time. Upheavals like Haymarket qualify our understanding of urbanization as an evolutionary process of increasing rationalization and discipline, specialization and interdependence, organization and control. In this respect, Haymarket is especially interesting as the focus of a sharply contested debate over the future direction of the United States at the very time the nation was becoming an urban, industrial society. More than any other element of the Haymarket Affair, the trial of the men held responsible for Degan's death provided the central forum for the discussion of what this violent civil unrest meant in terms of the development of the contemporary city.

Like many famous criminal and political trials, the Haymarket case was a grand performance in which the major characters addressed not each other but the world. In the days after the bombing, the police, under the opportunistic Captain Schaack and others, conducted a fiercely aggressive roundup of radical activists. Their investigation of these alleged subversives paid little regard to due process and civil rights. On May 27 the grand jury indicted ten anarchists (two avoided trial, one by testifying for the state, the other by fleeing the country). With difficulty the accused found legal counsel, and, despite their attempt to postpone the trial to a time when more calm and reasoned judgment might be possible, proceedings began in the Cook County Court House at Hubbard and Dearborn streets on June 21, less than seven weeks after the bombing.

The opening day witnessed one of the trial's most dramatic events, when defendant Albert Parsons came out of safe hiding in Wisconsin to declare his innocence and stand with the other accused. Parsons was the editor of the leading English-language anarchist newspaper, *The Alarm*, and, along with co-defendant August Spies, the most visibly active leader of the movement. From Parsons's surrender to the jury's verdict on August 20, the trial was so unfair and irregular that, apart from its other significance, it was one of the most shamefully handled cases in American legal history. It was a travesty that would have been appropriate to Gilbert and Sullivan or the Marx Brothers, were it not played with a real gallows at the end.

Jury selection took up almost half the time

of the trial, since bailiff Henry Ryce filled the pool with men who freely admitted their belief in the defendants' guilt. Judge Joseph E. Gary refused to dismiss such individuals for cause and even qualified two men who were friends or relatives of the murdered policemen, forcing the defense to use up its peremptory challenges and to accept a hostile middle-class jury. Gary then muzzled the defense and gave wide latitude to the prosecution, allowing the state to introduce highly questionable and sensational evidence, including the gory garments of the wounded policemen and an array of bombs and other terrorist devices with no bearing on the case at hand. The testimony of key prosecution "witnesses" was easily refuted, however, so that prosecutor Julius Grinnell finally had to concede that he could neither prove that any of the accused anarchists had thrown the bomb nor say conclusively who did. Instead, he and Gary convinced the willing jurors that they could convict the accused as conspirators who had encouraged the throwing of the murderous bomb, even though only two of them had anything to do with planning the meeting. (Those who actually showed up to speak were not the planners, only four of the accused had been at the meeting at all, and, most important, no one knew who threw the bomb or why he threw it.)

The trial was still the one place where the defendants had a chance to debate with the authorities what had happened at Haymarket. In court, each side tried to go beyond the immediate issue of guilt or innocence to discredit what it characterized as the social vision of the other. Both sides offered messages of alarm and reassurance, explaining why this awful event could take place and how the deeper dangers and dilemmas it revealed could be resolved. In so doing, they presented to the world competing conceptions of contemporary reality that included an analysis of the nature of order and disorder, and a definition of what constitutes normal and abnormal, acceptable and unacceptable social thought and action in the city.

Reminiscences of the trial indicate that the defendants and their attorneys disagreed over the tactics of their defense. The accused apparently wanted to turn the trial into a public forum in which they would explain their whole ideology in addition to answering the murder charge. Aware of the unpopularity of the anarchists' ideas and the flimsiness of the indictment, their lawyers advised that the trial was about the killing of Degan and concentrated on proving that their clients had no hand in this act. Any approach to their defense was certain to fail, but the anarchists' strategy was probably more to the point, for the strained legal arguments of the prosecution and judge reveal that the murder charge was a convenient hook on which to fasten the vague and unlegislated crime of radical dissent.

Even if the often violent public rhetoric of anarchism (which included the advocacy of armed force) in some was contributed to the Haymarket bloodshed, it is generally accepted by those who have examined the case that the state indicted the accused more for their beliefs than for their actions. But this analysis partly misses the mark, for they were characterized as representatives of a kind of anarchy they did not preach. In theory, at least, they advanced a carefully articulated constructive political program. Yet this was willfully ignored by the prosecution and jury, who in their frenzy insisted that the bombing could only be interpreted as an unjustified and senseless attack on the whole notion of society itself.

The fact that the murdered men were police — official representatives of law and order supposedly acting courageously to disperse an unruly mob — intensified this feeling and made this crime stand out above

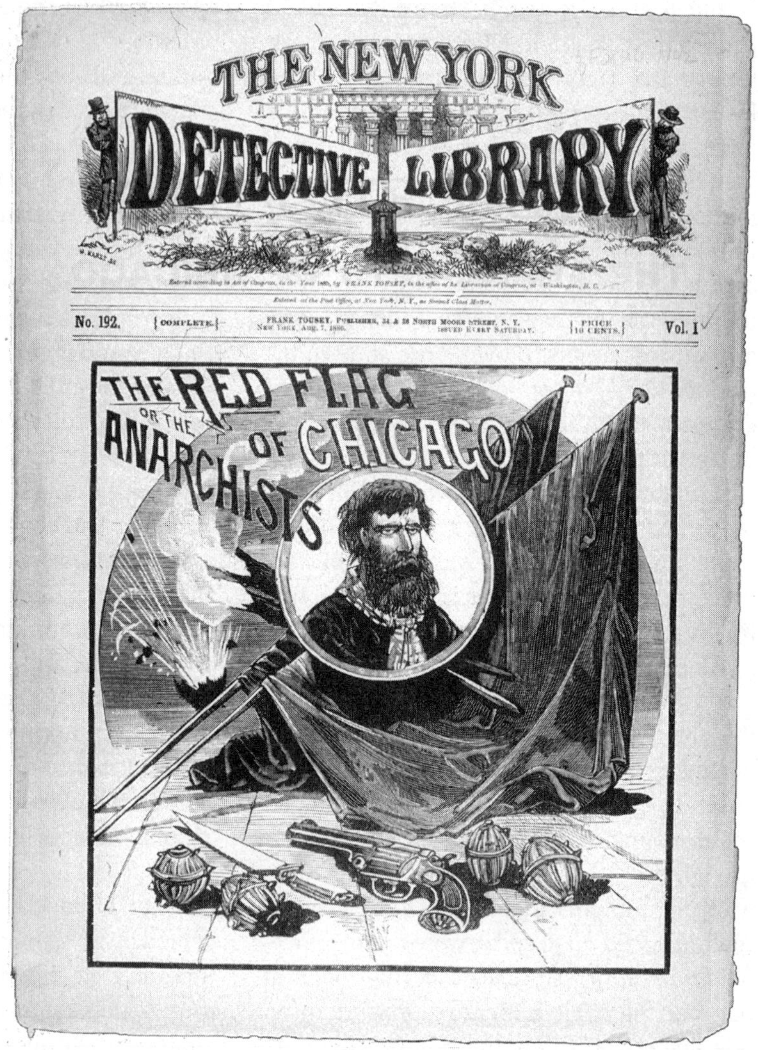

Writers used images associated with the Haymarket Affair to stir the public's imagination and to play on its fear of urban chaos, as in this depiction of the wild-eyed foreign agitator. *(CHS)*

other political acts of violence. It was irrelevant that in actuality the police had advanced without cause on an orderly gathering when all but a few hundred people had already left. Even Chicago Mayor Carter H. Harrison, who was present at Haymarket Square until shortly before the police arrived, considered what he saw and heard tame by contemporary standards. Grinnell as much as admitted that he charged the eight defendants mainly because they were representatives of a dangerous movement, and that by the same principle he could have prosecuted dozens more. He stated that the accused intended not to murder Mathias Degan, but to "kill the system — the system of law." Grinnell added, "Law is on trial; anarchy is on trial."

The prosecution defended the order of things in Chicago and America as beneficial to all. Society required law and order, and good citizens would discover their greatest chance for happiness and fulfillment by finding a useful and productive niche. The problem with the anarchists was that they refused to fit in. They were too lazy to work to earn the benefits that society promised. Assistant defense lawyer Moses Solomon argued that the evidence "shows conclusively that they are men of broad feelings of humanity, that their only desire has been, and their lives are consecrated to, the betterment of their fellow-men." But assistant state's attorney Francis Walker countered, "There is not one of them . . . that bears upon his face the stamp of sensibility or of heart, and there can be no argument made when they talk about the motive to justify murder and the advice of murder, only from the malignant heart." Seven years after the trial, Judge Gary defended his conduct by claiming that "the real passions at the bottom of the hearts of the anarchists were envy and hatred of all people whose condition in life was better than their own, who were more prosperous than themselves." For their evi-

The stern visage of Captain Michael Schaack offered a reassuring reminder of the strength of law and order.
(CHS)

dence, the defense offered the selfless dedication of the accused to the workingman. The prosecution presented the bomb.

The bomb, of course, was the one central fact that both sides had to explain. The prosecution placed it within an analysis of current events that saw order as a precarious ideal constantly threatened by these cowardly malcontents who would destroy what they foolishly and arrogantly refused to join. The value and vulnerability of the established order provided the rationale for taking harsh measures against those who would oppose it. Grinnell cited speeches and articles by the defendants (Parsons and Spies, editor of the German-language anarchist paper *Arbeiter-Zeitung,* were held accountable against their protests for every word published in the journals they edited) and anarchists in America and abroad that called for the use of dynamite and other violent means to overthrow the system.

This system, the prosecution argued, was based on reason, not just on law and order. The anarchists had conspired to violate sacred human principles, and the bomb was a monstrous affront to the sanctity of civilization. Six of the defendants were German, and one, Samuel Fielden, was British (only Parsons was native born), but it was their politics rather than their ethnic backgrounds that really made them "foreign" and removed any scruples about the proper methods of expunging them as a threat to society. Their highest crime was not murder but treason, a term with no legal meaning in this trial but which was nonetheless used repeatedly. In his opening remarks, Grinnell compared the throwing of the bomb to the firing on Fort Sumter, asserting that this later outrage was far worse since it involved cowardly terror tactics rather than open warfare.

The convicted men answered these broader charges personally in their final statements before sentencing in early October. For three extraordinary days, each of them in turn addressed the court. Their speeches, which were later published to help support their cause, varied greatly in length and tone. Parsons spoke last and longest, taking some eight hours over two days, pausing occasionally to ask without success for a brief rest. What they all tried to do, besides declare their innocence, was to put in the most positive terms the anarchist vision of society as it was and as it should be.

Parsons described anarchism as a form of socialism, which he defined, citing no less authoritative a source than Webster's dictionary, as "a theory of society which advocates *a more precise, more orderly, and more harmonious* arrangement of the social relations of mankind [than] that [which] has hitherto prevailed." (The emphases are Parson's.) He distinguished it from state socialism, or governmental control of everything, as a condition with "neither rulers nor lawmakers *of any kind.*" The anarchist, like the state socialist, "seeks to ameliorate and emancipate the wage laborers," but not by legislative enactment. Parsons continued, "The Anarchists seek the same ends by the abrogation of law, by the abolition of all government, leaving the people free to unite or disunite."

According to Parsons, he and his associates were strongly resistant to centralized control of any kind as inherently repressive and anti-democratic, but they were devoted to the very ideals that the state claimed it was protecting, notably peace, harmony, and order. The anarchists, however, desired a stable society based on free association between men and women who would regulate themselves without imposed rules. Anarchy promised an ultimate form of democratic equality based on natural law and free of a capitalist elite and exploitation, where urban variety was a source of vitality and strength. To the convicted men, the prosecution was in the service of a strictly hierarchical rather than horizontally organized society and a repressive government (and by definition every government was repressive). The ruling class forced its will on the worker through legislative law. Its institutions were the predatory corporation, the inhuman factory system, the Board of Trade, and paternalistic company towns like nearby Pullman.

Several of the accused downplayed the anarchist speeches, publications, and other documents produced as evidence of their armed opposition to authority. Of the eight defendants, Adolph Fischer and George Engel were the most active in their support of violent measures, and Louis Lingg proudly admitted to making bombs, but these three joined with the others in denying any connection to the Haymarket bombing. Spies and Parsons argued that they never committed such an action or advocated it in a specific instance. They claimed that they only urged workers to be prepared if the authorities resorted to force, citing how often this happened.

With greater rhetorical effect, they tried to prove how their accusers' own language encouraged deadly conflict. Spies cited stories on bombs from major Chicago papers that were no less inflammatory than those in the anarchist press. He pointed out that the *Arbeiter-Zeitung* on some occasions merely translated articles from the *Times* that advocated using dynamite against striking workers, and that the *Daily News* carried information on the making of explosives that was a more likely inspiration for the Haymarket bomb than any anarchist publication. Parsons recalled the violent statements of leading capitalists, asking, "Did not these monopolists bring about the inception of this language?" He sarcastically referred to a recent speech by Illinois Governor Richard Oglesby that described current conditions as a "social volcano." "What did he mean?" Parsons asked. "If he had made that remark at the Haymarket [meeting] he would be in this box here to-day, and turned over to the hangman." He maintained that the bomb was the work of an agent of capital, since it obviously aided the monopolists and hurt the workers. "Their speeches, their utterances, their newspapers openly counseled and advised by 'speech and print' just such things," Parsons explained, turning the judge's loose interpretation of conspiracy against the prominent figures he quoted: "The question, to use your honor's language, is 'not whether they did it with their own hands, but whether they (the monopolists) set causes at work which did end in the Haymarket tragedy?' By their own proposals I have shown you that they did."

As for the bomb itself, the anarchists placed it within an almost placidly fatalistic view of social cataclysm. They argued that what happened at Haymarket was a result and not a cause of social disorder, and that it was symptomatic of an advanced and warlike stage of industrial capitalism inherently doomed to catastrophe. It was wrong to accuse them since they prophesied rather than preached the inevitable collapse that must naturally come when force is all that holds society together. Spies compared social revolutions in their sources to earthquakes and cyclones as "the effect of certain causes and conditions." Society was in turmoil only because of the recalcitrance of capital. On the far side of the revolution awaited the happy tranquillity of democratic anarchy.

All the anarchists challenged the basic conventional vocabulary of the state and, in so doing, the assumptions behind the terms on which they were tried. This strategy employed the kind of reversals so familiar in the classic American anarchist text, *Walden*, by Henry David Thoreau. They did not simply state that anarchism was on the side of nature, reason, and harmony, but that the "system" was in fact opposed to its own official ideals. The sentence of the court, Parsons argued, "is the verdict of passion, born in passion, nurtured in passion, and is the sum totality of the organized passion of the city of Chicago." The police were criminals who had savagely attacked the crowd at Haymarket. Their order was disorder, their law was lawlessness. The preservation of the state, said Spies, "means the preservation of vice in every form. And last but not least, it means the preservation of the class struggle, of strikes, riots, and bloodshed." He indicted his accusers with the charges they raised against him: "You, who oppose the natural course of things, you are the real revolutionists. You and you alone are the conspirators and destructionists!"

In short, civilization was savagely uncivilized and barbarous, justifying itself through the ritual sacrifice of seven anarchists (the jury sentenced Oscar Neebe to fifteen years at hard labor while condemning the others to death) for the dead policemen. The police and the factory owners and the newspapers were guilty of conspiracy against the workers. It was they who were anarchists, if anarchy was simplistically equated with mindless terrorism. The language of the system was a network of lies since there was in the United States no free competition or individuality or progress as claimed, but monopoly and enforced obedience.

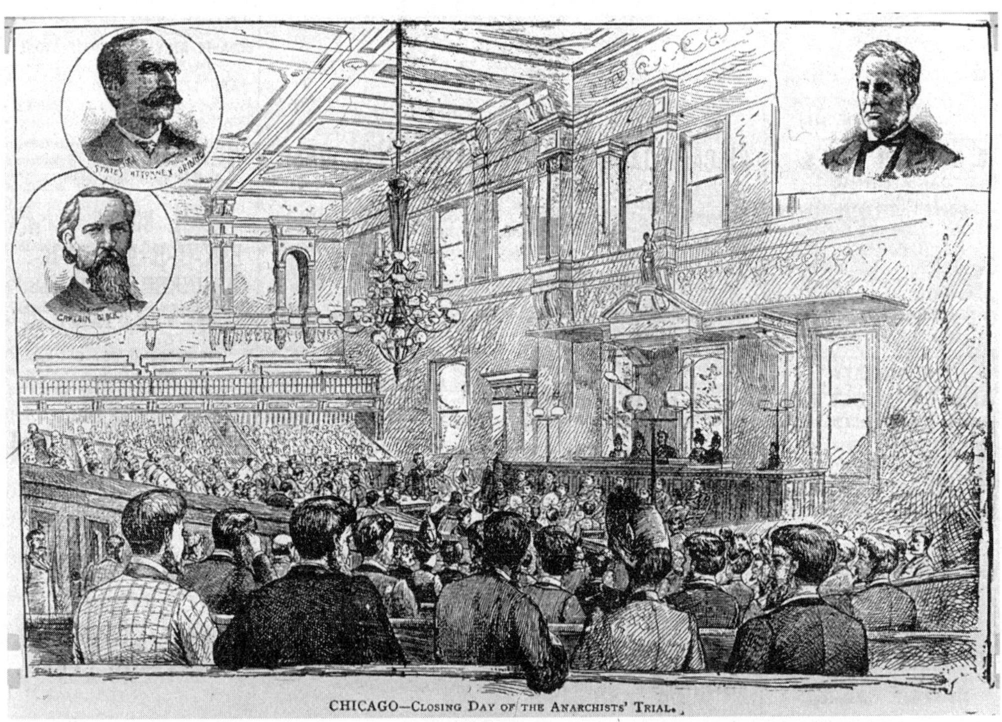

CHICAGO—Closing Day of the Anarchists' Trial.

From June 21 to August 20, 1886, Chicago and the world witnessed one of the century's most sensationalized trials. At issue was not just the guilt or innocence of the defendants, but two conflicting views of society. Followed closely in the press by a public eager for revenge, the trial was a travesty of justice. From the *Pictorial West,* November 1887.

(CHS)

It was the anarchists, furthermore, who were defending fundamental American values and had kept the democratic faith. Spies stated that they were sentenced to death "because they believed in a better future; because they had not lost their faith in the ultimate victory of liberty and justice!" George Engel claimed that his only crime was "[t]hat I have labored to bring about a system of society by which it is impossible for one to hoard millions, through the improvements in machinery, while the great masses sink to degradation and misery. . . . The statute laws we have are in opposition to the laws of nature, in that they rob the great masses of their rights to 'life, liberty, and the pursuit of happiness.' "

The language of this last remark, and of many others like it, answered the accusation of foreignness and treason by accusing the state itself of betraying hallowed national ideals. Spies repeatedly cited the links between anarchist ideology and the Declaration of Independence and other writings of the Founding Fathers, all of whom, he and the others claimed, would have been hanged in Judge Gary's court. "The nineteenth century commits the crime of killing its best friend," Samuel Fielden added. "It will live to repent it." Louis Lingg ended his short statement on a much more defiant note: "I despise you. I despise your order; your laws, your force-propped authority. HANG ME FOR IT!"

The conduct of the trial reflected the will of many prominent Chicago citizens, including George Pullman, Philip Armour, Marshall Field, and Cyrus McCormick, Jr. According to historian Paul Avrich, Pullman, Armour, and Field were among some three hundred Chicagoans who secretly pledged over $100,000 to aid the families of the policemen killed or injured at Haymarket and to help out the investigation and prosecution of anarchy and sedition. Schaack's history of the case, which placed Haymarket in the context of "the red terror and the social revolution in America and Europe," described such contributors as "public spirited citizens who wished the law vindicated and order preserved in Chicago." He explained that he spent their money to hire spies "who were familiar with the Anarchists and their haunts." McCormick, whose lockout of union workers in February of 1886 was an important step on the road to Haymarket, contributed large sums to the police over the next several years to support the investigation of subversives. The foreman of the jury was a salesman for Marshall Field, who used his considerable influence to block a movement for clemency among leaders of the business community in the days before the execution on November 11, 1887.

Grinnell and Gary were able jurists who acted as unreasonably as they did in this case because they, too, believed that men like the anarchists put the stability of the social order seriously at risk. To understand the paranoid and vindictive response to the accused, we should keep in mind how fluid and precarious this social order seemed to both social leaders and anarchists in 1886. The American economy was in an unpredictable and apparently uncontrollable rhythm of boom and bust that would not stabilize for another decade. Immigrants from abroad and throughout America were coming into urban centers in unprecedented numbers to produce and consume astonishing quantities of goods made with new machines and techniques. They found themselves working and living in an environment with no precedent — the modern industrial city — a wholly fabricated world of offices and industries, in which the measure of an individual's worth was his status within the system. In this new context, major civil disorders were part of the landscape. During the decade preceding Haymarket, Chicago had witnessed a series of violent outbreaks, the most traumatic being the battles between citizens, police, and soldiers during the Great Railroad Strike of 1877.

The mid-1880s were especially troubled times. In late April of 1885, protesters staged a major demonstration at the opening of the new Board of Trade building. This featured a procession singing the "Marseillaise" led by women carrying black and red flags. Parsons advised his listeners on this occasion to lay by their wages to buy guns and urged them to learn how to make and use dynamite. On May 4, 1885, a year to the day before Haymarket, the Illinois militia fired upon unarmed striking quarrymen at Lemont, southwest of the city, killing at least two people. The Haymarket meeting itself was called to protest what labor leaders saw as a murderous attack by police on workers who scuffled with scabs outside the McCormick plant on Blue Island Avenue on May 3.

Two days before the McCormick outbreak, Parsons had led 80,000 marchers along Michigan Avenue, under the close surveillance of the police, hired detectives, and the state militia. This parade, which is considered by many to be the first commemoration of May Day in honor of labor, was part of a nationwide strike for the eight-hour day. Behind these events lay countless other national and international demonstrations and conflicts, beginning at least as far back as the Paris Commune of 1871, the anniversary of which was religiously celebrated by the anarchists.

Chicago appeared to challenge any idea of social control. In the 1880s, the city's population grew from 500,000 to over a million. It is no wonder that the issue of foreignness was so important in the trial, for almost everyone involved had come from somewhere else, and each was trying to justify his own conception of the proper organization of society. Not only all eight defendants but virtually all twelve jurors, the prosecutor, and the judge were born and raised to adulthood somewhere else. Before sentencing, Spies pointed out that he had been a resident of Illinois "fully as long as Grinnell, and probably have been as good a citizen." Pullman came from upstate New York, Field from small-town Massachusetts. Even Mayor Harrison was a former Kentucky planter who was in his thirties when he settled in the city to practice law. At issue in the trial was the definition of the community they were all making together, and it is little wonder that the first-generation elite was so anxiously defensive and protective of the world it had made. Hanging the anarchists seemed to deal effectively with the doubts that all man-made social disorders raise, especially in a community lacking the confidence of a long history and firmly established traditions.

Regardless of what one thinks of the anarchists or their defense, there is truth in their claim that their trial demonstrated how desperate their accusers were to convict them at all costs. And the number of large-scale disruptions, including Haymarket, that befell America's cities in the late nineteenth century bears out their observation that modern industrial society, for all its organization, is constantly prone to the cataclysms and catastrophes that were so distressing to proponents of the established order. Major disasters whose causes lay outside human intention and agency — like the Chicago Fire or the San Francisco Earthquake — tested a city severely but could eventually be explained and mythologized in a way that interpreted them as blessings in disguise, as sources of unification and revitalization. Indeed, Chicago's and San Francisco's boosters bragged about the titanic scale of their natural catastrophes as evidence of their cities' irrepressible spirit and inevitable preeminence. But the aftershocks of man-made upheavals like Haymarket were harder to absorb, for they seemed to indicate something fundamentally wrong with the status quo.

While the prosecution tried to picture the accused as deviants and outlaws, the defense argued the unsettling point that the greatest danger to the community was from within, that its severest firetraps and fault lines were social. Haymarket furnished evidence for one of the paradoxical lessons of complex social organizations — that disorder cannot be excluded because it is part of the system itself, and that the effort to contain disruptions may have the opposite effect. A post-fire Chicago might cry to pass stricter building codes, but it could not fireproof against radicalism. Haymarket furthered the view of contemporary life as volatile, embattled, and perilous, and of dissent as a sign of weakness and danger to be met with suspicion and alarm. In respect to urban culture in particular, it contributed to the popular conception of the city as a place we enter expecting unpleasant confrontations and anonymous acts of meaningless violence, which, for all their apparent unnaturalness, are somehow more authentic than the civility that urbanity preaches.

In its own time Haymarket encouraged the already common practice of cultural critics to use metaphors of natural catastrophe to describe contemporary conditions. Observers of all sons were convinced that America was threatened by a social volcano, a tidal wave, a whirlpool, a pile of kindling about to ignite. They seemed to agree with Spies when he warned, "Here you will tread upon a spark, but there, and there, and behind you and in front of you, and everywhere, flames will blaze up. It is a subterranean fire. You cannot put it out. The ground is on fire upon which you stand."

In hanging the anarchists, the state was trying to stop the fire by smothering the "inflammatory" rhetoric of dissent. Such a means was ineffective in the long run. The condemned men, hoods over their heads, each shouted out a final declaration from the scaffold. Parsons, the last to speak, had just proclaimed, "Let the voice of the people be heard!" when the trap dropped, apparently quieting him and the others forever. But Spies's last words, which became the source of the inscription on the Waldheim monument were accurately prophetic: "The time will come when our silence will be more powerful than the voices you strangle today!"

The court did not accept Spies's politics, but it implicitly agreed with his assessment that society was in upheaval, which was why it had to assert its authority by taking his life. The immediate effect of Haymarket was to strengthen this authority. Appeals to the supreme courts of Illinois and of the United States failed, as did the attempt to secure reprieves for the five condemned men who refused to ask for clemency (Fielden and Michael Schwab did appeal to Governor Oglesby, who commuted their death sentences to life imprisonment). Schaack and John Bonfield, the police inspector who precipitated the bombing by ordering his men to advance on the peaceable rally in the Haymarket, eagerly fanned the fires of fear by inventing new conspiracies to advance their own ambitions. (Both, however, were soon cashiered for petty corruption, as was the officer who posed for the embattled police memorial.) And, in spite of Governor John Peter Altgeld's uncompromising full pardon of the three surviving defendants in 1893, the state won the rhetorical battle. Haymarket set the pattern for the subsequent repression of real and imagined subversives at times of cultural crisis and for the discrediting of philosophical anarchism as wild-eyed terrorism preached by crazy, lazy, bomb-hurling aliens.

Characterizing dissenters as dirty, foreign, and treacherous was an attempt to fortify and legitimize the institutions they questioned against even more moderate attack. The courts could not admit that there was any justice in the claims of the accused, for

The outcome of the trial reassured many Americans that the law was more powerful than the dynamite bomb thrown on Haymarket Square. Engraving from the *Graphic News,* June 5, 1886.
(CHS, ICHi-16071)

to do so would require a public acknowledgment that there were real problems with these institutions. In his pardon of Fielden, Neebe, and Schwab, Altgeld pointed out that the reaction to the anarchists far exceeded any physical danger actually posed by this small and disorganized group. The real threat was in the popular imagination, where the accused came to stand for the precariousness of social stability in an age of major dislocations, massive inequities, and unknown prospects. Put more simply, they were hanged because both injustice and dynamite existed, and, taken together, this was frightening. "What you see, and what you try to grasp," Spies told the court, "is nothing but the deceptive reflex of the stings of your bad conscience."

Part of the tragedy of Haymarket is how little was learned from it at the time. Refusing to explore the roots of social conflict and dreading wholesale chaos, most Chicagoans of power and influence retreated into the false security of an order based on fear rather than on positive principles. Reasonable reforms were delayed in the resort to simplistic explanations that would clarify in the least troubling way what had occurred on the evening of May 4, 1886. Altgeld displayed candor and courage when he explicitly rejected the request for mere executive clemency from "several thousand merchants, bankers, judges, lawyers, and other prominent citizens of Chicago" who "base their appeal on the ground that, assuming the prisoners to be guilty, they have been punished enough."

To have accepted this line of reasoning would have been to sustain the lie that there had been a fair trial, that justice had been served, and that the system was sound.

The legacy of Haymarket keeps coming back to the dramatic fact of the bomb. This modern force of dynamite, thrown by an undiscovered and hence inscrutable assailant, exploded with terrifying implications that refused to be explained away. Amoral and imprecise, dynamite was appallingly effective, a devastatingly democratic tool of instant reform. At the trial, Parsons pointed out that it could make any man equal to organized authority. He quoted military leaders, including army commander-in-chief Philip Sheridan, in proclaiming that this weapon altered the balance of power as much as had the invention of gunpowder. "The Pinkertons, the police, the militia, are absolutely worthless in the presence of dynamite," he warned, declaring, "Force is the law of the universe: force is the law of nature, and this newly discovered force makes all men equal and therefore free."

What Parsons did not acknowledge was that this force tore indiscriminately into all notions of civilized order — including an anarchist one — as readily as it tore apart the body of Mathias Degan. While not so calculated or cosmic as catastrophes such as the Great War, the Holocaust, or Hiroshima, the Haymarket bombing was one of those moments that demonstrated the terrible capabilities of man-made modernity as it irreversibly reshaped the temper of its time.

Upstairs-Downstairs in Chicago 1870-1907: The Glessner Household

Helen C. Callahan

In most large American cities in 1870, a majority of the employed women were domestic servants. By 1900, even though the proportion of women in manufacturing and office work had increased substantially, women employed in private households still outnumbered those in factories.

There were several advantages to domestic service: high among them were free food and lodging and a relatively low incidence of unemployment. An 1890 study by Lucy M. Salmon estimated that the national average wage for female servants was $3.25 per week, to which was added free bed and board worth more than the wage itself. The wage for female weavers in cotton mills — significant employers of women — ranged from $6.00 to $6.49 per week without additional benefits. Similarly, while fewer than 15% of female domestics were jobless at some time during June 1899 through May 1900, more than 22% of females in manufacturing found themselves in that situation.

To many women higher wages and greater security seemed insufficient compensation for the social inequality symbolized by the starched uniform and the limitations on personal freedom implicit in domestic service. But those willing to enter such employment found their labor in great demand.

Living and working conditions of domestics varied with the wealth, social standing, and personal idiosyncrasies of the employing family, but some generalizations can be made safely: working hours were long — from 14 to 17 hours per day; the workload fluctuated continually; and free time varied widely. This lengthy workday with few official breaks and a scattering of moments between jobs fully or partly free from work, encouraged disparate perceptions of the job on the part of employer and employee.

Prospective employers and servants were brought together through formal and informal means. Employers could interview and compare domestics at the "intelligence office": in exchange for the fee required from one or both parties, these employment agencies gave no guarantee and indeed were no more than a meeting place. Other employers might secure servants from welfare groups which placed girls in the homes of subscribing members as a favor to the latter. Many chose servants who had been recommended by either former employers or members of the existing household staff. Newspaper advertisement was a less attractive method because written references might be difficult to verify.

For many families, the first and only servant hired was the maid-of-all-work whose unspecified job might include cooking, washing, and waitressing. For a live-in servant, this was a particularly isolated life. A well-staffed city house might include a cook, one or more general maids, ladies' maids, and waitresses; there almost certainly would be a coachman. A family with children might hire a governess or hand over child care to one or more of the maids. The largest staffs included a housekeeper, a butler, and several footmen.

A cook would awaken by 6:00 A.M. to bake and broil a typically large nineteenth-century breakfast, to be served no later than 8:00. Dirty dishes were back in the kitchen by 9:00 and had to be cleaned before luncheon preparations began. A businessman was unlikely to be home for this 1:00 meal, but his wife often had guests. A substantial dinner, served at 6:00 P.M., would take most of the afternoon to prepare. Dishes were back in the kitchen by 7:30. At least ninety minutes would be required to return the kitchen to the order necessary for the next day's work. Somewhere in this period of time, the cook had to prepare the meals of the staff, who generally were provided with simple and unadorned food rather than with leftovers from their employer's table.

The functions of a general maid included housecleaning, serving food, and personal care of the mistress and her children. She could also be expected to do heavier work such as carrying in coal or wood to start the morning fires. Any of these functions could be transformed or expanded as the need arose. For example, a maid would also be "on call" for sudden tasks outside the house, such as clothes shopping. If an unexpected guest arrived, an additional meal might have to be improvised and served. A ladies' maid was technically restricted to the personal care of her mistress and a waitress to serving food; in most houses job differentiation was much less precise.

When a child was born to a well-to-do family, the services of a wet nurse would be secured for a limited time. Some such families might hire a governess as a nearly constant companion for the child up through adolescence, though in some households the governess was actually a maid who spent a good portion of her time with a child in addition to other household duties. Unlike a genuine governess, she might be in charge of a child's care but not its education.

A particularly large staff might be overseen by a housekeeper who was referred to by her last name preceded by "Mrs." She was not a servant and bristled at any such implication. If there were a butler, he was in charge. He also answered the door, kept accounts, and sometimes served at table. Butler, assistant butler, and footmen were added as the staff grew, but the coachman was probably the first male staff member hired. His duties included stable and carriage maintenance as well as driving. His lodgings were often above the carriage house.

In many homes servants resided in an attached but distinct area, generally above or beside the kitchen. A separate servants' entrance was usually located behind, on the side of, or at the basement level of the house. Servants' bedrooms, either in the attic or above the kitchen, were sparsely furnished with an iron bed, plain bureau, chair, and rug. If water pipes did not extend to that part of the house, the room might also contain an iron washstand. Toward the end of the century newer houses included servants' baths, but in older houses a servant might use a tub in the kitchen or, if the employer agreed, the family's bathroom.

Maids in uniform in the Leander Hamilton McCormick household, c. 1888.
(CHS, Prints and Photographs)

A servant's personal life had to be conducted primarily within the workplace. The female servant had little privacy, often sharing a room and sometimes a bed with another servant. She was potentially "on call" twenty-four hours a day. Factory work was oppressive, but as one twenty-three-year-old paper box maker explained, she and many other women had abandoned service because "it's freedom that we want when the day's work is done."

In 1870 nearly two-thirds of Chicago's female workers were domestics: by 1900 this proportion had fallen to just under a quarter. Yet domestic service remained the single largest occupation for females. The greatest proportional decline in service occurred between 1870 and 1880 — as it had nationally — partly matched by increases in dressmaking and tailoring. Unemployment in these occupations was much higher than in service.

For the census years 1890 and 1900 growth in the newer occupations of office and sales work was much greater in Chicago than nationally. Nevertheless, the combined total of female bookkeepers, clerks, saleswomen, and stenographers in 1900 still did not match the 35,340 women employed as servants and waitresses.

Except as statistics these women, generally young, unmarried, and foreign-born, remain unknown to us. Used carefully, the personal diary kept for almost fifty years by Frances Glessner, a wealthy and socially prominent Chicagoan, offers an unusually revealing glimpse of servants interacting with their employer and each other, particularly in the more relaxed atmosphere of rural Littleton, New Hampshire, where the family, including the two Glessner children Fanny and George, and the staff spent summers. Moreover, occasional letters from servants interspersed among the journal entries tell us something about their conception of their position in and out of service.

John Jacob Glessner, vice president of sales for Warder, Bushnell and Glessner, arrived in Chicago from Springfield, Ohio, in 1870 to establish a branch of the company he represented, Champion Reaping and Mowing Machines. In 1902, the company merged with other major producers to form International Harvester Company, which dominated the agricultural implements field. Glessner, a prominent member of a number of businessmen's clubs, was antiunion, favoring individual self-help among his industrial employees instead of organization. Although he promoted a scientific approach toward hiring industrial labor by the use of tests, that approach certainly was not taken in hiring servants.

The Glessners prospered as the commerce of Chicago boomed. Their first residence in late 1870 was a rented two-story frame house on the West Side near Union Park, the most fashionable district prior to the fire of 1871. After five years, they moved somewhat northeast to a more imposing two-story brick house with a large lawn. After twelve years there, the Glessners built their own home on Prairie Avenue, the center of Chicago's most exclusive residential area. The sturdy Romanesque-style building designed by H. H. Richardson provided privacy without imposing social isolation. Without lawn or front steps, its focus was a pleasant walled courtyard accessible only from inside. They also built a summer home, The Rocks, in Littleton, New Hampshire.

Frances Macbeth Glessner, a descendant of Peter Stuyvesant, first Dutch governor of New York, had grown up in a middle-class Ohio household which employed a governess, a seamstress, a cook, and a second girl until her father's food and dry goods stores failed in the mid-1840s. Unlike her husband, who did not attend college, Frances Macbeth graduated from a church-affiliated teaching school.

Once settled in Chicago, Frances Glessner enthusiastically pursued an active club life. She began an informal reading group in the 1880s which grew larger and more formal with the move to Prairie Avenue. This Monday Reading Circle, which continued to meet until about 1930, included approximately eighty women, half of them University of Chicago faculty wives. After depositing their coats downstairs, they proceeded to the library to sew while serious works were read to them for the first hour and lighter ones for the second. This was followed by luncheon in the large hall. Frances Glessner also helped found the Decorative Arts Society and was invited to join the exclusive 175-member Fortnightly Club in 1897.

Such club activities and a full social calendar made a live-in staff indispensable. At the same time, the presence of servants was to be disguised as much as possible. The long corridor on the 18th Street side of the Prairie Avenue house was designed specifically for that purpose. It allowed the butler or maid to walk from the rear service wing to the front door without passing through the main house. The kitchen, separated from the Glessner's formal dining room by the butler's pantry, was the center of work activity. The servants' dining area, on the other side of the kitchen, was the center of their free time activity. One-third the size of the main dining room, it contained a table, sideboard, writing desk, and little excess space.

On the second floor of the service wing,

three of the four bedrooms and a bath looked down on the grassy yard. On the opposite side of the house facing 18th Street and the northern light were an additional bedroom and a narrow porch. Servants who found time to relax on the latter were far from the pleasant courtyard where the Glessners enjoyed their own leisure in privacy.

A personal recommendation or a reputable agency were Frances Glessner's preferred methods for hiring servants, but she advertised when necessary in the *Chicago Tribune* and the German-language *Illinois Staats-Zeitung.* The wages she offered were slightly above the Chicago average. Her staff of two or three servants expanded in the 1880s to approximately five or six, including cook, housemaid, ladies' maid, waitress, butler, and coachman. The butler had nominal control over the staff, but when he became "disagreeable and overbearing," Frances Glessner stepped in.

From late 1870 through the end of 1907, the Glessners employed over one hundred servants. Throughout the period the turnover accelerated. The process can be followed by dividing the entire thirty-seven years into three unequal time periods on the

The front hall of the Glessner home at 1800 South Prairie Avenue.
(CHS, ICHi-17220)

basis of two significant events. The first period began in December 1870 when the Glessners arrived in Chicago; the second, in November 1887, with the move to the larger Prairie Avenue house, with its more distinct servants' quarters; and the third began in August 1891, after the entire staff quit.

Many females hired in the first period remained with the Glessners from three to nearly eight years, with more than half staying at least fifteen months. All but one woman hired in the second period stayed sixteen months or less.

Over half the females hired during the third period stayed eight months or less. But there were a handful who remained for between four and ten years. The only comparison possible in America is with the 1890 study of domestic service which calculated the average length of time spent in one job as less than eighteen months. Of course, this static figure does not tell us if the turnover was increasing. The Glessner figures seem to indicate two trends: one, a tendency toward shorter terms of employment for most servants; and the other, a very small core of servants who remained for at least four and probably more years.

The decreasing length of employment in the Glessner household was coupled with a more impersonal employer-servant relationship, which was reflected by the declining number of references to servants in Frances Glessner's journals. From the late 1880s on when servants were mentioned, it was usually by function rather than by name: Isabelle became "the maid" and Charles "the butler." Those servants who remained for years may have been lacking other marketable skills, been too old to leave one house for another, or may have been able to attain a significantly personal bond with their employer. When personal ties no longer seemed as pronounced as they had been in the first period, those servants who were able may have been more willing to leave. Because demand was high, servants who did not like an employer could move on with ease to another household. Others left service entirely either by taking up another profession or, more often, by marrying.

One particular source of tension between employer and servant was the different perception each had of free and work time. For servants, the only genuine free time was spent outside the house and away from the employing family: vacations and "the maid's day off." Because most of a servant's day was spent within the household, her co-workers were likely to be the friends she saw most often. But if she wanted to spend her holiday with them she could not, because vacations were staggered. A servant often spent those days with her family. Permission to extend such time had to be requested specifically, even in an emergency. At the employer's convenience, a one- or two-week vacation was liable to last-minute changes.

The maid's day off generally included one evening per week and every other Sunday. In 1889 when the Glessners had three maids and a butler, two of the four were given every other weekday evening and every other Sunday afternoon off. This meant that Glessner servants had more out-of-house, non-job time than the average, but a closer look at what constituted a day off is necessary.

The employer saw the day off as a privilege given on the condition that the day's work had already been done. A weekday off usually began after the morning work was done and ended when it was time to prepare dinner. Sometimes, it started after the early afternoon meal. There were often guests on Sunday; free time began after luncheon was served, dishes cleaned, and dinner prepared. Such a day off involved eight to eleven servant hours, but as the employer saw it, Sunday meant that the servant had "not much to do but heat the meals." A servant's

The Glessner family on the porch of their country home, The Rocks, in New Hampshire. *(CHS, ICHi-10452)*

scheduled days off could only be matched by another servant's equally irregular free time. Often servants spent most of that afternoon in the homes of married relatives.

Living in Littleton, New Hampshire, during the summer provided an opportunity for servants to mix with local people more often than they could in Chicago. The schedule for summer 1887, for instance, allowed

> two girls to go to town every Saturday evening — all to church Sunday morning — and for them to take turns about going to town to do the marketing — one goes Tuesday, one Wednesday, one Thursday. [July 23, 1887]

Only on one occasion during the summer were all servants relieved of duties including meal preparation: the servants' annual picnic. A carriage was rented, and the servants left for the day. Frances and Fanny Glessner indirectly benefited from the event because it gave them the rare opportunity to prepare their own dinner!

But even during non-job hours outside the home, the employer's influence did not cease. Employers felt the right and obligation to impose their own code of behavior on servants' morality. Some also proposed a dress code out of step with the clothing styles young working women admired. A time to return home was always specified if a servant went out for the evening.

A second category of free time was less clear: time spent outside the house with a member of the employing family in tasks which were not unequivocally work. This might include summer hours spent with Frances Glessner, who was quite fond of rerooting clematis vines and moving ferns from the nearby woods to the garden. The servant accompanying her was away from household duties but still on the job. Or it might include a trip to the circus with the Glessner children, George and Fanny. Time spent this way was open to conflicting interpretation. The employer considered it a free time privilege; but the servant was responsible for the children. Free time was often invaded by the presence of children, as one week in Littleton indicated:

> Tuesday George [Glessner] and Katie went to town. . . . Wednesday . . . I proposed to the girls that they go for a drive to the dairy. . . . Lizzie and Katie went taking Fanny [Glessner] with them. . . . Thursday I sent Katie, Lizzie and Fanny to the Twin [Mountain] to spend the day. [August 31, 1884]

Similarly, when Katie and her sister Lizzie [Fitzpatrick] went to church on Sunday mornings, the children often went along with them.

A third, equally unclear category was time spent inside the house but away from normal work duties: servants' self-created free time. An important part of this time would center around relations with other working people, deliverymen, and painters, for example, who passed through the house. This was a significant opportunity for servants to mix with members of the wider working-class culture. This category would also include time between tasks and chatting with others while working on a common job. Generally, it was limited to diversions which could be dropped quickly when a servant must appear to be working. This free time might be spent in the servants' dining room with the "simple but improving reading" provided by the employer — old magazines from the library upstairs or other "generally more diverting" literature the servants brought in. Because of the undefined nature of the workday, the employer might interpret these periods as time wasted, while the employee would find these moments highly necessary breaks in a long workday.

A fourth category was non-job time spent in the servants' quarters. Inviting a friend or family member to dinner required the employer's permission; even then, dinner might have to be rushed so that the servant could finish her other tasks. Technically free time, a significant portion of a domestics' social life had to be carried out within the employer's house, which gave rise to potential conflicts on proper behavior during time off. As Frances Glessner recorded one incident:

> In the evening there was so much noise and scuffling in the servants dining room [in Littleton] that I went through the playroom and opened the door just in time to see "Chet" Simpson [a local friend of the servants] and John Nelson [the coachman] scuffling with Mattie Williamson [a local person who would later become a Glessner servant] — both had their arms locked around her and were trying to get something away from her. I said, "I do not like this, and do not want you to do it anymore," then closed the door. They were much ashamed and all has been quiet since out there. [September 20, 1885]

Whether the culprits were indeed ashamed or merely appeared so is another matter. But servants could not openly question their employer's interference.

Different perceptions of free time were not the only source of confusion. There were also the problems of employer and servant expectations and responses to those expectations.

The Glessners rode out of their courtyard onto Prairie Avenue confident that every policeman for the next few blocks would stop traffic for their vehicle. Expecting deferential treatment was a pattern learned in childhood. Servants in their crisp uniforms embodied these expectations. Particularly on the occasion of the Glessners' twenty-fifth wedding anniversary, Frances Glessner recalled that the butler,

> Frederick [Reynolds] came in and in a graceful way asked me to accept two beautiful gravy ladles from the servants. With the spoons came a card "with the best wishes of the servants" followed by their names ar-

> ranged according to the length of time they have been with us. These gifts were all in the most perfect taste and touched us deeply. After dinner John called them in and thanked them for us both. [December 7, 1895]

On the other hand, service had much about it that was personal, and Frances Glessner took it as axiomatic that she should act decisively in the lives of her servants. But there were limits on the extent to which she could act simultaneously as intimate and employer.

In her seventh year of service, Katie Fitzpatrick confided to her employer that she had promised a week before to marry Chet Simpson, a widowed Littleton carpenter with children. Frances Glessner noted that Fitzpatrick "cried much — and seemed much distressed to leave her friends." A few days later both women went for a walk. Frances Glessner recorded: "I talked to Katie about Chet — and told her I would help all I could — but I rather think she will break it off."

During the next two weeks Fitzpatrick's indecision manifested itself in "miserable moodiness and bad temper," with the result that Frances Glessner had "a serious talk" with her. This lecture on demeanor may have prompted Fitzpatrick to reject her employer's counsel: "I advised her to wait a year but she told me the next morning she had concluded to remain here [in Littleton] and be married tomorrow." [October 9, 1886]

Fitzpatrick's decision to marry immediately was not only a means of asserting her separateness from her employer; it also provided a way out of domestic service. Nevertheless, she remained on good terms with Frances Glessner. From her new life as a wife and mother in a ready-made family in Littleton, the new Mrs. Simpson wrote a handful of letters to her former employer. These reveal some of her perceptions about her former and her new life.

In rural Littleton Katie Simpson was isolated from her old friends and the activity of Chicago. She welcomed the Chicago newspaper subscription Frances Glessner had sent. Her new house, though quite different from 1800 Prairie Avenue, was "very nicely laid out but . . . very plain and humble, [with] very little in it." [Letter, October 19, 1886]

A few years later, after Frances Glessner sent her some second-hand furnishings, Katie Simpson wrote her thanks: these pieces have "enabled me to have my home so much more comfortable than my husband's means would have been able to." [Letter, October 17, 1889]

Money was a problem. At the end of an early letter of thanks, Katie Simpson asked for her back wages, but went out of her way to avoid inconveniencing her former employer:

> I forgot to tell you Mrs. Glessner, I did not get my wages from Oct. 2, I Paid up every thing else there was no money left to get my wages. You can give it to Lizzie, she writes regularly to me. [Letter, November 3, 1886]

In the same letter, Simpson noted that her work schedule was heavier than it had been in domestic service, but "getting up at half past five washing, ironing, and all the new work comes as easy as if I had always done it."

For despite the acknowledged drawbacks of her new situation — more work, lack of comforts, economic difficulties, and isolation — Katie Simpson fully recognized and eloquently expressed what she had gained. Admitting that she missed the family and found it hard to believe that she was not filling her old place, she nevertheless confessed to feeling "free as if I were in a dream." [Letter, October 19, 1886]

Medical care for servants was provided by

some, though by no means all, employers. Those who did provide it avoided problems created by a resort to patent remedies, which might aggravate rather than cure a servant's illness and extend her unproductive time. In the Glessner household, servants who were ill were usually examined by the family's doctors, with the one important difference that those doctors were less likely to make house calls to see servants.

In one instance Frances Glessner was able to express her personal concern for one of her servants while exercising authority and displaying good sense. During a trip to New York City in 1887, Pauline Fisher, a servant traveling with Frances and Fanny Glessner, was diagnosed as having inflammatory rheumatism. At the doctor's suggestion, Frances Glessner went to the drugstore for necessary medicines and bathed her servant's pained joints. When the doctor decided on hospitalization, Frances Glessner later remembered:

> I came back to the hotel and told Pauline as gently as I knew how what the Doctor said. She cried and so did I. She said I was an angel and she was utterly unworthy of the kindness and care I had taken of her — that she would go anyplace or do anything I wanted her to do and make no fuss. [May 21, 1887]

While waiting for the ambulance,

> I put my calico wrapper on her, my slippers, her stockings and drawers — did up a change of clothes and then took care of her until the wagon came. . . . [May 22, 1887]

If in this instance the personal side of the employer-servant relationship triumphed, this was not always the case. On at least one occasion Frances Glessner felt that her benevolence had been sorely abused by all concerned.

Maggie Charles had worked for the Glessners for a year when she was severely burned in a gas explosion in the Chicago house while Frances Glessner was in New Hampshire. (John Glessner later joined his wife in Littleton, though he had been in the Chicago house at the time of the explosion). Charles remained in critical condition for a number of weeks but eventually recovered. Soon after returning to Chicago the Glessners had a lengthy discussion with her and with the other employees about what they believed had been an extreme abuse of privilege. As Frances Glessner chronicled it:

> The Doctor and nurse took every advantage of us possible in our absence — making the case as expensive as possible and using our house as badly and commonly as possible. The nurse staid longer than was necessary — ordered out our carriage for Maggie and when she found out it was not a victoria told Charles [Nelson, the butler] she would have one from the livery stable and charge it to us — the landau would not do.

As if that were not enough:

> The Doctor had luncheon served to him whenever he liked, cases of ginger ale were ordered — two quarts of French brandy consumed, — he was seen asleep on George's bed in the middle of the day — took his baths here, etc.

And for the final outrage:

> There were six women here to be fed and supported, all paid wages but two — one of those was Maggie's sister-in-law who imposed herself upon the family. [October 17, 1892]

There is no mention of a rebuke to the doctor.

When servants did not fulfill Frances Glessner's expectations, she perceived it in very personal terms, as seen in the particularly suggestive passage which follows. While out for a drive in New Hampshire, the Glessners passed another carriage containing the family's servants, who had decided on their own to take some hours off. Frances Glessner clearly saw this as a personal betrayal:

> Such breaches of trust make one's heart sick. We give these people every latitude, every comfort, confidence, and make them a part of our family, and yet when one of them refuses to do her duty, no one of the other four have enough respect and affection for us after all the kindness they receive at our hands, to look after our interests, and see that our wishes are carried out. It is sad indeed and dispiriting to have our confidence shaken in the whole of them. [August 6, 1886]

She felt much the same when she discovered from a new butler that the former butler, who had left her employ in a huff several months earlier, had been reading her journal surreptitiously during his years in the household.

The ambiguity pervading the employer-servant relationship in a household like the Glessners' is further evident in their celebration of Christmas. Servants were invited to watch the tree lighting but spent the rest of Christmas Day working. The staff generally received almost identical presents: in 1881, each servant was given $5 and a gold ring; in 1882, each maid received $5, a book of poems, and a handbag; in 1883, each re-

Frances Glessner with her two children, Frances (Fanny) and George, 1883. *(CHS, ICHi-10450)*

ceived a silver watch. 1884 was an exception — the favorite maid received $25.

In 1885 Mary Dempsey, the Glessners' cook, expressed her anger about the indignity of the Christmas gift-giving ceremony. Dempsey, who had been with the Glessners for three years, was enraged by the disregard with which presents were given to servants. That year the standard gifts were $5 in gold, an umbrella, and a fan.

> [Dempsey's] presents, all but the money, were afterwards laid on the dining table (by herself) and she told both children that she had an umbrella and had no use for the fan. Fanny had a cry over it. I have kept away from her until this evening when I sent for her and talked to her about how insulting she had been — and silly — when she told me she would leave if she couldn't suit me when I told her she most certainly would leave if she couldn't do her work in a pleasant spirit. [December 26, 1885]

Dempsey did not leave. She finally chose to depart two years later because she opposed the changes Frances Glessner tried to initiate when the family moved to Prairie Avenue. As Frances Glessner recorded the incident:

> I called Mary in to tell her I wanted the children called Miss Fanny and Master George and thought this a good time to commence it when I have new people coming in. She flew in a rage when I told her I wanted her to cooperate with me in seeing the beds were made in the servants' quarters before breakfast, etc. She was very impertinent and our talk ended in her flouncing out of the room saying she would leave, which she did. [November 8, 1887]

Frances Glessner's demands had exceeded Dempsey's limits of deference.

By 1894 Christmas presents had become cash payments of a month's wages to those who had worked since the previous Christmas and who had "faithfully performed their duties during the (previous) year." [Wage Journal] There was, by now, little ambiguity surrounding the Christmas ceremony.

Leaving a job, "giving notice," was the only work stoppage most domestics — and especially live-in servants — could carry out. Anything more overt than slowing down productivity could result in the loss of a place to live as well as a job. In some cases there were collective responses and, occasionally, a formally organized one. Contemporary periodicals mention strikes by household domestics and unions formed by domestic servants, such as the Household Union in Holyoke, Massachusetts, and the Servant Girls Union in Toledo, Ohio.

The ultimate expression of defiance within the Glessner household was a walkout by the entire staff in August 1891 while the family was in Littleton. The announcement was made after dinner when Frederick Cartledge, the butler,

> appeared with a document signed by all the five [servants] saying they would all leave as soon as they could be paid. John [J. Glessner] made out their accounts. The two men, Frederick and James, walked to town, brought out a dump cart and old white horse. They took their trunks and all five left the house at 6 o'clock — they got no traveling expenses — only wages. [August 2, 1891]

There had been continual friction between the servants and the custodian's family at The Rocks. The latter's version of the long-standing feud had been accepted, the servants felt, without a fair hearing for their side. Three of the five went to work in other prominent Chicago households; the butler, at least, received good references from Frances Glessner.

Emma Siniger, one of the maids, left with her fellow employees, but a month later tried to regain her former position by writing a letter of apology to Frances Glessner. She was unsuccessful, but wrote two more letters to explain her reasons for walking out. In the third letter, Siniger claimed the Littleton custodians had gone to the Glessners with lies about the servants' behavior. She boldly challenged her former employer:

> If you knew there was trouble going on Mrs. Glessner why did you not come and hear our story as well as you listened to Mr. Williamson's and the coachman's.

She went on to put the blame squarely on her employer's shoulders:

> It was too bad to have it [the walkout] happen so — but Mrs. Glessner, you could have prevented it if you wished. Why did you not give us an opportunity of having a plain understanding? But you would not. That day it seemed as if you purposely avoided us. Mr. Glessner listened to the stories down at the barn and believed them — you never thought that we had as much right to be listened to as they [the non-servants] had.

Frances Glessner expected personal loyalty from Siniger but had not given it in return.

After denying the custodian's allegations about her own behavior, Siniger set down her understanding of the loyalties and responsibilities of service.

> I never carried tales to you — no more did I carry tales from you and I know you do not believe that yourself. I was true to you and I did my work well. I was faithful to the girls as well. I could not be unfaithful to the rest of the help and stay right in with the lady of the house. I must choose my friends from working girls — and it would never do for me to give them up for my mistress. [Letter, September 28, 1891]

How articulate she was and how different from the way Frances Glessner described her on her first day of work three and a half years earlier:

> She is perfectly green, had never seen a water faucet or lighted the gas. She waited on the table today but the effect can hardly be described. [March 11, 1888]

Both employers and employees were invaded by ambivalent feelings and expectations. An employer expected a servant to be a silent and deferential attendant yet a personally loyal and occasionally intimate confidant. The loyalty the employer gave in exchange was limited; his or her obligations were more properly food, lodgings, and wages. Although servants were paid for work, deference was implicitly part of their job. But this obligation had limits beyond which they could not go without losing their self-respect. Some sort of personal relationship with the employer was attractive and, in fact, nearly impossible to avoid; but it was not the servant's sole personal relation or sole obligation within the household. When an employer demanded more from the relationship than the servant would give, the former perceived the latter's assertion of self not for what it was, but as defiance.

Chicago's Ethnics and the Politics of Accommodation

John D. Buenker

Chicago is a city of ethnics. It teems with the nation's largest concentration of Scandinavians, Poles, Czechs, Serbo-Croatians, and Lithuanians. It is second in the number of Germans, Greeks, Slovaks, Jews, and blacks who live here, and it has the country's third largest group of Italians. And they all have a good deal in common.

From the first Irishman to today's Spanish-speaking migrants, they became Chicagoans amid poverty, rejection, and discrimination, and they seized whatever means available to foster their economic well-being, to promote dignity and self-respect, and to defend their cultural and religious traditions.

No method has proved more popular or successful than political action. Politics, as turn-of-the-century writer Henry Jones Ford sagely observed, is "probably the secret of the powerful solvent influence which American civilization exerts upon the enormous deposits of alien populations thrown upon this country by the torrent of emigration." In Chicago, as elsewhere, the "bonds of Blood, Believer and Brother as strongly define political interest and conflict as do the bonds of class or locale."

Most ethnic Americans first turned to politics for economic survival. In a world where wages were too low, public welfare programs virtually nonexistent, and private charity inadequate or demeaning, the ward leader and the precinct captain functioned as the nation's "first social welfare agency." In exchange for political support, they distributed food, clothing, fuel, rent, and medical care to the needy, they settled family disputes, and they secured pardons, scholarships, pensions, and licenses. During the severe depression of the 1890s, saloon-keeper-politicians like "Hinky Dink" Mike Kenna, in his Workingmen's Exchange, fed thousands of the unemployed with free lunches. Politicians also helped save loved ones from "that awful horror of burial by the county"; Johnny Powers, notorious boss of the 19th Ward from the 1890s to the 1920s, financed so many funerals that he was nicknamed "The Mourner." Even more crucially, politics provided tens of thousands of jobs. William Lorimer, the "Blond Boss" of the West Side, secured 868 jobs for his Eastern European constituents through the Park Board in the month of November 1901 alone.

Powers had over one-third of his predominantly Italian voters on the city payroll. Mayor "Big Bill" Thompson hired so many black "temporary employees" that his enemies sarcastically referred to City Hall as "Uncle Tom's Cabin." "You and I know what a political machine is," a West Side committeeman once confided to a subordinate, "it's jobs and more jobs, and if you want to keep yours, you'd better come across with your precinct."

Many ward bosses lined their own pockets, but that rarely bothered those whom they helped when no one else would. Personal service, without condescension or bureaucracy, was the style of the ethnic politician. Lorimer's Eastern European constituents "came to my house and talked over their little troubles. . . . I helped them always." Despite her distaste for Johnny Powers's methods and morals, Jane Addams recognized that he inspired in his constituents "a sense of loyalty, a standing by the man who is good to you, who understands you, who gets you out of trouble." W. T. Stead, the English reformer and author of *If Christ Came to Chicago,* noted in 1895 that ward bosses stole "openly and good-naturedly," gave welfare benefits without red tape or embarrassment, and generally conducted themselves according to the "principle of human service." Under their tutelage, Chicago ethnics learned the rules of urban politics: (1) hold what you've got; (2) take care of your own; (3) get more benefits. In time, ethnic politicians and voters played a major role in shifting the nation from the path of the Protestant Ethic and of *laissez-faire* rugged individualism, to the concept of the welfare state. Their votes were instrumental in the adoption of such measures as child and women's labor laws, factory codes, workmen's compensation, old age pensions, medicare, and aid to dependent children, "underpinning," as Edgar Litt has observed, "the concept of collective economic and social responsibility inaugurated by the policies of the New Deal."

Politics also provided thousands of Chicago ethnics with a career ladder. Arriving without capital or marketable skills, and forced to abandon education for work at a tender age, most ethnics were doomed to a life of manual labor in the mills, factories, or stockyards. "A shovel was thrust into me hand," Mr. Dooley (Finley Peter Dunne) noted, "an I was pushed into a street excyvatin' as though I'd been born here." With professions and corporations beyond their reach, ethnics found that their only escape from dangerous, monotonous, and poorly compensated drudgery was in those areas which earlier arrivals disdained because of their questionable status and uncertain income — such as entertainment, athletics, gambling, saloonkeeping, real estate, contracting, and politics. Of six hundred Chicago precinct captains in 1935, Sonya Forthal reported, the vast majority were "from the second generation foreign stocks found in the city, with Irish, German, Jewish, Polish, British, Scandinavian, Italian, and Czech officials predominating. Seventy percent held some form of government job, illustrating the maxim that 'when a man works in politics, he ought to get paid.' " Political jobs resulted in valuable contacts which could be parlayed into business opportunities. Inside knowledge of zoning and franchise decisions made possible profits in real estate, insurance, contracting, or utilities, a practice popularly referred to as "honest graft." The income and security provided by public employment permitted higher education and a passage into the middle class for one's children.

Besides providing careers for thousands, the election or appointment of "one of our own" also constituted "a kind of group patronage." The increased material benefits

Bohemians posing proudly in front of a neighborhood saloon in the Pilsen district in the 1880s.
(CHS, ICHi-01705)

which resulted from having a friend at court were apparent enough, but of more importance were the psychological gains which "recognition politics" bestowed. To groups beset by hostility, ridicule, and discrimination, appointment to political office offered compensatory dignity and importance. The political advancement of a fellow immigrant proved to oneself and, indeed, to the world, that one's own group was as worthy as any. It helped the individual gain a vital sense of identity and integrity and avoid the antisocial behavior — alcoholism, drug addiction, violence, delinquency, divorce, and suicide — which often accompanied social uprooting. With socioeconomic and ideological differences between candidates and parties often blurred, Americans have relied to a great extent on ethnic and religious affiliations to determine their preferences. "For leadership in political discussion," the authors of *Voting* have concluded, "people mainly turn to others like themselves."

Blacks responded overwhelmingly to Alderman Edwin Wright's appeal in 1906 to vote "for the sake of the race of which you are a part . . . arouse from your slumber and realize that on your shoulder rests a responsibility as a man." Greeks were moved by exhortations to act "as descendants of the ancient Greeks and Pericles, the original author of the democratic form of government." When Woodrow Wilson campaigned for Italian votes after he had stated that Chinese made more valuable citizens, editor Oscar Durante told him "go to the Chinese to get votes." Whether it was Al Smith, "the Horatio Alger of the immigrants," running for president in 1928, or John Peter Altgeld, the first foreign-born governor of Illinois in 1892, or Mayor Anton Cermak in 1931, "renowned for his fairness to every race and his recognition of all our citizens in the matter of public affairs," the candidacy of an ethnic politician mobilized the political efforts of his fellows. Victory in a polyglot community meant giving proper recognition to candidates of all important ethnic groups. It was the greater astuteness of the Democrats in this area that led to the virtual demise of the Chicago Republican Party by the mid-Thirties.

Finally, Chicago ethnics undertook political action to protect their cultural and religious practices against pressures for conformity. The native-born Protestants who first settled Chicago often espoused a pietistic outlook which regarded most forms of physical pleasure as evil in themselves. They were disposed, James Timberlake remarked in *Prohibition and the Progressive Movement,* to "use the secular power of the state to transform culture so that the community of the faithful might be kept pure and the work of saving the unregenerate might be made easier." Through the United Order of Deputies, the American League, and the Chicago Law and Order League, the old settlers periodically sought to enact prohibition, Sunday blue laws, and anti-gambling and vice ordinances. They also sought to enforce Americanization by proscribing foreign languages in instruction, forcing attendance in public schools, and prohibiting non-Protestants from holding office.

Most Chicago ethnics, on the other hand, came from traditions which preferred to leave decisions about the use of fleshly pleasures to the Church and the individual conscience, and which permitted alcoholic beverages, Sunday recreation, and the mother tongue. To preserve these practices, ethnics voted for candidates from their own or similar backgrounds, or for understanding native Protestant Americans like Carter Harrison, William Lorimer, and "Big Bill" Thompson, who believed in the "fullest measure of personal liberty consistent with the maintenance of public order." The stage was set for the continuing struggle between what Nelson Algren referred to as the "Live and Let-Livers" and the "Do As I Sayers."

When state Superintendent of Public Instruction Richard Edwards tried to force the use of English in Illinois schools in 1890, ethnics protested that "to take my language away from me is to snatch the cradle I was born in from me." The resultant uproar led to the repeal of the law. Censorship of textbooks usually led to conflict between what has been termed a "Protestant–capitalist–native-American complex" and a "Catholic-labor-foreign complex." As late as 1923, a committee of public-school teachers urged voters to cast their ballots against Catholic Democrat William E. Dever unless "you want Rome to run our Public Schools." When Congress moved to restrict immigration by the odious National Origins Quota System in 1924, Chicago's ethnic politicians were in the vanguard of the opposition. Anton Cermak formed a joint committee of Southern and Eastern Europeans to organize protests, Jewish West Side alderman and future Democratic chairman Jacob Arvey led a delegation to testify before Congress; and, on the House floor, Chicago's "scrappy little Adolph Sabath," renowned in the greenhorn sections of every American city as the immigrant's Congressman, protested in Bohemian accents.

No issue so animated the political action of Chicago's ethnics as the liquor question. "Prohibition was the greatest ethnic issue," John Allswang has argued, "both for its precise aims and for the more general ethnic–native American conflict which it epitomized." Under Cermak's leadership, 1,087 separate ethnic organizations merged to form the United Societies for Local Self-Government, a powerful anti-prohibition coalition of 258,224 members. Ethnic newspapers denounced prohibition with invective seldom matched in the annals of journalism. Four times between 1919 and 1933, Chicago voters rejected prohibition in referendums. The ethnic vote made the decision overwhelming. Although Chicago voted 73 percent against prohibition in 1919, all the city's ethnic minorities except the Swedes opposed it by margins ranging up to 90 percent or more. Native-born Americans opposed it by only 58 percent, and prohibition actually carried Hyde Park, Woodlawn, Englewood, Beverly Hills, Rogers Park, and Uptown — "the higher rental areas where the native whites of native parentage live." University of Chicago political scientist Charles Merriam, a one-time alderman and mayoral candidate, observed that "almost no known dry has ever been elected mayor, prosecuting attorney or sheriff of Chicago or Cook County and many campaigns have turned chiefly upon the problem of comparative wetness." When Irish Catholic and wet Mayor Edward F. Dunne was pressured to close saloons on Sunday under threat of impeachment in 1906, ethnic voters rallied behind German-American Republican Fred Busse. When Mayor Dever moved against the gangster-controlled speakeasies in 1927, "Big Bill" Thompson won a large chunk of ethnic support and the election by promising to make Chicago "as wet as the Atlantic Ocean" and to "break any cop I catch on the trail of a lonesome pint into a man's house or car."

Successive waves of Chicago ethnic groups, then, have used political action to promote prosperity and security, to carve out careers, to achieve status and self-respect, and to defend their customs and traditions against nativist attack. Success in these areas constitutes the particulars of that most Chicago-like word, "clout." The pattern was first established by the Irish, the "pioneers on the

Eastern European Jews in the Maxwell Street area in 1906, buying wares from fellow countrymen too poor to rent shops.

(CHS, CRC 144 F)

urban frontier." Driven by the Great Hunger of the 1840s, Celtic peasants flocked to Chicago and crowded into shanties and tenements in Kerry Patch, Canaryville, Back-of-the-Yards, and Bridgeport. The last was originally so barren that native Chicagoans called it "Hardscrabble." Poor, unskilled, and victimized by the discrimination of "No Irish Need Apply," the "Paddies" and "Micks" still possessed certain political advantages. They spoke English. They had been deeply involved in politics at home, where they had learned to bargain for benefits from English overlords who despised them and their religion. They had a fierce ethnic and religious pride which bound them together against the outside world and made all political contests a case of "us against them." After bargaining for favors with "outside politicians," the Irish soon captured their own wards and precincts.

Because the nativist, anti-foreign, Know-Nothing movement of the 1850s was centered primarily in the Whig and Republican parties, the Irish became Democrats, even during the days of the Civil War and Reconstruction. By the 1880s the party was popularly referred to as "Mike McDonald's Democrats," after the notorious gambler and political boss. By the turn of the century, one-third of Chicago's aldermen and about two-thirds of the Democratic ward captains were Irish. Except for the two Carter Harrisons and William Randolph Hearst, party leadership was solidly in the hands of state chairman William O'Connell, boss Roger Sullivan, and Edward F. Dunne, who styled himself "a poor man but . . . the father of municipal ownership and thirteen children." Dunne became the first Irish Catholic mayor in 1906 and governor in 1912. In 1912, in fact, the Democrats presented an entire slate of Irish candidates for statewide offices and elected forty-three Celtics to the state legislature. Even when Irishmen began to move to the suburbs, their political influence endured. Perhaps, unlike the Yankees before them, they were unable to withdraw to such private power bases as foundations, universities, and corporations; but it was also a result of their continuing view of the Democratic Party as a medium by which to protect their hard-won gains. For the last half-century, except between 1927 and 1933, Irish mayors have governed Chicago. As late as 1962, Irishmen still held 51 seats in the state legislature, and there were 12 Irish aldermen, 21 Irish ward leaders, and 32 Irish states attorneys — when only about 10 percent of the city's population was Irish.

The other groups that composed the so-called Old Immigration (before 1890 and from Northwestern Europe) — the Germans and Scandinavians — were much less politically active. German Catholics generally became Democrats and German Protestants became Republicans, although cultural issues often drove German Lutherans into the Democratic camp. The Scandinavians were generally Republican, particularly the Swedes, whose religious preferences leaned toward pietism. By 1890, Chicago's political parties were fundamentally divided by a religious outlook. The Republicans were a coalition of native Americans, Scandinavians, and German Protestants; the Democrats were a combination of Irish and German Catholics; and the fluctuating Lutheran vote often decided the outcome of elections.

Then came the flood of New Immigrants — Poles, Czechs, Slovaks, Russian Jews, Lithuanians, Serbo-Croatians, Greeks, and Italians. The West Side became "a veritable babble of languages." The Newcomers were as poverty-stricken and despised as the Irish had been, spoke little English, and had almost no political experience, but for the next three decades they held the balance of political power in Chicago.

Since religious outlook was the deciding

political factor, the New Immigrants should have become instant Democrats, for the vast majority were either Catholics or Orthodox Jews. And the native leadership of the G.O.P. — the Medills, McCormicks, and Pattersons of the *Tribune,* Victor Lawson of the *News,* Herman Kohlsaat of the *Times-Herald,* and Governor Charles Deneen — seemingly did its best to accomplish that end by its stands on cultural issues. "A Republican is a man who wants you t' go t' church every Sunday," said Democratic boss "Bathhouse John" Coughlin in the 1890s. "A Democrat says if a man wants to have a glass of beer, he can have it." Lorimer, Thompson, and "Poor Swede" Fred Lundin, however, prevented the G.O.P. from committing political suicide. Although despised by the reform wing, they courted the New Immigrant vote by bestowing material benefits, playing recognition politics, and opposing forced Americanization.

Many Irish Democrats also aided the Republican cause by refusing to share their hard-won gains with the "Hunkies." Johnny Powers styled himself "Johnny DePow," and disdainfully boasted that he could buy all the Italian votes he needed for a glass of beer. By 1926, despite the fact that several New Immigrant groups outnumbered the Irish in the general population, 50 Democratic ward leaders and 25 of the party's 42 candidates were still Irish. Even when the party ran German Catholic Robert Sweitzer for mayor in 1919, other ethnics derided him as "the Irish Kaiser." As an exasperated black politician put it, "You Irish don't realize you're a minority group."

Under the circumstances, most New Immigrants fluctuated between the two parties until the 1930s, supporting whichever one gave them the most benefits or recognition, capturing scattered wards and precincts in both parties, and appearing as candidates for city and state offices. By 1903 there were three Poles in the state legislature. The Italians produced two aldermen and five assemblymen before 1920. The great breakthrough came in 1931 under the leadership of Anton Cermak, the canny Bohemian who was the most astute ethnic politician in the city's history. Ever since he formed the United Societies in 1906, Cermak had been plotting to wrest control of the Democratic Party from its Irish leadership. Skillfully he built alliances with other ethnic politicians and forced their inclusion on party tickets. He even courted such dissident Irishmen as Pat Nash, Ed Kelly, and Edward Dunne, who were chafing under the heavy-handed leadership of party boss George Brennan. When Brennan died in 1928, "the Bohunk" collected his political debts and bested Brennan's designated heirs, Michael Igoe and John Denvir. Finally ensconced as party leader, Cermak replaced many Irish ward bosses with New Immigrants and built ethnically balanced tickets, winning election as mayor in 1931 at the head of a "U.N. ticket" — Cermak, Kandl, Brady, Allegretti, and Smietanka. The following year, Jewish Henry Horner symbolized the political arrival of the New Immigrants by his election as governor.

When Cermak's opportunity to "ethnicize" the party was cut short by his assassination, and his party's leadership fell back into the hands of Irishmen Kelly, Nash, and Richard J. Daley, they now had to share their power with the New Immigrants. The Depression, combined with the Republicans' advocacy of prohibition and the restriction of immigration, had all but killed off the local G.O.P. The Democratic Party had become the sole arena in which ethnic groups could continue their struggle for clout. It was now, in John Allswang's phrase, "a house for all peoples."

But not quite "all peoples" yet. Chicago's blacks had arrived as Republicans, and the reception they received here reinforced that loyalty. As the New Immigrants moved inexorably toward the Democratic column, Republican "Big Bill" Thompson saw his opportunity and frantically courted the thousands of migrants pouring into the Black Belt from the South. "I'll give your people jobs," he promised, "and if you want to shoot craps, go ahead and do it." By 1930, Thompson had 2,785 blacks on the city payroll, a close approximation of their percentage in the general population. "Big Bill" assured black veterans of the Great War that "the black finger that is good enough to pull a trigger in defense of the American flag is good enough to mark a ballot." In his ill-fated 1931 reelection campaign against Cermak, he warned blacks to think about the upcoming World's Fair and "re-elect your friend Bill Thompson mayor if you want to go in the front gate, because if you elect that cracker you'll go in the back gate." Black leaders referred to Thompson almost reverently as "the second Lincoln," and Oscar DePriest, Chicago's first black alderman and the North's first black Congressman, insisted that "you must either vote for Thompson or else die." A more balanced judgment was rendered by Ralph Bunche in 1929, when he said Thompson had given Negroes "no little patronage and favor, a significant increase in recognition and influence, and a whole lot of bad government."

The Democrats helped Thompson's cause by blatantly racist election appeals. They accused "Big Bill" of being for "Africa First." They campaigned in racially changing neighborhoods to the tune of "Bye-Bye Blackbird," and Negro leaders warned their people to "elect Big Bill or it's going to be Bye-Bye Blackbird in Chicago." Even though Mayor Cermak generally eschewed outright racism, he fired thousands of black "temporary employees" and cracked down on Negro gambling houses and speakeasies. "The lid went on," a black politician moaned, "five minutes after it was certain Mayor Thompson had lost."

What political progress blacks had made up until then had been almost entirely within the G.O.P. Warren Harding got 95 percent of the city's black vote and Coolidge, 91. In 1920, Edwin Wright was selected as Republican chairman of the heavily black 2nd Ward. When Oscar DePriest was elected alderman in 1915, several blacks had already served in both houses of the state legislature. By the time DePriest was elected to Congress in 1928, however, the G.O.P.'s percentage of the black presidential vote had dropped off by 15 percentage points, and by 1936 it was down to 52 percent. Franklin Roosevelt became the first Democratic presidential candidate to carry the Black Belt four years later. Prominent Negro politicians Arthur Mitchell and William Dawson read the portents. They switched parties, and Mitchell defeated DePriest for Congress in 1934. By the Sixties, blacks were at least as Democratic as any other ethnic group in Chicago.

Despite their eventual conversion to the Democratic Party, blacks and Spanish-speaking Chicagoans seem unable to use the techniques of ethnic politics to advance themselves as rapidly as the earlier ethnic groups. The existence of one party dilutes their ability to maneuver for benefits as the New Immigrants did. The city's Republican Party is so moribund that there seems little future in capturing it, as the Irish did the minority party after the Civil War, and the risk of leaving the party from whom all good things flow is too great. Still, the Irish and the New Immigrants reserve few important positions for blacks or Latinos. When Oscar DePriest was elected to Congress in 1928, less than 10 percent of Chicago's population was black. Today, with better than one-third the population black, there are still only two black Representatives. Still, the black population is spreading, and there is more opportunity to capture new wards and

A sight familiar to Chicagoans — Mayor Richard J. Daley addressing a loyal ethnic group. The occasion, an election banquet in 1956 at the Prudential Plaza. *(CHS, ICHi-03593)*

elect new aldermen. Yet, even though Chicago, as the last "machine city," is less committed to civil service and "good government," there are still not nearly as many patronage jobs as there were in the heyday of the white ethnics. Moreover, the federalization and professionalization of welfare payments have destroyed much of the connection between politics and material benefits, placing a barrier of bureaucracy and red tape between the ward boss and his constituents.

Perhaps, in the long run, their frustrations may prove to be only as temporary as those suffered by the white ethnics. Perhaps Mayor Daley's eventual retirement will trigger a redistribution of political clout among ethnic groups similar to that of the early Thirties. If it does, Chicago may yet realize the ideal set forth by the Jewish philosopher Horace Kallen — "a democracy of nationalities" which will cooperatively achieve the self-realization of peoples of all origins.

PART III

THE PROGRESSIVE ERA

Everything under One Roof: World's Fairs and Department Stores in Paris and Chicago

Russell Lewis

In October 1889, Edward T. Jeffery, president of the Illinois Central Railroad, was sent to Paris by Chicago's Mayor Dewitt C. Creiger and the city's Citizen's Executive Committee to study the Universal Exposition of 1889. From Jeffery they hoped to learn what was involved in organizing, financing, and running a world's fair so they could prepare their proposal to host in Chicago the exposition celebrating the 400th anniversary of Columbus's discovery of America scheduled for 1892. Most important, they wanted a full and comprehensive account of the 1889 fair so that they could create an exposition that would surpass it. After six weeks of intensive research Jeffery submitted a detailed guide to securing exhibits, constructing buildings, financing, providing transportation, and managing the general business affairs involved in a world's fair. In his conclusion he offered this encouragement:

> Let the achievement of France in 1889 stimulate us to a similar though greater undertaking. If it be urged that time at our command is rather limited for its full accomplishment and complete presentment let us cast these doubts aside, and unhesitatingly believe that with our intense energy, our unbounded patriotism, our enthusiastic enterprise, our keen inventive genius, our vigorous industries, our unrivaled mechanical skill, our incomparable material resources, and our financial strength, we can push to a satisfactory completion "The World's Exposition of 1892. [Paris Universal Exposition, 1889]

The rest of the nation was not as confident as Jeffery that Chicago was capable of creating a world's fair that would be worthy of the Republic. While Chicago had the requisite energy, commitment, and money to complete the project, the city lacked refinement and experience with culture. Under French stewardship, aesthetic achievement had become one of the goals of exposition organizers. Indeed, fears were voiced that what would come about in Chicago would be only an enlarged western agricultural fair "with fat cattle, and prize pigs galore" instead of a proper tribute to the nation. A world's fair in Chicago, many easterners

Interior view of the Manufactures and Liberal Arts Building. Organized around a central clock tower at the intersection of the building's two major aisles, the exhibit space resembled a small city under one roof.

(Photograph by C. D. Arnold. CHS, ICHi-17532)

complained, would be a missed opportunity for America to make a good showing before the rest of the world.

But Chicago succeeded, and there was general agreement that the World's Columbian Exposition of 1893 had surpassed Paris's 1889 fair. "Every American can go and congratulate himself," announced *Frank Leslie's Illustrated Newspaper,* "that we have not only excelled, but in many respects surpassed the great expositions of the old world." Evidence of this achievement was found in the art and architecture of the fair. The Columbian Exposition was acclaimed unanimously as an aesthetic marvel, which created a vision of beauty and harmony unequaled in modern history. "And because the harmony thus revealed on so grand a scale," exclaimed contemporary art critic Mrs. Schuyler Van Rensselaer, and "because the items of beauty and impressiveness are SO many and varied yet so concordant . . . you will behold a sight which . . . has not been paralleled since the Rome of the emperors stood intact." For Arthur Sherburne Hardy, editor of *Cosmopolitan Magazine,* the fair was the greatest artistic achievement in the history of mankind: "But if history tells us any one conception more stupendous, or greater variety and unity, whose strength was more uplifting and beauty more entrancing than this — we do not believe it!"

To many Americans, the Columbian Exposition represented a momentous break with European traditions. It signaled the ebb of European dominance of the arts in America and the emergence of both an American appreciation for beauty and a distinct national art. For others there were not any new "American" contributions in the architecture of the fair; it was an eclectic amalgamation derived from classical and Renaissance styles.

Debate over its artistic achievement, if any, began immediately and still continues, but in fact other aspects of the fair were more important. The 1893 fair is a benchmark in the emergence of a consumer society whose history can best be understood through a study of the origins and development of the international exposition as a mass retailing institution in Europe in the second half of the nineteenth century. The growth of expositions is linked directly to a consumer revolution centered in Paris. Another modern urban institution, the department store, traces its origins to this revolution and, like the exposition, helped make Paris the consumption capital of the world. The Columbian Exposition, like its European predecessors, was also linked to the development of department stores, although the role these stores played in the development of urban life in Chicago was far different.

Expositions and the Consumer Revolution

The 1851 "Exhibition of Works of Industry of All Nations" in London's Hyde Park was the first attempt by any nation to gather together examples of engineering and decorative arts from around the world. Although Thomas Paxton's Crystal Palace, a novel construction of glass and iron, created a tremendous amount of popular appeal, the displays themselves were aimed to reach the more specialized audience composed of industrialists, investors, and engineers. Exhibits were organized according to the stages of production (extraction, manufacture, transportation, and trade). Prince Albert supported the exhibition enthusiastically in the hope that it would encourage the exchange of industrial knowledge and techniques among nations, for he believed that the growth of commerce and industry was a necessary step to creating a new era of world peace and prosperity. The many displays of British industrial powers were offered as instructive examples.

By focusing attention on the mechanics of production, the Great Exhibition in London was merely an international version of the national industrial shows common in France and England in the late eighteenth and first half of the nineteenth centuries. The first French exposition of international scope held in 1855, however, was a marked departure from the Crystal Palace exhibition. In Paris the focus shifted from the industrial revolution as seen in machinery and industrial processes to the consumer revolution as evidenced by a wealth of goods themselves. The origins of this consumer revolution are found in the movement of French court life in the eighteenth century from Versailles to the city of Paris and the changes that followed the rebuilding of Paris during the Second Empire. The enjoyment of discretionary spending was confined originally to nobility, something that Louis XIV and the court of Versailles in seventeenth-century France superbly expressed. Louis's court was also renowned for refined exquisite taste and impeccable manners, and in France especially consumption later became tied to specific ideas about taste, behavior, and fashion that formed another ideal of what it was to be civilized.

With the movement of the aristocracy from the country estate to the salons of Paris in the eighteenth century, the capital became the new center of both consumption and of court life, but it was court life increasingly opened to the bourgeoisie. Rosalind Williams has recently written in *Dream Worlds: Mass Consumption in Late Nineteenth Century France:*

> The salon provided an environment of consumption that united the brilliance of the court and the intimacy of the house . . . as a setting for social exchanges, salons did much to promote similarity in manners, ideas, tastes, and attitudes between nobles and bourgeoisie, two groups separated by legal distinctions and social origins, [but] united by economic privilege. . . . These two groups were slowly consolidating into a united upper class, largely because they came to share a common environment of consumption.

As a result, the ideal of courtly consumption not only survived the fall of the monarchy and the hereditary aristocracy in the French Revolution, but soon spread, embracing the middle classes in the early nineteenth century.

As greater numbers joined the ranks of the bourgeoisie, the demand for consumer goods increased, and Paris, which was underindustrialized (in large part because of a special tax on goods and raw materials entering the city), ironically became the city in which consumption began to flourish as a middle-class urban ideal. This can be attributed to the fact that not all goods were equally attractive to the bourgeoisie. Cheap mass-produced goods, like those from England, were not as desirable as the handmade, finely crafted products for which Paris was known, and which because of their uniqueness conferred on the buyer a greater sense of social status. These demands, along with the special tax discouraging industrialization in Paris, assured the proliferation of small workshops where skilled artisans produced specialty goods for the local market. In 1847-48, less than ten percent of Parisian-made goods were exported. Having grown in response to lavish aristocratic tastes, Parisian artisans supplied the French bourgeoisie's demands for luxury items. But the setting and the mechanics for their distribution were about to change.

The development of mass retailing techniques in the first half of the nineteenth century made shopping a more pleasant experience and encouraged greater consumption. The earliest changes came in the 1830s and 1840s, again in Paris, in dry goods stores called *magasins de nouveautes,* or novelty stores. These stores were very different from the small, guild-run, specialty stores that traditionally handled only a limited number of items and bargained with customers over prices. Increased production of goods enabled dry goods stores to buy in larger quantities and sell at low prices and still make substantial profits. They began to revolutionize retailing and consumption by carrying a greater variety of goods, introducing fixed prices, encouraging inspection of merchandise. and permitting the return of purchased items.

In spite of the Parisian bourgeoisie's growing commitment to consumption and luxury, the physical congestion of the city retarded the full realization of mass retailing and consumption as an urban ideal. Transport of goods and easy movement of customers across the city was almost impossible. and the clientele of the new dry goods stores, like traditional shops, was restricted to residents of the immediate vicinity. The center of Paris was still a medieval city when Louis Napoleon Bonaparte proclaimed himself emperor in 1851. The labyrinth of dark, narrow ancient streets on the Right Bank impeded the movement of air, people, and vehicles. Filthy streets and open sewers abounded, and the threat of infectious diseases (cholera broke out in 1832 and again in 1849) was always present. Public order was a problem too. Barricades were easily erected by dissident citizens in the narrow winding streets during insurrections, and congestion hampered the movement of troops to restore order. Such impediment could only be overcome by the physical transformation of the city which, when it finally occurred under Napoleon III and Baron Georges Haussmann during the 1850s and 1860s, greatly stimulated the growth of consumption and the development of new institutions of mass retailing.

The first result of the rebuilding of Paris was to make the malodorous, congested capital into a convenient, safe, and comfortable city. Between 1851 and 1871, large sections of the Right Bank's slums were demolished to make way for wide arteries that for the first time truly interconnected the city. The broad, straight, and long avenues that replaced the medieval streets increased the flow of traffic and helped to alleviate much of the congestion. They also eased the minds of the bourgeoisie about threats to the public order. Barricading became impractical, troop movement more rapid. Health conditions were greatly improved as well: the slum demolition made epidemics less likely and admitted more fresh air and sunlight to the city; an ambitious park program introduced open space to city dwellers; and a new sewer system and the supply of fresh water made the city far more livable. No longer a barrier to the bourgeois urban ideal, Paris quickly became the center for the efflorescence of a culture of consumption during the Second Empire.

In addition to making his capital healthier, safer, more convenient, and more comfortable, Napoleon III also wanted to make Paris the most beautiful city in the world, and many agreed that he succeeded. His rebuilding transformed the city into a display of material wealth and property that was not to be equaled in the nineteenth century. The pleasant parks with promenades and the magnificent tree-lined boulevards with their many cafes and restaurants made Paris the center of fashion and luxury. Its architecture in particular presented sumptuous and elaborate spectacles. Buildings like the new Louvre additions and the Opera were bombastic in their display of opulence and luxury. By making Paris his palace, Napoleon III made every citizen a participant in the display of national wealth and prosperity. The city itself became what the court at Versailles once was, the aristocracy was replaced by the bourgeoisie, and the ideal of civilization became dominated by the idea of consumption.

By the middle of the nineteenth century, it had become clear that industrial production would advance only as long as consumption continued to increase. Mass production required not only a system of retailing larger, more efficient, and more regularized than that of the traditional specialty shop, but also a form of advertising that would appeal to the consumers' curiosity, imagination, vanity, and pride. France, which had lagged behind more industrialized nations in the first half of the nineteenth century, took the lead in mass retailing and advertising during the latter half when selling rather than production was the primary economic problem. It was during this period that the international exposition and the department store evolved simultaneously in France in response to the consumer's demand for images of luxury and abundance, entertainment, and greater availability and variety of goods. Together they made Paris the world capital for consumption.

In 1855 the French opened their first international exposition. Unlike the English, they emphasized final products rather than the means of production. They featured the luxury goods for which Paris was famous, and stressed social progress and artistic achievement over industrial might. But the most important change was the policy that all items carry price tags, something that highlighted the new emphasis on sales, advertising, prizes, and other aspects of consumption.

Twelve years later, the 1867 Paris exposition represented a fuller expression of consumption and the display of prosperity that typified the Second Empire at its height. An ambitious plan to make it the most comprehensive exposition to date necessitated abandoning the 1855 Palais de l'Industrie as an exhibition space and building an entirely new structure. The new exhibition space, covering thirty-seven acres in the Champ de Mars, was an elliptical structure of glass and iron that was meant to be a model of the world (an earlier plan for a circular building was changed because of space limitations). The ellipse was formed by a series of concentric rings intersected at regular intervals by avenues radiating from an open oval court in the center to the outer circumference of the building. Each pie-shaped section was devoted to the exhibits of one nation, and in each ring were all the displays from each of the classifications of exhibits. Thus by walking the entire length of a ring one could see, for instance, all displays of furniture and other household objects, or clothing and fabrics.

The vast display of the great variety of articles available within any category was an exciting and stimulating experience for the consumer, who could walk the rings and do some comparative shopping. The elaborate display of elegant French products (almost half of the ellipse was devoted to French exhibits) highlighted France's achievements for the rest of the world and bolstered her reputation as the world's most prosperous nation. This display technique, with an emphasis on comparison of products from around the world, was a novel feature and a break with past expositions. By organizing the world by its products under one enormous roof, the 1867 exposition anticipated the development of the modern department store, and by its focus on the exotic, the exposition made entertainment and consumption increasingly synonymous activities.

This new type of exposition continued in Paris even after the demise of Napoleon III and the end of the Second Empire in 1871. In fact, the Paris world's fair of 1878 was more lavish and comprehensive than any previous exposition, covering more than 100 acres in the Champ de Mars. The elliptical form of the 1867 exposition was dropped in favor of a rectangular plan and more flamboyant architecture, and a new exposition building and exhibit area, the Palais de Trocadero, built across the Seine from the main exposition grounds. Whatever prestige France had lost in the Franco-Prussian War she regained through her undiminished displays of abundance.

Over the years these expositions put entertainment before education. By the 1889 fair, technology played an increasing role in the realization of novel fantasies and spectacles. The fair's greatest and most enduring monument was the Eiffel Tower, a 500-meter structure that straddled the Champ de Mars. A technical tour-de-force, the Eiffel Tower was quickly condemned by French artists and intellectuals as a disgrace to Paris, but it was adored by the public for the vista it offered and as a novel landmark. But the most fantastic spectacles at the 1889 fair were created with electricity. The magical land created by electricity, long before it had become a common fixture in homes and businesses, included illuminated fountains, falling rainbows, glittering jewels, and magnificent spotlights placed atop the Eiffel Tower that made every evening at the exposition a special event. The Rue de Caire, a replica of a street in Cairo complete with bazaars, Arabs, donkeys, and belly dancers, was a popular attraction that continued on a larger scale than before the practice of recreating exotic attractions for fairgoers. Architecturally, the 1889 exposition continued the emphasis on monumentality characteristic of previous expositions.

Department Stores and the Urban Ideal

Department stores developed in ways similar to expositions, for they too served the needs for new merchandising methods and met the demands of the consumer. Once Paris was transformed to allow for easy access to most parts of the city, several large stores opened to serve the entire city. They considered every citizen a potential customer. The Samaritaine opened in 1866, the Magasins Reunis in 1867, and the Belle Jardiniere in 1868. The Bon Marche, which first opened as a magasin de nouveautes in 1852, established itself as the first modern department store in Paris in 1869 when it moved to a larger and more elaborate building, designed to enhance mass retailing.

The purpose of the department store was not only to sell the goods off the shelf, but to sell the idea of consumption to the public. According to historian Michael B. Miller, the Bon Marche did both extremely well:

> Mass markets demanded a wizardry that could stir unrealized appetites, provoke overpowering urges, create new states of mind. Selling consumption was a matter of seduction and showmanship . . . that turned buying into an irresistible occasion. Dazzling and sensuous, the Bon Marche became a permanent fair, an institution, a fantasy world, a spectacle of extraordinary proportions so that going to the store became an event and an adventure. . . . This ambiance, in conjunction with the powerful temptation of vast display, was to be the great luring feature of the Bon Marche. [The Bon Marche, 1981]

Department stores provided comfort, pleasure, and amusement, every service and every desire under its all-encompassing roof. Customers visiting the Bon Marche, for instance, could visit the second floor reading room, painting gallery, or buffet, and prompt and courteous service was always guaranteed. But the fantastic and elaborate displays created for these stores were the most effective way to attract the public. Special sales in particular became occasions to use elaborate theatrical effects that would dramatically transform the interior of a store into an exotic setting from a distant land or a wonderful dream world. Patrons visited department stores out of the desire to gaze at the display of splendor. Going to these stores was a special excursion, and more often than not a purchase somewhere along the way would be part of the adventure. Department store owners like the Bon Marche's Aristide Boucciaut realized this and as early as 1872 actually began to promote his store as a tourist attraction. Significantly, Boucciaut also supported French fairs, which were good for his business and in which he often displayed merchandise.

Within the new Paris, department stores and expositions both served the same function of selling consumption to the public and developing an urban market. The department store became a principal urban institution and a focal point of the city for the bourgeoisie. It gave purpose to urban living by providing images of prosperity and luxury, comfortable surroundings, and entertainment and began to shape the character of bourgeois culture itself. French expositions, like the department store, were an extension of Parisian life, only they presented the urban ideal of consumption on a much grander scale and for all the world to see. The exposition was a great organ not only for advertising the material progress of France and other nations but also for promoting Paris as a model city.

Chicago department store owners, not surprisingly, were active supporters of the World's Columbian Exposition, and they saw in this event an opportunity for promotion by drawing attention to the similarities between their stores and the fair. Although Chicago department stores did not evolve simultaneously with expositions as was true in Paris, one key to understanding the place of the 1893 world's fair in the city's history nevertheless lies in the development of Chicago's department stores.

The development of Lake Street into something more than the typical nineteenth-century American mercantile center was due largely to Potter Palmer, who opened a dry goods store there in 1852. Not content to cater to the "pioneer taste" of Chicagoans, Palmer brought the latest fashions and "novelties" from the East to his store and displayed them invitingly. Within a few years his was widely acknowledged as the most fashionable dry goods store in Chicago. Palmer distinguished himself by making service on a grand scale the cornerstone of his business. The practice of guaranteeing satisfaction with each purchase, still uncommon at that time in America and virtually unknown in Chicago, was publicly announced in 1861 in *the Chicago Tribune.* Making shopping pleasurable was Palmer's goal, and he succeeded admirably by introducing moderate prices, a liberal credit policy, varied and plentiful goods, courteous and helpful clerks, and spacious and commodious surroundings. The store offered respite from the mud and general unpleasantness of Lake Street, and Palmer's store soon earned a reputation for attractiveness, convenience, and comfort. His business was enormously profitable and grew rapidly. He expanded into the wholesale business, opened a New York office, and in 1853 added the building next door to his Chicago store.

In failing health, Palmer sold his entire stock and business to two young and ambitious merchants, Levi Z. Leiter and Marshall Field, in January 1865 (Palmer had agreed to remain a partner until he could be bought out). Business prospered, and within two years the two young partners were able to assume complete ownership of the firm and introduce a new name to Palmer's old store: Field, Leiter & Co. This store continued Palmer's policy of serve the public with courtesy and reliable merchandise. Improvements to Lake Street over the years had helped the store make a more favorable impression on the public. The establishment of new street grades and the raising of most of the buildings on Lake Street above the level of the river channeled the flow of rainwater into the river instead of allowing it to collect in stagnant pools on the street. The paving of the street with Nicholson wood blocks vastly improved the appearance and cleanliness of the street, and the new store made a point to keep its street frontage swept. Yet mud still collected between the blocks on wet days, the stench of the river in summer was overpowering, and the street was always overcrowded.

At about the same time that Napoleon III was completing his rebuilding of Paris, Potter Palmer was busy engineering his own transformation of Chicago. Palmer had determined that Lake Street, though vastly improved since his arrival there, could not be developed much further. The river and the railroad line hemmed it in and limited expansion, and Palmer feared that a restriction on the growth of the mercantile and financial district might slow the commercial growth of the entire city and prevent Chicago from reaching its full potential. Through shrewd real estate speculation, Palmer hoped to engineer the transplanting of Chicago's main retail business center from Lake Street to State Street.

Though at that time State Street was little more than a narrow unpaved lane lined with poorly built wooden boardinghouses, saloons, and small shops, it still displayed potential for expansion into the commercial center of the city. Its main advantage was that the major South Side horsecar lines converged there with the major West Side lines, making it one of the most accessible points in the city. After buying most of the frontage property along a three-quarter-mile strip of State Street south from Lake Street, Palmer moved the buildings on his property back from the street and convinced other owners to follow his example. The result was a hundred-foot-wide boulevard that showed great potential for the kind of commercial development that would make shopping a more pleasurable experience.

Palmer's great plans for State Street became evident when he built the first of his magnificent Palmer House hotels at the corner of Quincy and State streets and a six-story, marble-fronted "dry goods palace" farther north at Washington. The shift from the old mercantile center to the new was symbolically complete when Palmer persuaded Field, Leiter & Co., who had succeeded Palmer as the most influential merchants in the city, to occupy his new State Street store. State Street was still unpaved when Field and Leiter opened in the new store in October 1868, but the stately appearance of the building made a grand impression. The interior was even more astounding. Richly decorated with plentiful gas lighting fixtures, frescoed walls, large mirrors, walnut counters, and large, carpeted areas, it was easily the most beautiful store in Chicago. The grand opening was a memorable event in Chicago's history, drawing thousands of curious visitors and a host of spectators along the street. "No institution in Chicago, whatever its character," proclaimed the *Chicago Times,* "ever drew so large an assemblage together at opening day." By 1871, thirty new marble-front buildings had been built along the new boulevard, and State Street was on its way to becoming one of the world's greatest shopping districts.

The consumer revolution, however, came much later to Chicago than to Paris. Despite all of Potter Palmer's efforts to introduce luxurious surroundings to Chicago and to promote shopping as entertainment, it was not until the 1880s that consumption became an important part of urban life. This was because wholesale business had taken precedence over retailing among Chicago merchants. In fact, many of the first major American department stores, including Marshall Field & Co., had begun as small adjuncts to large wholesale businesses. Retail sales were often limited to only one floor of the multi-story marble palaces along State Street. Chicago's central location along water routes, and later in the national railway network, had made it a major distribution center and had fostered the development of large-scale wholesale merchants. Chicago's wholesale market included small-town dry goods stores and rural general stores throughout the Midwest and the West. The rapid growth of urban markets in the 1880s, however, made retailing more profitable than wholesaling, and local merchants began to show more interest in the Chicago market.

The major obstacle to the development of mass retailing in Chicago was the city itself.

Women did not find Chicago's commercial district particularly attractive, and few ventured there despite attempts by merchants to lure them by promising comfortable stores and quality goods at bargain prices. The wholesale business, which came to dominate State Street in the late 1860s and 1870s, turned the street into a commercial thoroughfare rather than a promenade for shoppers. Wholesaling was a man's world. The buyers were not the ultimate domestic consumers, but businessmen comfortable with the great profusion of activity they saw in this commercial district. It was ugly, smoky, and dirty, and open vice and crime made it dangerous as well. These dangers, along with the unpleasantness and inconveniences of the commercial street, made shopping in the Loop a trying experience. Like the core of Paris before its transformation, Chicago's Loop was an impediment to the growth of consumption as an urban ideal.

With the expansion of retail business in the Loop, Chicago department stores began to offer more comforts and services to their clients to attract larger numbers of women customers. The courteous service and comfortable surroundings that had been the hallmark of merchants like Palmer, Leiter, and Field became even more important to the further development of mass retailing in Chicago. The introduction to the Loop of large stores devoted exclusively to retail sales enabled merchants to expand their services and create more comfortable surroundings.

The atrium of Marshall Field & Company's department store on Washington and State Streets. *(CHS, from* The Architectural Work of Graham, Anderson, Probst & White*)*

The ability to offer "everything for everybody, under one roof," as the Fair Store advertised itself, became an attraction to the public. Reception rooms where one could rest; reading rooms with writing desks, stationery, and reading materials; public lavatories; art galleries; cafes and tearooms; and eventually supervised nurseries became standard features of department stores.

The visual impression that the stores created was as important as the goods and services they offered. Once inside, the din and dirt of the street gave way to the soothing and comforting ambiance of luxury and elegance. The Marshall Field retail store built in 1879 featured, for example, an enormous grand rotunda in its center opening through all six floors with ornately designed columns and railings supporting and enclosing each floor surrounding the rotunda. An immense skylight flooded the store with light, which made the brilliant white interior appear even more dazzling. The Fair Store, another of the large State Street department stores, featured a grand amphitheater "with a great running fountain ornamented with vases, statuary, and flowers to refresh the vision."

Displays of merchandise also contributed to the special atmosphere of the department store. Separate departments were created for exotic items, like the oriental rugs in Mandel Brothers' Oriental Bazaar, or the Japanese wares in Carson Pirie Scott & Co.'s Art Decorative Department. The use of electric lights for display purposes produced an enchanted fairyland atmosphere. Thus, department stores in Chicago developed as havens from the city streets, and by offering comfortable and orderly surroundings, convenient services, and a chance to surround oneself in beauty and luxury, they were the agents whereby consumption became an increasingly important part of urban experience.

Although Chicago department stores sold similar goods and used the same kinds of mass retailing techniques as Parisian department stores, they had a much different role in the city. Like the theater and the hotel, the department store was a semi-public place, privately owned but open to the public. But even more than other such semi-public institutions, department stores offered the public what the city could not, and all under one roof: comfort, order, convenience, luxury, beauty, and entertainment. Thus consumption came to represent a host of amenities and urban ideals that promised to make the city more livable. Indeed, as public needs became increasingly synonymous with consumer demands, the department stores began to be seen as public servants. In the laissez-faire city of Chicago, the department store was one of the few examples of a planned and ordered environment, and more than any other city institution it offered the promise of what urban life might become.

By the time of the Columbian Exposition, mass retailing was well established in Chicago, and the department stores promoted themselves during the world's fair as if they were adjuncts to the event. Threatened by a growing financial panic, Chicago businessmen saw the opportunity to profit from the crowds that would be coming to Chicago. Months before the fair opened, stores tried to capitalize on the large number of visitors who were expected in the city by offering to supply Chicago homes with all the items necessary to meet the needs of the visitors. Department stores also promoted products manufactured especially for the fair. Marshall Field & Co. announced a special sale of fine fabrics, "which are particularly adapted for wear at the exposition" and offered a special assortment of shoes, as did Carson Pirie Scott & Co., who advertised theirs as " 'fine shoes for walking.' The extra walking which will be involved during the world's fair."

Among the conveniences designed to attract women shoppers to the new Marshall Field & Company department store was a tearoom, seen here in 1909.
(CHS, ICHi-01617)

Department stores extended their conveniences and amenities to out-of-town fair visitors both as a way to attract new patrons and as a public service. Stores like The Leader, Marshall Field's, the Fair Store, and Siegel, Cooper & Company invited the world's fair visitor to take advantage of their reception and retiring rooms and offered free information about the fair and the city. Siegel, Cooper & Company introduced a special international reading room during the fair that featured the principal newspapers of all the major foreign nations and promised that all visitors would receive a "Hearty, Honest, Cordial welcome." Marshall Field & Co. mixed the appeal of convenience with the attraction of sightseeing. In addition to courteous service, Field's retail store featured guides who spoke German, French, Spanish, and Italian to act as interpreters for foreigners making purchases and to give tours of the store and its facilities.

Chicago's department stores also drew attention to the similarities between their stores and the exposition. Special sales inaugurated during the fair were promoted as expositions of equal merit. One store boasted of the great time and expense it had devoted to an exhaustive search of Europe and America "to make the greatest collection of dress stuffs ever displayed in the greatest city of 1893" and added as a final note, "we look for no finer collection of dress stuffs even in the quickly approaching world's exhibition": The Fair Store proudly pointed to the value of its special sale: "As the great exposition will leave a lasting impression on the minds of all, likewise shall we make this sale a memorable one." Carson Pirie Scott & Co. advertised six new exhibits every Monday in their State Street store's windows, and the Schlesinger and Mayer department store promised wonderful object lessons in theirs. Siegel, Cooper & Company was more direct in its comparisons to the world's fair, bragging that the procession of visitors south to the fair "seems to find in the Big Store Chicago's grandest exposition." The similarities between the exposition and the department store were indeed great: both were international in scope and both were great attractions to visitors. But they were most alike in their meticulous attention to the needs of the public. The World's Columbian Exposition was in fact the idea of the department store applied to a city scale.

Commercialism and the White City

The "White City," as the Columbian Exposition was called, was the first world's fair to be compared to a city. The immensity of the fairgrounds by itself warranted this comparison, but the fair was also run like a separate municipality with its own street cleaning department, police and fire departments, electric light plant, and what corresponded to a mayor and board of aldermen. The cleanliness, orderliness, and beauty of the White City, however, were in sharp contrast to the dirt, confusion, and unsightliness of the host city. Above all, it was a public city. Noted Universalist clergyman John Coleman Adams wrote:

> The city was orderly and convenient. The plotting of the grounds, the manner of their development, the placing of the buildings, the communicative avenue and canals and bridges, all exhibited a pre-vision, a plan, a management of things with reference to each other . . . the mind was helped not hindered by the planning of the various paths. They seemed to be the details of an organization, not the mere units of an aggregation. The buildings were not a heap and huddle of walls and roofs. They were a noble sketch in architecture. The streets were not tangled thoroughfares representing individual preference or caprice; they were a system of avenues devised for the public's convenience. [*The New England Magazine*, March 14, 1896]

The exposition made comfort, conveniences and protection a priority for the fairgrounds and provided many of the same conveniences and services first pioneered by the department store. The Bureau of Public Comfort provided three stations on the fairgrounds where visitors could rest, eat lunch, and purchase inexpensive refreshments. The bureau's headquarters were located in the Terminal Station, where cool waiting rooms, wicker easy chairs, toilet rooms, a piano, and attendants were available. Nursing facilities were available in the Children's Building, where for a small fee a trained nurse would care for a child while its parents saw the fair. Nor were the basic amenities ignored. More than 20,000 linear feet of benches, capable of accommodating 50,000 people, were conveniently spread throughout the grounds for the tired sightseers. An abundance of daily filtered water was available free to anyone who had paid the fifty-cent admission to the fair, and hygeia water was available at one cent a glass. Dining facilities were plentiful as well. There were thirty-five restaurants on the grounds, and in each major building a lunch counter and special restaurant — all together more than 7,500 linear feet of lunch counter was provided. The fair management controlled the prices. Courteous service was also a feature of the fair. The Columbian Guards, the police force on the fairgrounds, were praised for their helpfulness in performing their duties "without any overofficiousness, brutality, and discourteousness that generally crops out in men dressed in of official garments and authority at the same time." In contrast to Chicago's Loop, the White City was comfortable, convenient, and orderly.

Architecturally, the Columbian Exposition continued the French exposition style that emphasized lavish display, heavy ornamentation, and images of luxury and prosperity. For the majority of visitors, the fairgrounds represented a novel spectacle rather than an aesthetic vision. Many descriptions of the fair pointed to the architectural unity of the exposition buildings as its most distinguishing feature, with the Court of Honor the focal point. But any suggestion of unity was overpowered by the architectural eclecticism of the buildings in the Court. The catalog of styles that each architect drew upon to individualize his work included neo-classical, Spanish-American, ancient Roman, Italian Renaissance, Venetian, Baroque, and Mannerism. Howe and Van Brunt's Electricity Building incorporated almost all of these styles.

Although the Court of Honor did not successfully achieve a vision of unity, neither did it dissolve into disharmony and chaos. Instead it reflected the merchant style of bombastic luxury and lavish splendor. Historian Henry Adams was not surprised that Chicago should choose this architectural style for the fair. "All trading cities had always shown trader's taste," he wrote of the fair buildings, "and, to the stern pursuit of religious faith, no art was thinner than Venetian Gothic. All traders' tastes smelled of bric-a-brac." Architectural critic Claude Bragdon wrote similarly, "All was simulacrum: the

Fair visitors could leave their children at the nursery in the Children's Building for an afternoon while touring the fairgrounds. *(CHS, ICHi-02232)*

buildings, the statues, and the bridges were not of enduring stone but lath and plaster . . . the crowds were composed not of free citizens of the place, but the slave . . . of the Aladdin's lamp of competitive commerce." What made the Court of Honor so enthralling was not the unity of the architecture, but the variety of styles that together created an overpowering emotional impression.

The creation of a dream-like fairyland environment added to the fair's attraction as a novel spectacle. This for many was the real reason for coming. The fair was an amusement, "a great exterior show of staged effects": Writing three years after the fair, well-known architectural critic Montgomery Schuyler described its architecture as "holiday building" compared to "work-a-day building." Although the monochromatic white color scheme of the fair buildings helped to sustain the illusion of architectural unity and harmony, it was more important for giving the exposition its ethereal quality. Fairyland imagery, one of the most popular mass retailing devices used in the late nineteenth century, conjured up a land of enchantment free from want and suffering. The effect was even more pronounced at night. More than 100,000 incandescent bulbs, 5,000 arc lights, and 20,000 glow lights every night presented, according to *Shepp's Worlds Fair Photographed,* a "fairy scene of inexpressionable splendor reminding one of the gorgeous descriptions in the Arabian Nights when Harun [*sic*] Al Rascha was Caliph."

It was the most extensive display of outdoor illumination the world had ever seen, surpassing the brilliant display at the Paris exposition of 1889. Although the Electricity Building contained many fascinating displays of the practical application of electricity to everyday life, it was the night illumination of the fairgrounds creating a novel entertaining spectacle that made the deepest impression on the public. Readers of Harper's Bazar learned what they stood to miss by not attending:

> One is never long at a loss for words in which to describe the marvels of the exposition. One may stumble and halt, to be sure, to take refuge in hyperbole, or content oneself with giving the ecstasy of the personal expression. Still, one can, with an effort, give the unhappy stay-at-home some idea of what he has missed at the fair. It is only when one comes to the wondrous enchantment of the night illumination that one fails for want of proper words. [September 9, 1893]

In addition to comfort, convenience, and entertainment, consumption defined the Chicago fair. "The Columbian Fair was large, immense, gigantic," wrote S. C. de Soissons of his Chicago visit in *A Parisian in America,* "but it was only a commercial fair, a larger shop than the others, that is all." The fair's Manufactures and Liberal Arts Building in particular fit de Soisson's description. It was Chicago's answer to Paris's Eiffel Tower (though it did not last as long), and what the building lacked in height it made up for in volume. Called the "main building," it was the largest structure in the world at the time, and visitors were frequently reminded that three buildings the size of St. Peter's in Rome could fit inside. Its vast six-acre central hall, the greatest unencumbered area ever enclosed under one roof, was made possible by an ingeniously engineered system of huge steel arched trusses. Yet, the Manufactures and Liberals Arts Building was not merely an engineering feat; there was a reason for its immense proportions. Indeed, more spectacular than the building itself were the exhibits displayed in its interior. The number and variety of manufactured articles displayed were staggering. More than 121 primary exhibit groups were further subdivided into 756 classes of goods, and within each class were hundreds of examples. Of the building's 6,000 exhibits, Japan alone had 2,089.

Organized around a central 135-foot-tall clock tower at the intersection of the two major aisles running through the building, the exhibit space resembled a small city under one roof: "Columbia Avenue, fifty feet wide, extends through the mammoth building longitudinally, and is crossed at right angles in the center by another thoroughfare of equal width. Parallel with these main roadways others are laid out in the usual rectangular form of a model city." The effect created was not unlike a city of stores with exotic structures and window displays to attract the public.

In their displays, exhibitors spared no expense. Many spent $20,000 to 530,000, and the white and gold Tiffany Pavilion was reported to have cost more than $100,000. A *Chicago Tribune* report quoted Director General Davis's estimate that the cost of all private exhibition in the main building would equal the cost of the building. It is likely that many of the Chicago exhibitors turned for help with their displays to the Drapery Department of Mandel Brothers, who had advertised "designs, complete in detail . . . always ready for immediate execution" and boasted that "some of the most striking exhibits of the Fair are the results of our efforts."

None better illustrated the general lavishness than the exhibit of the American Radiator Company. Designed by architect Charles B. Atwood, who also designed the Fine Arts Building, the Peristyle, the Terminal Station, and several other notable structures on the fairgrounds, this exhibit illustrated the kind of elegant environment created to highlight something as prosaic as a radiator:

> Four rows of graceful Corinthian columns formed the roof supports, the two interior rooms dividing the pavilion into two vestibules and an inner colonnade. The decorations were simple but effective and strictly in keeping with classic design. The entire pavilion was painted ivory with trimming of pure gold leaf. The ceiling was finished in a tint, varying from a creamy white to a warm rich pink, to harmonize with the satin paper on the walls. Delicate freehand decoration, representing Corinthian festoons and wreaths of laurel, adorned frieze and ceiling. The floor was of hardwood, adorned with numerous rich Turkish rugs. Furnishings strictly in keeping with the rich interior, and rare species of palms, completed the magnificent setting. [*The Economist*, January 1, 1894]

Wares displayed in the main building continued the French practice of including price tags. Commenting on the remarkably low price of ready-made clothing in the Belgian Pavilion, a *Chicago Tribune* report worried, "At the risk of leading Chicago people to break into the showcases it must be stated the prices pinned on those suits are . . . different from the prices paid for clothing in this part of the world." The importance of the fair as an opportunity to sell was evident in the controversy that developed over the disposition of exhibited wares. To prevent the dismantling of exhibits while the fair was still in progress, exposition rules stated explicitly that exhibited articles sold during the fair could not be delivered until after the close of the exposition. In a *Chicago Tribune* story, George Melaile from the French Pavilion expressed the view of many foreign exhibitors that the rule prohibiting delivery was harmful to sales:

> We are very much exercised about tales to visitors. We have incurred very heavy ex-

penses and we are exceedingly anxious to recoup ourselves by the sale of some of our wares. Moreover, our visitors are anxious to buy . . . we are allowed to sell anything we have provided we do not deliver it until the exposition is over. But that provision is a wet blanket on sales . . . the rules are designed ostensibly to prevent the weakening of the display by the removal of attractive exhibits. But we do not wish permission to sell the exhibits as we have an abundance of duplicates that are not on exhibition.

Before the end of the first month of the fair, rules were changed to allow exhibitions to sell and deliver their extra goods before the fair closed. And very likely many of these goods found their way to Chicago department stores. Mandel Brothers, for instance, purchased the complete exhibit of J. N. Richardson Sons' & Owden's linens.

The model city that the exposition suggested did not end when the fair closed its doors in October 1893. A movement to beautify cities with planned public buildings and spaces had been inspired by the White City and reached its peak in the first decade of the twentieth century. Plans made to rebuild sections of Washington, D.C., San Francisco, and Cleveland incorporated many of the ideas first introduced by the White City. In 1909, Daniel Burnham, Director of Works for the Columbian Exposition, submitted his Plan of Chicago, a vision of the city that was similar in design and ambition to Haussmann's transformation of Paris during the Second Empire. The most immediate impact of the White City's new urban vision, however, was on the department store. Marshall Field's Annex Building, designed by Charles B. Atwood and completed three months after the exposition opened, is the earliest example of White City ideals transferred to an urban setting, but a more complete realization came three years later in New York.

In September 1896, Chicago-based Siegel, Cooper & Company opened a new store in New York on Sixth Avenue between 18th and 19th streets. An immense seven-story structure complete with observatory tower and a searchlight visible ninety miles away, the building immediately became a landmark. With 798,000 feet of floor space — almost 17 acres — Siegel, Cooper & Company's New York "Big Store" surpassed Whitely's of London and Paris's Bon Marche to become the largest department store in the world. It clearly embodied the Columbian Exposition's vision of a city that was beautiful, comfortable, and convenient. Described as "A City in Itself" that offered "everything that man, woman or child can eat, wear or use in their homes," the Big Store promised more conveniences, more comforts, more privileges, more polite attendants than any other store." Indeed, the store gathered together services and amenities that made it like an ideal city: a doctor's office, drugstore, bank, information bureau, telegraph office, hair dressing parlors, conservatory, photograph gallery, nursery, bird and animal department, observation tower, and a New York post office branch.

The most telling evidence of the influence of the exposition was the thirteen-foot-tall gilded bronze replica of Daniel Chester French's statue *Republic* (the original graced the Chicago exposition's Court of Honor), which stood on a marble base set in a pool of water in the center of the store's ground floor. The pool was trimmed with palms, flowers and ferns, and four fountains shot water above the height of the second floor. The effect was made more spectacular by the use of colored lights that constantly changed the tint of the water. Whether in Paris, Chicago, or New York, the department store thus established itself as a powerful urban form. And in those cities and elsewhere it owed much and it gave much to the international exposition.

The World's Columbian Exposition itself represented only a grander expression of the French exposition style rather than a marked departure from the 1889 exposition in Paris. It was primarily a commercial event whose main goal was selling the idea of consumption to the public by creating elaborate images of luxury and prosperity and providing a comprehensive survey of the world's material wealth available for consumption. Both cities' expositions mirrored consumer revolutions, which gave increasing importance to selling products rather than merely producing them, to developing new techniques of mass retailing, and to creating new forms of entertainment.

Despite the similarities, however, the urban roles played by Chicago's and Paris's world's fair were different. French expositions followed an ambitious plan to transform nineteenth-century Paris into a safe, comfortable, and beautiful city. Indeed, the newly rebuilt city of Paris was the model for French world's fairs. Conversely, the Columbian Exposition was not inspired by the city of Chicago but was a model for the hoped-for transformation of the city. It was an extension not of urban reality but of urban ideals of public comfort, safety, and convenience that first had been introduced in department stores. Thus the fair offered a vision of what urban life in Chicago might become. When Chicago city officials sent Edward T. Jeffery to study the exposition of 1889 as a model for their own fair, they also chose Paris as a model for Chicago.

The Creation of Chicago's Sanitary District and Construction of the Sanitary and Ship Canal

Louis P. Cain

In the summer of 1879 heavy rains caused the sewage-befouled Chicago River to discharge into Lake Michigan for thirty consecutive days, polluting the city's water supply. The problem was not a new one. Cities situated on freshwater lakes generally used them both as sources of drinking water and as outlets for their waste, and this caused a high incidence of waterborne disease.

In the early 1850s outbreaks of dysentery and cholera had led the Illinois legislature to create the Chicago Board of Sewerage Commissioners, which engaged Ellis Sylvester Chesbrough, city engineer of Boston, to take the same post in Chicago. In 1855 Chesbrough submitted a comprehensive report outlining several alternatives for a sewage system which would "improve and preserve" the health of Chicago's residents. Before 1871 the flow of the Chicago River was reversed as part of the attempt to prevent waste from polluting the drinking supply. It was discovered that when the Illinois and Michigan Canal's Bridgeport pumps were in full operation, not only was polluted Chicago River water pumped into the canal but Lake Michigan water was pulled into the river, thereby reversing its flow and conserving the city's water supply. Under normal conditions this method proved effective. But the rains of 1879 were not normal.

As a result, the Citizens' Association of Chicago sponsored the formation of a committee "to devise a plan to dispose of the sewage of the city without contaminating the city water supply." The committee recommended a new, larger canal with dimensions comparable to those of the Chicago River. Like the Illinois and Michigan Canal, which had been built between 1822 and 1848, this new canal would carry the city's sewage and drainage away from Lake Michigan and over the low divide which separated the Great Lakes and Mississippi River drainage areas a few miles west of the city. The committee further recommended that all the city's sewage be emptied into the Chicago River and its branches. The river, especially the South Branch, would then be cleansed, because its current would be attracted by the strong current created by this "new river's" outflow.

A succession of dry seasons removed the impetus for further action. Then, in August 1885, the city was deluged by an unprecedented storm — "And a Flood Came," read a *Chicago Tribune* headline after more than 5½ inches of rain had fallen on the city in 19 hours. Not only did the sewers prove totally inadequate but the Des Plaines River overflowed into the canal, the canal overflowed into the Chicago River, and vast amounts of filth were carried into Lake Michigan and the city's water supply. The *Chicago Daily News* reported, "The rainfall . . . is . . . carrying out filth unspeakable and polluting the water far beyond the crib. This is what the majority of the people of Chicago will have to drink for days to come."

The subsequent outbreak of cholera, typhoid, and other waterborne diseases was estimated to have killed 12% of Chicago's population — one person out of every eight! The problem was clear: given Chicago's existing water supply–sewage disposal strategy, a heavy storm could kill!

The Citizens' Association committee now released a second report which proclaimed that the South Branch was "in an abominable condition of filth beyond the power of the pen to describe," and warned that the city was in danger whenever the Des Plaines River flooded. This second report "amplified and urged" the committee's previous proposal for the construction of a new canal but added a new twist by proposing a study by "a commission of experts" to put "a stop for all time to the unsanitary conditions which then existed." This report, as well as pressure from Chicago's leading citizens, forced the Chicago City Council to create a Drainage and Water Supply Commission in the spring of 1886.

The commission was to report by January 1887 in a "most full and comprehensive manner" including plans and maps as well as cost estimates for the proposed system. In January 1887 the commission made a preliminary report on the kind of legislation that would be necessary to implement any of several projects. The projects themselves were to be discussed in a final report which was never made because the City Council failed to make the necessary funds available.

The commission's mandate required solutions to two interdependent problems: (1) the protection of the city's water supply and (2) the abatement of the Chicago River's objectionable condition. No question was raised about the city's ultimate water supply source and no alternative to Lake Michigan was considered. Thus the problem was to keep pollution out of the lake on the one hand and to keep it from accumulating in the Chicago River on the other.

Three alternatives were considered: (1) to discharge the sewage into Lake Michigan at points as far removed from the water-supply intakes as possible; (2) to drain the sewage into artificial reservoirs to be pumped and used as fertilizer (a system known as sewage farming); and (3) to discharge sewage into the Des Plaines River, from which it would pass into the Illinois and Mississippi rivers. The study of these alternatives was divided into three classifications: topographic, hydrographic, and miscellaneous. The topographic surveys were to determine the feasibility of the third alternative. The hydrographic survey was to determine the rate of flow of the Des Plaines River and to consider the probable effects of diverting diluted sewage into it. The commission also investigated Lake Michigan currents and levels and lake and river deposits under the existing sewage system. Among the miscellaneous studies was an inquiry into the feasibility of sewage purification through filtration, and an estimate of the growth and distribution of the population of metropolitan Chicago.

The commission concluded that the first two alternatives only provided for a dry-weather sewage flow so that the only viable alternative was to divert the sewage into the Des Plaines River. Thus the commission report essentially agreed with the "new river" proposal put forth by the Citizens' Association committee.

The commission measured the maximum Chicago River flood flow at 10,000 cubic feet per second, and this was the crucial factor in determining the size of the proposed canal. It should be noted that cubic feet per second is a measure of the volume that passes by a spot in a particular time interval. The commission had to assume a drainage ratio in order to estimate the size, and hence the expense, of the proposed channel. A drainage ratio is simply the flow rate divided by the population, and in this case 4 cubic feet per second per 1,000 population was taken as the working estimate. This meant that a channel designed to handle 10,000 cubic feet per second flow would be sufficient to provide for a tributary population of 2.5 million people. The commission's estimates of the initial investment and annual costs (including interest) for each project are given in the table below. The *Tribune* reported that these estimates were generally believed to be high.

Cost Estimates of the Drainage and Water Supply Commission

Project	Initial Investment ($ millions)	Annual Cost
Lake Michigan disposal	$37	$2.4
Land disposal	58	3.0
Des Plaines River disposal	23-28	1.3

The recommended plan had the lowest estimated costs on both counts. Thus, there was an economic as well as a sanitary argument in favor of the "new river." The report also noted that the channel would provide a navigable waterway and a significant water-power source, which could be of great commercial value to the body responsible for its operation. Finally, the report noted that, because it would lower the level of the Des Plaines River over some sections, the proposed channel would have the effect of raising the level of the low-lying prairies contiguous to those sections, making the prairie less susceptible to damaging floods.

When the existing method functioned properly, the net results of both the existing and proposed methods were identical: diluted sewage discharged into the Illinois River valley. The proposed method, therefore, was one which removed the offenses of its predecessor while affording a greater degree of protection to the Lake Michigan water supply. In spite of the fact that a new channel would be required, this proposed continuation and improvement of Chicago's traditional sewage disposal strategy proved to be the least costly because it allowed the use of existing facilities and required no change in the city's water supply strategy. In fact, stripped to its essentials, the commission's proposal called for little more than a new, larger channel.

However, the commission's report failed to consider many important topics. Among these were the probable effects on the health and comfort of Des Plaines and Illinois River valley residents should the sewage be discharged into the Des Plaines River. It did not mention the possibility that this method might pollute St. Louis's water supply, as well as those of other Mississippi River towns. It said nothing about the possibility of filtering the water supply, even though slow sand filtration was an established, effective method. Nor did it discuss how and where the sewage would enter the Chicago River, or specify how to avoid sewage deposits and unsightly or malodorous conditions, other than to say that the sewage was to be diluted with lake water, and that the dilution could be regulated to help with these problems.

A small gathering celebrated the completion of the Main Channel on May 5, 1899. Downstream towns protested that the solution of Chicago's water problem would lead to the pollution of their own water supply.
(CHS, ICHi-05850)

The commission withheld from this preliminary report its opinion as to the proper degree of dilution "to provide immunity from offense" until tests could be conducted under variable weather conditions and in comparable bodies of water. It did not discuss the potentially serious consequences of the fact that industrial wastes were also being discharged into the Chicago River. Finally, the commission's report made no mention of state and federal government interests with respect to drainage via the Des Plaines River and the diversion of Lake Michigan water. This last omission became more significant in light of what became a long-running, continuous debate between the Sanitary District and the federal government when the district later began work on the Calumet-Sag Channel. That debate has continued to this day. It must be remembered, however, that the commission believed itself to be making a preliminary report only and expected to have a later opportunity to address details of this kind.

The Sanitary District Enabling Act of May 29, 1889, which went into effect July 1, 1889, was a direct result of the Drainage and Water Supply Commission's recommendations. This act was necessary for the implementation of the "new river" scheme since the proposed channel lay outside the boundaries of a single municipality. It permitted the creation of a regional governmental body that would encompass the entire area involved with maintaining "a common outlet for the drainage thereof." Chicago and its suburbs had identical water supply and sewage disposal problems; all benefited from the proposed scheme; and none could afford it.

The enabling act made it possible to create, administer, and finance the public utilities which the plan envisioned. The Illinois constitution limited a municipality's borrowing capacity to 5% of the total assessed taxable property within its corporate limits, and Chicago and its suburbs were all fully extended. The new district's financing powers consisted of property taxation and bond issues, with the same 5% maximum that applied to municipalities. Parenthetically, the Sanitary District of Chicago financed its projects primarily by construction bonds, with the remainder coming from excess tax revenues. Operating expenses, bonded indebtedness, interest, and the like were paid from district tax revenues. In November 1889, voters in affected areas carried a referendum for the creation of the Sanitary District of Chicago by a vote of 70,958 to 242.

The district's corporate authority was placed in a nine-member board of trustees, elected by the voters within the district. The act does not answer the question of why trustees were to be elected and not appointed, but there are several possible reasons. For one, since the district was granted taxing power, it was hoped that elected trustees would be more responsive to voting taxpayers than appointed trustees. Further, it was not clear who would otherwise be responsible for appointing trustees to a regional governmental body: since the area extended beyond the city of Chicago, but did not encompass all of Cook County, neither Chicago's mayor, its City Council, nor representatives of the county government represented all of the district's constituents and no one else.

The original area encompassed by the Sanitary District of Chicago was 185 square miles, but this was to increase greatly. In 1903 large additions were made in the Chicago River drainage basin to the north (the North Shore suburbs) and in the Calumet River drainage basin to the south (the Calumet region). The Illinois legislature, as part of the measure which authorized these annexations, provided that the annexed areas should be drained in like manner to the original area. This meant channels through which the sewage would flow with dilution water at a ratio equal to that of the district's original channel. Later, land was added to the west as well. By 1914 the area encompassed by the Sanitary District of Chicago had grown to 386 square miles, more than double the original area.

Today, the district known as the Metropolitan Sanitary District of Greater Chicago is legally limited to Cook County and encompasses almost all of the county. On the other hand, the Chicago metropolitan area extends over eight counties in two states.

The enabling act provided for the construction of the Chicago Sanitary and Ship Canal — also known as the Main Channel, or the "Big Ditch" — and its necessary adjuncts to collect the sewage and discharge it, diluted by Lake Michigan water, into the Des Plaines River. The law specified that the channel be large enough to allow for a minimum continuous flow of 3⅓ cubic feet per second per 1,000 population, ⅚ths of the amount assumed by the Drainage and Water Supply Commission. The dilution ratio enacted by the state appears to have been based on expedience rather than definite knowledge. The law also required that provision be made for a tributary population of three million. Thus, the Main Channel had to be capable of handling a flow of 10,000 cubic feet per second, the equivalent of the Chicago River's maximum measured flood flow.

The building of the Main Channel, the first construction work undertaken by the Sanitary District, was delayed for two years by administrative snarls and political conflicts among the trustees. There were disputes over routes, disputes with chief engineers — three were fired trying to resolve the conflicts — and controversial deliberations about savings costs by reducing the capacity of the channel by 42% and thus eliminating its use for navigation. But in the end, the capacity of the channel was not reduced.

The official start of construction was September 3, 1892, "Shovel Day," an occasion that the *Tribune* compared to the driving of the golden spike. In fact construction had commenced a few weeks earlier, so that Shovel Day was largely ceremonial. Around 1,200 people attended, "all in holiday attire, jubilant and enthusiastic." One thousand dignitaries were invited to the event and a special train carried "every one who is any-body in Chicago" to the site in the town of Lemont which was festively decorated for the occasion. First the ceremonial shovel, then an authentic blasting cap signified the beginning of the project that would take eight years to complete.

Chicago's open sewer approach to sewage disposal, utilizing the oxygen in a moving body of water to purify sewage, was dependent on two variables: the length of the receiving body and the volume of the flow.

The designed capacity of the 28-mile Main Channel was 10,000 cubic feet per second with a current of less than two miles per hour. The new canal and the Illinois and Michigan Canal were practically parallel from Chicago to Lockport. The Main Channel had a navigable depth in excess of 20 feet; the width varied between 110 and 201 feet; and the sides were either vertical or very slightly inclined. It was constructed in three distinct sections. An earth section between Robey Street (now Damen Avenue) and Summit was 7.8 miles long. An earth and rock section between Summit and Willow Springs was 5.3 miles long. Finally, a rock section from Willow Springs to Lockport was 15 miles long. The excavation required the removal of 28.5 million cubic yards of glacial drift and 12.9 million cubic yards of solid rock. The channel's retaining walls contained 880,000 cubic yards of stone.

Construction of the Main Channel demanded considerable dynamiting and the use of powerful earth-moving equipment to cut through millions of cubic yards of solid rock.
(CHS, ICHi-05852)

The remaining stone, from one of the most extensive quarrying operations of all time, was sold off.

The scale and nature of the undertaking necessitated innovations in the kind of equipment used. The soil was broken by machinery usually employed for railroad construction, and a specially developed grading machine pulled by twelve to sixteen horses threw the soil into a revolving apron which then discharged it into wagons driven alongside. Fifty steam shovels were used, one essentially a dredge on wheels. Its boom — 23 feet wide and 50 feet long — operated a dipper with a capacity of 2½ cubic yards. This machine was able to take rock from the cut and load it into trucks waiting on the top, but its advantage was reduced by the difficulty of moving it. The last two shovels placed in operation were also designed for the project and each weighed 72 tons.

On several sections excavated material was conveyed to the spoils banks or dump grounds by a machine known as the "Heidenreich Incline" (named for the contractor who devised it specifically for this project). The frame of the incline was mounted on tracks laid perpendicular to the lengthwise section of the incline. The platform at the base of the incline held the engine, boilers, hoisting machinery, and an electrical generator. The incline extended across the channel and traveled on tracks parallel to it with a trestle that extended down into the channel. Two cars were used for alternate loading and dumping. The incline and its approach were joined by wire cables so that the entire apparatus could be moved simultaneously. Later, Christie and Lowe refined the incline operation to include a double track that looped on the bridge, allowing side dumping of the cars.

Several other major earth-moving machines were also used during construction. The Mason and Hoover conveyor spanned the channel with a cantilever arm over the spoil area. This device, also named for the contractors who created it, was carried on tracks laid parallel to the channel on each bank. The conveyor was steam-powered by two 150-horsepower boilers which were mounted on a separate car and simultaneously powered a strong, double-ended plow which preceded the conveyor. The Bates conveyor had a hopper in which two cylinders containing intermeshed steel knives separated clay fed in by one of the steam shovels. Dredges were designed for the excavation of wet areas: channeling machines were designed to chisel the sides of the channel in the rock sections.

The *Tribune* described the mechanical work as evoking "the wonder and admiration of engineers throughout the world" and went on to say "engineers predict that these inventions will soon result in wonderful progress in the work of connecting oceans, lakes, and rivers, to the benefit of commerce and the advancement of civilization." This in fact turned out to be the case when the Panama Canal was constructed.

The Sanitary District believed that no restriction existed upon the maximum quantity which could be diverted from Lake Michigan and consequently chose to build a 10,000 cubic feet per second channel. There were legitimate grounds for this assumption, which was predicated on the belief that, since the new channel was an updated and enlarged version of the Illinois and Michigan Canal, it had all the rights granted to its predecessor; it was not the district's intention that the Main Channel maintain the maximum flow at all times.

Section 17 of the enabling act empowered the Sanitary District to "enter upon, use, widen, deepen and improve any navigable or other waterway, canal or lake" when it proved necessary. It indeed proved necessary to make improvements in the Chicago River

Engineers introduced important innovations in the equipment used for the construction of the Main Channel. Shown here is a bridge under construction.
(CHS, ICHi-05849)

so that the Main Channel could function properly. Although it had been dredged on numerous occasions, the river was only 17 feet deep and less than 100 feet wide in several places and if water was to pass between Lake Michigan and the Main Channel without obstructing navigation the river would have to be enlarged. This had been known from the outset. The fact that the district waited until after the Main Channel was well under construction to begin the Chicago River improvements had serious ramifications for Chicago's sanitary history.

In May 1895 a federal commission was appointed to investigate the Main Channel's effect on lake and harbor levels. Chicago's harbor, which had been under federal jurisdiction since the 1830s, included the Chicago River. Federal responsibility for harbors was lodged in the War Department, and the secretary of war, the chief of engineers, and Congress were all advised by the 1895 report that the proposed diversion would lower the levels of the Great Lakes by about six inches. The report also noted that without improvements to the Chicago River, a current hazardous to navigation might be introduced. The fact that the so-called "lake-levels controversy" played, and continues to play, an important role in the district's relationship with the federal government is sufficient reason to note that a diversion of 10,000 cubic feet per second would, according to today's best thinking, lower the water surface in the Michigan and Huron basins by less than three inches if all natural inflow into those basins were stopped for one year. Thus, as Jack L. Hough observed in *Geology of the Great Lakes* (1958), "it appears that the observed low-water periods were caused by climatic variations rather than by diversion of water."

The Sanitary District wrote the secretary of war requesting a permit to proceed with the proposed Chicago River improvements and enclosed full information and maps. The initial diversion was to be a volume of 5,000 cubic feet per second, to be expanded to the maximum of 10,000 cubic feet per second with increased demands upon the Main Channel. By comparison, the average flow in the lower Mississippi River today is in excess of 300,000 cubic feet per second; the flow in the Illinois and Michigan Canal after all enlargements was 1,000 cubic feet per second. The U.S. chief of engineers authorized the Chicago River improvements but raised questions about the effect of the diversion on lake levels and the current of the Chicago River. It should be noted that his only concern was with harbor rights — federal concern with pollution lay far in the future.

In July 1896, the acting secretary of war granted the Chicago River improvement permit subject to several conditions, the most important being that the authority was not to be construed as approval of the plan to induce a current in the Chicago River. This would be considered later. The government's opposition apparently was to the navigational features of the channel. Two reports, one by U.S. Army Engineer Captain W. L. Marshall in 1888 and another by U.S. Army Engineer D. C. Kingman in 1894, opposed the channel and argued that the current created for sewage would be injurious to navigation, and that the costs of the project would outweigh any transportation benefits. Moreover, Kingman's report noted, it was more important to make the Mississippi River navigable for deep-water ships. The Illinois River also needed improvements and did not become completely navigable until the last of five dams was completed in 1939.

In May 1899 the secretary of war, R. A. Alger, issued a permit which authorized the Sanitary District to open the Main Channel and make certain Chicago River improvements subject to three conditions. First, he intended to submit the question of the effects of the district's operations to Congress. Second, should the induced current in the Chicago River prove "obstructive to navigation or injurious to property," the secretary of war could stop or modify the diversion. Third, the district bore "all responsibility for damages to property and navigation interests" as a result of any induced current. The secretary's only evident concern was the effect the diversion might have on the current in the Chicago River. Alger apparently was reluctant to choose sides on the lake-levels question and hoped to pass that decision to Congress. That body took no action.

When the Main Channel was opened for the 5,000 cubic feet per second preliminary flow, it did indeed create a current in the Chicago River because the latter was so shallow. Federal permits were issued for additional river improvements in July 1900, six months after the channel opened. But because of an "excessive current" in the Chicago River, the secretary of war modified the original permit in December 1901, reducing the permissible diversion through the Chicago River to 4,167 cubic feet per second.*

The Sanitary District of Chicago was organized and its work planned and built with full disclosure of the district's intentions, and the federal government did not assume any real authority until shortly before the completed channel was opened, when it intervened to restrict the diversion in an unimproved section of the Chicago River so as to maintain a navigable velocity in that sec-

*In 1903 the permit was again modified to allow a maximum of 5,833 cubic feet per second during the season when the river was closed to navigation. These permits remained in effect until 1925.

tion. This restricted diversion remained in force after the Main Branch and the South Branch had been widened and deepened.

The river improvements were instituted to make possible the operation of the Main Channel according to the requirements of the state law because, as it was, the Chicago River could not handle the maximum diversion for which the Main Channel was designed. The Sanitary District spent in excess of twelve million dollars improving the Chicago River, and it seemed reasonable to assume that if this were done so that the necessary water volume could be diverted through the river without creating a current "unreasonably obstructive to navigation or injurious to property," the federal government would offer no objection to the diversion required under the state law. However, requests for a 10,000 cubic feet per second flow were denied, and the secretary of war undertook legal action in 1908 and 1912 to prohibit any total diversion greater than that specified by the federal permit. This controversy was not resolved until 1930 when the U.S. Supreme Court mandated the volume of water the district could divert for its operations.

The Sanitary District never recognized the federal government's "right" to fix the Lake Michigan diversion prior to 1930. The permit only recognized a maximum diversion of 4,167 cubic feet per second through the Chicago River, but the federal government attempted to change the permit's interpretation. The district built a conduit along 39th Street and placed a pumping station at the lake end to flush the South Branch's south fork, the infamous Bubbly Creek. The federal government always understood that the capacity of the Main Channel was the 10,000 cubic feet per second prescribed by state law. Public reports never mentioned a smaller figure. The Sanitary District diverted more water than the 4,167 cubic feet per second allowed by the federal permit and never denied that it was doing so. The district held that this was no violation of that permit, as no such requirement ever existed. The federal permit restricted the diversion through the Chicago River, not the total diversion from Lake Michigan. If water could be pumped into the Main Channel through the 39th Street pumping station, the district would abide by both federal permit and state law.

The change in the War Department's emphasis from regulating the flow through the Chicago River to regulating the total Lake Michigan diversion was undoubtedly influenced by the fact that several Great Lakes states had brought suits before the U.S. Supreme Court to restrain Chicago from diverting Lake Michigan water. These states argued that the district's diversion "damaged their riparian rights, navigation, agriculture, horticulture, and climate." The inclusion of Canada in this suit made this an international controversy. The Sanitary District assumed that the Chicago River improvements would remove the necessity for federal restriction. It also assumed that the lake-levels issue would not be raised. Both assumptions seemed reasonable. The diversion limitations in the May 1899 permit were based on navigational dangers in the Chicago River, and not on the fear of lower Great Lakes levels. The federal permit contained no condition that the diversion could be further limited because of lake-levels effects.

Over time as the district grew, the secretary of war issued additional permits as warranted, but each contained provisions similar to the May 1899 permit. In 1907 the War Department issued a permit for the construction of the North Shore Channel between the Wilmette lakeshore and the North Branch, and three years later it issued a permit for the building of the Calumet-Sag Channel, between the Calumet River and the Main Channel.

The fact was that the War Department was concerned with problems upstream from Lockport, not with problems created by flushing Chicago's sewage downstream. The Illinois River basin, into which the district's channel system emptied, contains about 50% of the area of Illinois, and, with Chicago, about 70% of the state's population, and it should have been predictable that Illinois River valley residents would resist having polluted water thrust upon them.

Both Joliet and Peoria raised objections. In the 1870s Joliet had suffered ill effects from Chicago's initial attempts to reverse the flow of the Chicago River. At that time the state legislature had to resolve the conflict that developed between the two cities. Peoria was well aware of Joliet's experience, and both feared the potential effects of the larger channel. On several occasions legislators from these cities attempted unsuccessfully to repeal the Sanitary District Enabling Act. But the Illinois River was a commercial waterway, and was little used for drinking water or recreation. Most river towns welcomed the diversion because the increased water volume solved the low-water navigational problems which had historically plagued the river. Initially, there was some concern about airborne health hazards, but an Illinois Board of Health investigation in the 1890s laid such fears to rest. However, though in-state residents did not complain about the Sanitary District, the city of St. Louis, Missouri, did.

St. Louis believed that the Sanitary District's strategy posed a threat to its Mississippi River water supply. It had been aware of the channel's construction but procrastinated about seeking an injunction until the

This cartoon caricatures the reaction of St. Louis, Missouri, citizens to Chicago's solution of its water pollution problems. *(CHS, from* Chicago Tribune, *January 4, 1900)*

last possible moment. But while the Sanitary District was able to avoid an injunction, it still had to answer St. Louis's objections in court.

In late 1898 the mayor St. Louis appointed a committee to investigate the potential effect of Chicago's sewage on the St. Louis water supply. This committee reported, in April 1899, that the Channel constituted a pollution threat. Consequently, in January 1900, Missouri petitioned the U.S. Supreme Court to enjoin the state of Illinois and the Sanitary District of Chicago from discharging sewage into the Main Channel.

But the Sanitary District had acted with dispatch and turned water into the Main Channel on January 2, 1900, two weeks before the filing of the St. Louis petition. There was no formal ceremony. The opening was kept quiet with only a few individuals in attendance, since the district feared that any prior notice might hasten St. Louis's attempt to get a federal injunction. Although the district had a federal permit from the War Department, it did not have the permission of Illinois's governor as required by state law.

The Sanitary District Enabling Act required the appointment of a three-man commission to advise the governor when all work was completed. Once its report was received, the governor could permit the start of operations. St. Louis's threatened suit led the district to request the commission to report in two steps: the first when all work upstream from Lockport was completed and the second when the downstream work was completed. By the end of 1899 the only major uncompleted work was river improvements near Joliet. The commission therefore refused the district's request. Nonetheless the district, to quote an unnamed trustee, "decided . . . to open at once."

> We [the district trustees] received pretty fair intimation [from the Governor's commission] . . . that if we took the bit in our teeth and went ahead we would not mortally offend the commission. In fact, we saw clearly that it would suit the commission to a dot if we took such a course. It relieved the commission of official responsibility, and at the same time prevented a charge that the Governor was standing in the way of great improvement. When so much was decided on we feared that if an announcement was made of our intentions somebody might get out an injunction. So we lost no time. The thing is done now, and I don't think anybody is the worse for it.

The "thing" was done with great discretion early in the morning. Only the trustees, a few friends, and two newspapermen witnessed the opening. The trustees initially attempted to shovel away the earth between river and channel at a point removed from a wooden dam that had been constructed to keep river water out of the channel, but the frozen earth would not yield to their shovels. Dynamite and dredging also proved ineffective. A fire had been built to provide some relief against the cold, and when all else failed, "into the fire went the structure which for . . . days had been pointed out as evidence of good faith in not opening the canal until the . . . commission had given its consent." Once the dam was ablaze, the assembled throng gathered for a picture — then the dredge took over. By noon the job was done.

The following day the *Tribune* editorialized that these events were "irrevocable," and the opening at the Lockport end for full operations would follow in short order: "Soon there will be an end to the bulletins of the Health department, notifying Chicagoans that the drinking water is in bad condition and must be boiled. The pure water era is near at hand." The paper also published the governor's statement that he had

had no prior knowledge of the trustees' actions and had not granted his permission.

Negotiations between trustees and commissioners continued while the channel filled. As the threat of an injunction intensified, the commissioners came to realize the importance of opening before such a suit could be filed. On Tuesday night, January 16, 1900, the trustees and two of the three commissioners boarded a special Santa Fe train and rode to Joliet to confer with the third commissioner. Word had been leaked that a formal opening of the Lockport end was planned for Saturday the 20th. During the pre-dawn hours of Wednesday the 17th, trustees and commissioners inspected the unfinished work at Joliet, then returned to a hotel to negotiate. By dawn a long distance call was placed to Governor Tanner notifying him that the commission approved the opening of the channel. Tanner gave his consent over the phone, and the Joliet contingent boarded a special train that had been standing by and rode back to Lockport.

By 11 A.M. on January 17, 1900, a "crowd of men, weary and worn from loss of sleep and looking haggard in the foggy morning light" were assembled to witness the opening of the bear-trap dam at the Lockport controlling works. By mid-afternoon the trustees were celebrating at a big lunch in Chicago as word came that St. Louis had filed for an injunction that morning.

Eventually the St. Louis suit was dismissed. A 1902 survey by a University of Illinois chemistry professor, Arthur W. Palmer, indicated that the Illinois River oxidized the sewage as it flowed toward the Mississippi so that the Illinois was clean by the time it reached Peoria and Pekin, where it was befouled once again by slaughterhouse and distillery wastes. It was these wastes, and not Chicago's, that were the principal polluters of the lower Illinois River. By the time the river reached the Mississippi, the water was clean once again — "little more than a harmless salt remained to tell of the enormous pollution 320 miles above." The water's physical appearance and the presence of a fishing industry also testified to the river's improvement. Indeed, the city of St. Louis found that the water in the Illinois River at its confluence with the Mississippi was purer than that in the latter river, and subsequently constructed purification works to remove the turbidity in the Mississippi supply.

Chicago, meanwhile, quickly felt the beneficial effects of the new channel, the city's mortality rate falling dramatically once it was opened. The typhoid death rate which had averaged 67 per 100,000 in the 1890s had fallen to 14 per 100,000 by 1910. The results validated Chicago's long-standing sanitary strategy. Expectations nurtured for twenty years had been realized; the pure water era was at hand.

Jens Jensen and Columbus Park

Malcolm Collier

In 1886, Jens Jensen, a young immigrant from Denmark, went to work for the West Chicago Parks as a day laborer. Thirty years later, he transformed 150 acres of land on Chicago's western boundary into Columbus Park, re-creating the Midwest landscape as he had experienced it in those thirty years.

Jensen never wrote an autobiography, but he often said that "there was a great story in those decades" of his life. It is the story of his personal experience with the Midwest and of his professional development within a group — other landscape architects, architects, writers, and others — who found something unique here and who generated a movement for its recognition. Jensen expressed his own recognition by creating beautiful landscapes in which he used native plants to re-create local forms and spaces. Those thirty years also tell the story of the development of Chicago's great urban parks, of which his own Columbus Park may have been the last. The two stories intertwine.

Jensen was born in Slesvig in 1860, into a prosperous Danish farm family. He attended agricultural school and served in the German army during a period of German domination of Slesvig. When he was twenty-four he sailed for America because he wanted to become neither a farmer nor a German subject. Anna, his Danish fiancée, also came. They married and began the immigrants' search for a place to settle. Their first attempts — a job on a Florida celery farm and on a farm in Iowa — failed. They moved on to the big city, to Chicago, where Jensen worked in a soap factory and then as a street sweeper in the West Chicago parks.

At least he was out of doors again, and the companionship of the Scandinavian community near Chicago's West Side parks must have helped. The Jensens, as it turned out, remained in Chicago for fifty years, until Mrs. Jensen's death in 1935. And during those fifty years, Jensen became an internationally noted conservationist and landscaper. He worked all over the Midwest, designing city parks, private estates, playgrounds, state park systems, and forest preserves. But landscape design is an almost anonymous art, and Jensen's name is now largely forgotten.

The story of Jensen's early personal and professional development, however, still exists in the memories of his friends and family and in scraps of information in park district documents. The larger story, the planning of spacious urban parks in which Jensen was to play so important a part, is part of the history of nineteenth-century America.

The first urban "country park" in the New World, planned by Frederick Law Olmsted and Calvert Vaux, was New York's Central Park, and the prodigious task of transforming those city acres was begun in 1858. Earlier, in 1841, Andrew Jackson Downing had published *A Treatise on the Theory and Practise of Landscape Gardening Adapted to North America* — a formidable title which went to six editions. Downing urged the development of public parks in America, for a curious reason — since Americans made great recreational use of the rural cemeteries on the outskirts of their cities, he reckoned that they would welcome public parks created for their leisure. He also found in the design of those cemeteries an emphasis on the "spirit or essence" of nature which seemed to him very much in the tradition of the eighteenth-century English landscape gardens.

Many nineteenth-century landscape architects shared his interest in the natural and informal. They also had social-welfare goals, seeing their work as barriers against rigid commercial developers who treated the land and the houses on it only as commodities. Olmsted expressed these goals in his writings; later, Jensen also wrote about his strong conviction that man's survival depended on his understanding that the soil is the source of all life.

It was in this spirit of naturalism and of social benefit that the first landscape architects had worked in Chicago. Olmsted and Vaux applied their social and environmental planning to the residential community of Riverside in 1868 and to Chicago's newly established South Park lands beginning in 1869. H. W. S. Cleveland moved from Massachusetts to Chicago, where his pamphlet *Public Grounds of Chicago: How to Give Them Character and Expression* was published in 1869. He believed that parks had "sanitary and moral purposes," and he advocated that their form be "simple and graceful." For Ossian C. Simonds, who lived in Chicago from 1878 until his death in 1931, the "guiding spirit was that respect for the quieter beauties of native vegetation." Graceland Cemetery, Lincoln Park, The Morton Arboretum, the University of Chicago Quadrangles, and other sites in the Midwest attest to Simonds's preoccupation with the visual and the horticultural aspects of his profession. His special gift was to emphasize native plants and "spatial design in harmony with the Middle Western landscape."

By the time Jens Jensen went to work as a day laborer in 1886, these talented and dedicated people had been working in Chicago for some years. Their architectural contemporaries were the vanguard of the movement which became the Chicago School. They were concerned with expressing the unique character of the Midwest, rather than with drawing on Eastern or European precedents. Of these architects, Dwight Perkins shared most completely the moral and social concerns which motivated the landscape architects.

Jensen's introduction to the special qualities of the Midwest began shortly after the family settled on Chicago's West Side. On family picnics, the Jensens explored the neighboring country and acquired a knowledge of the native plants. These trips into the countryside were made by wagon or streetcar, and the conductor was often reluctant to let the family board the car for the return trip, loaded as they were with baskets of flowers and plants. Within two years, Jensen had made use of these native plants in a new landscape in a corner of Union Park. He called it an "American Garden," perhaps to symbolize his new-found citizenship.

The early family excursions must have imprinted on Jensen's mind the form and com-

Jens Jensen.
(CHS, ICHi-10866)

position of Illinois countryside — the prairie, the streams, the rocky ledges and many-storied woods, the rolling meadows, and the distant horizon — as well as the associations among the plants. Later they became the elements of his great designs, his incredibly beautiful parks.

Jensen's particular skill in drawing on these elements in the execution of landscape designs developed over the years, but his industry and ability must have impressed his employers very early because they made him superintendent of Union Park in 1890, just four years after he started work as a sweeper. Union was a small park, but it was reasonably prominent in the 1890s because of its location in a somewhat fashionable neighborhood and because the West Chicago Parks Headquarters was located there. In 1894, he was promoted again — to the superintendency of Humboldt Park, two hundred acres of land on the West Side, only half landscaped. It must have seemed to the Jensens that they had found their place and their work.

Chicago had three thousand acres of park land in 1890, and a population of only a million and a half. This enviable proportion was due to the foresight of civic leaders who, as early as the 1850s, had envisioned a crescent of parks curving from Lake Michigan north of the city (at Lincoln Park), then west, south, and east again to the lake on the south (at Calumet). They viewed parks as important cultural facilities and as aesthetic improvements. Active recreation was far from their minds. In fact, an 1851 city ordinance stated that "No person shall play at ball, cricket, or at any other game or play whatsoever in any of the enclosed public parks or grounds in this city."

From the beginning, the development of parks was supported by men with quite different interests and purposes: real-estate speculators, doctors, civil engineers, politicians, and railway entrepreneurs. John S. Wright, called "The Prophet" of Chicago's parks, was the first of many real-estate speculators to promote the idea of acquiring land for future parks. The good business judgment of these men was confirmed in 1868 by reports which showed a very great increase in the value of land around New York's new parks. Early support for the parks movement came also from men who were building railroads and hoped to have added attractions along their rights of way. Each of Chicago's three divisions had its local promoters; they all hoped to improve the city and not to lose out in the process. More disinterested was a doctor, G. H. Rauch, secretary of the Illinois State Board of Health.

At a time when the bills creating the parks were pending and taxpayers needed to be reassured of the merit of such investments, Dr. Rauch addressed the Chicago Academy of Sciences on "Public Parks: Their Effect upon the Moral, Physical and Sanitary Conditions of the Inhabitants of Large Cities, with special reference to the City of Chicago." Like many of his contemporaries, Dr. Rauch was well informed about parks and urban arrangements in other cities, and he attributed much of the astonishing progress in landscape development in the preceding twenty-five years to Downing and the "impress of his genius visible everywhere." Rauch spoke of trees as protecting man's health by consuming carbon dioxide and by preventing the spread of cholera and malaria. Parks, he reasoned, also provided an opportunity to escape from everyday pressures, to relax, and to be protected from the corruption of the city. His was a nineteenth-century view.

"More parks" was also an early plea of Chicago's politicians. Mayor James Curtiss preceded even Prophet Wright by proclaiming, in 1847, that each division of the city should have at least one "public ground" of from ten to twenty acres. The bills that established the city's parks in 1869 reflected and enlarged upon his views. Three boards, independent of the city and independent of each other, were created. Later, when the city tried to regain control of the park administrations, which were obviously going to handle a great deal of money, the separate park districts were already entrenched.

The West Chicago Park Commissioners, appointed in April 1869, undertook the creation of three parks, connected by boulevards between about Fullerton Avenue on the north and 19th Street on the south — generally along the line of Western Avenue. The land was sandy desert and marshy prairie land, conditions which made it particularly appropriate that William LeBaron Jenney, engineer as well as architect, was appointed to work on these large tracts —

The lily ponds and sandstone bridge framed the receptory in Humboldt Park during Jensen's superintendency of the park.

(CHS, ICHi-03400)

called, ultimately, Humboldt, Garfield, and Douglas parks.

The task was enormous. Huge quantities of earth were moved, lakes were created, buildings constructed, woodlands planted, flower beds established, boulevards laid out. Work proceeded so well that in 1893 Andreas Simon wrote, in his *Chicago: The Garden City,* that "Nature had been tamed and her ruggedness and her softness woven into a garment for the earth."

Jenney was the first of many notable architects to work in Chicago's West Parks. The first greenhouse in Humboldt Park, built in 1886, was planned by Emil Frommann and Ernst Jebsen, who in 1896 designed the Receptory Building at the park's south end. The first refectory, completed in 1898, was the work of Jenney and William B. Mundie. The year Jensen created his American Garden in Union Park, 1888, Jenney and W. A. Otis designed the West Chicago Parks Headquarters building in the same park. Jensen worked with these men and knew their colleagues, several of whom later became his own colleagues. One of Jensen's qualities, observed by a later friend, was his ability to attract interesting and inspiring people. No doubt he did so as a young man.

During the 1890s, Jensen's circle of acquaintances widened to include other groups then active in Chicago. One of these was the group which gathered at Hull-House around Jane Addams. Jacob Riis spoke there in 1898 on the playground movement, inspiring a committee of Hull-House members to petition Mayor Carter H. Harrison II for playgrounds. And playgrounds became the next development, one in which Jensen was very active. Hull-House, like other settlement houses, was a crossroads where social workers, writers, architects, civic-minded citizens, and scientists met to share their interests. A number of these people, including Jensen, also gathered at Dwight Perkins's house for informal Sunday suppers. They shared a vision of civic responsibility and of the application of their talents to urban problems. Perkins called them The Committee on the Universe.

In 1892, the arrival of a large number of outstanding professionals who were helping William Rainey Harper build the University of Chicago added new academic and cultural emphasis to the life of the city. One of these, the botanist Henry C. Cowles, became Jensen's friend. Together, they explored the countryside around Chicago, studying the plants and the plant communities, a focus which Cowles described as "the science of plant housekeeping or, as some would say, plant sociology." Cowles and Jensen were really teaching themselves ecology, approaching it from their respective interests — Cowles's scientific analysis and Jensen's direct interest in form and life complementing each other.

Gradually, Jensen came to move among other groups — writers, financiers, and industrialists who also shared in the life of a very rich period in the city's history. The young immigrant emerged into a professional as the city emerged into an urban, industrialized center.

During those same years, of course, the West Chicago Park Commissioners were themselves an important influence on Jensen. Through the maze of official reports, auditors' figures, engineers' descriptions, legislation, and recorded rhetoric, Jensen's personal contacts may be traced. Two commissioners in particular may have been significant in Jensen's development: Edward G. Uihlein and C. C. Kohlsaat. Uihlein, a prominent businessman who served from 1894 through 1896, owned a greenhouse and a collection of tropical palms and orchids. About 1901, Jensen landscaped Uihlein's property on Wisconsin's Lake Geneva. Judge Kohlsaat, who served from 1884 to 1890, submitted a plan for a "natural park" north of Lake Street in Garfield Park. The idea was adjudged inappropriate for the 29-acre site available, but its submission indicates the growing interest in the new idea.

Joseph W. Suddard, who became president of the West Park Board in 1897, was also interested in the "natural park." He advocated creating small parks and a chain of outlying parks. In 1899, Suddard reported on "the sentiment that has been created during the last two years in favor of small parks in our populous districts and of an enlarged park system to provide for the future needs of our growing city." In 1900, he urged that the "newly created commission on small parks and playgrounds be given power to act." Suddard considered the valley of the Des Plaines especially suitable and urged action while the land was still available. "If acquired," he wrote, "but little expense would be necessary, as the lands should be preserved to retain as nearly as possible all their primitive beauty."

At that time, the park board and the city's most interested citizens seem to have been in accord. In view of Jensen's subsequent involvement with small parks and of his 1919 plan for "A Greater West Parks System," with a series of outlying parks in the same Des Plaines valley, the interaction among these men seems clear.

But before any extension of the West Side parks at all came about, Jensen was out of a job. As superintendent of Humboldt Park, he refused to accept short measure in the delivery of coal for the park buildings. His employers, accustomed to graft and patronage but not to moral challenges, simply fired him. Years later, one of Jensen's daughters told Leonard Eaton, Jensen's biographer, that the dismissal was the best thing that could have happened to her father. Probably she was right. It is hard to conceive of the West Parks as Jensen later redesigned them, or of Columbus Park as coming directly out of his first Humboldt Park period.

Jensen returned to the West Chicago Parks in 1905 as landscape architect and general superintendent of all the West Parks with complete authority and with superb support. In 1900, however, he was forty years old, had a family to support — and no job.

The years from 1900 to 1905 were as crucial for Jensen's professional development as they were for his family's finances, but information about these years is scarce. The landscaping job for Mr. Uihlein in 1901 was not extensive. In 1902, architect Jebsen designed a house for lumberman Herman Paepcke, and Jensen landscaped his twenty acres of Glencoe, Illinois, lakefront. The architect and landscaper had become acquainted, no doubt, because of Jebsen's buildings in Humboldt Park. Jensen landscaped two G. W. Maher houses in 1902 and 1903 — a house built for E. J. Mosser, an attorney living in Edgewater, and Harry Rubens's extensive estate in Glencoe.

Jensen's natural setting for the August Magnus house, designed by Robert Spencer in 1905, included native hawthorn, which Spencer also used as a design element in the windows. With this, Jensen seems literally to have been incorporated into the Chicago School of Architecture. In 1908, he landscaped Frank Lloyd Wright's house for the Coonley family, and in 1909, Louis Sullivan's famous Babson House in Riverside.

During the early 1900s, Jensen steadily moved into a wider sphere of action and relationships, including membership in civic and intellectual clubs, and an appointment to the recently created Special Parks Commission, of which Dwight Perkins was also a member. In 1903, Perkins was authorized to make an extensive survey for a metropolitan park plan — one of the goals toward which Perkins, Jensen, and their allies had been moving. The two men worked on the survey for a year, but without pay.

Recreation in the garden of Small Park No. 2 (now Stanford Park) at 14th and Jefferson Streets, shortly after it opened in 1909. Small Park No. 2 was one of a series of parks constructed on the West Side after Jensen became superintendent of the West Parks.

(CHS, ICHi-03489)

We also know some few but interesting smaller details about those five years. Between 1902 and 1903, Jensen started signing his plans "Jens," his Danish name, instead of "James," perhaps seeking a more special identity. He also began to dress more dramatically, wearing a neck scarf instead of a tie and a special cap which, he told Paepcke, "added to his character." His individuality became more pronounced, as did his emphasis on the Midwest landscape as his source of design. An assistant later said of him, "He knew he had to be different, found this notion [and] it turned out well."

Meanwhile, the West Parks were suffering financially and physically under the management of the self-serving politicians who had fired Jensen. Even the robust annual reports of over eighty pages shrank to twenty-seven. In 1904, however, when Charles S. Deneen was elected governor, he appointed Bernard A. Eckhart as president of the West Parks Board. Eckhart, a successful businessman known as a "student of subjects related to public welfare," was already familiar with park problems, having worked on the law for refunding the West Parks Board bonds from 1889 to 1891 as well as on some laws relating to drainage and water supply. He easily identified Jens Jensen as the man to restore the West Parks.

Jensen's appointment was enthusiastically reported in an August issue of the Chicago *Record-Herald:*

SPRINGTIME IN THE WEST SIDE PARKS

The announcement is made that Jens Jensen, formerly landscape gardener of the West

Side parks, has been offered and will accept the superintendency of the entire West Park system.

This brings all three of the large park systems of the city under expert administration. The South parks have long enjoyed that advantage. It was a great day for Lincoln Park when political administration ended and expert administration began. The West Side parks will henceforth receive similar benefits.

It is, of course, true that even the most capable professional park superintendent cannot get good results if he is subject to undue interference or if he is hampered by inefficient or loafing employees. No difficulties of this kind are to be expected on the West Side, as the new board of commissioners has made its policy known in emphatic manner. Mr. Jensen will have free scope for his skill, and he will have no workmen under him whom he does not desire to employ on the basis of their merits alone.

Though the dog days are approaching, it is springtime for the West Side parks.

Jensen held the position of superintendent and landscape architect from 1905 until 1909, at which time he became consulting architect in order to escape the burden of park administration and concentrate on private practice. But he continued to insist that park employees be trained to earn their pay, and, in 1920, Gov. Len Small, who preferred to use park jobs for political patronage, got rid of him by abolishing his position.

The years under Jensen and Eckhart were a very active period in the West Side parks. The work which Jenney and others had accomplished had fallen into disrepair and decay. Fortunately, the new men had more than their dedication to work with — a $3,000,000 budget which enabled Jensen to hire the best talent in Chicago. He created the Garfield Park Conservatory, the largest in the world. The prairie river winding through Humboldt Park, the rose garden there, and the very large "natural" garden west of it were a few of his many famous accomplishments. Still, they represented a transitional phase in Jensen's development as a designer. Prairie rivers appear again in Columbus Park and elsewhere, but the formal rose garden eventually became an embarrassment which Jensen would have preferred to disavow. The "natural" garden was really only informal; it was in his later gardens that he included more and more native plants. Today, that corner of Humboldt Park is a dismal sight: the prairie river is sluggish, the garden is a jungle of growth, and the rose garden is not, as Jensen wished, dug up. It is just neglected.

The palm house in the Garfield Park Conservatory.
(CHS, ICHi-03391)

During that same busy first decade of this century, Jensen was also planning playgrounds and urging the development of complexes of schools, gardens, and playgrounds. He was known in Europe for his conservatory, his playgrounds, and a paving compound he developed for park roads; indeed, his European reputation was as great as Frank Lloyd Wright's. He continued to promote a series of outlying parks and to maintain an active interest in civic and nature-related matters on a national scale.

The story of the land from which, in 1916, Jensen designed Columbus Park is interesting itself. Along Austin Avenue on the line between Chicago and Oak Park, Andrew J. Warren started farming 180 acres in 1872. His farm was called Warren's Woods. In 1890 his widow turned down an offer of $4,500 an acre for 150 acres of the woods from a Mr. Corrigan who wanted to build a racetrack; instead, she sold it to the Archbishopric in 1904 for $1,650 an acre as a site for a seminary. The seminary was never built, and in 1910 a man named W. E. Golden started agitating for the West Park commissioners to buy the land. In 1911, the General Assembly authorized the purchase for $560,000, over $3,370 an acre. The 150 acres thus became available to the West Parks.

Anyone who has followed Jensen's career thus far could anticipate the results. Columbus has been called "the finest and most complete of his parks." Jensen's statement on the design was published in the West Chicago Park Commissioners Annual Report for 1917. He wrote, in part:

> The motive that guided the landscape plan for Columbus Park is to be found in the general type of landscape in the immediate environment of Chicago. The greater part of the land has been left in its natural form. Water, in the way of a symbolized prairie river, has been introduced at the lower level. At the source of this river, the land has been slightly elevated. To the east of the river, an elevation or ridge has been built — this ridge skirts along the southern and western boundary of the Park. Along the river, it forms river bluffs, which are an important part of the landscape composition, and serve as a screen to shut out the city to the east.
>
> The bathing and swimming pools have been picturesquely designed in accordance with the rock ledges of our Illinois rivers, a laughing brook furnishing water for these pools. . . . To the south of the neighborhood house and near the source of the river is the players' green, dedicated to the drama and to music out-of-doors. This players' green consists of a slightly elevated spot, separated from the space for the audience by a brook. . . . The American dream is still in its making. The writer believes that its early expression will be in the out-of-doors, and he sincerely hopes that this simple but poetic place will become an inspiration that will help to create the great American drama.
>
> The center of the Park consists of a prairie, or large meadow, dedicated to golf and playfields. Several groves of trees break its monotony and furnish shade for the players, at the same time forming the oases in the prairie landscape. The major part of the planting is found on the Park borders, the river bluffs, and the elevated section south of the community house. It consists of material native to Illinois with a large assortment of plants that invite the birds. . . . Illinois hawthorns and crab apples are used in great profusion on the woodland border. These more than any other plant of this region express the landscape of northern Illinois, and with their stratified branches give a feeling of breadth and spaciousness, and repeat the horizontal lines of the prairies.

It is extraordinary prose to find in a municipal report.

Even today, despite tragic neglect and deterioration, anyone looking at the basic forms of space and planting in Columbus Park will agree that "The power of Jensen's park is the power of nature." It is certainly the essence of all the qualities which Jensen had found significant in the landscape of the Midwest and of all he had taught himself about ecology. And it embodies his principle that landscape design should refer to nature only, not to the culture of the people creating it.

Standing in Columbus Park, one can recapture its creator's vision:

> Looking west from the river bluffs at sundown across a quiet bit of meadow, one sees the prairie melt away into the stratified clouds above, touched with gold and purple and reflected in the river below. This gives a feeling of breadth and freedom that only a prairie landscape can give to the human soul.

Columbus Park is still a great park, exciting and intriguing enough to launch a career of search and speculation about the man who created it.

The Result of Honest Hard Work: Creating a Suburban Ethos for Evanston

Michael H. Ebner

"Shall Evanston be annexed to Chicago?" This question was posed by the *Evanston Index,* a weekly published since 1872 that had come to be acknowledged as the voice of the community's best people. It was answered on April 17, 1894, in the largest electoral turnout thus far in the North Shore suburb. Seventy-eight percent of the 2,093 men who voted said no. The balloting capped a series of measures taken by Evanstonians over four decades to establish and preserve a community identity separate from Chicago. Other Chicago suburbs were not as successful as Evanston. Chicago added 125 miles to its existing 49 in 1889, absorbing the entire South Side (including Hyde Park) in what remains the largest accretion of outlying land in the city's history. And in 1892, the village of Rogers Park to the south of Evanston also allowed itself to be consolidated with Chicago.

Evanston had struggled to maintain its village identity through its transformation into a suburb and then a city, and the annexation vote once again made Evanston's citizens conscious of the uniqueness of their suburb. The people of Evanston held their community in high esteem. "True Evanstonians," proclaimed Mayor Oscar Mann as he discussed his own opposition to annexation with Chicago, valued their community for its "individuality." Unlike some suburbs, such as Brookline, Massachusetts, whose sense of identity derived from being socially exclusive, Evanston's ethos, or communal character, was moral, and expressed in a strong stand in support of temperance. If most cities in nineteenth-century America were flawed morally and socially by the ramifications of the assorted vices associated with the sale and consumption of liquor, some of their suburbs, like Evanston, remained intent upon preserving their purity. As historian Perry Duis observes, this reinforcement of suburban sanctity symbolized "the triumph of moral geography."

If residents in some locales lacked a clear sense of the spirit of their community, the circumstances of Evanston's founding and development made it distinctive in that its ethos achieved an unusually well-defined ideological expression. Frances E. Willard, the legendary temperance and reform advocate, identified the singularly important precept underlying the Methodist founding of Evanston and Northwestern University in this way: "The happiest thought of those good men who founded our classic village was to incorporate in the university charter some provision that no intoxicating liquor should ever be sold within four miles of the campus." As to preserving this dictum, Willard deemed it the result of honest hard work. Keeping this moral ethos foremost in the community while it grew and changed was the difficult task the people of Evanston faced in the last half of the nineteenth century.

Visitors recognized and appreciated the unique character of Evanston. A handbook for travelers published in 1891 portrayed Evanston as "quiet, grave, and in part distinguished," attributing this "fame and prosperity" to the four-mile limit incorporated within the charter of Northwestern. A clergyman taking leave of his congregation in 1884 told an assembly: "When I think of Evanston, refined and cultured, and of the loving and kind people, it is hard to believe Old Adam and Original Sin and all the rest." Everett Chamberlin, in his post-fire guidebook *Chicago and Its Suburbs* (1874), instructed readers: "Evanston bears the stamp of its devoutly-inclined founders . . . its morals are as strict as those of a New England village." A pre-fire guide to metropolitan Chicago, James B. Runnion's *Out of Town* (1869), added: "The physical and architectural character of Evanston is peculiarly American. It is laid out at right angles, as rigidly as Methodism itself could demand."

The earliest settlement of this locale held

Evanston's special ethos began with education at Northwestern and the need to maintain an environment congenial to it. Heirs to that spirit, dignitaries here lay the cornerstone of Evanston's Central School in 1893, the year after Evanston shed its status as a village.

(Courtesy of the Evanston Historical Society)

few clues of the communal character that would eventually develop. It had been inhabited in 1826 by Stephen J. Scott, but more important was the arrival in 1834 of Abraham Hathaway. According to local historian J. Seymour Currey, Hathaway's log cabin served as something of a roadhouse or a "grocery" for travelers journeying to or from Chicago. Currey explains: "Here he kept liquor for sale and the place soon became the headquarters of counterfeiters and fugitives from justice, and generally speaking a vile resort." The area was not a suburb so much as it was an extramural settlement. By the mid-1850s, just before it officially became Evanston, several hundred persons inhabited the locale then known as Ridgeville Township, with timber the principal commodity. As the land was cleared it was given over to agriculture.

These scattered outposts existed just beyond the borders of cities — be it London, England, Sydney, Australia, or Chicago — occupied by those who were, as English historian H. J. Dyos tells it, "in every sense on the fringe of urban society." The function of these outlying regions changed as cities expanded physically and economically. In Chicago this burst of growth occurred in the mid-1840s, and Evanston owes much of its expansion in this period to the beginning of suburbanization (which in turn was related closely to innovations in transportation). However, its development unfolded, at least initially, according to a unique plan and in the service of an important mission.

We can find a starting place for both Evanston and its ethos with the founding of Northwestern University. On May 15, 1850, nine devout young men, representing the city's three Methodist Episcopal churches, convened in a law office over a hardware store at Lake and Dearborn streets in Chicago. Following prayer, they resolved that "the interests of sanctified learning required the immediate establishment of a University in the northwest under the patronage of the Methodist Episcopal Church." What came to be Northwestern University was chartered in January 1851; its board of trustees was drawn from the Methodist Episcopal conferences of the surrounding region, but no religious affiliation was required of prospective students or faculty.

Clark T. Hinman, first president and one of the founders of Northwestern, chose Evanston as the site of the university.
(EHS)

John B. Evans, a physician and entrepreneur, acknowledged as "the master spirit" in Northwestern's founding, clearly associated his vision of a great university serving the Middle West with the future of Chicago, and the trustees went so far as to purchase property within the city during 1852. But Clark T. Hinman, Northwestern's first president, objected. His motives are uncertain, but his influence prevailed. Hinman persuaded the site committee to explore "the suburbs on the line of some of the roads that are being built here, buy a farm and locate your institution, lay off a village to help build up the institution and sell lots."

The selection of the location — designated Evanston to honor Dr. Evans — owed much to the transportation revolution then transforming Chicago. Only ten miles of railway track entered the city in 1848, but by 1856, astonishingly, the figure exceeded 3,600 miles as eleven new lines were constructed. Essential to the development of Evanston was the railroad that began operating in January of 1855 (today known as the Chicago & North Western), proceeding due north of the city on an ascending ridge in close proximity to Lake Michigan. Meanwhile, the university's site committee, chaired by Orrington Lunt, explored a variety of possible situations between the border of Indiana and what would become Lake Forest. Lunt enthusiastically commended Evanston in mid-1853, and Dr. Evans verified that the projected railway line would in fact be laid near the site. In October 1853 the trustees acquired a 379-acre tract known as the Foster farm, and soon thereafter some additional parcels of land, which would contain the university as well as its accompanying village. Orrington Lunt tells of his initial reaction to the place: "It continued in my dreams all that night, and I could not rid myself of the fairy visions constantly pressing themselves upon my thoughts — fanciful, beauteous pictures of the gentle, waving lake, its pebbly shore and its beautiful bluffs." The visage also was heralded in a public announcement issued proudly by the Northwestern trustees as "affording the lovers of good taste every facility desirable for the most lovely residence in the country. . . ." A skeptical traveler, stopping to visit Evanston in late May 1855, concurred readily: "Our excursion yesterday convinced us that we were entirely mistaken and that all that has been said of its beauties is correct."

In considering the proliferation of newly established colleges and universities by the mid-nineteenth century, historian Daniel Boorstin once suggested that some existed to boost the economy of the surrounding communities while others — certainly Northwestern University amongst them — possessed a true "missionary spirit." In Evanston the purest expression of that spirit was temperance. "No spiritous, vinous, or fermented liquors shall be sold under license, or otherwise, within four miles of the location of said University, except for medicinal, mechanical, or sacramental purposes," declared an 1855 amendment to the university charter. This so-called *four-mile limit,* as it has been referred to since its adoption, readily came to embody the mission of Northwestern and its surrounding environs. The tone was set for the charter class of ten undergraduates enrolled for their freshman year: "The college bell tolled out the hours of recitation and devotion, and the beginnings of college life in Evanston were laid." Thus from the very beginning the relationship between town and gown was direct, immediate, and carefully defined. It was not a matter of chance. Evanston and Northwestern were altogether selfconscious as to their purpose and mission. "We have never seen a community anywhere," pronounced the official Northwestern catalog issued for 1858-59, "in which so large a preponderance of opinion was strictly moral and religious." With none too subtle indirection the catalog contrasted the merits of the four-mile limit and the evils associated with Chicago: "Parents may send their sons here with the utmost confidence that they will be placed at a distance from temptation and be brought under the most wholesome influence."

The sanctity of the four-mile limit was a central theme in local affairs. As early as 1858 a "liquor saloon" was shut down by a "midnight raid." From the beginning the limit faced a series of legal challenges. Most notably, the celebrated 1862 case of *John O'Leary* v. *The County of Cook.* Here the Supreme Court of Illinois judged constitutional the contested amendment to the university's charter. The resultant need for law enforcement contributed to Evanston's December 29, 1863, decision to incorporate as a town. This was quickly followed on January 6, 1864, by the election of five trustees. In 1869, however, the voters rejected 82 to 197 a proposition to advance Evanston's status to a city, fearing that the special legislative act for that purpose would diminish the legal strength of the limit.

Comparisons with other communities were fastened upon as a device for reminding residents of Evanston just how central the dictum was to their communal well-being. When a controversial statewide Sunday-closing law went into effect in mid-1872, the boast came forth: "Of course as Evanston had a thorough and effective law before, we do not notice the difference." When a particular community — Woodstock in McHenry County, Oak Park or Hyde Park at some distance, or adjacent places such as Wilmette, Gross Point, or Niles Center — enacted local legislation, be it for temperance or license, the new ordinance was dutifully called to the attention of the people of Evanston for the purpose of edification and reiteration. "We knew well that Wilmette was all right," was one such observation, following a vote by the trustees of the neighboring village to reject an application to license a saloon. And when a judicial election in Cook County ended in defeat for a "rowdy, free-whiskey, and no-Sabbath" slate, the electoral count in Evanston prompted the encomium: "We are more proud than ever of Evanston . . . sound clear to the core, every time."

By 1870 Evanston's population stood at 3,062. Its growth was gingerly but large enough to support six congregations. Northwestern University had dedicated its three-story University Hall in September 1869, its first modern building. A public school erected in 1860 had been enlarged twice by 1870, and two new school houses were planned. A public library association was incorporated, and a drainage commission was authorized in order to clear low-lying swampy ground for future development. The next year a locally owned and operated utility, Northwestern Gas-Light & Coke Company, initiated service on a limited scale to residents desiring gas illumination in their homes. As early as 1870 Evanston ranked with the townships of Hyde Park, Lake View, and New Trier as the status suburbs of Chicago. The per capita value of its property, the proportion of its population which was native born, and the proportion engaged in professional occupations were the highest of ten surrounding townships.

The Great Chicago Fire of October 1871 contributed significantly to the growth of Evanston. Within one month the newspaper reported on the "strangers" within Evanston as a result of the fire, concluding: "They are learning, now, how much cleaner and more quiet and pleasant is our village than the city, and how much better it is for their children." In early September 1872, the citizens of Evanston took the initiative that led to the adoption of a village charter late the next month. The electorate overwhelmingly approved, convinced that the Act of 1872 for Cities and Villages would now permit the enforcement of the four-mile limit. Six months later, in April of 1873, the Village of Evanston elected its first president and board.

Evanston's post-fire pace became frenetic. It had its own weekly, *The Index,* as of June 6, 1872, to chronicle the "rapidly unfolding life." The initial number, in true booster fashion, reported "many" residents "painting and pruning and dressing up their property this spring" and advised that its continuation would add value to local real estate. The township council ordered "about three miles of new sidewalks" and general street improvements. Evanston was said to have most everything required by a "respectable city" by the conclusion of 1872, including a variety of attractive retail stores, good railway facilities, a lakefront pier, the gas works, and a water plant scheduled for construction the next year. Upon the completion of the municipal water works in January 1875, citizens considered their quest for self-sufficiency within the metropolis complete. The new water plant and the four-mile limit soon were being touted as emblems of Evanston residents' safety from the dual ravages of fire and liquor.

Evanston is best labeled during this period as *discriminating* rather than *exclusive* in its estimation of its environs. Visitors, often groups on day excursions away from the city, sometimes received less than a warm welcome. "Chicago Takes a Vomit" reported *The Index* in one instance, adding: "Evanston was invaded . . . by the hardest and noisiest mob which has ever profaned the sacred atmosphere of this suburban

Wide but muddy thoroughfares were characteristic of early Evanston. As the town grew, civic attention divided betweeen matters of moral control, like temperance, to concern for ordinary urban amenities, like paved streets and public squares.

(Courtesy of the Evanston Historical Society)

Frances Willard, longtime president of the Women's Christian Temperance Union, made Evanston headquarters of a national movement against drink. Northwestern's "four-mile limit," which assured parents that their sons would be safely distant from temptation, also helped define Evanston as a haven from this symbolic city vice. *(Photograph by Mosher. CHS, ICHi-18255)*

Zion." Provided that decorum was maintained, however, no one was barred: "The colored folks, who came up from Chicago . . . and picnicked [*sic*] in our village parks, made a very fine appearance as they marched through Davis Street." As for excursions from Evanston to the surrounding countryside, beginning in 1876 the favored locale for the temperance minded and law abiding was the new Methodist-influenced camp meeting ground called Lake Bluff. On the shoreline immediately beyond Lake Forest, it was accessible by rail or lake steamer. "The near proximity of this Western Martha's Vineyard, about seventeen miles north," wrote its promoters, "will cause our citizens to be particularly interested in it. . . ."

The single most important force in perpetuating the distinctive self-identity of Evanston was the Women's Christian Temperance Union. It evolved out of a nationwide women's crusade motivated at least initially by liquor-related issues, and had taken hold in December 1873 at Hillsboro, Ohio. Locally it manifested itself on March 17, 1874, with the formation of a predecessor organization known as the Women's Temperance Alliance. Frances Willard, regarded as "unquestionably America's leading heroine to her contemporaries and the most famous woman of her day," served as the Union's national president from 1879 until her death in 1898. As a result of her prominent role, which over time earned her recognition of international proportions, many associated the WCTU with Evanston. And although Willard was not, in fact, among the founders, at home or beyond, historian Ruth Bordin estimates her importance to the movement as "a classic case of the right person, at the right place, at the right time."

The local objective of the Union was to transform Evanston, already idealized as a temperance village. The members sought to eliminate anything which suggested otherwise. "Let all our people be temperance people," *The Index* editorialized. Like it or not, every citizen would have to accept this notion. A "moral climate" was to be created in which temperance would thrive, and keen-eyed members of the WCTU would discourage or apprehend violators. Its youth organizations, such as the Star Band of Hope, started late in 1875 and offered "wild and wreckless" boys military drill to inculcate them with "good habits." What came to be known as the Illinois School for Girls, beginning in 1877 in South Evanston, assisted the "poor" requiring instruction in "temperance, industry, cleanliness, et cetera." Although the four-mile limit had been in effect for nineteen years when the temperance crusade reached Evanston in 1874, unanimity on the issue did not exist in the village. At that very time, in fact, came allegations that liquor could be purchased on Davis Street and the enactment of an ordinance by the village board strengthening the existing antiliquor provisions. Within two months, moreover, the newly organized Women's Temperance Alliance formed its own "committee on vigilance" to encourage citizens to cooperate with the authorities in pursuit of violators. Nonetheless, on two occasions in late summer of 1874 came further news of illegal sales. In 1877, despite the WCTU's creation of a new seven-member committee "to exercise all possible vigilance," violations continued. Little wonder that in the Union's annual report of 1878, Justine A. Pingree complained, "Many times do we hear the statement, 'O, there is nothing to do in Evanston.' " Likewise, an anonymous letter writer informed readers of *The Index* about "a good many large cracks in the moral fence." When a "traveling saloon," taking advantage of a legal loophole pertaining to delivery wagons, traversed the streets and avenues, a leader of the Union proclaimed: "The fair name of our town is but a hoax." In the face of still more claims, largely emanating from the WCTU about breaches of the law, Chief of Police William Carney wrote a public letter in January 1880 that was tinged with exasperation: "It can safely be said that there is not now a dram shop in the village, nor has there been anything in the shape of one during the last three years." No one was immune from criticism when it came to upholding the morality of Evanston. In the aftermath of allegations issued in 1881 that beer could be purchased on the streets of Evanston, Justine Pingree, speaking for the Union, even scolded the trustees of Northwestern University for shirking their responsibilities to uphold the four-mile limit.

By the early 1880s, however, organized temperance was changing. Nationally the Union was becoming less single-minded as Frances Willard focused on a range of social and economic issues. Locally the fervor of the 1870s evolved into an almost obligatory ritual. Temperance would only be invoked periodically when the village's historic legacy, encapsulated in the four-mile limit, appeared threatened. Indeed, the WCTU was now sharing its hold on the anti-liquor movement with three new organizations, The Citizen's League, a Prohibition Club, and The Four-Mile League, founded over a fourteen-year span beginning in 1882. Only in 1885 and 1886 would the intensity associated with the WCTU be resurrected, causing two successive village presidents to rebuke overzealous temperance proponents. The Lyman Bill, however, pending before the Illinois legislature in 1893, would have undermined the four-mile limit, and citizens responded with a vengeance. A delegation of prominent citizens, including the venerated Orrington Lunt, was formed to testify in opposition in Springfield. Evolving out of the furor over this proposed legislation (which met defeat) was the formation of The Four-Mile League at the call of President Henry Wade Rogers of Northwestern University, its objective being to stand vigilant against potential incursions in the future.

There were important changes in Evanston after 1880. Its population of 4,820 increased to 13,059 by 1890 and 19,259 by 1900. Enrollment at Northwestern University totalled 1,484 in 1890, with another 182 students attending Garrett Biblical institute. Evanston contained no less than twenty separate houses of worship as of 1894, a reflection of the diversity of its population.

This suggests Evanston's scale and complexity, which by the 1880s contributed to the diminished importance of its original ethos — maintained previously through the temperance movement — and the ascent of a new, more material set of concerns. Its famous anti-liquor crusade now stood a discrete step removed from the center, although ready at a moment's notice to return if required. Greater attention would be directed hereafter to the physical surroundings of the village, not human salvation or social purification. Addressing the issue of paved streets in 1889, *The Index* captured the spirit of those who advocated physical improvements: "Good roads are always the outcome of a high civilization, and nothing impresses the stranger more powerfully with the public spirit of a community. . . ." The *Evanston Real Estate News,* a one-time advertising supplement issued in 1886, admiringly labelled the village "the New Haven of the West" (while conveniently neglecting to mention that that university "town" had surpassed Hartford in 1860 as the largest *city* in Connecticut with a population of 40,000). Evanston's railroad connections, water supply, sewerage system, telephone service, educational institutions, churches, public library, post office, and health department gave it a privileged stature.

But the accelerated pace of progress troubled some residents. The Village Improvement Society, organized in 1881 and concerned for the most part with beautification, issued a timely and strenuous objection to telephone poles and overhead wires along principal thoroughfares; within days the village board ordered some of them relocated. When building permits were issued to construct apartment houses, forty-six in all between 1893 and 1899, this turn was carefully rationalized: they were already evident in prestigious locations around metropolitan Boston like Newton and Brookline and were "in every way adapted to suburban requirements." But as the village board debated terms of a franchise for an electric railway during the early 1890s — an issue which took almost a decade to resolve — misgivings were expressed. Excessive noise, unsightly overhead wires, destruction of trees adorning street parkways, and frightened teams of horses were common concerns of well-established suburbs and aesthetically minded cities faced with this latest technological innovation.

The founding of two country clubs in 1888 in many ways symbolizes the transformation of Evanston from sanctified village to domestic suburb. The Country Club and the Evanston Club were started within months of one another and given to pursuits social, athletic, and aesthetic. Golfing proved the foremost attraction, although within a decade polo and tennis also would attain popularity. *The Index,* as ever the voice of the best Evanston could offer, spoke of "clubdom" with unbridled enthusiasm. Pointedly distinguishing such affairs from the temperance-related pursuits which had brought the community its fame, the *Index* asserted that those "who are devoted wholly to church life, or to the art of instructing or building up the moral status of the world, will think this very foolish. . . ."

All this time as Evanston had been changing in important ways it remained a village in the eyes of the state of Illinois. Some residents considered this legal status a virtue. An outgoing president of the village board told those assembled at a testimonial dinner held to honor him during May 1891: "May it be long before the simplicity and beauty of our village are lost and, in government methods and character, we become transformed into the typical American city." But this opinion was not necessarily widely shared. Ever since 1874 when Evanston had consolidated with North Evanston, consideration had periodically been given to a union of Evanston and South Evanston. Some argued that the Village of Rogers Park, on the southern edge of South Evanston, should be included in this consolidation, but in the summer of 1892, Rogers Park joined with Chicago.

The long anticipated consolidation of Evanston and South Evanston, completing the unification of the "Triple Villages," fit into a familiar pattern. The key element was the frustration experienced by citizens of small communities that coveted the same level of

Railroads, especially the line that would become the Chicago and North Western, were key to the siting of Northwestern University and to Evanston's early growth. Seen here, the Chicago, Milwaukee, and St. Paul train station on Davis Street in Evanston, c. 1890.

(Courtesy of the Evanston Historical Society)

municipal services enjoyed by a larger, adjacent community. Dating back more than a decade, the village board of South Evanston (and those of Rogers Park and Wilmette) encountered what appeared insurmountable problems with drinking water and sewage disposal; between 1889 and 1891, tumultuous political campaigns were conducted as pro-improvement forces did battle with those who wished to minimize public expenditures. And those who favored further improvements could, and did, point to Evanston's high standards — symbolized by its water works, in continuous operation since 1875 — as the desired objective.

Some residents of South Evanston wondered whether their portion of the new city that would be formed by their union with Evanston would share equally in existing public services; others feared that such services would result in higher taxes. Exacerbating this debate was the revival of a long-standing controversy dating from the 1860s and the source of considerable litigation, as to the impact that Northwestern University's extensive tax-exempt real estate holdings had upon Evanston's tax structure. Inevitably, questions also arose about the loss of autonomy. Reservations also arose within Evanston. On the day preceding the vote an advertisement appeared entitled "Why We Are Opposed to Annexation"; it was signed by seventy-five Evanstonians, including the famed architect Daniel H. Burnham. The heart of this statement was that consolidation would not only fail to serve the best interests of South Evanston but would also foster "local jealousies" over municipal services and taxation.

Despite foreboding, on February 20, 1892, the proposition passed with the required consent of the electorate in each community. The union was approved by 57 percent in South Evanston and by 66 percent in Evanston. Then on March 29, in a follow-up election required by state law, almost 97 percent of the 810 voters approved adoption of a city charter for the newly constituted municipality. But what is most instructive about these events is what did not happen; virtually nothing had been said overtly about the question of liquor control. This is all the more important given the proclivity of segments of the population within South Evanston for circumventing the four-mile limit. Quite possibly the prevailing opinion within Evanston was that consolidating with South Evanston was the most effective means of exercising control over this problem. And surely, as some residents of Evanston recognized, this solution was preferable to the prospect of South Evanston eventually being absorbed by Chicago.

Conflict surrounded the first municipal election and confirmed misgivings some had had about the union of Evanston with South Evanston. A bitter campaign for Evanston's first mayor harkened back to issues concerning the origins and legacy of Evanston as a temperance village and divided the newly formed city. The two candidates were Oscar H. Mann and John R. Lindgren. Mann was a homeopathic physician who had been elected as president of Evanston's village board in 1891. He first had been elected to a seat on the village board as a pro-improvement candidate during the debate over whether Evanston should proceed with its water works. Lindgren was a partner in a Chicago investment banking firm. He came across as a high-minded public benefactor by virtue of his support for the public library, the Children's Aid Society, and Chicago's Apollo Music Club (which in recent years had turned its attention to offering performances before working-class audiences). Mann, whose political style can only be described as quixotic, intimated that the Lindgren candidacy reflected the designs of Northwestern University to enforce the four-mile limit and preserve the tax exempt status of its expansive real estate holdings. Another claim against Lindgren was that he was too much involved in the professional and charitable affairs of Chicago. As for Mann, according to Lindgren followers, he was *not* the choice of those citizens who wished to have a mayor who reflected the best attributes of Evanston.

The election was extremely close and a great disappointment to those who continued to subscribe to the visage of Evanston as "the classic village." Mann prevailed by a mere 25 out of 2,351 votes, a margin of 1 percent. Lindgren carried the original village of Evanston, his greatest strength drawn from the three lakefront wards which produced 50 percent of the city's total vote. Mann drew his support from the northern, western, and southern extremes — the newcomers. Lindgren supporters claimed to be "certain" that liquor had been offered to influence some voters; charges of ballot irregularities, including participation by aliens, also were issued. But it was the editorial estimation of the *Chicago Evening Post* that best told what had transpired in Evanston and what loomed ahead: "All the devices of older and hardened communities, the tricks of ward politics and subterfuges of the city heeler, instantly took root in that virgin soil. . . . The election yesterday was the first fruit of the new order."

Over the next months Evanston's citizens watched their new government become embroiled in a succession of controversies and minor scandals including the court-ordered reversal of the outcome of an aldermanic contest in the Fifth Ward because of fraudulent ballot counting. There was opposition to Mayor Mann's nominee for director of public works, an aldermanic committee was appointed to investigate allegations of bribery lodged against a member of the city council; and a dispute arose over the appropriation of $600 for the expense account of the mayor. "We are a city," editorialized *The Index* in a fit of frustration after the election, adding: "A number of things have occurred in connection with our own municipal affairs . . . giving evidence to that fact."

Embarrassing as this was to residents who prided themselves on Evanston's reputation, they marked only the beginning of their difficulties. In January 1894 a movement of uncertain origins pressed for the first serious consideration of union with Chicago. The results of the April 17 election have been mentioned; the impassioned and successful anti-annexation campaign at once made plain that most residents of Evanston — despite its growth and status as city — persisted in cherishing its independence and the oddities of a suburban ethos that stretched back to its pre–Civil War origins as a "sanctified village."

Compounding this question of identity was a petition submitted by the citizens of Wilmette seeking consolidation with Evanston. "There is no doubt," said a resident of Wilmette who had foreseen such a union in 1892, "that Evanston is the Athens of suburbs and united as it is with South Evanston would make it . . . one of the finest cities in the United States if Wilmette were added to it." Since the late 1880s Wilmette had been struggling, not unlike South Evanston and Rogers Park, over costly public improvements. The village's population had grown from 419 in 1880 to 1,458 by 1890. Consolidation, some claimed, would bring it improved public safety, more economical government, the enrollment of its student-age residents at the Evanston Township High School, and, of course, its residents would secure the advantages of the neighboring city's water works. *The Index* touched at the heart of the matter in an editorial advocating consolidation: "Every good work which Evanston is inter-

Fountain Square, Evanston, c. 1889.
(Courtesy of the Evanston Historical Society)

ested in, education, prohibition of liquor traffic, etc., would receive added support by the annexation of Wilmette." Not everyone proved as enthusiastic. An anti-annexation broadside issued by citizens of Wilmette stated: "We want to remain as we are, continue our good work, now more than two-thirds finished, until it would make your hearts rejoice at the lovely surroundings on every hand; beautiful walks, lovely shade trees, and smiling cheerful faces peering out from every window pane in all our happy homes. . . ."

The union of Wilmette and Evanston was never to be. Three times in 1894 the electorates of the two communities failed to achieve the necessary mutual consent. In the first round the citizens of Evanston approved consolidation but Wilmette rejected it; the decision was reversed in the next vote. On the third try the voters united in their opposition, disposing of the question once and for all. The best analysis of why the consolidation propositions failed is that the question became enmeshed with the matter of consolidation with Chicago. Also, at no time did a substantial majority of citizens in Wilmette support the union. Indeed, it may have been the specter of Evanston's difficult transition from village to city in 1892 that lingered in the minds of voters in Wilmette and influenced their decision.

The year 1894 constitutes a significant benchmark in the history of Evanston. Although much enlarged and now garbed as a city, the community remained much admired, envied, and even coveted; that year's thwarted designs of Chicago and Wilmette respectively for consolidation were the most recent affirmations of this fact. But the Evanston of old — ardently and proudly a temperance haven founded by those devoted Methodists from Chicago before the Civil War — had been transformed slowly over the ensuing half century. The manifest symbol of this change was the establishment of the Evanston Country Club in 1888. Shedding its status as a village and joining with South Evanston in 1892 was a further mark, more tangible in nature, in this progression. Still, the specter of absorption into Chicago — denying Evanston its autonomy, identity, and what remained of its original ethos — did prompt leaders of the community to resort to an invocation of its historic legacy, encapsulated in the words of Frances E. Willard as "the ideal temperance village." Old-fashioned and ill-fitting as this nostrum was in the face of contemporary circumstances, it reinforced those valued and trusted verities central to the original spirit and character of Evanston.

Walkout: The Chicago Men's Garment Workers' Strike, 1910-11

N. Sue Weiler

On September 22, 1910, Hannah Shapiro decided she could not accept 3¾ cents (a reduction from four cents) to sew a pocket into a pair of men's trousers. Hannah and sixteen other young women picked up their scissors and walked out of Shop No. 5 at 18th and Halsted streets, one of the forty-eight tailor shops owned by the Chicago firm of Hart, Schaffner & Marx. Thus began a strike that would last four and a half months, enlist strong support from progressive trade unionists and reformers, and bring about an investigation by the Illinois Senate.

The men's garment industry began in small workshops following the Great Fire of 1871 and grew rapidly in the course of the next forty years. Two types of manufacturing existed side by side in the city. By the turn of the century, a market for quality clothes had compelled the larger manufacturers to combine small shops into large factories as a way of assuring a standard product. At the same time, a growing market for ready-made clothes and the seasonal nature of the industry encouraged the continued proliferation of contract shops, also known as sweatshops.

The contract system continued to flourish alongside the large, fully integrated concerns primarily because of its elasticity. The existence of contractors meant that manufacturers did not have to add employees during the busy season but simply contracted for extra work. Sweaters continued to compete by providing small orders directly to retailers.

Whether the garment was produced from start to finish in a factory or partially made by contract labor, the initial stages of production were the same. The designing and cutting of the garments were done in the factory. If contractors were involved, the cut cloth was packed in bundles and delivered to the sweatshops. Here a succession of specialized machine operators (each doing a specified portion of the garment) did the sewing, helped by basters, who basted the unsewn pieces and removed the bastings from the sewn ones. Next the garments went to the button-holer (usually a subcontractor); the finisher (often working in her own home); and finally the presser, usually working in the factory in which the production process had begun. With this elaborate refinement in the division of labor, the sewing of a coat could be broken down into approximately 150 separate operations.

This division of the manufacturing process into self-contained operations was highly conducive to sweatshop production. Moreover, as little capital as fifty dollars and some knowledge of tailoring were enough to establish oneself as a contractor. A typical entrepreneur might buy half a dozen sewing machines, set them up in his apartment, and hire neighbors to operate them. Such tenement sweatshops dotted Chicago's West Side. So did the workshops of the country's largest clothing manufacturer, Hart, Schaffner & Marx.

The manufacturing firm of Hart, Schaffner & Marx had been organized in Chicago in 1887 by a family of retail merchants who wanted to produce suits for their own stores. At first the firm contracted orders to sweatshops, most of which were located in tenements employing an average of fifteen persons per shop. By 1905 the company had purchased forty-eight sweatshops, bringing production under its direct supervision. The contractors sold their equipment to the company and became foremen while the workers did similar work for a new employer.

Other large manufacturers of men's clothing in Chicago were The House of Kuppenheimer (founded in 1876 as a retail store), the Scotch Woolen Mills, Royal Tailors, and Society Brand. These Chicago clothing firms became pioneers in mass advertising, associating their trade names with quality clothing through advertisements in such national magazines as *Colliers* and the *Saturday Evening Post.*

By 1910, the men's clothing industry had become Chicago's largest employer — even larger than the stockyards — with a workforce of 38,000. Sixty-five percent of these clothing workers were foreign born, with another thirty-two percent having foreign-born fathers. The two largest ethnic groups were Polish Catholics and Bohemians, with substantial numbers of Italians and Eastern European Jews also working in the industry. Approximately half of these workers were women. Employers furnishing information to the Immigration Commission of 1910 explained that, "To [a] certain extent immigrants have been employed in the clothing trades of Chicago, because of their peculiar skill. This is more especially true of the Bo-

Factory inspectors checking a workshop, 1903. Small contract shops (sweatshops) flourished alongside factories, with the larger manufacturers contracting work out during the busy season.
(CHS, DN 1,246)

hemians, who are considered the best coat makers in the world; of the Scandinavians, who are the best workers on pants and vests; and of the Italians, who are the best hand sewers." After this lavish praise of foreign expertise, the report continued, "The chief explanation . . . given by the manufacturers . . . that American employees were not available [was that] . . . the Americans had a very marked prejudice against the business and refused to work at it."

In Chicago, as in other cities, the industry was concentrated in several distinct districts. The sales and general offices and the cutting and shipping rooms were usually located in the same building, close to the central business district. The Hart, Schaffner & Marx building on Franklin and Van Buren is the lone remaining representative of a once-flourishing garment district. The contract shops were located in surrounding areas near the workers' homes, mostly on Chicago's West Side, usually in ethnic enclaves.

Italian workers, who did most of the hand work, were squeezed into the area between Halsted Street and the Chicago River. Further south, between 16th Street and Roosevelt Road, thousands of Russian Jews opened some of the most crowded sweatshops in the city, specializing in coats and pants. Bohemians were located to the southwest between 17th and 22nd streets along Blue Island, where they produced coats. Sprinkled among them were Germans and Scandinavians, although these groups had almost disappeared from the industry by 1910. To the northwest was the large Polish district along Milwaukee Avenue between Ashland and Western, specializing in pants shops.

Sporadic attempts to organize garment workers in large cities had been only partially successful, though two national unions, the International Ladies Garment Workers Union (founded in 1900) and the United Garment Workers of America (founded in 1891 to coordinate the activities of local unions in the men's garment industry) showed promise. But attempts to organize the Chicago men's garment workers received a severe setback in the course of an eight and a half month strike in 1904. The strike, and subsequent care on the part of employers not to hire union members or sympathizers, decimated the ranks of the United Garment Workers in the city. Only two UGWA cutters locals with members working in a few of Chicago's small shops survived.

Employers, suffering from intense competition, were also consolidating and building cooperative organizations, one of whose purposes was to resist the organization of unions. Louis Kuppenheimer, one of the founders of the Chicago Wholesale Clothiers' Association, described that organization's purpose as exchanging credit information and facilitating the sale of goods. But the Chicago Wholesale Clothiers' Association, and the two national associations with which it was affiliated — the National Association of Clothiers and the National Association of Manufacturers — were also dedicated to resisting labor unions. Although the firm of Hart, Schaffner & Marx did not join these organizations, it shared their attitude toward unions, refusing to hire anyone suspected of union sympathies.

This was the atmosphere in which Hannah Shapiro (also known as Annie) and her coworkers decided to protest their employer's move — one that was by no means uncommon in the industry — to lower the piece rate agreed on in the negotiations at the start of the season.

* * *

At eighteen, Hannah Shapiro was a veteran of Chicago's garment industry. The oldest child of a Russian immigrant family, she had gone to work in a small shop making bow

A manufacturer checks an order in a contract shop. Since garment making could be broken down into many self-contained operations, such small shops specialized in one or two steps in the manufacturing process.
(CHS, DN, 205)

ties when she was thirteen. Two years later, she moved on to Hart, Schaffner & Marx, where she earned three dollars a week for ten-hour days pulling out bastings on coats. At one point she operated a pocket cutting machine, receiving her highest weekly wage of twelve dollars. But the rates on that task had also been reduced. In September of 1910 she was earning seven dollars a week seaming pockets.

In a 1976 interview, Hannah Shapiro Glick recalled that period of her life. In spite of her strike experience she did not remember the Hart, Schaffner & Marx workshop as a terrible place. She noted the advantage of being allowed passes to leave early on Friday and of not being forced to work on Saturday, which pleased her father, an orthodox Jew. Nor did she mind walking to the fifth floor, or the petty fines, which she was skilled enough to avoid. But inevitably, there were grievances, and because she was friendly with many of her coworkers — Polish, Rumanian, and Italian, as well as Jewish — and high spirited, Hannah often carried both their complaints and her own to the bosses. The cut in the piece rate was strongly resented, and despite the fear of what the consequences might be, Hannah Glick recalls, "We all went out; we had to be recognized as people."

Three weeks elapsed from the first walkout until most of the Hart, Schaffner, & Marx workers were on strike. Communications were slow: there were no leaders to make decisions, no mechanism to call a strike. Spontaneous walkouts by angry workers in sweatshops were common. Usually the contractor either met their demands or fired the few involved. Employment in larger factories gave workers a better opportunity to communicate with each other, but much of the work was still done in shops scattered throughout the area.

Within a week people from seven out of the ten West Side pants shops refused the work from Shop No. 5. Sidney Hillman, another recent arrival from Russia who worked in one of those shops, later recalled that at first the girls were a joke among the men, until finally some "bold spirits" decided to join them. Another worker, Jacob Potofsky,* attended a meeting of more than 500 people at Hull-House, where workers aired their grievances. The next day he talked about the meeting to the Bohemian, Polish, and Jewish women with whom he worked. When the 300 people in the workshop started to leave the room, the foreman shut

*Hillman and Potofsky would later become founding members and leaders of the Amalgamated Clothing Workers of America.

the doors in a vain effort to stop them. After three weeks at least 2,200 "bold spirits" were attending daily meetings at the West Side Auditorium.

Hart, Schaffner & Marx reacted to the walkout in a variety of ways. First the firm insisted that there was no strike. At the same time Harry Hart authorized a rate adjustment in the shop in which the trouble had started. But by now things had gone too far and there was no stopping the strike. By October 15 the firm admitted that it had been forced to hire private detectives "to protect the weak and foreign born employees from intimidation by strike agitators."

By the middle of October Hart, Schaffner & Marx strikers were being joined by workers from Kuppenheimer, Hirsch-Wickwire, and other clothing firms. Spokesmen for the Chicago Wholesale Clothiers' Association claimed that their workers had no grievances and were only striking out of sympathy for Hart, Schaffner & Marx workers or because they feared violence from agitators.

Although their workers were harassed by insults and bricks hurled at them through the factory's windows, Kuppenheimer managed to maintain production throughout the strike. Louis Kuppenheimer prided himself on the "moral" atmosphere of his factory, in which there was no mixing of girls and boys. Indeed, he claimed that many parents appealed to him to hire their daughters because of the protection thus afforded them.

Like most industrialists, Kuppenheimer refused to deal with a union because he claimed that workers were better off contracting as individuals. Furthermore, he considered open shops more American. As the strike continued, in addition to advertising for workers, he hired a New York agent to recruit strikebreakers. One entire floor of the factory was converted into sleeping and kitchen facilities to protect and isolate strikebreakers.

Nevertheless, the strike continued to spread. Strikers paraded past shops blowing whistles as a signal to workers to join them. One of the strikers, Clara Masilotti, later recalled that having heard about the signal she told the other workers in her shop: "The first whistle we hear . . . means for us to strike. You cannot work for twelve cents a coat and I cannot baste 35 coats a day." One day 200 persons appeared under the shop window at Blue Island and Polk whistling. Clara was the first to respond, and the "greenhorns" followed.

Born in the United States, Clara had been taken back to Italy by her family as an infant. She returned to Chicago in time to attend school for several years. At the age of thirteen she went to work in a date factory for thirty-two cents a day. Later she basted coats in a number of small shops, usually quitting after a disagreement with a foreman. In 1910 she was asked to be a forelady and teach the "greenhorns." She remembered that "the boss preferred Italians, Jews, all nationalities who can't speak English. They work like the devil for less wages."

Clara lost her position as a forelady when she refused to tell the workers that their wages had been cut, and she went back to doing piecework. In the course of the 1910 strike she became a leader in the Women's Trade Union League and continued as a union organizer.

* * *

At the time of the walkout, the strikers had approached Robert Noren, Chicago district president of the United Garment Workers of America. After consulting Thomas Rickert, the national president, Noren turned down their request for support. Rickert's reluctance stemmed from a "lack of faith in the possibility of organizing these people," and the assumption that "it was just an overnight strike."

Not until one month after the walkout did the UGWA finally issue a general strike call. Within a week of that call, on November 5, Thomas Rickert and Harry Hart signed a document agreeing on the selection of three persons to take up alleged grievances. The agreement also guaranteed that former employees could return to work without discrimination should they affiliate with the union. It specifically excluded the question of any shop organization. However, when the agreement was submitted to the strikers at a meeting at Hod Carriers' Hall, it was overwhelmingly rejected. The cutters — the aristocrats of the industry — had elected Sidney Hillman to explain why the settlement was unsatisfactory. Rickert was hooted with cries of "sold out," "betrayed," "traitor," and forced to flee from the hall. This episode was followed by a near riot when the UGWA was unable to honor 10,000 of its strike benefit vouchers.

In the meantime the strikers were seeking support from a variety of sources. A delegation of women had approached the Women's Trade Union League, founded in 1903 by social reformers and settlement house workers to support the efforts of working women to organize. Members of the League, moved by what they heard, promised to help if the Chicago Federation of Labor would endorse the strike. The League would provide aid to pickets, speakers for meetings, contact with the general public bringing favorable publicity, and relief aid.

After listening to an appeal by the strikers, the Chicago Federation of Labor delegates were moved to declare that "this firm [Hart, Schaffner & Marx] and others of like character were nothing more or less than slave driving institutions of the worst imaginable kind, and . . . gradually but surely, getting worse year by year." The day after the strikers rejected the Hart-Rickert agreement the Chicago Federation of Labor came out in support of the garment workers.

A Joint Strike Conference Board assumed leadership of the garment workers' strike. The Chicago Federation of Labor's president, John Fitzpatrick, became chairman; Edward

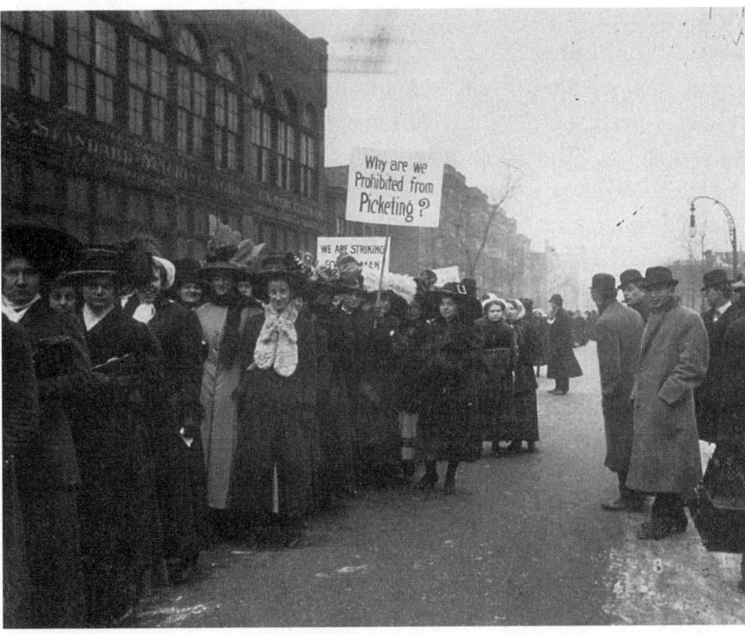

Garment workers parade during the 1910 strike.
(CHS, ICHi-04938)

Nockles, the second CFL representative, vice president; Agnes Nestor, a glove worker and president of the Chicago Women's Trade Union League, and Margaret Dreier Robins, social worker and president of the National WTUL and a member of the CFL Board, represented the WTUL; and Robert Noren and Samuel Landers represented the United Garment Workers of America. A committee of thirty-five, representing the workers, met with the Board to maintain liaison between it and the ranks. The Board unanimously adopted an agreement stipulating the need for a union shop, minimum hours with time and a half paid for overtime, and the establishment of grievance procedures.

Several other community groups rallied to support the struggling clothing workers, including the city's socialist organizations and a Citizens Committee. The *Chicago Daily Socialist* strongly supported the strikers and was credited with goading the UGWA into action. Two special strike editions were sold, earning over $3,000 for the strike fund as well as spreading the workers' story.

Chicago's prominent reformers formed a Citizens Committee chaired by Rabbi Emil Hirsch, whose congregation included some of the clothing manufacturers. A report prepared by the committee and given widespread attention by the press "revealed serious difficulties in all of the shops. . . ." The report denied that union agitators were responsible for the walkout and declared that the strike was justified. It went on to recommend some form of shop organization. Citizens Committee members became active in attempts to mediate the strike, often behind the scenes.

To sustain the strike through a blustery winter the Joint Conference Board commenced a massive fund drive, ultimately collecting $110,000. Approximately sixty-five percent of the funds came from organized labor, ten percent from socialist organizations, and the remainder in response to appeals organized by the Women's Trade Union League. In addition to financial aid, the Jewish Labor Federation donated $36,000 worth of meal tickets, while the Bakers Union contributed 60,000 loaves of bread.

Gertrude Barnum, Margaret Dreier Robins, and other WTUL members took "girl strikers" to meetings all over Chicago to plead for support. A meeting at Kings Restaurant, across from the old *Chicago Daily News* building on Wells Street, was well attended by newspapermen who frequented the restaurant. As one reporter wrote, "Over a simple little breakfast the girls talked their hearts out and explained their problems in natural fashion to a few friends." He went on to say that "Annie Shapiro . . . told her story in such a dramatic manner in broken English that her hearers were moved to tears." Clara Masilotti revealed that she had been coerced into working faster for less pay. And Bessie Abramovitz* explained that during rush periods she was often forced to work twelve or thirteen hours without extra pay, despite the Illinois ten-hour law, while during the slack periods she had to stay in the workshop all day for only one or two hours' pay.

Reporters learned that Anna Cassetteri carried additional material home to earn nine or ten dollars a week. Sixteen-year-old Anna Rudnitsky had been forced to sew slowly in order to keep her pay low. In spite of intimidation by the foreman, she led 300 young women out of Hart, Schaffner & Marx Shop No. 11. Mrs. Bina Wool testified that she had gone from place to place looking for better conditions, but found them all the same.

Hannah Shapiro did not confine herself to addressing society women and reporters: for the first time in her life she entered

*Later the wife of Sidney Hillman and a founding member of the Amalgamated Clothing Workers of America.

saloons to plead for her cause. One bartender contributed fifty cents, saying: "That's all I've got, little girl, for since the strike started nobody pays for a drink."

The most successful undertaking of the Joint Board was the operation of six commissary stores, providing appropriate fare for the different ethnic neighborhoods. The first two commissaries were opened in the Jewish Shelter House at 525 Maxwell Street and the Northwest Settlement in the Polish area at 1014 Noble. Jewish strikers were also served at 1853 Blue Island: Poles and Lithuanians at 1272 North Lincoln; Italians at 1015 Johnson Street; and Bohemians at 610 West 14th Street. Shop chairmen were responsible for distributing tickets for prepackaged weekly supplies. Reformers took advantage of the opportunity to educate the immigrants. Zelie P. Emerson and Katharine Coman, in a joint article written later, noted: "Many foreigners learned the nutritive value of articles of food hitherto unknown, such as beans and oatmeal. Hereafter, they will probably demand a higher class of ordinary groceries." Twenty-two carloads of food and 200,000 loaves of bread were distributed to over 11,000 families a week.

Of special concern were the 5,000 babies whose families were now unemployed. "Strike babies" — 1,250 were born during the strike — received layettes and milk through settlement houses. Appeals for financial aid were sent on postcards carrying the heading "Sacred Motherhood" and picturing a woman nursing a baby and working on a sewing machine while several small children played among unfinished garments.

The reformers were less successful in controlling the streets. Early efforts by the strikers to induce all the workers to join them were relatively calm. But as the weeks dragged on and employers began to import strikebreakers, violence on the part of strikers, non-strikers, and the Chicago police escalated.

A daily pattern was set by the end of the first month. Meetings were held in at least thirty-four halls scattered throughout the garment district. Some meetings were conducted in the native language of the particular group that worked there. More often speakers orated in several languages. Polish was spoken at Walsh's Hall on the Northwest Side; Italian and Yiddish in the West Side Auditorium; and Bohemian and Polish at Pilsen Park on the Southwest Side. After rousing speeches, cheering strikers left the halls in groups to march past tailor shops blowing whistles, enjoining workers to abandon their machines.

A Women's Trade Union League picket committee chaired by Emma Steghagen "undertook the twofold task of picketing with the girls and of patrolling the streets for their protection." After being handled roughly by the police, Steghagen and Ellen Gates Starr, the cofounder of Hull-House, officially and publicly protested. Starr had been grabbed insolently and told to go away or she would be sent to the station even if she were a social worker. Steghagen was given more specific instructions: "Go home and wash your dishes."

Just before Thanksgiving, strikebreakers attracted to the city by employers' agents and advertisements began to arrive in Chicago in large numbers. Pickets were sent to guard the railroad depots and clashes increased. Occasionally appeals to potential strikebreakers to go home succeeded — in one case the United Garment Workers paid the return fares of thirty-five arrivals. But more often the outcome was less peaceful. The Chicago Railroad Company appealed to the police for protection after twenty women set upon non-union Italians inside a streetcar.

Out-of-town strikebreakers were not the only source of trouble for the strikers. A sub-

Six policemen load a striker into a paddy wagon during the 1910-11 strike against the men's garment manufacturers of Chicago.
(CHS, ICHi-04939)

stantial number of garment workers had never joined the strikers and as the tension mounted many of these were chased and attacked by strikers on their way home. Private guards were hired by employers to escort strikebreakers to elevated stations and to their homes.

Alarmed by the mounting violence, City Council member and social reformer Professor Charles E. Merriam of the University of Chicago proposed that the City Council headed by Mayor Fred Busse mediate the strike. The Joint Conference Board and Hart, Schaffner & Marx cooperated with these efforts. It was hoped that if a settlement could be reached with the largest manufacturer, the others would follow. However, the representatives of the Chicago Wholesale Clothiers' Association persisted in their refusal to meet with union representatives.

Early in December a private detective shot and killed Charles Lazinskas, one of three strikers arguing with two young workers who were being escorted home. The detective barely escaped with his own life as an angry crowd quickly formed.

Approximately 30,000 strikers and sympathizers paraded through the West Side after Lazinskas's funeral, led by bands playing the rallying anthem of the French Revolution, the *Marseillaise.* They had been refused permission to march past the clothing firms' central offices in the Loop. In defiance of another police stipulation banning red flags, marchers carried red and white banners inscribed with rousing slogans. The marchers ended up at the West Side Ball Park, where they heard passionate oratory delivered in six languages. Charles Murphy, owner of the Chicago Cubs, donated coffee and sandwiches as well as the ballpark.

On December 15 a second striker, Frank Nagreckis, was killed and his companion severely injured by a policeman during a skirmish which broke out when strikebreakers tried to enter Kuppenheimer's. In both cases the crowds turned on the police and private detectives. Priests officiating at the funerals of the two Lithuanian workers asked for donations to the strike fund.

Joseph Schaffner and his partner, Harry Hart, appear to have been genuinely shocked by the outbreak of the strike. They had prided themselves on the modern, sanitary workshops provided for their workers, conditions that compared favorably with those prevailing in the sweatshops.

As the strike progressed, however, it became clear that while the physical surroundings of the workers might have been brought up to date, many of the oppressive conditions typical of the sweatshops had persisted. In 1916, testifying before the United States Industrial Regulations Commission, Schaffner declared: "The fundamental cause of the strike was that the workers had no satisfactory channel through which minor grievances, exactions and petty tyrannies of underbosses, etc., could be taken up and amicably adjusted."

While insisting that the strikers' grievances were minor in character, he admitted that they had been allowed to accumulate to the point of creating "a feeling of distrust and enmity toward their immediate superiors." Schaffner went so far as to confess that he had been "so badly informed of the conditions . . . [that he had] concluded that the strike should have occurred much sooner."

In another account published after Schaffner's death — *Joseph D. Schaffner, 1848-1919, Recollections and Impressions of His Associates* — an attempt was made to put the blame for the strike on the foremen, on the grounds that the owners were too absorbed in the merchandising aspects of their business to pay attention to what was happening in the workshops. The foremen, themselves working on a piece rate, and eager to produce more for less, imposed typical sweatshop conditions: erratic pay scales, speedups in production, and fines and petty persecutions.

By the time of Lazinskas's funeral, Hart, Schaffner & Marx had presented their proposal to the mediators. The reaction of the strikers surprised their leaders. After hearing funeral orations urging them to stick together until all the manufacturers conceded their rights, strikers went to their separate meeting halls. Workers who spoke in favor of settlement were drowned out by those opposed to it. Father Lawczyinski, of St. Mary's Independent Catholic Church, exhorted Polish workers to hold out for a closed shop, and holding up a crucifix called on them to make a solemn promise not to accept the terms.

At a meeting at Hod Carriers' Hall, emotions ran so high that John Fitzpatrick and Margaret Dreier Robins were unable to speak. Strikers at the meeting felt betrayed. Discussion was delayed until the agreement could be printed in nine languages and an educational campaign launched. After ten days the Joint Board acknowledged defeat in its efforts to settle the strike.

The violence accelerated. Just before Christmas John Donnelly was delivering a wagon filled with unfinished garments to home workers from a non-union tailor shop. Three men shot the eighteen-year-old to death, then disappeared into the crowd. According to his mother, he had been threatened before and intended to quit the next day.

Since people lived as well as worked in the neighborhoods in which such clashes were occurring, non-strikers became unwitting victims. Ferdinand Weiss was walking near a group of strikers arguing with strikebreakers and private detectives, when he was killed by a gunshot fired by a private detective. Mourning garment workers attended his funeral en masse. The fifth victim of the strike, Fred Reinhart, a guard at Hart, Schaffner & Marx, was apparently much hated by the strikers. On January 3 he was ambushed and killed by strikers while escorting two young strikebreakers home.

At the beginning of January two manufacturers who were members of the Chicago Wholesale Clothiers' Association agreed to sign contracts with the United Garment Workers of America, thus breaking the impasse. But the strike was far from over.

The settlement with Hart, Schaffner & Marx was accepted on January 14, 1911. It provided for the re-employment of all strikers and guaranteed that there would be no discrimination in favor of or against membership in the United Garment Workers. While no prior settlement on wages and working conditions was made, the agreement called for the establishment of an Arbitration Committee to settle current and future grievances. The Committee was to include one representative of the company, one of the workers, and a third chosen by the first two. No adjustment in wages or working conditions was to take place until after the workers returned to their jobs.

On January 17, Hannah Shapiro, Bessie Abramovitz, and 2,000 of their fellow workers were greeted by their foremen as they returned to their jobs at the Hart, Schaffner & Marx workshops. The approximately 18,000 people still on strike against Clothiers' Association members who had not settled attended meetings denouncing the agreement with Hart, Schaffner & Marx, the Chicago Federation of Labor, the Women's Trade Union League, and the United Garment Workers. Representatives of the radical International Workers of the World appeared at these meetings, hoping, according to one organizer, "to revitalize the strike."

On the other side, most of the members of the Chicago Wholesale Clothiers' Association refused to budge, in spite of tremendous public pressure and negative publicity, including an investigation by the Illinois Senate.

In the face of this intransigence Thomas Rickert, president of the United Garment Workers, took drastic action. On February 3, without consulting the Joint Strike Conference Board, let alone the strikers who were still attending meetings, he called off the strike. This time the leaders of the Chicago Federation of Labor and the Women's Trade Union League, as well as the strikers, felt betrayed. Margaret Dreier Robins called Rickert's action a "hunger bargain." As Sidney Hillman later recalled, the great majority of the workers:

> were forced to return to their old miserable conditions, through the back door; and happy were those who were taken back. Many who had participated in the 1910 strike were victimized for months afterward. They were forced to look for other employment and to wait until their record in the strike was forgotten. [*The Tailor Revisited*]

A new group of leaders had, however, been created by the strike, a more militant group than the leadership of the United Garment Workers. As Frank Rosenblum of the strike committee described the situation, the workers were "licked from a strike point of view [but] it did create a nucleus of an organization."

The long-range consequences became quite clear at the 1914 national convention of the United Garment Workers of America held in Nashville, Tennessee. Dissatisfied with the conservative leadership of the union, dissidents from Chicago, Philadelphia, and New York, the main centers of the men's garment industry, joined to form a new union — the Amalgamated Clothing Workers of America.

Under the leadership of veterans of the 1910 Chicago strike — Sidney Hillman, Jacob Potofsky, Bessie Abramovitz, and others — the Amalgamated went on to become one of the country's leading labor unions. The lessons of the Chicago strike were not forgotten.

Hull-House as Women's Space

Helen Lefkowitz Horowitz

Hull-House began as an educated woman's struggle to find meaning by immersing herself in the problems of an immigrant neighborhood. It emerged as a pioneer settlement house, offering a range of social services to the fragmented industrial city at the turn of the century. As Hull-House attracted residents, it became an alternative home that enabled educated women to live in the city and to link their work to reform. An exploration of the buildings of Hull-House reveals the settlement's complex and evolving purposes. The original Hull mansion offered the appealing vision of a cultured home in the slums. As Hull-House grew into a large institution, new buildings spread out from the original dwelling to shelter the developing social conscience of the settlement. Their Queen Anne and Prairie style exteriors suggested the settlement house's link to other buildings designed for progressive purposes, and their aesthetic interiors recalled the reformist hopes of the Arts and Crafts movement. For its college-educated women residents, the settlement remained home as well as workplace. In its plan and scale the expanded Hull mansion evoked the women's college dormitory, set incongruously, albeit appropriately, on the busy street of an immigrant neighborhood in a great city.

In September 1889, when Jane Addams moved with Ellen Gates Starr to the second floor of the former home of Charles Hull on Chicago's West Side, she was seeking a way out of the depression that had engulfed her since her father's death. The daughter of a prominent miller, leading citizen, and state senator from Cedarville, Illinois, Jane Addams had hoped to become a doctor. But her father's death immediately following her graduation from Rockford Academy in Illinois shattered her sense of purpose. Treatment by rest cure advocate S. Weir Mitchell in his hospital and at her sister's house, where she was "literally bound to a bed . . . for six months," was followed by seven years of spiritual wandering as Jane Addams attempted to live the life of the lady. After the family moved to Baltimore, Jane Addams's stepmother encouraged her in the proper pursuits of the leisured woman — a little charity, a lot of culture, and travel in Europe. The effort crippled her, and she remained deeply depressed. As she wrote to her friend Ellen Gates Starr in 1886, "I have found my faculties, memory[,] receptive faculties and all, perfectly inaccessible locked up away from me."

At the urging of her stepmother, Jane Addams made another trip to Europe. This time she found a purpose for her life that ultimately cured her depression, but it was not the one her stepmother envisioned. Jane Addams spent six weeks in London to observe the city's East End and Toynbee Hall, the original social settlement founded in 1884 in Whitechapel by Samuel A. Barnett, which located Oxford University men in the midst of London's poor. With her former schoolmate and traveling companion Ellen Starr, who had taught at Chicago's fashionable Kirkland School, she returned to America committed to a plan: the two would rent a house in the slums of some great city. They chose Chicago. Like many adventurous Midwesterners in the late nineteenth century, the two women were attracted by the sheer force and power of the new metropolis.

In the months before carrying out this scheme, Jane Addams visited various districts of Chicago and spoke to potentially interested audiences. At the Armour Mission she got a warm response from Allen Bartlit Pond, a young, socially conscious architect who taught there. The son of a Michigan journalist and prison warden, Allen Pond went to the University of Michigan and joined his older brother Irving in the office of S. S. Beman during the years of design and construction of the model town of Pullman. In 1886, the two established their own practice and, in the decades that followed, came to specialize in an architecture of social concern, especially settlement houses and student unions. Allen Pond eventually became an active force in many Chicago reform efforts. When he first met Jane Addams however, this remained far in the future. After her talk, Pond offered to walk with her around the neighborhood and help her find an appropriate place for a beginning.

A solid middle-class dwelling from an earlier Chicago appealed to the two. The original house built in 1856 for Charles J. Hull, as Pond later recalled,

Uncomfortable with traditional women's roles, Jane Addams moved to Hull-House in 1889 to take up settlement work.

(CHS, ICHi-09369)

> was spacious for that day and excellently built. In addition to the drawing-room, library, dining-room and the other usual apartments of a northern house of the period, there was an octagonal office in a one-story wing to the south, opening from the library and on to the veranda. The material was a purplish-red brick. . . . On three sides of the house were broad verandas; a low-gabled roof covered the high attic surmounting the second story, and the wide eaves were carried by heavily molded brackets. [*The Brickbuilder,* 1902]

As Chicago had grown and industrialized, the surrounding area, once the western edge of the city, became the zone bordering the downtown core: the wood dwellings which framed the Hull mansion now housed immigrants and their sweatshops and served as warehouses and small neighborhood businesses. "Dingy, forlorn and prematurely old, the first story was used as the office of a furniture factory . . . and the second story, drenched by the rains that poured through innumerable holes in the neglected tin roof, had long been the home of shifting and shiftless tenants." To the north of the Hull mansion, a shed served as an undertaking concern; to the south, "toppling and decayed frame buildings used by dealers in coal, hay and feed and second-hand bottles" had upper floors which served as tenements. The house, however, "still preserved a conspicuous individuality" and appealed to Pond "as the first bit of historic background . . . which he had found in Chicago," a survivor of the Fire of 1871. At this juncture, the house must have struck Jane Addams as the proper expression of her still vague scheme. Behind its rather tattered appearance, it had a solid construction and fine features, contrasting markedly with its somewhat disreputable neighbors.

Jane Addams and Ellen Gates Starr originally intended the house to provide a handsome home for women of culture. Addams herself described the beginnings:

> We furnished the house as we would have furnished it were it in another part of the city, with the photographs and other impedimenta we had collected in Europe, and with a few bits of family mahogany. While all the new furniture which was brought was enduring in quality, we were careful to keep it in character with the fine old residence. Probably no young matron ever placed her own things in her own house with more pleasure. [*Twenty Years at Hull-House,* 1910]

Yet unlike other women of her class, Jane Addams never expected merely to enjoy privately the pleasures of a cultivated life. She wanted to share that life with her impoverished immigrant neighborhood. As she wrote in her 1895 essay "The Subjective Necessity for Social Settlements": "The blessings which we associate with a life of refinement and cultivation can be made universal and must be made universal if they are to be permanent." Thus the two women invited into Hull House their neighbors — immigrants from Germany, Italy, Poland, and Bohemia — for a reading of George Eliot's *Romola.* As they responded to the needs of their surroundings, Jane Addams and Ellen Starr stretched their sense of neighborliness to include a wide range of social services and reform activities, but they never lost the sense of the importance of creating a cultured home and extending it to others.

Other middle-class women in Chicago had lost the ability to meet as neighbors with those outside their limited world. In the decades after the Civil War, the rapid growth of Chicago, industrialization, and the great influx of immigrants had reordered the city. A new, fragmented geography divided urban space into functional areas. Commerce seized the center of the city. Around its core lived the poorest residents, who sought work in factories. Those able to pay for transportation chose residences, in the developing suburbs, at increasing distances. Jane Addams reflected on the changes: Hull-House itself had "once stood in the suburbs, but the city has steadily grown up around it and its site now has corners on three or four foreign colonies." Physical conditions had become miserable.

> The streets are inexpressibly dirty, . . . sanitary legislation unenforced, the street lighting bad, the paving miserable and altogether lacking in the alleys and smaller streets, and the stables foul beyond description. . . . Rear tenements flourish: many houses have no

> water supply save the faucet in the back yard, there are no fire escapes, the garbage and ashes are placed in wooden boxes which are fastened to the street pavements. [*Twenty Years at Hull-House*, 1910]

Nothing alleviated the plight of the poor. They lived apart from institutions and from those with "the social tact and training, the large houses, and the traditions and customs of hospitality." They had no open spaces of green, no libraries or art galleries, no gymnasia, no club rooms or places for festivity outside the saloons. Hull-House cut through the social geography of the city to offer those spaces for cultural and social activity that the immigrant quarters lacked.

In choosing to live in the Nineteenth Ward, Jane Addams and Ellen Starr drew on the English precedents of Toynbee Hall and the creation of novelist Walter Besant's imagination, the Palace of Delight. In Besant's novel *All Sorts and Conditions of Men,* Angela Messenger, the heiress of a brewery fortune, decided to create in London's East End a Palace of Delight, a large structure with a ballroom, theater, gymnasium, library, club rooms, coffee and tea rooms, and a school for music and the arts and crafts. She planned it as a place within the poor's "reach, at no cost whatsoever, absolutely free for all, the same enjoyments as are purchased by the rich." Though the attempt in London to bring into reality a Palace of Delight failed,

Ellen Gates Starr, co-founder of Hull-House. *(CHS, DN 62,288)*

Jane Addams drew on its example for Hull-House. Walter Besant did not specify the architectural style of his East End Palace. He described the theater as similar to those of the ancient Romans, suggesting that Beaux Arts classicism might have expressed his vision, an impression reinforced by the axial symmetry of the plan for the main building. But as they shaped Hull-House, Jane Addams and Allen Pond worked from the very different aesthetic of John Ruskin and his Arts and Crafts followers, and visually Hull-House resembled Toynbee Hall.

The founders of Toynbee Hall thought to set down a bit of Oxford in the slum of London's East End. Its architecture of simplified Gothic in collegiate quadrangle form reflected these intentions. Both the architect and the client of Hull-House knew Toynbee Hall at first hand, and Allen Pond himself favored the quadrangle as the best expression of the settlement impulse. Yet Jane Addams felt that Hull-House ought to be oriented toward the neighborhood more than a traditional quadrangle allowed. As Hull-House added building after building, it surrounded a small enclosed yard, giving a much needed patch of green. Yet this did not create a real quadrangle because the surrounding buildings opened not only on the inner court but also onto the street. While residents always needed some sense of retreat, they wanted the neighbors to have easy access. When the first two buildings were added onto each side of the original house, the three structures formed an open court, which became a play area for neighborhood children. In 1896, a resident suggested that such "open spaces, bare or bricked as they are, defend the mass of buildings from the dread likeness to an institution. The playground porches of the Children's Building, where there are flowers up to the last moment, and the easy-going aspect of the outside benches and their frequenters, help out the welcome."

But an institution Hull-House became, and one of sizeable dimensions. Over the course of sixteen years, beginning in 1891, Hull-House added twelve buildings to provide places for the neighborhood to congregate, play, meet, and study. The complex of thirteen buildings covered one square block of approximately five acres. When the original terms of the sublease expired, Jane Addams entered into an ever-widening series of lease agreements with the owner, Helen Culver, the niece of Charles J. Hull. As the lease time lengthened, the property widened, and philanthropic monies became available, Addams felt freer to build. The settlement erected the Butler Art Gallery (1891), the coffeehouse and gymnasium (1893), a third story on the original Hull mansion and the Children's House (1896), the Jane Club for working women (1898), a new coffeehouse with theater above (1899), an apartment building with a men's club on the first floor (1902), a Women's Club building (1904), a residents' dining hall (1905), a Boy's Club (1906), and a nursery (1907). In each case, client and architect worked closely, united by a shared sense of settlement purposes. As Jane Addams put it, "We always went over the scheme together before anything was said in regard to the building."

When Irving Pond wrote of the work of his partnership with his brother, he conveyed no consciousness of working within any architectural style. He regarded architecture as "an art . . . the beautified expression, of life." Its forms "to be vital . . . must be fused in the fire of individuality." Consciously or not, however, the Ponds worked largely within the Queen Anne idiom as architects were applying it in England.

The Queen Anne style combined a number of seemingly irreconcilable elements: a taste for English vernacular buildings of the seventeenth and eighteenth centuries; a renewed interest in Renaissance and Georgian detail; and complex, asymmetrical massing of forms. As Mark Girouard, the recent chronicler of the Queen Anne aesthetic, has put it, the style served both "sweetness and light." The sons and daughters of the Victorians cultivated a conscious aesthetic attitude, and they commissioned "sweetness" in the dainty houses designed by Richard Norman Shaw. But they also sought "light" in the temperance movement, the London board schools, and the education of women. From 1873 through the 1890s (even to 1910 in Newnham College, Cambridge), Queen Anne gave architectural expression to progressive ideas.

While a certain extravagance accompanied many Queen Anne buildings, the brick public buildings took a plainer style. In the 1870s, London board school architects E. R. Robson and Basil Champneys designed basic rectangular block schools with steeply pitched roofs, dormer windows, prominent chimney stacks, multi-paned windows, and an occasional Flemish gable. They used contrasting bricks enlivened by white woodwork. Many of the buildings that the Ponds designed for Hull-House were a pared-down version of this style.

The turn-of-the-century view of Hull-House from Halsted and Polk that Irving Pond favored shows the strong influence of Queen Anne. By then, the Butler Art Gallery had its third story with its steeply pitched roof pierced by dormers. The decorative brickwork of the second story conveyed a Flemish feeling, emphasized by the diamond-paned, leaded windows. Pond repeated this brickwork as he added to the original mansion a "hooded top story of fanciful brick." The Children's House, given by Mary Rozet Smith, with its large welcoming veranda, continued many of these decorative elements, while adding Palladian windows, a small cupola, and pilasters along the Polk Street side. Each Hull-House building assumed an independent form, but brickwork and a common floor height marked frequently by stringcourses united the complex. Pond added variety through differing roof treatments and decorative details. As seen from the internal quadrangle, the gables, the steeply pitched roofs, and the octagonal study intensified the picturesque quality of Hull-House.

Whether consciously chosen or not, the Queen Anne style fit Hull-House's aims. In the England of the 1870s, progressive thought favored the style. To American reformers in the 1890s, the Pond brothers' Queen Anne designs must have looked absolutely right.

While Queen Anne governed the shape of the exterior of much of Hull-House, the ideas of John Ruskin and the Arts and Crafts movement influenced the design of its interior spaces. Ruskin had a profound impact on both the philosophy and the appearance of Hull-House. His writings deeply affected Jane Addams and Ellen Starr, and some of their most powerful statements read like glosses on his work. Ruskin's works taught the original residents the need for the elite to bring culture to the masses as well as opened their eyes to the horrors of industrial society and its loss of meaningful work.

Hull-House led the Arts and Crafts movement in Chicago in the mid-1890s. On October 22, 1897, the Chicago Arts and Crafts Society was founded at Hull-House and included among its active architect members the Pond brothers. Talented craftsmen set up metal and woodworking shops at Hull-House. Ellen Gates Starr went to England to study traditional bookbinding in the 1890s and returned to set up a bookbindery in the settlement. A Labor Museum opened in 1900 as a working demonstration of arts and crafts principles.

The interior decoration of the Labor Museum expressed the Arts and Crafts aes-

View of Hull-House complex, c. 1900, from Halsted and Ewing Streets. The Queen Anne style favored by architects Allen and Irving Pond is evident in the pitched roofs, dormer windows, and decorative brickwork. Both Jane Addams and the Pond brothers were influenced greatly by the design of London's Toynbee Hall Settlement.

(Photograph by Barnes Crosby. CHS, ICHi-19288)

thetic. A photograph, probably from the early 1890s, shows Ellen Starr and Jane Addams taking tea at a small table in the Labor Museum beside a generous bricked fireplace with shelves above holding decorative crockery and a vase of lilies arranged after the style of the Pre-Raphaelites. This scene captured the cozy atmosphere of an English country cottage as it was reinterpreted and idealized in the late nineteenth century by the Arts and Crafts movement. The Hull-House coffeehouse took this revivalism even further. A scene painting of an English country inn etched on its street side decorated the simple block building.

The settlement's Arts and Crafts aestheticism sometimes conflicted with its social goals. Hull-House intended the coffeehouse to serve both as the dispensary of hot food and as a gathering place for the neighborhood. However, the decor intimidated some of those the settlement hoped to attract. A contemporary observer explained,

> When the coffee house was opened, with its stained rafters, its fine photographs, and its rows of blue china mugs, it had a reflective visit from one of its neighbors. He looked it over thoroughly and without prejudice, and said decisively: 'Yez kin hev de shovel gang or yez kin hev de office gang, but yez can't hev 'em both in the same room at the same toime.' Time has shown the exactness of the statement. Its clientele . . . have selected themselves, and it is not the man in overalls who is the constant visitor, but the teacher,

> the clerk, and the smaller employer of the region. The laboring man sends his children for bread and soup and prepared food, but seldom comes himself, however well within his means the fare may be. [Dorothea Moore, "A Day at Hull House," *The American Journal of Sociology*, 1897]

When the settlement outgrew the original coffeehouse, Hull-House built a second one with a more conventional exterior.

The Chicago Arts and Crafts Society played a critical role in the development of Chicago's second great architectural style, the Prairie school, and later Hull-House buildings expressed its aesthetic. After 1900 the hold of Queen Anne gradually loosened in successive Hull-House buildings, and the cleaner lines of the Prairie style came to dominate. This spareness and horizontality of decorative treatment corresponded to the movement of Hull-House into the twentieth century. Along Polk Street, box-like forms with flat roofs enclosed the gymnasium, the Women's Club, and the Boy's Club. As Hull-House residents became more involved in social reform, its architecture carried forward the innovative architectural tendencies at work in the city. Reform, which at the end of the nineteenth century had a Queen Anne face, took on a Prairie school exterior in the twentieth century.

The coffeehouse did not attract workers to linger, but it provided a source of inexpensive, nutritious food that they could purchase and take home, potentially freeing the women of the neighboring households of some of the obligation of food preparation. While the coffeehouse's nostalgic architecture looked back to the past, its purpose confronted resolutely, if ineffectively, the present. The coffeehouse initiated Hull-House's efforts to confront the social needs of its immigrant neighborhood. The settlement carefully set up the public kitchen.

> First the neighborhood dietaries were thoroughly investigated to see whether the need for better food and less sketchy preparation actually existed, and why the people were paying for what they ate. Then one of the residents went down to Boston, and took a training-course in public kitchen management and supervision. When she returned, she worked out all details carefully, simple shining ovens, glittering copper tanks, and ingenious, convenient containers for distribution of her wares.

The effort met with only a modest response that hardly matched the hopes of the settlement. The neighbors "preferred what they were used to eating, and what 'they'd ruther,' to the nutritious."

A more ambitious and successful plan began simply in 1891 when Jane Addams went to Mary Kenney, an Irish working woman and trade union organizer, to ask her to form a cooperative boarding club for unmarried working women. Addams offered to donate furnishings and the first month's rent. The club of six, which then hired a cook and general worker, grew rapidly in number and, in 1898, the settlement erected the Jane Club building. While officially the Jane Club was not a part of Hull-House, the Ponds designed the building, a Hull-House benefactor paid for it, and the rent that the women paid went to the settlement.

The women lived in twenty single and four double rooms, unusually private quarters for working women at the turn of the century. In addition, the three-story structure housed a laundry, trunk room, kitchen, serving room, dining room, drawing room, library, and bath and toilet rooms. While groups such as the YWCA also tried to provide housing for working women at the turn of the century, the Jane Club differed in at least one important way: the women themselves formed the cooperative enterprise.

They had no housemother or external supervision: the group made their own rules. And the cooperative allowed men to visit in its pleasant wicker parlor.

Jane Addams never approved of working mothers, but she had to face the realities of the immigrant community in which she lived — a living wage required the labor of more than a single household breadwinner. In response Hull-House created a crèche — a nursery for very young children — and in 1895 built the Children's House. The crèche had two bedrooms, a dining room, kitchen, toilet room, and "sunshine porch" protected by wire netting on the second floor. The kindergarten took the third floor, music classes the fourth, and the boys' club the first.

In 1907, the Crane Nursery, adjacent to the playground fronting on Ewing Street, superseded the Children's House. Originally, the settlement hoped to include within this complex Hull-House's most daring social experiment. It planned twenty-six flats for "the poorest families that can pay rent at all" to adjoin the crèche and kindergarten. The apartments had an unusual design, for each contained a "stair hall, living room, bedroom and bathroom which opens directly on the outer air," unlike the typical tenement, ventilated only by an airshaft. Hull-House, however, never constructed the apartments.

These attempts to meet the economic needs of Chicago's Nineteenth Ward by providing a food dispensary, a nursery, and housing for working women found expression in separate buildings. Hull-House provided appropriate space within its many structures for almost all of its efforts to improve the surrounding immigrant neighborhood and Chicago itself: the clinic for medical care, meeting rooms for labor and reform groups, apartments for investigators of urban conditions, and the dining hall and parlors for debates on the ideas and methods of social change.

Hull-House moved into ever widening areas of reform because it attracted extraordinary women who pushed Jane Addams to develop a more comprehensive understanding of her task. In 1890, Julia Lathrop moved to Hull-House to begin a long career of social service; and in 1891, factory reformer Florence Kelley became a resident. Other settlements in Chicago — such as the Chicago Commons and the University Settlement — and settlements in other cities provided stimulation and the challenge of new approaches. As dynamic reformers came to Hull-House, they attracted others. By 1894, interest grew to such an extent that the residents limited their numbers to twenty. The settlement grew constantly, however, and by 1929 there were seventy residents.

Two kinds of women came to Hull-House to live. Some, like Jane Addams, had been well educated but lacked a clear direction. Others, such as Dr. Alice Hamilton, had surmounted obstacles to become the first generation of professional women. For each group, Hull-House served different but complementary needs.

Jane Addams always understood that the settlement served not only the neighborhood but women like herself. In her essay "The Subjective Necessity for Social Settlements," she reflected on those women whose world closed in on them after leaving school. Imbued with a sense of service and knowledgeable about the world, "the daughter comes back from college and begins to recognize her social claim to the 'submerged tenth.'" It was then that "the family claim is strenuously asserted; she is told that she is unjustified, ill-advised in her efforts. . . . The girl loses something vital out of her life which she is entitled to. She is restricted and unhappy." The settlement offered the necessary outlet for the energies of these young women, a place where they might escape from the constraints of the traditional feminine role and encounter the broader society. For those "cultivated into unnourished, over-sensitive lives," Hull-House promised the "solace of daily activity."

Alice Hamilton already had found meaningful work: she came to Chicago as a medical doctor to work at Rush Laboratory and then as a professor at Women's Medical College of Northwestern University. She turned to public health to link her practice to the service of others, and, in time, became the leading authority on industrial diseases and the first woman professor at Harvard Medical School. At Hull-House she directed her professional skills toward social reform. For a busy single woman practicing in a rough and bustling city, the settlement offered itself as a haven and promised commitment and community. A place of cooperative living, the settlement lightened the burdens of the late nineteenth-century household. Unlike the single family house, it offered the larger sociability and fellowship of a female community — especially vital to women whose emotional world revolved around other women.

The women residents shared the original Hull mansion. (Those not accommodated in the house lived in apartments around the court.) It is unclear whether residents shared rooms with one another or lived singly, whether they thought of their rooms as individuals' personal property or rotated them. There is no floor plan of the upper two stories of the house illustrating how the rooms flowed into each other. In 1895, when Allen Pond enlarged the house, he created fourteen bedrooms and four bathrooms on the second and third floors. In 1902, he redesigned a suite of two rooms and adjoining bath for Jane Addams's personal use. She insisted, however, that the bathroom have an opening onto the hallway for the other residents. This suggests that the women of Hull-House consciously chose to live in a home-like atmosphere. As buildings filled out the Hull-House complex, other living possibilities, such as separate apartments or hotel rooms strung along a corridor, certainly existed, but these alternatives did not provide the women of Hull-House with the living arrangements that they sought.

In 1898, Beatrice and Sidney Webb, founders of English parliamentary socialism, visited Hull-House. Beatrice Webb shared the usual admiration of Jane Addams, but she did not enjoy her stay. Although the sore throat and fever she had contracted may have contributed to her distaste, she found the physical and social setting of the settlement a trial to be endured. "Hull-House itself," she wrote in her diary, "is a spacious mansion, with all its rooms opening, American fashion, into each other. There are not doors, or, more exactly, no *shut* doors: the residents wander from room to room, visitors wander here, there and everywhere; the whole ground floor is, in fact, one continuous passage leading nowhere in particular."

The women residents of Hull-House not only sought a set of tasks and a commitment to the wider society, but they chose to live together in a communal setting. "The restless movements of the residents from room to room" that so bothered Beatrice Webb was central to Hull-House women's shared lives. As Edith Abbott, resident with her sister Grace from 1908 until the 1920s, remembered, "We were a kind of family group together — a very argumentative family group, for we often disagreed."

In addition to the residents' library, parlor, and the main reception hall, the downstairs held the octagonal office where the head residents transacted the main business of the settlement. Unlike the increasing separation during the nineteenth century of home and office with their opposing values of nurture and marketplace, at Hull-House the two were reunited. Living in the house meant a full union of work and life.

The dinner table dramatically demonstrated this union. Residents took breakfast at their table in the coffeehouse, a restaurant intended both for them and for the neighborhood. To accommodate those whose rounds began early or whose work kept them up late, no set hour governed breakfast. "We argued," Edith Abbott recalled, "in relays, over the morning newspaper." Residents had lunch and dinner communally in the dining hall, a separate room serviced by the coffeehouse kitchen. Originally the residents sat around an oval table. Dinner, served at six, was "the meeting ground of the day," a time for the transaction of business and the thrashing out of issues. As the numbers increased, the settlement built a new dining hall where the residents ate at long, rectangular tables under chandeliers. As Edith Abbott remembered it:

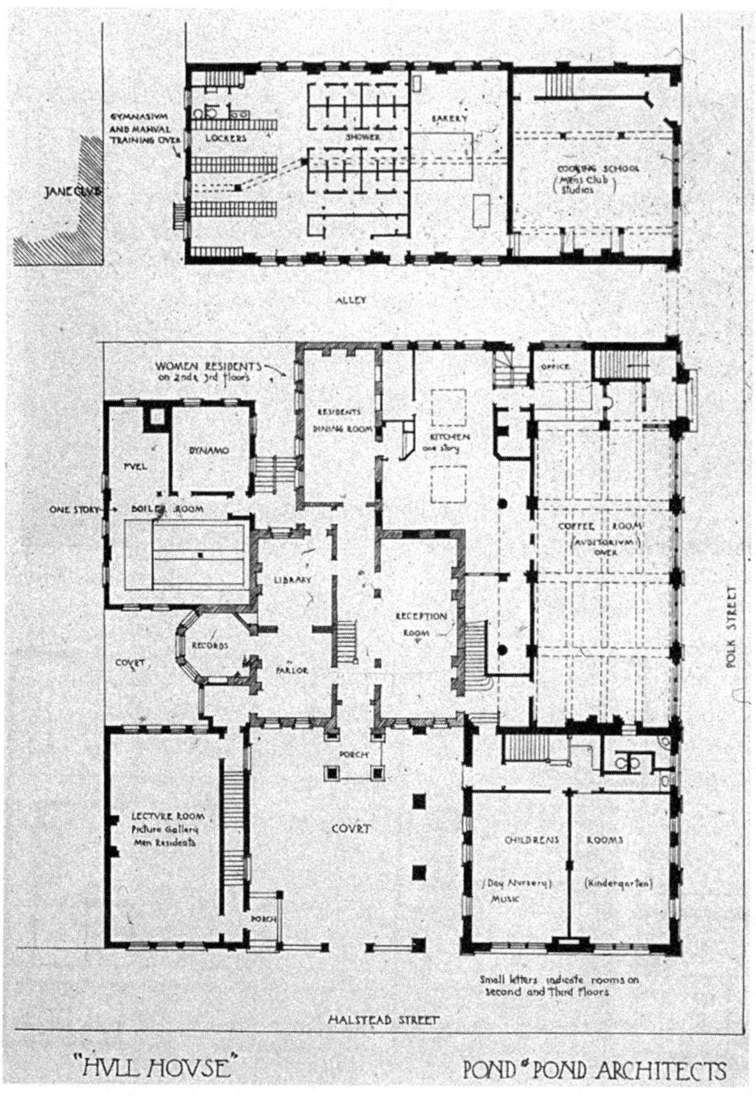

Pond and Pond's floor plan of Hull-House appeared in the Chicago Architectural Club's exhibition in 1900 and was reproduced in the exhibition catalog. By 1907, the Hull-House complex covered a full square block.
(CHS Library)

> Miss Addams liked to have dinner a more formal occasion than the residents made of the breakfast table. In the large and quite beautiful dining-room with a great fireplace at one end and a very large old mahogany sideboard at the other end, there were three long mahogany tables, each of which could seat fourteen persons. But even when all the tables were used, the room still seemed very spacious. We tried to be prompt for a six o'clock dinner, for the dining-room, like every other common room in the House, was used in the evening for a club or a class, and we were expected to leave before the club arrived. Miss Addams usually sat at the head of the middle table, and during the dinner hour she often rapped on her glass for attention while she told us something that she thought was new and important . . . or she read a letter from someone like Lillian Wald of New York, or Mrs. Barnett of London. [*Social Service Review,* 1950]

As the settlement attracted the interested and curious as guests, dinner became a time of intellectual and political controversy. Visitors agreed that Hull-House was one of the best salons in America for discussing current issues.

Beatrice Webb did not agree. Her comments about the "terrific ordeal" of her first evening at Hull-House convey the tenor of that life as seen by English middle-class standards. "First an uncomfortable dinner, a large party served, higglede-piggledy." Then the ongoing stream of visitors who all had to be introduced, then a lecture followed by "a severe heckling." Beyond this harsh beginning, she described the "rough and ready restaurant" with its "unappetizing food," and the "scanty service" of the settlement, exemplified by the residents themselves answering the front door.

Beatrice Webb disliked the informality of Hull-House life and its sharing of certain domestic tasks. James Weber Linn, Jane Addams's nephew, biographer, and Hull-House resident, recalled, "Every resident did what came to hand in the House as out of it — cooked and cleaned and washed windows and replaced furniture that was constantly shoved here and there and everywhere." Florence Kelley remembered her introduction to Hull-House on an early snowy midwinter morning. She waited in the company of a Kickapoo Indian for the door to open. "It was Miss Addams who opened it, holding on her left arm a singularly unattractive, fat, pudgy baby belonging to the cook, who was behindhand with breakfast. Miss Addams was a little hindered in her movements by a super-energetic kindergarten child, left by its mother while she went to a sweatshop for a bundle of cloaks to be finished." The open and casual manner of Hull-House was a fond memory to Florence Kelley, who then moved in to stay for more than seven years; it was "scanty service" to Beatrice Webb.

However received, the informal atmosphere of self-help was intentional. Edith Abbott recalled that Jane Addams refused to get a switchboard

> because she liked to have the arrangements simple and "like a home, not like an institution." One of the long time neighborhood friends was employed to answer the telephone during the day but after five o'clock the residents took charge of answering both the doorbell and the telephone. We all enjoyed our evenings "on door," for the neighbors came in with news and with requests of many kinds. [*Social Service Review,* 1950]

Jane Addams did not have a secretary in the early years and parcelled out the mail that needed answering at breakfast. While the residents ate when it best suited them, they "all liked to be there when Miss Addams appeared with her bundle of mail. . . . Miss Addams had a gay, pleasant, friendly way with her that made life interesting for all of us."

While the public quality of Hull-House grated on Beatrice Webb's nerves, it was what Alice Hamilton wanted. A resident from 1898 until 1919, Alice Hamilton stayed at Hull-House because "the life there satisfied every longing, for companionship, for the excitement of new experiences, for constant intellectual stimulation, and for the sense of being caught up in a big movement which enlisted my enthusiastic loyalty." Both her mother and her sister joined her at the settlement.

Hull-House was a busy, public place. While most of its residents could have lived as sheltered middle-class women, they perceived such lives as enervating and futile. By acts of will, they chose a life of action and community, and the shared life in the settlement that they created sustained their choice. It freed women from both the family claim and the demands of housekeeping, it created an extended family of like-minded women, and it reached out to include an ongoing stream of visitors who represented the vital social movements of the time.

Though primarily a women's place of work and residence, Hull-House always included men, at least in supporting roles. This is in contrast to other women's institutions of the same era, which more strictly separated the genders. In several of the eastern women's colleges, academic women lived and worked in communities of women. Women's college faculty and alumnae formed the College Settlement Association, implicitly limiting it to women. While Jane Addams formed her most intense friendships with other women — Ellen Starr and later Mary Rozet Smith — she never attempted to limit her public world to women. Originally the male residents lived in a cottage on Polk Street and dined at Hull-House. They came into the settlement when the third floor was added to the Butler Art Gallery. In 1902, Hull-House built apartments for married couples.

Some Hull-House women consciously chose a world which welcomed men. Edith Abbott had tried teaching at a women's college but found that, like her sister, she "believed in coeducation." She enjoyed the "vigorous activity of Chicago's Halsted Street," so different from "the cool aloofness of a New England college for women." She liked the argumentativeness, the bustle, and even the evening dances organized for Greek neighbors which attracted "so few Greek women that the women residents, young and old, were called in 'to help the Greeks dance.' "

Women dominated Hull-House, however. It is in terms of their needs in the American industrial city that the settlement can best be understood. An unmarried middle-class woman at the turn of the century remained an anomaly. If she chose to live an active life away from the home she had known as a child, she needed an alternative that the city did not offer. First of all, she required a place where she could live respectably. In a world that divided those of her sex into "true women" and "loose women," she needed to keep the protection that a middle-class home afforded. A woman with work in the world had to find freedom from the demanding burden of a single-family establishment. In separating herself from the familial and social world she had known, she needed a nurturing community. Her commitment to the issues of her time required her to make a connection between her work and the broader social questions of the city.

Hull-House met these needs. As it did, it drew on an alternative familiar to these women: the college. Many of the settlement workers had been among the pioneers who went to college in the years after the Civil War. Jane Addams and Ellen Starr attended

Rockford Seminary, which gained collegiate status a few years after they graduated; Julia Lathrop went to Vassar; Florence Kelley, Cornell. In the settlement these women recreated critical elements of the life that they had known.

Until the 1960s, American colleges treated their women students quite differently from their men. While men often enjoyed the freedom of college towns, women lived in residence halls that shared common characteristics. Unlike a men's dormitory, the building itself — whether designed for 25 at Smith or 400 at Vassar — took the form of a house. Public rooms were grouped around a central entrance on the first floor; a stairway separated the private rooms on the upper floors. Until the 1920s, college women generally lived in suites and shared common bathrooms, an arrangement that fostered intimacy. In many seminaries and colleges, women students performed a limited amount of domestic work to cut costs. Unlike the work of a household, this involved clearly defined duties of approximately an hour each day. College women also took their meals communally, sitting at long tables headed by teachers. While students in the years after World War I found such arrangements confining and offensive to their sense of privacy, those who preceded them experienced college life as liberating and transforming. College offered to women in the late nineteenth century an alternative world of meaning and purpose and gave to that world the physical structure of the residence hall.

Hull-House recreated this college world for adult women in the city. It took the form of a nineteenth-century women's dormitory — the house plan, with its separation of downstairs public space and upstairs familial private space, was expanded to accommodate twenty to fifty women. While minimizing domestic work, it required some shared tasks, such as being "on door." In the dining hall, residents took communal meals, and Jane Addams headed the central table and made announcements and reported news. As the buildings spread around the city block, first in Queen Anne, then in Prairie style architecture, and created courtyards, many residents must have recalled their alma maters. Yet in two critical respects, the settlement differed from the college. While the dominant experience for college women was the women's college with its all-female community, Hull-House included men at mealtime and in common work. While college life provided an alternative world for women, it was one cut off from the political, economic, and social realities of the day. Connection and integration provided the very reason for Hull-House. The settlement linked the private lives of reform-minded women to the harsh facts of the nineteenth-century city. Breaking through the geography of industrial Chicago, it attempted to offer to an impoverished immigrant neighborhood the amenities available to the middle class. By the twentieth century, the settlement added efforts to meet basic needs of food, child care, and shelter for working women, as well as to serve as the center for varied reform efforts. In creating the settlement, the women of Hull-House rejected any notions of seclusion to plunge into the life of their time. They placed their dormitory not on a country estate outside Poughkeepsie, but on Halsted Street in the heart of Chicago.

Samuel Insull and the Electric City

Harold L. Platt

Arriving in Chicago at the time of the World's Columbian Exposition of 1893 was a young Englishman named Samuel Insull. The thirty-five-year-old immigrant had come to take over the fast-growing but troubled Chicago Edison Company. Insull arrived at an opportune moment because the exposition was revealing for the first time the potential of electricity to improve urban life. Visitors to the exposition were amazed by the seemingly endless applications of electricity, which included whirring dynamos and motors, dancing fountains and spotlights, futuristic kitchens, powerboats, and an elevated railway. And "the wondrous enchantment of the night illumination" was the most spectacular sight at the fair, which featured dazzling displays from all over the world.

The widespread use of electricity at the world's fair underscored the dilemmas confronting Insull after he became president of the local Edison Company. The new energy source promised a better life for Americans through the triumph of technology over nature. Like the computers of recent years, electrical devices a century ago were almost mystical in their power to evoke visions of a future free of drudgery. Abundance and leisure would spread among all the people, fulfilling America's democratic ideals. However, electric supply companies were plagued by technological flaws that kept rates at luxury levels and distribution grids confined to only the most concentrated business districts. In fact, the White City's 100,000 incandescent

Samuel Insull in 1894, the year after his arrival in Chicago. Insull emerged as a leading spokesman for the electrical industry in the 1890s.

(CHS, ICHi-13727)

bulbs, 20,000 decorative "glow lights," and 5,000 brilliant arc lamps were more than twice the lighting supplied by the Edison Company to the real city in the mid-nineties.

To provide electricity for a majority of Chicagoans, Insull faced two problems. First, he had to create a technology to supply electricity cheaply and efficiently to the average household. Second, he had to sell electrical energy to people who were enjoying lower-priced gas services. The story of Insull's solutions to these problems illustrates how technology shaped Chicago's patterns of physical growth and social change. More than anyone else in the United States and Europe, Samuel Insull put electrical technology on a sound economic footing. During his first five years in Chicago, he emphasized the problems of supply, the ability of the utility company to bring energy to the consumer at a reasonable cost. In 1898 Insull combined promising technical innovations with new economic concepts to formulate a plan for the "massing of production." In other words, Insull believed that large-scale generators would cut utility rates down to a point where everyone would use electricity instead of alternative sources of light, heat, and power. He boldly sponsored the construction of the world's first steam turbine generator station and turned the Commonwealth Edison Company into the nation's leading electric supply business. During the next decade, electric rates fell dramatically as Insull installed a unified network of large plants and distributor lines across the city. In 1911 Insull began building another generation of "superpower" generator stations and transmission lines to meet the growing demand for energy. By World War I, he had interconnected a 6,000-square-mile territory, creating a regional network of power.

After 1898 Insull devoted more time to the "engineering of selling." A study of his marketing strategy reveals how energy consumption affected changing styles of domestic architecture and the daily routines of the twentieth-century family. To be sure, constantly falling rates, improved light bulbs, and more household appliances helped introduce electric service into Chicago's homes. But in developing a systematic sales campaign, Insull also strove to link electricity to notions of progress, modernity, and class status. Influential reformers of domestic life such as the Prairie School architects and home economics experts reinforced these ideas by extensively using electricity in their model plans. During the 1920s, city dwellers and suburbanites burned their lights longer and discovered new ways to consume energy. Electricity became an important feature of modern American life. New methods of refrigeration significantly improved nutritional standards, and the radio helped change the routines of daily life while reshaping the popular culture of a region. By the time of the Great Depression and Insull's fall from grace, Chicago had become an energy-intensive society.

Samuel Insull emerged in the 1890s as a leading spokesman for the electrical industry. Born in London, England, in 1859, he kept close ties to Europe, where many of the most important advances in electrical technology originated. Starting as an office boy, the ambitious young man learned shorthand, landed a job at London's first Edison telephone exchange, and in 1880 became Thomas Edison's personal secretary. The immigrant landed in New York City just as the "Wizard" was perfecting his incandescent lighting system. At the very center of the whirlwind, Insull learned the new industry from its top to its bottom, everything from making deals in the board rooms of Edison's financial backers to laying cables under the streets. In 1886 the rising young executive was sent to Schenectady, New York, to set up factories for Edison lighting equipment. Six years later Edison and

Thomas Edison hired Samuel Insull to be his personal secretary in 1880. During the next decade, Insull learned the industry of incandescent lighting from top to bottom, gaining experience in the technical, financial, and manufacturing aspects of the business.
(From Central City Electric Service, CHS)

the rival Thomson-Houston Company merged; Insull became second-in-command of the new General Electric Company. Armed with his technical, financial, and manufacturing experience, he put his own name forward in 1892 to become chief executive of the fledgling Chicago utility. After visiting the Dream City in 1893, he put its dramatic lessons to work in the real city.

When Insull came to Chicago, electrical services were in a state of technological uncertainty and economic disarray. Although the Edison venture had inaugurated central station service in 1887, the company faced stiff competition from other electric utilities as well as from its own isolated plants. A multitude of these small, inefficient generators illuminated about 75,000 bulbs in stores, hotels, and theaters, while Chicago Edison used two central stations at full capacity to power 50,000 lights. Two problems prevented the central station from beating the competition with cheaper rates, making the continued proliferation of these small systems seem inevitable. The first great constraint on the supply of electricity was the expense of a system of copper circuits, which limited the distribution area of an Edison station to a mile-and-a-half radius and to the most concentrated sections of the city. Chicago Edison originally spent $200,000 to lay nineteen miles of copper wiring in the Loop, an investment equal to building and equipping its central station. The cost of copper prohibited the extension of services into the city's residential neighborhoods. In Edison's direct current (DC) system, electricity flowed one way around a circuit. Its low voltage, or pressure, worked best with the early lamps, bulbs, batteries, and motors, but it suffered high energy losses when transmitted any distance. To offset these losses, the diameter of the expensive copper conduits had to be increased in the same way as a city's water mains might be enlarged. (As the pipes grow in diameter, more water can be pumped at a constant pressure to a distant point.) In DC systems the use of large copper wiring added dearly to utility rates.

A second technical drawback of the central station kept the shoestring operators and isolated plants in business. The small generators and the steam engines that drove them minimized fuel savings and kept labor expenses above the cost of operating isolated plants. Central stations were mere agglomerations of the same small-scale equipment sold to private individuals. Since many of Chicago's commercial and manufacturing buildings already had steam boilers and engines for heat, hot water, and power, extra attachments such as dynamos for electric lighting cost little. Lacking reliable meters and other measuring devices, Chicago Edison had a hard time convincing consumers that the central station supplied the cheapest service. On the contrary, utility salesmen had to resort to offering secret discounts, free wiring schemes, and other incentives to lure potential customers away from buying their own isolated plants. Restricted distribution areas and small-scale equipment kept electrical energy a luxury item twenty years after its introduction.

The high price of electricity explains why the new technology immediately became identified with class status, modernity, and urban life. In most respects, these images of urban elitism represented a continuing tradition of big-city leadership in culture and fashion. Regardless of cost, the exclusive hotels, shops, and homes were the first to obtain the most up-to-date amenities. In the 1880s electricity became the new status symbol of the elite. Only Chicago's merchant princes and Edison Company directors John Doane and Marshall Field could afford to spend $7,000 to $8,000 for a complete isolated plant to illuminate their Prairie Avenue homes. The glittering lights of the world's fair reinforced the link between technology and progress, thus increasing the demands of city dwellers for electricity.

The electrical system at the Columbian Exposition helped Insull solve his two technological problems. Although the General Electric Company's Tower of Light stole the show as the most spectacular electrical industry exhibit, newcomer George Westinghouse supplied power to the fair. Westinghouse had shrewdly underbid the industry leader to give a practical demonstration of his alternating current (AC) system. Unlike the circular flow of DC, alternating current reversed its flow many times per second. Using transformers, AC could be increased to high voltage and transmitted efficiently at great distances over relatively thin wires to substations. Transformers would then reduce the voltage for local distribution. At the fair, Westinghouse used transformers and a second device, the rotary converter, in tandem to supply power for a wide variety of different voltages and for AC and DC as well. Invented in 1888 by Charles S. Bradley, the rotary converter changed AC into DC, or the reverse. Insull immediately realized the potential of coupling transformers and converters together to create a universal system of distribution across the entire city. During the next five years, he built a hierarchical network with a new large generator station, AC transmission lines, and several substations where high voltages were transformed and converted to serve each district.

Now that Insull could pursue his dream for the massing of production, he acquired every electric company in the city. By 1896 he controlled, through Chicago Edison, all the central stations in the city and all the patent rights to the manufacturers' equipment. These patent licenses put Insull one step ahead of the "grey wolves" in the city council who attempted to blackmail Chicago Edison into buying their paper creation, the Commonwealth Electric Company. Instead, the aldermen sold it and its valuable fifty-year franchise at a bargain price to Insull after failing to obtain equipment to carry out their threatened competition. In 1907 Insull consolidated his monopoly under this favorable grant as the Commonwealth Edison Company.

Insull's international contacts informed the Chicago businessman about another recent invention that helped solve the problems of a small-scale technology. While visiting England in 1894, he discovered a meter that measured not only energy consumption but also peak demand. The "demand meter" offered an indirect albeit ingenious way to correlate consumer rates and utility costs. Insull used the meter to restructure the company's rates from a flat charge per kilowatt hour to a two-tiered system. A customer's peak demand reflected his share of the utility's capital investment costs for facilities and equipment. Customers paid a fee based on this "readiness to serve," and a second fee for their energy consumption. The charge for each kilowatt of demand was the same for all customers; a sliding scale of rates gave discounts to large consumers. This system gave residential customers an immediate 30 percent rate cut.

The demand meter alone did not directly result in the massing of production, but it helped Insull understand the economics of electrical technology. In 1898 he became the first utility operator in the United States to recognize that marketing strategy was more important than production technology. The use of the meter revealed that electric companies needed aggressive sales campaigns to attract a highly diverse range of customers. Especially desirable were those who used electricity during off-peak hours, such as all-night restaurants and ice makers. As Insull explained, the average workman "is unable to run a tool in the shop, go down in the elevator which takes him to the street, travel on a streetcar and use electric lights in his home all at the same time." Building the company's energy load by filling the daytime and evening valleys between the rush hour peaks kept otherwise idle equipment operating. It also reduced unit costs and increased stockholder dividends.

In 1898 Insull's conclusion that "low rates may mean good business" marked a watershed in home electrification. The economics of consumption replaced the technology of production as the pivotal issue. He argued that "the way you sell the electric current has more bearing on costs and profits . . . than whether you have the alternating or direct current system, or a more economical or less economical steam generating plant." For the next dozen years, Commonwealth Edison led the industry in marketing electricity at low rates while increasing its residential customers. Insull's reputation as a "system builder" derives from this period when he perfected the techniques of energy production and sales on a metropolitan scale. Residential service grew from a few thousand to more than fifty thousand households as rates fell steadily to half the original costs. Falling rates encouraged home consumers to burn their lights longer and to use appliances such as irons, fans, sewing machine motors, and hot plates. Frank Lloyd Wright and other Prairie School architects took advantage of electricity in their redesigns of the interior lighting and the kitchens of model suburban homes. Electricity became a cultural symbol of modernity for the Chicago-area middle class.

Elimination of isolated plants helped provide cheap residential electric service for Chicagoans. After 1898 Insull concentrated on lowering rates for the single largest consumer of electricity, the street and elevated railways. Accounting for nearly three-fourths of total consumption, the railway companies had generated their own power since the onset of rapid transit in Chicago in 1893. In 1903 Insull secured a contract with the Chi-

Central generating stations, such as the Fisk Street Station, were key to Insull's regional network of power. This "invisible world" of energy transformed Chicago's physical environment and the daily lives of citizens.

(From Central City Electric Service, CHS)

cago and Oak Park Railroad Company by offering them unbelievably low rates. Even selling power to the transit firms at cost, he could reap handsome profits from all his other business during off-peak hours. The contract helped Insull finance the highly risky venture of building the world's first steam turbine generator station. The new technology, which is still in use today in both nuclear and fossil-fuel stations, made the large-scale generation of electricity possible. During the next four years, Insull signed similar contracts with all of the city's transit companies.

Besides securing the transit contracts, the utility executive achieved similar success with commercial enterprises. Since electric lighting had become identified with elite status and urbanity, nearly all retailers, hotels, restaurants, clubs, and other places of amusement acquired modern services. Distribution lines spread rapidly along trolley routes, which were often located in neighborhood business strips. To convince the merchant skeptical of higher costs, Insull began in 1906 to offer a low-priced electric light fixture with a cluster of new tungsten filament bulbs that produced three times more illumination than the old ones. By 1911 electric lighting had replaced gas in Chicago's businesses. The installation of electricity in commercial establishments also helped to introduce the householder to the advantages of central station service. The stores gave Chicagoans firsthand experience with the advantages of the light bulb over the gas jet and the kerosene lamp: electricity was brighter, cleaner, and less subject to fire or explosion.

Insull used special incentives in building his sophisticated approach to selling electricity to residents. He offered these inducements to secure the initial installation, even at a short-term loss to the company. Chief salesman John Gilchrist explained: "You must get him [the prospective customer] to use the current first, get him into a familiarity with the advantageous points of your electrical system, and you must do it by a method that attracts him strongly." After the householder was hooked or, more properly, hooked up, the family's increasing use of lights and appliances would become profitable for the company.

In the 1900s Insull and his lieutenants built a sales organization that transformed this marketing strategy into a coordinated mass-merchandising campaign. An advertising department established in 1901 developed into a major enterprise of its own with daily newspaper appeals and a free publication called *Electric City Magazine.* The company also created a chain of fancy appliance stores, and it sent out a small army of door-to-door solicitors armed with free giveaways. Readers of the daily press were told that "A home without ELECTRIC LIGHT is like a coat without a lining — unfinished, incomplete." And in 1908 solicitors canvassed the neighborhoods to give 10,000 housewives the free use of G.E. irons for six months. Liberal installment plans stretched the cost of wiring the house and paying for the appliance over a two-year period. This kind of incentive, or "entering wedge," as one solicitor called it, usually worked, "so that almost before the householder realized it, he [was] relying on electricity for his light and various other needs and wondering how he could have gone without it for so long."

The industry's marketing experts used special psychological appeals in selling to women. A close examination of the *Electrical Solicitors Handbook,* the salesman's bible, provides fascinating insights into sexist attitudes about housewives. To persuade the men, the 1909 training manual recommended the use of hard facts; but it suggested a "keeping-up-with-the-Joneses" approach to convince the women. "In interviewing the lady of the house," it advised,

> it is a good plan to mention what her neighbors are doing, and so play upon her social pride, insinuating in a delicate way that if they can afford it, she can. Explain how miss so-and-so has now a lovely electric kettle for her afternoon teas . . . and declare she "could not live without it". . . .

Other strategists took this psychology of envy to its logical conclusion by proposing that women solicitors could better implant the seeds of desire in the housewife's heart than their male counterparts. "Then you know the result," a saleswoman confided, "the new house has certainly got to be wired, and no further argument [to convince her husband] is necessary."

Insull's vigorous campaign to wire the residential sections of Chicago extended into the suburbs. In the early 1890s small jerry-built companies had begun to supply these communities with evening service from dusk to 11:00 P.M. By 1902 the integration of the electric interurban lines along the affluent North Shore allowed Insull to test his system of supplying a diverse mix of energy consumers from a unified network of efficient central stations. The social environment of the suburbs was ripe for the extensive application of electricity in the new homes erected by Prairie School architects. As Gwendolyn Wright observes in her study of these housing reformers, "New domestic technology was central to the aesthetic and the cultural redefinition of the model home." Although the wiring of the suburbs was minimal in 1910, the electric home and kitchen were already well-established symbols of modernity to middle-class families. A year later, Insull prepared to fulfill their vision of the suburban ideal when he consolidated the five largest gas and electric companies outside the city into the Public Service Company of Northern Illinois (PSCNI).

In building a regional network of power, Insull achieved his goal of supplying electricity to Chicago's homes. From 1911 to 1925, his perfected system of energy promotion grew into a persistent campaign spanning a 6,000-square-mile territory. In the city, Commonwealth Edison's residential customers increased from 80,000 to 680,000, or about 93 percent of Chicago's families. In 1925 the average family was also consuming twice as much electricity as it had in 1911. Irons and other appliances were commonly used, even in working-class households. In the suburbs, the successful PSCNI provided electricity to almost 175,000 homes in 212 localities, in addition to gas service to 53 of the built-up suburbs close to the city.

Electricity helped facilitate an exodus to the suburbs by supplying a level of modern convenience the middle class had come to expect in the city. Electric lines and poles also symbolized a better life for those who already had suburban homes, since gas service was generally unavailable in these outlying communities. Increasing numbers of new homes were built with electrical wiring, while older houses were retrofitted. Subdividers had long since learned that extra amenities often enhanced the attractiveness and the value of their properties. Many owners of older homes initially feared installing new wires and fixtures, but these fears were calmed once workmen learned how to avoid destroying interior decorations. The PSCNI wired 600 older houses in 1910. This number grew annually to 10,200 installations in 1915, when the job of retrofitting was about half finished.

For residents of both new and old houses, the desire for better lighting remained the greatest source of demand for electrical energy. Ironically, leaders in the gas industry were first to notice how the light bulb had sharply raised standards of interior lighting. The brilliant illumination of downtown stores and public places made people feel like they were living in the dark. These changing perceptions gave rise to the profession of the illuminating engineer, as well as a new style of domestic architecture. Frank Lloyd Wright best demonstrated the new sensitivity to light in his prairie houses with their ribbons of art glass, picture windows, and indirect lighting fixtures. Although few could afford one of Wright's "city man's country houses," more and more Chicagoans considered home electric lighting a necessity of modern life. In 1912, for instance, the builders of working-class dwellings used this argument in appeals to Insull for an economy lighting package. He responded by offering to wire these houses for $12, an additional fee of $2.50 for each outlet, and $1.75 to $6 for various lighting fixtures. In comparison, the cost of wiring more affluent dwellings ranged from $100 to $300.

Household appliances were of secondary importance in the spread of electricity into the home. After 1911 G.E., Westinghouse, and other manufacturers created more mass-consumer products for cooking and cleaning. Lighting, however, still accounted for 85 percent of the electricity used in the average household of the mid-1920s. As late as 1927, the majority of homeowners used only the iron and the vacuum cleaner. The next two most popular appliances, the washing machine and the toaster, appeared in far fewer homes, 42 percent and 30 percent respectively. Insull's emphasis on appliances in advertising suggests that they were used primarily as an extra incentive to persuade the doubters to install service. Before World War I, ads usually depicted appliances being used by servants, further suggesting the absence of a fully established mass market for their products.

Although residential demand for electricity was usually limited to better lighting, the growth of all types of energy consumption profoundly affected the city and its inhabitants. The emergence of a highly diverse community of energy consumers on a regional scale was a powerful influence on the physical growth of the city. After 1910 housing surveys of Chicago show two outstanding trends: the coming of high-rise apartments in the center and the spread of bungalow-style houses at the periphery. The architecture of the skyscraper relied on electricity for elevator and utility services as well as for construction. While affluent urbanites sought the fashionable life as cliff dwellers, blue-collar workers pursued the more traditional dream of owning a single family house. As the trolley lines opened up cheaper land at the city's edge, the subsequent boom in construction replaced the worker's cottage with the bungalow. On a smaller scale, it incorporated many of the design innovations of the Prairie School architects, including more windows, modern kitchens, and the replacement of the parlor with the living room. The bungalow boom of the twenties suggests that the process of suburbanization was not confined entirely to areas beyond city borders.

In these outlying communities, Insull's regional network of power helped move people and businesses out of the congested metropolitan core. Cheap rapid transportation carried the masses to homes, shops, and factories now supplied with levels of light, heat, and power previously found only in the central city. During the 1920s the use of more energy narrowed the differences between the city and the suburbs in the delivery of modern services. The rich had long used servants to elevate domestic life in the country from rural squalor to city-like comfort. Middle-class residents who could not afford servants found a technological

To encourage homeowners to have their houses wired for electricity, Commonwealth Edison offered a two-year installment plan to stretch out the cost of wiring. *(CHS, ICHi-20010)*

substitute in electricity. Electrical services thus encouraged suburbanization by providing the comforts of the city while retaining the advantages of the country.

Besides helping Chicago to grow, increasing energy use significantly affected the daily routines of its residents. From 1909 to 1919, for example, the per capita consumption of electricity increased by 171 percent. An "invisible world" of energy was emerging, a world we take for granted today. In the new-style home of this period, electrical appliances acted as modernizing agents that fulfilled cultural ideals of scientific management and home economics. Advertising genius Bruce Barton expressed his faith in technology as the engine of progress in newspapers, promising that

> the home of the future will lay all of its tiresome, routine burdens on the shoulders of electrical machines, freeing mothers for their real work, which is motherhood. The mothers of the future will live to a good old age and keep their youth and beauty to the end.

Recent studies by Ruth S. Cowan and other historians seriously question whether machines really liberated the housewife. She argues that they simply added new shackles by creating higher standards of house cleaning and mothering, as Barton's advertisement unintentionally suggests. Yet Cowan does not deny that electrical devices removed much of the physical drudgery from housework.

The effects of electrification on the lives of Chicagoans were often subtle, barely noticeable changes that gradually transformed domestic routines into an energy-intensive style of life. Perhaps the best example of this influence was the growing use of artificial refrigeration. It was applied to every step in the commercial food chain, including transporting fresh meat and produce, cold storage and processing plants, new-style "supermarkets" with self-serve refrigerator units, and home iceboxes. Making a wider selection of fresh foods available at lower prices, the use of energy changed the diets and the nutritional standards of the average family.

The phenomenal success of the radio during the late 1920s shows that Chicagoans had become dependent on electricity to maintain a new energy-intensive life. Of course, the link between electric consumption, technology, and leisure activities had formed decades before with the lighting of downtown theaters, the rise of amusement parks, and the spread of motion picture palaces throughout the metropolitan area. But the radio brought this new world of urban popular culture into the home. Perfected during World War I, the radio became a mass-consumer item in 1923 when commercial production began in earnest. Two years later, nightly network programs were changing the rhythms of everyday life. Insull remarked that "the widespread use of radio receiving sets is . . . a factor in the increased use of electricity for residential lighting." In 1930 the radio became Chicago's most popular home appliance, surpassing the iron in only seven years. A 1934 survey of local utility customers confirmed that 94 percent had a radio receiving set.

During the 1920s, the growing demand for energy became so powerful that even the Great Depression failed to halt the increase of residential consumption. Despite the economic crisis, the average Chicagoan continued to use more electricity in the home, setting yearly records until the oil embargo of the mid-1970s. In contrast, electric consumption by industry and commerce closely followed general economic trends. These patterns reflect the pervasive influence of energy on the city. By 1930 economic activity and employment had become inseparably linked with electric-powered mechanical technologies. In the home, shop, and factory; Chicagoans had created a world based on the intensive use of energy.

While the Great Depression did not interrupt the growth of energy consumption in the home, it ended Sam Insull's career as the world's greatest salesman of electricity. His prominence during the business boom of the 1920s made him the perfect scapegoat for its collapse in the 1930s, especially after his pyramid of holding companies came crashing down like a house of cards. In 1932 Franklin D. Roosevelt campaigned against "Ishmaels and Insulls," and the president's men soon levied charges of fraud against the aging utility executive, forcing him to flee the country. Hunted down and brought back to face federal and state indictments, Insull easily won acquittals from juries after taking the stand in his own defense. He had made some terrible mistakes in attempting to maintain absolute control of his utility empire through stock manipulations, but he was no crook. To the contrary, Insull the system builder had made many contributions to Chicago and its people.

Being Born in Chicago

Susan Sessions Rugh

Parents today are searching for an alternative to conventional birth in a hospital delivery room, but do not want to give up the hospitals' resources if they should be needed. Now, childbirth in a warm, homelike setting, with all the resources of a modern hospital, are offered with the Birthing Center at Chicago Osteopathic Medical Center. A birthing bed, pictures on the wall and patterned drapes give the Birthing Room the feeling of a bedroom at home, where the mother can experience an extra measure of security and comfort during childbirth. This homelike atmosphere helps make childbirth what it is meant to be — a family affair.

Chicago Osteopathic Medical Center, "Caring," March 1986

Current childbearing practices center around the concept of natural childbirth, and prime value is placed on the emotional comfort of the mother and her control of pain through breathing routines and mental exercises. With safe medical practice assured, strong emphasis is given to choice of practitioner, birthing style, and environment; and hospitals compete to offer the most homelike atmosphere. As hospitals today try to rival home comforts, one wonders why women began to leave the home setting to give birth in hospitals.

Indeed, by the 1920s more expectant mothers were checking into hospitals. In 1900 less than 5 percent of urban women were delivering their babies in hospitals; by 1939 that number had increased to 75 percent. Poor women, admitted as charity cases, had given birth in hospitals before the twenties, and wealthy women had been among the first to accept hospital delivery. The rapid increase in hospital births after 1920 occurred mostly among middle-class families.

The genesis of the conventional hospital birth can be traced in large part to events in Chicago. Obstetrician Joseph Bolivar DeLee, founder of Chicago Lying-in Hospital, worked to popularize the medically managed birth. Dr. Morris Fishbein of the Chicago-based American Medical Association (AMA) urged pregnant women to seek professional obstetrical attention; Herman N. Bundesen channeled his energies as commissioner of Chicago's health department into promoting prenatal and pediatric health care. Such professional, promotional, and educational efforts focused national attention on the issues surrounding maternal and infant health and helped to make hospital birth an increasingly attractive alternative for America's expectant mothers.

This dramatic shift to hospital birth was part of a larger trend toward general hospital care, especially in the cities. In the early twentieth century, the urban population continued to grow rapidly: Chicago mushroomed from just over 1 million people in 1890 to 3.4 million in 1930. More unattached people were living in the city, seeking independence as lodgers rather than boarding family-style. With population density increasing and rents rising, fewer urbanites could afford to live in an apartment with space for a sickroom or servants. The growing number of women working away from home also meant that fewer women could stay home to nurse an ill family member. As traditional family-centered care became impractical, the sick turned increasingly to hospitals for help. Improvements in transportation, especially the widening use of the automobile, meant that patients and doctors could reach the hospital more easily for medical care.

Medical factors also played a major role in the rising popularity of hospitals. As an outgrowth of broader academic reforms, medical education shifted away from the low standards of profit-oriented commercial medical colleges to more costly, exclusive, and exacting graduate medical schools affiliated with prestigious universities. The American Medical Association contributed to medical reform by implementing stricter professional standards through its control of state licensing boards. Scientific and technological advances in medicine encouraged specialization by physicians. These specialists needed patients for training purposes, and as internship programs expanded, changes in medical technology made the hospital a more efficient place to provide care. Safer antiseptic standards prevailed at the hospital, and anesthesia was readily available. As more sophisticated equipment came into use, medical treatment became less mobile, confined almost exclusively to the hospital.

Of the three types of hospitals — municipal, denominational, and voluntary — the latter responded with the most flexibility to these changes, courting both patient and doctor to remain financially solvent. The cost of caring for charity patients, admitted in part to provide teaching and research opportunities for specialists, was subsidized by donations and paying patients, who were lured by hotel-like hospital rooms scaled to economic class. Private physicians were recruited to bring in patients, and by the end of the 1920s most physicians had affiliated with a hospital. This increasing number of hospital doctors resulted in more auxiliary medical personnel, such as anesthetists, dieticians, and social workers. The number of hospital beds increased from 42,065 in 1909 to 892,924 in 1928.

In the meantime, the first reliable maternal and infant mortality statistics were issued in 1915 and received wide publicity. These rates were distressingly high; they showed that 61 women died for every 10,000 live births. (By 1980 fewer than one woman in every 10,000 died in childbirth.) Rates remained high throughout the 1920s, and by 1930 the United States placed last among twenty-five countries as a safe place to have a baby. Three solutions emerged: legislation, health education, and medical prevention.

The Sheppard-Towner Act of 1921 allotted federal funds to the states to promote prenatal care under the administration of the Children's Bureau in the Department of Labor. A newly enfranchised female voting public had lobbied unstintingly for federal

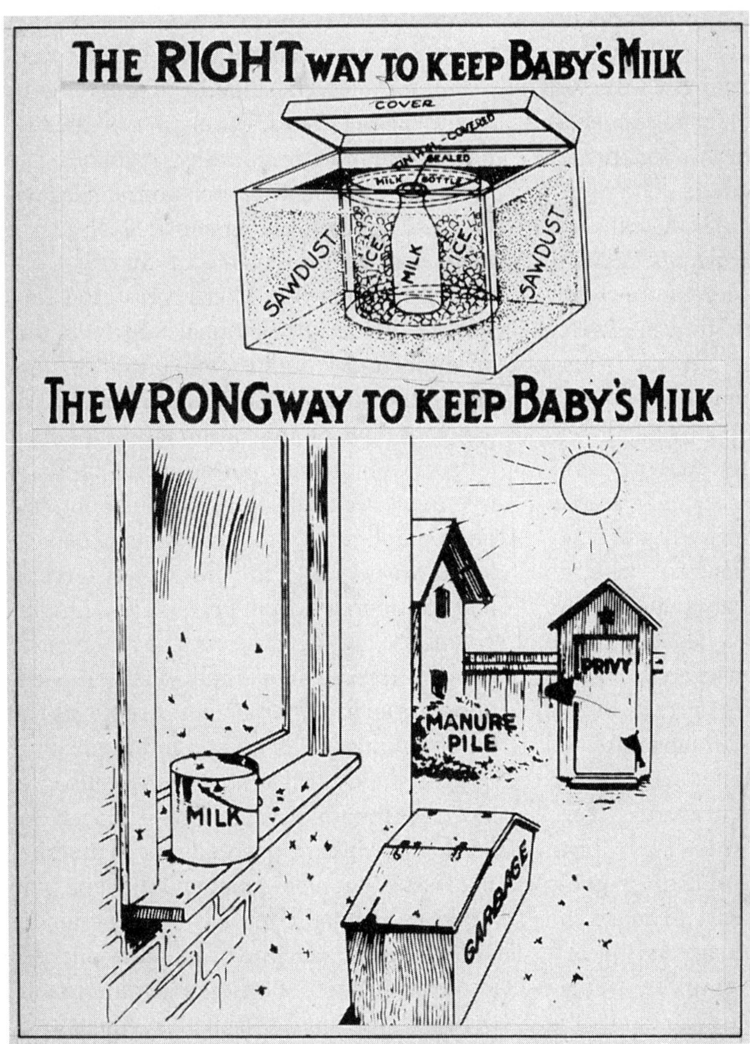

Scientific discoveries in the late nineteenth century revealed that germs could be transported through the air, contaminating unprotected food. In what became one of many reform movements of the Progressive Era, the Infant Welfare Society of Chicago waged a pure milk campaign to educate mothers about the proper storage and preparation of milk.
(CHS, ICHi-20209)

legislation to address the national disgrace of high infant and maternal mortality rates. Under the aegis of Sheppard-Towner, health authorities established nearly 3,000 prenatal care centers, distributed a massive number of prenatal care pamphlets, and made more than 3 million home visits. Although infant mortality figures had dropped 40 percent by 1933, maternal mortality rates were only beginning to decline by that time. Charging that it infringed on states' rights and raising the specter of "state medicine," the American Medical Association successfully opposed the act as a threat to the financial base of medical practice. The legislation lasted only the decade.

The effort to lower mortality rates through education was part of the wider movement to popularize good health. Professional health educators and public health workers superseded doctors and scientists as popular health authorities. They advocated "health for its own sake" by inculcating proper health habits.

In Chicago, health department commissioner Herman N. Bundesen made child and maternal welfare a veritable crusade between 1923 and 1927. Bundesen, physician and father of six, was a health advocate well known nationwide. In 1928 he admonished, "My plea is that you live health, talk health, sell health, and think health." Through a weekly health bulletin with 20,000 readers in 1925, Bundesen sold good health habits to Chicagoans. The bulletin addressed a variety of prenatal and infant care topics, offering simple advice: avoid large crowds, restrict the use of the sewing machine, and take a bath "at least once a week." Good health was good for business, and lowered mortality and morbidity rates were used as a tool in health boosterism. A 1928 department study published in the bulletin boasted, "Chicago has provided many necessary child welfare advantages which make it a desirable place in which to live and rear children."

Bundesen seemed most proud of his health care booklets, two of which addressed maternal and infant welfare. *Our Babies,* published in 1925, was sent to every Chicago family and distributed with each birth certificate. The author of the 72-page guide stated that "Pains were taken to make the bulletin as simple in language as the text would permit keeping in mind the average mentality of mothers into whose hands the booklet was intended to fall." He published a second booklet, *Before the Baby Comes,* to educate women because "we feel that this terrible slaughter of the innocents can be greatly reduced as it is due almost entirely to public ignorance."

Educational efforts encompassed ice and pure milk campaigns, and the department cooperated with volunteer groups to staff infant welfare stations throughout Chicago. At these stations physicians and public health workers examined children and advised mothers on health care. Leading hospitals such as Michael Reese, Presbyterian, and Chicago Lying-in cooperated with the Infant Welfare Society by providing free health care for those who could not afford a physician.

But for many, hospital birth and the protection it offered were the answers to the maternal and infant mortality problem. The American Medical Association advocated hospital delivery to the public in *Hygeia,* a magazine for the lay reader that first appeared in 1923. It publicized Hospital Day, May 12 (Florence Nightingale's birthday), as an opportunity for the public to "view the equipment and to learn of the system of organization which makes the modern hospital such an efficient place for the care and treatment of the ill." In 1925 the caption to a photograph of "A Bunch of Bouncing Babies" asked why so few of the previous generation had considered hospital birth. The AMA answered: "Now the maternity hospitals, with their equipment to take care of all complications, are an important factor in reducing the number of deaths of babies and mothers."

Even fiction was rallied to the cause. Dr. Morris Fishbein's "Neighbors — A Story for Mothers," which appeared in the September 1923 issue, has a poignant and didactic plot: a mature woman contrasts the experiences of her two new neighbors, one of whom uses an obstetrician; the other, a general practitioner. The former has a joyful, medically uneventful birth while the latter, who waited years to have a child, suffers eclampsia, which goes unrecognized by her doctor. She experiences convulsions, goes partially blind, and loses the baby. The bereaved father remarks in the closing paragraph of the story, "We've found out that when a fellow [the general practitioner] claims too much he can't give value received. We've found out that there's something to being prepared and that prevention saves a lot of trouble." The message — that going to a general practitioner was a risky investment of the resources of the tragic couple — was quite clear. But in case the reader missed the point, just below the story was a reminder that 200,000 babies and 20,000 mothers died in 1920.

Women's magazines such as *Ladies Home Journal* addressed the issue of how to pay for hospital delivery with budgets and advice "about how to make the best birth buy." In "Babies While We're Young: They Cost Less Than the Cheapest Automobile," which appeared in September 1926, Margaret Matlack responded to "articles decrying the low birth rate among the educated classes" by estimating the costs of having a baby and suggesting a family savings plan. She expressed clear preference for hospital birth, with its advantages of "preparation for any emergency, completely sterile equipment, the most efficient care for mother and baby, [and] complete detachment from household worries." For the modern young couple, hospital birth should be given the attention devoted to the purchase of a car.

Among doctors, prophylactic or preventive obstetrics emerged as the professional remedy to the problem of maternal and infant mortality. Medically managed delivery relied heavily

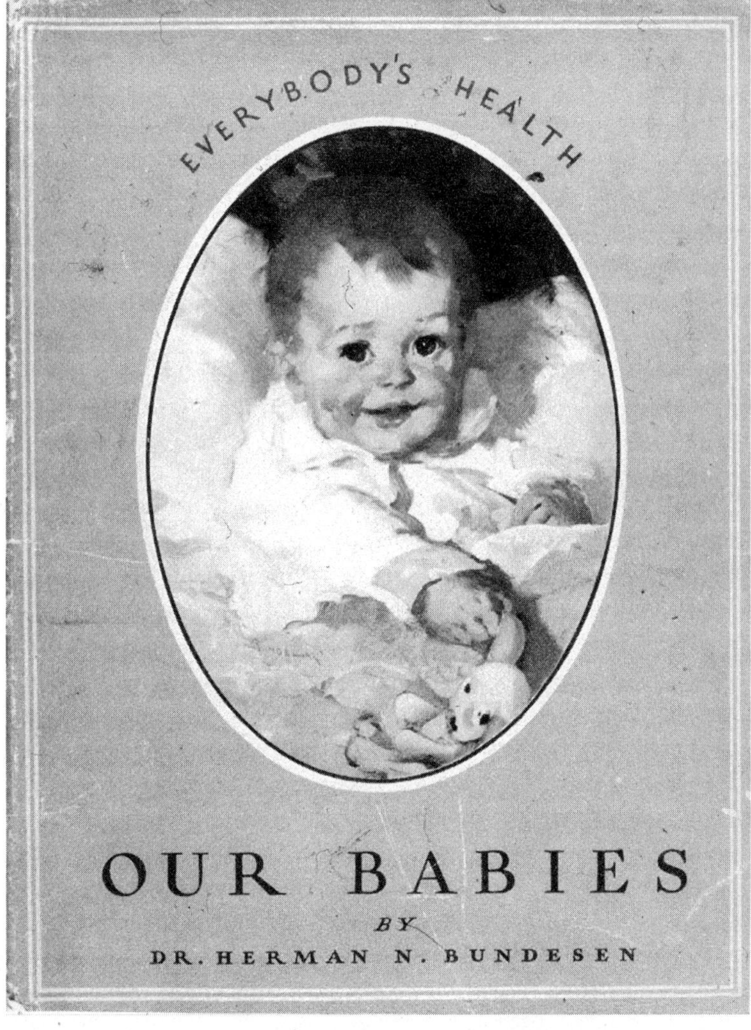

Dr. Herman N. Bundesen, commissioner of Chicago's health department, promoted good health habits in his 1925 booklet *Our Babies,* sent to every Chicago family and distributed with each birth certificate.
(CHS)

upon the routine use of anesthesia and forceps to control the birth process. Although physicians were by this time the accepted birth attendants at most home deliveries, this interventionist approach mandated hospital care by a specialist. (A campaign by the health department and doctors to eradicate midwifery had dominated the maternity care scene throughout the 1910s. By 1926 only 14 percent of births were attended by midwives, and the figure dropped to a negligible 6 percent by 1932.) According to medical historian Morris Vogel, "Redefining childbirth as unnatural facilitated its transfer out of the home and to the unnatural setting of the hospital." Dr. Joseph B. DeLee was a leading obstetrician who played a major role in the development of preventive obstetrics and the popularization of hospital birth.

DeLee has been described as one of two "titans" of obstetrics, along with his contemporary, Dr. J. Whitridge Williams of Johns Hopkins University. According to sociologist William Ray Arney, DeLee and his followers "wanted obstetrics to be a super-profession, and all of this group's rhetoric and recommendations for practice followed from this position." His motivations for this stance stemmed largely from his obsession with earning the professional respect accorded surgeons. He felt that "not until the pathologic dignity of obstetrics is fully recognized may we hope for any considerable reduction of the mortality and morbidity of childbirth." Williams led the other faction for a broader profession that would include the general practitioner. The establishment of the American Board of Obstetrics and Gynecology in 1930, however, legitimized the separatist obstetricians' domination of the profession. DeLee achieved national renown and even appeared on the cover of *Time* magazine on May 25, 1936, as the "No. 1 U.S. obstetrician because he founded Chicago's great Lying-in Hospital, helped make obstetrics a learned and respected profession, [and] demonstrated methods to prevent women from dying in childbirth."

Joseph B. DeLee (1870-1942) trained at Chicago Medical College and Cook County Hospital and studied throughout Europe. During his internship he had been deeply disturbed by the sight of new mothers giving up their babies to orphanages, and he resolved to help poor women. In 1895 he opened the one-room Chicago Lying-in Hospital and Dispensary near Jane Addams's Hull-House. He modeled it after the New York Lying-In Hospital and its Broome Street Dispensary that he had visited. His initial aim was to deliver the babies of poor women in their homes at no charge. After several years, with the early support of Jewish charitable organizations and individual contributions, he had a steady stream of patients and could afford larger facilities. From these modest beginnings the hospital acquired wider community support, built a strong women's board to administer its day-to-day affairs, and attracted nurses and doctors for advanced obstetrical training. In 1909, after moving twice to successively larger rented facilities, plans were made to build a new hospital with a separate pavilion for infectious maternity cases. The pavilion was to be paid for with funds raised by Mother's Aid, a Jewish women's sewing auxiliary founded by DeLee's sister, Ruth Newman, in 1904. The outbreak of World War I delayed construction, and Chicago Lying-in Hospital did not open until August 15, 1917. A six-story brick building at the corner of Vincennes Avenue and 51st Street was the main facility (until 1932 the Dispensary still operated as part of Lying-in), with 120 beds. In 1931 Chicago Lying-in (CLI) moved to a new building on the University of Chicago campus, two years after its official affiliation with the university's new medical school.

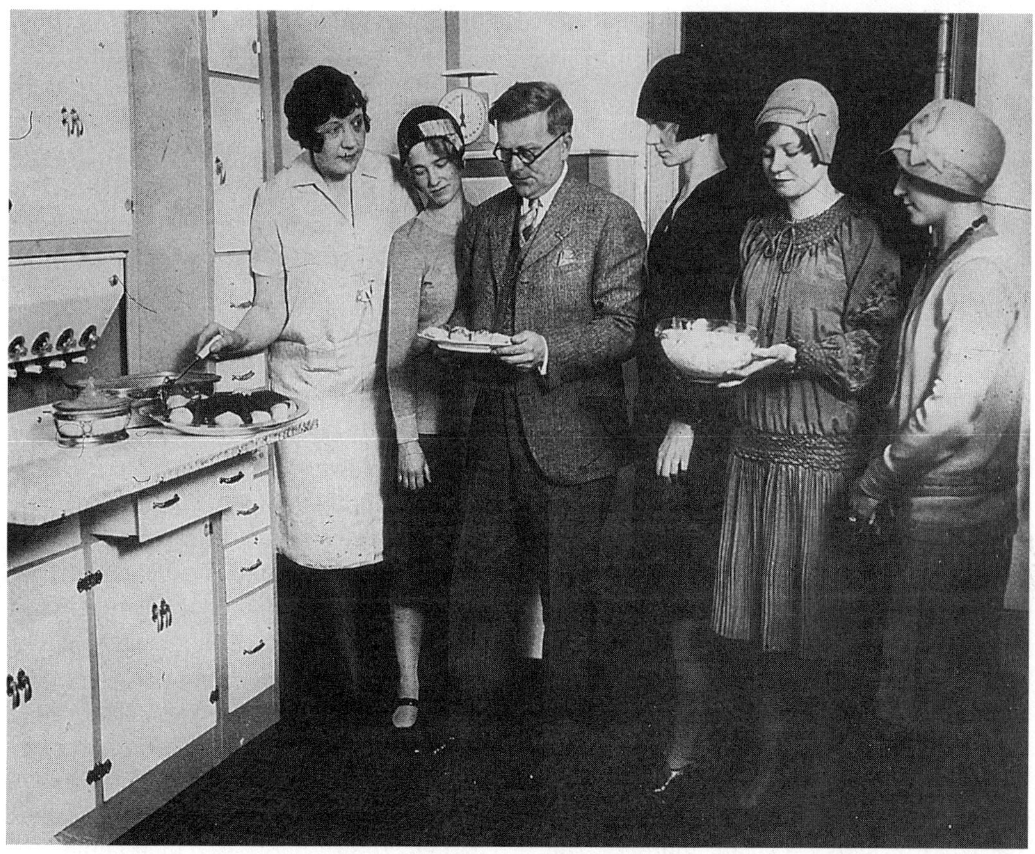

Dr. Bundesen, concerned with all aspects of public health, teaches a cooking class in 1929.
(CHS, ICHi-20211)

DeLee's own hospital gave him a proving ground for his medical practices, while offering reputable maternity care to Chicago women. The best known of these practices was described in an article appearing in the first issue of *The American Journal of Obstetrics and Gynecology* in 1920. In this article DeLee described the prophylactic forceps delivery that would characterize conventional hospital birth for many years. He claimed that this operation, by which the physician could speed up delivery by extracting the baby with forceps from a surgically enlarged vaginal opening, "saves the woman the debilitating effects of suffering," and anatomically "virginal conditions are often restored." He argued that it also preserved the baby's brain from injury from constant pounding against the pelvic floor. He asked rhetorically, "if you believe that a woman after delivery should be as healthy, as well, as anatomically perfect as she was before, and that the child should be undamaged, then you will have to agree with me that labor is pathogenic, because experience has proved such ideal results exceedingly rare."

DeLee's prophylactic forceps operation was widely used by the house obstetricians at CLI. If the patient was delivering her first baby, she usually received an episiotomy to enlarge the vaginal opening and hasten the birth. During the twenties 42 percent of the patients received episiotomies, and forceps were used in 21 percent of the deliveries. More severe complications could be solved with a low Cesarean section that DeLee popularized. These operative strategies resulted in a maternal mortality rate of 26.4 per 10,000 for the period 1918-31, as compared to about 65 per 10,000 for the United States as a whole. The fetal mortality rate was 3.6 percent, compared to 6.4 percent nationally. The success of CLI in this regard was aided by prenatal clinics which were established as early as 1921 to detect eclampsia and other pregnancy disorders. DeLee's operative approach to childbirth also proved to be an effective tool in demarcating obstetrics as a medical preserve for the specialists, and Chicago Lying-in's attachment to a major university brought to fruition DeLee's earlier efforts to earn respect for the obstetrical profession.

By 1931 CLI was the hospital of choice for many of Chicago's expectant mothers. The women's board that administered the hospital and raised most of the funds for its expansion brought not only money but recognition to CLI, making it the fashionable place to have a baby. According to one upper-class patient who remembers the twenties, "It was a wonderful period. Everybody went to Lying-in." But who was the "everybody" who went to CLI? A look at hospital statistics reveals clients from varying economic backgrounds evenly distributed by religion. For any class of patient, CLI offered a safe, convenient birth.

A safe, convenient birth was what Louise Hulley Turner wanted in 1924. In her letters to family members now housed in the Chicago Historical Society and in an article she wrote which was published in *Century Magazine* in 1926, we get a firsthand view of Chicago childbirth. In "The Other Side of the Baby Budget: There Are Still Perfectly Good Forty-Dollar Babies," the young matron explained how she obtained a bargain price at Chicago Lying-in for the birth of her first son. Satisfied with her hospital experience, she argued that the educated classes, or as she called them, "the gently bred," could begin their families if they were willing to accept financial help from the hospital.

Louise Chrisfield Hulley Turner was indeed "one of the gently bred." Born in Pennsylvania in 1896 to Lincoln and Eloise Mayham Hulley, her family was oriented toward education. She was educated at Stetson University in Florida (where her father was president), and received an M.A. degree in 1918 from Radcliffe. She studied education during the school year 1922-23 at the University of Chicago, where she met her husband, James Haskew Turner, a recent graduate of the University of Chicago Law School. They were married on August 18, 1923. While these letters surround the birth of their first child, a son, in 1924, the Turners eventually had six children. The Turners raised their family and lived near the University of Chicago until their deaths in the mid-1970s.

The Turners started their family immediately after marriage, before they could accumulate much savings from the $35 a week James earned in his practice. Louise Turner made inquiries of her friends as to where to have the baby. While one friend argued against maternity hospitals because "they're so expensive and so strict," another, who was a nurse, told her she could probably afford CLI "if I did not mind entering a ward and being attended by a house physician." In the 1920s about half the patients at CLI were part pay, about one-third were full pay, and the rest received care free of charge. While all CLI patients were entitled to the most advanced obstetrical care in the country, the quality of attention they received was based on their ability to pay. A full-paying patient either came to the hospital on her own or at the request of her doctor. If she had a private room, she was required to have her own doctor, whom she paid in addition to hospital room charges. Private nursing care could add a substantial amount to hospital charges for the private room patient who chose to hire her own nurses. Private room patients were valuable for the revenue they brought the hospital, and it was thought that they kept the standards of the hospital at a high level. A full-paying patient could be housed more economically in either a semi-private room (two beds) or in a ward with three or four beds in a room. In this case she did not need her own doctor and was cared for by the house staff.

Part-paying patients were admitted to the hospital through the Social Services Department after they had filled out a form assessing their financial needs. The patient then decided how much she could pay; and the hospital absorbed the balance. In that way, DeLee idealized, "the wives of wage earners can . . . obtain the same highly specialized attention given to the wealthy patients." Part-paying clients were not eligible for private rooms unless medically necessary. In that case they were entitled to a private room even if there was a shortage of private rooms for full-paying patients. Charity patients were not refused unless the hospital was full. They were accommodated in the three- or four-bed wards at no cost, and "the fact that the patient is a charity case is known only to the office of the Hospital, unless she tells the other patients herself." However, a wealthy patient could be easily identified by whether or not she was dependent on the house staff for medical and nursing care. Ability to pay even determined the patient's hygiene; private patients were to have baths every day, those in semi-private rooms every other day, and "ward patients on first, fifth and tenth days."

Hospital rates remained stable during the 1920s. Wards cost $4 a day, semi-private rooms $5 a day, and private rooms $7 to $14 a day depending on location. Additional fees were charged for the birth room ($5 to $20) and the nursery ($1 a day). All payments were due weekly in advance with extra charges for telephone service, newspapers, drugs, special anesthesia, and laboratory work.

Special nursing care was available at the rate of $7 for a 12-hour day, which could nearly double the cost of hospitalization in private rooms. The services of interns and house nurses were included in the basic hospital rate. If a patient was to utilize the house staff and stay in a ward, her total bill would have been approximately $60, a good deal less than the national going rate of $85.

After arranging her fee through the Social Services Department (she received a discount of $1 a day), and withstanding what she termed the "hoi polloi" in the free prenatal clinic, Louise Turner decided on CLI. She concluded that the low price would more than offset the inconvenience of "wildly picturesque room-mates."

Louise Turner's letters to her parents and sister Harriet about her son's birth cover one year beginning in December 1923. Her first letter complained of the "fussiness" of her stomach and that she had decided to have the baby at Chicago Lying-in. She noted with surprise, "You don't have to take a thing to the hospital except clothes for yourself and your little baby to go home in. They furnish everything. And they keep you about ten days." She attended the free hospital clinic weekly near the end of her pregnancy. She also commented on her monotonous maternity wardrobe. Although maternity clothes were available from the Lane Bryant store downtown, she coped by simply buying bigger sizes of a few things to wear.

May 1 found the Turners in a new apartment on East 67th Street which wasn't quite finished, three weeks before her due date. She confessed, "Moving is Jimmy's idea. I let him do all the deciding for the family." She watched the carpenters finish the apartment while she hemmed diapers to add to the two dozen she had purchased. She sewed petticoats and nightgowns for the baby, and sheets and a quilt for the baby bed that she thought might be too big for the small apartment. With the baby underthings she borrowed from her sister and the buggy she bought, she was ready for the arrival of the baby. During the last few weeks of her pregnancy she felt well enough to see a musical downtown with her husband. They also walked across Jackson Park to the lagoon and toured the replica of Columbus's boat left over from the World's Columbian Exposition.

Her labor began at home about 5:30 Sunday evening May 26, and she spent until midnight readying the apartment for her absence. "I cooked things for Jimmy, washed and ironed his things, packed mine, scrubbed and straightened the house a bit, even to the sink, bathtub and stove, changed the linens, etc. for I wanted to have Jimmy as comfortable as possible." She dropped on the bed every five minutes when the pains came and was grateful that her husband was home so he could accompany her to the hospital. She needed an escort, for she had to ride two streetcars and walk eight blocks to CLI.

Once at the hospital she seemed ill-prepared for the medical routines preceding delivery. "I didn't realize the doctors had to make examinations to see your progress and I tho't they were just practising on me and I resented it so and of course it hurt cruelly." She remarked that one intern was particularly insensitive when she said she couldn't turn over in the middle of a contraction. "Oh, you could if you wanted to well enough" was his response, and he told a nurse she was "another lazy one." Her account of the delivery indicates it was a classic DeLee prophylactic forceps procedure with ether as the anesthesia. "I tried to do what they said but I couldn't help bring the little baby. I guess my bones were too hard and wouldn't move. Anyway — they gave me ether and I swallowed quarts of it (heavenly stuff — it surely saves your life, doesn't it?) and then they took the little baby with instruments without a scar and sewed me up." She recounted, "After the usual baptism of fire and several hours of unconsciousness, I drifted back through a confused world to find my husband sitting beside me." Only then did she find out the baby was a boy, whom she did not see until 9:30 P.M., more than six hours after the 3:07 P.M. delivery.

It is striking that such a well-educated woman had so little information about the physical processes of labor and how to physically cooperate with the doctor. She probably didn't feel it necessary or important to prepare for the labor experience since most likely she would be sedated. It is also important to note that she apparently wasn't treated with much personal respect by the medical staff, quite possibly because of her paying status. Her economies meant she was delivered by a house physician, Dr. Anna Ross Lapham, who boasted that Turner would not have a scar from the episiotomy. Medical pride of performance was intact, but by today's standards her account shows a lack of concern for personal dignity.

Yet Turner was grateful for her care and quite satisfied with its quality. Her letters from this time are filled with testimonials to maternity hospitals and obstetricians. Of CLI she said, "they never lose a baby or a mother here and the care is excellent. . . . If I'd gone to any old doctor as I intended to he'd have ruined me and my baby likely." She reiterated in another letter, "I can never be too thankful that I didn't go to any old hospital and any old doctor. . . . I'm thoroly [*sic*] converted to an obstetrician and a baby hospital. Never anything else for us." She advised her pregnant sister, "I want you to have the best care in a regular *baby* hospital by a *baby* doctor." She had delivered safely, she was assured that she would heal without a scar, not "ruined," and the baby was healthy. She obviously felt that the emotional bewilderment and physical pain of the delivery experience were amply compensated for by the medical safety and comforts of her stay.

After the birth, proud fathers were allowed to visit nearly all day; other visitors, from 11 A.M. to 1 P.M. and 3 to 8:30 P.M. in private rooms. Ward visiting hours were much shorter, only 3 to 3:30 P.M. and 7 to 8 P.M. Two visitors were allowed per day in addition to the husband. Rules were printed for visitors, warning them not to upset the mothers with startling news, because "then the milk supply is affected and the baby suffers. Even the dairymen could tell you this." The rules reflected the attitudes of the day that "childbirth is hard at best, and the mothers need rest and generous opportunity to recuperate." Visitors were warned that if they did not observe the rules "then you are unjust and unkind to those who are entitled to most tender consideration." Well-wishers brought or sent flowers which were cut and arranged in vases in a special flower room near the patient rooms. Visitors could pick

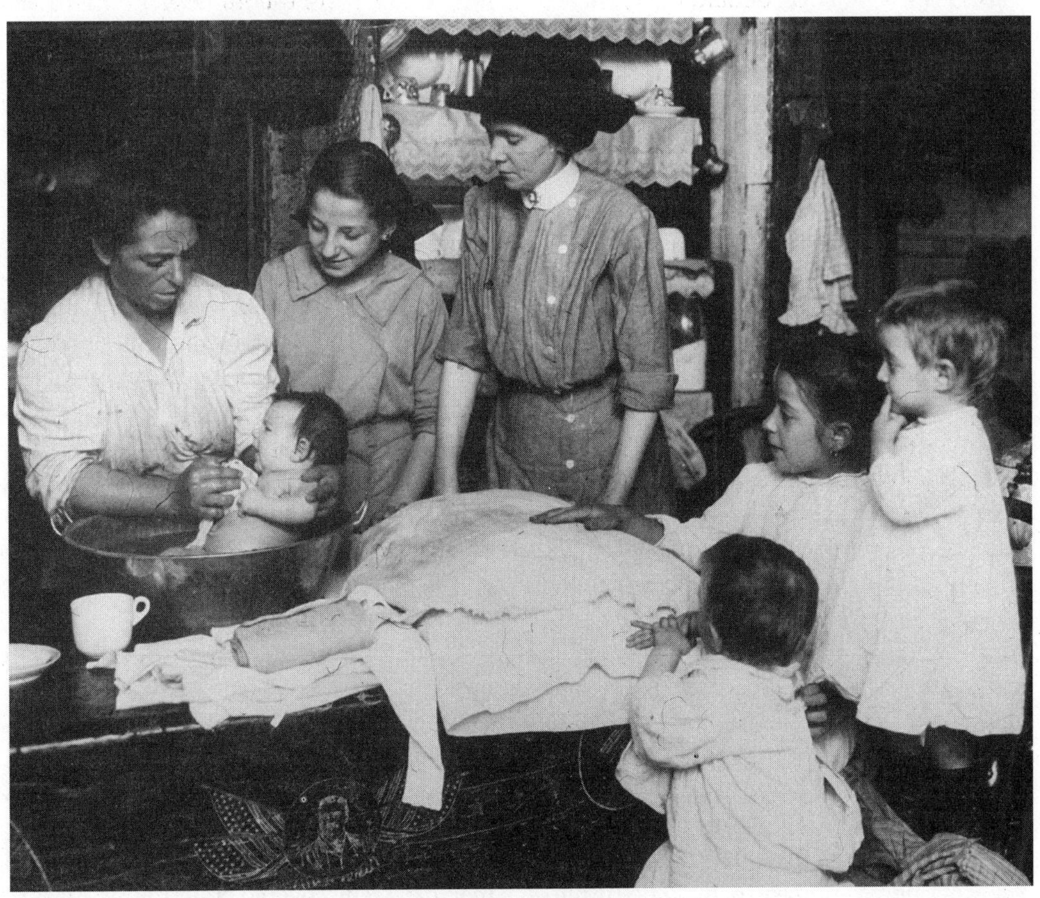

An Infant Welfare Society nurse shows a new mother how to bathe her infant.
(CHS, ICHi-20214)

up a present in the gift shop, perhaps a copy of *Baby's First Seven Years*, an elaborate baby record book first published in 1928 by Mother's Aid to raise hospital funds.

Mother and baby were discharged from the hospital any time from ten to fourteen days after delivery. They might return to the hospital for a postpartum checkup at eight weeks. When reminded by a post card, over two-thirds returned for clinical care. Beginning in 1921 baby clinics offered pediatric care. Patients who could afford it were visited at home by a private pediatrician. Wealthy patients retained nurses to help them adjust to the duties of motherhood.

Louise Turner's ten days in the hospital were spent resting, reading, and writing letters. She remarked that it was difficult to write lying down because she wasn't yet allowed to sit up. "The hospital routine keeps me busy enough — meals, the baby, my toilette and Jimmy's visit." She saw her baby "only five times a day, half an hour or less each time and it's not half enough. I'll be glad to get him at home where I can gaze at him all day." The baby was an enthusiastic nurser, "a little gormand [*sic*]" except for the feeding he skipped after he was fortified for his circumcision with whiskey in water.

Turner stayed in a ward room with three other women. Her room was "pleasant, in good taste, and spotlessly clean." The subdued decor of gray ceiling, faint pink walls, and brown furniture must have been planned with rest in mind. She discovered the congeniality of roommates to be an advantage in her recovery. Even if she wasn't allowed to walk around in "pretty negligees" like the private patients, at least she was not lonesome. She felt her care was excellent and thought her stay "on the whole, a most restful and satisfactory experience." Her bill came to $47.50, "truly a very cheap baby." The Turners splurged on a cab to bring the baby home.

An analysis of the style of childbirth in the city of the 1920s makes it clear that both medical and social change led to adaptations in the birth-giving process. The press and public health workers publicized high infant and maternal mortality rates, and the nation responded with legislative action. The hospital emerged as the most efficient place for medical care, where medical specialists had all resources at hand. Led by DeLee, obstetricians wooed the public and defined their profession by characterizing birth as abnormal or unnatural. This allowed them to take control or manage the delivery through efficient intervention. In a quest for professional legitimacy, they set out to slay the dragon of maternal and infant mortality with prophylactic childbirth. Today's medically managed birth descends from the practices popularized in the 1920s.

A middle-class maternity patient in the 1980s need not worry about standards of medical care or how to pay the hospital bill. Instead, the focus is now on amenities, matters of taste that she controls to make her feel emotionally "at home" as she faces the cathartic struggle of giving birth. Similarly, the urban parents of the twenties sought the safety of hospital delivery as a wise investment of their resources. However, it was the medical management of the hospital delivery that appealed to them, not its emotional aspects. They were willing to sacrifice personal comfort to obtain that scientific guarantee.

Certainly the changes in hospital birth over the last sixty years have been profoundly affected by changes in our understanding of the roles of men and women, mothers and fathers. The bulk of change has taken place in the last decade as women have moved toward greater independence and men have rediscovered fathering. As styles of life change, so do styles of birth.

Antilabor Mercenaries or Defenders of Public Order

Clayton D. Laurie

By early July 1894, Chicago had endured more than fifty days of a strike that disrupted all rail traffic coming to and from the city. The presence of hundreds of policemen, U.S. deputy marshals, and contingents of federal troops had failed to reopen the railroads or convince strikers and mobs of the unemployed to cease unlawful activities. Tensions ran high. On July 6, the violence and destruction reached the first of many peaks when an agent of the Illinois Central Railroad shot and killed two rioters in the city's Panhandle Yards near Fiftieth Street. In the aftermath of this act, a mob of six thousand destroyed an estimated seven thousand rail cars and other property valued at $340,000. Mobs even burned six buildings on the grounds of the World's Columbian Exposition, which took place in Chicago the previous summer. Faced with increasingly uncontrollable disorders, Chicago mayor John Hopkins appealed to Illinois governor John P. Altgeld to intervene with state troops.

While prepared to intervene instantly, Altgeld was nonetheless chagrined to find that U.S. Attorney General Richard Olney had usurped his authority and prerogatives for restoring order. Olney was determined to use federal military power to end the nationwide strike and destroy the Chicago-based American Railway Union (ARU), which supported it. Federal troops were deployed during the summer of 1894 as a partisan strikebreaking force in an unprecedented abuse of federal military power. The army, although following the orders of its civilian superiors, including the U.S. Attorney General, gained a negative reputation among labor that took decades to overcome. Olney's actions during the spring and summer of 1894 added fuel to the raging controversy over the proper domestic role, if any, of federal troops, especially in relation to disorders arising from labor disputes. The Chicago deployment was the largest intervention of federal soldiers for riot duty since the Civil War, and it prompted the army's first attempt to develop a doctrine on handling civil disturbances.

The Pullman Strike grew from disorders that began in May 1894 in the company town of Pullman, Illinois, then twelve miles south of Chicago. Founded in 1880 by George M. Pullman as the site of the Pullman Palace Car

George Pullman created the town of Pullman to house the workers at his Pullman Palace Car Works.
(CHS, ICHi-01922)

Company, the town was intended to be a worker's paradise "where all that is ugly and discordant and demoralizing is eliminated." The company's slick advertising brochures, however, did not present the entire truth about the company town. While the twelve thousand employees and their families had company-provided amenities, such as housing, a hotel, a post office, a bank, a church, general stores, schools, and utilities, all were company-owned and financed by deductions from workers' wages. The rates were calculated to return to the company 67 percent annually on the money spent to construct and maintain them. Prices and rents in Pullman were often 20 to 25 percent higher than those in surrounding communities, and sometimes wage deductions consumed all of an employee's pay, forcing them into debt to the company. While workers were not compelled to live in Pullman, only residents could count on steady employment in hard times.

In the year after the Panic of 1893, George Pullman, seeking to avoid the worst effects of the bad economic times, followed the lead of other industrialists and reduced employee wages between 25 and 45 percent. He did not, however, reduce rents, prices for goods and services in Pullman, or the salaries of managers and superintendents. The Pullman Company continued to pay stock dividends of between 8 and 9.5 percent, as it had since its founding in 1867, and had managed to maintain a surplus of twenty-five million dollars despite bad economic times. Pullman later claimed that the company was operating at a loss during the reductions and strike, but a later investigation by the United States Strike Commission found the opposite to be true.

Seeking relief from the hardships caused by the wage reductions, a committee representing Pullman employees met with George Pullman on May 9, 1894, to request a reduction in rents and a restoration of predepression wages. Pullman claimed that wage cuts were necessary to keep the factories open, but he promised to investigate. The next day, however, three members of the committee were summarily fired. Outraged at what they perceived as Pullman's bad faith, the remaining members of the committee met and voted to strike on May 11 unless the company reinstated the terminated workers, reduced rents, and restored wages to pre-1893 levels. In a preemptive move, Pullman declared an indefinite lockout, putting all four thousand employees out of work. A peaceful strike and stalemate ensued for the next three weeks, while repeated attempts by Pullman employees to reach a negotiated settlement failed.

The dispute in Pullman would probably have remained local had its existence not become known to two larger organizations whose rivalry escalated the conflict into a national one. The American Railway Union, formed by Eugene V. Debs in June 1893, had 150,000 members, including several thousand Pullman employees. Opposing the ARU was the eight-year-old General Manager's Association of Chicago (GMA), a business association consisting of the Pullman Company and twenty-four railroads, among them the giants of the rail industry. After Pullman management rebuffed employee attempts at a compromise solution, the ARU took up the cause and presented the Pullman Company with an ultimatum: unless its representatives agreed to arbitration by June 26, the union would begin a nationwide rail strike and would boycott any train carrying a Pullman car. Since most major railroads used Pullman cars, the national rail system would be paralyzed. When George Pullman ignored the ARU's ultimatum, the strike began.

The GMA quickly came to the defense of the Pullman Company. Railroad company lawyers called for court injunctions against the strike and ordered nonstriking employees to place Pullman cars on as many trains as possible, calculating that widespread disruption of passenger, freight, and mail traffic would provoke a public outcry, cause federal intervention, and tarnish the ARU's image. For the same reasons, the GMA avoided calling on municipal authorities or the Illinois state militia between June 26 and July 2 to break what was initially a peaceful and orderly strike, hoping instead for decisive federal actions to destroy the ARU.

The railroads had a powerful friend and ally in U.S. Attorney General Richard Olney. Before and during his tenure at the Justice Department, Olney served as a director or a legal adviser to several railroads that were members of the GMA. At the same time that he earned an annual salary of eight thousand dollars as attorney general, he received more than ten thousand dollars annually as a retainer for his services to the Chicago, Burlington, & Quincy Railroad. Olney agreed that the ARU constituted an implacable foe of business to be curbed by all possible methods, and he believed that its leadership and policies presented revolutionary threats to federal authority. According to historian Jerry M. Cooper, Olney worked to break the strike primarily to destroy the ARU, to discredit Eugene Debs, and to intimidate other national labor organizations into submission.

Olney, in attempting to involve the federal government in the strike, first appointed attorney Edwin Walker as special counsel and strike adviser to Thomas E. Milchrist, the U.S. District Attorney for the Northern District of Illinois. As a former railroad lawyer and the GMA's own choice to lead antistrike efforts, Walker, like Olney, was well suited for the task ahead. Olney's second step was to convince President Grover Cleveland of the need to act. The events developing in Chicago troubled Cleveland, but he hesitated to commit federal troops until their presence was necessary to prevent lawlessness. As Olney pointed out, however, Cleveland had the legal authority to intervene militarily under Revised Statute 5298, a law allowing the president to use army regulars to enforce federal laws and protect federal property. Cleveland could also intervene under the various railroad acts intended to protect the mail and interstate commerce. While the president mulled over the events and his options, Olney directed Walker and Milchrist to initiate court injunctions to get rail traffic moving and to break the strike.

Earlier in 1894, Olney had used federal court injunctions to allow federal intervention in disputes with Jacob Coxey's Commonwealth of Christ and other "industrial armies" that hijacked trains to the East. This tactic, however, applied only to railroads in federal receivership. But in July 1894, this now-familiar federal tactic no longer worked because few eastern railroads were financially insolvent. Instead, Olney sought to use two other justifications for federal injunctions — to prevent interference with the U.S. mail and interstate commerce. During an earlier strike against the Great Northern Railroad, Olney's solicitor general had determined that any train hauling at least one mail car was a mail train. Olney reasoned that efforts to remove the mail car, or any car, on the same train constituted interference with the U.S. mail. On June 28, he instructed Edwin Walker to obtain federal court injunctions so that "passage of regular trains carrying U.S. mails in the usual and ordinary way . . . [would not be] obstructed." As an added antistrike measure, the GMA pressed Olney to invoke the Sherman Anti-Trust Act, a law originally intended as a device to control industrial and business monopolies but now used against trusts or conspiracies of organized laborers. Olney readily complied with GMA requests.

Having selected protection of the mail and interstate commerce and invoking antitrust legislation as grounds for intervention, Olney sought a blanket injunction, citing all three justifications, that would render ARU interference with rail traffic in the Chicago area virtually impossible. Although neither city nor state officials had yet requested federal aid during what had thus far been a peaceful strike, U.S. Circuit Court Judge William A. Woods and U.S. District Court Judge Peter S. Grosscup issued, on July 2, at Olney's behest, an injunction of such breadth that labor leaders denounced it as a "Gatling gun on paper." It prohibited ARU members from interfering with mail trains or trains engaged in interstate commerce and forbade union members from persuading others to join the strike or encouraging those already engaged in the boycott. If Debs complied with the injunction, the strike would end immediately, and the future of the ARU would be jeopardized. The injunction, however, as Olney and the GMA understood, meant little without enforcement power.

Federal marshals had already been unsuccessful at controlling what little disorder existed, which unemployed persons unconnected with the strike or the ARU had instigated, and they now appeared unable to enforce the injunction as well. Under Olney's orders since June 26, U.S. Marshal John W. Arnold had appointed three thousand men as deputies in the Chicago area. Some were white-collar or nonstriking railroad workers volunteered by their companies, but most were thugs, derelicts, drunks, and other disreputable persons who made needless arrests, brutalized citizens, and, in some cases, plundered the very property they were hired to protect. All were paid, armed, and deployed at the direction of the GMA. Edwin Walker complained to Olney that the marshal appointed a "mob of deputies" who were "worse than useless," and who, rather than assuring law and order, were provoking strikers and the unemployed to violence.

The apparent failure of federal marshals, deputies, and local police to maintain law and order left only two alternatives: Illinois's National Guard forces or federal troops. At the outset of the boycott, Illinois's forty-seven-year-old, liberal, and prolabor governor, John P. Altgeld, had deployed portions of the state's national guard at trouble spots in Danville, Decatur, and Cairo, but as conditions worsened he prepared to concentrate the entire force near Chicago. Despite his readiness to intervene, Altgeld was unsympathetic to the railroads, had refused to accept GMA favors or succumb to their influence, and believed that the cause of the Pullman workers was basically just. Above all he was unwilling to position state forces as GMA-supporting strikebreakers.

Altgeld's attitudes did not surprise the GMA or federal officials. Area businessmen and local and federal authorities had long distrusted the self-educated and self-made Altgeld because of his German-immigrant, working-class background, his Populist leanings, and his past support for radical causes. Already considered a political outsider, Altgeld increased the suspicions of those uncomfortable with his philosophies by pardoning the surviving Haymarket Affair anarchists soon after taking office. Railroad owners had little trouble convincing Walker and Milchrist that if Altgeld used state troops in Chicago, the troops would be restricted to restoring order and would not break the strike.

The actions against the industrial armies in the spring had eroded Olney's confidence in state militias and in the law enforcement capabilities of his own marshal force. From the beginning of the Pullman boycott, Olney sought to employ federal troops. To do this, he needed to demonstrate to President Cleveland, as required by Revised Statute 5298, that it had become impracticable "to enforce the law by the ordinary course of judicial proceedings" with the resources at hand.

Olney's first opportunity to persuade Cleveland to send troops to Chicago came on July 1, 1894. When a mob of two thousand strikers at Chicago's Blue Island rail yard defied Arnold's orders to disperse, the U.S. marshal wired Olney that it was "impossible," even with a force of 125 deputies, "to move trains here without having the Fifteenth Infantry from Ft. Sheridan ordered here now." Although news reporters, the Chicago chief of police, and Mayor Hopkins all later testified that no significant disturbances had taken place at Blue Island or in Chicago before July 2, Olney used Arnold's telegram to convince Cleveland of the need for federal military intervention. Anticipating presidential orders, the army's commanding general, John M. Schofield, alerted the Department of the Missouri to prepare to move the entire garrison at Fort Sheridan by steamer or rail to Chicago's Lake Front Park. Despite Olney's and Arnold's pleas and Schofield's preparations, Cleveland decided not to follow the precedent set during the Coxey episode and not to deploy troops until he received a joint statement from officials in Chicago that proved soldiers were needed.

Moving quickly, Olney instructed Walker on July 3 to forward a request for federal troops, signed jointly by Milchrist and Grosscup, and with this statement Olney persuaded Cleveland to commit federal forces. Schofield was summoned to the White House. After locating the commander of the Department of the Missouri on Long Island, where he was allegedly vacationing, Schofield ushered Maj. Gen. Nelson A. Miles into a White House conference with himself, President Cleveland, Secretary of State Walter Gresham, and Secretary of War Daniel Lamont. After some discussion, Schofield recounted that Miles and Gresham balked at sending federal troops to the city; they deemed them unnecessary and believed that they might provoke further violence. The other members of the conference, however, convinced by Olney, who waved Arnold's telegram as proof of the existing danger, overruled them and convinced the president that immediate federal military assistance was crucial.

The conference brought to the fore a longstanding rivalry between Miles and Schofield that was to have an enervating effect on the federal military intervention in Chicago. Their respective memoirs differ sharply on the sequence of events at the conference but do indicate some of the subtle hostility the two officers had long held toward each other. Miles claimed that he "happened to be on important duty in the east" when the crisis erupted, while Schofield wrote that Miles's "staff officers didn't know his whereabouts nor did the Adjutant General of the Army." Miles later claimed in his memoirs that he favored sending troops to Chicago immediately to put down a radical revolution, while Schofield portrayed Miles as "not having anticipated any emergency which would require or justify . . . use of troops in his department." According to Schofield, "In [Miles's] opinion the U.S. troops ought not be employed in the city of Chicago at that time."

Miles's view that troops were unnecessary upset Schofield, who already considered Miles derelict in his duty for not ending his vacation and returning to Chicago earlier. The two generals had previously clashed over Miles's slowness in responding to orders from Schofield and his proclivity either to change or to ignore orders altogether. Earlier in the spring, during the coal miners' strike in Indian territory, Miles took nearly a month to comply with Schofield's order to send troops to evict strikers from coal mines on federal property.

Schofield and Miles's strained relations reflected both a personality clash and differences in interpretation regarding the role of the army in civil disorders. Schofield, at age sixty-three, had had a long and varied career that included both combat service and civil affairs duty. An 1853 graduate of the U.S. Military Academy with a subsequently earned law degree from the University of Chicago, he saw active duty in the Third Seminole War and commanded Union volunteers in Civil War battles at Atlanta, Franklin, and Nashville. Schofield helped implement Reconstruction programs in the South and briefly served as secretary of war and as commandant at West Point. A highly erudite man, Schofield taught natural philosophy at West Point and, for a brief period, physics at Washington University in St. Louis. Unlike most officers of his generation, he had broad experience in civil-military relations gained in a variety of posts where he had served in daily contact with government officials and civilians. Now within two years of mandatory retirement, Schofield faced a series of domestic disorders and a recalcitrant and obstinate subordinate in Nelson Appleton Miles.

The man destined to oversee federal troops in Chicago was different from his commander in both background and temperament. General Miles, fifty-three years old in 1894, was a self-educated, hardened combat veteran with little experience in civil-military affairs. As a commander of volunteers, he had seen action in many major campaigns of the Civil War and had won the Medal of Honor for gallantry at Chancellorsville, where he was severely wounded. By age twenty-five, Miles, known as one of the "boy generals," had commanded a corps of twenty-six thousand men. After the Civil War, his active combat service continued on the frontier, where he fought the Comanche, Kiowa, Nez Percés,

Arapaho, Sioux, Cheyenne, and Apache between 1866 and 1894. Unlike Schofield, Miles had little formal education and none at the university level, but he could count on valuable family military and political contacts to compensate. His wife was a niece of Ohio senator John Sherman and of Gen. William T. Sherman, Civil War legend and former Commanding General of the Army. Accustomed to the independence of frontier commands and sure of his connections, power, and capabilities, Miles grew restive under Schofield's attempts to control the federal military intervention in Chicago. Schofield, convinced that a rapid and decisive military response was needed and similarly convinced of his own power and responsibility, overruled his strong-willed subordinate and ordered troops to be deployed in the Midwest.

After personally putting Miles on the next train west, Schofield instructed Miles's adjutant in Chicago, Lt. Col. James P. Martin, to concentrate all the forces from Fort Sheridan at Lake Front Park. As soon as the encampment was complete, its commander, Col. Robert E. A. Crofton, Fifteenth Infantry, was to confer with Arnold, Milchrist, and Walker on how to best deploy the troops to enforce federal laws and facilitate transport of the mail.

Early on the evening of July 3, Crofton entered Chicago with eight companies of the Fifteenth Infantry, two troops of the

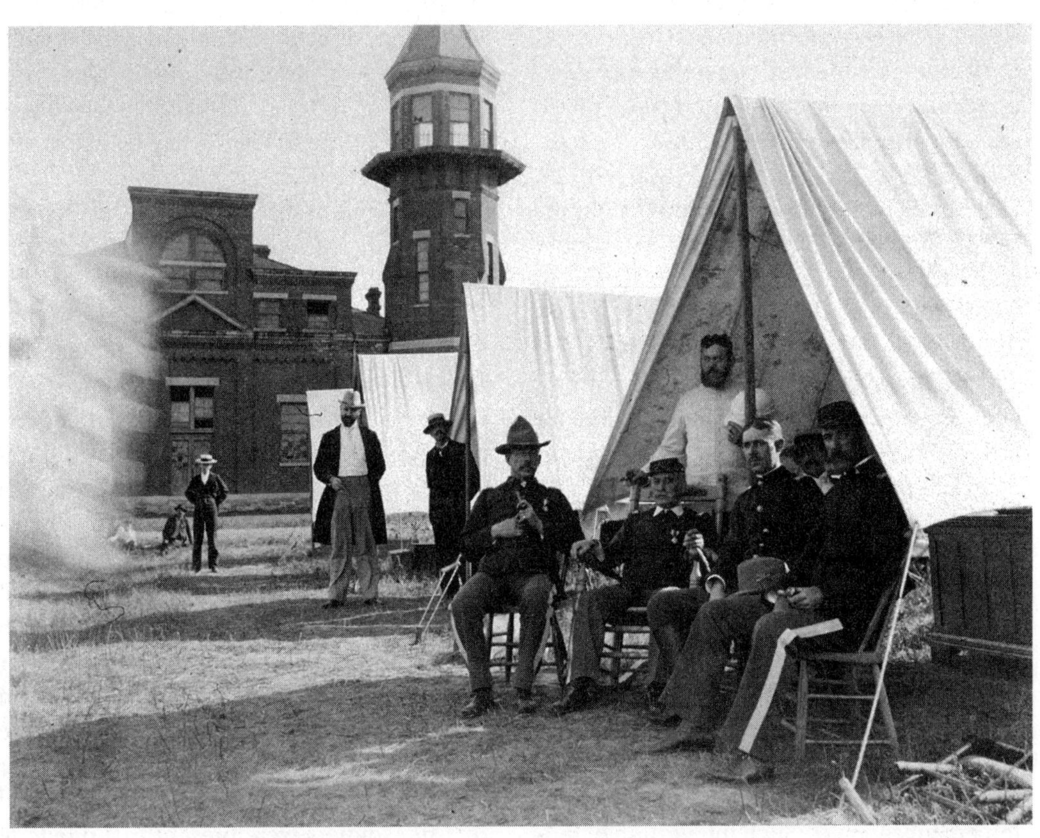

A rare photograph showing troops stationed in Pullman during the strike.

(CHS, ICHi-22928)

Seventh Cavalry, and one light battery of the First Artillery. Upon consultation with Arnold, Martin, Milchrist, and John M. Egan, chairman of the GMA — but ignoring both Chicago and Illinois civil and military officials — Crofton decided to deploy his men throughout the city rather than concentrate them at Lake Front Park as ordered. He sent four companies of infantry to Blue Island, two companies to the Union Stock Yards, and two companies to the Grand Crossing. The next morning, he reinforced the regulars at the stockyards with two cavalry troops and an artillery battery. He then set up headquarters downtown where he could take advantage of telegraph facilities.

These initial federal deployments were not enough. On the recommendation of Arnold, Crofton subsequently broke up the large federal troop formations to form scores of small detachments of ten to twenty men, assigning them to work alongside police squads and posses throughout the city. Walker later advised Arnold that certain army units would assist the deputies in arresting offenders and therefore he should place deputies where the federal troops were stationed.

By deploying federal forces in small squads to work with police and deputies, Crofton showed a lack of appreciation for Schofield's policy (and that of Gen. Winfield Scott Hancock during the 1877 Great Railway Strike) that troops should always remain in large formations under exclusive military control. In General Order 15 issued on May 25, 1894, Schofield had told departmental commanders explicitly that federal regulars were to operate only as coherent tactical units under the direct orders of their military superiors, not as reinforcements integrated into the posses of federal and local law enforcement agencies. Such integration of federal troops under control of municipal and state civil authorities, as opposed to their own officers, constituted a direct violation of the 1878 Posse Comitatus Act, which forbade such use. Like Hancock, Schofield believed that civil authorities, in asking for military aid, confessed their own inability to restore order and should therefore allow the military to direct events.

There were sound tactical reasons to avoid the use of scattered detachments of soldiers. The sight of small numbers of federal troops accompanying policemen and deputy marshals on July 4 had failed to intimidate the Chicago mobs. That evening, ten thousand people, including strikers, the unemployed, youths, and thrill-seekers, roamed the rail yard at Blue Island and the stockyards, tampering with signal lights, overturning rail cars, and setting fires. Restrained by Schofield's standing orders not to fire unless directly threatened with assault, federal troops attempted to disperse the mobs from railroad property that evening and most of the following day by using rifle butts and bayonets.

Meanwhile, Miles arrived at the Department of the Missouri Headquarters in the Pullman Building at Michigan Avenue and Adams Street. Several troubling issues awaited him, the first of which concerned troop deployments. The legal questions raised by Crofton's assignment of federal troops as reinforcements for posses did not concern Miles as much as the potential danger of scattered units being overwhelmed by mobs that might take advantage of the restrictions placed on the use of lethal force. Even more troubling, Miles was forced to confront newspaper reporters, labor groups, and Governor Altgeld, all of whom criticized federal actions and charged the army with protecting the Pullman Palace Car Company and the railroads. Miles explained that the soldiers were present to aid federal marshals, to protect federal property, to reopen interstate commerce and mail service, and to aid state militia and local police forces if they were in danger of being overwhelmed, as authorized under Revised Statute 5298. Federal troops were not sent to restore order per se, this being a task of state and local forces. The strikers, however, were not convinced. Hostility toward the federal troops was intense; "time and again, troops were met with boos, jeers, and curses." One army officer stated that his "men bore patiently the vilest abuse and vilification," while a newspaper correspondent wrote that the strikers "seemed to take it as a personal insult that the soldiers were there."

Undaunted by this seeming lack of public support, federal troops continued to do their duty. Learning that mobs were converging upon federal units along the Rock Island line at Blue Island and at the stockyards, Miles authorized Crofton to disperse them by warnings, pickets, and guards — and if these methods failed, by use of firearms. While such measures enhanced the security of his troops, they did little to reopen blocked rail lines. Without directly menacing the troops and risking federal firepower, large mobs continued to obstruct the tracks and destroy railroad property. On July 5, the federal soldiers at the stockyards repeatedly tried to disperse the estimated five thousand rioters from the tracks but were unable to move the trains and soon withdrew, with the mob still controlling the area. At Blue Island, the attempts of regulars to clear the tracks and get trains moving again were also thwarted.

Miles interpreted these initial failings as an indication that reinforcements were needed, and he sent for seven companies from Fort Leavenworth, Kansas, and Fort Brady, Michigan. On July 5, he telegraphed Schofield:

> The injunction of the United States Court is openly defied and unless the mobs are dispersed by action of police or fired upon by U.S. troops (whether menaced or not), more serious trouble may be expected. Mob is increasing and becoming more defiant. Shall I give the order for troops to fire on mobs obstructing trains?

To prepare for any eventuality and to enhance his firepower, Miles ordered a battery of Hotchkiss revolving guns and three batteries of artillery from Fort Riley, Kansas.

Schofield's messages to Miles indicated a growing dissatisfaction with the latter's handling of affairs in Chicago, especially his tacit approval of Crofton's tactic of dividing federal forces into small detachments to aid civil authorities. In his haste to reproach Miles, Schofield temporarily ignored the question of firepower: "Troops should not be scattered or diverted into small detachments nor should they attempt to perform services in several places at the same time." Schofield further reminded Miles that his first duty was to protect federal property. The preservation of private property and the restoration of public order were the duties of state and local authorities. Schofield later commented that he had difficulty believing that a "Major General of the Army could be so ignorant of the duty devolved upon the troops when ordered by the President to enforce the laws of the United States."

Miles ignored Schofield's instructions about the distribution of troops for another day. Even after five companies of regulars from Fort Leavenworth and two companies from Fort Brady arrived on July 6, Miles continued to deploy federal troops (now numbering 930) in company-size or smaller detachments. In addition to assigning two companies to guard the federal building at Adams and Jackson streets, he sent a detachment to each of the city's six major rail depots. These detachments escorted deputy marshals to make arrests and accompanied rail crews while they repaired tracks within the city. Miles hoped these efforts would clear the railroads and city streets of rioters and obstructions. Since most of the tracks traversed Chicago's working-class residential areas, however, success was limited and brief. As soon as trains bearing troops passed, mobs of residents, strikers, and the unemployed reappeared. Realizing the futility of these tactics, Miles belatedly complied with Schofield's order to reconcentrate federal forces. Later, on July 6, eight companies of infantry, one battery of artillery, and one troop of cavalry were sent back to Lake Front Park to reinforce the other seven companies of infantry and one cavalry troop still active downtown.

While Miles was rearranging his troops and seeking freer use of their firepower, the destruction of railroad property reached a peak. When an Illinois Central agent shot and killed two rioters on July 6, an angry mob of six thousand went on a rampage and burned nearly seven thousand rail cars in the Fiftieth Street Panhandle Yards, causing an estimated $340,000 worth of damage, as compared to an average of $4,000 for each of the previous days of the strike. Mobs destroyed railroad property elsewhere as well and forced non-striking railroad workers to flee their job sites. It was now obvious to all, even to Debs and the ARU leaders, that what had started as a peaceful attempt to aid the Pullman strikers had now become a wild, uncontrolled spree involving thousands of strikers and the unemployed, a spree that even federal troops could not quell. Critics in the media (such as the *Chicago Times*) and labor and management groups were quick to point out, to the disappointment of Olney and the GMA, that the troops under Miles had failed to clear the tracks, ostensibly the main reason for summoning that force to the city. After all, impatient businessmen complained, John Egan had predicted that the presence of regulars would "bring peace with a short, sharp jerk." Instead violence and disorder had escalated to alarming levels. Distressed at the inability of police, U.S. marshals, or federal troops to quell the violence and cognizant of press reports stating that Chicago was at the mercy of the mob, Mayor John Hopkins asked Governor Altgeld to intervene with state troops.

Altgeld, increasingly angry with the federal government and the city, had impatiently waited for Hopkins's call since July 4. He had protested that federal troops were not initially needed or wanted, especially since neither local authorities nor Olney had requested that he commit state forces, the traditional first recourse in such cases. Although not wanting to appear to be turning a blind eye to lawlessness, or to be helping either the strikers, with whom he sympathized, or the GMA, with whom he did not, he continued to be one of the loudest critics of federal military involvement. In a strongly worded telegram to President Cleveland, Altgeld protested the unilateral and gratuitous commitment of federal troops to the city without his knowledge, consent, or input. He contended that the railroad's inability to hire enough non-striking workers to run the trains was due to a lack of public sympathy and not the interference of strikers or of unruly mobs. Altgeld added that the restoration of order was his responsibility as governor, not Cleveland's, and that if either Cook County or the railroad owners had requested state aid he could have promptly provided three regiments of infantry, one troop of cavalry, and one battery of artillery.

To Altgeld's arguments Cleveland tersely replied that he had ordered federal troops to Chicago in strict accordance with the Constitution and federal statutes and had issued, somewhat belatedly, a cease and desist proclamation to the rioters. Every action was perfectly legal and, under the circumstances, justified. Events in Chicago, Cleveland maintained, were nothing more than simple issues of law and order. Altgeld nonetheless remained convinced that federal actions constituted an illegal usurpation of state prerogatives.

Determined to assert gubernatorial authority at last, Altgeld answered Mayor Hopkins's request for aid on July 6 by sending four thousand Illinois National Guardsmen to the city — a fourth force operating independently to restore order. Repeating Crofton's earlier error, however, Hopkins scattered the Illinois guardsmen in small units to clear tracks and protect railroad property at key points throughout the city. This dispersal encouraged confrontations between militiamen and the mob, with tragic results. On the afternoon of July 7, while furnishing protection to a wrecking train on the Grand Trunk rail line at Forty-ninth and Loomis streets, Company H of the Second Regiment of the Illinois National Guard became involved in the bloodiest encounter of the strike. As the train stopped to raise an overturned car, the crowd cursed and threw stones at the escorting guardsmen. The commanding junior officer ordered the mob to disperse and his men to load their rifles. The crowd thinned as many women and children left. Reduced to its most militant members, the mob grew more threatening and continued throwing rocks. The officer then ordered a bayonet charge that wounded several people but again failed to disperse the crowd. When the mob retaliated by throwing more rocks, one of which struck the officer on the head, and by firing a few scattered gunshots, the officer, fearing for the safety of his men and despairing of receiving reinforcements, ordered his command to fire at will and to make every shot count. After firing one hundred rounds in several volleys, killing or wounding at least twenty people, the mob milled around in confusion until dispersed by Chicago police officers wielding revolvers and clubs.

The intensity of the mob violence on July 7 prompted Miles once again to scatter his forces, contrary to orders, to protect the railroads from threatened attacks. By now he had become convinced that Chicago was on the verge of revolution, the result of a labor conspiracy led by the ARU and involving heavily armed radicals. Miles was further convinced that only he could save the city from a bloodbath. He wrote Schofield that "the masses want peace but the agitators [are] very ugly and say they must have civil war." On Miles's orders, Crofton sent two companies to the Dearborn Station, two to Union Depot, and one each to the depots of the Illinois Central, Rock Island, Grand Central, and Chicago & North Western railroads. His orders directed his subordinates to aid U.S. marshals in arresting trespassers and those "obstructing or destroying lines of communication" along the railways and to open fire if mobs attacked trains or federal troops.

By late evening on July 7, Chicago was an armed camp containing 13,430 men sworn to protect property and uphold local, state, or federal laws: 3,500 Chicago policemen, 5,000 U.S. marshals and deputies, 930 federal troops, and 4,000 Illinois National Guardsmen. Between July 6 and 10, 1,000 additional federal troops arrived in Chicago, including infantry, cavalry, and artillery from Fort Leavenworth and other western posts and the Ninth Infantry from Madison Barracks, New York. Initially each of these groups operated independently with only slight efforts at coordination between city police and state guardsmen or between U.S. marshals and deputies and federal troops. At times, several forces would respond simultaneously to the same disturbance but rarely accomplished anything because they lacked common leadership, goals, or a plan of action. Seeing the folly of such endeavors, U.S. Marshal Arnold placed his deputies at Miles's dis-

The rioting of July 6 and 7 changed the Pullman Strike from a standoff between management and labor to a wild and violent spree that troops could not control. Drawing by G. W. Peters from a sketch by G. A. Coffin. *Harper's Weekly*, July 28, 1894

posal. The two men then arranged a division of responsibility, with troops protecting deputies as the latter made arrests.

Disappointed at the slow pace of police, deputies, and troops acting separately to end the rioting, the GMA sent John Egan to consult with Mayor Hopkins and General Miles about consolidating all forces under one commander, preferably Miles. Hopkins initially declined the proposal, prompting Miles to inform his officers that if state and local governments failed to "maintain peace and good order within the territory of their jurisdiction, military forces would assist them, but not to the extent of leaving unprotected property belonging to or under the protection of the United States." Three days later, on July 10, Hopkins finally agreed to coordinate efforts; Chicago police and Illinois's guardsmen would concentrate on restoring order while federal forces reopened rail traffic. Each force, however, remained under the leadership of its own respective civil or military commander.

Yet lack of coordination persisted, and city police and state militia officials refused to share intelligence on mob activities with each other or with federal forces. Miles turned to GMA chairman Egan for assistance. Egan had organized a network of informants to report on the activities and plans of the ARU and had created a central intelligence agency for disbursing information on all strike-related incidents and activities. Whenever beleaguered railroad officials needed federal troops to prevent or quell mob activity, looting, or vandalism, Egan informed Miles, who sent federal troops to support deputy marshals as they arrested mob or strike leaders. (Miles later denied in sworn testimony before the U.S. Strike Commission that he had any such contact with Egan or that he acted on GMA orders, but documents in the files of the Department of the Missouri proved he was in daily contact with Egan by memorandums and telephone.) Miles's own reports and troop deployments clearly reflected the information and ideas gathered by Egan and his informants.

As Egan developed the intelligence framework needed for planning, Schofield issued a general order that became the foundation of army civil disturbance doctrine and for the first time set forth tactical guidelines for riot operations. Soon incorporated in army regulations, the wording of the general order remained almost unchanged until 1937. Issued on July 9, 1894, General Order 23 read that "a mob, . . . resisting or obstructing the execution of the laws . . . or attempting to destroy property . . . is a public enemy" and how troops deal with this public enemy is "purely a tactical question." It was up to the commander and troops at the scene to determine when and how to quell mobs and with what weapons, either "the fire of musketry and artillery or . . . the use of the bayonet and saber." Army officers were ordered to bear in mind that innocent bystanders were often intermingled with rioters in any crowd, and that the fire of troops should be held until adequate warning was given for "the innocent to separate themselves from the guilty." After this warning, however, "the actions of the troops should be governed solely by the tactical considerations involved." U.S. Army soldiers were told not to "consider how great may be the losses inflicted on the public enemy" by military action, but to concentrate on making "their blows so effective as to promptly suppress all resistance." Punishment of the rioters, the order concluded, "belongs not to the troops but to the courts of justice."

Miles agreed completely with the contents of General Order 23. Strongly supportive of the railroads, federal authority, and law and order, he now believed that labor unions, especially the ARU, were in league with anarchists, Communists, and Socialists. When Egan's spies reported that Eugene Debs was orchestrating a general strike in Chicago, Miles was certain that this was the expected bloody revolution that had as its goal the overthrow of the federal government. In reality, however, the now desperate Debs sought the support of Chicago's utility workers whose absence from their jobs would effectively shut down the city. This condition of paralysis, he reasoned, could be used as a negotiating point to get state and federal troops withdrawn from the city so the strike could proceed unhindered.

Debs's utility workers' strike never occurred. The increasingly desperate economic situation of the strikers forced them to submit. More important, Debs and the other top ARU leaders had ignored the July 2 federal court injunction and were arrested on charges of contempt of court, conspiracy, and interference with the mail, all prohibited by the Sherman Anti-Trust Act. Denied leadership, the ARU, on the advice of American Federation of Labor president Samuel Gompers, ended the Chicago strike on August 5.

Chicago's labor dispute had cost the railroads and local, state, and federal governments an estimated $685,308 in direct damages and costs for law enforcement. Strikers lost an estimated $1.4 million in wages and gained nothing in return. At least 13 people were killed, 53 were wounded or otherwise injured, and 190 were arrested by federal officials. None of the deaths or serious injuries was caused by federal troops.

Shortly after Debs's arrest, Schofield directed Miles to confer with Arnold and other officials to determine whether the army needed to stay in the city. He also instructed Miles to inquire if Hopkins and Altgeld could substitute police and state militia for regulars protecting federal courts in which strikers were being tried for obstruction of the mail. Miles vigorously and repeatedly protested these orders. He believed withdrawal of troops from a city on the verge of open rebellion to be premature and dangerous. While Walker and Arnold initially agreed that troops could be safely withdrawn from the city in mid-July, pressure from the GMA forced them to change their opinion, and they concurred with Miles. It took an explicit telegram from Secretary of War Lamont ordering a federal withdrawal, and a further telegram from Schofield directly ordering Miles to act, to make the latter acquiesce. The withdrawal of the Ninth Infantry to Madison Barracks and the temporary removal of all other troops to Fort Sheridan on July 18 ended the federal military intervention, even though the strike would drag on nonviolently for another two weeks.

The loss of effective leadership after the arrest of Debs and his chief lieutenants and the crippling effect of the omnibus injunctions best explained the ARU's decision to end the Pullman Strike. Under escort of federal troops, deputy marshals had arrested scores of strikers and mob members on charges of contempt of court, while state militiamen similarly aided city police and deputy sheriffs in arresting an additional 515 strikers and mob members on charges of murder, arson, burglary, assault, intimidation, riot, conspiracy, and incitement to riot. On December 14, 1894, five months after the strike ended, the U.S. District Court for the Northern District of Illinois found Debs guilty of conspiracy to restrain interstate commerce, in violation of the Sherman Anti-Trust Act. After an unsuccessful U.S. Supreme Court appeal, Debs served a six-month prison term.

Subsequent court rulings vindicated the actions of Attorney General Olney, President Cleveland, and federal officials in Chicago. In the landmark decision of May 27, 1895, In re *Debs,* the U.S. Supreme Court denied Debs's petition for a writ of habeas corpus, ruling that even without the permission of state governments, "the strong arm of the National Government may brush aside all obstructions to the freedom of interstate commerce or transportation of the mails. If the emergency arises, the Army of the nation, and all its militias, are at the service of the nation to compel obedience to its laws." This precedent-setting decision authorized and confirmed presidential power to use federal military force domestically, under the restrictions of the Posse Comitatus Act, in any strike involving either the transportation of mail or the movement of interstate commerce.

In late July 1894, President Cleveland appointed a three-man commission to investigate the causes of the strike and to offer suggestions for the prevention of future railroad upheavals. The U.S. Strike Commission's controversial findings, issued in November 1894, were praised by labor and denounced by railroad interests. The commission claimed that the Pullman Company was unduly harsh in its relations with its laborers; that the GMA illegally usurped civil power; and that Pullman's refusal to arbitrate its differences with its own workers and with the

ARU was largely responsible for the strike's length and the intensity of the violence. The commission recommended that railroad companies recognize unions, which already existed and were unlikely to disappear, and that they ban all labor contracts forbidding union membership. A final suggestion called for compulsory negotiation and arbitration to settle labor disputes. While the recommendations of the commission were initially ignored, in 1898 Congress passed the Railroad Arbitration Act, the first of many pieces of legislation intended to prevent nationwide rail strikes. Richard Olney, at that time a private citizen, was its author.

The effectiveness of the federal military response in the Pullman Strike was beyond doubt. Although many workers believed that the army broke the strike, in fact Miles concentrated the army's efforts on guarding fed-

Eugene V. Debs, leader of the American Railway Union. For his role in the strike, Debs was convicted of conspiracy to restrain interstate commerce. *(CHS, ICHi-0990)*

eral buildings and railroad depots. Once the threat subsided, the army withdrew federal troops from the city in mid-July even though the ARU did not call off the strike until early August. Illinois guardsmen and city police were actually the forces responsible for crushing riotous mobs and ending the strike. Federal troops, however, maintained a high profile in the city and were repeatedly deployed to guard bridges, clear tracks, and aid deputy marshals in arresting union leaders for conspiracy to interfere with the mail, hinder interstate commerce, or block military roads, as authorized under Revised Statute 5298. The army's presence in Chicago, although it was not technically charged with quelling the riot, proved that the government's will would ultimately prevail and order would be restored.

The riot and strike duty performed in 1894 affected the army's image, organization, and doctrine significantly. On one hand, the federal military intervention confirmed labor's suspicions, held since at least 1877, that the army and various state militias were sympathetic to big business and corporate interests, if not tools under their direct control. Many commanders did in fact share the beliefs of business and civic leaders and found railroad officials most gracious and generous in furnishing transportation, lodging, supplies, and intelligence for army operations. President Cleveland's intention in committing federal troops, however, was to uphold federal laws and remove obstructions to the federal mail and to western railroads under federal receivership. In reaching these goals, federal troops indirectly prevented the ARU from successfully conducting their strike and in effect aided the GMA in breaking both the boycott and the union. The inability of the union to prevent disorder unleashed by the strike was a critical factor in enabling Attorney General Olney to persuade the president to intervene. The strike was in no sense peaceful, and mob violence, by whatever parties, gave Olney the opportunity he sought to secure military forces to break the ARU, a group he considered revolutionary.

As did their predecessors after the Great Railway Strike of 1877, Secretary of War Lamont and General Schofield quickly took advantage of the army's new popularity with the government and with the conservative urban middle and upper classes to ask Congress to finance two artillery and two cavalry regiments to secure the cities and railroads against future labor unrest. But congressmen refused to augment the size of the army, preferring to fund an improved state militia system composed of their own congressional constituencies rather than a larger standing army. Critics justified this approach by pointing out that Miles's troops merely protected trains and federal property while Altgeld's state militia actually broke and suppressed the mobs. Congress continued to vote only enough in appropriations to maintain the army at twenty-eight thousand men.

Denied funds for expansion, the War Department increasingly relied on consolidating existing units to meet the demands of future labor disorders. By the end of 1894, the army, as part of an ongoing process undertaken for many reasons, reduced the number of posts from ninety-five to eighty. By 1900, sixteen garrisons of regimental strength remained, twenty-two of from four to seven companies each, and fourteen posts of two companies each. The experience of 1894 further convinced the army that large garrisons should be located near urban centers and railroad junctions where they were readily available to quell labor-related violence.

Yet the consolidation of limited army manpower near urban areas failed to reassure military leaders of their ability to react to future disorders effectively. In an era when the fear of social revolution was strong, Schofield inaugurated a major shift in civil disturbance tactical doctrine. Whereas during the Whiskey Rebellion of 1794 President Washington had directed a massive show of force to intimidate rioters, a practice used frequently after the Great Railway Strike of 1877, Schofield and his successors began to frame army regulations to emphasize a greater reliance on firepower to make up for the lack of numbers. General Order 23 of July 9, 1894, and its variations over the next half-century, treated the use of sabers, bayonets, rifles, and artillery as purely tactical questions, and mobs of rioting citizens as public enemies "beyond the pale of protection against military violence accorded to the general public." Paradoxically, however, this emphasis on firepower and tactical force for domestic disturbances was accompanied by an increasing policy of restraint, which has characterized most federal military interventions in labor disputes since the Pullman Strike.

"Don't Shake — Salute!"

David E. Ruth

In his *Report on an Epidemic of Influenza in the Fall of 1918,* Chicago Health Commissioner John Dill Robertson counted among his achievements newspaper photographs in which he demonstrated to a vulnerable public the use of a protective gauze mask. Not only did masks fail to prevent the disease from devastating thousands of families in Chicago, but Commissioner Robertson knew they failed. "For my part," he later quipped to a group of colleagues, "let them wear a rabbit's foot on a watch-chain."

The exceptional virulence of the influenza strain of 1918 first became apparent during August outbreaks in Africa, Europe, and North America. No other modern strain of influenza led so frequently to deadly pneumonia. Young adults were most susceptible, and general good health provided no defense against the disease. Wartime mobilization of soldiers and civilians created optimal conditions for the spread of the virus. Global fatalities exceeded twenty million and may have approached forty million. Influenza and pneumonia deaths in excess of the annual average surpassed half a million in the United States. According to one historian, "Nothing else — no infection, no war, no famine — has ever killed so many in as short a period."

In Chicago influenza took a terrible toll. More than fourteen thousand people succumbed between mid-September of 1918 and March of 1919. Over half the dead were between twenty and forty years of age, and most of those were under thirty. Southern and eastern European immigrants, who were the most recent arrivals and who generally lacked inoculative exposure to similar influenza strains, suffered the highest mortality. The annualized weekly death rate leaped from 10.8 per thousand in early September to 63.0 per thousand in late October. Mortality peaked on October 17, with 381 deaths attributed to influenza or pneumonia. The death rate dropped during the remainder of the month and through November, only to flare again in December. Influenza and pneumonia deaths exceeded 8,500 between September 22 and November 16, which city officials considered to be the epidemic period. During that period the Department of Health received reports of 37,921 influenza cases and 13,109 pneumonia cases. Officials acknowledged, however, that sickness was far more widespread than their statistics indicated. Thousands of cases went unreported.

Medical science offered neither prevention nor cure. The great public health achievements of the previous three decades — against typhoid, diphtheria, and tuberculosis — were grounded in advances in bacteriology and immunology. Microbiology had made the health officer the effective agent of modern science. But most experts realized that the vaccines developed to protect people against influenza were useless and that doctors could do little even to relieve pain. Nevertheless, as Commissioner Robertson's duplicitous demonstration of masks indicated, officials were unwilling to discard their claims to scientific authority.

In the absence of specific medical solutions, officials bestowed the mantle of science on traditional explanations for sickness and health. American anti-influenza campaigns combined general scientific principles with a rich mixture of social and moral values. To ward off infection, to assign blame, and to explain death, Chicago health officials drew on their most deeply held beliefs about the proper organization of American society. Not only the control of an epidemic, but the nature of public order and authority in American society seemed to be at stake.

Because it apparently required far-reaching action, the wartime epidemic — a crisis within a crisis — seemed to present leaders with a unique opportunity to recast society in their ideal molds. Leaders attempted to create a hierarchical social structure headed by public officials and experts from government, business, and science who would make policy decisions; they expected ordinary men and women to follow their reasoned policies without challenge. This corporatist ideology, invoking a managerial approach to public administration and social ills, embraced middle-class values of work, moderation, and sobriety. Ultimately the elite leadership hoped to replace the authority of unbridled individualism, neighborhood tradition, ethnic custom, and working-class values with a carefully engineered program that was to be administered through a highly efficient bureaucracy run by middle-class managers.

The coercive power of government and the persuasive power of mass publicity — both greatly enhanced during the war — provided potent tools for implementing the

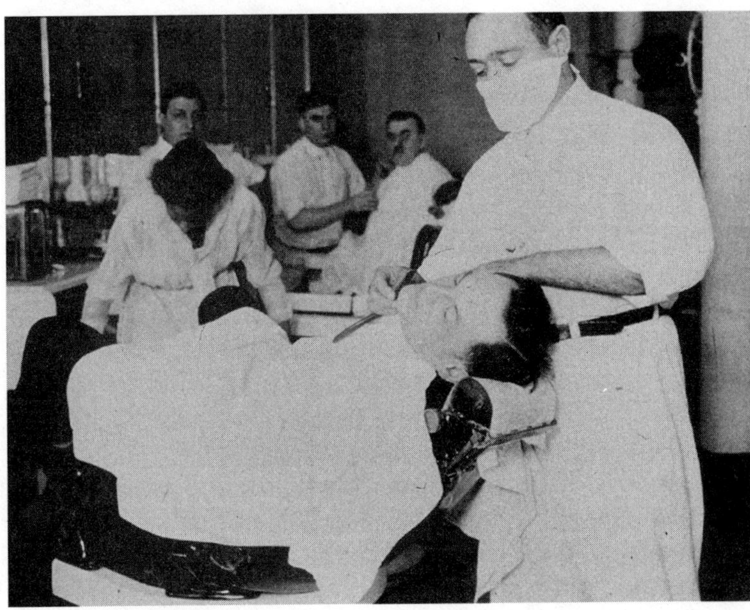

Masks were among the many items and products that supposedly prevented influenza.

official vision. The corporatist ideology and the official anti-influenza campaign, however, did not go unchallenged in the fall of 1918. Diverse groups of Chicagoans ignored, resented, or rebelled against official decrees about how to avoid or overcome influenza. Doctors, patients, and other Chicagoans of every racial, economic, and ethnic group refused to play their assigned roles. Embedded in their acts of resistance were many positions about the proper nature of American society and the place of individuals and groups within it.

From the start the official campaign against influenza owed less to any analysis of the disease's course than it did to accepted middle-class notions of healthy living. Like other public officials across the country, Chicago and Illinois authorities acted in accordance with guidelines set forth by United States Surgeon General Rupert Blue, the most comprehensive of which urged "a proper proportion of work, play and rest." Officials implemented the policy recommendation of the Illinois Influenza Commission, which was composed of Robertson, State Commissioner of Public Health, C. St. Clair Drake, and representatives of the federal Public Health Service, the army and navy, the American Red Cross, and the American Public Health Association. Authorities banned public dancing, restricted funeral attendance, prohibited smoking on trains, and ordered motormen to keep doors open on train cars to improve ventilation. At the height of the epidemic, they issued orders to close all movie houses, theaters, social lodges, and night schools. Later orders prohibited lectures, debates, recitals, social and club activities, athletic events, cabaret performances, banquets, and conventions not approved by the State Council of National Defense — in short, according to Drake, "all public gatherings of a social nature not essential to the war."

The men and women who implemented this program reflected the development of progressive social values that occurred during the first two decades of this century. The proliferation of professional, scientific, and business associations signaled the emergence of a class of occupational specialists who espoused scientific and bureaucratic approaches to urban problems such as education, welfare relief, and public health. If government and professionals cooperated, the progressives believed, the people needed only to be told of a program's rationality to give their full backing. Spurring the desires for a managed social order was a new recognition of human interdependence and a consequent decline of the individualistic ethos that had prevailed in the nineteenth century. The complex relations of modern society made the well-being of all seem dependent on carefully coordinated responses to common problems.

Chicago health authorities organized their campaign against influenza in accordance with the new recognition of interdependence. Only a united effort, rooted in the expertise and bureaucratic structures of the new professional class, they reasoned, could protect the modern city. Health officials demanded cooperation from professional associations, social welfare organizations, and civic clubs. Middle- and upper-class women, who were believed to possess unusual competence in caring for the sick, received a special summons to service. Cooperation from schools and from clergy who might work "the healing powers of fresh air and sunshine into the theme of their regular sermons" seemed essential. Officials expected other businessmen to emulate movie theater managers who, before officials closed the theaters, preceded shows with two-minute talks on "How to Escape the Influenza," which were modeled after the Liberty Loan appeals of the "Four-Minute Men" that often delayed wartime shows.

The new managerial values required that a strong, visible leader head the coalition of government and private groups. During the epidemic weeks, Commissioner Robertson played the part. Like other wartime officials — exemplified by Herbert Hoover, whose program of meatless and wheatless days created a nation of "hooverizers," people who skimped so that the boys in the trenches would not have to — Robertson personified efficiency, authority, and social unity. The *Chicago Tribune*'s sardonic references to "his highness" and "his eminence," made only after the influenza had receded, suggested the extent of his dominion in earlier weeks.

Robertson's most important task was to rally popular support for the public health campaign. Yet the nature of cooperation he expected reflected a social vision that separated Chicagoans into a powerful minority and a passive majority. While medical and social workers were to lend their expertise and civic leaders were to use their influence for the public good, the proper role for most men and women was merely to obey. The extensive publicity campaign testified to the belief that ordinary people were amenable to instruction and would defer to the supposed expertise of public health officials. Authorities perceived that diverse media were powerful tools that they could use to shape public action. Daily articles in the city's newspapers intoned the sanctioned program of treatment and prevention. The main tenets of this regimen — deference to physicians, isolation of patients, avoidance of crowds, attention to diet and rest, temperance, and the salubrious value of sunshine and fresh air — could not have remained unfamiliar to any newspaper-reading Chicagoan. "Healthgrams" in trains warned that coughing, spitting, and sneezing had resulted in the deaths of no fewer than 10,220 Chicagoans the previous year and admonished passengers to stifle coughs and sneezes "to keep Chicago healthy." Police stenciled "No Spitting" on city sidewalks and posted "Spitting Arrested and Prosecuted!" signs in streetcars, train stations, theaters, and public buildings. Hundreds of thousands of pamphlets, cards, and foreign-language circulars proclaimed the virtues of rest, baths, and regular bowels. Robertson, recognizing that written appeals failed to sway much of the public, urged physicians to "impress the fact that influenza is a serious disease and if neglected not infrequently terminates in death."

The society of managerial leaders and obedient followers envisioned by health officials had, at its core, a traditional, corporatist ideology that the crisis of war made especially compelling. In pure form the corporatist ideology assumed the interests of all Americans to be identical. Because the institutions of American society were essentially sound, according to the corporatist ideology, business, government, and professional leadership represented the aristocracy of ability best suited to serve those interests. Disputes about public policy could occur only when men and women disagreed with their leaders. When everyone properly deferred to authority and observed traditional morals, harmony would prevail.

The guardians of Chicago's health fervently believed that unified leadership was fundamental to any cohesive society. Harmony emanated down the social order. Thus authorities and cooperative newspapers found reassurance in the support promised by "representatives of virtually every big organization in the city," who voted "to control influenza in every possible way." According to the Department of Health, "The great reason that Chicago . . . followed a safe and sane course, was due to the great civic, social and commercial organizations of this city which immediately mobilized and stood squarely behind the Health Department, allaying fear and advising people to heed . . . the health authorities."

This assessment, however, praised ideologically appealing images rather than medically effective actions. Though some business and civic groups did provide tangible assistance, the contributions of most organizations were more symbolic than substantial. Newspapers enthusiastically reported the show of unity, but their pages mentioned no specific deeds. Organizational publications of the time indicate that most groups lent the campaign against influenza little beyond vocal support. Yet the pageant of society's leaders gladdened officials because they assumed that Chicagoans would follow their natural leaders in support of the Department of Health. Unity seemed to depend on hierarchy and deference to authority.

The institutional closings, by far the most prominent public health intrusion into the lives of ordinary Chicagoans, showed much about which pursuits officials deemed healthy to society. Physical health became a metaphor for social fitness. Activities that remained acceptable were either beyond the sphere of public health authority or had some recognized moral value, or both. Manufacturing, commerce, the Liberty Loan war bond drive, and military mobilization were exempt from interference. The business of a nation at war had to continue. Moreover, officials implied that the healthy city was vibrant and productive. The Department of Health boasted that aside from "the closing of places of public amusement . . . Chicago's great loop district was otherwise as crowded as normally." "In a great city like Chicago," Robertson wrote, "in which one-fortieth of the population of the entire nation resides, and in war time, when it is absolutely essential . . . to keep the arteries of business open, the plan of closing business and stopping commerce could not be considered for one moment." To restrict Chicago's industriousness — its greatness — would have been to sap its vitality. The middle-class work ethic helped cement society.

Churches and schools remained open because officials believed they promulgated the public health message, allayed panic, and fostered social cohesion. Although they clearly offered ample opportunity for the spread of germs, worship and learning seemed to be healthful activities. The Influenza Commission reportedly allowed churches to remain open "on the theory that religious activity is essential to the morale of the community." Schools replaced parental incompetence with expert oversight. According to the *Tribune,* "It was thought that children would be safer if they were in school, looked over by teachers, nurses, and school physicians. Had the schools been dismissed the supervised contacts of the schools would have been replaced by the unsupervised contacts of the playgrounds, streets, and vacant lots."

Health officials discerned no similar redeeming value in the activities they banned. Instead, in closing dance halls, theaters, and cabarets, they aimed a traditional weapon of social control — enforced adherence to a middle-class moral code — at the new realm of commercial leisure. Much of the closing list reads like a decade-old catalog of the targets of moral reform. Activities that had recently shed their lower-class stigma and had gained middle-class acceptance, or at least toleration, became unacceptably pernicious during the emergency. The healthy society was austere; frivolity invited disaster.

The first commercial amusement that the Influenza Commission prohibited, public dancing, set the sexual code of the working-class young apart from that of the middle class. During the years just before the war, reformers had conceded that commercial dance halls, properly regulated, might pro-

Victrolas were presented as ways to cope with the temporary closings and the resulting dearth of entertainment.

vide useful recreation and socialization for urban youth. The influenza epidemic reversed this step. "There is no greater menace than dancing," Robertson announced early in October. "Not only do the dancers become overheated and make themselves susceptible to colds, but the close contact and unusually heavy breathing while dancing make for contagion." Movie theaters were natural targets for the closings. Only in the past few years had feature-length films and palatial theaters transformed movie-going into a favorite activity of the middle-class. Rowdy working-class audiences continued to flout middle-class behavioral norms in crowded neighborhood theaters. Insecurity caused by the epidemic tapped old prejudices. The primary motivation for closing the theaters, Robertson admitted, was not to control the spread of germs, but "to discourage the late hours kept by most adults." After most establishments reopened, the acting chief of police refused to allow cabarets — unlike "the legitimate restaurants, the bona fide eating houses" — to operate for several more days. Like dance halls, cabarets had been the objects of the city's moral reformers. Suggestive jazz music, indiscriminate mixing of audience and performers, and, occasionally, interracial patronage made these clubs seem particularly dangerous.

Though health authorities subscribed to the germ theory of disease, their constant championing of moral prophylaxis in conjunction with the closing orders revealed that they sought to control not an elusive, inscrutable microbe, but the visible, clearly imperfect individual. "Immunity from influenza," the Department of Health asserted, "is largely a matter of individual conduct and action." According to the Department of Health *Bulletin,* "The fact should never be lost sight of that disease is not an accident nor a visitation of providence, but is the result of ignorance, carelessness and improper living."

The social agendas of some observers were evident in their hopeful assessments of the effects of the closings. Robertson noted "a decided falling off in vice and crime during the time when restrictions were placed upon public amusements, dance halls and assemblies of various kinds." He concluded with evident satisfaction, "So far as vicious conduct and immorality are concerned, it would seem that 'to keep the home fires burning' and to stay off the streets late at night lessen the number of misdemeanors and misconduct of every kind." Similarly, the *Chicago Daily News* reported enthusiastically that laid-off show girls, promising to make their loss "the country's gain," had traded stage for munitions factory. Discipline redeemed all.

Yet officials acknowledged that the closings did little to slow the spread of germs. Discussing the orders, Robertson admitted that "the ideal of quarantine is chimerical and impossible of realization in the complicated life of a modern city." But the closings had an important educational value. Though the medical utility of the closing order was "problematical," Robertson concluded that "it surely did have the effect of getting information regarding the disease to every individual in the City of Chicago and it impressed upon the public that care was necessary." Like the national campaign to save peach pits for use in gas masks or the knitting of socks for soldiers that drew American women into the war effort, the forgoing of popular amusements was a gesture of dubious direct value that officials used to create an impression of public utility. The moral code that the closings enforced provided a basis for cohesion. The Department of Health linked cooperation, efficiency, patriotism, and fortifying self-denial:

> The closing of the theaters of the City of Chicago means more than preventing the spread of communicable diseases. It means that people will be preserving their vital powers. It means that the people, instead of going to the theater evenings after a day of strenuous activity, will probably seek their beds around 10 o'clock at night, or earlier, and will thus conserve their physical powers and energies for the next day's battle of life.
>
> The great big thing for human beings in the fight against disease is to be able to meet its attacks. Those whose physical powers are high probably will escape. But the present is not the time to waste bodily energy. It should be the duty of every citizen to conserve every ounce of his physical strength. You are well today. Tomorrow you may be stricken.

Enlist, the message read, and be saved.

The martial tone of this exhortation was significant. During the war, old values had acquired new dress, and Chicago's leaders modeled their campaign against influenza on the crisp lines of military order. The modern army epitomized the corporatist ideal. Strong leaders, a clear hierarchy of experts, and disciplined followers all united in a just cause: the American Expeditionary Force provided a compelling example to men and women who advocated a bold extension of public authority. Before reports revealed that influenza had begun to ravage military training camps, leaders drew both moral and policy lessons from the apparent good health on the bases. Society could easily withstand the epidemic, one observer wrote wistfully, "if only the methods and regime of camp life could be applied to civil communities."

The military model was readily available in November of 1918. Since the start of the war, American leaders worked to cultivate martial fervor on the home front. On their urging, families tended victory gardens, children scavenged for valuable material, and young men registered for the draft. Virtually all college men donned the uniform of the Students' Army Training Corps. Programs to conserve food and gasoline shaped the dinner menu and eliminated the Sunday pleasure drive. The Committee on Public Information's "Four-Minute Men," recruited from all over the country, delivered increasingly vitriolic rhetoric to crowds on street corners and in theaters. The Treasury Department relied on giant rallies — and the pressure of neighbors and co-workers — to sell the Liberty Loan bonds that financed the war. With mobilization came repression, justified by a war-inflamed rhetoric of intolerant American patriotism.

War shaped public discourse about the influenza epidemic, and authorities and reporters were fluent in military jargon. A *Tribune* photograph of health workers in gauze masks carried the caption, "Wearing 'Gas Masks' in Chicago." Germs became "deadly bombs," and sneezes "explosions." "Talk about bullets sprayed from machine guns," quipped a cartoon on the danger of uncovered sneezing. "Who is going to be next?" asked the Chicago Medical Society. "Everybody is waiting for the blow. . . . Preparation is the greater part of the battle. Germany almost demonstrated this. It is well for the profession to lay its forces for the onslaught. We have every reason to expect an attack."

The blend of military metaphor and public health necessity made cooperation a matter of patriotic duty. "Chicago is winning her fight against influenza and pneumonia," a letter read at theaters asserted, "and it is up to you, Mr. Citizen, to continue the fight and stamp it out entirely." The Department of Health compared the influenza death list to the "terrible toll of human lives on the battlefield" and urged Chicagoans to help in a winnable fight. The Red Cross appealed for volunteers "from the many willing and patriotic workers who have yet to find their definite places in the 'Win the War' program." "Hold the Home Lines," the United Charities urged. Service against influenza became yet another test of loyalty in a society obsessed with differentiating between loyal and disloyal, dutiful worker and slacker, 100 percent American and treacherous ethnic. Like war, the fight against influenza demanded devotion, valor, and, above all, obedience.

Public enlistment and the military ideal culminated in a late October campaign to replace the handshake with the salute. The newspapers ran front-page announcements: "Don't Shake — Salute!" They elaborated on the transmission of disease by dirty hands. "When a custom becomes a menace to public health," the Department of Health *Bulletin* explained, "an enlightened and progressive community should be able to find a substitute. . . . Let society pull down the sen-

World War I schoolchildren's war garden. The cooperation, patriotism, and fortifying self-denial that the war demanded were also asked of citizens in the anti-influenza campaign.
(CHS, DN 70,397)

timent that keeps up handshaking and insist on the salute instead."

But the salute did not replace the handshake. Everywhere the preachers of harmony heard dissonance. Competing ideals of behavior remained strong. Resentment of public authority and resistance to its dictates suggested that many people neither saw themselves as obedient followers nor believed that their leaders possessed unchallengeable knowledge. In the absence of credible scientific solutions, nonsanctioned methods flourished. Turning their backs on the new bureaucratic order, thousands of dissenters drew instead on an array of individual, neighborhood, and ethnic values.

Scattered evidence reveals widespread dissatisfaction with the emergency regulations. Many men and women expressed opinions despite their lack of expertise and questioned whether the health authorities had any basis for their actions. A *Chicago Daily News* reader argued that the closings had no value and that, indeed, people "so left to brood over the idea of disease" would prove more susceptible than if they had been diverted by entertainment. Amusement, not austerity, offered health. Orders regulating trains generated considerable dissent. The *Daily News* reported that "while church, school, and other anti-smoking elements" supported the ban on smoking, most commuters "strongly opposed" it. During cold weather, train operators had to nail open car doors to comply with the order for adequate ventilation after passengers ignored signs to leave the doors open. A *Daily News* reader provided a striking image of shivering passengers cursing the authorities who claimed to know what was best for them. "Wouldn't it be just as well to advise people — nay compel them — to sit all day on the benches in Jackson park?" he asked. "The people do not want these autocratic conditions on the street cars. We are fighting for democracy. May we not have a little foretaste of it at this time?"

The circumscribed nature of public authority gave additional evidence of opposition to the health officials. Large public funerals for at least two prominent city residents, a former mayor, John P. Hopkins, and a former school board superintendent, Ella Flagg Young, took place in defiance of the emergency orders. And while leaders turned out to honor their dead, Chicagoans on the other end of the social spectrum honored their traditions in the city's thousands of saloons. Police raids and repeated warnings to saloon keepers to eliminate filth, overcrowding, and poor ventilation gave evidence of leaders' distaste for the poor man's club. Leaders weighed their desire to close the saloons against the consequences of alienating Chicago's working people. Despite several members' desire to include saloons in the closing orders, the Influenza Commission recommended only that overcrowding be prohibited. The incongruity of open saloons and closed theaters, dance halls, and cabarets reflected not an official endorsement of the workingman's favorite pastime, but a frank recognition of the limits of public authority.

Working-class saloon going during the epidemic weeks revealed values fundamentally different from those of the guardians of health. Historian Roy Rosenzweig has shown that in ethnic saloons workingmen constructed an "alternative culture" that rejected middle-class conventions and values. Raucous, male-dominated saloons changed the middle-class ideal of mixed-gender entertainment, drinking challenged middle-class temperance, gambling challenged the legal system, and the mutuality of treating fellow drinkers to rounds challenged capitalist individualism. Workers used their leisure hours to forge a culture that enabled them to cope with urban life. Coping often meant ignoring middle-class mores, and during the epidemic these mores seemed no more compelling than before.

Many Chicagoans, particularly among the poor, disregarded or never heard the official message. "In many instances," one report conceded, "the information has reached only those who are least in need of such instruction, while the foreign population and economically dependent classes have not been reached at all effectively." And many who heard refused to follow. When scientific medicine failed to provide favorable results, even the most aggressive publicity campaign could do little to keep people from older methods of prevention and treatment. Parents kept healthy children home from school because they had done so in previous epidemics. In late October truancy peaked at over 30 percent, and in the poorest neighborhoods it exceeded 50 percent. These parents did not entrust their children's health to teachers and the supposed wisdom of experts who urged school attendance. Home seemed to offer not disease but sanctuary.

Many people put their faith in folk remedies and nonsanctioned doctors. The campaign against supposed quacks and nostrums was such an essential part of the public health message that the acceptance of them by many signaled either a failure of publicity or a renunciation of public authority and the corporatist vision. Insisting that the only rational precaution was "all the fresh air and sunlight you can get," the Department of Health ridiculed the (no less efficacious) medicinal use of sulfur, asafetida, cucumbers, and potatoes. "Every one seemed to be jumping about frantically for some panacea," a homeopath wrote; "many will accept charlatan advice of the worst kind possible." Dr. A. Wilberforce Williams, medical columnist for the *Chicago Defender,* a newspaper serving the black community, warned, "The fogies and fakers are reaping a very rich harvest in dispensing and disposing their 'sure cures' for influenza. Many people are so dull and ignorant that they will accept the uneducated, the unscientific, the untrained advice." Doctors attacked foreign-language newspapers for carrying bald advertisements for sure cures and miracle healers. African-Americans and immigrants seemed dangerously isolated from the new authority.

But dozens of advertisements suggest that the middle-class readers of the mainstream daily newspapers were also receptive to the appeals of popular medicine. Gordon's Mustard Oil Cream proclaimed boldly, "Prevents Spanish 'Flu' Wards Off Pneumonia." "Influenza Germ Smoked Out," promised Smo-ko Tobaccoless Cigarettes, which medicated "the air passages that cannot be reached any other way." "Cream Applied in Nostrils May Prevent Spanish Influenza," announced an unusually tentative advertisement for Ely's Cream Balm. The producers of Kolynos Dental Cream, which "evolved under the influence of bacteriology . . . [and is] a truly scientific dentifrice," asserted that "a small amount of the dental cream — about half the size of a pea — in the entrance of each nostril" would *"filter the air you breathe* and . . . have a distinct germicidal action." Purchasers ignored the persistent refrain that only doctors could prescribe effective medicine.

Nonsanctioned methods of treatment and prevention often came from the regular medical profession itself. Training and experience carried more weight than an intrusive bureaucracy. Dr. William Brady, medical columnist for the *Daily News,* became the most visible critic of official policy when he advocated keeping children home from

The authority of the U.S. Army's surgeon general was called upon in this mouthwash advertisement, reflecting faith in both medicine and the military. Merchants were asked to play their part in controlling the epidemic by stocking the mouthwash.

school and ridiculed both the city fumigation campaign and Commissioner Robertson's admonition to avoid wet feet. The prescription of narcotics during the epidemic revealed the Department of Health's failure to implement army-like discipline over doctors. Surgeon General Rupert Blue and the Influenza Commission warned against prescribing narcotics, and medical journals claimed that opiates predisposed influenza patients to pneumonia. Nevertheless, a survey of city pharmacies revealed that 103,980 influenza prescriptions, about a quarter of the total for influenza patients, contained codeine, heroin, opium, morphine, or other powerful narcotics.

More generally, many Chicagoans failed to take their assigned places behind public officials in the campaigns. Most of the middle-class ignored its putative public duty. While hundreds of women served as unpaid nurses, attendants, and cooks, most refused to assist. Fewer than a quarter of the women with Red Cross first-aid training answered the organization's appeal. The total corps of volunteers was no more than a few thousand, though the Women's Committee of the State Council of National Defense alone called upon twenty thousand women who had earlier registered for volunteer duty.

After praising the accomplishments of volunteers, nearly all observers agreed on the need for more nurses and assistants. A report from the Chicago Commons Settlement, located in the city's crowded Near North Side, noted that "nurses or helpers were so scarce that only the most emergent cases could be cared for." The superintendent of the Visiting Nurses Association wrote that the epidemic showed "the lack of neighborliness in a big city like Chicago. . . . The shortage of physicians, nurses and other trained workers was bad, but the shortage of relatives and neighbors was worse." "Any community," she declared, "ought to be able to handle neighborhood needs better than most of them were handled." A homeopath noted "the lack of volunteers from the hundreds of those women who were so anxious to rush into the four Red Cross courses in nursing in 1917, when it was the fad of the hour to do so." Their notions of service, he charged, were "much more romantic . . . than to nurse dirty Russian Jews in the Ghetto." Despite the equation of public health with military service, authorities had only limited success in transferring the organization of the battlefield to the neighborhood. Fear, private obligations, or a simple lack of public-spiritedness kept most of the middle-class from enlisting.

Many doctors also resisted their role in the bureaucratic order. Upholding individualistic values in defiance of the corporatist ideology, physicians chafed against the subordination of the private practitioner to the general good that the public health program seemed to imply. Physicians particularly resented the assumption of broad public authority by the Volunteer Medical Service Corps, a private organization formed to maintain a pool of doctors willing to perform emergency military or public health service. During the epidemic the corps used the rhetoric of wartime loyalty to recruit doctors for service in the public health campaign. The organization's opponents, led by the Chicago Medical Society, the powerful local chapter of the increasingly privatistic American Medical Association, accused the corps of overstepping its bounds and attacked its manipulation of nationalist hysteria to bolster semiofficial authority. "It is no reflection on a physician's patriotism if he does not join this organization," a society editorial concluded. "If failure to join signifies anything, it shows some independence of spirit and a disposition not to be awed by a pseudo-military demand, and not to desire to camouflage one's willingness to serve by a pseudo-military rank." Individualistic values remained strong.

By the middle of November, newspapers gave scant attention to influenza. Though the daily death rate remained high, the epidemic had crested. In the flush of victory over Germany, most Chicagoans turned their thoughts from the fading influenza crisis. Yet on November 13, a bizarre *Tribune* story seemed to summarize Chicago's experience with the epidemic. "Slicker Julia Finds Wealth as Flu Nurse" told of a "woman of diamonds and furs, silken ankles and jails, gem studded fingers and aliases by the dozen" who had fleeced at least seven and possibly fifty stricken families. Disease-ridden Chicago proved susceptible to the scam. "While influenza patients died or lived," the *Tribune* reported, "Julia, clad in a nurse's uniform, plundered their homes." Disarmed by "her rose lipped smile and pearly teeth," victims paid her for useless medicines and exorbitantly priced supplies. For one sufferer she called "an M.D. known to the police as a dope seller and narcotic supplier." The patient's family paid her twenty-two dollars to fill the prescription — and received a bottle of what later proved to be Cherryola, a soft drink. Julia avoided arrest, once by convincing a future victim, who then convinced a detective, that he had known her as a little girl who hitched onto his wagons. Finally, police arrested her and uncovered three mysterious associates: her fiancé, identified as "Charlie the Greek," Eva Jacobs, "a girl of the shady world," and "Suicide Bess," apparently alive and well, keeper of "a hangout for thieves."

A dope-dealing doctor, hopes for easy cures, disappointment, a vaguely threatening foreigner, a criminal underworld made even more corrupt by the gender of some of its denizens, the persistent strength of a sentimental tie, the sacrifice of virtue to the false pleasures of a seductive face: the story resonated because it spoke to the concerns of many Chicagoans during the epidemic of 1918. The attempt to create a more cohesive society — led by a united elite of experts and public officials, peopled by a receptive citizenry, and organized around a middle-class moral code — had largely failed. Fissures ran too deep, especially along ethnic and class lines. The elite themselves proved fractious. Of course the visions of hierarchical unity did not die, nor did the use of science in the service of traditional morality die, as the nation's response to AIDS reminds us now. But in 1918 Chicagoans showed themselves in varying measures too self-centered, independent, and stubborn to fall into line.

PART IV

THE CHICAGO CULTURAL RENAISSANCE

Pleasure Garden on the Midway

Paul Kruty

The name "Midway Gardens" evokes dual images — of fairground and park, carnival and café, public spectacle and private enjoyment. To Chicagoans it was once all of these things and more. Like Chicago itself, it was a "city in a garden." The idea of Midway Gardens stirred the imagination of its architect, Frank Lloyd Wright, and elicited one of the most extravagant designs of his career. It prompted a real estate speculator, Edward C. Waller, Jr.; an amateur musician, Charles H. Matthews; and a builder, Paul F. P. Mueller, to join forces. This difficult, underfinanced project, planned for an unlikely part of the city, promised almost no hope of financial success.

Yet Midway Gardens *was* built. During the fifteen years it existed, 1914-29, it was home to a first-class restaurant, a private club, a symphony orchestra, and a jazz band. It hosted a ballet company, many society dinner parties, the annual balls of an avant-garde art group, and countless vaudeville acts. Chicago's urban concert garden not only stands as one of the undisputed masterpieces of its architect, it also holds a significant place in the histories of American classical and popular music, dining in Chicago, and the fight over Prohibition.

The developments that led to this extraordinary building are as numerous as they are diverse. Traditionally, Midway Gardens has been appreciated almost exclusively as the product of its architect's imagination. Certainly it is Wright's genius that has secured a place for Midway Gardens in the history of modern architecture. But the building can be fully understood only by studying its contemporary sources: its relationship to outdoor parks and beer halls in Chicago and to the city's music scene, its legacy from the World's Columbian Exposition, and the intentions of Wright's original clients. Wright's ideas were greatly influenced by each of these factors. He also drew upon his own earlier projects for amusement buildings. Finally, he was able to respond to the dream of his clients because of his personal experiences in Europe in 1910. Regardless of Wright's great design, without the dedication and sacrifice of the contractor, Paul Mueller, the building could not have been constructed. Midway Gardens was the result of a shared vision and the complete collaboration of client, architect, and builder.

Midway Gardens was designed and built in 1913-14. The large complex, 300 feet on each side, consisted of an outdoor bandshell

Several thousand people arrived at Midway Gardens for the grand opening on Saturday, June 27, 1914, and almost as many more were turned away.
(Photograph by J. W. Taylor. CHS, ICHi-01436)

and a restaurant building facing one another across an open terraced summer garden courtyard. Contained within the larger winter garden block was a three-story hall with tiers and balconies for dining, flanked by a private club and a tavern. Above the main hall, supported by steel trusses, was a roof garden. Wright decorated the reinforced-concrete building with murals and sculpture, ornamented some of the cream-colored brick walls with a veneer of thin concrete blocks, and trimmed the cantilevered eaves with a decorated metal facia.

The main pavilion fronted on the west side of Cottage Grove Avenue south of 60th Street. Although Midway Gardens was a symmetrical building, Wright did not provide an entranceway at the center as one would expect. Instead, he designed access at the corners, marking each with a tower or "belvedere." From the north belvedere at 60th and Cottage Grove, visitors could enter the dining hall by walking south through a galleried promenade. They entered the summer garden by walking west along the covered walkway a short distance, and, as they turned left, the whole garden opened in full view. Concert-goers continued to the end of the covered walkway, where they descended directly to the seats set before the stage. The five levels of the summer garden were separated by planters of bushes and flowers.

Midway Gardens bordered upon Frederick Law Olmsted's Washington Park and Midway Plaisance — the same Midway then associated in most Chicagoans' minds with the carnival district at the World's Columbian Exposition twenty years before. Within sight of the University of Chicago and the intellectual community of Hyde Park, Midway Gardens was surrounded by the working-class Woodlawn neighborhood, which contained beer halls and two amusement parks, including White City several blocks south.

The block bordered by 60th Street, 61st Street, Cottage Grove Avenue, and Langley Avenue had been the site of entertainment concessions long before Midway Gardens. During the Columbian Exposition the Ferdinand and Isabella Pavilion and Theater stood on the southeast corner of the block, while on the north end of the property, the Garden City Observation Wheel Company maintained a rival to the great Ferris wheel that stood on the Midway. Standing in 1895 on the corner where the Gardens would be built was Old Vienna, a restaurant and beer garden whose name recalled one of the star attractions on the Midway during the world's fair. The Forty-Niners Mining Camp occupied another part of the largely undeveloped parcel of land.

In 1898 the Chicago City Railway Company acquired the whole city block and announced the creation of a casino and pavilion called Sans Souci (carefree), named after Frederick the Great's pleasure park outside of Berlin. Located between Washington Park and the Washington Park Race Track, Sans Souci was well served by public transportation, and it prospered. By 1908 a full complement of structures had been added to the original buildings, including Wonderland, Midgetland, Laughing Gallery, Odeon, a Japanese building, a bandstand, a miniature railway, a merry-go-round, and a penny arcade. In 1912 a rival amusement park, White City, opened a few blocks away. But with the race track now gone and the competition stiff, the management of Sans Souci was unable to retire a five-year mortgage on a $100,000 loan, and the park was closed.

In January 1913 Edward C. Waller, Jr. and his partner Oscar J. Friedman bought the Sans Souci property. Friedman was a Hyde Park florist whose only contribution to the partnership appears to have been financial. Ed Waller was the son of one of Wright's most important early clients, Chicago developer Edward C. Waller. While the elder Waller had established his business through careful investment, young Waller was an impetuous entrepreneur who saw his fortune come and go several times in his life.

Waller did not bring Wright, who was in Japan buying prints (and winning the commission for the Imperial Hotel in the process), into the project for another six months. In the meantime, he made preliminary plans to retain and lease six of the amusement buildings on the south half of the property and replace the rest with some sort of beer garden. Because Sans Souci had been famous for its summer band concerts, Waller wanted his new garden to exploit Sans Souci's reputation for lively musical entertainment.

Waller often dined at the University Club on Michigan Avenue with a group of amateur musicians that included Livingston Fairbank, an heir to one of Chicago's meatpacking families, and Charles H. Matthews. "Music-mad Charlie," as Wright later called him, had lived in Dresden, studied conducting in Germany and Austria, and was a friend of composer Richard Wagner's son, Siegfried. He suggested that Waller use the north half of the property for "a German concert garden, not a beer garden with incidental music." This kind of garden would necessitate, he explained, a full symphony orchestra that could play throughout the summer months. The men's enthusiasm mounted by the day until they all agreed to become financial partners and, as Matthews said, make "a go of it!" Incorporated in West Virginia in 1913, the Midway Gardens Company included Waller and Friedman, presidents; Fairbank, vice-president; and Matthews, treasurer.

In the early teens Chicago hosted a wide range of summer entertainment gardens for all tastes and classes. Local beer halls abounded, often with a few tables in back. Several beer gardens, however, were elaborate affairs. One of the largest was the Green Mill Sunken Gardens at Broadway and Lawrence Avenue, with a central open courtyard separated from the street by arcaded walkways and an enclosed restaurant building. While each beer garden usually had a small band, Green Mill used an ensemble of twenty-five players. The oldest and most popular beer garden in Chicago was the Bismarck Garden, "that attractive bit of Vienna or Berlin" (as the *Evening Post* described it in 1914) at Broadway and Halsted Street. This establishment served the large German population as a haven of "gemütlichkeit" since 1895. Fearing competition from its new South Side rival, the Bismarck added a fifty-piece orchestra for its 1914 season. Both the Green Mill and the Bismarck were remodeled and enlarged extensively that same season.

Ravinia Park on the North Shore, summer home to the Chicago Symphony Orchestra since 1905, was then a decade old. It was in a different class from other entertainment gardens. Its ample grounds, casino, concert hall, and outdoor pavilion made it the summer pilgrimage spot for Chicago's serious music lovers as well as its social elite. Midway Gardens was planned to combine the best elements of all of these parks — formal and informal dining, public bar and private club, background music and serious classical concerts.

In planning Midway Gardens, Frank Lloyd Wright, like Waller and Matthews, had the Green Mill Gardens, Bismarck Garden, and Ravinia to borrow from and improve upon. Wright, however, had his own dreams about the possibilities of an entertainment park such as Midway Gardens. For twenty years, he had retained vivid memories of the Columbian Exposition — of crowds strolling past festive buildings, of colonnades reflected in pools of water, of flags flying and music playing in open-air bandstands. Although he often decried the architectural style of the fair's buildings, Wright employed elements of plan and organization from the fair in several public commissions before Midway Gardens. These included a large project with pavilions and a bandstand for Cheltenham Beach, located south of Jackson Park, at 79th Street, which he designed in the mid-1890s. Two years later, he created a small beer garden called Mozart Gardens at 55th and State streets and an immense development on Wolf Lake near the Indiana border combining restaurants, piers, casinos, and an enormous water chute.

When approached by Waller about the Midway Gardens project, Wright not only had experience designing pleasure parks, he also had personal knowledge of the type of concert garden that Matthews was urging Waller to build. While in Berlin three years earlier, Wright had the opportunity to dine at many outdoor concert gardens, such as the Terrassen am Hallensee (Terraces on Lake Hallen), a twin-towered, three-level outdoor restaurant on one of Berlin's suburban lakes that presented nightly orchestral concerts. During this same trip Wright also had become intrigued by the extent to which his European colleagues used sculpture and mural decoration to enhance their buildings.

The commission for Midway Gardens provided the perfect opportunity to combine all of Wright's interests in the complete work of art and the chance to restore his name and reputation in Chicago, which he had so badly tarnished by his love affair with Mrs. Cheney.

Although Wright later recounted that he shook the scheme out of his sleeve in a single weekend, evidence suggests that the building had a much longer genesis. Among almost two hundred surviving drawings for Midway Gardens are three separate versions of the concert garden, as well as a remodeling plan for Sans Souci. In these drawings, it is possible to trace Wright's changing conception of the project and his response to Waller's continuing budget reductions as the great cost became apparent.

In Wright's first scheme, which he completed during the last part of 1913, long covered walkways leading to separate buildings (presumably facing Washington Park) encompassed fully half of the Sans Souci property. A freestanding bandstand was to be surrounded with an artificial lake. The plans changed in early 1914. Although the entire north half of the block had been cleared, it was decided to build the Gardens only on the northeast corner of the property. At first this somewhat reduced plan of the Gardens was left open at its inside corner and connected by covered walkways to the remaining Sans Souci buildings. For the final design, completed by mid-February, Wright created a self-contained structure facing Cottage Grove Avenue that was closed to the rest of the block. A bandshell now replaced the bandstand. As in the earlier plans, water was to be an important part of the scheme — a narrow reflecting pool would separate the orchestra from the audience.

Wright immediately assigned his trusted builder, general contractor Paul Mueller, to the project, and Mueller started hiring subcontractors. Mueller had already erected the Larkin Building and Unity Temple for Wright. (After the completion of Midway Gardens he would supervise construction of the Imperial Hotel in Tokyo.) Wright began to assemble his team of artists. For sculpture, he first turned to his long-time associate, Richard Bock. Bock recommended hiring Stanislaus Szukalski, a young Polish emigré studying at the Art Institute who later became one of the city's most radical artists, but the meeting between Wright and Szukalski ended in mutual rejection. Wright's son John then suggested a California acquaintance and pupil of sculptor Gutzon Borglum, Alfonso Iannelli, who was hired in mid-February. Decisions about muralists were put off for several months.

During March and April, Wright and his staff worked furiously to complete the models and presentation and working drawings. At his home and studio near Spring Green, Wisconsin, Wright created sketch after sketch, and his talented draftsman Emil Brodelle turned them into elegant perspective drawings. Architect Harry Robinson ran Wright's Orchestra Hall office in Chicago, while at the construction site John Lloyd Wright acted as supervisor to Paul Mueller. When the annual exhibition of the Chicago Architectural Club opened on April 9, the public saw a large display of Wright's latest work, including many drawings and models for Midway Gardens. In the *Chicago Tribune*, an excited Harriet Monroe, editor of *Poetry* magazine, called Midway Gardens "perhaps the most complete opportunity which Mr. Wright has had as yet to express his ideas in a group of buildings."

Meanwhile, Matthews and Waller were arranging for the entertainment and food services. By the winter of 1914, Charlie Matthews had convinced Max Bendix to shoulder the task of organizing the new orchestra. Bendix, who was in New York pursuing a dual career as conductor and violinist, had a long association with Chicago. He began his career in Cincinnati, worked in Philadelphia and New York, and then came to Chicago in 1886, performing with the Theodore Thomas Orchestra in the Interstate Industrial Exposition Building in what is now Grant Park. He had been concertmaster of that orchestra during its famous engagement at the 1893 world's fair. Since then he had taken up conducting as well. News of Bendix's appointment appeared in the press on February 20. By May *Musical America* reported that the best players of the Chicago Opera orchestra had joined Bendix's new National Symphony Orchestra. Fondly recalling his first days in Chicago, Bendix announced he would present music "such as no one has heard on summer nights in Chicago since the old days of Theodore Thomas in the Exposition Building." The first trial concerts were held in early June at the Auditorium Theatre, and on June 20 the group moved to the busy construction site that was Midway Gardens. That evening, the first trial concert in the bandshell opened with the prelude to Wagner's *Die Meistersinger*.

Matthews formed a board to administer the orchestra that included Chicago composer John Alden Carpenter and his brother Benjamin (who was Fairbank's brother-in-law), businessman and composer Edson Keith, and lawyer Arthur Dyrenforth, all members of the University Club. Matthews also acquired notable music libraries from two conductors — Anton Seidl, Wagnerian conductor at New York's Metropolitan Opera, and recently deceased Chevalier N. B. Emanuel, a local conductor and music collector. Matthews helped Bendix locate musicians for the orchestra and began consulting on possible designs for the bandshell. While Matthews was providing for first-rate musical fare, Ed Waller contracted with a well-known restaurateur, John Z. Vogelsang, to manage the food service, which was to include a restaurant, bar, private club, and outdoor dining.

Work began at the construction site in early April. Wright remembered that "soon all of old Sans Souci there was left in plain sight was a rusty old steel-tower." Meanwhile, Bock and Iannelli worked in a tarpaper shack along with craftsman and Italian immigrant Ezio Orlandi of the Orlandi Statuary Company, whom Bock had enlisted to create the molds for Wright's elaborate ornament and to cast the sculpture as well. As the number of decorated concrete pieces began to mount into the hundreds, a special sprinkler system had to be installed in the yard to cure them properly before they were set in place. Soon rows of smiling sprites screened the two sunken gardens, their abstracted, faceted forms matching the geometric patterns on the walls, while the winged figure called the "Queen of the Garden" framed both the interior and exterior facades of the winter garden, as well as the bandshell. Four freestanding sprites dominated the space in the main hall, each based on a geometric form — female figures of circles and triangles, and males of cubes and dodecahedrons.

As work progressed, Wright turned his attention to the interior murals and hired two teachers from the Chicago Academy of Fine Arts, John W. Norton and William P. Henderson. Henderson brought his best pupil, Katherine Dudley, to join the ensemble. Last of all, Wright secured the services of Chicago's "post-impressionist," Jerome Blum, although he could not induce Blum's friend, cubist painter Manierre Dawson, to work on the Garden's murals. As with his sculptors, Wright clearly made attempts to find the most innovative artists in Chicago to create designs that would harmonize with his building. Both Norton and Henderson created schematic human figures based on squares, circles, and triangles and placed them in idyllic settings mirroring the outdoor scenes soon to occur in the summer garden.

In addition to his plans for the grounds and buildings, Wright also designed furniture, fixtures, and dinnerware for Midway Gardens. None of Wright's several designs for furniture was ever realized. Instead, the place was furnished with white-painted wooden tables and chairs similar to those found in the Bismarck and Green Mill gardens — or in almost any contemporary German beer or concert garden. But Wright's lamp design was produced, and his patterns for china were turned over to the Chicago representative of Bauscher Porcelain, Arthur Schiller, who had them applied to stock forms and cast in Weiden, German.

When Matthews returned from "run[ning] around the United States interviewing musicians," as Wright later described his client's efforts, he began giving the architect advice about the bandshell to insure proper acoustics. While Wright had designed several bandstands (none of them ever built), this was his first bandshell. The two men quarreled over the height and sides of the shell and about the possible canvas tent. Wright was furious about the effect alterations would have on his design, but he worked out a compromise with Matthews and made changes nevertheless. Music critic Felix Borowski reported the row in the *Tribune:* "There can be no doubt, however, that whatever the orchestra shell may do to diminish the artistic effect of the remainder of the architecture, the acoustic results are of the most admirable kind." Wright himself was so pleased with the result that for the rest of his life he remembered the bandshell design as his own idea.

Construction continued at a frantic pace, and the inspired Wright made numerous changes at the site without new drawings. The morning before the official opening, Saturday, June 27, the *Tribune* reported that the grind of concrete mixers and the shouts of the gang bosses drowned out the rehearsing orchestra. The few visitors who succeeded in dodging the long trail of wheelbarrows carrying rubbish out and flowers in were too interested in the construction work to pay much attention to Mr. Bendix. Instead they watched William Henderson and John Norton putting the first strokes on the mural panels.

By evening an audience of several thousand had arrived for the opening festivities, while almost as many more were turned away. By July 19, the *Tribune* reported that attendance figures for the first three weeks were "almost frightening. Last Saturday and Sunday, we are told, a total of more than 17,000 persons crowded into the place." In addition to a healthy dose of Richard Wagner (as well as a weekly "Wagner Night" on Friday), Bendix included his own music on the programs. He even urged Charlie Matthews to conduct now and again. Calling Midway Gardens "the final word in al-fresco amusement retreats," the *Evening Post* explained that "it has the metropolitan charm of Bismarck Garden and the musical quality of Ravinia." The *Music News* was happy to report that what made Midway Gardens different from "Bismarck Garden, Riverview, White City and other summer gardens," was the unique seating arrangement — the "650 seats for those who wish to listen to music merely, [where] the audience can sit in peace, unoffended by obstreperous waiters and undisturbed by the chatter of people at tables."

Midway Gardens opened during one of Chicago's most exciting musical seasons. *Musical America* reported with amazement one Sunday in April when there were "Nine Concerts in One Day in Chicago," including recitals by Mischa Elman and Dame Clara Butt and the world premiere of Leo Sowerby's violin sonata. The sixth North Shore Festival opened in Evanston in June with international stars such as Alma Gluck and Herbert Witherspoon. Dancer Ruth St. Denis began the season at Ravinia. On the popular side, the *Tribune* reported that although

> a few years ago there were not more than forty theaters in all Chicago, now there are 750, and in at least 200 of them vaudeville performers are employed to help our moving pictures. In addition, there are well paid engagements for 100 or more performers in the downtown restaurants, while outside the loop almost every eating place in town — to say nothing of the big summer parks — employs musicians and singers. . . . Never was the demand so insistent for noise and constant motion.

At Midway Gardens, work continued on the interiors until September. They were never decorated as Wright intended them, however. His relationship with the muralists was disastrous. Many of the wall dimensions for Norton's and Henderson's designs were changed during construction, and their carefully planned compositions no longer fit. Wright painted over other murals even though he had approved them. Finally, the architect decided to create his own murals. In early August he produced two compositions that eliminated all representational forms, however abstract, and used only circles of varying sizes and colors. On August 15, 1914, with these panels drawn, Wright received the horrific news that the cook at his home in Wisconsin had murdered his

Although Wright would later take full credit for the excellent acoustics of the bandshell, they were actually the result of a compromise between Wright and Matthews, who insisted that the architect modify his original design.

(CHS)

beloved Mrs. Cheney, her children, and members of his staff, and had burnt down part of Taliesin. His personal life devastated, Wright's involvement with Midway Gardens thus came to an abrupt end. It was left to his son John to transfer the two designs (using oil stains and gold leaf) to the end walls of the tavern room.

Ed Waller was having his own less tragic troubles. There simply was no money. When Paul Mueller realized that Waller had begun construction with about $70,000 instead of $250,000 as he had claimed, Mueller agreed to continue on credit. The subcontractors were not so generous, however, and started filing liens as early as July. By December, nineteen such suits had been filed. Creditors lost faith by October and tried to foreclose. Heated negotiations led in late December to a $200,000 loan in the form of 455 promissory notes, guaranteed by Chicago Title and Trust Company.

Throughout these troubles, the Gardens stayed open and busy, playing to full houses and rave reviews. After Bendix's last concert on September 7, *Music News* lamented the dispersal of the National Symphony. Announcing that "there is room for a second symphony orchestra in Chicago" (especially one whose talented conductor had studied with Theodore Thomas), it pleaded, "Bendix, 'blieb bei uns, und geh' nicht fort!' [Stay with us and don't go away!]"

The first winter schedule went into effect with the outdoor garden closed. In the winter garden building, now billed as the "Rendezvous of the Smart Set," entertainment included vaudeville acts and instruction in the latest society dances led by Carlos Sebastian and his wife, Dorothy Bentley. Miss Georgene Faulkner, Hyde Park's "Story Lady," read to children, and Mme. Rosa Olitzka, contralto at the Met, sang to their parents. And, of course, Vogelsang's served its famous cuisine to, among others, guests at a private banquet for Mrs. Potter Palmer. Special events in the winter garden included an "Artist's Night" in May 1915, hosted by Lorado Taft, a fashion show that July, and an automobile fair in September with a guest appearance by dancing "superstar" Vernon Castle.

In spring of 1915 the Midway Gardens managers scored a major coup when they signed Russian ballerina Anna Pavlova, who had danced at the Auditorium Theatre on April 25, to appear as part of their summer program. Dance critic Percy Hammond reported breathlessly in the *Tribune* that they had arranged to have Pavlova "beautify further their oasis on the south side by dancing there throughout July. If this Midway Gardens is not, during July, the most joyous site in the middle west I shall be cynically serene in my belief that Chicago is the Caliban of cities."

After two weeks of rehearsing and a complete reconstruction of the stage, Pavlova began her four-week engagement on July 3 before an audience of 4,500. The next day she signed a contract with Universal Films to make a movie of Auber's opera *La Muette de Portici.* Two days later, behind the Midway Gardens bandshell in the rubble of Sans Souci, Anna Pavlova's only movie began its filming. Pavlova's engagement became the stuff of which legends are made. By the third week, the *Evening Post* reported that the episode had attracted visitors from "the four corners of Chicago and within a radius of many hundred miles." Fifteen-year-old Ruth Page, who later became one of Chicago's most renowned dancers, traveled from Indianapolis to see her idol.

Despite the phenomenal success of Pavlova's run, Midway Gardens had encountered more bad luck the second season. In June, the gala reopening of the summer garden had been twice rained out, the wardrobe concession had sued the management, and the notorious James "Toronto Jimmy" Johnson and his band of "yeggmen" blew the safe and stole $12,000. After Pavlova's performances the rain returned to further dampen attendance figures despite Max Bendix's best efforts to program inviting concerts. The end of the 1915 summer season saw the return of what Wright called "ugly suspicions" about funds.

On October 5, 1915, a month after the second winter season had begun, Mayor William Hale Thompson decided to enforce an old Sunday closing law concerning the sale of alcohol. This political skirmish between the "wets" and the "drys" effectively closed establishments such as Midway Gardens on one of their busiest days. The next day the *Tribune* reported that Thompson's order "has had the immediate effect of driving the Midway Gardens into a receivership." The following day a judge ordered the gates padlocked.

As new lawsuits appeared, including one filed by Clarence Darrow on behalf of disgruntled members of the private Garden Club, Waller became reconciled to the impossibility of resurrecting Midway Gardens. Failing to solve the problems during the winter of 1915-16, Waller filed for bankruptcy on March 31, 1916. In May the property was quietly acquired from the three principal stockholders by Schoenhofen Brewery as an outlet for their Edelweiss Beer. Workers began remodeling small portions of the interior in early June.

The neighborhoods of Hyde Park and Kenwood had been dry for many years. Since 1896 the Hyde Park Protective Association had been waging legal battles with liquor establishments bordering the dry areas. Extended lawsuits were fought with the Germania Beer Garden and the original Edelweiss Garden, both on the north side of Washington Park. When news of Midway Gardens had appeared in February 1914, long-time prohibitionist Rev. M. P. Boynton of Woodlawn led the protest, fearing that yet another cheap beer garden was coming to the borders of Washington Park. Although opposition had subsided and Midway Gardens had flourished for two seasons, some circles met the closing of the Gardens with a sense of relief. With the reappearance of the Schoenhofen Company, the opposition prepared for a new confrontation.

In mid-June 1916 the new management made an enormous publicity blunder when it announced that it was changing the name of Midway Gardens to Edelweiss Gardens, the name of the old Washington Park beer garden. The incredulous *Tribune* explained, "Memories of the old Edelweiss summer garden at the northwest corner of 51st Street and Cottage Grove Avenue, which disappeared in a reform wave years ago, are recalled by the announcement that the now closed Midway Gardens will be renamed 'Edelweiss Gardens.'" The "drys" were mobilized and succeeded in having an amusement license denied.

Schoenhofen Brewery apparently wished to continue to attract the clientele of the original garden. Arthur Dunham, a respected conductor, composer, and organist, was hired to organize a new orchestra. In publicity statements, Dunham even repeated Bendix's enticing promise that the programs were to be "modeled on the old Theodore Thomas programs which were given in the Exposition building." A strange state of affairs continued for a month, with protesters decrying the Garden's adverse moral effect on the young, while Dunham's orchestra played Beethoven and Brahms nightly to a "very fashionable audience" who had to be admitted free of charge until a license was issued. Mayor Thompson finally solved the problem in a democratic way by local plebiscite. The "wets" won overwhelmingly, and the license was granted.

To Frank Lloyd Wright all of this was unimportant compared to the harm about to come to his building. In early July, John Norton reported to William Henderson that he had recently seen Wright, who talked of the fate of the Gardens. Wright had said that it was "to be painted over," and that he was going "to sue to stop them." But in the end, he was powerless to prevent these changes. Wright later bemoaned the new management's desire to "add obnoxious features out of balance and nasty" and explained that "the whole effect was cheapened to suit a hearty bourgeois taste."

Although this was not the proprietor's original intention, it is, indeed, what happened during their tenancy. For the second season, Dunham's orchestra was replaced by Francisco Ferullo's band. The new "hearty bourgeois" attractions of the 1917 season also included "four fountains [which] have been placed in a bed of rocks surrounded by vines and trees, [and] three open dance pavilions" as well as a "new elaborate lighting system" and "rustic decorations."

As a local center for vaudeville, cabaret, and ragtime, Edelweiss Gardens thrived. Novelist Edna Ferber, living in Hyde Park at the time, reveled in the Gardens' ambience. In *The Girls* (1921), Ferber captured the flavor of her favorite terraces: "It was deliciously cool there in that great unroofed space. There was even a breeze, miraculously caught within the four walls of the Garden. . . . A row of slim trees showed a fairy frieze above the tiled balcony." Chicago novelist Robert Herrick also frequented the Gardens and its terraces. In *Waste* (1924), Herrick used the building (calling it "Bellevue Gardens") as the model for the masterpiece of the novel's hero, an embattled architect.

After a wartime hiatus during 1918, Edelweiss reopened for two more years. Contrary to modern accounts, it remained extremely popular and surprisingly did not close after the passage of Prohibition. Edelweiss weathered the 1920 season as a dry establishment. Perhaps Ted Lewis, with his "famous aggregation of 'jazzists,'" temporarily made the difference.

Edelweiss Gardens closed, however, in 1921. After the Midway Automobile Tire and Supply Company acquired the property, owner Edward C. Dietrich announced plans in August to convert the winter garden building into a ballroom, remove the restaurant, and enclose the summer garden. This ambitious undertaking was apparently infeasible. Two years later work did begin on a more modest remodeling of the winter garden, including a makeshift cloakroom at the north entrance. By September of the following year, 1924, the building inspector could report that the hall was occupied, although work was not complete. The "Midway Dancing Gardens," as new signs proclaimed, was ready to dazzle Chicagoans with the latest in popular dance music.

A second "Golden Age" had already arrived, although Matthews, Bendix, Dunham, or even Wright probably would not have recognized it as such. When the Gardens reopened, the new ballroom hosted Art Kassel's band, "Kassels in the Air." As early as December 1923, Kassel's "Midway Gardens Orchestra" was making its first records. Kassel's dance band included several jazz players. When fifteen-year-old Benny Goodman joined them for the summer of 1924, a new hot sound flowed through the hall and its balconies, much to Kassel's amusement and his audience's pleasure. The following summer, Bix Beiderbecke sat in with the group to lighten the spirit of Iannelli's concrete sprites.

The winter garden, remodeled as a ballroom, was the site of several fund-raising dances sponsored by Chicago's radical art group, the No-Jury Society of Artists. "Cubist

Balls," attended by artists dressed as works of abstract art, were held at the Gardens on October 13, 1924, and January 29, 1926, on the eves of the third and fourth exhibitions of the society.

During the tenancy of Midway Dancing Gardens, German architect Eric Mendelsohn visited Chicago. In November 1924 Wright's former pupil, Barry Byrne, took Mendelsohn on a tour of Wright's buildings. After visiting the Coonley house in Riverside, they traveled to the Midway Gardens dance hall, which to the ecstatic Mendelsohn symbolized the Dionysian side of Wright's genius. In its battered state in the mid-1920s, however, Midway Gardens did not inspire the same feelings in its changing clientele. To Studs Lonigan, the protagonist of James Farrell's famous novel set in the neighborhood around Washington Park, Midway Gardens had become little more than a good place to pick up girls.

In 1926 Floyd Towne and his band took over music making at the Gardens. Towne's associates included famous jazzmen such as Muggsy Spanier, Frank Teschemacher, and Jess Stacy. When Stacy first arrived on a cold winter evening, Spanier directed him to one of the upper balconies because "we got all the gin upstairs." Spanier recalled that the band lasted "for two glorious years" before quitting in a row over music and uniforms. He also claimed that "as soon as we left business fell off. It got so bad that in no time at all the place was torn down and turned into a garage."

Whatever the reason for the decline of Midway Dancing Gardens, Edward Dietrich gave up trying to recover his investment and closed the doors. Social historian Lewis Mumford, traveling to see Chicago's architectural masterpieces, found the Gardens boarded up. Finally, in the spring of 1929, Dietrich leased the corner to the Sinclair Refining Company who, according to the terms of the lease, agreed to "completely wreck and remove the building commonly known as the 'Midway Gardens Building.' "

When demolition was nearly complete in October, Wright was contacted by the *Daily News*. He evoked an image of his all-but-forgotten concert garden as it should have been by then:

> [Its walls] would be covered with the climbing ivy the scheme craved with a natural hunger. The solidly built place would now be polished, mellowed, enriched by years of good care, hallowed by pleasant associations — a proud possession of any great city.

Wright ended by asking the questions that so many have asked since: Is there no Chicago honor for such love as made the Midway Gardens an oasis of beauty? In the wilderness of smoky dens, car tracks, and drug stores, is there no place for a rendezvous such as its backers knew Chicago needed and believed Chicago wanted?

By the spring of 1930, a gas station stood on the corner of Cottage Grove Avenue and 60th Street. At the back of the lot, a forgotten remnant of wall stood for another quarter of a century. Today only bits and pieces of Midway Gardens survive in various collections around the country.

Given this commission by cosmopolitan friends, Wright had created a setting for relaxed dining and serious listening. Tailored to the Chicago society that the architect knew so well, it reflected at the same time Wright's encounters with new forms of Old World culture and pleasure. Chicago responded heartily to the great dream of Wright, Waller, and Matthews, but when the dream turned into a financial nightmare, no worthy Maecenas stepped forward to its rescue. A decade later, a second chance to salvage and restore the remnants of Midway Gardens was met with silence, and Chicago's great concert garden disappeared. In 1915 Prairie School architect John Van Bergen, another student of Wright's, had proclaimed Midway Gardens "the most vital, living example of American architecture of this class yet produced . . . a monument which will stand unparalleled for many years." Midway Gardens is long vanished, but its design remains "unparalleled" in uniting all the arts in the creation of an architecture of pleasure.

H. L. Mencken and Literary Chicago

Anthony Grosch

With characteristic boldness and zest, H. L. Mencken in 1917 and again in 1920 startled the literary world with, of all things, accolades to Chicago. The praise came in two newspaper columns, one called "Civilized Chicago," which first appeared in the *New York Evening Mail,* and the other, "The Literary Capital of the United States," in London's *The Nation.* The Chicago of Mencken's heyday abounded with literary and intellectual vitality, independence, and strength. Chicago was still new, and Mencken relished its spirit and its remarkable literary bloom.

To Mencken, Chicago represented honesty, freshness, and the true national spirit. Lying out on the prairie at the edge of a giant freshwater lake, Chicago was the center of the hinterland, a word Mencken used with alacrity. Deep in the interior of the continent, Chicago lay in apparent isolation from the refined or dainty influences of the East and beyond. Even its name, having come into American English through the French from the Indian, sounded un-European, un-English, foreign, exotic. The city rose from native soil like the plant from which comes its name — the sturdy and stinky wild onion. The city also grew like a weed, within a wink of history, leading the novelist Henry Blake Fuller to observe in 1895 that Chicago had risen "from an Indian village to a metropolis of two millions within the lifetime of a single individual." Conceived and nourished by the American nation, Chicago — for Mencken — best exemplified the national culture. In "Civilized Chicago" he boldly asserted: "A culture is bogus unless it be honest, which means unless it be truly national — the naif and untinctured expression of a national mind and soul."

In antebellum Chicago, Yankee New Englanders and New Yorkers had begun a civilization. Almost as soon as it had been established, into Yankee Chicago teemed the youth of the rural Midwest and the immigrants from across the ocean. The city manifested the din and grime of factories, the bellow and stench of stockyards, the bustle and clatter of streetcars and drays, the steam and soot of engines and trains. Disparate people mixed with disparate things to make a powerful but often discordant society. The result was that Chicago, Mencken declared, "is overgrown, it is oafish, it shows many of the characters of the upstart and the bounder, but under its surface there is a genuine earnestness, a real interest in ideas, a sound curiosity about the prodigal and colorful life of the people of the republic." So from the bowels and babble of raucous Chicago emerged refinement too — a great university, an orchestra, museums, libraries, buildings — the spirit of all this shown off so splendidly at the World's Columbian Exposition of 1893.

Perhaps the exposition was the finest monument to Yankee Chicago, and Mencken may have too eagerly dismissed the New England influence on the city when he said that "the sharp winds from the lake seem to be a perpetual antidote to that Puritan mugginess of soul which wars with civilization in all American cities." Despite Mencken's frequent blasts at the Puritans, the professors, and all who represented genteel America, the people who belonged to this very class produced in Chicago not only the city's achievements in commerce and industry, but also its first flowering in arts and letters.

In the 1890s — often called Chicago's golden decade — there seemed a harmony in civic culture that has never been recaptured. Then the tycoons of railroads, lumber, grain, and meat shared an association with architects, writers, painters, sculptors, and poets. It was a time when after a Friday afternoon concert by Theodore Thomas's symphony orchestra in the Auditorium, artists and their patrons walked down Michigan Avenue to the Fine Arts Building to join for tea and conversation in an informal gathering called the "Little Room." Here assembled many of Chicago's cultural forebears: Mrs. Arthur Aldis, Mrs. William Armour, Hobart Chatfield-Taylor, Mr. and Mrs. Eugene Field, Henry Blake Fuller, Hamlin Garland, Francis Hackett, Major and Mrs. Joseph Kirkland, General and Mrs. A. C. McClurg, Harriet Monroe, Lucy Monroe, Anna Morgan, Mr. and Mrs. Potter Palmer, William Morton Payne, Ralph Fletcher Seymour, Louis Sullivan, Lorado Taft, and many others.

One of the fruits of this first phase of the Chicago Renaissance in the nineties had a profound effect on the young Mencken in Baltimore. This was an avant-garde little magazine called *The Chap-Book,* which boasted among its contributors the likes of Charles T. Copeland, Ralph Adams Cram, Eugene Field, Henry James, H. G. Wells, Max Beerbohm, Paul Verlaine, George Santayana, and Joseph Pennell. Aubrey Beardsley and Will Bradley were frequent illustrators.

In 1921 Mencken enthusiastically remembered *The Chap-Book* and called it a leader in "the movement against the Puritan (and especially New England) hegemony which got under way in Chicago in the middle 90's." But ironically, *The Chap-Book* was started by two young men of New England pedigree: Herbert S. Stone, whose father had founded the *Chicago Daily News,* and H. I. Kimball, whose father was a representative in the South for the Pullman Company. Before publishing in Chicago, Stone and Kimball had met and begun *The Chap-Book* at no place other than Harvard University, the institution that nurtured and spawned Mencken's bitter enemies of the professoriat — Irving Babbitt, Paul Elmer More, and Stuart Pratt Sherman. Mencken was to fight and win the battle against the oppression of the genteel tradition, but even he was indebted in a strange way to it — at least as it was transmitted in Chicago.

The weakness of the genteel writers was a reluctance to depict the indecorous aspects of society and the more disturbing elements of human character. Like Macbeth, they believed in the efficacy of suppression: "Stars, hide your fires,/Let not light see my black and deep desires." Yet their strength was in their responsibility to the community and in their notion that literature ought to influence human conduct for the better. Writers of the genteel tradition dominated the latter nineteenth century in America and

Chicago, and the literary history of Chicago's first century offers several remarkable and noteworthy examples.

In 1856 Juliette Kinzie published an eloquent autobiography called *Wau-Bun* (an Ojibwa word that means "the dawn" or "the break of day"). The book was subtitled *The Early Day in the Northwest.* Kinzie had come to Chicago from Connecticut in 1831 as the bride of John H. Kinzie, whose father had settled across the Chicago River from Fort Dearborn in 1804. Remembering the frontier settlement of her youth, Kinzie recalled her hope that in Chicago a civilization might arise in which "Education and Christianity should go hand in hand, to make the 'wilderness blossom as the rose.' "

In 1872, the year after the Chicago Fire, Edward Payson Roe, a Presbyterian minister originally from upstate New York, published a novel called *Barriers Burned Away.* The book depicts scenes of the Great Fire, during which a German immigrant says: "Men who meet this great disaster with courage and fortitude . . . possess an inherent nobility such as no king or kaiser could bestow." In 1895 Henry Blake Fuller published a novel about Chicago's ruling class called *With the Procession.* Born in 1857 in Chicago, Fuller was the last male descendant of Samuel Fuller, who had sailed on the Mayflower. Immediately following the dose of the 1893 world's fair, a character in the novel looks at the exposition buildings and notes "the universal expectation that the spirit of the White City was but just transferred to the body of the great Black City close at hand, over which it was to hover as an enlightenment — through which it might permeate as an informing force." Also in 1895 Hamlin Garland, who had grown up on midwestern farms, published *Rose of Dutcher's Coolly,* a novel about a Wisconsin farm girl who pursues a writing career in Chicago, where she becomes part of a cultural circle reminiscent of the Little Room. Here we read that Chicago is "the Napoleon of cities. A city of colossal vices and colossal virtues." Implying that virtue will triumph, the speaker predicts that in 1920 [Chicago] will be the mightiest center of the English speaking race."

In 1892 when William Rainey Harper organized the University of Chicago, he persuaded Robert Herrick, a Harvard-educated professor at MIT, to come to the new university. Herrick, whose New England antecedents dated back to the 1630s, taught for thirty years at Chicago. He also began publishing novels in the 1890s. In *Chimes,* an autobiographical novel published in 1926, Herrick asserted that the university ought to be "the home of the human spirit, . . . the one withdrawn place of modern life where all the manifestations of humanity could be gathered in essence and — handed on! . . . The enduring, the significant thing was — the Idea, the university itself!" — which was to give its students "the desire to understand, to grope onwards deeper and deeper into the mystery of existence."

Obviously people don't write like that anymore, and we read such things today with some incredulousness. So did Mencken. He, and we, seem more comfortable with what followed from other writers less intent on uplift than a realistic portrayal of lives they had fled (often in the rural Midwest) and of new lives they had found (typically in Chicago). Not that these realists were necessarily better writers or that they took literature more seriously; it was just that they saw the world rather differently — and to Mencken rather refreshingly.

Willa Cather, for example, grew up in the prairie village of Red Cloud, Nebraska. The rails of the Chicago, Burlington and Quincy linked Red Cloud to Chicago, and a memorable event of Cather's youth occurred when a salesman from Marshall Field's arrived with a huge box of fireworks for the Fourth of July.

Versatile Ben Hecht, seen above in 1915, was an integral part of Chicago's "literary renaissance." Acting as war correspondent and reporter for the *Chicago News* between 1914 and 1923, he was also publishing stories in the *Little Review* and *The Smart Set.* As a playwright his most famous work, *The Front Page,* was a collaboration with Charles MacArthur. *(CHS, DN 64757)*

As a young woman Cather visited Chicago to attend the opera, and "in the spring of 1895 . . . she stayed for a week and went to the opera every night." From such experiences came a great novel in 1915 about a prairie girl who moves to Chicago and rises to become a celebrated Wagnerian soprano. Cather called it *The Song of the Lark,* after Jules Breton's painting in The Art Institute of Chicago.

In Floyd Dell's 1921 novel *Moon-Calf,* a young writer turns his back on small-town Illinois and yearns for Chicago:

> He saw again in his mind's eye . . . a picture of the map on the wall of the railway station — the map with a picture of iron roads from all over the Middle West centering in a dark blotch in the corner. . . .
>
> "Chicago!" he said to himself. . . . the rhythm of [the] word . . . said itself over and over in his mind: "Chicago! Chicago!"

So the literary young scattered throughout the Midwest found their way to Chicago: George Ade from Kentland, Indiana; Edgar Lee Masters from Lewistown, Illinois; Theodore Dreiser from Warsaw, Indiana; Sherwood Anderson from Clyde, Ohio; Vachel Lindsay from Springfield, Illinois; Edna Ferber from Kalamazoo, Michigan; Ben Hecht from Racine, Wisconsin; George Cram Cook from Davenport, Iowa; Ring Lardner from Niles, Michigan; and Carl Sandburg from Galesburg, Illinois. Like Mencken himself, many began writing for newspapers, where they learned to record the authentic sights and sounds of the city. Their titles suggest their subject and style: *Fables in Slang, Chicago Poems, Gullible's Travels, 1001 Afternoons in Chicago, Tales of Chicago Streets.* In such Chicago writing Mencken began to hear the true speech of the people.

But it remained for Theodore Dreiser, in the first year of the century, to present distinctively new content and a thoroughly new attitude in fiction. In his novel *Sister Carrie,* a young girl comes from Wisconsin to Chicago, lives with a traveling salesman, leaves for New York with a married man, and rises to become a prominent actress almost through pure chance and without any admirable qualities of character. Because such frankness was repugnant to the genteel tradition, *Sister Carrie* was suppressed — very few copies were circulated — and Dreiser mightily discouraged. Mencken read *Sister Carrie* in 1900 and was bowled over: "It made a colossal impression upon me . . . and I became a Dreiserista at once." It stuck with him, and in 1924 he still declared that the American writers of the twentieth century "owe both their opportunity and their method to the revolution that followed *Sister Carrie.*"

Mencken's own influence on Chicago writers was various. As a writer himself, he was admired and imitated, especially by newspapermen like Ben Hecht. In his reviews, Mencken often commended Chicago writers and writing set in Chicago. He said that *The Song of the Lark* was proof that Willa Cather "was a true professional [novelist]." Mencken likened Sherwood Anderson's *Windy McPherson's Son* to Dreiser's *The Titan,* finding the same "gusto of a true artist in it." Of Dreiser's *Jennie Gerhardt,* Mencken wrote: "And the scene in which she is set is brilliantly national too. The Chicago of those great days of feverish money-grabbing and crazy aspiration may well stand as the epitome of America. In his essays, Mencken battled hostile academic critics such as Paul Elmer More of Harvard, who called the Chicago writers "uneducated people" and said that Dreiser "got most of his education in the streets of Chicago and from the free libraries of this and that town" and that Anderson "apparently [owed] his acquaintance with the alphabet to the grace of God."

As an editor too, Mencken was receptive to the Chicago writers. Between 1916 and 1923 *The Smart Set,* which he edited with George Jean Nathan, published work by Dreiser, Cather, Anderson, Masters, and Hecht. As a public defender, Mencken benefited all writers in America with his relentless championing of artistic freedom. He extended all his resources to writers under attack. A notable example was his action when the New York Society for the Suppression of Vice had Dreiser's novel *The "Genius"* banned in 1916. Mencken worked to persuade "the more conservative and famous authors" in America to oppose the ban. He attracted about four hundred signatures to his protest, which drew national attention to the evils of censorship.

And Mencken was a friend. His encouragement and suggestions were invaluable to Dreiser, who told Mencken about many of the other promising writers in Chicago. Dreiser had been befriended by Floyd Dell, who introduced him to many of the habitués of the South Side bohemia at Fifty-seventh Street and Stony Island Avenue. Dreiser then encouraged Mencken to do what he could on their behalf. Mencken's famous salutes to Chicago resulted.

The question arises whether these accolades to Chicago were sincere and not just more of Mencken's spoofery. Fanny Butcher, longtime Chicago literary journalist, recalled that "Ben Hecht told me once that Mencken's labeling of Chicago . . . as the literary capital of the United States was one of his best jokes — a slap at the complacency of New York." It is true that his title provoked controversy and infuriated New York; it was classic Mencken mischief. Yet he meant what he said. He discovered in Chicago the city that best personified America. In Chicago stories and novels, Mencken read credible tales of national life in the American vernacular.

In both "Civilized Chicago" and "The Literary Capital of the United States" Mencken stressed a fundamental point: that in the first two decades of the twentieth century Chicago had made a remarkable contribution to

American arts and letters. He cited George Ade's *Fables in Slang,* Edgar Lee Masters's *Spoon River Anthology,* Theodore Dreiser's *Sister Carrie,* and Sherwood Anderson's *Winesburg, Ohio.* He mentioned in passing Finley Peter Dunne, Joseph Medill Patterson, and Robert Herrick. In his typically outrageous manner, Mencken announced: "It was Chicago that turned out Ring Lardner, the first American author to write in the American Language." Continuing, he proclaimed: "It was Chicago that produced Henry B. Fuller, the pioneer of the modem American novel. It was Chicago that inspired and developed Frank Norris, its first practitioner of genius. And it was Chicago that produced Dreiser, undoubtedly the greatest artist of them all."

Discerning that activities of historic significance had occurred recently in Chicago, Mencken summarized the city's achievements in theater, poetry, publishing, painting, music, and architecture:

The first and best Little theater in America was set up in Chicago [by Maurice Browne in 1912].

Out in Chicago you will still find the first magazine [*Poetry,* founded by Harriet Monroe in 1912] ever devoted to . . . new verse, and either the actual corpse or the plain tracks of four-fifths of its best professors, from Vachel Lindsay to Carl Sandburg, and from Harriet Monroe to Edgar Lee Masters.

It was Chicago . . . that launched the Chap Book saturnalia of the nineties — the first of her endless efforts to break down formalism in the national letters and let in the national spirit. It was Chicago that produced the "Little Review" [Margaret Anderson's famous literary magazine begun in 1914].

And so in painting, in play writing, in music, even in architecture. The only architectural novelty that America has ever achieved, the skyscraper, was born in Chicago — the fact almost goes without saying.

Harriet Monroe encouraged Carl Sandburg by publishing him in her newly founded journal *Poetry: A Magazine of Verse,* beginning around 1913. Surrounding Sandburg in this 1933 photograph are his wife *(seated, left),* author Mrs. Julia Peterkin *(seated, right),* and *(standing left to right)* Mrs. Carl Hendrickson, literary critic Fanny Butcher, and Harriet Monroe. *(CHS, ICHi-19377)*

With his sagacity about America, Mencken recognized the Chicago Renaissance at a time when most of its makers confess they were unaware of it. His two articles remain fresh today, filled with wit and spark as well as observations quoted again and again by writers seeking to capture Chicago. Two quotations are especially memorable. The first, from the beginnings of "The Literary Capital of the United States":

> Chicago the unspeakable and incomparable, at once the most hospitably cosmopolitan and the most thoroughly American of American cities.

The second, from the closing words of "Civilized Chicago";

> I give you Chicago. It is not London-and-Harvard. It is not Paris-and-buttermilk. It is American in every chitling and sparerib, and it is alive from snout to tail.

These animated words ended Mencken's applause for Chicago both in a material and in a spiritual sense. Never again did Mencken himself write about the culture and literature of Chicago. It was partly because by the early 1920s, the vitality he admired in Chicago had dissipated, and many of the writers earlier associated with the city had moved away. But it was also partly Mencken himself. It is well known that when he left *The Smart Set* in 1923 and began the *American Mercury* in 1924 his interest in literature declined as his interest in social and political issues rose. As this happened his attitude toward Chicago changed, and through the pages of the *American Mercury,* the erstwhile "literary capital of the United States" felt his sting.

It came via a young newspaperman named Samuel Putnam, who had been writing art and literary criticism for the *Chicago Evening Post* and lamenting Chicago's cultural deficiencies. One day he received a letter from Mencken, which asked, "Why don't you do an article for the *Mercury,* showing up those phonies out there?" Putnam, in 1947, recalled:

> In those days it was "Mencken giveth and Mencken taketh away." Having crowned Chicago as the literary capital in the first place, he had decided that it was now time to dethrone it, and, in accordance with the *Mercury*'s policy, he preferred a local hatchet man for the job. I was elected and I accepted. An interesting correspondence followed in which Henry L. became very specific, and as the proofs came through, I found that he had thought of still more victims whom he wished me to add to the list. There were certain scalps that he wanted, chiefly those of the *Daily News*–Schlogl crowd. [Schlogl's was a tavern that was the haunt of newspapermen and other Chicago literary figures in the 1920s and was the subject of Harry Hansen's recollections in *Midwest Portraits* (1923).] He was especially bitter toward the late Keith Preston, then columnist on the *News,* who it seemed had been guilty of *lèse-majesté.*
>
> When my article finally appeared in the August 1926 *Mercury,* it bore the startling caption: "Chicago: An Obituary." The effect was instantaneous and bordered on riot. I was assailed by columnists and literary organizations all over town. A mass meeting was held at which I was all but lynched in effigy and I was read out of the Press Club for my remarks about that institution. . . .

Anyone who reads "Chicago: An Obituary" can see why the local writers were inflamed. The article lists thirty-six writers who left the city. Following were the names of forty-eight who remained with the rhetorical question: "How does this list compare with that of the emigrés?" So in 1926 Mencken abruptly withdrew the title, "The Literary Capital of the United States," which he had bestowed in 1920, thus ending his formal relationship with literary Chicago.

But his spirit remained to inspire the next generation of young Chicago writers. Because of Mencken, they faced fewer of the taboos that had bedeviled their elders. Although close enough in time to be deeply touched by Mencken's influence, the Chicago writers who came of age between the world wars were neither reviewed nor published by him. In 1938 Mencken himself noted that he read fiction with "decreasing interest." His friendship with Dreiser had cooled, and he had lost touch with novelists generally. An exception was James T. Farrell, whose *Studs Lonigan* may have reminded Mencken of Dreiser's "naturalism." Farrell and Mencken corresponded, and in his letters Mencken praised and encouraged Farrell. Yet Mencken never reviewed any of Farrell's books. In a 1940 interview Mencken remarked: "Wonderful stuff in those Chicago tales. Whoever doesn't like Farrell is an idiot or a liar." Mencken was undoubtedly pleased and amused by the fact that his name actually found its way into an episode of *Studs Lonigan.* Preaching a sermon to the young adults of Studs's parish on the South Side, a priest denounces the books of that fake sage of Baltimore, that man who profits by telling youth to read Nietzsche. I refer to H. L. Mencken. Who is H. L. Mencken? He is a noisy, vociferous, and half-baked little man. What does he say? He says: "Read Nietzsche!"

Mencken was delighted.

The Chicago writers of the 1930s and 40s and of subsequent years possessed characteristics Mencken would have approved. They were often not of Anglo-Saxon stock; they wrote the language as spoken by actual Chicagoans; and they never looked back to the genteel tradition. Unlike earlier writers, who were pilgrims from the hinterland, these writers were often either born in Chicago or reared as youths in its neighborhoods. They tended to find Chicago both depressing and stimulating. Yet Mencken's indirect or direct influence persisted with them too. Saul Bellow recalls that in the 1930s he went to the public library to read the novels and poems of Sherwood Anderson, Theodore Dreiser, Edgar Lee Masters, and Vachel Lindsay. These were people who had resisted the material weight of American society and who proved — what was not immediately obvious — that the life lived in great manufacturing, shipping, and banking centers, with their slaughter stink, their great slums, prisons, hospitals, and schools, was also a human life. It appeared to me that this one thing, so intimately known that not only nerves, senses, mind, but also my very bones wanted to put it into words, might contain elements that not even Dreiser, whom I admired most, had yet reached.

Today, in Bellow's novels stands the evidence of the longings of a boy on the Jewish West Side who received the Chicago literary heritage and went on to make of it more than he had received.

And Richard Wright, who came in his late teens from the Deep South to Chicago as part of the great black migration north, felt it too. In *Black Boy,* his terse autobiography, Wright tells of the impact of Mencken on him. As an adolescent in Memphis, Wright had by chance come across an editorial denouncing Mencken. He was curious about the kind of man the *Memphis Commercial Appeal* would castigate publicly, and he determined to learn more. Because the Jim Crow laws prevented blacks from using the public library, Wright had to borrow a card from a sympathetic white man, forge a note, and pose as an errand boy even to have the chance to read Mencken. Wright recalls: "I opened *A Book of Prefaces* and began to read. I was jarred and shocked by the style, the clear,

Vachel Linsday's poetry was fraught with symbolism and written to be chanted, which he did in performances while vagabonding around the country.
(CHS, ICHi-11547)

clean, sweeping sentences. Why did he write like that? And how did one write like that?" His reading set Wright to using a dictionary and to asking, "Who were these men about whom Mencken was talking so passionately?" Under Mencken's influence, Wright — for the first time in his life — began to read seriously. He started reading many of the writers discussed by Mencken. "I read Dreiser's *Jennie Gerhardt* and *Sister Carrie,*" says Wright, "and they revived in me a vivid sense of my mother's suffering; I was overwhelmed. I grew silent, wondering about the life around me." Later, Wright remembers, "I bought a ream of paper and tried to write." Such were the lonely beginnings of Wright's novel of Chicago's Black Belt, *Native Son,* published in 1940.

With the novels of Farrell and Wright, Chicago fiction moved into an exceptional period of literary naturalism. Despite Mencken's retirement from literature, his early feelings toward Chicago carried an implied prediction of literary continuity. "In Chicago," Mencken had said in 1920, "there is the mysterious something that makes for individuality, personality, charm; in Chicago a spirit broods upon the face of the waters." This spirit infused Willard Motley's 1947 novel of life on West Madison Street, *Knock on Any Door,* in which Nick "Pretty Boy" Romano goes to his death in the most poignant electric chair scene in American literature and leaves the reader with the chilling words: "Live fast, die young and have a good-looking corpse!" Nelson Algren in 1949 published *The Man with the Golden Arm,* which depicted the perverse beauty of West Division Street and the plight of a drug-addicted gambler, Frankie Machine, whose poetic epitaph goes:

It's all in the wrist, with a deck or a cue,
And Frankie Machine had the touch.
He had the touch, and a golden arm —
"Hold up, Arm," he would plead,
Kissing his rosary once for help
With the faders sweating it out and —
Zing — there it was — Little Joe or Eighter from Decatur,
Double trey the hard way, dice be nice
When you get a hunch bet a bunch,
It don't mean a thing if it don't cross that string,
Make me five to keep me alive,
Tell 'em where you got it'n how easy it was —
We remember Frankie Machine
And the arm that always held up.

The notion exists that Chicago literature stopped, if not in the 1920s, then certainly at the end of the 1940s, after the great years of naturalism. By mid-century all seemed finished. Or such was the impression conveyed by Nelson Algren in his ardent yet caustic work of 1951, *Chicago: City on the Make,* and by A. J. Liebling in his famous *New Yorker* articles collected and published in 1952 as *Chicago: The Second City.* Algren lamented that Chicago "used to be a writer's town," and Liebling remarked: "For a city where, I am credibly informed, you couldn't throw an egg in 1925 without braining a great poet, Chicago is hard up for writers."

Mencken said that he saw in Chicago "the whole gross, glittering, excessively dynamic, infinitely grotesque, incredibly stupendous drama of American life." And he saw clearly enough. In the 1950s and 1960s writers representing the city's mixture of racial, religious, and ethnic groups continued to render the variegated life of Chicago — novels such as Arthur Meeker's story of Chicago's wealthy in *Prairie Avenue,* Gwendolyn Brooks's lyric expression of black womanhood in *Maud Martha,* Meyer Levin's sensitive interpretation of the Leopold and Loeb case in *Compulsion,* Harry Mark Petrakis's story of the Greek immigrants on Halsted Street in *The Odyssey of Kostas Volakis,* and Ronald L. Fair's narrative of racial violence on the South Side in *Hog Butcher.*

In the 1970s and 1980s the stream continued, including Cyrus Colter's account of black family life in *The Rivers of Eros,* Mark Smith's panorama of social classes and neighborhoods in *The Death of the Detective,* John R. Powers's rendition of a South Side boyhood in *The Last Catholic in America,* Saul Bellow's chronicle of a literary intellectual in *Humboldt's Gift,* John Mella's surrealistic vision of the city in *Transformations* (whose narrator, incidentally, asserted that The Newberry Library "housed, deep in its bowels, . . . a revolutionary clinic for the study and cure of language disorders, a class of ailments that, among the literate population, was becoming increasingly common"), William Brashler's portrait of Uptown in *City Dogs,* Shirley Nelson's depiction of the Moody Bible Institute in *The Last Year of the War,* and Tony Ardizzone's story of growing up on Fullerton Avenue in *In the Name of the Father.*

Further evidence — thus far in the 1980s — in novels, short stories, essays, poems, and plays and in the numerous recent books on architecture, politics, history, and social conditions shows an impressive body of writing on Chicago. Almost seven decades after Mencken first told the world about literary Chicago, the city and its writing hold much promise. Indeed, Chicago may be enjoying another renaissance. Of course, if he were alive today and writing as he had in the first quarter of the century, Mencken in his inimitable style would exuberantly and ruthlessly expose the bogus elements of Chicago's life and letters. Yet Mencken's dominant interest was the American people and their republic, and Chicago served only as a brief and passing example in the corpus of his writing. At the height of his powers Mencken aimed to wrest control of the national culture from those he deemed "*Boobus americanus:* the most timorous, sniveling, poltroonish, ignominious mob of serfs and goose-steppers ever gathered under one flag in Christendom since the end of the Middle Ages." Mencken found in Dreiser and other literary realists, many of whom were linked to Chicago, fighters warring against the ignorance and oppression of puritanical America.

Today, because of Mencken, the hostility expressed early in the century by the publishing and critical establishment toward Dreiser seems absurd. As testimony to his genius, an observation by Mencken about

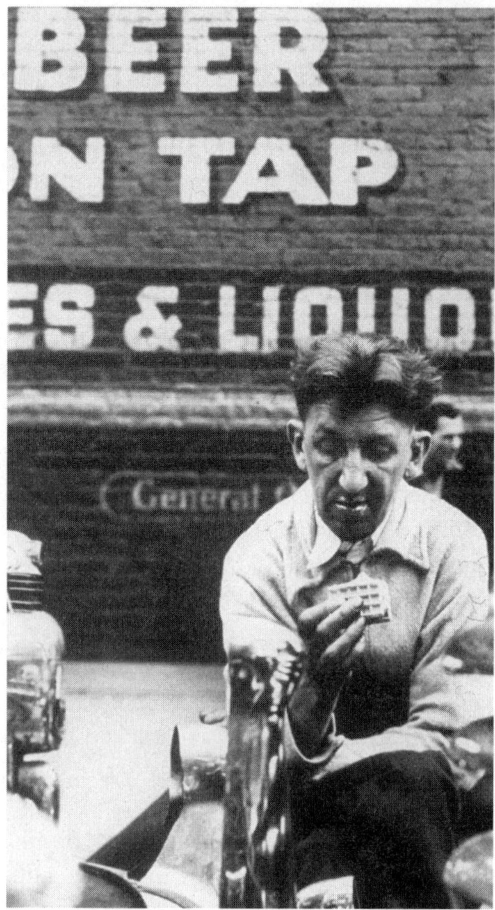

Nelson Algren on North Clark Street, late 1940s. Photograph by Arthur Siegel.
(CHS, ICHi-19378)

Chicago in 1920 remains true today and will surely last as long as there is a breath of spirit in the city. It might well be taken as an enduring civic motto: "[Chicago] is colossally rich; it is ever-changing; it yearns for distinction."

The following pages offer glimpses of Chicago, both literary and pictorial. The excerpts come from a variety of works of diverse styles.

Nelson Algren (1909-1981)

When the peke-and-pansy season is past they get one fleeting glint of the City of Light like their world-city out of the books — and know, in that swift homesick moment, that they're as close to home, and as far, as ever they'll be.

For Paris and London and New York and Rome are all of a piece, their tendrils deep in the black loam of the centuries; like so many all-year-round ferns tethered fast in good iron pots and leaning always, as a natural plant ought, toward what little light there is. But Chicago is some sort of mottled offshoot, with trailers only in swamp and shadow, twisting toward twilight rather than to sun, a loosely jointed sport too hardy for any pot. Yet with that strange malarial cast down its stem. . . .

But Hustlertown keeps spreading itself all over the prairie grass, always wider and whiter: the high broken horizon of its towers overlooks this inland sea with more dignity than Athens' and more majesty than Troy's. Yet the caissons below the towers somehow never secure a strong natural grip on the prairie grasses.

A town that can look, in the earliest morning light, like the fanciest all-round job since Babylon. And by that same night, south down State or north on Clark or west on Madison, seem as though the Pottawattomies had been the wisest after all.

Chicago: City on the Make, 1951

Sherwood Anderson (1876-1941)

It was a wonderful place, that South Water Street in Chicago where Sam came to make his business start in the city, and it was proof of the dry unresponsiveness in him that he did not sense more fully its meaning and its message. All day the food stuff of a vast city flowed through the narrow streets. Blue-shirted, broad-shouldered teamsters from the tops of high piled wagons bawled at scurrying pedestrians. On the sidewalks in boxes, bags, and barrels, lay oranges from Florida and California, figs from Arabia, bananas from Jamaica, nuts from the hills of Spain and the plains of Africa, cabbages from Ohio, beans from Michigan, corn and potatoes from Iowa. In December, fur-coated men hurried through the forests of northern Michigan gathering Christmas trees that found their way to warm firesides through the street. And summer and winter a million hens laid the eggs that were gathered there, and the cattle on a thousand hills sent their yellow butter fat packed in tubs and piled upon trucks to add to the confusion.

Windy McPherson's Son, 1916

Henry Blake Fuller (1857-1929)

The grimy lattice-work of the drawbridge swung to slowly, the steam-tug blackened the dull air and roiled the turbid water as it dragged its schooner on towards the lumber-yards of the South Branch, and a long line of waiting vehicles took up their interrupted course through the smoke and the stench as they filed across the stream into the thick of business beyond: first a yellow street-car; then a robust truck laden with rattling sheet-iron, or piled high with fresh wooden pails and willow baskets; then a junk-cart bearing a pair of dwarfed and bearded Poles, who bumped in unison with the jars of its clattering springs; then, perhaps, a bespattered buggy, with reins jerked by a pair of sinewy and impatient hands. Then more street-cars: then a butcher's cart loaded with the carcasses of calves — red, black, piebald — or an express wagon with a yellow cur yelping from its rear; then, it may be, an insolently venturesome landau, with crested panel and top-booted coachman. Then drays and omnibuses and more street-cars. . . .

With the Procession, 1894

Robert Herrick (1868-1938)

"I'll give you fifteen to drive a wagon," he said offhand. . . .

In that way I made the second round of the ladder, and went whistling out of Dround's packing-house into the murky daylight of the Stock Yards.

I liked it all. Something told me that here was my field — this square plot of prairie, where is carried on the largest commissariat business of the world. In spite of its filth and its ugly look, it fired my blood to be a part of it. There's something pretty close to the earth in all of us, if we have the stomach to do the world's work: men of bone and sinew and rich blood, the strong men who do the deeds at the head of the ranks, feed close to the earth. The lowing cattle in the pens, the squealing hogs in the cars, the smell of the fat carcasses in the heavy wagons drawn by the sleek Percherons — it all made me think of the soft, fertile fields from which we take the grain — the blood and flesh that enter into our being.

The bigness of it all! The one sure fact before every son and daughter of woman is the need of daily bread and meat. To feed the people of the earth — that is a man's business. My part was to drive a wagon for Dround at fifteen a week, but I walked out of the Yards with the swagger of a packer!

The Memoirs of an American Citizen, 1905

Willard Motley (1912-1965)

Nick turned onto Maxwell Street. Before him stretched the Maxwell Street Market extending between low, weather-grimed buildings that knelt to the sidewalk on their sagging foundations. On the sidewalk were long rows of stands set one next to the other as far as he could see. On the stands were dumped anything you wanted to buy: overalls, dresses, trinkets, old clocks, ties, gloves — anything. On what space was left near the curb were pushcarts that could be wheeled away at night. There were still other rough stands — just planks set up across loose-jointed wooden horses: hats for a quarter apiece, vegetables, curtains, pyramid-piled stacks of shoes tied together by their laces — everything. From wooden beams over store fronts, over the ragged awnings, hung overcoats, dresses, suits and aprons waving in the air like pennants. The noises were radios tuned as high as they could go, recordshop victrolas playing a few circles of a song before being switched to another, men and women shouting their wares in hoarse, rasping voices, Jewish words, Italian words, Polish and Russian words, Spanish, mixed-up English. And once in a while you heard a chicken cackling or a baby crying. The smells were hot dog, garlic, fish, steam table, cheese, pickle, garbage can, mould and urine smells.

Knock on Any Door, 1947

Theodore Dreiser (1871-1945)

There is nothing in this world more delightful than that middle state in which we mentally balance at times, possessed of the means, lured by desire, and yet deterred by conscience or want of decision. When Carrie began wandering around the store amid the fine displays she was in this mood. Her original experience in this same place had given her a high opinion of its merits. Now she paused at each individual bit of finery, where before she had hurried on. Her woman's heart was warm with desire for them. How would she look in this, how charming that would make her! She came upon the corset counter and paused in rich reverie as she noted the dainty concoctions of colour and lace there displayed. If she would only make up her mind, she could have one of those now. She lingered in the jewelry department. She saw the earrings, the bracelets, the pins, the chains. What would she not have given if she could have had them all! She would look fine too, if only she had some of these things.

Sister Carrie, 1900

"Ain't We Got Fun?"

Lewis A. Erenberg

Although the world's Columbian Exposition of 1893 is regarded as one of Chicago's greatest artistic achievements, the fair was also important to the development of the city's entertainment and amusement industry and to twentieth-century urban life. The organization of the fair demonstrated two very different attitudes about leisure and amusement. To reflect the official goals of the exposition — the pursuit of culture, gentility, and refined leisure — planners laid out chaste white Beaux Arts buildings, graceful walkways, and romantic lagoons throughout the Jackson Park fairgrounds. These aesthetic wonders were created to satisfy the middle class's longing for a vision of harmony and unity; as well as to inspire, uplift, and educate the masses. The vision of the White City as an orderly and disciplined community trumpeted technology, culture, and women as the foundation of a new American urban society. But the fair organizers also realized that less elegant amusements were necessary to attract crowds to the fairgrounds to see the official vision. The Midway, a mile-long amusement zone separate from the fairgrounds (but officially part of the exposition), offered the public the thrilling Ferris wheel, exotic oriental belly dancers, and many more elaborate and titillating attractions and amusements. The Midway gave people what they really wanted — amusements without relation to culture, body without refinement.

The Columbian Exposition juxtaposed these two conflicting views of leisure. It reaffirmed the dominant Victorian ideal of culture, a feminine perspective that stressed activities of the mind over base pleasures of the body. Advocates of this view embraced values of work and industry, restraint and order, home and family. The fair also legitimized the amusements of the Midway. These male-oriented entertainments promoted sensuality and frivolity, thrills and danger, anarchy and impulse. The appearance of these two worlds side by side at the fair portended an important change in the development of Chicago's urban culture. For the next thirty years, these "lower" amusements steadily gained popular support and began to play an important role in urban life. At the same time, Chicago's elites would pursue genteel leisure, struggling to maintain family standards of entertainment.

Throughout most of the nineteenth century, Chicagoans experienced a double standard that permitted men of all classes many public freedoms denied to women. This was especially true of amusements, a world largely of men who lived outside official familial values. Here, Chicago's anarchic life of gambling, rough-and-tumble politics, and aggressive business thrived.

The saloon, a lower-class male preserve offering liquor, sports, politics, and informal entertainments such as singing and dancing, was the center of this world. Providing a loose atmosphere that allowed men to indulge as they pleased, the saloon functioned as a male sanctuary from the growing world of domesticity. Chicago had many kinds of saloons. As historian Perry Duis shows, exclusively ethnic saloons were found in Polish and Italian neighborhoods, while more cosmopolitan institutions were run by the Germans and the Irish throughout the city. The latter were especially popular downtown. Some hotel saloons, such as the Tremont House's Men's Cafe, were considered "nice" affairs. But typical rowdy male saloon behavior — informal mixing, drinking, and camaraderie — was hardly genteel. Saloons were off limits to proper women; consequently, women who frequented them were considered prostitutes. The German beer garden was an exception to this rule. Drinking beer in a garden-like setting was part of the German continental Sunday. Women and children were welcome to join the beer garden festivities (there was sometimes a band), but they were only allowed to participate *en famille.* No unescorted women were admitted into the beer garden, thus eliminating the possibility of informal mixing with women outside familial control. Disturbed at first by the beer drinking, native-born Americans soon came to accept the beer garden as a respectable place to spend leisure time.

Variety was another male entertainment linked to alcoholic intimacy, and thus it too was considered disreputable by genteel Victorians. Performed in saloon music halls, variety shows attracted lower-class men with drink, dancing, singing, and comedy sketches. Often located in a red-light district, the rowdy variety hall featured performer-audience interaction: patrons hissed, jeered, stamped, and shouted at low comedians. Variety catered to a largely male audience until the late 1880s when it, along with dime museums, was transformed into vaudeville to attract a family trade.

The public dance hall was considered an equally dangerous threat to Victorian values of work, order, and restraint. The upper and middle classes danced in the privacy of their own homes, where they could insure that women would not mix with men of questionable backgrounds. Until the 1890s, lower- and working-class dances were also largely private affairs. Ethnic and voluntary benefit societies, religious groups, and social clubs rented space in halls adjacent to or above saloons. They sold tickets to the public, but these groups still tried to control the gatherings, especially their youthful attendees. A new influx of poor immigrants in the 1890s, however, opened public dance halls to anyone with the price of admission.

The most notorious dance halls crowded the red-light districts. The Levee roared, as did its predecessors, largely because Chicago was a wide-open town, and the traditions of democratic anarchy were strong. The dance halls, saloons, gambling dens, sporting houses, and brothels of the Levee provided the most intimate forms of public amusement and thus were prime attractions for visiting businessmen, sailors, transport workers, and men living in the city. A relief from domesticity, the Levee supported male mingling, rough equality, and anarchic behavior longer than any other part of the city. Although the Levee was never officially condoned, middle-class citizens tended to look the other way, allowing the district to flourish, because the Levee centralized vice into one clearly marked space separate from respectable wards and respectable women, Even after the Levee closed in the 1910s, Chicago's city fathers continued to protect prostitution, a testament to the durability of strong male underworld traditions and resistance to formal civilization. For those unable to uphold the official standards of Victorian culture, red-light districts thus offered a "safe" outlet for anarchic male behavior.

Not all traditionally male amusements remained closed to women. By the late nineteenth century, circuses, melodrama, and minstrelsy, in particular, began to present family entertainment. Theater owners created a less informal and more hospitable theater atmosphere to attract a different clientele. As part of this campaign, prostitutes and drinking, eating, and yelling by patrons were prohibited. Women and children soon became the backbone of the matinee theater audience.

Blackface minstrelsy was frequently featured in Chicago theaters. Dating from the 1840s, it was popular with the transient male society of mining communities and industrial cities. Cavorting as the characters "Tambo" and "Bones," white men in blackened faces acted out their interpretation of the black race. Minstrelsy portrayed northern blacks, or "Jim Dandies," as self-indulgent, uppity folks, incapable of self-control. Their bodily impulses, not their minds, dictated their actions. Plantation blacks were depicted as relatively happy because the plantation owners imposed control over their lives. Indulgent in body, with gross lips, eyes, and legs that seemed to dance out of control, black men were seen in minstrelsy as the opposite of whites, whose sturdy producer values working class audiences identified as their own. Yet in wearing the black mask, whites could step outside the boundaries of acceptable behavior and act out the dangerous impulses they denied themselves as they struggled to maintain self-control and genteel standards. By the 1870s, women were admitted to minstrel shows.

Circuses portrayed the rural roots of American life. Beginning in the late nineteenth century, circuses barred prostitutes from their premises and cleaned up their "gyp joint" atmosphere to attract the family trade. The themes of the acts became more suitable for middle-class audiences. Featuring dramatic encounters between beasts and courageous animal trainers and the derring-do of equestrian artists, the drama of the circus highlighted the triumph of morally and physically courageous men over nature. Circus performers demonstrated self-control as a key value, for one slip could send an artist to a certain death. The introduction of three rings to the big top in the 1880s not only symbolized the taming and subduing of nature, but it also structured the audience's experience; it defused the anarchic impulse of the crowd and made it more orderly and decorous.

Melodrama, which broadcast the official values of the age within a sentimental mold, also promoted proper self-control as a standard of Victorian culture and civilization. Attracting both men and women, melodrama featured male heroes who won social success by saving chaste heroines from evil villains. The will power and rationalism expressed in the deeds of heroes in late nineteenth-century plays like *Rip Van Winkle, Davy Crockett, East Lynne,* and *Sherlock Holmes* set the hero apart from the villains, who were either rich and self-indulgent or poor and vicious. By drawing on his "natural" internal morality to depose harsh external authority symbolized by the villain, the hero served just society better. The key to winning the woman was the hero's commitment to gentility. Even rough-hewn Davy Crockett married and con-

Variety show theaters, considered rowdy and disreputable by Victorians, evolved into more respectable houses of entertainment suitable for families by 1900. This combined theater and dime museum was located on State Street between Van Buren and Congress Streets. *(CHS, ICHi-04793)*

tributed to a stable home life. In keeping with the value placed on sexual restraint, heroes and heroines never enjoyed the debilitating fruits of victory.

Beginning in the 1890s Chicago amusements began to change dramatically. The demand for different forms of entertainment came from the two poles of society, the upper and working classes, who questioned the restrictions of Victorian standards. The growing identification of success with money, consumption, and pleasure gave the rich and the poor, not the middle class, the power to shape institutions of amusement. In their search for new values and identities, this generation of urbanites turned to mass entertainment. Finding themselves in increasingly mechanized jobs, children of recent immigrants from southern and eastern Europe sought alternative ways to express their creativity. Caught between European culture and the culture of the United States, they found in amusements some definition of their identity as Americans. Similarly, as more young women of varied backgrounds began working in factories, offices, and department stores, they felt a similar need, and now they had money to develop their personal lives. On the other end of the spectrum, some wealthy turn-of-the-century

Chicagoans found formal etiquette, expensive lifestyles, and European culture unfulfilling. The sons and daughters of Chicago's elite depended on the captains of industry for their existence. Following the social and economic ravages of the 1890s, wealthy young men seeking leadership roles in society emerged from their private lives to spend more time in public. Many young women explored their personalities through new kinds of leisure without having to break from their class and their parents' expectations. Elegant hotels in the Loop catered to upper-class men and women seeking a more public (and publicized) leisure life.

By the 1890s many working-class people had begun to find the circus, minstrelsy, and melodrama too confining and genteel. New forms of amusement emphasizing fewer formal rules of behavior and more audience involvement began to develop. Offering an unusual array of entertainment, along with food, drink, and dance casinos, the amusement park emerged in the twentieth century as a place where ordinary folk learned to spend their money, indulge their impulses, and just enjoy themselves. Steeplechase Park, which opened in 1896 on New York's Coney Island, was followed in 1903 by Chicago's Riverview Park, built by the wealthy

Amusement parks such as Chicago's Riverview allowed visitors to pit themselves against and attempt to master the machines that dominated everyday life. *(CHS, DN 64,657)*

George Schmidt. Modeled after European parks such as Denmark's Tivoli Gardens, Riverview covered seventy-two acres of the city's North Side at Belmont and Western avenues. Intended solely as amusement for the masses — not for educating them to higher culture, contemplating nature, or creating harmony between labor and capital — Riverview departed from the uplifting vision of the 1893 fair and earlier city park plans. In the place of aesthetic marvels and scenic landscaping, Riverview Park offered thrills, excitement, and new experiences in an urban setting. Made easily accessible to all parts of the city by the elevated and street railways, Riverview was soon joined by White City and Midway amusement parks on Chicago's South Side.

Set apart from everyday life, the amusement park gave visitors the chance to test themselves against the machines that dominated urban life. Mastery of technology, not the natural world, was the key to securing human enjoyment in the modern American city. The Scenic Railway at Riverview, for example, a roller coaster installed in 1907, was never intended to be scenic. It was a parody of Chicago's elevated railroads that gave riders a chance to take a risk under relatively safe conditions and to enjoy a minor catharsis of the noise and confusion of the industrial world. By surviving the ride, one mastered the machine. Amusement parks also provided chances for sexual encounters. The frightening, heart-pounding experience of rides often threw men and women into each other's arms, and in the tunnel of love or in the fun house a young couple could elude parents to pet and kiss. Release rather than restraint was the order of the day. At the amusement park, the formal rules of public behavior and the exclusive patterns of one's social and ethnic group could be temporarily suspended.

As it developed in the 1890s, vaudeville replaced the rural roots of minstrelsy, melodrama, and the circus with new urban myths. The new vaudeville circuits, Keith-Albee and Orpheum, aimed to uplift their theaters and present ethnic entertainers to mixed audiences — working-class families, lower middle-class clerks, white-collar employees, and even the elite in the top-dollar houses.

These new entertainment entrepreneurs gilded their theaters and made them into plush agencies of luxury; every patron thus had access to the trappings of wealth. Ushers treated every woman as a lady as part of a special effort to attract women and make them comfortable. The great variety of acts presented on the vaudeville stage reflected the tremendous diversity and abundance of city life: circus acts played out rural roots, minstrel acts portrayed racial stereotypes, and dialect comedians, fancy dancers, monologists, and singers of snappy songs satisfied every taste. To appeal to immigrant groups, many vaudeville acts manipulated the language to portray the audience's difficulty in adjusting to a new country. Like the city, vaudeville was also highly specialized. Vaudeville bills, according to historian Albert F. McLean, were organized with extreme care so that no act would be duplicated. Starting with a dance or animal act, the first half of the bill climaxed with the sub-headliner, usually a comedian. In the second half, the bill might include a magician — such as Harry Houdini — a singer, a dancer, or perhaps a playlet. Strategically located at the end of the show was the headliner, distinguished in the public's mind by his or her salary.

Vaudeville interpreted the material world of technology, money, and enjoyment for urban audiences, redefining success to mean consumption of wealth rather than its pursuit through work. Performers like Houdini escaped from handcuffs, jails, water tanks, and boilers through human strength and

Vaudeville became much more respectable during the 1890s when managers upgraded their theaters to plush, luxurious agencies like the Chicago Opera House.
(CHS, ICHi-19861)

technical knowledge rather than by reliance on the spirit world. Their escapes demonstrated that technology need not be a trap. Vaudeville's animal acts, unlike the ferocious beasts of the circus, showed that nature could be domesticated: trick horses counted, dogs "spoke," and monkeys rollerskated. Finally, Eva Tanguay (the "I Don't Care Girl"), Sophie Tucker, and other women performers offered new and daring perspectives on female sexuality. Chicago's vaudeville theaters were the second major stop on the national circuits, and by the second decade of the twentieth century the city sported two theaters — the Majestic and the Palace — featuring headliners only.

By the 1910s movies competed with live vaudeville for middle-class audiences. Introduced according to legend at the Columbian Exposition as an educational device, movies were soon put to other uses. Cheap and accessible storefront nickelodeons opened in working-class areas, increasing in number and spreading rapidly. Between 1907 and 1908 the number of licensed theaters jumped from 116 to 320; the new amusement reached its zenith in 1913 with 606 nickelodeons in operation. Poor audiences who could little afford transportation costs found them conveniently strung along major thoroughfares like South State Street, Milwaukee Avenue, North Avenue, and South Halsted Street. Abraham Balaban started his movie empire in 1908 on Kedzie Avenue and 12th Street, the heart of the Jewish district, and in the 1910s he opened his first palaces, the Central Park (1917) and the Riviera (1918).

Before the rise of Hollywood, Chicago played an important role in filmmaking.

Among its most notable studios were Essanay and Selig Polyscope. William Selig, a magician interested in projections, built the world's first movie studio. Opening in 1897, it produced *Tramp and Dog* in Rogers Park. In 1907 Selig's studio at Irving Park Road and Western Avenue was the largest in the country. Founded the same year, Essanay studios grew out of George K. Spoor's interest in Edison's Kineloscope, which he had seen at the Columbian Exposition, and out of his partnership with cowboy star Broncho Billy Anderson. Because of the large number of theater personnel in Chicago, both companies initially prospered, employing stars such as Tom Mix, Broncho Billy Anderson, Gloria Swanson, Francis X. Bushman, Wallace Beery, and, for a time, Charlie Chaplin. But two factors eventually destroyed Chicago's moving picture industry. California's weather was better for year-round production, and the Motion Picture Patents Company, of which both studios were members, had its exclusive right to motion picture patents ruled unconstitutional by the courts. New independent companies entered the market, and the dominion of the old studios waned by World War I.

Hailed as democratic drama available to a broad audience at egalitarian prices, the movies capitalized on the principle of simultaneity. Anyone could be watching the same movie anywhere in the land at the same time. With this nationwide reach, movies were a powerful threat to traditional Victorian assumptions about sex and class. Women out shopping could drop into a movie theater unchaperoned; couples might seek the dark for petting. The movies had a strong Americanizing influence on immigrants. The transformation of nickelodeons into full-scale palatial theaters by the late 1910s and 1920s brought the luxuries of the rich to them, and because the films were silent, immigrant children could learn about American life. Like Houdini escaping from confinement, movie audiences were freed from the constraints of their neighborhood and ethnicity to experience a richer life through the power of technology. Whether immigrant or native born, the ordinary moviegoer retreated to the voluptuous surroundings of the theater to transcend the barriers of time, space, and class.

Many urban reformers and moralists questioned how American culture was portrayed in films. The immorality, sexual high jinks, and crime-dramas that characterized many movie plots discouraged middle-class patronage and prompted the reform and censorship activities of Jane Addams, the Juvenile Protective Association, City Club, Chicago Women's Club, Hull-House, Chicago Commons, the Northwestern University Settlement, the Vice Commission, and the Committee of Fifteen, an anti-vice organization comprised of leading citizens. Largely members of old Chicago and midwestern Protestant families, reformers worried that movies would promote vice. A typical pattern, according to Addams, consisted of rural and immigrant children coming to the city, finding jobs in factories, and losing the creative appreciation of work. Instead they found excitement and meaning on the city streets and in low amusements. Many reformers believed that the inhospitable industrial environment destroyed the character of young boys and girls, that the family was being undermined, and that greedy amusement men took advantage of a primitive desire for adventure, amusement, and companionship.

In 1907 Addams tried to prevent outright censorship by using Hull-House as a theater to show films with a moral message. According to Kathleen McCarthy, the poor response to her effort forced her to abandon her plans to use technology for positive reform and moved her closer to her colleagues' censorship position. The reformers demanded police permits for films shown in Chicago and prohibition of all "immoral and obscene" films. They won an eleven-person censorship commission in 1909 to aid the police board, and by 1914 had established a salaried civilian commission, comprised of five men and five women, with sole authority over movie censorship. Under the guidance of reformers, films containing immoral and antiauthority themes and overt sexuality were banned. Because Chicago was a major market, studios submitted films in advance for the board's approval. The success of movie censorship in Chicago established a model followed by other cities.

The drive to reform movies was part of a larger concern with the degeneration of public life in the Progressive period. Fearing the spread of decadence from the rich and vice from the poor, the anxious middle class worried about the future of proper leisure. Seeking to uplift the movie "experience," movie men sought more "respectable" patrons. They cleaned up their theaters, met ventilation laws to make their buildings more comfortable, installed paramilitary ushers to protect women and insure order, and removed objectionable films. Elaborate movie palaces, such as the Uptown on the North Side, and the Chicago and Oriental theaters in the Loop, connected movies to ideals of success rather than to lower-class values. The quality of films improved as they evolved from the peephole dramas of 1907 to longer playlets, serious historical dramas, and, ultimately, full-fledged star vehicles in the 1910s. D. W. Griffith's classic productions, *Birth of a Nation* and *Intolerance,* were attempts to make an art of film drama. Griffith's films spoke to the anxieties of the day. In *Birth of a Nation,* a three-hour extravaganza, a southern family is saved from impassioned and unruly blacks by the Ku Klux Klan. Although banned in Chicago through the efforts of the NAACP, Griffith's masterpiece played on fears that the restrained family, responsible democracy, and success were being destroyed by the ravages of passionate newcomers. The artistic treatment of these themes in this and other films helped draw middle-class patrons to the theaters and legitimize the movies.

By the middle 1910s, other films played on the anxieties of urban life felt by the middle class. Theda Bara introduced the vamp, a woman who expressed her sexuality in a dangerous guise. In other films, historian Larry May asserts in *Screening Out the Past,* positive heroes and heroines like Douglas Fairbanks and Mary Pickford showed the middle class that the pitfalls of urban life — class, industrialization, and the corporation — need not entrap men and women. Usually playing the son of a rich tycoon, Fairbanks typically seeks to escape entrapment in his father's corporation, which is rife with the temptations of luxury and degeneration. Through his athletic prowess and the love of a new kind of woman, Fairbanks reaffirmed a traditional ideal of success and a moral basis for leisure. "Our Mary," meanwhile, played an orphan or an exotic character such as a gypsy, a Hindu, or an Indian, who is eventually saved by an appropriate hero who marries her. Thus, upward social mobility was still assured, and the experiences of women in the modern city could be utilized to enliven modern marriage. It is not surprising that these two stars married at the end of the decade and were the first to play out the cinematic values of personality, vivaciousness, and popularity off the screen. The modern star system was established.

By the 1920s, with movies legitimized, the off- and on-screen lives of stars became guides to personal and private behavior. They represented life lived to the fullest, vitality, and the ability to live safely off the corporate system without being destroyed by it.

As model consumers on screen, they demonstrated new clothes, cosmetics, new ways to dance, and courtship and marriage behavior. Fan magazines printed their advice on love, discussed their marriages and divorces, and published photographs of them spending money. Clara Bow, the "IT" girl, possessed an indefinable quality that attracted men, while Rudolph Valentino portrayed a Latin sensuality that women might have desired in ordinary men. Joan Crawford's films captured a growing youth culture which, by the 1920s, faced the dilemma of how far good girls could go in sexual matters and still maintain their reputations. This moral balancing act suggests how important movies and their stars had become in establishing a new set of values for Americans. Ironically, this infatuation with the star also tended to standardize taste because movies were a form of mass entertainment.

The evolution of the dance hall into a respectable amusement followed a course similar to that of the movies. Because of their close association with saloons and prostitution, dance halls were slow to gain public acceptance. To increase liquor sales, saloonkeepers opened annexes for dancing. By the turn of the century, the number of dance halls had increased with the growing working-class population. According to Jane Addams, young working-class people patronized dance halls for the same reason they patronized movies: for release from the dullness of their factory lives. Throughout the 1910s, drinking at dance halls was a problem. Reform groups made numerous attempts to eliminate alcohol consumption, regulate the types of dances allowed (especially troublesome were rag dances that featured close holds and animal movements), and open municipal halls as alternative spaces for dances. Settlement houses held closely chaperoned dances to safeguard women, but there were too few settlements and too many young women who considered dancing their favorite recreation to make such reform measures effective.

These attempts at regulation alerted private entrepreneurs to the dance hall's commercial potential. By refusing to serve liquor and decorating their dance halls in elegant fashion, they hoped to blunt moral opposition and attract huge numbers of respectable people. In 1922 the Karzas Brothers opened the Trianon at 63rd Street and Cottage Grove Avenue, conveniently located near elevated lines and major bus routes. It opened with a major society gala and continued a "no jazz" policy through the 1920s. Like its North Side sister, the Aragon, which opened in 1926 on Lawrence Avenue off Broadway, the Trianon attracted lower-middle-class clientele as well as working-class folks. Free from the lower-class and disreputable associations that had won the notice of reformers, both the Trianon and the Aragon employed floor spotters to prohibit "disreputable" behavior and patronage. Often designed to evoke the splendor of Louis XIV's palace at Versailles, these dance halls prided themselves on their "high-class" aura. The new ballrooms thus permitted ordinary people to indulge in fantasies formerly limited to the wealthy. Like movie palace patrons they could live out the themes of consumption in their own private dreams filled with romance and aristocratic luxury. In the palatial Trianon, moreover, the sumptuous aristocratic-like surroundings uplifted the sexual atmosphere of the lowly dance hall to new heights of romance. The Aragon's starlit sky and sultry Spanish decor paralleled the better-known movie theaters. It still stands today, a testament to the human desire for release from the everyday world.

Movie palaces and dance halls became firmly established in the 1920s as popular amusements, but the cabaret, or nightclub, became the leading symbol of the Jazz Age.

Rooted in the music halls of the 1880s and the dance halls that boomed after 1900, most early cabarets of the 1910s were part of saloons. Forced to compete with new forms of amusement, saloonkeepers cleared away tables, created dance floors, and hired novelty variety entertainment. Hundreds of saloons soon added small stages and platforms.

Two features gave the cabaret its unique character. One, it offered informal and intimate entertainment in a public setting. Doing turns on the "floor" and among the

To upgrade the reputation of pre-1910 movies, entrepreneurs built luxurious motion picture palaces such as the Chicago Theatre in the Loop.
(CHS, ICHi-19819)

tables, entertainers broke down the barrier between performer and audience. Successful entertainers relied on personal appeal as much as their acts to attract the attention of patrons amid all the clatter and distraction of the saloon. Two, the cabaret also provided a place where the public could dance, eat, and drink under one roof. The anonymity of the cabaret crowd gave Chicagoans a chance to experience and display public intimacy through the dance. The dances were active, based on the shuffle walk-step of black music, and intimate, emphasizing close holds and tight embraces as in the bunny hug or turkey trot. That dancing patrons shared the floor with entertainers suggests that members of the audience were exploring their own "performing selves."

Chicago's cabarets had a much rougher image than those in New York. This was partially a carry-over of the city's strong anarchic tradition and the continuing influence of the underworld and red-light districts. Many of the early cabarets were located in the Levee, attracting lone males out for a good time, the more cosmopolitan movie and theater crowds, and prostitutes. When the Levee closed, the cabarets grew in popularity as places of assignation. Like other amusements, the cabaret developed as a place where men and women could explore new sensations and desirable experiences. Beginning in the 1910s more reputable spots began presenting public dancing. The Edelweiss Gardens, formerly the Midway Gardens (designed by Frank Lloyd Wright), presented "Dining, Dancing and Entertainment" and advertised "the most charming environment, where the cuisine is unexcelled, and the entertainment is unequalled." Attempting to erase the red-light connection, the Edleweiss presented high-class dance acts such as Mr. and Mrs. Carlos Sebastian. The College Inn, located in the Sherman Hotel in the Loop, did the same after about 1911 during the rage for ragtime dancing. Even movie palace mogul A. J. Balaban opened a cabaret, the Movie Inn, at 17 N. Wabash Avenue in 1915, to cash in on the craze for public dancing. Frequented by many Essanay actors, the Movie Inn was divided into booths named for movie stars and decorated with numerous photographs of stars. Within a year, however, the cafe ran into trouble with city authorities as part of a general cabaret crackdown. Too many "gay" blades appeared regularly in the afternoons with young married women from Balaban's own neighborhood. Reformers were concerned about casual mixing between entertainers — especially female — and audience members and the nature of the dances; the issue of afternoon dancing aroused a storm of protest.

As part of a general nationwide scare, the Juvenile Protective Association, the Law and Order League, and other reform groups urged the city council to take action against the cabaret. On July 30, 1913, the association ordered entertainers to restrict their performances to the stage, outlawed the wearing of tights by performers, and ended public dancing. However, there were enough respectable venues featuring public dancing to force the issue into the courts. When police threatened to arrest the Drake's wealthy dance patrons, the hotel challenged the law. In 1916 the Illinois Supreme Court declared the city ordinance unconstitutional, ruling that because the hotel did not charge admission, its dance floor was more private than public, and therefore exempt from amusement licensing of any kind.

The rapid proliferation of cabarets and nightclubs in the 1920s paralleled the rise of speakeasies during the Prohibition era. These "peephole" spots exuded an aura of illegality and danger, prime features of the nightclub as it expanded in the 1920s. Gangsters gained control of the clubs because of their ability to supply illegal alcohol. Al Capone controlled many of the clubs on the South Side; Bugs Moran, the North. The attractions of risk, danger, public intimacy, and a chance to see a good show and rub elbows with celebrities out to play appealed to enough of the public to make the clubs profitable. Youth culture, an outgrowth of the expanding college population, included new forms of courting and dating that coincided with the introduction of women into fast amusements. Young men and women could find privacy in public, and they could also break the conventional bonds of behavior in a fast and intimate atmosphere where money made the wheels of pleasure go round.

Nightlife flourished all over town. In Uptown, one of the trendiest sections of Chicago in the 1920s, movie theaters, ballrooms, and nightspots vied with each other for patrons. The Green Mill Gardens, a gangster hangout on North Broadway, presented Sophie Tucker, Joe E. Lewis, and other celebrities. Rainbo Gardens at Clark Street and Lawrence Avenue enjoyed brief success. Tower Town, north of the river, had dives for the underworld and transients who inhabited the furnished rooms west of Clark as well as Rush Street, an entertainment strip populated by Gold Coast residents. Interspersed were "bohemian" places banking on free love and homosexuality to draw tourists. In the Loop, major clubs inaugurated a revue show policy. The Friars Inn, Ciro's, the Terrace Room of the Hotel Morrison, the Blackhawk, and numerous other nightspots made the Loop as important for nightclubs as it had been for theaters and movie palaces. Chicago was jumping. Women went out as much as men; public dancing and drinking abounded.

The South Side also boomed. The Stroll, the area around South State and 35th streets, had been famous as a nightclub zone since the turn of the century. The Pekin and Vendome theaters presented both film and live entertainment to black audiences. Numerous dance halls and cafes also occupied the zone, including the Dreamland Ballroom, the Entertainer's Cafe, the Sunset, Plantation, and numerous other spots. Although black and tans (clubs where whites and blacks mixed) existed there, the Stroll catered to blacks, largely because they were excluded from white amusements. Loop vaudeville and movie theaters restricted blacks to the balcony, colloquially dubbed "Nigger Heaven." Similarly, white ballrooms, hotels, and cabarets remained segregated. While immigrant whites were allowed to participate in amusements that helped Americanize them, blacks received a different message: remain in the balcony of America forever.

Because the two zones remained largely segregated, passing between them heightened the white nightclub-goer's sense of danger and risk. Jazz in particular attracted whites to the black clubs. Beginning in 1917, Chicago became an important jazz town as numerous exiles from New Orleans made the city their second home, adding to the stock of itinerant piano players and entertainers already in town. King Oliver and Louis Armstrong, appearing at the Lincoln Gardens in 1922 and 1923, presented Chicago with the best jazz in the land. At the Lorraine Gardens was Freddie Keppard's Four. By 1926, the South Side was bursting with jazz activity, and numerous bands such as Sam Wooding's formed here and then left to play in Europe. The Theater Owners' Booking Association (TOBA) circuit broke up and re-formed in the city, making Chicago an important stop on the jazz circuit. King Oliver moved over to the Plantation; across the street, the Sunset hired Carroll Dickerson's large orchestra featuring Louis Armstrong, Earl Hines, and

Zutty Singleton. Yet, while all of these groups played and recorded, Chicago itself was not hospitable to jazz. The best salaries went first to the white sweet orchestras, featuring string instruments and melodic music, that dominated the best ballrooms, such as the Trianon and Aragon, and to black society orchestras (Dave Payton, Charles Elgar, Erskin Tate) second. While the hot New Orleans players became famous enough through recordings to earn a living, they had to play in the more conservative large black orchestras or not work at all.

Yet the chance to hear unadulterated jazz brought numerous white pleasure seekers to black clubs. Crossing the racial barriers, they enjoyed finding exotic entertainment and unbridled sexuality. While these "slummers" sought the utmost in pleasure, white jazz players absorbed, used, and spread the music itself. King Oliver and Louis Armstrong delighted and educated young Chicago musicians. According to Eddie Condon, wherever Oliver, Armstrong, Jimmy Noone, or the Dodds (Baby and Johnny) were playing, young white jazz players could also be found. The Austin High Gang, Dave Tough, Jimmy McPartland, Bix Beiderbecke, Eddie Condon, Mezz Mezzrow, Benny Goodman, and numerous others, adopted black musicians' emphasis on solo playing to a background of collective improvisation. Idealizing black players as natural musicians, many of Chicago's white jazz artists gloried in their own release from the restrictions and conventions of music and from the conservatism of their midwestern families. But they had a rough time of it in Chicago. A conservative Catholic and rural-based city, Chicago glorified the waltz at the Aragon in the personage of Wayne King. The white jazz musicians' pursuit of spontaneous, *personal* freedom in their music was not welcome in the large popular music clubs. Instead, they played the all-male underworld clubs along North Clark Street or the second-rate ballrooms around town. By 1928 most had left for New York, pursuing more lucrative jobs. By then Chicago, like other jazz towns, was a musical colony dominated by New York's music scene. And within a decade these white and black Chicagoans became the backbone of swing music.

From the 1890s through the 1920s, Chicago enjoyed a renaissance of popular culture. Movies, amusement parks, vaudeville, nightclubs, dance halls, and music came to dominate both neighborhood and downtown in the 1920s, a time commonly called the Jazz Age. These new amusements redefined success to include pleasure and consumption. They became mixed-sex activities, but on terms vastly different from the hero-heroine model of early melodrama. Entertainment entrepreneurs won the respect of the middle class for their luxurious and sophisticated establishments and for upholding familial values. These new amusements also created new ways for men and women to court, and they established greater equality for women in leisure activities. Technology, long the bane of the working class, was glorified as an agency for human pleasure and consumption. In all of these entertainments, money was portrayed as the key to success and pleasure.

It was considered dangerous for blacks and whites to mix. Blacks represented the underclass, and therefore were kept outside the influences of Americanization that immigrants enjoyed. Segregated from white amusements, blacks pioneered their own. Their creative revenge was jazz. No matter how unappreciative Chicago was of the new music, the city became one of its centers, and found itself in the midst of a new culture emphasizing pleasure, impulse, and release. The Great Depression of the

1930s closed many dance halls, hotels, movie houses, theaters, and nightclubs, halting the explosion of popular amusements for a time. They would reopen in different forms by 1933 and 1934, but their outline and essence had already been established in Chicago in the preceding decades.

The Saloon in a Changing Chicago

Perry Duis

For some, the old-time saloon was a
gathering place,
A home away from home, or a place to
bring the family;
For others, just a place to stop for a quick
bracer;
For still others, a den of vice.
It was all these things, and a free lunch to
boot.

The afternoon had witnessed strange activities in downtown Chicago. People scurried about carrying small boxes from store basements and back rooms. Limousines backed up to the Fidelity Safety Vault Company on Randolph Street, where uniformed chauffeurs carried out carefully wrapped bottles, and less well-heeled citizens toted bags or carts and even pressed baby carriages into service. It was January 16, 1920. Prohibition would begin at 12:01 a.m., but whatever alcohol Chicagoans could gather inside their homes would be a legal possession.

As evening settled upon the city, things were unusually quiet. The Celtic Bar in the Sherman House was dark, as was Righeimer's luxurious place. Moran's, a downtown landmark since 1883, and Stillson's bar had already been transformed into coffee shops. Hick's Café had in its window a small coffin banked with flowers; in it was a bottle of whiskey. One of the few farewell parties for Demon Rum took place at the Stevens Restaurant, but those celebrants were teetotalers, the same that tomorrow would travel from one former saloon to another drinking victorious toasts of grape juice. The very term "saloon" is still illegal in Chicago.

What disappeared that evening was more than a retail business. It was also a unique social institution, as much a part of Chicago's history as the Water Tower or Hull-House. For more than a century, the corner saloon and its proprietor had been the center of a bitter debate. Temperance folk viewed the saloonkeeper as a plague, a thief who took workingmen's wages and left their families to starve. His substantial girth and diamond stickpin symbolized a prosperity based on Satan's Commerce. Everything that proper citizens viewed as evil in urban society — crime, civil unrest, and corruption — could ultimately be blamed on the "liquor trust."

To the saloonkeeper's friends, on the other hand, a bar was a retreat from the hectic world, a place of relaxation where clocks and traffic jams did not exist, and the barkeep was a professor of common sense and an expert on everything from the rules of card games to city politics to international finance. When Finley Peter Dunne began his newspaper column of biting social commentary in 1893, he chose a mythical saloonkeeper, Martin J. Dooley, as his philosopher.

Whatever one's own view, the saloon and its proprietor demonstrated an important principle in the history of urban social institutions; that the ability to adapt to massive and rapid changes was necessary to survival in nineteenth-century America. Especially in Chicago, that principle was obvious. Few cities in the world grew as rapidly. Few welcomed as many different ethnic groups; in few did the local economy grow and diversify as rapidly; and few witnessed such a swift transformation of outlying rural villages into residential, then commercial, and, finally, industrial neighborhoods. The changes came with lightning speed, and only the ability of the saloonkeeper to adjust to his environment and tailor his service to new customers insured his survival. His adaptability also made the liquor business a durable foe, one which temperance interests were able to conquer only through a constitutional amendment.

The friendly bar on a Chicago corner was the product of years of adaptive evolution, its roots deep in three liquor-selling businesses of the nineteenth century. One was the familiar inn or tavern. The first, the Miller House, opened in 1827, but Samuel Miller and Archibald Clybourne had a competitor only two years later, when James Kinzie and Archibald Caldwell opened the Wolf Tavern. Thus began the liquor dealer's greatest problem: attracting customers away from his rivals. Still these were almost primitive hostelries. As one old-timer, Charles Cleaver, remembered years later:

> The outer door opens into a large room used as a sitting-room for the men folks, and also as a barroom, for in one corner, generally in the angle, you will see a cupboard with two or three shelves. . . . From this room you would enter the family sitting-room, also used as a dining-room for travelers. . . . The upper story, although sometimes divided into two rooms, was often left in one, with beds arranged along the sides. Once in a while you might find a curtain drawn across the further end of the room, affording a little privacy to the female portion of the occupants, but often not even that, the beds being occupied promiscuously, on the first-come-first-served principle.

Although more sophisticated hotels appeared in later decades, and they continued to operate barrooms, the hotels had begun to encounter new types of competitors by the 1850s — the grocers and the wholesale liquor dealers. Both concentrated on bulk sales — barrels and jugs — and their involvement in the retail trade came about almost by accident. Wise customers demanded a sample of the spirits or wine they were about to purchase, so dealers set up small "sample rooms" for tasting. Before long, such facilities began attracting people who were more interested in drinking than in making a purchase to carry home. A number of retail-only places called themselves "sample rooms" and, by the end of the 1850s, that term had become merely another name for a saloon.

Indeed, by the 1850s, retail liquor sales had become a specialized business, and by the end of the Civil War, most barrooms had no connection with groceries, hotels, or wholesale dealerships. Lacking these sidelines, saloonkeepers also began to adapt their businesses to particular areas of the city or to particular groups of customers. The North Division of the city had several beer gardens to cater to the German immigrants who brought their families along, while Irish

An unidentified tavern in Chicago. The saloon was an important social institution in nineteenth- and early twentieth-century Chicago, serving variously as a gathering place, a home away from home, a political forum, and an employment agency. Temperance advocates considered them dens of vice.
(CHS, ICHi-01691)

neighborhoods had dimly lit stand-up bars that sold mostly whiskey and which no "decent" woman would enter. A few downtown places were attractively furnished, and drinks there cost more than in the unadorned neighborhood bars. Between 1860 and 1880, the saloon trade prospered and seemed destined for further prosperity along the same lines.

But a change was in the making. Although the German immigrants, with their taste for lager beer, established only a few breweries in the city before the Civil War, lager became Chicago's most popular drink after 1870. It was light and effervescent, it could quench a parched throat faster than the heavier ale and porter, and its manufacture was simple and inexpensive. Moreover, everything needed to make Chicago a major brewing center was handy. Talented immigrant brewmasters arrived by the dozen. The limestone ridges in some parts of the area made excellent cold-storage cellars, and Lake Michigan's abundant ice made it easy to construct substitutes. Finally, Chicago lay in the center of a major grain and hops market, making those raw materials both plentiful and inexpensive.

The result was a prolific expansion of the lager beer industry after 1870. By the turn of the century, there were over fifty Chicago brewers competing for customers and contending with products shipped in from other cities. Milwaukee brewers had first established major Chicago markets during the disruption caused by the Great Fire of 1871. The widespread adoption of pasteurization, which made it possible to ship chilled beer hundreds of miles without spoilage, allowed Anheuser-Busch of St. Louis to move its brew into Chicago in rubber-lined refrigerator cars. As the wholesale price of beer began to fall, the competition became chaotic. Saloonkeepers in New York or Boston in 1880 paid $15 for a fifty-five gallon barrel of medium-grade beer, but in Chicago, because of the competition between city and outside brewers, saloonkeepers paid only $3.50 and got back a rebate of fifty cents. Such low beer prices could not help but change Chicago's retail liquor business. Low wholesale costs meant inflated retail profits, which allowed many marginally profitable barrooms to remain open. As a result, Chicago became notorious for the number of its saloons.

In the 1870s, the desperate brewers began to employ many gimmicks to win the loyalty of saloonkeepers and thus assure themselves of retail outlets for their beer. They gave away large murals, many of them the infamous saloon nudes, as well as brightly decorated mirrors, steins, and trays, and a few of the larger brewers furnished large glass signs to hang over the front door. Their salesmen promised loans for remodeling and time payments for beer purchases. But it seemed like a losing battle; no deal, however good, legally bound a saloonkeeper to one brewery or prevented him from accepting gifts and buying beer from others. It was Illinois' temperance reformers who unwittingly delivered the individual proprietors into the hands of the brewers.

During the 1880s, the so-called "high license" idea swept the nation. Not a new idea — it had been tried in 1855 — the plan was a simple panacea for the evils of the proliferating saloon. And saloons had indeed proliferated, primarily in Chicago. In 1882, for example, there were 3,759 of them to slake the thirst of 580,693 residents — one pair of swinging doors for every 149 men, women, and children. In some areas, like the old 16th and 17th wards at the lower end of Milwaukee Avenue, there was a liquor license for every dozen drinkers.

A tenfold increase in the license fee, the reformers believed, would close down the worst of the "low dives," slum groggeries that propped up their ailing beer and liquor business with gambling and prostitution. The additional municipal revenue that was generated would finance a larger police department, pay for new streets, and underwrite other city services. After prolonged debate, the Illinois General Assembly passed the Harper High License Act of 1883.

Within a year, it was clear that the new law was having an unforeseen effect. Saloonkeepers who were unable to pay $500 for a license turned to the brewers who, in turn, began purchasing the permits and furnishing them to the retailers. In return, the beermaker demanded that the saloonkeeper sell only one brand of beer and that he purchase it at an inflated figure. Most proprietors had little choice.

The new arrangement permanently altered the retail business in a number of other ways. It initiated an extensive brewery investment in saloons. The larger companies established real-estate offices and began renting prime locations and subletting to licensees. They conducted surveys of traffic patterns in order to locate their saloons on the most profitable sites. They bought buildings when they could, and later even began to construct their own saloon buildings. The handsome structures that remain today on the South Side at 94th Street and Ewing Avenue and Front Avenue between 113th and 115th streets and, on the North Side, at Belmont and Southport avenues are visible reminders of the involvement that the Schlitz Brewing Company once had in the retail business.

Financial control of the saloons by the brewers also transformed the saloonkeeper from an entrepreneur to an employee. By the turn of the century nearly three-quarters of all Chicago barrooms were dominated by the brewers. A prospective proprietor would invest only $50 or $75. In return he received a storefront, fixtures, a supply of whiskey and beer, and glasses. The fixtures, which were turned out in brewery woodshops, were standardized, much as they are in chain groceries. Most important, the decision as to whether the saloonkeeper had failed or succeeded was no longer his. The failure to have enough nickels at the day's end might mean instant foreclosure. He might find himself locked out in the morning. Moreover, his failure often worked to the advantage of the brewer, who could retain only the most talented barkeeps and keep enough licenses and fixtures available to serve the needs of new ethnic groups as they entered the city.

A third of the hopefuls failed each year, and those who survived did so only by attracting new customers, by encouraging loyal ones to drink more, or by adding sidelines. The sidelines included a variety of crimes, almost all of which were unofficially supported by the community. Almost everyone ignored the midnight closing law, for example; when reformers tried to have it enforced, the City Council moved the time back to 1 a.m. Few obeyed that law, either. Public opinion also went counter to the Sabbath law. Mayor Levi Boone, who had advocated Sunday closings along with the high license fee in the mid-1850s, had thereby helped to precipitate the Lager Beer Riot of 1855. Joseph Medill had ordered a crackdown during his post-fire administration. So in 1874, the City Council simply passed a new law requiring that the front door be locked and the shades drawn, leaving the rear and side doors open to the thirsty. Not only did this nullify the idea of Sunday closing, but it also placed a premium on corner locations. After that, no mayor until "Big Bill" Thompson in 1915 dared to demand a quiet Sabbath.

Some saloonkeepers — perhaps 5 percent — became entangled in more serious offenses. The public, however, had its own

An unidentified Chicago saloon. When the saloon license fee rose in the 1880s, many independent saloonkeepers could not afford to stay in business. To keep saloons open and ensure a market for their product, breweries purchased the permits and furnished them to the retailers.
(CHS, ICHi-17433)

definition of crime. Prior to the 1890s, gambling and prostitution were widely thought to be incorrigible masculine weaknesses. Most brothels were accordingly confined to the three vice districts where the north, south, and west streetcar lines entered the Loop, and there was an open gambling district on Clark Street, just north of Madison Street. It was not until 1894 that the Citizens' Association, a group of reformer-businessmen, drove the gambling saloon into secrecy, and the red-light districts did not suffer the same fate until two decades later.

Although Chicago's vice resorts and their unsavory owners attracted most of the attention, most male and a few dozen female proprietors survived legitimately by trying to anticipate the needs of their customers and by adjusting to changes in the neighborhood. Competition caused them to provide more than liquor, and their saloons became important social institutions. The free lunch was an important service: the better the lunch and the more services offered to the patrons, the more nickels in the cash register. And that meant survival.

The variety of saloons seemed endless. Some catered to transients in the city's three skid-row districts. Bars along West Madison Street and on Clark Street at the north and south ends of the Loop doubled as flophouses and cheap dives. Day-labor agencies were located either inside the saloons or nearby, and many of the quarters that the tramps earned passed over the bar. Many of these places for transients were impersonal, quickly ushering into the street those who had run out of money. The free lunch was coarse and unattractive, usually made up of crackers, cheese, and the cheaper cuts of pork and beef.

The saloonkeeper in Chicago's tenement district served a very different constituency and performed other services. His free lunch often fed whole families; unemployed patrons brought along their wives and children. Other neighborhood tragedies called for someone to pass the hat or organize some other form of informal charity. In happy times, the barroom served as a pleasant annex to everyone's crowded tenements. The back room could be reserved for special occasions, and many blushing brides emerged from receptions held there. On quieter evenings, card games and serious discussions of politics were held in many of Chicago's neighborhood saloons.

The neighborhood saloon also served as a kind of communications center. It was stocked with newspapers for those who could read but not afford to buy them. For illiterates who had to depend on verbal information, the saloon, like the grocery store, the clothesline, and the front stoop, was an important meeting place.

The barroom was also a portal to the outside world. The man at the bar could tell you how to get downtown or where to find a job. Many of his neighbors moved frequently and used his place as a permanent mailing address, making it an informal post office. And when relatives arrived from the old country, the address that they nervously clutched belonged to a pair of swinging doors. The man behind the bar would lead them to their families.

This knowledge of the neighborhood and the trust of his customers made the saloonkeeper a natural politician. Many voters assumed that a man who could arbitrate disputed card games could make laws; similarly, if they could trust him to keep their valuables in his safe, they could give him control of the city treasury. And it was obviously in the saloonkeeper's own best interest to become involved in politics. Seven out of thirty-six aldermen in 1886 were saloonkeepers; they could fend off new laws that would damage the business, and their connections were useful in controlling the

Drawing from the *Chicago Tribune*, 1898. Reformers frowned upon women who frequented saloons, suggesting that they were prostitutes. In some neighborhoods, however, families — men, women, and children — gathered together in saloons.
(CHS)

police and manipulating the judicial system when necessary.

Barkeeps were among the city's most colorful politicians. On South Clark Street stood the famous Workingmen's Exchange, presided over by "Hinky Dink" Kenna, whose free lunch could compete with the heartiest restaurant fare. Years later, one of his former customers could still remember the meal: a pair of large pork chops, a heap of fried potatoes, and four slices of toast. From 1891 until 1913, John J. Brennan wielded his "inflooance" as alderman of the 18th Ward on the West Side. His barroom was adjacent to a police precinct station, and his secondary job as a bail bondsman earned many votes from those he saved from a night in jail. Brennan also provided food and lodging in exchange for votes at each year's elections, prompting Raymond Robins, the director of the Municipal Lodging House, to comment that:

> John Brennan comes nearer to living up to the teachings of the scripture than a great many who make greater pretentions to morality. He controls the people of his ward, not because he is base and corrupt, but because he is simple and democratic. He had saved more people from evictions, given more food to hungry men and sent more people to hospitals and kept them there than perhaps any other man in Chicago.

Most of the saloonkeeper-aldermen thrived on chicanery. Nonresident "repeaters" were transported from precinct to precinct on election day, bribed by a free drink. But men like Edward F. Cullerton and John Powers were also able to survive because they could adapt to the ethnic transitions in their own neighborhoods. Both had started out in politics when their constituents were primarily Irish, but when Powers retired his ward was heavily Italian, and Cullerton's Lower West Side neighborhood was predominantly Czech and Polish. Both had to bring the new nationalities into their organizations and adjust to new languages and new customs. Like the barrooms they ran, they had to reflect the characteristics of their surroundings.

Thousands of Chicago liquor dealers faced that same problem. Neighborhoods changed quickly, and each nationality had its own variety of saloon. We have already mentioned the different drinking habits of the Germans and the Irish. Later groups also had their preferences. Poles enjoyed whiskey, but they proudly bought beer made by their countrymen's White Eagle Brewery; Italians drank wine and played cards; Bohemians held weekend dances in rented halls. Other ethnic groups, notably the Greeks and Jews, preferred coffeehouses and other community meeting places and did not generally frequent saloons.

Ethnic changes meant that a saloonkeeper had to decide whether to stay where he was or try to follow his customers. If his trade was large enough, he might try to hire an additional bartender from the incoming nationality, someone who could converse with the newcomers and prepare their favorite delicacies for the sideboard. Or the owner might try to survive the change on his own, counting on the trade of former residents who occasionally returned to the old neighborhood. If he moved out, his replacement would start out with high hopes and financial backing from a brewery.

Many departing saloonkeepers moved into factory districts. There were major clusters of bars near such neighborhoods in Roseland and in Kensington, adjacent to George Pullman's saloonless town; along Ashland Avenue's "Whiskey Row" near the stockyards, and at the gates to the South Chicago steel mills. Such trade also had special requirements. The workingmen demanded a hearty lunch, and the noon-hour traffic was especially brisk. Neighborhood boys toted in dozens of growlers — homely tin pails — for workers who stayed outside. These saloons also cashed the men's paychecks, a service that required the handling of large amounts of cash and increased the risk of holdups. Many places furnished halls for union meetings. There was never any rental charge — provided, of course, the men patronized the bar.

Some proprietors moved onto busy thoroughfares, where service tended to be less personal, and the reputation of the owner was secondary to the location. Spots near park entrances were desirable, although the trade was seasonal and varied with the days of the week. Streetcar transfer corners were the best: riders caught in winter snow or summer heat were easily lured through nearby swinging doors. Many people also came in to use the washrooms, although etiquette required the user to return the favor by patronizing the bar — a practice which convinced temperance leaders that thousands of unwary men had been led to ruin because of simple biological need. Women's clubs demanded that the city erect drinking fountains and washrooms in parks, elevated stations, and other public places. In 1911, the City Council finally gave in, and the publicity that greeted the new City Hall focused as much on the toilet facilities as on any other aspect of the new building. But despite the fanfare surrounding its new rivals, the saloon restroom continued to serve the commuting public.

Saloonkeepers at the edge of town also dealt with strangers. Places which clustered near the entrances of cemeteries served mourners on their way back to town. On the far Southwest Side, the community now known as Mount Greenwood began as a row of bars on 111th Street, opposite the cemetery of the same name. Other roadhouses catered to the weekend carriage trade. During the 1880s, when social groups planned "tally-ho" outings in old twenty-passenger coaches, the ultimate destination was often an old country inn that had become a suburban saloon. When the bicycle fad hit Chicago during the next decade, members of exclusive cycling clubs toured the countryside in caravans and stopped to hold parties in the same bucolic barrooms. During the week, many of these places also hosted farmers on their way to and from the city markets.

In the outlying areas, one could also find liquor in commercialized amusement areas; most of these had begun as beer gardens that added bands and games to attract crowds. During the 1880s, Grenier's Garden, at Madison and Throop streets, held six-day bicycle races on its grounds, and Rudolph Voss's place, on the Southeast Side, had a model coal mine and a village blacksmith shop in full operation. The Relic House, which opened near Lincoln Park soon after the Great Fire, housed hundreds of melted mementos. Finally, after the turn of the century, amusement parks like Sans Souci, White City, and Riverview continued the tradition. Although mechanized rides had replaced the German bands and the patrons arrived on the "El," even these large places could trace their ancestry back to the enterprising saloonkeepers of earlier generations.

From the 1880s on, when the first attractive saloons opened downtown, the great ambition of many barkeeps was to open such a place. A downtown operation, however, required not only money, but also an ability to adjust to a different clientele and to great variations in the hours of peak patronage. Bars near the train station served "bracers" to commuters hurrying to work; the same people stopped by on their way home in the evening. Noontime brought the heaviest trade. The fancier places, fitted like private clubs, had private dining rooms, billiard parlors and barrooms fitted with onyx wainscotting, matched veneers, and uniformed bartenders. There were also bars like Jim McGary's, which catered to politicians, and ex-Alderman Billy Mangler's place, which, during one period, served as a hideaway for newspaper reporters. It was in Mangler's back room that George Ade, Finley Peter Dunne, John T. McCutcheon, and other members of the famous Whitechapel Club gathered to drink, sing, and trade stories.

Many of the downtown saloons had reputations that extended far beyond Chicago's borders. Henrici's and the Berghoff were considered fine restaurants. Both Chapin & Gore and Hannah & Hogg were distilling and bottling companies that operated chains of saloons. Each richly furnished outlet owned by Chapin & Gore had large caricatures of famous Chicagoans on its walls, and Hannah & Hogg set large stone statues of people and animals on the sidewalk in front of its branches. But none could compare with the attractions of Heinegabubeler's, on State Street, where "Mutographoscopes" — a kind of Kinetoscope — showed such treats as Night at Vassar and Midnight in Paris in "natural motion." Heinegabubeler's had a gymnasium and reading rooms, but it was most famous for making "greenhorns" the butt of pranks. Holes in their mugs leaked beer on their shirts. The vending machines dispensed rubber gum, and the washroom bowl collapsed. Customers who complained were ushered to the sidewalk, but those who could laugh at their own plight were treated to free food and drink while they watched the misadventures of the next victim.

Despite the standardizing influences of brewery ownership, there were, as we have seen, almost as many types of saloons as neighborhoods in Chicago. Each proprietor could still shape his business to his clientele — if he did not, his competitors would soon put him out of business. Such adaptability and aggressiveness enabled the liquor business to survive decades of criticism. Still, by the turn of the century, trouble, as well as beer, was brewing.

All of the individual dealers depended on cheap wholesale beer prices, but, as the 1900s began, grain shortages nearly tripled the cost of making beer. The saloonkeeper, trapped in the tradition of "nickel beer," had to absorb the increase. In 1906, the brewers quietly joined with temperance forces to raise the annual license to $1,000 and freeze the number of permits issued. The beer-makers were anxious to squeeze out the remaining independent saloonkeepers, and many of the smaller places did indeed close up, but the major effect of the new laws was to increase the operating expenses of the average proprietor. He now had to pay back twice as much to the brewer.

Thus, in 1907, the General Assembly enacted a local option law, enabling individual precincts and wards to enact their own prohibition laws. Within two years, two-thirds of the city had outlawed the saloon. Brewers moved their licenses to the "wet" central wards, but there were too many dealers competing for too little trade. The rate of bankruptcy increased so rapidly that the municipal judicial system had to establish a special "license court" to arbitrate disputes between evicted saloonkeepers and the brewing companies, and the trade journals began publishing lists of closings so that whiskey salesmen and food purveyors could keep track.

Even the politics of the situation were changing. Membership in the Liquor Dealers' Protective Association dwindled to a fraction of its size in the 1890s. Shortly after, Anton Cermak's United Societies for Local Self Government emerged as the leading defender of the immigrant's "personal liberty" to drink. The United Societies, a union of athletic clubs and singing societies, displaced the saloonkeepers themselves as the most prominent spokesmen for the liquor trade, undoubtedly with the industry's aid and assistance, and only a few barkeeps remained in the City Council. The anti-vice crusades which ultimately closed the red-light Levee district in 1912 had given all saloonkeepers a bad name. "Respectable" people did not want to be seen drinking in public. Public health officials claimed that the liquor served in saloons was adulterated with artificial coloring and even fusel oil. The health department attacked the traditional flyspecks on the free lunch, demanded that the food be covered, warned against the common serving forks, and outlawed the unwashed mustache towel.

Ultimately, the saloonkeepers also began

"Rushing the Growler," was one of the many masterpieces in Sigmund Krausz's *Street Types of Chicago*, published in 1891.

(CHS, ICHi-3135)

to encounter changes in Chicago's social life to which they could not adapt. One was the rise of the automobile. During its first years, this invention was considered a toy, a recreation for the wealthy, but by 1910 increasing numbers of the middle class had come to regard it as an ideal means of daily transportation. Faster and more comfortable than a streetcar, it also removed saloon customers from the street corner and made it more convenient for them to drink at home. Delivery service brought bottled goods directly to their homes. Hip flasks came into vogue. Meanwhile, the nickelodeons — another form of the Kinetoscope — invaded the working class neighborhoods. There were 606 of them in 1913, and many men found that they could entertain the whole family for less than the cost of an evening's drinks in a saloon.

The last few years of legal liquor proved even more agonizing for the survivors. Anti-German sentiment during World War I made beer drinking appear to be unpatriotic, and wartime measures to conserve grain limited and then ended the production of alcoholic beverages. By 1915, the saloonkeepers' political influence had evaporated, and Mayor Big Bill Thompson felt he could safely defy Cermak's United Societies. He announced that he would enforce the ancient Illinois Sunday closing law. Big Bill accomplished the feat — not without protest, to be sure, but without a riot.

Still, the honorable profession of saloonkeeping survived. There were fewer and fewer saloons in Chicago as the years wore on, but the survivors demonstrated an important characteristic of social institutions: they adapted to economic, social, and physical changes. The one or two saloons that remained open in a neighborhood where there had been twenty became that much more important to the neighborhood. The result was a business that mirrored its environment and that was almost impossible to eradicate.

Until the cold night of January 16, 1920, when even the survivors perished.

Claude A. Barnett and the Associated Negro Press

Linda J. Evans

The Associated Negro Press (ANP) was the oldest and largest black press service in the United States. Founded in Chicago in 1919 by Claude A. Barnett, a young, black entrepreneur who remained its director for the next four and a half decades, the Associated Negro Press supplied news stories on affairs concerning black citizens, opinion columns, feature essays, poetry, book and record reviews, cartoons, and occasionally photographs to black newspapers throughout the country. The ANP's service enabled its members, which included nearly all of the major black newspapers in the United States as well as many of the smaller ones, to offer their readers detailed coverage of activities within black communities across the country and the latest news about national trends and events. In the 1960s the World News Service division of the ANP served more than one hundred African newspapers as well.

Yet the significance of the ANP was not widely recognized in its own time, and it usually receives only passing reference today in the growing number of scholarly studies of the black press. This neglect arises, in part, from the nature of the organization itself. The Associated Negro Press was a nationwide channel for news about black Americans, but it rarely drew attention to its own operations. Each of the member newspapers of the ANP was free to shorten, rewrite, or ignore the many news items that it received from the press service every week. ANP articles did not necessarily appear in identical form from city to city, and newspapers often failed to include a credit line when they printed stories or columns provided by the ANP. Many readers did not know that some of the articles in their local newspapers were provided by the Associated Negro Press.

Although he was not a well-known public figure, Claude Barnett was one of the outstanding journalists of mid-twentieth-century America. As founder and director of the Associated Negro Press, he provided a unique service for the black community through forty-five years of enormous change. He established the ANP with almost no capital investment and maintained it for years on little more than personal promotion and will power. It was never a commercial success, but it served other purposes. The ANP helped create a national black culture and increased

As a student at Alabama's Tuskegee Institute, Claude Barnett came to admire Booker T. Washington and his teachings.
(CHS, ICHi-17330)

black awareness of trends and events in the nation at large. It provided a national forum for black leaders, set professional standards of news writing for the black press, helped to stabilize many small black newspapers, and enabled many black journalists to gain reporting experience at the beginning of their careers. The ANP was successful in another way as well: it placed Claude Barnett at the center of a national information network, introduced him to black leaders throughout the country, and thus made him a valuable ally to those who sought to shape modern black life.

Claude Barnett was born in Florida in 1889 to William Barnett, a hotel worker who divided his time between Florida and Chicago, and Celena Anderson Barnett, who supported herself and Claude by working as a housekeeper in the homes of wealthy Chicagoans. While growing up, Claude attended elementary schools in Chicago and in Mattoon, Illinois, where he lived for varying periods with his mother's family. Thus he derived his sense of close family ties from his mother's relatives.

Between 1902 and 1904, Claude attended Oak Park High School while he worked as a houseboy in the home of Richard W. Sears, co-founder of Sears, Roebuck & Company. Mr. Sears favored the youth with extra privileges, such as tickets to plays and concerts, and later arranged a job for Barnett with his company. But Celena wanted her son to continue his education, and in September 1904 she sent him to Tuskegee Institute in Alabama.

At Tuskegee, Barnett finished the advanced course in only two years, but one can scarcely overestimate the influence of Tuskegee on the rest of his life. During his time there, he came to share his mother's admiration for Tuskegee's founder and president, Booker T. Washington, and the principles he taught: self-help, moderation, respectability, vocational training, and black capitalism. Barnett also gained a heightened awareness of the rural agricultural heritage of many of his classmates and the majority of the southern black population. Coming from an urban background, Barnett otherwise might never have learned to understand the rural poverty and humble aspirations which prevailed among many black people who looked to Tuskegee for leadership. In time Barnett began to identify with the goal that united all of Washington's disciples — the building of a firm economic foundation for black equality in the United States. Other Tuskegeeans who shared the approach to racial progress — classmates, staff, and alumni — formed a network of associates that Barnett would find congenial and helpful throughout his career. After graduation, Barnett returned to Chicago and took a job with the post office, where his duties included sorting the many publications sent regularly through the mail. Later he would write that the time he perused the newspapers and magazines was well spent, for he developed an eye for good writing and advertising that proved invaluable in his journalism career. When a bout of ill health forced him to leave the post office in 1916, Barnett tried his hand at several ventures. He set up his own advertising agency; dabbled in sales of photographs of famous black men and beautiful black women; and helped organize the Kashmir Chemical Company, manufacturer of Nile Queen cosmetics. While most of his partners' investments were financial, Barnett's contribution was his advertising acumen gained from his years with the postal service.

In 1918, his talents were again useful when he attempted to pay for a visit to California, where his mother was living with her second husband, by selling advertising on commission for the *Chicago Defender* at train stops along the way. On that trip, he sought out black editors throughout the Midwest and West and discussed their needs. When he returned to Chicago, he opened the Associated Negro Press. The ANP symbol, an owl holding a scroll bearing the words "Progress, Loyalty, Truth," aptly summarized the path that Barnett marked out for his organization.

The creation of a news service like the ANP was almost inevitable. Since the turn of the twentieth century, the black migration from the rural South to New York, Chicago, and other cities had generated new concentrations of black population and new financial and cultural resources. Before and during World War I, the *Chicago Defender* heavily promoted the opportunities in Chicago for well-paying jobs and social dignity. Wherever the *Defender*, the *Pittsburgh Courier*, and other major black newspapers circulated in rural areas and across the South, black people read about different patterns of race relations, an emerging black urban culture, and accomplishments by black men and women. Chicago's black population had grown by more than 250 percent, from 30,150 in 1900 to 109,458 in 1920, making it one of the nation's major centers of black culture. A new middle class made up of black business and professional people responded to this expanding population, eager to provide the services demanded by the largely segregated black community. A similar process throughout the country was producing new or greatly enlarged institutions controlled by black leaders and serving a black constituency: businesses; schools; hospitals; professional, fraternal, and political organizations; churches; and newspapers. Some of the most successful new enterprises, especially the life insurance and cosmetics companies, greatly boosted the advertising income of the black press.

By the end of World War I, black newspapers were firmly established in many centers of black population. Some of these were among the most influential publications of the next fifty years. Besides the *Defender* and the *Courier,* they included the *Norfolk Journal and Guide,* the *New York Age,* the *Amsterdam News* (New York City), the *Afro American* (Baltimore and other cities), the *Philadelphia Tribune,* the *Houston Informer,* and the *Black Dispatch* (Oklahoma City). In addition,

Shipping room, Kashmir Chemical Company, Chicago. Early in his career, Barnett was a partner in this company, where he developed advertising for Nile Queen cosmetics, the firm's major product line.

(CHS, ICHi-17328)

many small black communities throughout the country supported local black newspapers with more limited circulations. As their readers grew more prosperous, better educated, and more cosmopolitan, these newspapers both reflected and helped to shape a new social milieu.

Because most of the black newspapers published once a week, the ANP was a mail service rather than a wire service. The ANP's Chicago office sent news releases to ANP member newspapers two or, in later years, three times a week in order to meet their weekly deadlines. In return, the members agreed to pay a modest fee for the service, to print an ANP credit line with each news item from the releases that they published, and to act as a local correspondent for the Chicago office of the Associated Negro Press.

At their offices on Chicago's South Side, Barnett's small staff of experienced journalists sifted information from these reciprocal reports and from the daily newspapers, black newspapers, government news releases, public relations announcements from foundations and organizations, and reports from ANP correspondents throughout the country. For background information they referred to the ANPs morgue containing topical files of clippings from old newspapers and from past ANP releases. From these sources they compiled the ANP's news releases, which varied in format from fifteen to forty or more legal-size mimeographed sheets of typewritten articles. ANP members received much more material than any single newspaper was likely to publish.

These news releases included two somewhat different types of news. First the ANP tried to cover events, trends, and personalities within the black community that would interest a national audience. This material included news about black churches (particularly the National Baptist Conventions and the African Methodist Episcopal Church), colleges, fraternal organizations, politicians, social leaders, athletes, criminals, inventors, entertainers, business men and women, and union organizers. Claude Barnett was always partial to success stories — the first, best, newest, oldest, the "most" of any respectable achievement — these were held up as examples for racial pride and emulation.

The other kind of news that the ANP supplied to its membership was similar to the news articles found in the daily press, except that the ANP always focused on the aspects of the important news of the day which affected black people. In later years, when the daily newspapers were reporting on New Deal relief and recovery programs, the Associated Negro Press carried stories on the number of blacks employed in the programs and the kinds of jobs they were allotted. While the dailies reported a massive flood relief effort in the South, the ANP surveyed the distribution of aid to black families. When Congress passed new legislation, the black press wanted to know what black politicians thought about it, whether black civil servants would be involved in administering it, and if it would affect blacks substantially.

Claude Barnett wrote a number of the stories contained in the ANP news releases using his many contacts to verify details or check on interpretations of reports received by the editorial office. But much of his time was spent in routine administration, arranging for local correspondents to cover conventions and other news events around the country, cajoling publishers to pay overdue service fees, soothing irate editors, recruiting new reporters and columnists, and persuading new publications to join the Associated Negro Press. In addition, he traveled extensively and served on numerous political, philanthropic, social, and educational committees. Barnett relied heavily, therefore, on the ANP's editors and on Irene Roland, who was his secretary for nearly thirty years, to run the office during his absences.*

In the beginning, the press service met with a wide range of reactions, as quoted in the ANP *Annual* of 1920, the first and only annual report published by the ANP. A number of white as well as black leaders praised the service's constructive attitude, patriotism, and usefulness. Prominent among ANP supporters were Secretary of War Newton D. Baker, the editors of several major newspapers, and Robert R. Moton, who had succeeded Booker T. Washington as president of Tuskegee Institute. William Pickens wrote a terse statement on the significance of the black press:

> The truth never will be told about a disadvantaged minority by the general press of any country, whether that minority be racial, political, or religious — Negroes in Georgia, Socialists in New York or Jews in Russia. If such a minority does not express itself thru organs of its own, it will not be expressed.
>
> The Associated Negro Press, therefore, belongs, in interest, to every colored person of the country. It is our only hope of shoveling ourselves out from under the avalanche of lies that are annually let loose upon us.
>
> Every Negro who is financially able and refuses to take at least one of his local Negro papers and one of the big national Negro periodicals is a slacker in the ranks.

*In the 1920s, ANP editor Percival L. Prattis carried much of the day-to-day burden of running the ANP. Prattis was responsible also for promoting *The National News Gravure,* a weekly rotogravure supplement for black newspapers. Other ANP editors over the years included Frank Marshall Davis, a respected poet and jazz expert; Albert G. Barnett, son of Chicago's first black editor, Ferdinand Barnett of the *Conservator,* and Ida B. Wells Barnett (but no relation to Claude); and in the 1950s and 1960s, Eddie L. Madison, J. H. Randall, Enoc Waters, and Lee Blackwell.

The *Annual* also carried U.S. Attorney General A. Mitchell Palmer's caveat denouncing "agitators of the Radical Socialist Revolutionary conspiracy [who] have devoted time, money, and thought toward stirring up the spirit of sedition among the Negroes in America."

The little pamphlet was really a public relations piece rather than an analysis of the ANP's financial structure. All of the report's testimonials were carefully phrased not only to impress black editors — who presumably could judge the quality of ANP service for themselves — but also to reassure white leaders as well as blacks that a national channel of communication devoted to the interests of blacks did not pose a threat to national well-being. Barnett launched his press in 1919, in the midst of a period of labor and racial unrest and the Red Scare following World War I. In that year, 76 black men were lynched across the nation, and there were some 20 race riots, the largest of which occurred in Chicago, where an estimated 38 persons died and more than 500 were injured.

By the end of its first year, the ANP claimed eighty-eight member newspapers, including some of the larger ones. Other members were little more than newsletters, and a few were nearly identical newspapers issued by a single publisher for distribution in several different towns under local titles. By 1944, Barnett estimated that ANP member newspapers had a combined circulation of more than 800,000 with about 2,400,000 readers a week — the readership being considerably larger than the number of newspapers sold because the major, big-city newspapers often circulated informally from hand to hand, like popular magazines, in small towns.

Even with a growing membership, the success of the ANP was not assured. Barnett usually had difficulty collecting his service

This idealized vision of the Negro press as a beacon of black achievement appeared in the ANP's first and only annual report, published in 1920.

(CHS)

fees, and as late as 1927, he claimed that the ANP produced so little revenue that every worker in the Chicago office held an extra job in order to earn a living. He managed to institute a graduated fee structure by which the newspapers with larger circulation paid higher rates for service, but the larger, well-managed newspapers would not support ANP expansion. They were nearly always unwilling to contribute extra funds for coverage of special events. For them, the ANP was only a convenient adjunct to their regular news sources. Indeed, several newspapers maintained their own national network similar to the ANP's system of stringers and voluntary local correspondents.

One of Barnett's special concerns was the ANP's relationship with the *Chicago Defender.* The ANP drew some of its editors from the staff of the *Defender,* and this is one explanation for the friction between the two organizations. It was logical for him to seek new employees from the pool of talent provided by the great national black newspaper with offices just down the street. Whether or not he lured them with the promise of higher salaries is unclear. Certainly a significant attraction of the ANP editorship was the vision of what the service might become if it could afford to offer its members extensive coverage similar to that of the AP or the UPI.

Despite sincere and strenuous efforts by

many men and women in the black press, black newspapers never achieved the kind of harmonious arrangements enjoyed by AP or UPI. Paradoxically, the better the ANP became, the greater the challenge it posed to the *Chicago Defender,* the *Pittsburgh Courier,* and the handful of other newspapers that circulated nationally among blacks; maintained their own networks of correspondents throughout the country; and in effect competed with the small, local newspapers that depended heavily upon the ANP for their national news reports. This conflict of interests surfaced frequently in the relations of the ANP and the *Chicago Defender.* In the 1920s, the *Defender* cancelled all ties to the Associated Negro Press and refused to renew them, a situation analogous to a major daily paper such as the *New York Times* refusing to cooperate with a wire service like the UPI. In the mid-1930s, Barnett was one of a group of investors who hoped to buy the *Chicago Defender* — until the publisher arranged to continue his family's control of the newspaper.

In the early 1940s, Barnett attempted to arrange a merger of the ANP and the Negro Newspaper Publishers Association in order to expand the news service. Negotiations broke down when it appeared to Barnett that some of the larger newspapers hoped to absorb the ANP, alter the rate structure to favor themselves, and generally revamp operating procedures so as to make the press service commercially viable at the expense of the small newspapers that Barnett had carried for many years. The NNPA then set up its own news service in competition with the ANP. It lasted only a few years. Later, some of the larger publishers organized a different NNPA — the National Newspaper Publishers Association — and established another press service, which closed in 1960. During all of this jostling for position, the ANP lost few members to the rival organizations. Some newspapers belonged to both, with the ANP retaining the larger membership.

In addition to the ANPs Chicago staff, Barnett employed a Washington, D.C., correspondent on a regular salary, plus correspondents in Hollywood, New York, and other cities who were paid space-rates according to the number of inches of publishable material they submitted. There were also voluntary correspondents scattered throughout the country who contributed occasional stories on local events in exchange for the privilege of carrying an ANP card and the gratification of seeing their writing in print.

In 1939, when Alvin E. White became the ANP's first full-time Washington, D.C., representative, Barnett began applying for Congressional press gallery credentials for the ANP but was denied. During World War II, Ernest Johnson represented the ANP in Washington, also without full credentials. It was not until 1947, after Alice Dunnigan had taken over the ANP position, that black press representatives were regularly accredited to the White House and the Congressional press galleries. Louis R. Lautier, the Washington representative of the NNPA, was the first black press representative admitted to the Congressional press galleries; Alice Dunningan of the ANP was the first accredited at the White House.

The ANP also distributed by-lined opinion columns with the kind of personal commentary on current events that it tried to avoid in its regular news stories. Many authors of these columns received no pay for their contributions; yet the ANP attracted a variety of distinguished writers who sought a national forum for their ideas. One of the most provocative was William L. Pickens, field secretary of the NAACP, whose articulate, seemingly uninhibited, and often witty commentary on American race relations made his articles a popular ANP feature. Gordon B. Hancock, a Baptist minister and leader in founding the Southern Regional Council, wrote an ANP column entitled "Between the Lines" for twenty-five years. Other columnists included President Frederick D. Patterson of Tuskegee Institute, founder of the United Negro College Fund; noted sociologist and president of Fisk University, Charles S. Johnson; and in later years, Barnett's old colleague, P. L. Prattis of the *Pittsburgh Courier*.

Although Barnett managed to draw upon many talented journalists and black leaders for contributions, the wide variety of articles provided by the ANP was not enough to keep all of its members satisfied. The black press was traditionally an advocacy press whose purpose was to speak for as well as to the black community. It was often strident and contentious, and there was little agreement among the various newspaper publishers on editorial policy. Naturally they were concerned with thorough and accurate reporting. But they also sought to promote the welfare of the black community as they perceived it — and sometimes to advance their own personal influence or political ambitions as well. Many publishers saw their newspapers as vehicles for advancing their own power and prestige as well as the more general aspirations of the black community.

The editors of the ANP themselves, however, could not afford the luxury of using the news service for personal aggrandizement. To keep the ANP's diverse membership satisfied, ANP news coverage had to conform to objective, middle-of-the-road standards (although its signed opinion columns frequently offered more controversial fare). The ANP release of November 14, 1932, boasted:

> The staff of the Associated Negro Press takes pardonable pride in calling the attention of the membership papers whom we serve to the type of service rendered during the past political campaign. We endeavored and we think succeeded in presenting the news, views and opinions of all parties, groups, and factions so that editors might choose and pick that which suited the editorial policies of their papers. . . . On our staff is a Republican, a socialist, a Democrat, and a communist, but so far as the service was concerned no partisanship obtruded.

This exuberant editorial note probably revealed more about the personal opinions of the ANP staff than Barnett considered appropriate. Later editorial comments merely asserted that the ANP was nonpartisan.

Even after taking such conciliatory measures as these, all of Barnett's skills of personal diplomacy were required to hold his organization together. The member newspapers were quick to suspect bias. They accused Barnett of favoring large newspapers over small ones in its membership privileges, or of distributing news stories that favored Republicans over Democrats; northern interests over southern; sophisticated urban attitudes over small-town and rural concerns; sensational crime over respectable achievements; civil rights demonstrations over coverage of the regular social, fraternal, church, and college activities in the black community — and vice versa. The essence of Barnett's achievement lay in his ability to balance the rival interests that challenged the ANP.

Barnett never forgot that the ANP needed the support of many of the smaller black newspapers as well as the larger ones in order to survive. Unfortunately, many small newspapers operated on a very slim margin of profit and were beset by the difficulties that commonly plagued small businesses — undercapitalization, low credit ratings, and a lack of basic training in bookkeeping. In some cases, a small, part-time staff with little journalism experience put together each issue of the newspaper from whatever sources were available in their town, and they depended on the ANP for their national news coverage. Barnett was generally reluctant to cut off membership for nonpayment of service fees, and carried many members on credit for months. The ANP survived its early years because Claude Barnett added a key innovation: he linked the press service to an advertising exchange. While most newspapers did not have ready cash, nearly all had "white space," unused advertising space in their publications which they readily allocated to Barnett in return for ANP service. Barnett then sold this space to advertisers through other companies that he owned — the Associated Publishers' Representative and, later, the National Feature Service.

Barnett looked to the black community and its new black companies for advertising business. At first he arranged an advertising exchange with his own firm, the Kashmir Chemical Company. But when Kashmir failed after a dispute with the manufacturer of Cashmere Bouquet toiletries over their similar brand names, Poro College beauty products, one of the first million-dollar black cosmetics companies, replaced it as Barnett's first major advertising client. His advertising service attracted more clients, including several other black cosmetics companies. Through this exchange system, advertisers reached local markets wherever the black population was large enough to support its own newspapers. The newspaper enjoyed the benefits of ANP service in return for publishing the advertisements, and the ANP secured a steady income from the advertisers — who could pay — rather than from the newspapers — who often could not.

Barnett worked assiduously to expand the amount of advertising carried by the black press and to promote black business in general. Because black magazines and newspapers attracted far less advertising revenue than "white" or general audience publications, black publishers were more dependent on income from subscriptions and newsstand sales. To improve the quantity and quality of its services to the black community, the black press needed a stronger financial base.

In 1925, Claude Barnett persuaded Secretary of Commerce Herbert Hoover, whom he knew through work with the Republican party, to create a position in his department for a black adviser to small business. Barnett's hand-picked candidate got the job. Barnett also participated actively in the National Negro Business League, which was headed by his old friend Albon Holsey of Tuskegee Institute. They saw the 1930 federal census as a chance to document the considerable economic gains made by black citizens over the previous decades and thus to gather official evidence that a substantial Negro market existed in the United States. Because census takers usually missed a significant portion of the black population, Barnett coordinated an informal effort by black advisers in predominantly black areas across the country to make the census as complete as possible. He hoped that better statistics would persuade major national advertisers that they could reach a worthwhile audience of potential consumers by placing their ads in the black press.

Unfortunately, the Depression deepened and cut short this expansion program, and soon Barnett relinquished his own advertising companies. Poro College beauty products went bankrupt. A lawsuit against Barnett by the W. B. Ziff Company of Chicago, which was then the main clearinghouse for advertising in black newspapers, was settled out of court in 1934. Barnett's advertising exchange was dead. In later years the ANP continued to receive a little income from public relations programs, but Barnett carefully protected the reputation of his news service by insisting that products or services that advertisers asked him to mention in ANP releases have some sort of news value.

Despite the fact that his own direct financial stake in promoting advertising had declined, Barnett continued to believe that increasing this source of income was essential for the black press in general. In the early 1950s, Barnett finally achieved some success with a new version of his efforts to interest national advertisers in the Negro market. He persuaded Liggett and Myers to finance a series of short films on Negro achievements in education, science, entertainment, and other noteworthy activities. The films also contained ads of prominent black Americans, including Claude Barnett, praising Chesterfield cigarettes (much to the amusement of Barnett's friends who knew that he preferred cigars).

As his advertising income dwindled in the 1930s, Barnett reorganized his news service to become eligible for new forms of financial aid. By registering the ANP as a not-for-profit agency and clarifying its tax status with the IRS, Barnett qualified to receive donations and grants from various organizations and individuals who were usually designated "associate members" of the ANP. In return, these supporters received ANP news releases (although not as frequently as the newspapers because there was no need to meet a publishing deadline) and, occasionally, Barnett's advice on their public relations programs as well. The associate members included Tuskegee Institute, North Carolina

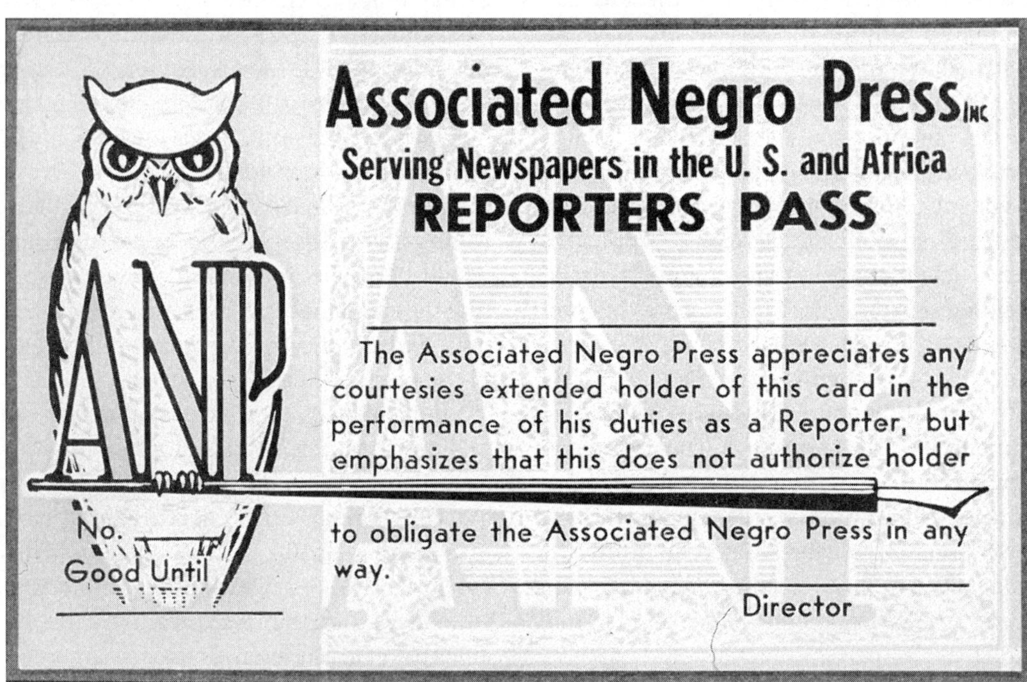
Associated Negro Press INC
Serving Newspapers in the U. S. and Africa
REPORTERS PASS

The Associated Negro Press appreciates any courtesies extended holder of this card in the performance of his duties as a Reporter, but emphasizes that this does not authorize holder to obligate the Associated Negro Press in any way.

Director

No.
Good Until

Volunteer correspondents throughout the nation contributed local news stories in exchange for the privilege of carrying an ANP reporter's pass.

(CHS)

College at Durham, and other schools, philanthropists, several churches, and fraternal groups. Often the administrators of these organizations were Barnett's friends, persons whom he had met in the course of many years of political and philanthropic activities. This arrangement created potential conflict of interest problems for the ANP. It could not afford to appear biased. Above all other considerations, the Associated Negro Press had to assure its member newspapers that ANP news releases were reliable.

As the ANP's reputation grew, Barnett broadened the scope of his own activities. The ANP's first editor, Nahum D. Brascher, had introduced Barnett in 1920 to the world of black Republican politics. Since the era of the Civil War, the Republican party had been more open to black participation than the Democratic party, accrediting black delegates to its national conventions and later appointing blacks as national committeemen and committeewomen. At the 1920 Republican National Convention, held in Chicago, Brascher and Barnett campaigned so effectively for candidate Leonard Wood that even though he did not receive the nomination, they attracted favorable notice from party leaders. Barnett's Republican party activities culminated in 1928 when he served as secretary of the national publicity committee of the Colored Voters Division of the Republican National Committee during Herbert Hoover's presidential campaign. In 1932, Claude Barnett was elected a trustee of Tuskegee Institute. He and Richard H. Harris of Montgomery, who was chosen the same day, shared the honor of being the first graduates of Tuskegee to sit on its board of trustees, on which Barnett would serve for the next thirty-three years.

In the 1930s, Barnett's other activities continued to expand. He served as president of the board of trustees of Chicago's Provident Hospital, became a director of Supreme Liberty Life Insurance Company, and devoted considerable time to inspection tours of the South as an unpaid adviser to the Agricultural Adjustment Administration on the impact of government programs on black farmers. He also persuaded the Conference of Presidents of Negro Land Grant Colleges to sponsor a comparative study of the amounts of government money distributed to black and white colleges. The report, compiled in 1936 by Horace Mann Bond, documented inequities more clearly than ever before.

In 1934, Claude Barnett married Etta Moten, a well-known concert singer and actress. Her career immediately became another factor in his many travels and promotions. Prominent black men and women whom Barnett met through the ANP, Tuskegee Institute, the National Negro Business League, and other organizations often sponsored her annual concert tours. Although her career soon outgrew his ability to manage it on a part-time basis, he continued to offer suggestions to her professional theatrical agents. For several months in the early 1940s, the Barnetts lived in New York while Mrs. Barnett sang the lead in *Porgy and Bess* on Broadway.

During World War II, Barnett expanded ANP news coverage, emphasizing black participation in the war effort. The ANP, like most of the black press, publicized cases of racial discrimination in the armed forces in hopes of pressuring the government to modify its policies. Barnett defended only two segregated facilities: the black veterans hospital and the air corps training base located at Tuskegee, Alabama. The pilot training program at Tuskegee was segregated, he acknowledged, but even a segregated opportunity seemed better than none at all. Claude Barnett also worked on local national Red Cross committees and later served on the Red Cross's national board of governors.

The subject that claimed much of his attention during the war years was federal agricultural policy. Tuskegee Institute and several other black universities in the South trained and sponsored local agricultural extension agents. In 1942, the U.S. Secretary of Agriculture appointed Claude Barnett and President F. D. Patterson of Tuskegee Institute to serve as his special assistants. Barnett and Patterson used their inside knowledge to improve black access to USDA jobs; to educational, health, and insurance programs for farmers; and to federal aid for agricultural colleges. Renewed by succeeding secretaries, their appointment finally expired in 1952 with the outgoing Democratic administration.

Also during the war years, Barnett became a trustee of the Phelps-Stokes Fund. This foundation sponsors programs for better race relations in the United States and helps support the Booker T. Washington Institute in Liberia. In 1947 Claude Barnett made his first trip to Africa, primarily to inspect the Liberian school (which was set up originally with assistance from Tuskegee Institute advisers), and he and his wife traveled extensively on the African continent. Their enthusiasm for African art and culture — as well as for business opportunities in Africa's developing nations — was overwhelming. Barnett reported to the Phelps-Stokes Fund on his impressions of the Africans he had met: "They look like us — they act like us — they are us." The Barnetts began to collect and exhibit African art — eventually donating much of it to Tuskegee Institute. Mrs. Barnett added African songs and costumes to her concert repertoire, and the Barnetts gave many speeches about Africa before American civic, religious, and fraternal groups.

Over the next seventeen years Barnett traveled to Africa fifteen times and gathered a wide range of friends and acquaintances among African political leaders, educators, clergymen, editors, and businessmen, and American diplomats and businessmen stationed abroad. The Associated Negro Press began to carry more news stories on African affairs — so many, in fact, that a few of the ANP member newspapers complained that they could not possibly devote so much of their space to foreign events. In 1959-60, Claude Barnett organized some of his many African contacts into a World News Service (WNS). This service, operating out of the Associated Negro Press offices in Chicago, provided African newspapers with news releases in English or French. It lasted three and a half years.

By the early 1960s, the Associated Negro Press faced growing pressure as the entire structure of the national news media changed. During the years of the civil rights movement, television news as well as newspapers began to offer more extensive coverage of events involving black Americans. Some of the more prosperous black newspapers joined the wire services and thus had immediate access to the latest news. In 1956, the *Chicago Defender* began to publish a daily edition, and the *Afro American* published twice weekly. Other black newspapers that were unable to compete with the dailies in national news coverage tried to retain their audience by emphasizing purely local news that was not available anywhere else, even in the ANP news releases.

The ANP's biweekly news releases were still useful, of course. They not only covered the national news — including the civil rights movement in considerable detail — but they also provided copy that was edited to focus on black interests, and it was ready to print. Barnett estimated that ANP releases could save a member newspaper the equivalent of one employee's time in rewriting news stories from other sources. Yet, one by one, the ANP's members were falling away or failing to pay their fees. Although Barnett's editors attempted to revitalize the organization, it became ever clearer that, ultimately, the fate of the Associated Negro Press depended on the man who had bargained, arranged, cajoled, and maneuvered to maintain it for nearly half a century.

In 1963, *Ebony* magazine ranked Barnett among the one hundred most influential black Americans, yet at seventy-four years of age, Claude Barnett suffered increasingly from ill health and could no longer personally call on the vast range of contacts that had enabled him to sustain the ANP for so many years. His wife and friends urged him to lighten his workload and enjoy the rich memories of his exceptional career. Thus, when Claude Barnett reluctantly retired in July 1964, the Associated Negro Press closed its doors. He began writing an autobiography and traveled again to Africa, but his health problems continued, and he suffered partial paralysis from a stroke that kept him home in Chicago. He died on August 2, 1967.

Although Claude Barnett's continual involvement in promotions of one sort or another — publishing, advertising, and politics — might seem to imply something of a freewheeling character, his contemporaries described him very differently. To them he appeared to be a quiet, dignified man who was basically conservative in his beliefs and actions. Much of his success came from his ability to balance innovative ideas with tactful but persistent advocacy. He used publicity to spotlight cases of racial discrimination whenever he thought public attention could improve the situation, but fundamentally, Claude Barnett was a pragmatist who inclined toward quiet diplomacy rather than public confrontation.

James T. Farrell and Washington Park: The Novel as Social History

Charles Fanning and Ellen Skerrett

The people of Washington Park are special — they have lived twice: once in their own guise, in the streets and apartments of their community, and again in the thousands of pages of fiction that James Thomas Farrell has created in the course of the past fifty years. Washington Park and its environs have been the source and setting for a major portion of this writer's remarkable body of work, which constitutes one of the most sustained productions in twentieth-century America of fiction in the realistic tradition.

James T. Farrell was born on the South Side on February 27, 1904. He left Chicago in 1931, firmly committed to the "lifework" that he himself has defined as "a panoramic story of our days and years, a story which would continue through as many books as I would be able to write." Since then, although he has lived mostly in Paris and New York, Chicago has continued periodically to fire his imagination. Like James Joyce, who boasted from his self-imposed exile in Europe that a tourist could negotiate Dublin with a copy of *Ulysses* as guide, Farrell has made good use of the perspective on his native city to be gained by distance. As a result, within his large and varied *oeuvre* (which fills, to date, some fifty-two volumes) there is no fuller, more accurately detailed, or more compassionate creation than Chicago's South Side. Washington Park emerges in Farrell's fiction as a realized world, as whole and coherent as Joyce's Dublin or William Faulkner's northern Mississippi.

Running like mountain ranges through Farrell's twenty-two novels and 250 short stories are four major fictional cycles: the *Studs Lonigan* trilogy, the O'Neill-O'Flaherty pentalogy, the Bernard trilogy, and, in progress since 1958, the *Universe of Time* series, of which eight volumes of a heroic projection of thirty have been published so far. Our focus here will be the first two cycles, which make up what we call the "Washington Park novels": *Young Lonigan* (1932), *The Young Manhood of Studs Lonigan* (1934), and *Judgment Day* (1935); *A World I Never Made* (1936), *No Star is Lost* (1938), *Father and Son* (1940), *My Days of Anger* (1945), and *The Face of Time* (1953).

By focusing on these eight novels, we hope to suggest an added dimension to the accomplishment of this son and grandson of

A lazy game of croquet in Washington Park around the turn of the century. *(CHS, ICHi-03499)*

Irish Catholic teamsters. Farrell is, of course, first and foremost an American realist — fiercely and scrupulously honest, immune to sentimentality, and pioneering in his commitment to the serious literary consideration of the "common life" of urban working- and middle-class communities. At the same time, and in addition to their undisputed value as literature, we suggest that the Washington Park novels can be read as social history, corroborating and clarifying more traditional sources of information about Chicago neighborhood life in the early twentieth century. Through his careful, detailed presentation, Farrell demonstrates that Washington Park is a world in itself, with four clear reference points like the markings on a compass: the Street, the Park, the Church, and the Home.

Much more than simply a locale for unsupervised leisure time, the Street and the Park emerge in Farrell's fiction as mutually exclusive choices for the city child. Each represents a possible way of growing up, and each has its ideal models to engage a child's imagination. In the course of the Washington Park novels, Farrell depicts this powerful opposition in the contrasting development of the two young protagonists, Studs Lonigan and Danny O'Neill. The Street is a destructive element, characterized by gang life with its brutalization of the finer instincts and its pressures to conform: to fight, to drink, and to dissipate time and energy in order to be "strong, and tough, and the real stuff." The center of street life in Washington Park is Charley Bathcellar's poolroom on 58th Street near the "L" station: its heroes are the gamblers, drinkers, and loafers who congregate there.

The Park, on the other hand, is a creative and liberating element, offering release from the disorder of street life and the confinement of the home. The center of the park is the athletic field, which to the city child is a kind of paradise — a lined-out grassy place where rules are clear and enforced, and success and failure are unambiguous. Its heroes are sports figures, from park league stars to the Chicago White Sox, the pride of the South Side.

Danny O'Neill, after watching a no-hitter pitched by the White Sox's Ed Walsh, chooses the Park as his milieu, resolving to become a professional baseball player. He practices by the hour — mostly alone — and devises elaborate games with penny baseball cards. Baseball is at once the most beautiful sport to watch and one of the least team-oriented of team sports. Thus it is not surprising that it so fascinates the young boy who is something of a lonely dreamer, and in whom the detachment of a budding artist is evolving.

It is no more surprising that Studs Lonigan chooses the Street. A normally inquisitive boy, he shows signs of intelligence, even imagination, in the early scenes of *Young Lonigan.* And yet he is weak-willed and easily led, and he assumes the facile and corrupting "tough guy" values of the street-corner society to which he is drawn after graduation from eighth grade. He joins the 58th Street Gang and takes as his models the hustlers of the poolroom and the gangsters of the silver screen. But, significantly, the recurring dream of Studs's short, unhappy adulthood is of his one afternoon in the park with Lucy Scanlan during their eighth-grade summer. So the opposition of Street and Park is central to Farrell's delineation of the complex mixture of character and environment that brings Danny to his vocation as an artist and Studs to his grave at the age of twenty-nine.

For Farrell's Irish Catholic characters, the familiar world is an even smaller unit than the neighborhood of Washington Park — it is the parish. Farrell's presentation of the Catholic Church and parish is crucial to his full evocation of what life was like for the South Side Irish. Moreover, his depiction of urban Catholic culture was among the first such efforts in American literature.

The parish provided continuity with Ireland on the one hand and help in adjusting to America on the other. And it provided spiritual guidance and solace for its members. Catholicism remained the tacitly accepted center of life for immigrants such as Mary and Tom O'Flaherty (Danny O'Neill's grandparents) and in varying degrees for their American-born descendants. Studs Lonigan

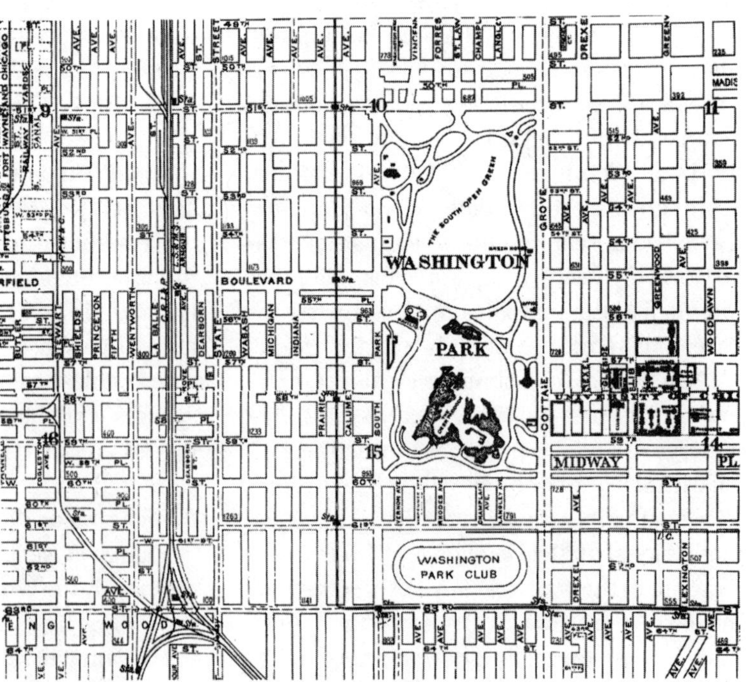

James T. Farrell grew up in Washington Park and attended St. Anselm's grammar school there. The neighborhood formed the setting for many of his novels, in which St. Anselm's became "St. Patrick's." This map shows the neighborhood in 1904.
(CHS, ICHi-13895)

and Danny O'Neill go different ways in their attitude toward the religion in which they were raised and educated. For all his flirtations with street life, Studs remains a conventional Catholic, never questioning the teachings and prohibitions of the Church, and reacting typically right up to his death. Indeed, when Studs tries to pull his sinking life together he does so by joining parish organizations; his fevered deathbed dreams reveal him as a believer in heaven and hell and the Catholic way of deciding who goes where.

With his intelligence and artistic bent, Danny O'Neill's reactions to the Church are more complex. As a sensitive, highly imaginative child, he is terrorized by the fear of hell instilled in him by his family and the nuns of Crucifixion School. Later, he tries to force himself into a vocation in the priesthood in order to please his grandmother and the nuns. Yet there are positive aspects to Danny's exposure to Catholic culture. His seventh-grade nun is the first person to push him toward an intellectual life, and some of his priest-teachers at St. Stanislaus High School encourage him further toward learning and writing. Catholicism provides Danny with models of educated and dedicated men and women; in addition, it gives what is unavailable to him elsewhere — a sense of order, of historical continuity, and of mystery. Thus, the Church remains a powerful presence throughout these novels, from Studs's graduation from St. Patrick grammar school in *Young Lonigan* to the funeral mass for Jim O'Neill at the end of *Father and Son.*

After the Street, the Park, and the Church, the fourth cardinal point in the world of Washington Park is the Home, which for most residents of the neighborhood meant, and still means, apartment life. Through the three main families of his Washington Park novels, Farrell describes a range of South Side styles of living, from the struggling O'Neills to the comfortably middle-class Lonigans, with the O'Flahertys fluctuating somewhere in between. Their homes and home lives are depicted in meticulous day-by-day detail, recording for posterity how ordinary people lived in Chicago in the 1910s and 1920s.

The O'Flaherty family's move from an immigrant neighborhood near Blue Island Avenue to a "big apartment" in the 4700 block of S. Indiana Avenue was typical of the route taken by thousands of upwardly mobile Chicago Irish. In telling the story of the O'Flahertys, Farrell documents the means by which the majority of marginally middle-class families got ahead — pooling resources. Young people lived at home, contributing their earnings to the family until they married. By the time old Tom O'Flaherty retires from his job as a teamster his children — Al, Ned, Margaret, and Louise — are earning enough to maintain a decent standard of living.

The O'Flaherty apartment on Indiana Avenue is situated in "a good neighborhood," Grand Boulevard, located just north of Washington Park. In such a place the O'Flahertys qualified as "steam heat Irish," a description compounded of jealousy mingled with derision. It is to this apartment on Indiana Avenue that five-year-old Danny O'Neill comes to live with his grandparents in 1909 because his father doesn't earn enough money to support the growing O'Neill family.

In 1911 the O'Flahertys move three blocks south, to an apartment at 50th Street and Calumet Avenue near "Crucifixion Church and School" (Farrell's name for the Corpus Christi parish complex at 49th Street and Grand Boulevard [later South Parkway], where Danny O'Neill begins his education).* The family moves again in 1912, to 157½

*Farrell himself attended the Corpus Christi school from 1911 to 1915.

Attackers stand over a black man stoned to death by the mob in the Race Riot of 1919. *(Photograph by Jun Fujita. CHS)*

S. Prairie Avenue, one block south in the same parish.

The O'Flahertys live on Prairie Avenue until the conclusion of *No Star Is Lost* in the spring or summer of 1915, when they move once more — to 57th Street and Indiana Avenue in "St. Patrick parish" in Washington Park. On moving day, walking along 58th Street for the first time, eleven-year-old Danny O'Neill is challenged by two older boys who are checking him out as a newcomer to their territory. Their names are Johnny O'Brien and Studs Lonigan.

In 1918, Jim and Lizz O'Neill, Danny's parents, move their family from a frame cottage at 45th and Wells streets to an apartment building at 58th and Calumet Avenue. In the opening page of *Father and Son* Jim surveys his new apartment, which, unlike the cottage, has "a bathroom inside, running hot and cold water, steam heat, gas and electricity." The O'Neill family finally seems to be out of the woods, and Jim is proud to have caught up with his wife's family: Lizz's parents, the O'Flahertys, live only a block away.

By 1918 the O'Flahertys have made their last move — to 5812½ South Park Avenue (now Dr. Martin Luther King, Jr. Drive). The view over Washington Park makes this their most attractive apartment. Here — as reflected in the major action of *Father and Son* and *My Days of Anger* — Danny O'Neill becomes an adult. He attends "St. Stanislaus" High School, graduating in 1923, and takes pre-legal courses at "St. Vincent's night school. Finally he enrolls at the University of Chicago, just across Washington Park, but an intellectual world away from South Park Avenue. (These steps parallel Farrell's own education at St. Cyril College, the night school at DePaul University, and the University of Chicago.) And most important for his growth, Danny experiences the deaths of his father in 1923 and his grandmother Mary O'Flaherty in 1927. Eventually he decides to leave Chicago for New York and a writing career.

Farrell's beautifully structured five-volume narrative of Danny O'Neill's coming of age is a moving "portrait of the artist as a young man" and one of the first American portraits of a young artist emerging from a Catholic working-class environment. In this respect, then, the O'Neill-O'Flaherty series is a pioneering accomplishment of the first order.

In the O'Neill-O'Flaherty novels, Farrell chronicles the migratory patterns of a segment of Chicago's Irish community. In *Studs Lonigan,* he documents the response of some Irish families to the "Great Migration" of blacks to the South Side. Farrell's treatment of this important event provides a more specific example of his particular method of blending history and fiction.

The South Side began to change during World War I when thousands of black people moved north to Chicago from the South, both in search of jobs and to escape Jim Crow laws. At first these migrants settled in the clearly defined "Black Belt" that stretched south along both sides of State Street from the old black ghetto around 16th Street. In 1910, when blacks constituted two percent of the city's population, the center of black Chicago had been 31st and State streets. As their numbers grew, blacks moved east and south from the increasingly congested Black Belt into adjoining neighborhoods which had been, up to then, entirely white. The terrible race riots of July 1919 were the first overt and unignorable sign of the tensions created by this movement. New neighborhood groups were formed and old ones redirected for the purpose of keeping blacks out of white neighborhoods.

Blacks had lived in Washington Park as early as the 1880s, but until the twentieth century they had been confined to the area west of State Street, and eventually State came to be considered a "natural" boundary line between the races. But by 1915 blacks had begun to settle in apartments south of Garfield Boulevard and east of State Street. Neither vigilantism, riots, nor local neighborhood action could divert the course of the expanding Black Belt. The whites of Grand Boulevard and Washington Park, confused and frightened by what they saw as a threat to their established way of life, elected to flee wholesale.

Many moved east to Hyde Park, hoping (not without cause) that the University of Chicago would help shelter them from integrated living. Others went south and east to the newer and somewhat fancier area known as South Shore, which boasted a country club and proximity to Lake Michigan. In the wake of this mass exodus, black people moved into the old neighborhoods. The census figures are dramatic: in 1920 the Washington Park area had 38,076 residents, 15 percent of them black; in 1930, 92 percent of the area's population of 44,016 was black. Equally dramatic are the figures for the smaller square of territory bounded by Garfield Boulevard (55th Street), 59th Street, State Street, and South Park Avenue, within which the fictitious O'Neills, O'Flahertys, and Lonigans lived in 1920. At that time, the area housed 11,825 whites and 848 blacks; by 1930 there were 426 whites and 14,475 blacks.

In a 1948 article, "Testimony on Censorship," Farrell replied to the critics of his explicit rendering, in the *Studs Lonigan* trilogy, of the fears and prejudices of Washington Park residents:

> a number of people who had lived in this neighborhood, say, as far back as 1916, when *Studs Lonigan* began, felt that they had become settled for life, and they did not realize that under their feet the growth of Chicago, the change of Chicago, was going on, and that whole neighborhood was going to

> change, and all that they felt secure was going to crumble. . . . I attempted to register that change more directly in terms of the reactions of the characters. Those residents were not exactly correct in terms of any clear analysis of why the change was, but it was their ideas. For instance, the most common view in white neighborhoods is that Jewish people and colored people caused the change, so that it exacerbated prejudice. So that is put down plainly and directly in the book.

As the trilogy opens, Studs's father, Patrick Lonigan, sits on the back porch of his home in the 5700 block of South Wabash Avenue on a June evening in 1916. Looking around, he finds that life is good. His business as a painting contractor is booming; soon he'll be worth "a cool hundred thousand berries." He owns his own building in this respectable middle-class neighborhood, and has been here since before his son's birth. His pleasant associations with the area go back even further; among his most cherished memories is one of a Sunday afternoon while he was courting his wife, when he had rented a buggy at no small expense and "they had driven way out south," to find that "Fifty-eighth Street was nothing but a wilderness," and "it was nearly all trees and woods out here." He looks back with self-satisfaction on his childhood as the son of "pauperized greenhorns" from Ireland: like Tom and Mary O'Flaherty, Patrick Lonigan had grown up near what Finley Peter Dunne's "Mr. Dooley" called "Archey Road," located in the heart of Bridgeport.

The only one of his brothers and sisters to become successful — an outcome he attributes to persistence — Patrick also recalls his days as "a young buck in Canaryville" (the neighborhood around St. Gabriel Church at 45th Street and Lowe Avenue). Like the O'Neills and O'Flahertys, he had made a series of moves south before ending up in Washington Park as a prosperous homeowner. This evening's occasion, Studs's graduation from St. Patrick grammar school, completes Lonigan's happiness and our picture of his situation: he is a Catholic family man and supporter of his parish institutions, a typical middle-class Chicagoan whose success and identity are embodied in his position and property in St. Patrick parish, Washington Park.

But Patrick Lonigan is far from secure. Even on this happy evening, his complacent reverie is interrupted by the thought that

> the family would have to be moving soon. When he'd bought this building Wabash Avenue had been a nice, decent, respectable street for a self-respecting man to live with his family. But now, well, the niggers and kikes were getting in, and they were dirty. . . . And when they got into a neighborhood property values went blooey. He'd sell and get out . . . and when he did, he was going to get a pretty penny on the sale.

As the novel continues, signs of unrest grow as the ethnic and racial makeup of Washington Park changes. Old man O'Brien predicts as early as 1916 that "one of these days, we're gonna have a race riot." When the riots come in July 1919, Studs and his 58th Street Gang roam the border streets between their turf and the newest black areas near Garfield Boulevard. In search of blacks to avenge the death of a white boy from 61st Street, they find only a single ten-year-old, whom they strip and terrorize. Another sign of the times is the repeated bombing of the home of Abraham Clarkson, "the leading colored banker of Chicago" (modeled after Jesse Binga, the first black in the 5900 block of South Park Avenue) and an earnest, contributing member of St. Patrick parish.

Partly because he has worked so hard to

get there, Patrick Lonigan is unwilling to leave Washington Park, despite the steady movement of blacks into the area from the north and west, and the equally steady exodus of his friends. In 1922 the family moves one block east to a new building on Michigan Avenue, and Patrick Lonigan digs in his heels — this is his last move, he contends, and rejects a $90,000 offer for his building, even though his daughter declares that "the best people . . . are moving over to Hyde Park or out in South Shore. Soon," she says, "I'll be ashamed to admit I live around here."

What follows now in the lives of the Lonigan family is based in large measure on what in fact happened in the parish of St. Anselm, where Farrell spent his childhood. Bounded by 57th Street, 63rd Street, State Street, and St. Lawrence Avenue, St. Anselm had been organized in 1909 by Rev. Michael S. Gilmartin in the new residential district adjoining Washington Park. Within a year, the Irish-born priest had financed the construction of a combination church-school-parish hall, rectory, and convent. As his parish grew, Father Gilmartin began to save for a new church, but by 1924, when ground was finally broken, many of his parishioners had already moved farther south. Between 1925 and 1930 enrollment in the parish school dropped from 400 to 100. In 1932 Father Gilmartin was transferred to another parish while the order of the Divine Word Fathers assumed the care of St. Anselm's, which soon became a thriving black parish.

In its reincarnation in the Studs Lonigan series this course of events is used to depict the feelings of a man like Patrick Lonigan,

The tracks of the Cottage Grove Avenue streetcar line and the Jackson Park elevated station at 63rd and Cottage Grove are visible in this view of one of the major business streets serving Washington Park, 1930.

(CHS, ICHi-04169)

who once believed that Washington Park would be his last home in Chicago, and in his fictional rendering of this complex and sensitive historical situation Farrell contributes much to our understanding of the roots of interracial tension in Chicago following World War I.

In the book, Father Gilhooley has decided to build St. Patrick's Church on the corner of 61st and Michigan. The pastor has assured his parish that Michigan Avenue will become "a boulevard straight through," and Lonigan believes that the new church will keep the neighborhood white and double the value of his building at the same time. Two years later, Studs attends a fund-raising meeting for the new church, which is still being seen as the potential salvation of the neighborhood. Now that the present buildings are free of debt, the parishioners of St. Patrick parish are urged to contribute to a church that will be "one of the most beautiful . . . in this city," and "the fondest dream of your pastor."

Around this time, Studs and some of his friends hear a lecture at the Bug Club (Washington Park's answer to London's Hyde Park Speakers' Corner) on the inevitability of black migration to the South Side of Chicago as an "outgrowth of social and economic forces . . . a pressure stronger than individual wills." But it makes little sense to them and merely leaves them puzzled at "an Irishman being a nigger-lover." (The speaker is John Connolly, a well-known local radical.) In a few months it becomes clear to all that the new church has not stopped or even slowed the influx of blacks to the area, and many disillusioned parishioners, including the Lonigans, begin blaming Father Gilhooley. A stronger pastor, they contend, would not have "built a beautiful new church, and then let his parish go to the dogs. . . . He'd have organized things like vigilance committees to prevent it."

Eventually Patrick Lonigan also gives up on his neighborhood. Reluctantly selling his building to a black man, he moves his family to South Shore (around 71st Street and Jeffery Boulevard) in 1928. What happens at the old house on moving day reveals the emotional cost of such moves and enables us to understand the overall design of the *Studs Lonigan* trilogy.

Patrick Lonigan knows that he has lost his last real home; he is simply too old to make another. "You know, Bill," he confides to Studs in the empty parlor on Michigan Avenue, "your mother and I are gettin' old now, and, well, we sort of got used to this neighborhood. . . . they were all nearby, and they all sort *of* knew us, and we knew them, and you see, well, this neighborhood was kind of like home. We sort of felt about it the same way I feel about Ireland, where I was born." The thought of moving to South Shore brings no comfort, for "out there there'll only be about ten buildings in our block, the rest's all prairie," and "we're not what we used to be, and it'll be lonesome there some times." From this point on, both Patrick Lonigan and his son are permanently displaced persons.

Taken out of his familiar neighborhood, Studs becomes even more of an aimless drifter. No more at home on South Shore than is his father, Studs complains that there is "no place to hang out" there. Five months after moving away he returns to Washington Park and finds his gang's "old corner" at 58th and Prairie Avenue looking "like Thirty-fifth and State" (the center of the Black Belt). The playground, school, and church are strange to him already, and even Washington Park itself seems like alien territory: "It had used *to* be his park. He almost felt as if his memories were in it, walking about like ghosts." Later that night, a drunken Studs goes back to the park looking for the tree he had sat in with Lucy Scanlan twelve years before. He can't find it and gets lost trying.

Later, on the New Year's Eve that ends *The Young Manhood of Studs Lonigan,* the 58th Street Gang throws a wild reunion party — not in one of the neighborhoods in which they now live, but "at a disreputable hotel on Grand Boulevard [now Dr. Martin Luther King, Jr., Drive] in the black belt." Their night of debauched drinking results in the permanent ruin of Studs's health, and he ends up, in "the dirty gray dawn" of January 1, 1929, passed *out* beside a fireplug back at 58th and Prairie Avenue. It looks as though, in his semi-conscious stupor, he has been trying to go home again.

On the day of his son's death in the Depression year of 1931, Patrick Lonigan embarks on his own sad odyssey, literally retracing the steps of his life. He drives from South Shore to Washington Park, stopping to take a look at his old building and to say a prayer in St. Patrick Church, then on to Bridgeport "to look at places where he had lived and played as a shaver." Far from finding solace in the familiar streets of Bridgeport, Lonigan is reminded instead of the poverty of his youth and his current financial problems.

Patrick Lonigan's disillusionment is complete. All that he had believed to be stable has crumbled; he has lost his son, his home, and much of his hard-won financial security. By the end of *Judgment Day,* in a pathetic search for meaning, he has come under the influence of the anti-Semitic radio priest "Father Moylan," based, it seems, on Father Charles Coughlin. Finding no other way to explain what has happened to him, Lonigan blames his troubles on "Jew real estate men" and a "conspiracy" of "Jew international bankers."

As with James Joyce's departure from Dublin, Farrell's from Chicago was a leave-taking in body but not in spirit. As we have seen, Chicago became the inspiration for the first, amazingly prolific phase of his career. In the eleven years ending with the appearance of *My Days of Anger* in 1943, Farrell published the *Studs Lonigan* trilogy and four of the O'Neill-O'Flaherty novels, two other Chicago-based novels *(Gas-House McGinty* and *Ellen Rogers),* and over fifty Chicago short stories.

In his later fiction he has made frequent returns to the South Side, especially in several volumes of his monumental work-in-progress, the *Universe of Time.* Using the character of Eddie Ryan, a Chicago writer (born, like his creator and Danny O'Neill, in 1904), Farrell reexamines the experience of the artist in the modern world. In Farrell's latest novel, *The Death of Nora Ryan,* it is 1946 and Eddie has returned to Chicago because his mother is dying. As he keeps vigil he knows that in time he will turn the experience into art:

> What was happening now, this present, would be the past and would be in his memory. The experience would have crystallized in his unconscious mind. . . . One morning he would wake up, sit at his desk, and start writing about it.

He wonders about the "simple purposes" of his mother's life, but concludes "Yes, it mattered. Nora Ryan's life was a world. For Nora Ryan. These thoughts brought back his most familiar and important ideas. He must one day dignify his mother's suffering in the consciousness." The importance of Nora's life and of her son's depiction of lives like hers is brought home when Nora's night nurse reads one of Eddie's novels and responds with surprised pleasure, thinking:

> The book was so much like life. She knew the people in this book. . . . She had known these people all of her fifty-three years. They were her own kind. She had never expected

to read a book like this. She had never thought that books like this were written.

Because books like this are indeed written, have been written for fifty years, and continue to be written, at least three generations of American readers owe a debt of profound gratitude to their author, James T. Farrell. Chicagoans, of course, owe him even more, and the South Side Irish owe him the most of all. He has dignified their lives in the consciousness.

PART V

CHICAGO IN MODERN TIMES

The Enduring Chicago Machine

Richard C. Wade

The urban political machine is uniquely American. It appeared in the nineteenth century, the product of a peculiar mixture of American democratic institutions and the first explosive growth of the nation's cities. A machine developed in almost every sizable American city, be it old or new, North or South, growing or declining. Almost universally deplored by the best-known observers of American institutions, the machine was widely believed to be corrupt, exploitative, undemocratic, and ironically, "un-American." In 1889 Lord Bryce made his famous judgment "There is no denying that the government of cities is the one conspicuous failure of the United States. The deficiencies of the National government tell but little for evil on the welfare of the people. The faults of the State governments are insignificant compared with the extravagances, corruptions and mismanagement which mark the administrations of most of the great cities." Bailey Aldrich, one of the country's leading literary figures, noted the ethnic flavor of some machines by referring to their performance as "a despotism of the alien, by the alien, for the alien, tempered by occasional insurrections of the decent folk." A Harvard political scientist wrote an article on "The Irish Captivity of American Cities"; Lincoln Steffens's *The Shame of the Cities* summed up the popular view of the governance of the nation's municipalities.

After the decline and virtual disappearance of the institution following the Great Depression, a nostalgic literature grew up around the boss and his machine, arguing that for all their shortcomings they at least provided leadership and (presumably) eliminated untidy primaries and messy public disagreements over policy and budgets. This benign view was popularized by Edwin O'Connor's charming *Last Hurrah,* but finds a genial respectability among academics, columnists, and political observers. Nearly every election evokes the "good old days" when party bosses would get together and choose a slate, and the well-disciplined organization would march willing citizens to the polls to vote for superior candidates and acceptable programs. In the process of revision, a machine system scarcely recognizable to most historians has been created.

Chicagoans have always believed their city is the peculiar home of the machine and boss system. Yet this form of municipal politics stemmed from roots common to most large (and some small) cities. But if it

Two of Chicago's most notorious bosses, Alderman Michael "Hinky Dink" Kenna (left) and "Bathhouse" John Coughlin, pose at the 1924 Democratic Convention in New York. In exchange for political support, Chicago's political bosses provided jobs and other services for the residents of their wards. Coughlin earned his nickname by promoting a number of public bathhouses in the city's First Ward. *(CHS, ICHi-10927)*

did not invent the machine, Chicago did elevate it to an envious level of technological perfection in the post-depression period, establishing a national reputation for machine efficiency. An eastern journalist remarked after a visit to Chicago: "I have seen the past, and it works." Yet, the Cook County organization is not the most successful. That accolade belongs to Albany, New York, where the venerable Erastus Corning had been mayor continuously from 1943 to 1982. In his last years he charmingly explained his success by observing that, despite rampant inflation, "the five dollar vote still stands in Albany." Nor was Chicago's machine ever as criminal as Hague's Jersey City, or as corrupt as Jim Curley's Boston, or as racially venal as Crump's Memphis. Michael "Hinky Dink" Kenna, boss of Chicago's First Ward, acknowledged this, observing that "we never go for the big stuff" because it was "too risky" and instead settle on the incremental emoluments of the "small stuff."

Nonetheless, Chicago's machine has had a wide reputation for its effectiveness and endurance, and its present disarray strikes observers as novel and unexpected. The historian's perspective, however, is different. The proper question is not why it has collapsed, but rather why it lasted so long. For one can only understand Chicago's recent experience in the context of the origins of the

American urban machine and of its decline during the past two generations.

The boss system emerged out of the peculiar conditions created by America's great urban explosion of the nineteenth century. Wave after wave of immigrants piled into the inner cities, and young people streamed in from the American countryside, creating unprecedented residential congestion. In New York's Tenth Ward, the density approached 300,000 people per square mile; in Chicago some areas exceeded 100,000. No other city in the world could match these population density figures. No matter what their origins, the newcomers faced the same conditions — wretched housing, scarce jobs, inadequate schools, littered streets, anemic public services, high crime rates, and endemic disorders.

Indeed, today's urban problems are not new. Photographer Jacob Riis coined the phrase "how the other half lives" nearly a hundred years ago. Harvard professor Joseph Mayer Rice examined the nation's school system and found that dropping out, truancy, overcrowding, and poor teaching were rampant. Chicago's Board of Health reported that three out of five children born in the First Ward died by the age of one year. In late nineteenth-century Chicago hundreds of trains, all puffing soft coal, jammed into downtown; horse manure dirtied the streets, and sanitation carts made irregular garbage pickups in the city's alleys. Children frolicked in contaminated creeks, soiled streets, and dangerous lots. At best, municipal governments responded to this broad range of problems with concern and well-meaning yet ineffective programs, but more usually with neglect, indifference, or even exploitation.

People living in the inner cities managed as best they could. Women sought sanctuary from the crowding and chaos in churches and temples, which offered peace and quiet under the genial and forgiving eye of a priest or rabbi. For the men, there was the saloon. Here, too, was an urban oasis well lit, clean, convivial — where people knew each other's first names. Here everyone has somebody. And there was always the street. Although jammed at times, it was a place away from home and job, where friends chatted and new acquaintances were made. Yet, the broader institutional adjustment of the inner city to the predicament of its vulnerable people was political. The machine and the boss system gave public expression to the life of the people who occupied the most difficult parts *of* the American city.

The machine hardly had noble origins. It sprang from the plight and ambitions of second-generation newcomers to the city. Young, ambitious, and often talented, they grew up tantalized by society's promises of success and frustrated by the contradictions of upward mobility: they could not go into business because they had no money; they could not go into the professions because they had no education; they could not go into high finance or commerce because they had no family connections. What they did have were numbers and the right to vote. This was the loophole in the system. Everywhere else numbers were the curse of the neighborhood — too many mouths to feed at home, too many apartments in the building, too many tenements on the block. Yet in politics numbers were an asset; indeed, here *only* numbers counted. If used shrewdly, they could transform the source of difficulty into an instrument of protection and strength. Political power could cushion the worst effects of the dreadful conditions in the inner-city neighborhoods.

Given this opportunity, members of the second generation took it. Without personal resources, they organized themselves loosely, were sought out by party functionaries who rewarded them with jobs, and found their way onto party slates. Organized in gangs, they occupied the netherland between legal and illegal activity. Their general behavior, often involving brawling and limited violence, contributed to the low reputation of political organizations in "tenderloin" wards of most American cities. But their cohesiveness made them attractive to political factions seeking votes on primary or election day.

Thus, it must be stated at the outset that the machine was never a charity organization or a social settlement. Indeed, it is not surprising that bossism's methods and objectives were disreputable. It sought exemptions from the law: permitting saloons to operate on Sundays, protecting gambling and prostitution, winking at building code violations. On another level, it merely sought leniency for those caught in the web of the law: posting bail for an old drunk, attesting to the character of a truant student, postponing rent evictions, and reducing the cost of a hospital bill. All of these activities frustrated or skirted the law, but they also aided those unable to manage their own affairs.

Most of all, the machine acted as a primitive employment agency. Later generations would see this function simply as patronage on the public payroll. But the boss had a

Chicago tenement dwellers, c. 1912. Immigrants in America's large cities in the nineteenth and early twentieth centuries faced wretched housing and crowded living conditions, a shortage of jobs, inadequate schools, littered streets, anemic public services, and high crime rates. *(CHS, ICHi-03847)*

much longer reach that included all employment even marginally connected with public expenditures. Such employment was not inconsiderable, for machine power reached its apex between 1880 and 1930 as cities were building what is now called the "urban infrastructure." This included streets, sewers, bridges, tunnels, and water and electrical systems, as well as innumerable schools, hospitals, parks, and transit systems. Private construction matched public building, and nearly all of it was done manually, which required tough hands and strong backs. Employers depending on franchises, building codes, and ordinances had to indulge, if not co-opt, political power. They needed labor; the machine provided it. The neighborhood depended on jobs: the political system had special access to them.

Since this was a period of unprecedented urban expansion, jobs were plentiful — but by contemporary standards, not by ours. Though no one kept accurate statistics at the time, it is unlikely that unemployment ever fell below 20 percent. And the machine produced only a modest cushion for the depression years that occurred relentlessly every decade. The slim margins meant that all members of the family entered the labor force — wives and children of both sexes and all ages above six or seven. This depressed wages, creating competition even within families.

The local outpost of the machine was the clubhouse. It was to the boss system what the coffeehouse was to the merchant or the social club to the business community. Located in the heart of a troubled neighborhood, it became the focus of local political life. Its long bar beckoned, and its bright lights filled the room, softened only by sawdust on the floor. Card tables dotted the back room; there were usually some pool tables, and in the larger clubhouses perhaps even a boxing ring. In the further recesses or upstairs the boss and his associates conducted the neighborhood's business — discussing a few jobs, agreeing to see the judge about a disorderly conduct charge, chatting with prospective candidates for the slate. Downstairs bustled with conviviality, unbuttoned small talk, and engaging braggadocio. Here, in this relaxed setting among friends, a neighbor was somebody. Though he was just another body on the job, and he was lost in the crowd on his block and in his building, at the political club he counted. Friends called him by his first name, and he ran into people who were well known. The district leader gave him a political task to do; he could even joke about owing money to a friend or the bartender, And, just as satisfying, candidates and reporters paid their respects with a visit on election day.

To survive, the machine had to learn how to care for those without jobs and those whose wages did not cover rent, food, and clothing. This meant somehow postponing or finessing hospital bills, picking up funeral costs, getting coal when it was short or expensive, and providing turkeys for the destitute at Christmas and Thanksgiving. Nostalgic literature has romanticized this function, but it was, in reality, of considerable importance to the neighborhood. Every February, for example, "Big" Tim Sullivan, New York's boss of the Bowery, distributed shoes to the children in the school district. To be sure, Sullivan shook down the local merchants for the shoes, and his largess stopped at the ward boundary. Reformers did not believe his gift constituted scientific charity, but the criticism only enhanced "Big" Tim's reputation for caring for his people.

Yet personal favoritism was never a very secure base for the machine. More and more, the boss performed services for the block or the district: a small park here, a school or playground then a new sewer or better pavement in one place, a fire station in another.

The saloon served as a political clubhouse where bosses and their associates conducted their business in a relaxed and friendly atmosphere. A place where men went for jobs and other political favors as well as companionship, the saloon was an important link between the machine and the ordinary citizen.

(CHS, ICHi-20009)

Bathhouses sprang up everywhere, providing hygienic facilities in congested neighborhoods where there was no indoor plumbing. Indeed, Chicago's First Ward boss John Coughlin promoted so many that it earned him the sobriquet "Bathhouse John." Even an annual family trip to the country brought escape from the urban cauldron and many thanks to its sponsors. The politicians who ran the machine took their cuts along the way. They contributed handsomely to the rampant corruption of the political process, participated in boodle and bribery as a matter of course, continually raised taxes, indulged special business interests, and protected gambling and prostitution. And men who held only modest jobs on the public payroll suddenly became rich. Reformers and the newspapers harped on the sordid aspects of the boss system. But neighborhood residents accepted machine shenanigans as a matter of course. After all, if your own politicians would not protect you and provide even the most basic services, who would? Machine corruption and a ballot cast on election day seemed a small price to pay for the benefits received.

Ironically, the machine's opponents unwittingly promoted the bosses' role. In this period the "best people" supported movements to "clean up" city government by lowering taxes, balancing budgets, and encouraging nonpartisan employment and business efficiency. To them, "reform" meant temperance (if not prohibition), women's rights, and civil service reform (thus adding an educational factor to public employment). They believed issues such as poverty, health, housing, and consumer protection belonged to private agencies or the market economy. In short, they believed in a limited role for government and a large measure of self-reliance for all — rich and poor, strong and weak.

The machine and boss system evolved out of this gap between the needs of the vulnerable people in the inner-city neighborhoods and the indifference and often hostility of the older residents, most of whom had moved to the outer residential edges of the city while maintaining an economic stake in the business downtown. Reform reflected the politics of the successful residents on the city's periphery, while the boss and the machine expressed the plight of those caught up in the dreadful conditions in the older neighborhoods. As the metropolis grew, so did the numbers on both sides. The split widened, and the issue of boss and machine rule dominated the nation's political dialogue.

The contest was nationwide and included nearly every major city. And it was nonpartisan. In some places, like Philadelphia, the machine was Republican. In others, like Boston, it was Democratic. In Chicago, the division existed in both parties. Although Americans today associate machines with the Democratic party, the connection has only developed since the Great Depression. The political affiliation of a machine was unimportant. The Democratic and Republican parties were primarily national in their focus; their ideology and policies mattered little to the city politician. Even the party in power in Washington mattered little to most city dwellers. There was no income tax of any significance, no draft, no social security, no health programs, and no unemployment insurance. Only the postal system connected Washington to its metropolitan reaches. He who presided at City Hall was more important than the occupant of the White House. Indeed, local elections often attracted more voters than presidential contests.

The struggle between machine and reform characterized American politics for a half century. Each side enjoyed a share of the successes. In the process, the machine tempered its grossest practices, and reformers softened many of their moral judgments of the people who lived in the congested downtown areas. This accommodation was accelerated by the exodus of second- and third-generation inner-city dwellers, who moved to the pleasant residential areas previously occupied by older inhabitants. But this unique era of American politics came to an end. The Great Depression hit the cities harder than any previous economic panic. It lasted a decade and ultimately redefined American urban, and hence national, politics.

The depression was as much a watershed in the history of cities as of the country. For more than two hundred years, cities had managed their own affairs. Chicago, for example, built the Sanitary and Ship Canal, which reversed the flow of the river. It created one of the most extensive park systems in the world, it reshaped the lake shoreline, and it provided water for its suburban neighbors. The city established an extensive mass-transit system, educated its growing school population, and pioneered the social settlement. All of this was accomplished without aid from either Springfield or Washington; indeed, Chicago had enough money left over to send some to both. The Great Depression marked the end of this urban self-sufficiency; in the modern period cities would come to depend increasingly on state and federal funds. As a result, even where the machine hung on, it no longer controlled the money, the policy, or the jobs.

The New Deal, propelled by persistent unemployment, widening poverty, and growing desperation, began to provide nationally the programs for ordinary people that the boss system could only produce sporadically and inadequately. Jobs offering the minimum wage and unemployment compensation emanated from Washington through the Works Progress Administration (WPA) and the Public Works Administration (PWA), and from countless local public works. The Social Security Act provided help to the elderly, school-work programs and conservation projects kept young people busy, and public housing and the Federal Housing Administration furnished shelter for the homeless and security for homeowners. In short, what the machine had provided on a primitive level and with obligations was now provided by the federal government as a matter of right. Thus, few people noticed as the whole rationale for the boss system slipped slowly away.

The fact that the bosses supported Franklin D. Roosevelt and his New Deal concealed the erosion of their power. City governments were initially the only government agencies available to administer relief and new programs; the machines seemed to prosper, and

Workmen pave LaSalle Street with creosoted wood blocks, c. 1910. The neighborhood political machine acted as a primitive employment for workers helping to build America's urban infrastructure — streets, sewers, bridges, and water and electrical systems — between 1880 and 1930.

(CHS, ICHi-20005)

their power appeared enhanced. In Chicago the Kelly-Nash machine loomed larger than before, even though its old reform nemeses Harold Ickes, Henry Horner, and Charles Merriam held high positions in Springfield and Washington. Inevitably, the locus of authority shifted to Washington, and the most effective mendicants proved the ablest bosses.

Washington's authority eroded the base and autonomy of local political organizations. But the New Deal's sponsorship of unions also undermined the private patronage historically available to the machine. The unions now found the jobs, exercised discipline in the workplace, protected the employed worker, and, along with the federal government, took care of him during slack times. The union hall replaced the old political clubhouse. Here were the bar, the meeting rooms, pool and bowling, and even family recreation. At the union bank, workers cashed checks, saved for vacations, and, later, paid their medical hills. It was not uncommon for unions to lead their new members in a charge against their old machine benefactors even when Roosevelt was still alive. The famous phrase of the Democratic convention in Chicago in 1940 was "clear it with Sidney"; "Sidney" was Sidney Hillman, the head of the Amalgamated Clothing Workers, not a political boss.

By the end of the war, the Kelly-Nash machine gave way to Jake Arvey, a shrewd observer who understood that the old ways were over. To survive at all, it was necessary to ally with "clean," if not "reform," candidates. Under his tutelage, the machine supported Martin Kennelly for mayor and later put Paul Douglas and Adlai Stevenson at the top of the Democratic state ticket. This nimbleness left the machine intact, if not very powerful. Across the country, boss systems collapsed. In Philadelphia, the GOP's most durable machine dissolved amid scandal; elsewhere the dominoes tumbled. Memphis, Jersey City. Seattle, Atlanta, Minneapolis, St. Louis, and New York replaced the old system with "New Look" mayors.

Chicago, among the major cities, seemed immune to the new forces. Yet Richard J. Daley was never a boss in the classic sense. He did, in fact, inherit some substantial remnants of the old Kelly-Nash machine, and the local press found it easier to cast him in the old mode than to analyze him in the context of the new conditions. Indeed, he often reveled mischievously in past illusions and suffered the swagger of loudmouthed but pint-sized ward "leaders." He even referred to the city council as "an independent legislative body" and made embarrassing appointments of hacks to important offices. But he also knew the "good old days" of machine rule were over. His success depended on presenting quality candidates, at least at the top of the ticket, and on controlling the roughest edges of what he liked to call "the organization." While a few disreputable candidates might sneak in as lower judges, Daley preferred to be associated with the Douglases, Stevensons, and Kennedys for the most visible nominations.

Daley's unique power rested in his combined role as the city's highest elected official and chairman of the Cook County Democratic Party. Thus his popularity discouraged even ambitious rivals, and his control of the organization virtually eliminated serious primaries. This conjunction of public and party leadership permitted Richard Daley almost a quarter century of dominion over Chicago politics and explains the longevity of the Chicago machine. Just as important to his success was the mayor's keen sense of the limitations of his power in a complex metropolis laced with minor baronies beyond his control. Parky Cullerton and Tom Keane, for example, had their own constituencies immune to all but the courts. The organized business community was beyond reach but not accommodation, and Daley prided himself in keeping Chicago a "union town" and so enjoyed continuous labor support. He reduced his opposition to a predictable number of "independents," mostly from the lakefront wards; and even there his capacity to co-opt was respected.

Yet, for all his power and shrewdness, Daley could not handle the most compelling issue of his time and his city — race. His problem was neither indifference nor bigotry, for he always believed that blacks were simply the newest ethnic group to be drawn to Chicago. As such, they would go through the same immigrant experience as their European predecessors. That experience in Chicago was clear. The newcomers gathered in the center city, discovered their numbers, somehow found jobs, and then dispersed to the pleasant residential areas beyond the urban interior. Irish, Germans, Italians, Poles, and others could be found, even if in modest numbers, throughout the city and in the suburbs as proof of successful mobility.

Though blacks did gather at the center and found a few jobs, they never moved their homes beyond the original settlements. Instead the ghetto simply oozed out, block after block, until the South and West sides of Chicago contained monolithic concentrations previously unknown in the city. The black ghetto, unlike the temporary immigrant ghetto, seemed increasingly permanent and therefore intolerable to its residents.

Initially, Daley resorted to the old machine remedy — jobs. Indeed, some white leaders complained that his appointments discriminated against them. But postwar America bred a black middle class that expected more — equal opportunities for jobs in the private sector, open housing, and a larger share of elected officials and high appointments. Daley never grasped the complete ramifications of this demand. "Why don't they act like the Poles, Jews, Italians, and Germans?" he once asked quizzically. He never understood that because they hadn't been treated like earlier groups, a new approach was necessary. Yet as flames ate through the West Side, as old black allies defected, and as a new black middle class continuously enlarged, he clung to what he considered the American system — the incorporation of all groups, no matter what race or religion, into the country's, and certainly Chicago's, metropolitan mainstream. But the acids of the race question soon eroded the established Daley assumptions. Even before his death, this issue was eroding the machine's power.

Within a few years of Daley's death, the machine faltered, and the election of anti-machine candidate Jane Byrne in 1979 left disarrayed debris. Ironically, and with no historical instincts, she tried to remold the organization around her through old-fashioned patronage. The result was a reelection bid that defied even Chicago's flamboyant past. A three-candidate race in the Democratic primary resulted in a narrow victory for black candidate Harold Washington against the incumbent mayor and the son of Richard J. Daley. In a rare and nasty election, white Republican Bernard Epton came within a few votes of defeating Washington. Chicago had its first black mayor.

Washington's administration has been less than tranquil. White aldermen have girded themselves from the outset against the new reality, and untidiness has replaced Chicago's reputation for party discipline. New accommodations have become more important every day, and it is imperative that all ethnic and racial groups in the city come to understand that their futures are bound up in cooperation rather than confrontation. If by chance this happened, an eastern journalist could return to New York from Chicago and announce, "I have seen the future, and it works."

“Rent Reasonable to Right Parties”: Gold Coast Apartment Buildings, 1906-29

Celia Hilliard

In October of 1906 the first tenants moved into the new Marshall Apartments at the northwest corner of Cedar Street and Lake Shore Drive. The nine-story building, in a simple colonial style of vitrified brick, contained eight elaborately fitted apartments of about 4,000 square feet each. Rent for each unit was an unprecedented $4,200 per year, but even before the land on which the building would stand had been purchased, every apartment was spoken for by families listed in the Chicago Blue Book.

Since 1882, when Potter Palmer built his baronial mansion on the newly created Lake Shore Drive, the Gold Coast had become an increasingly popular site for the homes of wealthy Chicagoans. This area is bounded by Oak Street on the south, Lake Shore Drive on the east, North Avenue on the north, and Dearborn Street on the west. As contractors filled in the swamp east of Michigan Avenue, East Lake Shore Drive acquired the same elite aura. By the time the Marshall Apartments building was ready for its first occupants in 1906, the Gold Coast was firmly established as Chicago's finest residential district.

The Marshall was not the first example of multiple housing on the Gold Coast. The Maison du Nord, a large rooming house in what is now the 1200 block of Astor Street, rented to fifteen boarders as early as 1896, and the Ormonde, down the block, advertised large flats “high grade in every way” with “rent reasonable to right parties.” Nor was the Marshall the first to feature large rooms or expensive appointments. The Raymond, at Walton Street and Michigan Avenue, contained fourteen-room apartments and a top floor ballroom thirty-six by forty feet, and the McConnell Apartments on Astor Street offered four varieties of wood paneling and one unit with four fireplaces. All of these establishments — and many hotels and apartments in other parts of the city — housed families of high social standing.

Nevertheless, the Marshall Apartments set an important precedent in Chicago's residential history. Its layout, elegantly labeled in French and geared to grand-scale entertaining, set the pre-Depression standard for luxury apartments in Chicago and established its architect, Benjamin Marshall, as the city's foremost designer of apartments. Indeed, the very fact that the Marshall was built at all not only signaled the end of the Potter Palmer family's tight control of that prime strip of real estate, but reflected a fundamental change in the status of apartment houses. Formerly considered no more than a dwelling place for transients, the apartment as a luxury home for the wealthy would come into its own during the next two decades.

The Marshall Apartments, at 23 (later renumbered 1100) Lake Shore Drive, was described in the *Chicago Evening Post* as an "ultra high class apartment building" developed "largely for entertaining purposes like the quarters of many wealthy residents of New York." The land cost $45,000, and the structure cost between $250,000 and $300,000 to build.

The floors were of oak, and the walls were finished in English oak, mahogany, and enamel. The floor plan for each apartment was a soon-to-be-typical H-shape and included a twelve- by twenty-five-foot reception hall, a large salon, an octagonal dining room, an "orangerie" (greenhouse), a versatile library/billiards/morning room, three large bedrooms, three maids' rooms (a butler's room could be rented on the first floor for an additional twenty dollars a month), a kitchen, a pantry, a servants' parlor, a completely equipped laundry, a silver vault, cedar closets, fruit and wine closets, a cooling room, a trunk room, and five baths. One visitor, the novelist E. M. Delafield, found just the array of taps in her bathroom so bewildering that a splash of tap water turned into a "quite involuntary shower." The "ascenseur" (elevator) was decorated with French grillwork, painted panels, and beveled glass, and was operated by liveried attendants on duty twenty-four hours a day. A "completely unobtrusive freight elevator" was used as the service entrance.

The first tenants included the families of Frank Frazier (a wealthy broker), Warren M. Salisbury (the president of a leather goods and rubber belting company), W. G. Beale (Robert Todd Lincoln's law partner), Cobb Coleman (heir to a prospecting fortune), Benjamin LaFon Winchell (president of the Rock Island Lines), Samuel Insull (president of Commonwealth Edison), Joy Morton (founder of Morton Salt), and W. J. Chalmers (a major owner of the largest mining machinery works in the world). A few years later Marshall Field's sister moved in.

While most of these tenants also had large suburban homes, farms, or summer "cottages" on Lake Geneva or the New England seacoast, apartment living nevertheless altered relationships between family members, servants, and neighbors. In his memoir *Chicago, With Love,* writer Arthur Meeker summarizes the sort of changes that took place after his family moved into the Marshall:

> For the first time in our history we found ourselves in a flat, all on one floor, in close proximity to one another. In the beginning Father didn't much like it; he felt that, in spite of twelve rooms and five baths, it was a step down in the world to share a roof and front door with seven other families; what finally reconciled him, I believe, was that the Samuel Insulls, then at the peak of their prosperity, our neighbors again, were one of the families. Mother liked it very much; she said it was like living in a hotel; enjoyed exploring her kitchen, a room she'd never seen before, and took to coming in a negligé to the breakfast table. What was pleasanter than that tryst over coffee and bacon and eggs, with Michigan's waves dancing in the

Lake Shore Drive as it appeared in 1928, looking north from Oak Street.
(CHS, ICHi-04326)

sun outside our east windows, and the first post on the letter-tray — imagine it now! — punctually at half past eight? The result was that, from then on, we were a great deal more often together.

The success of the Marshall Apartments inspired Benjamin Marshall to complete several similar projects, each on the same theme — spacious layouts with ever bigger rooms, more baths, more fireplaces, more elaborate kitchen equipment, and more space for servants. Exteriors also became more elaborate, with a surplus of pillars, balustrades, twisted columns, pediments, crests, and fancy stonework topped by an awkward assortment of smokestacks, elevator penthouses, pipes, and water tanks.

Though never formally trained as an architect, Marshall seemed to have an instinctive sense of line, proportion, and detail. After leaving school at the age of seventeen and a short stint as a fabric cutter and garment designer, he joined the architectural office of H. R. Wilson. By the time he was twenty-one, he had a half interest in the firm.

In the course of his career he designed more than half the apartment buildings erected on Lake Shore Drive before the Depression, as well as the Blackstone, Drake, and Edgewater Beach hotels and many of the famous clubs and restaurants within their walls.

Marshall's flamboyant style enhanced the dramatic appeal of his buildings. Colleagues recalled that he liked to drive up to a construction site in his white Packard convertible, sporting a white suit, white shoes, and Panama hat, and with two or three beautiful women on each arm. The pink stucco mansion he built in Wilmette was equipped with many "unusual contrivances," including a satin-covered mattress floor and a goldfish pond installed in a ceiling. Another talented Chicago architect remembered, "I used to sit out in front of the Drake Hotel and watch him with his girls and his wealthy clients and wonder, 'What does he have that I don't have?' "

In the years before World War I, Marshall designed 999 E. Lake Shore Drive, a ten-story building which faced the lake in two directions. Simulating the Second Empire style, the structure had red brick spandrels, white limestone, rounded oriels, and intimate balconies. He drew the plans for the Stewart

Apartments at 1200 Lake Shore Drive, which featured eighteen-room apartments of about 8,000 square feet each (including a wine cellar ten by nineteen feet). His magnificent building at 1550 N. State Parkway provided the best view in Chicago — the lake to the east and the park to the north, and its salons and dining rooms opened into each other to create an entertainment area 100 feet wide.

While in 1899 Potter Palmer had reportedly tried to block construction of the Raymond Apartments at Michigan and Walton, after his death in 1902 there was little further opposition to multiple housing on the Gold Coast. Other prominent architects were engaged to design apartment houses too, and they created memorable spaces for both their tenants and themselves. Howard Van Doren Shaw, the Lake Forest "estate architect," completed the Elm Street Apartments at 1130 Lake Shore Drive in 1910. The apartment he designed for himself in the building featured marble floors, elaborate ironwork Gothic and Renaissance tapestries, and a library with a sixteen-foot vaulted ceiling which was entirely lit by candles. Describing one of Shaw's interiors, Frank Lloyd Wright once remarked, "I utterly failed to imagine entering it other than in costume."

William Ernest Walker designed two buildings at 936 and 942 Lake Shore Drive (they have since been torn down) which featured two- and three-story units. Atop the structure at 936 he built a $40,000 rooftop "bungalow," a twelve-room house of white cement (probably the first penthouse in Chicago) for himself and his family. There was a vine-shaded pergola with a fireplace underneath it, and an attic beneath the sloping roof which was completely outfitted as a gymnasium. A woman guest remembered, "It was all very cool and fresh up there. You felt you were on vacation. There were no flies or piles of dirt like we have now. I went up to the attic and looked out at the stars through oval oriel windows. It was just like Paris."

Although there were at least a dozen and a half apartment buildings constructed on the Gold Coast before World War I, the character of the neighborhood remained the same. Lake Shore Drive was still a two-lane avenue with gas street lamps and leafy elm trees on either side. Except in Streeterville — the section of lakeshore east of Michigan Avenue at Oak Street — buildings were at least a block apart, heights did not rise beyond ten or twelve stories, and apartment units were, for the most part, one or two to a floor. Nevertheless, a feeling still persisted among the older generation that even an eighteen-room apartment was somehow second best.

But after the completion of the Michigan Avenue Bridge in 1920 doubled and tripled North Side land values; after postwar inflation and income taxes raised the price for bricklayers, carpenters, and cooks to the point that pinched the pockets even of the rich; after promoters discovered a whole generation of widows with North Side mansions for sale — then Gold Coast apartment building became a boomtime business. One cynic ventured to guess that the area was called the Gold Coast because of the presence of so many prospectors.

Once the trend accelerated, selling fever spread over the whole neighborhood. Properties changed hands by the year, by the month, by the week. James Deering died at sea in 1925, and within two years a twenty-three-story building stood on the site of his Lake Shore Drive home. The old Chapin house at the southwest corner of Goethe and Astor streets was sold for $150,000 one April and resold for $200,000 in May. Strings of townhouses lining the neighborhood's side streets were purchased and torn down. A house on Cedar Street was sold for $42,500. Five months later the adjoining house was sold for $50,000. The following year the next house brought $65,000 and the one next to that $75,000.

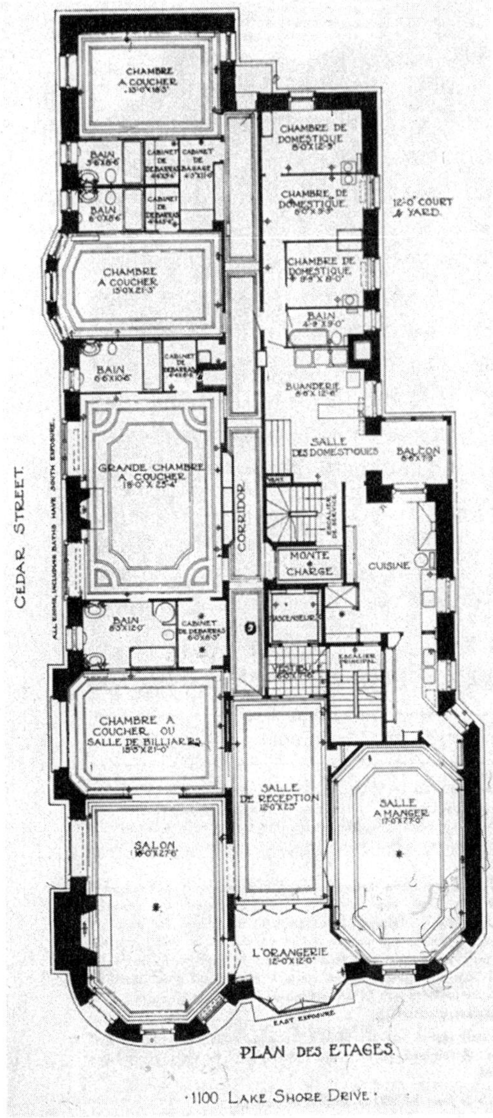

Benjamin Marshall's floor plan for 1100 North Lake Shore Drive, from Albert Pardridge's Directory to Apartments of the Better Class along the North Side of Chicago, 1917.

(CHS Library)

In spite of the shortage of materials, which nearly doubled building costs in the 1920s, developers had located a potential gold mine on the Drive. In the entire city 80 percent of the construction permits issued during the 1920s were issued for apartment units, but on the Gold Coast this percentage was nearly 100. By January of 1928 there were over 700 apartment units on Lake Shore Drive, representing an investment of well over $25 million. Gold Coast "prospecting" hit an all-time high when a syndicate which owned the land on Lake Shore Drive between Banks and Goethe streets announced plans to build a $15 million apartment complex there pending favorable court action on some necessary property adjustments. Whether the judge or the economy intervened first is not known, but the plan was never carried out.

Never host to assembly-line housing, the Gold Coast featured an extreme version of every current apartment-building trend. Apartments ranged from one to twenty-two rooms. Some, like the units at 900 N. Michigan, had big, high-ceilinged rooms, though not too many of them. Sometimes lobbies were reduced to tiny reception rooms; sometimes expanded, they assumed new magnitude. The lobby at 900 N. Michigan was inspired by a dining room in a Versailles palace. The lobby at 1400 Lake Shore Drive was like the first floor of a hotel, complete with barbershop, commissary, florist, newsstand, beauty shop, restaurant, cigar store, valet service, drugstore, and gift shop (as well as a small golf course with its own full-time instructor).

Uncertain about the future popularity of apartment living, the developers of the Park Dearborn at Goethe and Dearborn accepted a hotel-like design of 400 rooms with 400 baths which offered one-, two-, and three-room apartments. One real estate writer assured the public, "Tenants will be able to spend most of their time in the bathtubs . . . for even the two-room suite has two bathrooms and we presume the three-room apartment has a trio of bathing boudoirs for the fresh water fans."

With Gold Coast real estate at a premium, buildings were erected closer together, and the ideal of a four-sided structure which could be viewed from every angle gave way to a cheaper reality. New structures displayed "the Queen Anne front and the Betty Ann back" — while expensive stone trimmed the façade, and the sides and back were of common red or yellow brick. An apartment hotel at 1220 N. State, for example, featured Bedford stone on the first few floors, plain stone a little farther up, and finally, as the façade rose beyond pedestrian vision, simple brick.

Architects experimented with color. At State and Elm streets, B. Leo Steif designed an eye-catching exterior. The first floor was faced with dark French blue terra-cotta; the second, third, and fourth with terra-cotta of a light blue green (almost robin's egg) color; from there on up the building was constructed of delicately shaded salmon-colored brick.

Eventually, buildings on upper Michigan Avenue were designed to combine shops, doctors' offices, artists' studios, dressmakers' rooms, business headquarters, and apartments, until it seemed that there wasn't a structure standing without a chic little suite hidden away in it somewhere. Everybody wanted one, and the universal popularity of apartments was made manifest in advertisements for suburban houses. "This lovely home," one advertiser boasted, "features all the comforts of a flat."

In publicity brochures, the latest apartment house was often pictured rising through a mist, the photograph captioned with quotations from some great thinker. "Simple was the noble architecture," Voltaire is anachronistically quoted on the virtues of 1320 N. State. "The House reveals the Man," says Emerson of the same building. Some lesser thinkers got into the act too: "Beautiful originality rises above the mobs — not with the freak who strives for attractive shams, but with the personality of refined genuineness."

All the money and ingenuity that prosperous Chicagoans had concentrated on estates with large grounds a few decades earlier was now lavished on their Gold Coast apartments. The popularity of cooperative ownership, a system whereby tenants bought their apartments (more exactly, relative shares in the building corporation), encouraged tenants to spend money expressing their personal preferences and tastes in their apartments. In a few instances groups of friends banded together to create their own apartment building.

In many buildings, layouts and appointments varied from floor to floor, and sometimes different architects were brought in to design special apartments. The exterior of 1301 Astor Street is the work of Philip B. Maher, but several of its first tenants hired David Adler to design individual interiors. A woman whose family rented an apartment there during the 1930s recalled that "the variety was great, but too many hands on the blueprints caused problems too. You could never get cold water in the bathroom because that pipe was right next to somebody else's hot water pipe."

Furnishings and materials veered toward the exotic — parquet floors inlaid with pewter, marble foyers, alabaster urns, ivory walls, oak timbers, floor to ceiling fireplaces. Architect Jarvis Hunt had a living room with rough granite walls, a twenty-foot ceiling, and a fireplace "big enough for a small oak tree as a back log." Fifteen feet above the floor hung the head of a white rhinoceros. "Shot this rhino myself," Hunt would explain, "with my pocketbook, in a taxidermist's shop."

One apartment featured jungle murals and tiger skins on the floor. A woman in another had a photograph of the Taj Mahal enlarged twenty-five times and fitted into a six-foot-wide alcove. The artist Frederic C. Bartlett painted his apartment throughout with *trompe l'oeil* murals, including striped chairs, balconies, and staircases. He painted his dining room walls with a whole row of ancient busts on a Roman landscape. "I remember the first time I had dinner in that room," a guest recalled:

> I was staring at eyes of the Roman heads and suddenly I noticed the eyes were moving. That's kind of a shock right in the middle of soup. Then I realized it was another trick of his. There were holes bored in the walls, and that was the maid seeing whether she should pick up the plates. It didn't bother me so much because when I came in I took one of those painted chairs for real and dumped my coat on the floor.

Mrs. Cyrus McCormick had workmen create faces from Bible scenes on her bathroom walls. Kate Buckingham installed an entire room from a fine old Gothic castle in her parlor. An apartment at 209 E. Lake Shore Drive contained all-over murals of centurions overlooking a Moorish city, pashas, priests, shepherds, lavishly clothed women, and a deep pool with a jewel-like bottom. Elsewhere in the same building was a master bedroom with arched windows of thick stained glass portraying Faith, Hope, Prudence, and Chastity. Twin beds were placed on an oak dais surrounded by heavy copper-colored velvet drapes, hanging candelabra, and Romanesque columns.

If there was one building that seemed to epitomize the 1920s luxury apartment house, it was 1500 N. Lake Shore Drive. Built on the site of the Victor Lawson* mansion at a record-high cost of $5.5 million (not counting interiors), it included one twenty-two-room apartment, duplex units with winding staircases, two ground floor "maisonettes" with their own entrances, and a penthouse with a bell tower and a tea garden. Buyers included the William Wrigleys, the J. Russell Forgans, the George Woodruffs, and leading executives of such firms as Standard Oil, U.S. Gypsum, Peoples Gas, and the Chicago Trust Company. Observers concluded that the building "had an air of superiority baked into every brick."

In an interview, the building's architect, J. Edwin Quinn, recalled the start of the project:

> We 'flatters' — that's what they called us in those days — had plenty of competition for the good buildings. I heard about the Victor Lawson property being torn up, and I knew it would come up for sale. I talked to a guy at the bank, and he said, "There will be plenty of people after that spot. The bidding will start low, but you come up with a million dollars and it's yours."
>
> I didn't have any million dollars, but I got my friend Pete Reynolds the builder to come up on the bus and talk about it. He was leery of the deal because of the price, but I arranged ahead for the motorman to find something wrong with the bus when we got to the corner of Lake Shore and Burton, and in that extra time I gave him a big pep talk on the site.

Reynolds bought the land and resold it to a syndicate of developers (of which he was the head) to create the biggest, most ambitious apartment project on the Gold Coast.

*Victor Fremont Lawson published the *Chicago Daily News* from 1876, and was its editor from 1888 until his death in 1925.

Fine woodwork frames a view through William Wrigley's twenty-two-room duplex apartment at 1500 North Lake Shore Drive, c. 1927. Although wealthy Chicagoans stopped building castles on Prairie Avenue and Washington Boulevard, they maintained their foothold in the city by moving into luxury apartments such as this on the Gold Coast.
(CHS Prints and Photographs, Trowbridge collection)

A New York construction company was hired to build it, a New York real estate firm was hired to advise on selling and managing the apartments, and a New York architect was called in to advise on the design. "That was the thinking at the time," Quinn remembered, "anybody from New York is better than somebody in Chicago. So they paid New Yorkers money to get involved, and then we home-grown fellows showed them how to turn that whole design around and make more money on it."

From the start of the project the participants tried to make money, and ended up spending it instead. The wreckers intended to clear their part of the fortune by selling the brickwork of the Lawson house for 20¢ a brick. But when they started to demolish the walls, they found the bricks were set in imperishable cement and the potentially profitable structure had to be blown up with dynamite.

The architects didn't make any money either. "The fee was just based on putting up the building," explained Quinn. It did not include the custom arrangements and designs expected by owners who purchased co-ops before construction started. Quinn continued:

> They say we're all just glorified draftsmen, the real architect is the client's wife. Boy, if you don't think you don't get sour on women.

I had to allow for them to change their minds sixteen times before I let a painter or a plasterer touch the place. They'd want a vent pipe here, an outlet there, next day it was something different. There is almost nothing worse than a babe who is married to a guy with a lot of money. And the men weren't that great either. A banker was taking an apartment in that building and wanted a choice of layouts. I worked hard on some sketches and brought them over before the weekend. He went on a boat trip with some of his high class friends, and when he got back he told me the sketches blew out to sea and could I do another set. I said no, I could not.

The neighbors were sometimes as troublesome as the clients. The townhouses of Colonel Robert McCormick, publisher of the *Chicago Tribune*, and of a neighbor, Bertha Baur, were directly behind the rising apartment structure. A multi-storied garage with two spaces per apartment was going up at the rear of the building, looming right over the alley. Quinn reminisced:

> I was already seven stories up on the building when Colonel McCosmic — that's what I called him — decides the garage is spoiling the atmosphere in his garden. Bertha Baur joined up with him, and they tried to get the thing torn down. Garages were considered so low class then. Nobody wanted the noise and the gasoline pumps near their living room. . . . I finally called Bill Wrigley and said, "Say, your friend the Colonel doesn't

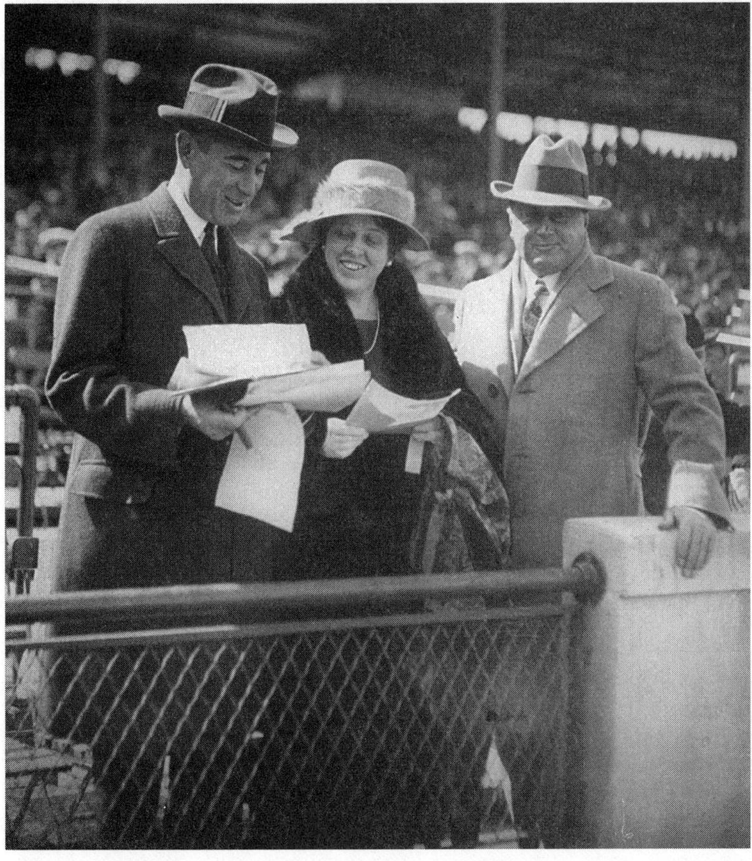

William Wrigley (right) at Cubs Park with Albert Lasker and Mrs. Fred Upham.
(CHS, DN 75,967)

want you to have space in the building for your cars." "The hell he doesn't," Wrigley said and the problem got solved.

Despite the setbacks, 1500 N. Lake Shore Drive emerged as a premier Chicago apartment house. "It's still the most beautiful apartment building in Chicago," says Quinn. "It's the most beautifully made. When you work with people, you ask them what work they like to do. Because then it's fun, it's not work. The moldings, the woodwork, everything is first class. I found a couple of Italians who just lived to make pictures in plaster. The leaded copper downspouts, the ironwork, that bronze lantern at the door — they were all made by people who loved their work and they're more beautiful now than they were fifty years ago."

The interiors matched the fine exterior. Tenants imported a wealth of decorative materials including Italian murals, Gothic organ lofts, and paneling from Continental castles. William Wrigley's twenty-two-room duplex in the building was one of the most glamorous apartments ever designed in Chicago, a masterpiece of craftsmanship with moldings, cornices, carved arches, built-in glass cases, and parquet floors. The dining room was designed to seat the twenty-two-member Cubs team. Even the master bathroom had an elaborately plastered ceiling, a glittering chandelier, and carved woodwork around the medicine cabinet. A second-floor sauna kept Wrigley tanned all year round. "He paid $13,000 to some interior decorator for an old pot-bellied stove too," Quinn recalled. "He was a very romantic guy, and when he did something he went all out."

But with the stock market crash of 1929 the era of "going all out" came to a famous and rapid close. Buildings under construction on the Gold Coast were completed, but projects still in the planning stages were scrapped. Mortgages were foreclosed, and co-ops reverted to rentals. Some apartments were broken up into smaller units. Benjamin Marshall was forced to sell 1100 N. Lake Shore Drive to his tenants for $10 and their agreement to assume two years of back taxes and a mortgage of $225,000.

But though the Depression years and World War II put an end to Gold Coast "flatting," almost all of the early apartment houses have survived. The building at 1100 N. Lake Shore Drive is a regrettable exception. But much more than the oversized, overstuffed mansions which preceded them, the Gold Coast apartment buildings of this era have retained, through significant social and economic changes, their aesthetic value and their enduring romantic appeal.

Crisis and Community: The Back of the Yards 1921

Dominic A. Pacyga

The history of the Chicago stockyards was marked by labor troubles almost from the start. The Knights of Labor were the first to attempt to organize the packinghouse workers, in 1886, but an unsuccessful strike that year proved their undoing. In 1894 stockyard workers struck in a show of sympathy for the Pullman workers. But this strike was poorly organized and also petered out. The most significant strike by these workers in the pre–World War I period was organized in 1904 under the banner of the Amalgamated Meat Cutters and Butcher Workmen of North America. Led by the American Federation of Labor (AFL), it was directed at improving the conditions of the unskilled workers in the industry. But once again the combined strength of the great packers defeated the strikers. No further attempts at organization took place for the next thirteen years.

A successful organizational drive during the war brought most of the packinghouse workers into the fold of the Amalgamated Meat Cutters. And war also brought a degree of prosperity to the neighborhoods surrounding the square mile of slaughterhouses and pens located on Chicago's South Side. It was to protect the gains made during the war that the union called a strike in 1921.

This conflict lasted a little more than a month, but the bitterness engendered in its course would take more than a decade to fade. However, the strike represented an important stage in the development of the community based in what was known as the Back of the Yards. To the surprise of those who had always considered the immigrant districts as merely chaotic and disorganized conglomerations of people, the residents of the area stood together in the face of common problems and showed a cohesiveness and self-awareness that had not been anticipated.

By 1921 the packing industry was firmly entrenched on the South Side of Chicago. The Union Stock Yards, established in 1865, had proven to be the most successful of the western livestock markets and had, therefore, attracted the greatest names in meat packing to the area. In 1921 the yards stretched over more than a square mile and employed approximately forty thousand workers in the industry. The Big Four, as the major packers were known, dominated the industry: Armour, Swift, Morris, and Wilson had their main plants and general offices in the Chicago stockyards and set the pace for the smaller packers. An earlier attempt by Gustavus Swift to consolidate the major packers into the National Packing Company had been prevented by the intervention of the federal government. But although the attempt to set up a corporation that would have been comparable to United States Steel had failed, the industry, by 1921, showed clear signs of oligopoly.

With the continuing growth of the packing industry, the need for a source of cheap labor became more and more acute. The development of the residential area directly adjoining the stockyards was a direct response to the needs of the industry. The neighborhood known as the Back of the Yards, roughly a mile-and-a-half square to the south and southwest of the Yards, contained dun-colored, two- and three-story frame tenements interlaced with an occasional brick flat. The district had originally been settled in the 1870s and 1880s by the Irish and Germans, but by the turn of the century Slavic immigrants and their children had begun to predominate in the area.

The East European experience had left a strong impression on the community and helped shape the attitudes of the neighborhood during crisis periods. This was demonstrated in the reaction of one of the Slavic groups, the Poles, during the industrial crisis of 1921. Following the arrival of the first Poles in the area in 1877, the community had grown rapidly. In 1884 Poles were introduced into the stockyards on a large scale for the first time as strikebreakers in an Irish and German walkout. After that incident, Poles settled in the area and organized the first permanent Polish Parish, St. Joseph's, in 1889. With the turn of the century, when Polish immigration into the district reached its peak, other parishes were founded to the east and north of St. Joseph's.

By 1921, the Slavic settlement of the Back of the Yards was more or less complete. The parishioners of ten of the thirteen churches in the area were Slavic or East European in origin. Indeed by then, the last Polish parish to have been organized — in 1911 — the Sacred Heart of Jesus, had already paid off its debt. Besides the parishes other types of ethnic organizations had sprung up in the area, including local chapters of larger fraternal groups such as the Polish Roman Catholic Union and the Polish National Alliance. A series of informal organizations also enjoyed considerable support, including youth gangs and, perhaps most significantly, the peasant commune. This was an attempt to re-create in America, despite vastly differing conditions, the Eastern European village structure within which many of the immigrants had been reared.

Once firmly established in the area, the Poles began to set down roots in the industry as well as in the neighborhood. The AFL affiliated Amalgamated Meat Cutters and Butcher Workmen of North America began a drive to organize the stockyards and packinghouses in 1900. This campaign was aimed at the non-English-speaking workers — especially the Poles and Bohemians — who now predominated in the industry. Fortunately for the Amalgamated Meat Cutters, the charter granted it by the American Federation of Labor in 1897 virtually made it an industrial union. The AFL resolution concerning the Amalgamated stated

> That the jurisdiction of the Amalgamated Meat Cutters and Butcher Workmen of North America should include every wage earner from the man who takes the bullock at the house until it goes into the hand of the consumer.

In 1900 the Chicago-based Journeymen Butchers Union of America, a local skilled-

The el and one of the major packinghouses dominate this southwest view of the stockyards, c. 1910.
(CHS, ICHi-04085)

craft union, joined with the Amalgamated, and the great drive to organize the Chicago stockyards was on. President Michael Donnelly of the Amalgamated Meat Cutters personally led the campaign in Chicago. The union attempted to organize on an industrial rather than on the traditional craft basis. Donnelly also began a deliberate interracial policy. The union leaders realized that the demands of the workers would never be met by the packers if different ethnic or racial groups could be relied upon to act as strikebreakers. This might be especially true if, because of their ethnic or racial background, they had been excluded from the union in the first place. The Meat Cutters used bilingual organizers and started ethnic locals.

Organized labor often feared the East Europeans, believing them to be unorganizable and a fruitful source of strikebreakers. Yet in 1904 the Poles had flocked to join the Meat Cutters union, and they returned in large numbers during the World War I organizational drive which eventually culminated in the Packinghouse Strike of 1921. Why? The most obvious reason for the growth of a union organization in America was simply self-interest. Numerous private and public investigations of the industry and of the residential area had reached the same conclusion, namely, that living and working conditions in the area were terrible.

Indeed, living conditions were so bad that even a packer representative stated in 1918: "The only remedy is the absolute destruction of the district, burn all the houses." Earlier, Upton Sinclair in his novel *The Jungle* (1906) had written:

> The most uncanny thing about the neighborhood was the number of children; you thought there must be a school out, and it was only after a long acquaintance that you were able to realize that there was no school, but that these were the children of the neighborhood — that there were so many children to the block in Packingtown that nowhere on its streets could a horse or a buggy move faster than a walk.

> It could not move faster anyhow, on account of the state of the streets. Those through which Jurgis and Ona [characters in the novel] were walking resembled streets less than they did a tiny topographical map. The roadway was commonly several feet lower than the level of the houses, which were sometimes joined by boardwalks; there were no pavements — there were mountains and valleys and rivers, gullies and ditches, and great hollows full of stinking green water.

By 1920, not much had changed. Schools were still inadequate, though according to the census fully one third of the population of the Back of the Yards was under the age of ten. The poverty of the area was only slightly relieved by wartime prosperity. In the fifteen years since Sinclair's observations some improvements had been made in the streets and sewerage system, but the area remained bleak. One notable change was the growing commitment of the immigrant community to the neighborhood. About 57 percent of the homes in the area were now owned by residents, and about 90 percent of these houses were owned by immigrants rather than native born, although immigrants made up only 50 percent of the total population. Actually, 60.7 percent of immigrant-occupied dwellings were owned by immigrants.

Dangerous working conditions and appalling health conditions persisted in the stockyards and packinghouses long after the 1904 strike. Between June 1907 and December 1910, thirteen men died in the Chicago Swift plant alone. Nevertheless safety conditions failed to improve, and in 1917 the packing industry still had one of the highest accident rates in manufacturing. The general health conditions were also frightening. In the period from 1894 to 1900, tuberculosis and pneumonia accounted for 20 percent of the deaths in the stockyard district. A government investigation of the industry in 1906 blamed the meat packers:

> The lack of consideration for the health and comfort of the laborers in the Chicago Stock Yards seems to be a direct consequence of the system of administration that prevails. . . . the unsanitary conditions in which the laborers work and the feverish pace which they are forced to maintain inevitably affect their health. Physicians state that tuberculosis is disproportionally prevalent in the stockyards, and the victims of this disease expectorate on the spongy wooden floors of the dark workrooms, from which falling scraps of meat are later shoveled up to be converted into food products. . . .
>
> The neglect on the part of their employers to recognize or provide for the requirements of cleanliness and decency of the employees must have an influence that cannot be exaggerated in lowering the morals and discouraging cleanliness on the part of the workers employed in the packinghouses.

Fifteen years later, in 1921, the tuberculosis death rate among Poles and other East Europeans was still the highest in the city of Chicago. Many of these deaths were directly attributable to the working conditions found in the plants of the major packers.

There is little doubt that the Poles of the Back of the Yards hoped that the union might be able to do something about the conditions that continued to prevail in the industry and the district. Prior to World War I, the meat packers had been involved in an intensive drive to cut costs and increase profits. The most obvious way to achieve this was to lower wages. This proved easy enough in the days before the war because of the great surplus of labor in Chicago. During the war, however, the disruption of immigration and the manpower demands of the U.S. military forces ended the packers' advantage.

But the big break for the workers lay in the fact that the industry was important to the war effort.

From the defeat of the 1904 strike until the outbreak of the war, the meat-packing industry had been characterized by wildly increasing production and profits while wages remained frozen. Common labor rates in the stockyards remained at 17½¢ an hour — the rate paid just after the 1904 strike — throughout the prewar period, while Swift's national sales more than doubled ($200,000,000 to $425,000,000), as did earnings ($4,000,000 to $9,000,000) and dividends ($2,000,000 to $5,000,000). Lack of organization since the defeat of the 1904 strike left the workers powerless in the face of this ironic situation. The war crisis brought an immediate and drastic change. Now production accelerated even more, but labor was in short supply.

Other factors also helped. The Democratic administration of Woodrow Wilson had a more liberal labor policy than previous administrations and was also most anxious to avoid problems in so important an industry as meat-packing during wartime. Fearing crippling strikes, the government set up an arbitration board for settling labor problems in the meat-packing industry. Federal Judge Samuel Alschuler was appointed to investigate conditions and settle wage disputes between the workers and management. And, most significantly, Alschuler in effect recognized the Amalgamated Meat Cutters as the official representative of the packinghouse workers.

Judge Alschuler's first award, announced in March 1918, granted a basic eight-hour day and a basic forty-hour week, wage increases, and pay for overtime. The changes

The canning department of Morris & Co. in 1917. Wartime brought a boom to the industry and higher wages to the workers.

(CHS, DN 69,087)

had long been asked for and greatly affected the lives of the workers and conditions in the Back of the Yards. Over a three-year period Alschuler granted roughly a 50 percent pay increase to the packinghouse workers. On December 8, 1920, a final wage increase awarded 100,000 employees an average of $27.50 in retroactive pay. The combination of effective union recognition and wage awards during this period led to a growth in the membership of the Amalgamated Meat Cutters from approximately seventy-five hundred retail butchers in 1916 to a nationwide membership of one hundred thousand, including most of the workers in the large meatpacking centers, by 1920.

Then, on February 26, 1921, the Big Four packers notified the government that they would no longer be able to abide by the wartime arbitration agreements. In March the packers agreed to a compromise which kept the arbitration agreement in effect until November 28, 1921, and reduced wages. On July 4 of that year, the Chicago packers asked the Alschuler arbitration court for another wage cut of five cents an hour, claiming that wages constituted 45 percent of their production costs and that they were still losing millions of dollars. The unions, of course, reacted negatively to the reduction, and the 1921 AFL convention in Denver backed the workers in their protest. The convention charged that the packers were taking advantage of the postwar slack by reasserting the prewar open-shop policy.

The arguments went on for several months until, on November 1, 1921, the *New York Times* reported that the Amalgamated Meat Cutters had voted to strike on November 15. The union claimed a national membership of 100,000 workers, 40,000 of them in Chicago alone. The Big Four responded on November 9 by proposing further wage cuts. They claimed, moreover, that an Amalgamated Meat Cutters' strike would not affect their operations, since the vast majority of their workers were content with conditions and nonunion status. Louis F. Swift, who was the major spokesman for the packers, claimed that Swift workers earned $5.70 more per week than steel workers, and $6.70 more per week than cotton workers. The *New York Times* quoted his appeal to the workers, "It must be apparent to you, to your foremen and to your workmen, that this step, wage cuts, must be taken."

These announcements on November 9 were followed by the convocation of plant congresses at the plants of the Big Four. The plant congress had originally been devised by Swift and Company as a form of company union and was supposed to serve as a representative council and grievance forum for the workers. The idea had by now been adopted by the other packers as well.

On November 18, 1921, word came that the Swift plant congress had voted to cut the pay scale, leaving the details of the adjustment to the company. At the same time, it was announced that representatives of 26,000 Armour employees had voted for, and fixed, a reduction which would become effective November 28. Wilson and Company was expected to declare a cut the next day. The new agreement would affect all plants throughout the West. The reports stressed that the workers had agreed voluntarily to the wage cuts. The reaction of the Amalgamated was quick and predictable. Union secretary Burns was quoted as saying: "We gave to our national officials the right to call a strike in October. If a working agreement satisfactory to the organization as a whole cannot be reached, a strike will be the result."

The stage was now set. Swift and the other packers were banking on the belief that the workers would not support a strike, but the Amalgamated Meat Cutters responded by calling a nationwide strike. On December 5,

Photographing the Stock Yards strike in 1921.
(CHS, DN 74,749)

1921, the union claimed that more than twelve thousand Chicago packinghouse workers had walked out. The packers, however, claimed that only a thousand workers were on strike. The next day the packers admitted that the number was higher but claimed that the total was still only twenty-five hundred out of an estimated forty thousand workers.

On December 7, the *New York Times* published an editorial expressing the packers' viewpoint. "The strike is not caused by the 10% reduction in wages, but by a determined effort on the part of the old line labor leaders to destroy the shop representation plan."

On that day, the Back of the Yards was the scene of fierce rioting as crowds of workers attacked the high fences surrounding the yards and were repeatedly driven back by the Chicago police. The strikers fought with stones, bricks, and clubs, while the police fired volleys into the air and used their nightsticks freely and effectively. But although the mounted police charged into the crowds repeatedly, the demonstrators refused to disperse. The most serious confrontation took place on West 44th between Ashland Avenue and Marshfield Street. Here as more that 2,500 residents of Back of the Yards struggled with the police, two men were seriously wounded by gunshot and another half dozen injured.

A mob of stickers grabbed a black whom they identified as a strikebreaker and dragged him to Bubbly Creek where they threw him in and pelted him with stones and bricks until he disappeared below the crusty and polluted water of the West Fork. Such violence forced the packers to keep their workers inside the plants, even though it meant providing them with shelter and food for the duration.

The *Chicago Tribune* of December 8 carried the sensational headlines:

STRIKERS STORM "L" TRAIN
9 SHOT, 27 HURT IN YESTERDAY'S RIOTS AT YARDS

Claiming that the rioting was the most serious since the race riot of 1919, the *Tribune* reported that 1,000 extra police had been put on duty to reinforce the regular 500 Stock Yard District police.

As Chicago read the December 8 headlines, the Stock Yard District went hack to war. The riots were renewed, and sniper fire was reported up and down the streets of the Back of the Yards. Around one hundred fifty people were injured in the December 8 riots when, according to the *Tribune,* "Mounted Policemen repeatedly charged into mobs of strikers and their adherents which congregated despite efforts of half the city's police force in strategic corners near the exits of the stockyards."

At the same time, the *Tribune* reported the solidarity with which the community responded to the events. The women emerged as the most radical and violent in their stand. Among the first to confront the police, they threw red pepper into the eyes of horses and the mounted police and devised various tactics to block the motorcycle police. The entire Back of the Yards became a battlefield. Non-striking workers often found mobs of strikers in front of their houses chanting and throwing bricks and sometimes starting fires. At Davis Square, a small park located near the 43rd Street and Ashland Avenue entrance to Packingtown, the rioters chanted at the police, calling them Cossacks and pelting them with bottles and bricks. Over 1,000 police took part in the rioting at Davis Square. This was the high point of the violence.

On the day of the Davis Square riot, Judge Dennis Sullivan handed down an injunction against the strikers, noting "All rights are relative; the line comes when the actions are a benefit to themselves and an injury to others." On December 9, the Amalgamated Meat Cutters asked for a parley while local leaders planned to expand the strike. It was reported that more than eight thousand strikebreakers had been imported into Packingtown, yet the union remained optimistic. Union leader Dennis Lane claimed, "We will win if the men stick. Things are looking better than they ever did."

These brave words supposed a continuation of widespread community support and dedication, but the bitter economic realities of the time proved too much for the people of the Back of the Yards. As the harsh winter days dragged on with no settlement in view, it became clear that the choice was one of starve or go back to work. The spirit of defiance waned. By January 9, 1922, a spokesman for Armour and Company announced, "There is no matter of dispute between the management and employees." In effect, the strike was over.

But the worst was still to come for many of the strikers, for when they attempted to return to the plants they found that their jobs were no longer available: non-striking workers who had proved their loyalty to the company and strikebreakers imported for the occasion had taken their place. The immigrant strikers (most of those named in the Chicago papers as participating in the riots were Slavic or Lithuanian) were quick to learn the realities of the American labor market in 1921.

But why had a community which had itself been accused of strikebreaking by earlier generations of stockyard workers rallied so faithfully and, indeed, violently in support of this strike? The fact is that even though the success of the Amalgamated Meat Cutters in organizing the stockyards during the war was in good part due to the special circumstances created by that emergency, it is unlikely that the unionization drive would have been as successful had it not been for the recently achieved stability of the immigrant community.

The Poles and other immigrant groups in the Back of the Yards had by 1921 passed the first crucial test of settling into the community. By then the initial stage in the adaptation of a population which had come from predominantly rural areas in Eastern Europe to the unfamiliar industrial environment of America had been successfully accomplished. This process was by no means automatic, but once the settlement had taken on the outward appearance of stability the establishment of various ethnic parishes had made the transition much easier.

A great many of the Poles who came to the Back of the Yards were probably from the region of Galicia, which was then part of the Austro-Hungarian Empire. More specifically, many of the stockyard Poles came from the High Tatra Mountains. These mountaineers, or *gorale,* shared a long cultural tradition that embraced the notion of the extended family and fostered a deep feeling of community. While the outlook of the *gorale* most certainly underwent many changes as they

A typical scene in the Back of the Yards district in the 1920s.

(CHS, ICHi-03924)

traveled the world in search of *chleb* (bread), their basic behavioral patterns survived.

In their monumental study *The Polish Peasant in Europe and America* (1921) W. I. Thomas and Florian Znaniecki pointed to the disruptive effects that migration had had both on individuals and the community. They saw the traditional peasant family as on the verge of extinction and concluded that the Polish community in America was merely a transitory sociological phenomenon. Yet at the very moment that Thomas and Znaniecki were putting their study together, the stockyard Poles were organizing as a group with shared goals and displaying a strong sense of social cohesion which grew out of the tradition that the authors considered moribund.

From shortly before World War I until many years later, much of the leadership of the community came from the Polish Catholic church. Three priests in particular — Fr. Louis Grudzinski, Fr. Stanislaus Cholewinski, and Fr. Francis Karabasz, pastors of the three Polish parishes in the Back of the Yards — offered much guidance. Father Grudzinski, with the cooperation of his two colleagues, had organized Guardian Angel Nursery and Home for Working Women in Back of the Yards in the early 1900s. The nursery, which might more appropriately have been called a settlement house, provided the neighborhood with a day-care center, a women's hotel, and a dispensary, as well as a cultural institution to help preserve the *Polsko's'c,* or Polishness, of the people. Located on the corner of the district's notorious Whiskey Point, Guardian Angel was in direct competition with the University of Chicago Settlement House, just down the block.

The Polish settlement was only a small part of the attempt to preserve the ethnicity of the immigrant group. As the large fraternal organizations, like the Polish National Alliance and the Polish Roman Catholic Union, expanded their activities and as the Archdiocese of Chicago became more interested in the social welfare of the community, the proliferation of ethnic institutions continued. Perhaps the most interesting of the local cultural institutions were the neighborhood libraries. Most successful in Back of the Yards was the Julius Slowacki Library, which carried books in the Polish language. When the demand for Polish reading material became even greater, the various parishes also opened libraries to cater to the tastes of the community. These religious and cultural institutions, along with various entrepreneurial ventures such as a community store and tavern as well as Polish banks, commercial clubs, and even theaters, had been permanently established by World War I. In other words, what might in 1900 have been described as a conglomeration of Poles living in a certain district had by 1921 become a stable community with a network of interlacing institutions and a high degree of self-awareness.

When the moment of crisis came, this basically conservative community mobilized all its resources in self-defense. The strikers did not regard themselves as radical opponents of the capitalist system. They were members of a community whose very livelihood was under attack. The prospect of a 25 percent wage reduction was a direct threat to the viability of the entire community. That is why it reacted as a whole and why such conservative institutions as the Roman Catholic Church and the Polish Roman Catholic Union continued to give their support to the Amalgamated Meat Cutters, even after the violence of early December.

This radical response of basically conservative social institutions reflected the dichotomy of being both Catholic and working-class in America in the early twentieth century — a dichotomy that affected not only the Back of the Yards but the labor movement of the entire country.

The Brotherhood

Beth Tompkins Bates

In 1925, the Brotherhood of Sleeping Car Porters (BSCP), a union recently formed in New York City, began organizing Pullman sleeping car porters and maids on Chicago's South Side. The principal target of the BSCP was the Employee Representation Plan, a union created by the Pullman Company for its porters and maids. The Brotherhood said the porters and maids needed the BSCP because it would represent their interests, not those of the Pullman Company. BSCP organizers soon discovered, however, that before they could represent the interests of porters and maids, they had to gain recognition and support from the middle-class black community on the South Side of Chicago. Not only did this elite dislike labor unions, but the majority regarded the Pullman Company as a friend of black Chicagoans. Since the black middle class controlled institutions in the black community such as the press and larger churches, their opinions mattered.

The Pullman Company started performing "good works" and pouring money into the black community on the South Side during the last decade of the nineteenth century. Florence Pullman, daughter of George Pullman, founder of the Pullman Palace Car Company, contributed a large sum of money to help found Provident Hospital in 1891. The country's first interracial hospital, Provident not only received black citizens on an equal basis with whites, but both its advisory board and medical staff were interracial, giving the black neighborhood unprecedented control over health care. Florence Pullman continued to make contributions during the hospital's periodic tough times. In 1896, George Pullman and Marshall Field purchased land adjoining Provident Hospital for a nursing school, which by World War I was training an average of twenty-five nurses a year.

Pullman Company executives also provided significant financial backing for the Wabash Avenue Young Men's Christian Association (YMCA) and the Chicago Urban League. Both the Wabash Avenue YMCA, established because the downtown branch did not admit blacks, and the Urban League were important in shaping work habits of black Chicagoans as well as placing them in jobs.

Around 1900, the Reverend Archibald James Carey saved Quinn Chapel, the largest African Methodist Episcopal (AME) church in Chicago, from foreclosure, establishing his reputation as a capable financial manager. Several prominent families, including the

Pullmans and the Swifts, noticed his success and promoted his rise in both political and ecclesiastical circles. The Reverend Carey, considered one of the most influential political voices on the South Side, was appointed AME Bishop by 1920.

The Reverend Carey also expanded the multiple roles of the black church further than most ministers when he established an employment service for black workers. Carey's employment service linked the interests of black workers, discriminated against by the city's trade unions, with wealthy white families such as the Pullmans and the Swifts. When Carey announced positions with the Pullman Company from his pulpit, the company appeared to be a benevolent friend of black workers. The arrangement made sense to the black elite, who thought employers had done much more for black workers than the generally racially exclusive white trade unions. Consequently, these leaders advised black workers to support management and eschew unions.

The Reverend Carey felt so strongly that economic opportunity for black workers would result from cooperation with industrial magnates rather than solidarity between black and white workers that he forbade the congregations in his bishopric in Chicago to allow A. Philip Randolph, national leader of the BSCP, or Milton P. Webster, head of the Chicago division of the BSCP, to speak before them. Carey's comprehensive approach to ministering, with its reliance upon the Pullman Company's benevolence, helped strengthen the company's ties to the black community.

While not everyone's faith in the goodwill of the Pullman Company was as strong as that of the Reverend Carey, the black middle class generally agreed with Claude Barnett, founder of the Associated Negro Press, that it would be "difficult to overestimate the economic value to the entire colored group that the business of 'pullman portering' has been" to the backbone of the community. The roster of defenders of the Pullman Company, the largest private employer of black workers nationally, in its struggle against the upstart union of porters and maids read like a Who's Who within the black community. It included Jesse Binga, head of Binga State Bank, most ministers, and Robert S. Abbott, publisher and editor of the *Chicago Defender*.

Moreover, the black middle class must have wondered why union porters and maids thought they stood a chance against the Pullman Company. When the BSCP threw down its gauntlet, it landed at the feet of a giant American corporation, an opponent with more than sufficient resources to combat union porters and maids. Finally, it was difficult to ignore the Pullman Company's success in defeating unions in the past.

Yet, despite the overwhelming odds against the BSCP effort to gain support for its labor union, the attitudes of the black middle class and elite were not as homogeneous as some scholars have argued. In December 1925, while most ministers, the press, and politicians ignored or spoke against the BSCP, the Chicago and Northern District Association of Colored Women, one of the premier women's clubs in Chicago at the time, invited A. Philip Randolph, head of the BSCP, to speak to them.

Two weeks later, the Woman's Forum, a Sunday evening civic and social discussion group at the Metropolitan Community Church, heard Randolph speak in Ida B. Wells-Barnett's home. She told Randolph that they wanted to hear his side of the story since they had not been able "to find anything in our press favorable to this movement" and had heard so much propaganda against it. Wells-Barnett had hoped to hold the meeting at the Appomattox Club, a social and fraternal club for professional and politically con-

In his hours on duty, a porter was always on call, attending to passengers' needs. Here, a Pullman porter stands by as passengers board a train, c. 1915. *(CHS, ICHi-26271)*

nected men, rather than in her home. The Appomattox Club, however, told Wells-Barnett they could not "afford to have Mr. Randolph speak" on its premises because so many of "the men who are opposing him are members here and it would embarrass them with the Pullman Company." To the twenty-five business and professional women gathered at her home Wells-Barnett said, "I can hardly conceive of Negro leaders taking such a narrow and selfish view of such vital problems affecting the race." After Randolph's remarks about the aims and purposes of the BSCP, the women endorsed the Brotherhood and asked, "What can the Woman's Forum do to help this great movement?"

Milton P. Webster, head of the Chicago division of the BSCP, wrote Wells-Barnett, seeking to expand the opening the Woman's Forum provided. He suggested that Wells-Barnett give the BSCP a copy of the membership list of the Ida B. Wells Club, a civic club formed in 1893 by Wells-Barnett, so that the BSCP could "send out publicity to the women direct." Webster also asked Wells-Barnett to encourage the women to attend BSCP meetings. The women, he hoped, would serve as a conduit within the black community to advertise and educate others about the Brotherhood's cause. The Ida B. Wells Club women would act as a counter to the weight of "hostility of our local newspapers against this movement."

Webster emphasized that the Brotherhood was not just a labor organization, but a social movement. "In the Brotherhood of Sleeping Car Porters the Race has a staunch, progressive, militant movement, which will ever be on the alert to wield its power whenever the interests of the Race demands," he wrote Wells-Barnett. Her club members were important to the larger goal of getting the Brotherhood's message on "economic subjects of vital importance to Negro workers" out to the community, despite all attempts of the press to silence the BSCP.

To a large extent, Webster's proposal and the civic interests of members of the black clubwomen's movement in Chicago converged. The key issue uniting them was that of fuller citizenship rights for all African-Americans, for which the BSCP employed the idiom of "manhood rights." Black women, active in the fight for the Nineteenth Amendment, viewed the struggle for manhood rights as part of the broader efforts to claim full citizenship for all African-Americans. A larger political role for black women was part of the struggle for fuller freedom for the entire black community. Fuller freedom entailed moving out from under white control and enjoying rights of first-class citizenship — achieving equality with white Americans. The work of Ida B. Wells-Barnett illustrates this point.

Ida B. Wells-Barnett began the black women's club movement in Chicago in the 1890s, in order to defend the "manhood of her race" through her anti-lynching crusade. Wells-Barnett did not neglect black women when she thought of advocating brotherly consideration; nor did she imagine only males when she and others in that era used the term "manhood." For Wells-Barnett, women's enfranchisement was necessary to stop lynching. The vote for women would give added weight to the quest for full citizenship for both women and men. Wells-Barnett drew upon her network of clubwomen to work for suffrage for women, as well as other issues that would strengthen the black community, bringing African-Americans more control over the direction of their lives.

Passage of the Nineteenth Amendment did not eclipse the political activism of black middle-class clubwomen. Those who had been involved in the movement for suffrage continued to focus on issues that plagued both black men and black women, a pattern that distinguished their agenda from that of their white sisters. Working with the BSCP merely broadened their agenda to include the importance of claiming economic as well as political rights. When the BSCP appealed to clubwomen to carry the BSCP message deep into the black community, these women probably envisioned a chance to be in the vanguard of a social movement designed to strengthen the overall ability of the black community to claim first-class citizenship.

The BSCP suffused its labor rhetoric, aimed at porters and maids, with the idea of manhood and manhood rights, implying self-reliance, standing tall, and moving out from under the paternalistic control of whites. In a widely circulated poster under the banner, "Reasons Why Pullman porters and maids should join the Brotherhood of Sleeping Car Porters Now," organizer Ashley Totten wrote: "We appeal to that spark of manhood; that willingness to take the position of a man and not a coward." Within the larger community, BSCP flyers, handbills, and literature revived

Ida B. Wells-Barnett, seen here in 1920, invited Milton P. Webster to speak to the Woman's Forum at a meeting in her home.
(CHS, ICHi-12867)

the nineteenth-century usage, articulated by Frederick Douglass and W. E. B. DuBois, that equated manhood with full humanity and first-class citizenship.

The local black press addressed slavery, freedom, and citizenship on a regular basis. The articles, however, usually portrayed progress as a straight line flowing from slavery toward human dignity. When Randolph, Webster, and other BSCP organizers discussed full-fledged "Americanism" and citizenship, they used these terms to question just what progress had been made and on whose terms. A company union denied the porters and maids the fundamental right to organize and to choose their own leaders. Similarly, black leaders in the wider community were usually chosen by white patrons. Black politicians found that the best way to contest racial exclusion was through political inclusion in what scholar Charles Branham called a "preexisting political culture," which rewarded those who learned how to adapt to machine politics.

To the porters and maids, clubwomen, and the general public, the BSCP raised the issue of the "unfinished task of emancipation," asking them to "rededicate [their] hearts and minds" to the spirit of Denmark Vesey, Nat Turner, Sojourner Truth, Harriet Tubman, and Frederick Douglass, who "shall not have died in vain." Black Americans had to assert their manhood rights to first-class citizenship and throw off what *The Messenger,* A. Philip Randolph's magazine, called the "grip of the old slave psychology." Claude Barnett, Bishop Carey, and Robert S. Abbott were condemned in one issue for having "a wish-bone where a backbone ought to be." With such leaders, it continued, "one can hear the clank of the slave's chain" in all they say and do. *The Messenger* reminded its readers that "New Negroes" had the backbone to demand full civil rights. A popular handbill harked back to nineteenth-century manhood rhetoric with a sketch of Frederick Douglass and a caption that said: "Douglass fought for the abolition of chattel slavery, and today we fight for economic freedom. The time has passed when a grown-up black man should beg a grown-up white man for anything."

To promote this outlook, the Chicago division of the BSCP began working with a committee of citizens, largely leaders from the Ida B. Wells clubs and the Chicago and Northern District Association of Colored Women. The first test of the ability of this network to overcome the opposition of Chicago newspapers and ministers came in October 1926. By that time, Irene Goins, another pioneer in women's social activism in Illinois, actively worked for the BSCP. As president of both the Chicago and Northern District Federation of Colored Women and the Federated Women's Club, Goins helped expand the base of active clubwomen demanding social justice for all black Chicagoans. She influenced state politics as founder of the Women's Republican Club.

But Goins also had ties to the black working class. The first African-American woman in the Midwest to take an active part in the labor movement, she worked for several years on the eight-hour-day bill with Agnes Nestor, president of the International Glove Workers Union. During World War I she organized the Woman's Labor Union at the stockyards, continuing her efforts to organize black women workers at the Chicago Stock Yards after the war. She also served on the executive council of the Chicago Women's Trade Union League from 1917 to 1922. Clearly, Goins could carry the Brotherhood's labor message beyond middle-class club circles.

By the fall of 1926, the BSCP also gained the support of Mary McDowell. First president of the Chicago branch of the Women's Trade Union League (WTUL) and a Univer-

This undated photograph shows one of the mass meetings so important to the success of the BSCP.
(CHS, ICHi-22640)

sity of Chicago settlement-house worker, she was the only white person among the Chicago citizens contesting the politics of Pullman paternalism alongside BSCP organizers in the early years. McDowell, along with Wells-Barnett and Webster, promoted the mass meeting of October 3, 1926, in the community. Webster and Randolph gave much thought to details such as the quality of paper used for advertising the mass meeting as well as the character of the images projected to the black community, for Webster vowed to "mobilize all of the forces in Chicago, religious, social, fraternal and otherwise," to bring out a crowd.

The fall 1926 mass meeting was a success in terms of publicity. Webster doubted that the Brotherhood could have "bought the same publicity in Chicago with the expenditure of a thousand dollars." The Brotherhood program and movement was, Webster believed, "the talk of the town." If so, it was partially the result of the efforts of McDowell and Wells-Barnett, along with the Wells Club members, to broadcast the BSCP message to the larger community.

Nevertheless, the majority of representatives from the black press and pulpit — most notably the *Chicago Defender* — continued to speak against the BSCP, when they mentioned the Brotherhood at all. Despite this continuing lack of support, the BSCP did gain, little by little, additional recognition. Lula E. Lawson, executive secretary of the South Parkway Young Women's Christian Association (YWCA), opened up the YWCA network to the BSCP when she endorsed their goals in 1928. By the 1920s, the YWCA emphasized collective action and the importance of participation in "group work" as a means to give the individual a greater sense of self-worth and a connection with large-scale social change. The YWCA strove to revitalize the community, which it believed was fragmented through forces of modern life, such as migration and industrialization. Lula Lawson brought this perspective and experience to the BSCP. Her ability to interest individuals in the merits of a larger community vision opposed to Pullman philanthropy and patronage politics must have been valuable to the BSCP.

Dr. William D. Cook, minister of the Metropolitan Community Church, was the first minister to open his church to the Brotherhood. His support was not surprising since, as Webster told one scholar, Cook was "kind of an outlaw preacher," who once headed one of the largest and most prominent churches — Bethel AME — of Chicago. Cook's church had a history that stretched back to World War I of social and political leanings "not in harmony" with a majority of the AME churches in the Chicago area. Shortly after the Reverend A. J. Carey was appointed AME Bishop of Chicago in 1920, he removed Cook from Bethel forever. Out of that turmoil came the People's Community Church of Christ and Metropolitan Community Center, dedicated to the service of humanity and the welfare of the community. Under Cook's leadership, the church, generally known as Metropolitan Community Church, sponsored activities such as educational programs and seminars on industrial relations. Cook found and rented office space for the porters and maids during the first crucial two years of the union's existence and, until his death in 1930, addressed many of the Brotherhood's meetings.

Dr. J. C. Austin opened up the Pilgrim Baptist Church for mass meetings of the Brotherhood soon after he came to Chicago from Pittsburgh in 1926. Known nationally as a "dynamic personality" and business leader as well as minister, Austin, as an outsider to Chicago politics, was not entangled in patronage nor paternalistic relations. He arrived with a vision of uplifting the race and

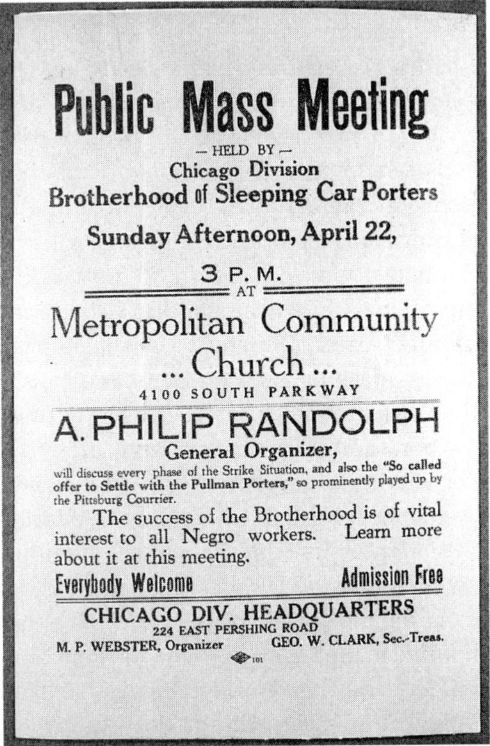

Unlike more conservative black churches, the Metropolitan Community Church supported the work of the BSCP. This broadside advertises a mass meeting held at this church.

(CHS, ICHi-06236)

building a progressive church in Chicago. Offering protection and advice to workers was just one of the church-sponsored services that Austin initiated to put uplift into practice. Pilgrim's stated mission was to reach the unreached, upon the "highway and in the hedges." Apparently, this approach to Christian ministry filled a need, for by 1930 the church had attracted more than nine thousand members, becoming one of the largest and most prosperous of the hundreds of churches on the South Side. Meanwhile, Bishop Carey continued to ban the Brotherhood from AME churches, reminding AME ministers of their responsibility to warn their membership against the evil influence of labor leaders.

Also joining forces with the BSCP was Dr. Charles Wesley Burton, minister of the Lincoln Memorial Congregational Church until he began practicing law in 1926. Webster considered Burton to have a "world of experience in the various social problems that concern the Negro." When Burton took over the ministry of the Lincoln Memorial Congregational Church, he started a strong community outreach program on social issues.

At a mass meeting on October 30, 1927, the BSCP made significant gains in terms of support and recognition from the black community when more than two thousand people heard the BSCP rebuke the *Chicago Defender* for its editorial stance. Randolph charged that the *Defender* had surrendered to "gold and power." Earlier the BSCP had referred to the *Defender* as the Chicago "Surrender" and the "World's Greatest Weakly." Many of those who packed Cook's Metropolitan Community Church to hear the BSCP leaders lash out at the *Defender* were drawn to the meeting through the clubwomen's network and the distribution of more than five thousand circulars throughout the black neighborhoods on the South Side. The BSCP featured its fight against a company union, which it pictured as a fight against whites choosing black leaders. As a result of the meeting, a large number of citizens delivered a "bushel basket of mail" to the *Defender* demanding an explanation for its failure to cover news of the BSCP.

Pullman Company detectives, reporting to executives about the Brotherhood's activities, noted the increased attention the community showed toward the Brotherhood by the fall of 1927. The *Defender* staff also noticed: with the November 19, 1927, issue, they began supporting the Brotherhood. The change in policy was nothing if not abrupt. Roi Ottley, biographer of Robert Abbott, publisher and editor of the *Defender*, said Abbott changed his policy toward the union in response to both decreased circulation and charges that black editors supporting Pullman were "traitors to their race."

Although the Pullman Company fired or otherwise punished the porters and maids identified with the unions, sentiment within the black community was shifting toward the BSCP, thanks in part to the efforts of Dr. Cook, Dr. Austin, Ida B. Wells-Barnett, Lula Lawson, and Mary McDowell. The Brotherhood held meetings several nights a week, with as many as fifty to sixty porters and maids showing up. Larger "mass" meetings, aimed at the community, were held about once a month, commanding good publicity because organizers would blanket key parts of the community using their friendly networks.

In December 1927, Webster formalized the group of supportive citizens into the Citizens' Committee. He added new members at the same time. Perhaps the most important addition was Irene McCoy Gaines, leading clubwoman and industrial secretary of the South Parkway YWCA. In her role as industrial secretary of the YWCA from 1920 to 1925, she advocated a labor-oriented approach to civil rights. In addition, Gaines and her husband, Harris Barrett Gaines, formerly a representative in the Illinois State Legislature and Assistant State's Attorney, had access to the social and political world of upper-class black Chicagoans. From 1924 to 1935, Irene Gaines served as president of the Illinois Federation of Republican Colored Women's Clubs, a group that she helped to organize. In January 1928, Webster appointed Gaines secretary of the Citizens' Committee.

Key members of the Lincoln Community Men's Club may have influenced the breakdown of opposition during the next couple of years among middle-class professional black men not normally familiar with the merits of labor organizing. In 1928, Dr. Burton, of Lincoln Memorial Congregational Church, became chairman of the Citizens' Committee. Burton probably encouraged David W. Johnson, president of the church's Lincoln Community Men's Club, to join the committee. Johnson helped the Brotherhood by writing letters to citizens, and encouraging other members of the Men's Club to do the same.

George Cleveland Hall lent his support to the BSCP in 1928, revealing that even within the Chicago Urban League, a bastion of pro-employer sentiment, differences could be found on the issue of unionism. Hall, one of the League's founders and a well-known physician, became a member of the Citizens' Committee of the BSCP despite the fact that the Pullman Company had always contributed to the Urban League. Hall hardly fit, however, the profile of a New Negro economic radical.

Considered one of the most articulate business leaders in the early part of the century, Hall in many respects appeared to be out of the Booker T. Washington camp, which believed black Americans should accept the status quo and not directly challenge second-class citizenship. Indeed, he and his wife had been personal friends of Washington. Hall promoted black business in Chicago and, in 1912, became the president of the Chicago branch of Washington's National Negro Business League, which believed capitalism was color blind. Simultaneously, however, he was one of two active black leaders of the National Association for the Advancement of Colored People (NAACP) and participated in its committee on grievances. The contradiction implied by active membership in both a Washington and a DuBois organization at the same time — one advocating an accommodating approach, the other a more direct, militant approach — did not seem to upset Hall. While he may have supported Washington out of personal loyalty or even because he subscribed to certain aspects of self-help, he did not believe in accommodating to the status of a second-class citizen. He thought that black Americans had to fight white prejudice and discrimination directly and move out from white control of black institutions, which seems to be the issue that connected Hall with the Brotherhood.

The Citizens' Committee became the official sponsor, beginning in 1928, of the Brotherhood of Sleeping Car Porters' Labor Conferences, annual meetings to educate porters and the public about labor and civil rights issues. Some members of the Citizens' Committee spoke at the conferences; others used civic and political clubs to advance the BSCP's labor point of view. Still others, such as Mary McDowell, worked with black and white labor networks and used the pages of the *Federation News* to discuss the BSCP approach to reform and advancement through labor organization.

By the 1930s, the BSCP, through the Citizens' Committee, influenced the protest agenda of many club members and leaders on Chicago's South Side. The Reverend Harold M. Kingsley, pastor of the Church of the Good Shepherd, described by one interviewer as "preaching to the white collar class," spoke at Brotherhood mass meetings and at its annual labor conference. His sermons emphasized the virtue and value of labor. But at the 1930 Negro Labor Conference, sponsored by the Citizens' Committee, he said the black church of the late 1920s ignored the plight of the working class just as the Russian church had before the Russian Revolution of 1917. "The Church is the one institution that gets more of the people together than any other institution," he said, but it needed to be "educated up to the economic conditions of the workers." Frederic Robb, president of the Washington Intercollegiate Club, spoke at that same labor conference and focused on the need for black workers to educate students "up to their responsibilities" and for "students to quit criticizing the worker and get in harmony with him." Finally, Robb also admonished the churches to "foster a labor psychology."

Labor leader A. Philip Randolph, seen here in the early 1930s, headed the BSCP from its founding in 1925 until 1968. Though he never worked as a porter, he understood the difficult conditions these men faced.
(CHS, ICHi-12255)

The Brotherhood's need for outreach into Chicago's black community did not disappear when the Pullman Company finally recognized the BSCP as the bargaining agent for porters and maids in 1935. A loosely organized group still existed as a reserve army to counter adverse publicity put out by Pullman within key community networks. But the active years of the Citizens' Committee were between 1927 and 1933, when the BSCP needed help mobilizing support in its attack on the culture of Pullman paternalism. The Citizens' Committee raised questions about the value of a political culture that denied black Chicagoans — as workers and as citizens — rights of first-class citizenship. But it also put workers' interests and unionization on the agenda of civic clubs, helping to bridge the gap between the middle and working class, and introducing labor issues into civic discourse. Finally, the work of the Chicago Citizens' Committee of the BSCP foreshadowed alliances of the mid-to-late 1930s between groups such as the Chicago chapter of the National Negro Congress (NNC), which focused primarily on labor issues, and middle-class groups like the Chicago Council of Negro Organizations, which focused on securing civil rights for black Chicagoans. In 1939, Irene McCoy Gaines headed the Chicago Council of Negro Organizations, leading joint efforts with the left-leaning NNC local to support workers' rights. Without the labor education provided to the black middle class through networks of the Citizens' Committee, alliances uniting left-wingers and more conservative groups in protests against second-class citizenship might have been harder to form.

The Giant Jewel: Chicago's 1933-34 World's Fair

Susan Talbot-Stanaway

During the summers of 1933 and 1934, over forty-eight million Americans stepped out of the depression and into a "veritable bombardment of color and light — a giant jewel, its myriad facets flashing countless rays of beauty" — the Century of Progress Exposition. Although the country was shrouded by the gray pall of the depression, fair organizers proceeded with plans to host a great world's fair to celebrate the one-hundredth anniversary of the city's incorporation.

The *Official Guide of the Fair* described the city as "undaunted" by years "of recent memory, when the economic scheme seemed to go awry, and the steady march of progress appeared, to many, halted." Out of the disasters of the depression, the fair sought "to bring assurance . . . that the forces of progress sweep on. They are forces of science, linked with the forces of industry." Through the financial power and merchandising acumen of the industrialists who planned the fair, Chicago could "jubilate over her own birthday, so peculiarly eloquent of progress." The writer compares the city of 1933 to that of 1893, which was just emerging from financial panic and widespread unemployment and was still rebuilding from the fire of 1871. He states that Chicago turned her "face toward the morning of new day just as she had done in '93. She invited the world to observe with her the victories of a glorious past and the promise of a more glorious future." The face that the city presented to the world for this celebration was flamboyantly painted with the colors of modernism.

A writer for *Fortune* magazine wrote that the fair could succeed because of the depression, explaining:

> [It will] attract many mid-western families who in more prosperous times would vacation in the mountains or at the seashore but who this summer will content themselves with piling into the family car and setting off to spend a few inexpensive days at the fairgrounds. . . . To attract the 350,000 people who are expected to swarm into the fairgrounds each day Messrs. Dawes and their colleagues have played heavily on two potent American fetishes: Progress and Education. These are the keynotes of their fair.

To demonstrate American progress and education, the Century of Progress organiz-

Aerial view of the General Motors and Ford Buildings at the 1933-34 A Century of Progress International Exposition. More than 48 million visitors attended the fair.

(CHS, ICHi-17552)

ers embraced modernist concepts in art and architecture. By doing so they intended to surpass the impact of the World's Columbian Exposition forty years earlier. The pristine classical architecture of that fair, colored only at night by electric lighting, was its most memorable and influential feature. Caught in the shadow of the White City, progressive architects like Louis Sullivan were destroyed. But in 1933, an "exuberantly youthful Chicago," to express the "adventurous aspirations . . . and freedom from old inhibitions" of her citizens, "has turned her thought toward the tomorrow of humanity rather than back upon yesterday." Fair architects chose the role of prophet rather than that of historian, exploiting raw geometry in a plethora of upbeat hues. Dr. Allen Diehl Albert, honorary secretary of the fair's Architectural Commission, summarized: "The Century of Progress might well be termed a preview of the architecture of the future. Millions of people will view it and become mentally alert to the new conception — the material, form, mass, silhouette, and color."

The Century of Progress Architectural Commission consisted of ten prominent national architects: Raymond Hood, Harvey Wiley Corbett, Ralph T. Walker, and Albert Geiffert, Jr., of New York, Paul Phillipe Cret of Philadelphia, and Arthur Brown, Jr., of San Francisco. Chicago architects included Hubert

Burnham, John A. Holabird, Nathanial Owings, and Louis Skidmore. (For reasons that are unclear Frank Lloyd Wright, Chicago's most internationally famous architect, was entirely excluded from the fair.) In 1928, the commission announced that the architectural keynotes of the fair would be new elements of construction, the potential of artificial lighting, new construction materials, and an attempt to "illustrate the beauty of form and detail" of contemporary architectural styles.

The onset of the depression forced the commission to eliminate some exciting but grandiose architectural schemes, a situation that underscored the importance of color as a progressive feature and economic expedient. In fact, a coloristic aesthetic was facilitated by new materials and methods. In place of the expensive stainless steel, bronze, and fine woods of twentieth-century European fairs, reclaimable asbestos cement board, sheet metal, masonite, gypsum board, and plywood were assembled in prefabricated units and fastened over web-and-timber skeleton frames of lightweight steel. Clip fasteners and reversible screws replaced nails on many buildings. The need to construct the building by the most economical methods determined style and decoration to some extent. According to a member of the Department of Works, "The simplest and most inexpensive machine production led to units of flat surface. Hence the architectural characteristic of the buildings is walls of flat surfaces, with mass effect rather than detail ornamentation." Color applied as paint, therefore, made excellent aesthetic and economic sense.

The commission's decision to color the fair was unique in American architectural history. The fair's variously designed, but mostly modernistic, buildings were to be coordinated and enlivened by means of a single color program. The commission chose architect and stage designer Joseph Urban to create and implement the color program. He selected a palette of twenty-four intense hues, which were applied to the facades of every building, fence, flagpole, and ticket booth. This scheme was intended to "achieve harmony," to "fit the architectural scheme of utilitarian modernity, and to play its part in a joyous festival." At the same time, it was intended to "express the Exposition's deeper, more lasting implications and purposes." The guidebook writer mused:

> Were one to pose as a prophet, he might well say that here is suggestion of a future American color harmony, distinctive, bold, that could change neutral sections of cities and towns, bring cheer and liveliness to workers in factories, perhaps revolutionize in time the conceptions of color effects in homes.

Aesthetics and depression-induced budget cuts, however, were only part of the reason for painting the fair in brilliant hues. The close correlation between the intense, jazzy color applied to buildings and the similar shades used in consumer goods and advertising suggests that the bright colors served a fundamental purpose: to sell the products displayed at the fair. Two of the chief movers behind the fair were Charles Gates Dawes and Rufus C. Dawes, two brothers who owned the Pure Oil Company as well as a number of utilities. Among the principal financial guarantors were Julius Rosenwald of Sears, Roebuck and Company, Philip K. Wrigley, the chewing gum king, and other oil and utility magnates. In addition, as with previous and subsequent world's fairs, most of the buildings and exhibits were designed to sell products. Among the largest of the buildings were those of Ford, General Motors, Chrysler, Firestone, Sears, Time-Fortune, and Western Union. The Hall of Science and the Travel and Transportation buildings, for example, included numerous concession booths and displays sponsored by industry and commercial firms. Color could increase attendance, create an upbeat mood in visitors, and make them receptive to the sales messages of exhibitors. In the building sponsored by the A&P grocery store chain, for example, visiting homemakers were urged to paint their kitchens in the brilliant hues used on the company's coffee packages so they could have a "carnival . . . all the year round" in their own homes.

Color effects inside homes had already been manipulated through the twin brushes of advertising and marketing. Although fair organizers, supporters, and critics would have vigorously denied it, Joseph Urban's color scheme corresponded with the development of color as a design tool in advertising and of a multitude of color variations in commercial products — everything from cars to bathroom fixtures. For at least a decade, manufacturers and advertising designers had sought to introduce a sense of changing, ever-better style in their products through the use of color. The first issue of *Fortune* magazine, which appeared in 1930, contained an article celebrating the use of color. The *Fortune* commentator began:

> Consider, for a moment, a red bed. Red is a common color and a bed is a fundamental article of furniture. Yet the combination of the two had, until very recently, almost a startling effect. Grandmother, perhaps, would have thought a red bed immoral. Mother would have considered it at least

In addition to satisfying new requirements for residences, the architects of the House of Tomorrow offered an optimistic vision of the future of home life. The house stood three stories high and had a concrete foundation, steel frame, glass walls, and air conditioning. Photograph by Kaufmann and Fabry.

(CHS, ICHi-22838)

> peculiar. Nearly anyone in, say, 1920, would have expected to find only a Red in a red bed. Yet, within the past five or six years, thousands of red beds have blossomed in corresponding thousands of American bedrooms. Also have arrived blue beds, green beds, yellow beds, mauve beds, and blue, green, yellow, purple, and mauve bedspreads to cover them. There is now nothing startling about color in the bedroom — although architecture remains drably monotone.

By the early 1930s, automobiles, telephones, and household appliances had become "fashion goods." General Motors introduced automobiles in several colors in 1924. About the same time, Martex came out with colored and decorated bath towels — at four times the price of plain white. By the end of the 1920s, Kohler Company of Wisconsin offered bathroom fixtures in gray, lavender, blue, green, brown, and ivory. Another company made toilet paper available in various hues, such as green. A sink manufacturer with a romantic imagination offered sinks in Tang Red, Orchid of Vincennes, Royal Copenhagen Blue, St. Porchaire Brown, Rose du Barry, Ionian Black, and Meissen White. The kitchen could be transformed by electric refrigerators, sold in 1928 by one firm "in four intriguing colors," gas ranges (which were said "to blossom riotously in rainbow hues"), and Hoosier kitchen cabinets in "Venetian green and Oriental red interior." Furnaces such as the "Redflash" boiler invigorated the basement.

Clothing advertising in particular promised self-transformation through color. In an Arrow Shirts advertisement in the November 18, 1933, issue of *Collier's*, a young man declared, "I've decided I need more color in my life," and then explained, "A man gets so little chance to go a bit gay in his dress, that I'm mighty pleased with the swing toward colored and patterned shirts. It's giving me an opportunity to enjoy some brightness and color for a change." The ad concludes with "How about a little more color in *your* life?"

Commercial transportation companies incorporated color into their vehicles. Colonial Airways Corporation vaunted airplanes with bright blue bodies and bright orange wings. Railroads would not be outdone; the Chicago & Alton's *Alton, Ltd.*, which plied a route between Chicago and St. Louis, was pulled by red and maroon locomotives One writer noted that the "Iron Horse has become most piebald on the Denver & Rio Grande Western Railroad, which running through the Grand Canyon, has decorated its cars in colors 'symptomatic of the Grand Canyon sunset.' "

Color appeared most dramatically and most visibly in Hollywood movies. In 1921, Technicolor, Inc., produced its first commercial movie, *Toll of the Sea*. In 1929 Warner Bros. produced the all-color movies *On with the Show* and *Gold Diggers of Broadway. Gold Diggers* grossed $3.5 million and resulted in a popular vogue for color. The vast changes in film-making required by color, however, and the lack of cash in the early 1930s led to a virtual halt in the making of color movies. Nonetheless, the use of color had captured Americans' imaginations.

In advertising, color stood out amid the black-and-white pages of magazines and stimulated interest in products no matter what their color. In 1927, a writer for *Printer's Ink*, the journal of printing and graphic design, declared that color is "the sex appeal of business." Another writer commented that color "promised therapeutic feelings of emotion or sensuous excitement." Rich color and glitzy foils for images and type were frequent in magazine advertisements in the 1920s, although by 1933 such expensive ads had declined to a few pages per issue. But color would have certainly remained in the public

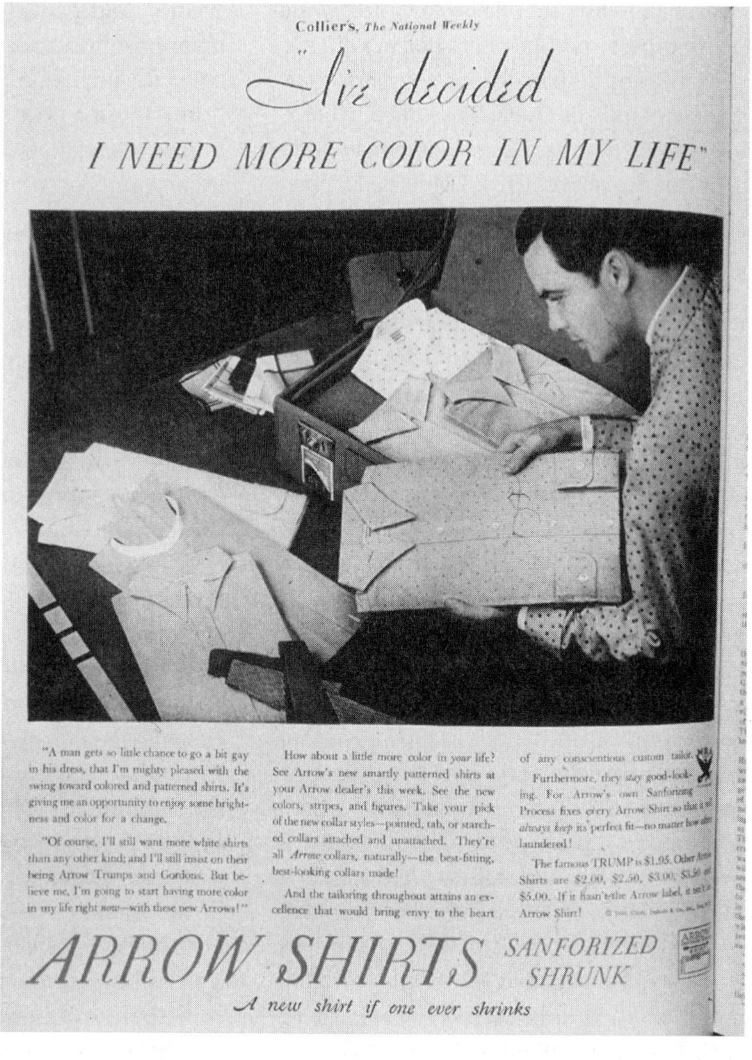

Clothing advertising urged consumers to transform their lives with bright colors and patterns. This ad posed the question: "How about a little more color in your life?" From *Collier's*, November 18, 1933.

view as a reminder of the material prosperity and optimism of the 1920s. Color epitomized what was new and desirable, and it was an essential characteristic of modernism in consumer goods.

Thus by the time the Century of Progress organizers began their planning, color had pervaded consumer culture and popular entertainment. It also characterized modernism in the fine and decorative arts. As one recent historian has suggested, "Modernism is best considered as a conceptual approach rather than a style." Its overwhelming force in our century has been found in "its ability to create memorable imagery and a vocabulary of form and detail that are, to a greater or lesser extent, appropriate to the present." Modernism was an approach to the twentieth century's new experiences and unique dilemmas that embraced their newness and found solutions in innovative imagery, technology, and materials. These solutions, however, did not create a uniform or cohesive style. Instead, visual artists and designers explored new urban tensions and pleasures with new forms and expressive color. In painting and sculpture, for example, the early twentieth century brought the coloristic explosions of fauvism in France, expressionism in Germany, and futurism in Italy. The use of color in the decorative arts was apparent at Paris's 1925 Exposition International des Arts Decoratifs Modernes, which introduced art deco as stylistic language. Art deco's predecessor, art nouveau, was characterized by pastels and the soft hues of nature, while deco designers often chose strong colors in their work. The influence of color on modern art soon reached America. In the catalogue for the epochal Machine-Age Exposition of 1927, Louis Lozowick described a new art with "shapes and colors not paralleled in nature," and art that would encompass the "flowing rhythm of modern America."

Joseph Urban, the designer chosen to color the fair, was influenced by these new uses of color. From 1918 to 1933, he designed and directed the majority of the stage productions for New York's Metropolitan Opera. There he created a new style of scenery that served as a medium for the reception of colored light. Deeply hued light was enormously effective in setting and shifting mood; this factor would have been of great importance to fair organizers. Indeed, they would have seen color used to such effect in the Urban Room at Chicago's Congress Hotel, where the designer had arranged that the entire room could be bathed alternatively in red, blue, yellow, or white light.

At the fair, Urban used color to unify buildings designed by various architects and to establish the moods and relationships prescribed by the commission and the fair organizers. He selected a palette of twenty-four intense colors: one green, two blue-greens, six blues, two yellows, three reds, four oranges, two grays, and white, black, silver, and gold. Most buildings were painted three or four colors; some accommodated five or more. On large buildings, like the Electrical Group, Urban used a number of colors to separate the building's masses and link the building with nearby structures. Such focus and transition were described by one of Urban's assistants:

> Passing into the east court of the Hall of Science an entirely new mood, a new key, is established. The main mass of deep orange with its wings of lighter orange rests on a series of blue and white horizontally striped terraces stretching out toward the water, and is pinned to earth by the main tower which picks up the blue of terraces and whose perpendicular function is emphasized by a vertical strip of the deep blue already encountered in the avenue of approach. The bridge of the General Exhibits Building is white, picking up the white of the lower terraces of the Hall of Science. . . . The fins and plates at the semicircular ends of the wings toward the lagoon culminate in a blaze of clear yellow, cobalt blue and white. . . . In this way three distinct units forming a natural sequence have been treated in three different color moods which resolve with easy transitions into each other.

Urban carefully chose overall percentages of colors for the entire fair — 20 percent white, 20 percent blue, 20 percent orange, 15 percent black, and the remaining 25 percent divided among the reds, yellows, greens, and grays. These percentages provided the required unity and interest without dissonance. At night, the color program was intensified through hidden neon tubes, colored floodlights, and shifting colored searchlights. Urban believed that "it becomes a function of color to realize that artistic possibility which gives a building its architectural value" and "to give the required sense of size, playfulness or mystery in each particular case." He also felt that "the atmosphere of daily life should be lost the moment one entered the fair grounds, that the visitors should forget their cares and troubles and be conscious of the joy of living."

Urban became ill at the end of 1932 and died in July of 1933. Otto Teegen, Urban's assistant, assumed the immense task of selecting the type of paint, seeing it colored to Urban's specifications, and supervising the application of all fifteen thousand gallons within a period of thirty-three days. A special casein paint was chosen as it would dry quickly, adhere well to gypsum board, plywood, and masonite, and stand up to Chicago's severe weather.

The coloring of the fair elicited a variety of reactions. For Teegen, the fair was the culmination of a dream. He commented: "How many of us, looking out of our Pullman window as we are carried past the small characterless cities along the line, have not wished that the skies might some day rain paint, millions of gallons of paint, no matter what color, just to give life to those dreary forms." One member of the Architectural Commission expressed the hope that color like that used at the fair could reintroduce the innocent joys of nature into a machine-tooled society:

> One of the needs of American life . . . was the free use of color. The tendency among us has been to make our barns red and houses white. Wherefore on these broad spaces of buildings . . . one sees yellow as bright as buttercups, blue as deep as the sky, red as flaming as fire, green as green as the new leaves on the forest in springtime.

Perhaps the most dramatic reaction came from a writer who experienced an epiphany on viewing the fair for the first time, recording his impressions in musical terms: "The symphonic crash of colors suggests the great moment in Wagner's *Rheingold* when Thor strikes the rock from which leaps the rainbow bridge spanning the Rhine." Others found that color had truly fulfilled the goals set for it by the Architectural Commission. Paul Cret wrote that he had seen "conservative people gasp at the violent pigments covering a whole facade, and then, when they left the fair grounds, wonder why the streets of the city were so dreadfully drab and gray."

Most of the participating architects, as can be expected, commented favorably. Albert Kahn gushed, "A pageant of indescribable beauty has been created." Ely Jacques Kahn affirmed the vital role that color played:

> Urban's color scheme for the entire exhibition has done at least one vital thing. Being unable to assimilate the varied degrees of good and bad taste of individual designers, he has whipped the whole scheme into a picture of sparkling color that is intriguing to say the least. He has avoided the restrained and chaste pastel inanities for a palette that is restricted to primary colors and a severely limited number of related tones. The result is bold, fresh and masculine. By judicious use of dark blues and blacks, he has embalmed various architectural experiments that are fortunately hidden to the average visitor. . . . It would seem to me that this color statement is by all odds the most vital contribution to a new architecture.

Some outside reviewers, however, were less enthusiastic. Douglas Haskell, writing for London's *Architectural Review,* declared, "Only tinted glasses can give this palette . . . any unification. It 'knocks your eye out.'" In Haskell's opinion, Urban's color "pulled apart the individual buildings. . . . What had not already been fretted away in the jagged forms was frazzled by the disparate hues." Haskell concluded that "the result is hence

The Havoline Thermometer, which towered above the Havoline Motor Building, exemplified the advertising-driven architecture of the fair. *(Photograph by Kaufmann and Fabry. CHS, ICHi-02121)*

more curious than beautiful." The health columnist for the *Chicago Sunday Tribune* even identified an optical problem caused by the colors and suggested a solution:

> It may be noticed that severe eye strain causes a sort of pus formation which is generally corrected with either glasses or covering the eyes for a period. This is generally noticed in snow blindness . . . or 'World's Fair' visiting. In the latter case this is caused by the riot of colors on the buildings. . . . Here again we have something that may call for attention. . . . It is best to use glasses of the black, blue, blue-green or green variety, rather than the popular amber. . . . [These] will not cause headaches or eye fatigue, as was commonly noted during last year.

To Frank Lloyd Wright, who was not asked to help plan the fair, "the whole performance is petty, strident and base. . . . Nothing has happened except gesture and gaudy — something bawdy — self-indulgence." Only R. Buckminster Fuller, the maverick architect later famous for his geodesic domes, seems to have identified the relationship between Urban's color and popular and commercial media and debunked the "garish advertising-mania architecture . . . designed to restimulate 'business' . . . rather than serving as a copyable composition for the current generations."

Was Urban's color program "gaudy" or "garish" or simply a monumental variant of the red bed that had found acceptance in American bedrooms? In 1930 *Fortune* declared that "old suppressions had been released" in consumer products but believed that color in architecture was "still held to be advanced and possibly dangerous thinking. . . . America has not yet seen a major architectural effort in which color has been unreservedly and intelligently used." The Century of Progress Architectural Commission had hoped to educate the architectural palate of visitors and convince the world that Chicago could lead the nation into the beckoning sunrise beyond the depression. What was in fact achieved was a brief moment in which the art of architecture met and assimilated the flamboyant language of contemporary mass entertainment, advertising, and product design.

Chicago's "giant jewel" glimmered for two summers beside the lake with twentieth-century America's true colors. The fair was a welcome respite from depression drab and an advertising man's dream. *Fortune*'s commentator, close to the pulse of American business, wistfully anticipated:

> Alone among the arts which serve industry, architecture lags behind in the rush to know and use color. When at length it comes into its stride, it can make the most spectacular exhibition of all. The splendid Jain temples of Jaipur, gorgeous with their emeralds and rubies and sapphires, will pale beside a green and orchid tower, vaulting a fifth of a mile into the air. We shall outdo the barbarians. And our poets will applaud.

Chicago and the Bungalow Boom of the 1920s

Daniel J. Prosser

For those who grew up between Halsted and Ashland on the Far South Side or in the outlying sections of Jefferson Park, the bungalow is as familiar as an old green and white CTA car. Even suburbanites who travel through the Northwest Side on the Milwaukee Road can hardly fail to notice the small, hip-roofed brick houses which line block after block of the area. For good reason, more than one observer has referred to the "bungalow belt" bordering long stretches of the city limits.

These clusters of single-family houses were one of the primary results of Chicago's great building boom of the 1920s. Constructed on land made accessible by the extension of streetcar lines and by an increase in automobile ownership, they were direct descendants of the nineteenth-century workers' cottages so prevalent in older parts of the city. They enabled the solid working class to fulfill its dream of a free-standing house on a privately owned plot of land.

At the same time, the bungalow brought to mass housing many innovations in design and household convenience: the latest in wiring and plumbing, the newest in bathroom and kitchen equipment, and improved interior arrangements. A few bungalow builders even attempted to adopt the innovative exterior design of architect Frank Lloyd Wright and other members of the Prairie School.

Like many Midwestern cities, Chicago contains a large proportion of detached, single-family houses, including many which were designed specifically for the workingman's pocketbook. As early as the 1850s, many of the city's streets were lined with long, narrow, one-story frame cottages built specifically to house workers. Early versions featured spare and elegant Greek Revival detailing, while later examples were decorated with heavy Victorian bracketing and scrollwork, but underneath these surface variations the basic character of the cottage remained untouched. It might be raised to allow for a full-height basement at grade, it might be divided into apartments, or it might be moved to the rear of the lot so that another cottage or two-flat could be placed in front. The cottage was infinitely flexible.

With the rapid growth of the city in the late 1800s, new cottages were built in outly-

The bungalow was a direct descendant of the nineteenth-century worker's cottage. This 1883 broadside shows a floor plan typical of those used in constructing cottages throughout the Chicago area.
(CHS, ICHi-06577)

ing areas — including suburbs and villages which were later annexed to the city — while older ones in the close-in neighborhoods served as housing for the most recently arrived immigrant groups. Even today many of these workers' cottages can still be found, and they continue to provide adequate, if somewhat spartan, housing for a large segment of the city's working class.

This tradition of single-family house construction on the outskirts reached new heights during the prosperous 1920s. Homer Hoyt, in *One Hundred Years of Land Values in Chicago* (1933), placed the total construction of bungalows throughout Cook County during the decade at 100,000. Within the city limits, construction of single-family houses, most of which were bungalows, reached 2,058 in 1920, 7,852 in 1923, peaked at 9,371 in 1925, and declined to 2,931 in 1929.

By this time "bungalow" had come to replace the term "cottage." Originally the word had been used specifically for small houses in California, but by the second decade of the twentieth century it was commonly applied to any cottage of single-story plan and simple design. Thus the bungalow boom of the 1920s was simply another wave of cottage building. The bungalows may have *looked* different, but they were hardly unprecedented.

The boom was a result of several things. The lack of private construction during the war produced a pent-up demand, and when building resumed in earnest in the early 1920s, entire blocks of bungalows went up at once. This trend continued well into the decade as Chicago attracted a growing number of new residents (census figures show a 25 percent increase in population from 1920 to 1930) and enjoyed the fruits of postwar prosperity.

Prospective buyers who had accumulated some wartime saving often turned to local building and loan associations, which played an important role in channeling funds into housing. On both the Northwest and Southwest sides, for example, savings banks serving Polish immigrants and their descendants were deeply involved in home financing. In his study of Polish-Americans, Julius Ozog attributed the growth of home ownership in Chicago directly to the more than a hundred Polish building and loan associations whose combined assets totaled nearly $336,720,000 by 1928.

Even more important was the availability of land. It was, in fact, precisely the opening of large subdivisions which made bungalow construction economically feasible. The older neighborhoods had developed as new transportation facilities brought previously isolated land within convenient reach of the Loop, and the same pattern was repeated in the 1920s. The electric trolley system had reached its point of maturity just before the war, serving virtually all sections within the city and often connecting with the systems of nearby suburbs. The elevated railways had been extended to new areas of the West Side along the Douglas Park line, which was initially projected to run all the way to Westchester. Interurban electric railways like the Aurora and Elgin and the South Shore augmented the older and equally important steam commuter railroads which served nearby towns and villages. There was even some motorbus service on the North and Far South sides for areas which were not included in the regular trolley routes.

Finally, and in the long run most significantly, the automobile made accessible land between fixed transportation routes. Within the city limits alone, passenger car registration increased from 89,973 in 1920 to 222,557 in 1923, and to 408,260 by 1929. By the mid-twenties, the influence of the automobile was readily apparent in newspaper advertisements for bungalow developments: many contained detailed instructions for potential buyers who wished to visit the site by car — and announced that a garage was included with every house.

This expansion of transportation into previously undeveloped areas made real estate subdivision a popular business. According to the Tax Assessor's Office, Chicago had more than half a million vacant lots in 1921, and even after the boom had passed its high point in 1928 an estimated 30 percent of the total lots in the city were still vacant. As a consequence, the price of land remained low, keeping the cost of bungalows competitive with rent. In 1926 the average price was $5,500, and the larger developers provided financing.

While bungalow construction took place in virtually every part of the city in which there was vacant land, certain areas of the South, Southwest, West, and Northwest sides were particularly well populated with these homes. This bungalow belt ran generally from south of 87th Street on the South Side to west of Western Avenue on the Southwest Side, out to the suburbs on the West Side, and west of Crawford (now Pulaski) Avenue on the Northwest Side. Four districts contained particularly high concentrations: the areas bounded by Halsted, Ashland, 87th, and 99th streets on the South Side; Western, Kedzie, 51st, and 63rd streets on the Southwest Side; Central, Ridgeland, Roosevelt, and 26th Street in the western suburb of Cicero; and Crawford, Cicero, North, and Diversey on the Northwest Side.

Bungalow construction was carried out in several ways. Some owners preferred to buy their lots and choose an independent contractor to build a house patterned after one of the contractor's plans. Or, if they wished, clients could present their contractors with plans purchased from one of many companies which sold prepared working drawings. A prospective homeowner need only scan the classified pages of his favorite newspaper to find a contractor to match his needs. And a number of national companies — including Sears, Roebuck — sold pre-cut houses in a variety of bungalow designs for assembly on the owner's lot. Sears even devised a mortgage plan which allowed customers to use a lot instead of a down payment as collateral for purchasing a house on credit.

Many contractors specialized in serving particular parts of the city. Grauer Brothers of 6006 W. North Avenue constructed bungalows for the Northwest Side, while the Stanton Construction Company, located on Western Avenue near 63rd Street, did a lively business on the South and Southwest sides. Often these firms offered convenient financing arrangements. In 1925, for example, the Lake Cement Construction Company, with headquarters in the 5700 block of S. Robie Avenue, promised to build a five-room brick bungalow on the owner's lot for $4,950, complete and ready for occupancy for $1,000 down and a balance comparable to rent.

Customers who lacked the time or inclination to deal with a contractor directly could go to one of the many real estate developers who offered to construct a house selected from one of several stock plans. Here, too, the classified pages of the newspapers attest to the popularity of such schemes throughout the city and suburbs.

A row of bungalows built during the late 1920s in the 9100 block of South Colfax Avenue. Such clusters were one outcome of Chicago's great building boom of the 1920s. Photograph by Ralph Tower. *(CHS, ICHi-01341)*

W. D. McIntosh, one of the largest developers, promised easy financing for a bungalow in Oak Park to any customer who bought a lot for $350 (a typical price for a narrow lot in the 1920s). John Bain and Company of the 6200 block of S. Ashland Avenue proposed the same arrangement on the Southwest Side. H. H. Barbour, operating on the Northwest Side, offered to build wooden bungalows for $6,500 if the customer purchased one of his lots in a subdivision along Lawrence near Milwaukee Avenue. Frank DeLugach, located on the Far South Side near 103rd Street and Princeton Avenue, preferred to advertise locally, exhorting steelworkers from the surrounding mills to examine his new brick bungalows and take advantage of the "most liberal offer ever made to workingmen!" John R. Robertson and Company made an even more direct appeal to South and West siders who had sufficient manual dexterity to build bungalows from do-it-yourself assembly kits.

Finally, one could buy a finished bungalow from a small-scale developer. This had been a common pattern of housing construction and marketing in the nineteenth century, and was responsible for the typical bungalow neighborhood in the city: a group of identical houses stretching perhaps as far as a block and differing only in trim or color of face brick, if at all. One of the more active builders was the Loeb-Hammel firm, which worked on the Northwest Side. At one point it had two clusters (one of eight and one of fifteen) under construction at the same time. But more typical was the smaller entrepreneur who would undertake the building of two or three bungalows, sell them, and use the profit to construct a few more.

Although the average bungalow builder was a relatively small-scale investor, a handful of businessmen specialized in large tracts designed for mass production and high-volume sale. Some of these tracts included as many as a hundred or more units built to a standard plan but featuring a limited variety of facades. Thus, instead of a block of identical bungalows, the customer would find several blocks of dwellings, all basically the same but distinguished from one another by different exteriors.

The best example of this was the Westwood project, built by the Mills and Sons Company in Elmwood Park, adjacent to the city's Northwest Side. The initial complex, opened in 1927, consisted of sixty small brick bungalows with four basic floor plans and ten different facades. By April of that year, Mills opened a similar complex lying just west of the first and advertised an attractive financing package for the basic $8,750 price. By September Mills was calling Westwood "The World's Largest Bungalow Development," and by the spring of 1929 the advertisement proclaimed that more than one thousand families had settled in the area.

In addition to introducing a range of styles and floor plans, Mills departed from the customary grid arrangement by experimenting with curvilinear streets and grassy open spaces. Just off Grand Boulevard, where the development began, Mills placed a large circular park from which the residential streets radiated in a pattern which resembled one-quarter of a wagon wheel, with the park as the hub and the streets as slightly arched spokes. His goal was to convince businesses to cluster around this park and thereby form a village at the entrance to Westwood.

The bungalow has not been treated gently by architectural critics. One defined it as a "house that looks as if it had been built for less money than it actually costs." Yet for the blue-collar worker with a steady income or the young independent businessman just getting started, it afforded a degree of comfort and style which was well within reach of his modest resources. It was a "cottage with class."

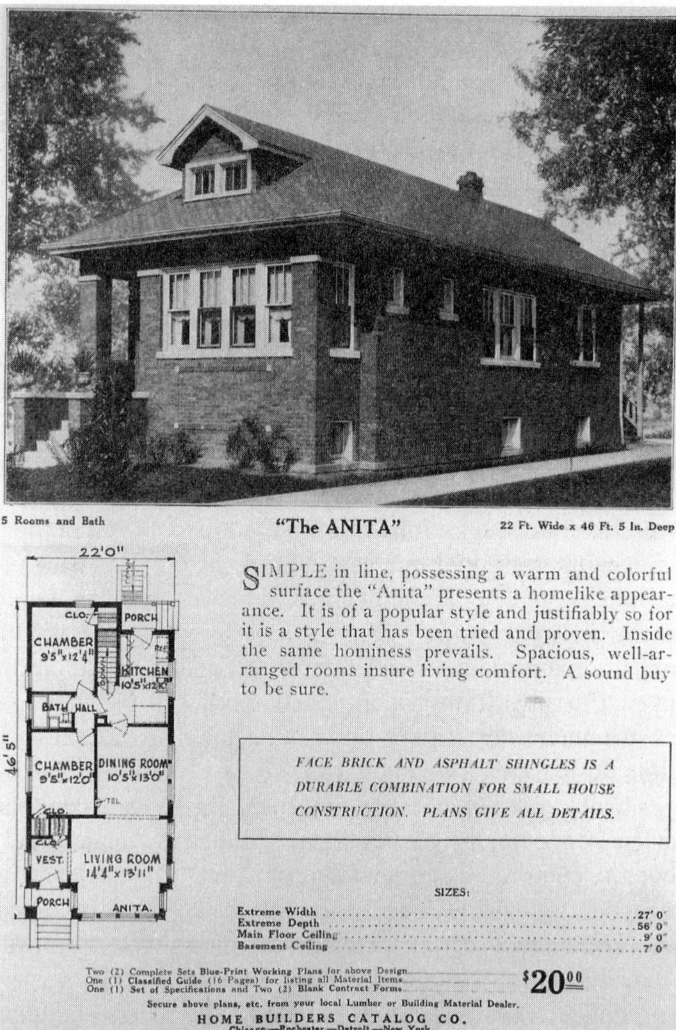

Advertisement for "The Anita," which embodied many elements typical of Chicago bungalows and their floor plans. Note the long, narrow dimensions — 22 by 46 feet — which were scaled to the requirements of a narrow city lot. From *Home Builders Catalog*, 1926.
(CHS, ICHi-15887)

To be sure, the bungalow's layout was shaped by the same long, narrow city lot which had originally given rise to the old worker's cottage. The classic cottage layout had remained generally unchanged throughout the nineteenth century — the parlor and a small bedroom at the front, the kitchen directly behind the parlor, and a second bedroom behind the first. Larger versions included a dining room between the parlor and kitchen and a third bedroom between the other two. These layouts were subsequently used in the construction of many Chicago area bungalows.

There were, however, some distinct improvements. Perhaps the most notable was the more prominent role assigned to the living room. Up through World War I, many families still regarded the front room as a space to be reserved for special occasions, and family living centered around the dining room and kitchen. In the bungalow plans of the 1920s, however, the front room is clearly labeled "living room" and is made distinctly larger than the dining room. Often, this was accomplished by moving the front bedroom back to allow the living room to stretch almost the entire width of the house.

Another improvement was the addition of a central hallway. The nineteenth-century cottage dispensed with this luxury, and simply allowed bedrooms to open directly into the kitchen, dining room, or parlor. As bathrooms became common toward the end of the 1800s, builders merely boxed off a corner of the kitchen and installed conveniences there. But the bungalows of the 1920s featured circulation spaces which allowed the residents to pass directly from the bedrooms to the bathroom. This gesture toward privacy may seem small, but it was quite a concession from contractors obsessed with wringing every square inch of space from their product.

Perhaps most appealing to the potential homeowner was the emphasis on mechanization and convenience. Advertisements stressed that the builders had incorporated the latest innovations in plumbing and wiring, not to mention such features as sparkling ceramic tile bathrooms, built-in cupboard space, and closets for every bedroom. What had been perceived as luxuries by the previous generation now became available to the stable working class of the 1920s. Outside stood the Model T; inside there was an electric chandelier in the dining room and a porcelain lavatory in the bathroom.

No room was more drastically altered by the emergence of new household devices than the kitchen. Most obvious, of course, was the electric refrigerator, introduced in the 1920s as a welcome alternative to the messy icebox. Other innovations included the improvement of sink traps, gas ranges, and a variety of electrical devices such as toasters which transformed the kitchen from a place of drudgery to what the commentators of the day liked to call a "cooking laboratory." As bungalows were specifically designed for servantless families, their promoters made much of these advancements.

There were other improvements over the cottage as well. The common building material was brick rather than wood. Moreover, the walls were often solid masonry rather than brick veneer, as became common in post–World War II construction. Central heating — hot air, hot water, or steam — was standard. And many of the larger developments, such as Westwood, came complete with streets, sidewalks, and utilities already installed.

Yet it was in exterior design that the bungalow differed most from the cottage. The nineteenth-century cottage had been built in whatever style was fashionable at the time, from Greek Revival to High Victorian Italianate. In the early twentieth century it was built in a style adapted from Chicago's own Prairie School of architecture, an adaptation which required a radical change in appearance. It was this change which made the shift in name from "cottage" to "bungalow" so significant. Instead of being just another cottage built in the 1920s, the bungalow acquired a distinctive appearance.

The basic characteristics of the Prairie style of Frank Lloyd Wright and his followers are familiar: long horizontal lines, low-pitched roofs, deep overhangs, broad windows which mirrored the contours of the Midwestern terrain, and a distinctive mode of ornamentation in which piers and moldings were used to divide the facade into a set of complementary horizontal and vertical elements. This new style was developed by Wright and his disciples during the first years of the twentieth century and is best exemplified in commissions for large suburban houses set in open surroundings.

Yet several other architects also attempted to adapt the Prairie style to smaller dwellings. The firm of Tallmadge and Watson, for instance, constructed several houses which served as influential models of the bungalow style. Writing in 1911, architectural critic Henry Saylor identified a distinct "Chicago School" bungalow and concluded that it was "almost a new style in the architectural types of the world." Compared to the typical cottage or bungalow, however, these were relatively extended structures on large lots.

During the decade prior to World War I, bits and pieces of the Prairie style began to appear on mass-produced dwellings. By 1920, stock plan companies which sold working drawings to contractors, such as the Home Builders Catalog Company of Chicago, advertised designs with hipped roofs, deep overhangs, wide front openings of grouped windows, piers supporting porches and imbedded in walls as pilasters, and belt courses to emphasize the horizontal dimension. At the same time, there were some interesting variations in detailing. For example, one might find a full-arched porch entrance breaking with the right-angled regularity of the facade, or a segmental-arched basement window, complete with keystone, poking up at the foundation level. In fact it was not unusual for the entire facade to bow out in a half octagon bay. Builders were well aware of the difficulties of achieving architectural purity on a budget and frequently took liberties in modifying the style for a mass market.

Nor could the attempt to transform the bungalow into a Prairie style house disguise the fact that it remained in essence a nineteenth-century cottage. The long, low lines and earth-hugging quality of the Prairie house simply could not be transplanted to a 35-foot-wide lot. The bungalow required a high narrow facade with an elevated basement and a high attic with a dormer window. These had become standard with the old cottage as devices for providing additional space, and the public would hardly sacrifice this space for the sake of aesthetics. Thus even the purest of the bungalow designs was an awkward cousin twice removed from the great Prairie houses.

Unidentified Chicago neighborhood, c. 1900. Such cottages housed large numbers of the city's workers throughout the nineteenth century.

(CHS, ICHi-00855)

The peak of bungalow construction was reached in 1926-27. At a time when the market was becoming saturated because those who could afford it had already made the transition to home ownership it took easy credit terms to attract a second level of purchasers in order to maintain construction levels. In retrospect it can be seen that some of these purchasers were not really in a position to invest in housing, since the relatively high rates and short payback periods of mortgages in those pre–Federal Housing Administration days obligated marginal buyers to terms they would have had difficulty meeting during the best of times. With the onset of the Depression at the end of the decade, default and forfeiture became endemic and many lost their homes.

Nonetheless, the bungalow boom had had a beneficial effect on the city and its inhabitants. It provided Chicago with a stock of solid housing in the single-family mode which allowed families to attain their ideal of owning their own home. It also provided them with the electrical and mechanical devices of the 1920s which made housekeeping less of a chore. And it enabled them to become owners of part of Chicago's unique architectural heritage.

"Big Red in Bronzeville": Mayor Ed Kelly Reels in the Black Vote

Roger Biles

For fourteen years, the longest tenure of any Chicago mayor prior to the rule of Richard J. Daley, Edward J. Kelly served as chief executive of the nation's second city. With Pat Nash, he ran the most powerful — and probably the most infamous — political machine in the nation. Along with his contemporaries, men like Jersey City's Frank Hague, Kansas City's Tom Pendergast, Boston's James Michael Curley, Memphis's Ed Crump, and the Bronx's Ed Flynn, Kelly represented the last of a vanishing breed — the autocratic big city boss who controlled not only the affairs of his city, but to a considerable degree those of his state and the nation as well. A household name throughout America in his day, Ed Kelly has been largely forgotten in the aftermath of the Daley years.

Known chiefly as the first of the Bridgeport mayors, Kelly has been dismissed as no more than a custodian for the political machine assembled by Anton Cermak and perfected by Daley. But this fails to acknowledge Kelly's role in attracting to the local Democratic machine the substantial black vote which had traditionally gone to the Republican party.

A popular saying of the twentieth century — "The Republican party is the ship, all else the sea" — accurately described the passionate commitment of the nation's blacks to the party of Lincoln. As one of the first politicians to actively court the black vote, Chicago Mayor William Hale ("Big Bill") Thompson, a Republican, amassed huge majorities in the city's Bronzeville. In the bitterly contested campaign of 1919, Thompson's narrow victory was attributed to his support by black voters, and in 1927 he received an amazing 93 percent of the black vote. Even when he lost to Democrat Anton Cermak in 1931, receiving only 42 percent of the popular vote, Thompson still garnered a formidable 84 percent of the Bronzeville vote. Although the Democrats had wrenched the mayoralty away from the Republicans, they had failed to disengage the G.O.P.'s stranglehold on the black electorate.

Aware of the party's ineffectiveness on the black South Side, Cermak immediately went to work to alter the political balance of power there. The day he took office, the new mayor fired 2,260 temporary employees, many of whom were black. At the same time he served notice that gambling, prostitution, and other illegal activities, formerly ignored by the Thompson administration, would cease in Bronzeville. The *Chicago Defender*, the city's most influential and widely read black newspaper, observed that the city "closed up like a drum. The lid went on five minutes after it was certain that former Mayor Thompson had lost his fight for a fourth term as Chicago mayor."

Cermak transferred Police Captain John Stege to the South Wabash station, located in the midst of the black community, telling him to "raise all the hell you can with the policy gang." Stege's men arrested some two hundred a day, cramming them into jail cells so tightly that no one could sit down. They randomly stopped automobiles to search for evidence of gambling and raided private homes to break up games of whist and bingo. Police arrest records for 1931 showed that 87 percent of the locations raided that year fell within the black belt; the number of blacks arrested that year tripled. The *Defender* called the South Side raids "political persecution" and Cermak's police "Cossacks." The mayor clearly indicated that such actions would cease if blacks switched their allegiance to the Democratic party.

In addition to these heavy-handed tactics, Cermak also began the task of constructing a black Democratic political organization on the South Side. The mayor served notice of his intentions by installing Michael Sneed, a precinct captain in the Thomas Nash organization, as the first black Democratic committeeman of the Third Ward. Joe Tittinger, the white committeeman of the heavily black Second Ward, also received instructions from City Hall to organize a black Democratic contingent in his domain. Cermak's death after only two years in office cut short his plan and left to his successor, Edward J. Kelly, the bulk of the task yet undone.

Ed Kelly, a second-generation Irishman from the South Side, had come late to Chicago politics. For most of his adult life he worked for the Chicago Sanitary District, rising from an unskilled laborer to the post of chief engineer. He also served on the South Park Board, eventually becoming its president. It was during his presidency that Chicago's Grant Park was landscaped and Soldier Field, the Shedd Aquarium, and the Adler Planetarium added to the lakefront. When Mayor Anton Cermak fell victim to an assassin's bullet in 1933 after only two years in office, Cook County Democratic Chairman Pat Nash shepherded legislation through the Illinois General Assembly permitting the City Council to go outside of the city government to choose an interim mayor. He chose Kelly, an old friend and business associate who had never held an elective office.

In seeking to attract black votes to the Democratic machine, Kelly took a very different tack from that followed by his predecessor. He quickly repudiated the coercive methods employed by Cermak's police and returned the official policy to one of benign neglect toward gambling and vice on the South Side. Despite his repeated and vehement protests to the contrary, Mayor Kelly's police allowed the black vice lords a free hand. Originally a nickel and dime operation, the policy game had become a multimillion dollar operation by the 1930s and the chief source of capital within Bronzeville. As a result, some of the richest and most powerful men in the area were policy kings, operating on sufferance of the local authorities. Just as it had achieved a comfortable working relationship with the previous Republican administration, so the black underworld now reached a rapprochement with its Democratic successor.

The Jones brothers, the South Side's most powerful gambling kings, actively participated in the operation of the Third Ward Democratic Organization and soon became precinct captains as well. Illy Kelly, noted policy chieftain and the son-in-law of former Republican alderman, Louis B. Anderson, ran unsuccessfully for Second Ward Democratic Committeeman in 1934. And as the leaders of black syndicates offered their allegiance to the Democratic machine, they brought with them considerable sources of manpower. As University of Chicago sociologist Harold F. Gosnell reported, one gambling operation dispatched 1,500 policy writers to the South Side streets to canvass for the Democratic ticket at election time. With their considerable financial and human resources, the black underworld bosses exerted a significant influence on political participation in Chicago's Bronzeville.

At the same time that he cultivated the seedier elements of the South Side, Kelly accelerated the process of constructing a black Democratic organization. Spurning threats and intimidation, Kelly sought to attract blacks by demonstrating that as the party in power, the Democrats had much to offer those who cooperated. He did this by making available more patronage jobs than the number previously offered by the much beloved Big Bill Thompson. The subsequent advent of New Deal–created federal jobs would increase the patronage Kelly could offer black Chicagoans, but even before the WPA boom, blacks received city jobs in unprecedented numbers under the Kelly regime.

In addition to increasing the quantity of jobs available to blacks, Kelly also improved their quality, elevating blacks to high positions in city government and appointing them to prestigious committees and panels. Some of the important appointive positions held by blacks under Kelly included those of Civil Service Commissioner, Assistant Corporation Counsel, Assistant City Prosecutor, Deputy Coroner, Assistant Traction Attorney, Assistant Attorney General, Assistant State's Attorney, Chairman of the Chicago Housing Authority, member of the School Board, and Judge of the Municipal Court. He also broke down the barriers to advancement within the police department, paving the way for blacks to rise to the rank of captain. And the mayor appointed Robert S. Abbott, editor of the *Chicago Defender,* to several important positions, including the Board of Commissioners of the Chicago World's Fair, the Committee on the Chicago Exposition, and the Chicago Jubilee Committee.

Kelly worked assiduously to present a good image to black voters and succeeded in establishing a reputation as a friend of "the Race." The mayor prohibited the showing of the film *Birth of a Nation* in Chicago because of its explicit racism. He honored successful black Americans for their achievements (making Joe Louis "mayor for ten minutes" in an elaborate city hall ceremony, for example) and made numerous personal appearances at South Side functions. "Big Red," as blacks affectionately called the mayor, attended the annual Tuskeegee-Wilberforce football games at Soldier Field and endorsed Governor Henry Horner's refusal to extradite a fugitive black man to an almost certain lynching in Arkansas. He espoused his belief in integration and pledged to expedite the process:

> I am afraid that the colored people have segregated themselves too much and have not taken advantage of the opportunities offered them to mingle freely in different public places of amusement that would contribute to their culture and refinement and general betterment. . . . As long as I am mayor of the city of Chicago I intend to be mayor of all the people, and I expect to see to it that each and every person and every group of people have an equal opportunity, as far as I am able in my capacity as executive of the city.

Mayor Kelly welcomes heavyweight boxing champion Joe Louis to Chicago. Kelly attended the civic and social functions in the black community as faithfully as he did those of other ethnic groups.
(CHS, DN-78,179)

At the dedication of the new Wendell Phillips High School, Mayor Kelly affirmed his commitment "that the public school system in Chicago, so long as he is mayor, shall be conducted in accordance with law and order applicable alike to all nationalities." He concluded by pledging his administration to the quest for racial justice, saying "the time is not far away when we shall forget the color of a man's skin and see him only in the light of intelligence of his mind and soul."

In the second year of Kelly's mayoralty, events on Chicago's South Side tested his ambitious rhetoric. In October 1934 Kelly met with a grievance committee of Morgan Park blacks to discuss the de facto segregation of the local high school, a supposedly integrated facility. The black parents protested to the mayor that two branch schools set up near the high school, ostensibly to relieve crowded conditions, actually were being used to separate black and white students. (White freshmen went to Clissold, while their black counterparts attended Shoop.) At the same time, they complained, school officials had brought hundreds of white pupils into the Morgan Park district, while neighborhood black students could not attend the local school. Amidst howls of protest from whites, Kelly rescinded the Board of Education's edict commanding black students to attend Shoop and ordered them readmitted to Morgan Park High School.

On the Monday following Kelly's action, more than 2,000 white students, a majority of Morgan Park High School's enrollment, walked out in protest. When an estimated 200 aggrieved white parents stormed the mayor's office demanding segregation, Kelly dispatched them and refused to reconsider. Following his threat of police action against the strikers, the protest died out and the recalcitrant white students returned to school. The *Defender* praised Kelly for his courageous stand: "In this answer the Mayor of Chicago vindicated his right to the respect and confidence of every citizen of every color and creed whose mind is not blinded by hate, prejudice, and bigotry." In 1945 white students struck at Englewood and Calumet high schools in opposition to integration, and again Kelly stood firm in his commitment to open schools.

Kelly's soaring popularity in the black community manifested itself in the political realm. The first indication came in 1934 when the Democrats selected a black candidate, Arthur W. Mitchell, to contest Oscar DePriest's congressional seat from Illinois's

First District. The popular DePriest, a three-term incumbent and nationally renowned as the first black Republican to sit in Congress since 1901, had the endorsement of the black press, including the influential *Defender.* But with the aid of the Kelly-Nash machine, Mitchell won a narrow victory, becoming the first black to serve as a Democrat in the House of Representatives.

On the heels of this electoral triumph came the 1935 mayoral election, the outcome of which substantiated Kelly's tremendous popularity among black voters. The mayor received the enthusiastic endorsement of the *Defender,* which observed, "Black people believe in Kelly and in fact say that the only difference between him and Bill Thompson in respect to them is the name." He not only enjoyed the support of Bronzeville Democrats but of many black Republicans as well. Both William L. Dawson, alderman of the Second Ward, and Robert Jackson, alderman of the Third Ward, ran for reelection that year as Republicans but publicly backed the incumbent mayor. Berthold Cronson, Republican alderman of the Fourth Ward, came out for Kelly as well. The mayor, in turn, endorsed the black Republican aldermen of the three South Side wards. The margin of victory for the incumbent far exceeded even the Democrats' expectations; Kelly received 80.5 percent of the vote in the black Second, Third, and Fourth wards.

The dramatic change in the voting of Chicago blacks from 1931 to 1935 reflected not only a burgeoning attachment to Ed Kelly but also a realistic assessment of political realities in the city. The blacks' desertion of the Republican party in 1935 represented only part of a huger, city-wide defection as Republicans and independents alike forsook the hapless G.O.P. candidate Emil Wetten. Recognizing the certainty of the outcome, South Side blacks jumped on the victorious Kelly bandwagon well in advance of the post-election reckoning time. As the *Defender* reminded its readers:

> If you leave it to the West, North, and far South Side to elect the mayor then don't be

Arthur W. Mitchell *(standing)* addresses a meeting of the Second Ward Organization. Kelly's endorsement of Mitchell in the Illinois First Congressional District race signaled the local machine's decision to appeal to the city's black voters. *(CHS, ICHi-15832)*

surprised when those things you are likely to want are left to them. Politics is a business; there is no sentiment involved; support is given for support.

In the 1936 gubernatorial primary, black voters demonstrated their fealty to the Kelly-Nash machine by supporting the organization candidate, Dr. Herman Bundesen. In the predominantly black Second and Third wards, Bundesen's plurality exceeded 8,300 votes; in nearby wards in which blacks compromised a minority of the population, the Fifth, Sixth, Seventh, and Eighth, Horner defeated the challenger by more than 4,000 votes. The *Defender* explained, "Members of the Race who voted in the Democratic primaries had nothing personally against Governor Horner, they were following the leadership of Mayor Edward Kelly, who had proven himself their friend." In the general election later that year, South Side blacks followed the lead of other Chicago Democrats and supported Homer against his Republican opponent.

In 1939 black support for Kelly failed to equal the standard set four years earlier, but the South Side vote remained substantially Democratic. Kelly's appointments of Wendell Green to the Civil Service Commission and Robert Taylor to the Chicago Housing Authority solicited praise from the black community. Again the *Defender* gave Kelly its hearty endorsement, saying that "Mayor Kelly has faced all issues fairly and equally when the rights of our race are involved." Republican mayoral candidate Dwight Green argued that little progress had been made in combating the school board's segregationist policies, but Kelly's stand for open schools, most notably in the Morgan Park incident, negated the attack. Kelly received 59.5 percent of the black vote, as compared to 56.1 percent of the total city vote. In a reasonably close, hard-fought contest, Kelly's success in Bronzeville exceeded his city-wide performance.

Kelly's critics groused that his following among black voters resulted primarily from the popularity of the national Democratic party and Franklin D. Roosevelt in particular. Certainly blacks throughout the nation found much to their liking in Roosevelt's New Deal. Hard hit by the Great Depression, urban blacks found the work and relief programs sponsored by the federal government a godsend. A popular blues song of the time illustrated black dependence upon such programs:

> Please, Mr. President, listen to what I've
> got to say:
> You can take away all of the alphabet,
> but please leave that WPA.
> Now I went to the poll and voted,
> I know I voted the right way —
> So I'm asking you, Mr. President, don't take
> away that WPA!

The exhortation of one black preacher — "Let Jesus lead you and Roosevelt feed you!" — typified the high regard in which Roosevelt came to be held by black Americans in the thirties, Indeed, by 1940 the previously Republican *Defender* had become a staunch supporter of the Democratic party, repenting its earlier "blind, child-like faith" in the G.O.P. and lauding Roosevelt as the "greatest champion of the cause of the common people." As one political analyst wrote, "Harry Hopkins (Roosevelt's chief relief administrator) really turned Lincoln's picture to the wall."

But to assume that Roosevelt's popularity — and Kelly's, in turn — depended solely upon federal welfare programs would be to oversimplify and distort a complex phenomenon. In the 1932 presidential election Roosevelt and his vice-presidential running mate, Southerner John Nance Garner, re-

Mayor Kelly talks to the press in Washington, D.C., after conferring with WPA Administrator Harry Hopkins (with hat). For Chicago's hard-hit black community the WPA jobs and federal relief, dispensed ostentatiously by the Democratic Party, were a godsend.
(CHS, ICHi-15879)

ceived only 23 percent of Chicago's black vote. In 1936 that percentage more than doubled to 48.9 percent, and rose again to 52 percent in 1940. While the popularity of relief programs undoubtedly accounted for much of the increase, that was only one of a number of factors which coalesced during this decade to attract blacks to the Democratic party. As Harold F. Gosnell and Elmer W. Henderson have detailed, other considerations were vitally important. The urbanization of blacks in the preceding decades engendered psychological changes which broke down stereotyped, traditional allegiances. Blacks became dissatisfied with the Republicans who took their support for granted. Increased exposure to labor movements and radical ideology encouraged a growing class consciousness among blacks. The more enlightened Democratic party of Roosevelt benefited from the reputations of such noted "race liberals" as Eleanor Roosevelt, Aubrey Williams, and Harold Ickes. Roosevelt, like Kelly, broke new ground by appointing blacks in ever-increasing numbers to prestigious federal positions. And finally, the successful wooing of black votes by local Democratic leaders aided the quest of the national party.

This last point underscores the fact that Kelly's support in Chicago's South Side was not simply a microcosm of Roosevelt's national following. While the vote totals for the president rose steadily, Chicago blacks never supported the national Democratic ticket as completely as they did Kelly. The Chicago Democratic machine's attempts to recruit blacks predated the Roosevelt administration's similar action. Clearly, efforts by both local and national Democrats complemented each other, and each benefited from the successes of its counterpart. Kelly brazenly claimed the virtues of the Roosevelt administration as his own and never ceased to emphasize the importance of federal relief to depression-stricken blacks. But stressing the Roosevelt connection constituted but one firearm in the mayor's arsenal; his sustained success with black voters rested upon the construction of a robust organization in the South Side subservient to, and patterned after, the larger city Democratic machine.

The man who ultimately came to rule the black Democratic submachine was William L. Dawson. Kelly initially chose Dawson for one very specific purpose, to take control of one troublesome ward. In the words of a politician close to Dawson:

> Kelly did not build Dawson by pre-arranged plan into *the* South Side boss; he made him head of the second ward, and after that Dawson just grew. In each showdown, Dawson was seen to be the better man and was supported.

Born in Georgia, William Levi Dawson attended Fisk University and Northwestern Law School, served with distinction in the army during World War I, and settled in Chicago ,where he became a lawyer. He entered politics as a Republican and became a precinct captain. He was elected alderman of the Second Ward with the backing of Congressman Oscar DePriest in 1933. In the City Council Dawson acquired the reputation of a maverick who frequently voted against his fellow Republicans. Dawson and the Democratic mayor became good friends, and the Second Ward alderman became known as "Kelly's man" in the council. Along with several other Republicans, Dawson openly supported Kelly-Nash candidates in municipal elections. Many disgruntled South Siders charged that Dawson was a Republican in name only.

Events within the Republican party on the South Side served to obstruct Dawson's ambitions. William E. King, the Second Ward committeeman, feared that Dawson intended to assume complete control of the ward and therefore disavowed any connection with the alderman. With the control of patronage for the ward and the support of Congressman DePriest, King staved off Dawson's challenge in 1936 and kept the office of committeeman. The year after his successful reelection as alderman in 1937, Dawson shifted his sights to the congressional seat taken away from DePriest by Arthur Mitchell. In the Republican primary, Dawson bested Louis B. Anderson and Oscar DePriest, thanks in part to the aid of First Ward Republican Committeeman Daniel Serritella, who operated under the orders of Democratic County Chairman Pat Nash. In the general election, however, he lost to the popular Mitchell by a 30,207 to 26,396 vote. With avenues for advancement blocked within the G.O.P., an inability to assume control of the Second Ward organization, and a healthy relationship with the powerful Kelly-Nash machine, Dawson, by the end of the 1930s, began to look to the Democratic party for the fulfillment of his aspirations as a political leader.

Fortunately for Dawson, an upheaval in the Democratic Second Ward Organization created an opening for someone of his ambitions. For several years blacks had been complaining about the dictatorial, insensitive leadership of the white committeeman, Joseph Tittinger, who distributed almost all of his patronage jobs to the few whites living on the eastern edge of the ward and even imported whites from neighboring wards to supervise employment assignments. He had a black precinct captain removed from a patronage job to make way for his own son, kept segregated office hours at party headquarters for what he referred to as "colored" constituents, and moved his personal residence to an area governed by a restrictive covenant. Impervious to complaints by his black constituents, Tittinger pledged to remain as committeeman as long as there was "a single white vote in the ward."

In June 1939, 53 precinct captains from the Second Ward presented Kelly and Nash with a petition of grievances requesting the removal of Tittinger as committeeman. The *Defender* warned that if the Democrats failed to take action "The belief is current that the Republican forces will come back into power in the next election." Tittinger responded to the criticism by firing the precinct captains from their patronage jobs. Many of these then banded together to form an independent organization to oppose him in the upcoming 1940 election. Faced with a disintegrating ward organization and the threat of a black Democratic faction hostile to the Kelly-Nash regime, the mayor resolved to oust Tittinger and replace him with a black politician.

Speculation about the new boss of the Second Ward revolved around three men: Christopher Wimbish, Bryant Hammond, and William Dawson. Wimbish, a former Republican assistant state's attorney, had joined the Democrats in the mid-thirties as a member of State's Attorney Thomas Courtney's anti-Kelly faction and had been instrumental in challenging Tittinger's control of the ward. Hammond, a Democrat of longer standing, supported Cermak in the 1931

Republican Oscar DePriest, a leading black politician, 1917, posting bond prior to an election. This was required of all candidates to insure that they would fulfill the duties of public office if elected.

(CHS, DN-67,731)

mayoral election and ran a strong race against William E. King for state senator in 1934. Unlike Wimbish, Hammond had long been a staunch Kelly loyalist and an outspoken critic of Courtney in the 1939 primary. But as Kelly's champion in the City Council, Dawson held the inside track, the only drawback being his party affiliation. He was, after all, still a Republican — at least until 1939.

In the February aldermanic elections that year, Dawson finished third behind Democrat Earl B. Dickerson and Republican William E. King. When the closeness of the contest necessitated a runoff between the top two finishers, Dawson threw his support to Dickerson, who subsequently won the election. Dawson met with Kelly, informing him of his decision to switch to the Democratic party. Kelly, who had been advised to choose Dawson as Tittinger's replacement by several influential black citizens, solicited Dickerson's approval and announced the change in late November.

Not everyone among the Democrats welcomed Dawson with open arms, the chief obstructionist being County Chairman Pat Nash. Always a stalwart party man, Nash did not trust anyone who would switch parties for what he suspected to be personal gain. He remembered Dawson as an enemy in the bitter struggle for control of the Second Ward, and while it was permissible to help a friend from the City Council in a Republican primary, it seemed quite another matter to aid the same individual against lifelong, proven Democrats. Therefore, Nash stood by Tittinger and promised him continued control of the ward's county patronage. Kelly stuck with Dawson, granting the new Democrat access to state and local patronage. Kelly finally won the Cook County Central Committee over to his side, and by December 1939 Dawson had officially received the blessing of the Democratic machine. His biggest problem now lay in consolidating his power within the Second Ward.

Initially Dawson faced two complex problems — how to convince his former Republican supporters to follow him into the rival camp and how to assuage the fears of Second Ward Democrats that they would be supplanted by a wave of renegade Republicans. By his own account, the first problem proved the more difficult of the two. For years Dawson had been preaching partisan loyalty to black Republicans and denigrating Democrats. Now he had to explain his dramatic reversal and encourage others to make the same move. He pointed to bankrupt Republican promises, the Democratic record as the party of the downtrodden, the friendly Kelly administration, and the great progress enjoyed by blacks during Roosevelt's two terms. Many followed Dawson into the Democratic ranks, a situation that gave pause to established Democrats in the ward. Dawson reassured them that they would lose neither their high standing in the party hierarchy nor their jobs; they had, in fact, few jobs to lose, and after the dictatorial reign of Tittinger, Dawson readily won over the fearful.

In a short period of time, the new ward chief proved himself an able and energetic administrator. He instituted strict discipline into what had always been a loosely structured ward organization, formed women's and young people's Democratic clubs, and kept his office open at all times to all residents of the ward. Recognizing the great number of women working as precinct captains, he appointed three black women to senatorial committeemanships. He appointed rival Christopher Wimbish president of the ward organization. And to appease the few white residents of the ward, Dawson slated Tittinger for state representative. The newcomer was securing his hold on the Second Ward, but his control would remain incomplete because of the uneasy alliance with Alderman Dickerson.

Trouble between the two men commenced even before Dawson's official acceptance by the Cook County Central Committee. Mayor Kelly named Dawson and Dickerson to co-chair a fund-raising drive for his annual Christmas charity. Dawson's workers sponsored a benefit which raised $500 to buy clothes for distribution at Christmas. Dickerson claimed credit for work which Dawson felt had been done by his staff alone. The incident, in which both men strove to impress the mayor, indicated the tension between the rivals for control of the ward. Dawson's refusal to endorse Dickerson in his bid for the 1940 Democratic nomination for congressman further exacerbated their uneasy relationship. Dawson had earlier promised that support in exchange for the alderman's backing against Tittinger, but in 1940 he stood behind the incumbent, Arthur Mitchell. Meanwhile Dawson worked to isolate Dickerson from the center of power in the Second Ward; he "forgot" to invite the alderman to meetings and regularly called him to the podium to speak at political rallies with only a few minutes left on the program.

Frustrated by his committeeman's machinations against him, Dickerson also found himself increasingly alienated from city hall. Feeling betrayed by Dawson in 1940, Dickerson refused to campaign for Mitchell — a decision very unpopular with Kelly and Nash, who demanded complete support of the ticket by all Democrats. Kelly also disapproved of Dickerson's incipient radicalism: the alderman became an outspoken proponent of organized labor, a more militant spokesman for black rights, president of the Chicago Urban League, and worst of all, along with Paul Douglas and John Boyle, a persistent critic of the Kelly administration in the City Council. Particularly galling to the mayor was Dickerson's opposition to a traction ordinance favored by Kelly, on the grounds that it allowed unions to discriminate on the basis of color. Dawson observed, "he was always raising the race issue and antagonizing people. . . . Me, I never raise the race issue, even in Congress, and I certainly didn't in the Council. . . ."

The events of 1942 sealed Dickerson's fate as a pariah. Congressman Arthur W. Mitchell decided not to run for reelection that year (although he gave his wife's failing health as the reason many believed that his decision reflected a surrender to the expanding Dawson machine), and the Democratic organization chose Dawson to replace him. Dickerson resolved to run as an independent in the primary, finally severing the cord that bound him to the Kelly-Nash machine. He campaigned ardently as a New Dealer and criticized Dawson for replacing Democratic jobholders with his former Republican cronies. Defending his radicalism, Dickerson predicted that Dawson "can at best be another weak-kneed Mitchell owing allegiance to a machine rather than the people." But despite a valiant campaign, Dickerson lost to Dawson by an overwhelming margin, 14,638 to 4,521. Dawson's subsequent victory over the Republican candidate William E. King elevated him to a new pinnacle in the South Side political arena.

In 1943 Dickerson lost his City Council seat to Dawson's cohort, William H. Harvey, assuring Dawson complete control of the Second Ward. That same year Benjamin Grant, elected as the first black Democratic alderman from the Third Ward in 1939, lost to Republican Oscar DePriest; this signaled the death knell for Michael Sneed's decaying Third Ward Organization. It also paved the way for Dawson, whose subordinate, Christopher Wimbish, succeeded Sneed as ward committeeman. Secure in his own bailiwick, Dawson added the neighboring ward to his expanding fiefdom.

In the following years Dawson would repeat this pattern of infiltration, so that by the mid-fifties his domain would span five wards on the predominantly black South Side. Into the Twentieth Ward he installed Kenneth Campbell as committeeman; into the Fourth, Claude Holman; into the Sixth, Robert Miller; and later, when Wimbish faltered, Ralph Metcalfe into the Third. As blacks moved into these previously white wards, Dawson's men, political organizers and canvassers, came in as well, laying the groundwork for the takeover. When the white bosses lost an election, Dawson approached the city Democratic leadership — Ed Kelly, Pat Nash, and later Jacob Arvey and Joe Gill — and pleaded to try his hand. In each case his superior organization produced healthy vote totals for the machine and vindicated his claims.

Dawson built a submachine within the larger Chicago Democratic machine, whereby he controlled the votes of an estimated quarter of a million people by 1950. This can only be explained as a by-product, and not the design, of Ed Kelly's decision to install the former Republican into the seat of power in the Second Ward. Dawson's ability to produce for the machine, the electoral success in each of the wards he controlled, guaranteed his continued support from city hall. As political scientist James Q. Wilson noted, "Had a weaker or less effective man than Dawson set out to be the Negro leader, it is possible that in a series of challenges others would have triumphed and no single Negro machine would have emerged." Despite the fact that Kelly had not foreseen the direction in which Dawson's leadership would take the South Side, his strategy must be viewed as successful. Dawson, an organizational genius, brought discipline and order to a traditional trouble spot, so that Kelly and countless other Democrats benefited on election day.

In short, Ed Kelly's successful cultivation of the black vote proved a great boon to Chicago's Democratic machine. Unlike Cermak, who chose the stick rather than the carrot, Kelly astutely proselytized blacks by offering them unprecedented recognition and increased patronage. He used the availability of federal jobs and the popularity of Franklin D. Roosevelt to add to the luster of the local machine. And while some machine critics questioned his sincerity — Dickerson maintained that Kelly really "was never a friend of the Negro people" — and skeptics called the mayor's commitment to blacks solely political, his administration struck a positively progressive chord in the realm of race relations. His sustained advocacy of integrated schools and defense of open housing, reaffirmed in the post–World War II years, rankled much of his predominantly white constituency in Chicago. While Democratic politicians covered the black vote, Kelly's "liberalism" on the race question often exceeded the bounds of political expediency. Clearly, the black community, as well as the Democratic organization, benefited from the alliance forged by Kelly.

The Siting of the University of Illinois at Chicago Circle: A Struggle of the 1950s and 1960s

George Rosen

In 1909 the long-awaited Burnham Plan for the city of Chicago was made public. One of its most important recommendations for the improvement of the downtown area was the widening of Congress Street and the development of a new civic center just southwest of the Loop. Surrounded by a grand public square, the projected center was to become "the very embodiment of civic life" — and Congress Street, transformed into a broad thoroughfare, was to "furnish opportunities for the highest class of adornment known to civic art." Twelfth Street (now Roosevelt Road) was also to be widened to create another boulevard parallel to the new Congress Street.

Sixty years later Congress Street *was* widened — to form the Eisenhower Expressway. Roosevelt Road was also widened. But instead of flanking a civic center, the streets now lead into the heart of the major auto expressway system into and out of the city — the Chicago Circle interchange of the Eisenhower, Kennedy, and Dan Ryan expressways. Just west of this Circle lies the new campus of the University of Illinois at Chicago Circle. The Near West Side neighborhood around that campus has also changed significantly, both from what it was before the campus was built and from what its inhabitants had hoped it might become.

The decision to place the UICC campus at that location has a history that dates back to 1946. When it was finally made in 1961, it touched off one of the sharpest battles in Richard J. Daley's long term as mayor of Chicago. Indeed, the siting of the Circle campus was, in the opinions of both Mayor Daley and David Dodds Henry, then president of the university, among the most significant actions of their respective and lengthy administrations.

In the early stages of the decision-making process, from 1946 to 1956, the University of Illinois was the major actor. During that period the university decided to build an undergraduate four-year campus in the Chicago area and selected a suburban site. What were the goals which the university sought to achieve by those decisions? The large number of World War II veterans returning to college on the G.I. bill made it clear that the educational responsibilities of the university in the postwar period would severely tax the existing capacity of the Urbana campus. It was also apparent that a large proportion of the prospective students would be from Chicago and its surrounding area. The immediate responsibility of educating war veterans was met in 1946 when the university set up a temporary campus at Chicago's Navy Pier to provide veterans with the first two years of undergraduate training. A second temporary campus was set up in the town of Galesburg, 170 miles southwest of Chicago. The latter campus was closed by 1949, but the Chicago Undergraduate Division at Navy Pier continued to function until 1965.

The opening of the Navy Pier campus not only provided the university with an entry into undergraduate education in the Chicago area, but created a demand from the late 1940s onward to convert the temporary two-year campus into a permanent four-year school. This came from various groups: Chicago-area students who wished to save on the costs of education by commuting to school; from the faculty at the temporary campus; and from Chicago civic, business, and trade union groups whose members would benefit from having a large, state-supported university in the community. Their arguments were voiced at public meetings, in the newspapers, and by leading political figures in the city and state

The University of Illinois's first Chicago home: Municipal (now Navy) Pier, leased from the city in 1946. Shown here in 1958, it continued to house university classes until 1965.

(Photograph by J. Sherwin Murphy. CHS, ICHi-26525)

legislatures, including State Senator Richard J. Daley.

The university was initially ambivalent toward this demand. After the great wave of returning veterans subsided, there was a period of slackening enrollment which reflected the decline in birth rates during the depression of the 1930s. More important, this was the period when the president of the university, George B. Stoddard, was making a major effort to develop the Urbana campus into one of the leading educational institutions in the country. He was worried that a Chicago campus would divert scarce resources from Urbana, an opinion shared by other administrators and faculty members who were reluctant to face competition from academic departments at a new sister institution. President Stoddard publicly acknowledged the desirability of building a University of Illinois campus sometime in the future, and even suggested placing it north of Congress Street near the university's medical school, which had been located in Chicago since the turn of the century.

Yet this vision of a future campus did not satisfy local advocates. There were public confrontations between President Stoddard and the faculty at the Pier, culminating in faculty and student protests before the Board of Trustees. These incidents in turn contributed to the unexpected Board vote of no confidence in President Stoddard in July 1953 and his resignation immediately thereafter. Before this vote, however, the Board had also set up a committee headed by Wayne Johnston, a Board member from the Chicago area and president of the Illinois Central Railroad, to consider the immediate establishment of a permanent four-year campus in Chicago. Originally set up on a temporary basis, the committee became a permanent part of the Board until the issue was resolved. Wayne Johnston was to play a major role in the entire process.

But the issue of a Chicago campus drew unfavorable reactions from several sources. There was significant opposition from the Champaign-Urbana community and its legislators, including State Senator Everett Peters, a strong proponent of the university in legislative battles and an influential figure in the state Republican party. While Urbana people feared the loss of business, there was also resistance from some of the private universities in the Chicago area, which feared the presence of a University of Illinois campus of high academic stature but low, state-subsidized tuition. Finally, the university position was influenced by the changing organization of public education in Illinois and the conversion of various public colleges into universities during and immediately after the war. These new universities, especially Southern Illinois University, aspired to high academic standing and lobbied so persuasively that they could make it difficult for the University of Illinois to get its budget requests through the legislature. A public university in Chicago would strengthen this capability.

Following President Stoddard's resignation, his immediate acting successor, Lloyd Morey, set up an internal committee to examine the entire issue of a campus in the Chicago area for the university. At about the same time the General Assembly set up the Randolph Committee, headed by Paul Randolph, the state representative from the Navy Pier district and the most active proponent of the Chicago campus in the legislature, to consider the same issue.

Both committees sought to estimate the potential student demand for college education in the state over the next several decades, and the implications of this for future enrollments in both the University of Illinois and in the private universities in the Chicago area. The demographic projections showed that by the early 1960s, the increasing birth rates of the postwar period and the expected higher incomes would create a need for a permanent public campus in the Chicago area without reducing enrollments in the private institutions. On the basis of these projections the university committee reported in favor of a Chicago-area campus. Underlying this report was the fear that if the University of Illinois did not take the initiative one of the other state universities, or even the city, would. If that happened, the University of Illinois would have lost both the potential support of the Chicago political organization in the state legislature and the ability to influence the future direction of what would be a potential rival. If the University of Illinois did set up such a Chicago campus, it might achieve both those results.

Another internal committee then examined the building and space requirements for a new campus. Its report estimated a minimum requirement of 130 acres for a low-rise campus with enough space for buildings, parking, athletic, and service facilities. This space estimate was a fixed requirement not to be sacrificed because of a high price of land, and remained the minimum need in all the following discussion and negotiation.

On the basis of these reports the Board of Trustees hired the Real Estate Research Corporation, a private Chicago-based firm, to recommend a site in an area of low or medium density population. Reporting to the Board in 1955, the Corporation set forth criteria for the choice of a site: adequate transportation for potential students; immediate availability of land to build enough facilities to house the two-year undergraduate program by 1963; a minimum area of 140 acres plus additional space for expansion; a maximum land price of $5.00 per square foot; and, finally, consistency of the site plans with community plans for land development in the selected area. The report examined 69 potential sites; of these, the slum-clearance sites were ruled out on grounds of the difficulty of relocating inhabitants and of potential political opposition. Two alternatives were recommended: one, an island of 150 acres to be built in the lake off the Adler Planetarium; and the second, a 300-acre suburban site, Miller Meadows, immediately to the west of the city off the Eisenhower Expressway, which was owned by the Forest Preserve District. The internal university committee preferred Miller Meadows because it was larger and would cost less, but there were also some preliminary discussions with the Illinois Institute of Technology concerning construction of a campus in cooperation with, and near, the existing IIT campus. This second possibility was ruled out because it involved a slum clearance site.

In reviewing this progress, Lloyd Morey, in one of his speeches before the permanent University of Illinois president took office in September 1955, urged the people of Champaign-Urbana to support a new Chicago campus; otherwise, he feared a "separate school establishment under separate controls," with "uncoordinated development of other public institutions in Illinois" in response to a "tidal wave of students." Meanwhile the Randolph Committee had reported to the General Assembly also favoring a four-year Chicago campus, and several bills were presented to the legislature to appropriate money for such a campus in the Chicago area. The university opposed those bills on the grounds that it had neither determined the need for, nor the location of the campus, and the measures were defeated.

David Dodds Henry, the new president, came to the University of Illinois with a background of urban university administration at Wayne (later Wayne State) University in Detroit and at New York University in New York City. He recognized the need and accepted the political importance of a Chicago campus, and during his first year in office reviewed the previous studies, initiated additional research, and developed a strategy that he thought would achieve the necessary political support for the new campus. The additional research confirmed the preference for a low-rise campus and its 130-acre minimum space requirement. At the high price of city land this would rule out a city campus since the same acreage could be purchased in the suburbs at a far lower cost. As expressed in a memo written in early 1956 by Charles Havens, the university's director of physical plant and one of President Henry's chief lieutenants on the campus issue, "[the] objective is to relocate the present two-year program now offered at the Pier . . . to procure enough ground to take care of two to three times the [8000] students planned for in the first phase and to progress to a four-year school when there is a need for such. . . ." The target date for opening the new two-year campus was September 1963, and President Henry anticipated that by that time the need for an expanded program would be so obvious that no one would oppose it. In July 1956, acting on Henry's recommendation, the Board of Trustees voted in favor of the Miller Meadows location and directed the president to acquire that site.

But the university failed in its effort to buy this suburban acreage, which was owned directly by the Forest Preserve District and indirectly by the Cook County Board of Commissioners. Both agencies fought the sale, and the new mayor of Chicago, Richard J. Daley, elected in April 1955, was unwilling to support it publicly. Daley's political ally Dan Ryan, chairman of the Cook County Board, also opposed Miller Meadows, as did some of the state legislators from Chicago.

At the same session the university successfully blocked independent action by legislators to appropriate money for specific Chicago-area campus sites as part of the university's budget. The Board of Trustees strongly objected to the legislature making a location decision that the Board felt was its prerogative, and an appropriation from the regular budget would divert funds from the resources available at the Urbana campus. But in 1957, at Governor Stratton's urging and with university support, the legislature passed a large bond issue bill for university and hospital construction throughout the state, which included $35 million for a Chicago-area campus. If approved by public vote in the 1958 election, the bill would separate the financing of the new campus from that of Urbana; and this prospect helped allay many of the financial fears among faculty and administrators at the downstate university.

Up to this time the university had simply kept the mayor of Chicago informed of its ideas and plans. Mayor Martin H. Kennelly was apparently satisfied with such consultation, but his successor was determined to play a much more active role. Daley was deeply interested in the redevelopment of the city and urged the protection of the Loop as a key to maintaining Chicago's position as a major center of business and industry. He also favored the establishment of a public university in the city, and believed that a University of Illinois–Chicago campus would contribute greatly to the welfare of Chicago. Undoubtedly he also believed that it would contribute to his own political success, especially in his campaigns for reelection. But even though Daley combined the posts of mayor and chairman of the Cook County Democratic party, he did not yet have the unrivaled political power he was to wield in later years. He recognized the aims and opinions of other important political allies in the city, such as Dan Ryan, and could not easily oppose them, especially when they headed or served on legally independent bodies.

After the university failed to acquire the Miller Meadows site, President Henry lost

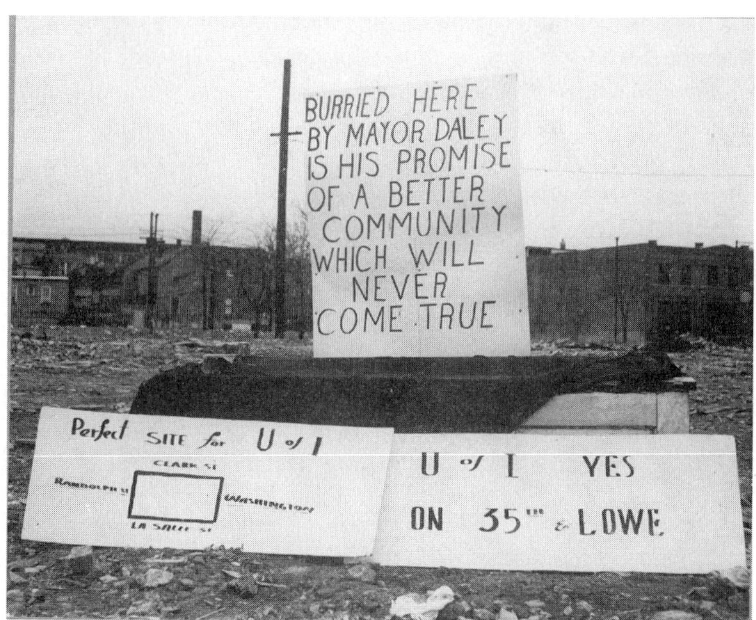

Although many UICC sites had been considered, angry West Side residents could think of at least two more possibilities: City Hall and Mayor Daley's home in Bridgeport.
(Photograph by Larry E. Hemenway. CHS, ICHi-14396)

little time in soliciting Daley's involvement. In a July 1957 memo to Wayne Johnston, Henry wrote that "since we are bound pretty largely by what the Mayor [of Chicago] will help us do, we had better start with him and stay with him in our planning." Acting on that awareness, the university began a continuous series of negotiations with the mayor and his officials, and the city administration became as powerful an actor as the university in the site selection process.

Within the city of Chicago various groups favored different sites. The Central Loop Area Committee, representing many of the largest downtown business firms, publicly urged that the university locate its campus in or near the Loop. Hoping to secure the central area of the city against the threat of deterioration, the committee suggested three possible locations. Two of these had already been ruled out by the university, but one, the railroad terminal land extending from Congress Street to Roosevelt Road east of the Chicago River, seemed promising, although there were problems concerning the cost and availability of property in this area. The land was owned by the railroads, and since it was not subject to eminent domain, the railroads would have to give or sell the land to the university or the city.

The residents and business firms in the Garfield Park region strongly pressed for the location of the campus in that community to preserve the area west of the park against encroachments by blacks. The state legislators from the district took a prominent part in supporting legislation for a Chicago campus. The university officials suggested several sites on the lakeshore and in outlying neighborhoods. The city officials seemed partial to the terminal site but mentioned other possibilities as well.

In early 1958 the university's Board of Trustees again asked the Real Estate Research Corporation to review and recommend possible sites. The criteria were similar to those used in the first review, and the results were not dissimilar. Urban clearance sites were ruled out; the four sites urged by various proponents were considered outstanding, and two were recommended. The outstanding sites were Riverside Golf Club (still in the suburbs next to Miller Meadows, but privately owned and subject to eminent domain), Meigs Field on Northerly Island, the Railroad Terminal area, and Garfield Park. Each site averaged about 130 acres in size, of which one quarter would be available for parking. The university preferred the first two, the city administration the third one, and the local community the fourth. The report favored the first two of these possibilities.

The second report was received on the eve of the November 1958 elections in which the proposed bond issue failed to receive the required public vote, and in which three Republican members of the university Board of Trustees were defeated, ensuring a Democratic majority after March 1959. The defeat of the bond issue put the entire financing of the campus in jeopardy unless another measure were to be passed by the legislature and approved by the public. The change to a Democratic Board of Trustees confirmed the greater likelihood of a city rather than a suburban location, since the new majority would be more likely to agree with the mayor on this matter, provided a city site could be selected.

In order to meet certain deadlines for requesting funds for the new campus, the "lame duck" Board of Trustees had to act on the report of the Real Estate Research Corporation. In February 1959 that board voted in favor of the Riverside Golf Club because of its low cost and quick availability, with Meigs Field as a preferred alternative if that site could be obtained in the near future. This decision aroused strong protest among inhabitants of the club area, Chicago legislators, and Chicago interest groups, and Mayor Daley asked the university to delay its plans in order to reconsider the railroad terminal site. On February 23, 1959, he informed the trustees that "the city would be willing to defray any extraordinary costs which would arise out of the selection of a site in Chicago."

The university had been waiting for just such a commitment, and the Board of Trustees agreed to delay action on the Riverside site. President Henry also directed university officials, in making their budget estimates, to assume the same purchase price to the university of any land for a site in Chicago as for Riverside, i.e., approximately $1 per square foot and a total cost of $4.3 million. But now the burden of finding a site was placed on the city, which became the major actor in the decision-making, although the final acceptance remained with the Board.

In early 1959 Governor Stratton again urged the passage of a new bond issue bill for the six state universities, and in June the legislature approved a measure earmarking $50 million for the University of Illinois's Chicago campus as well as $25 million for the Edwardsville campus of Southern Illinois University to assure downstate support. This time all the elements of a successful political coalition had been assembled. If the 1960 election favored the new bond issue, funds would be available without reducing the budgets of existing institutions. It was also clear that private universities could not expand to meet the expected demand for higher education in Chicago. Mayor Daley strongly supported the campus; the governor favored it; and the opposition of Senator Peters and other downstate legislators had been reversed by the provision of funds for SIU. Champaign-Urbana residents were comforted by the fact that a city campus without dormitories and a football field would be less of a threat to Urbana-area businesses; and the greater demand for university facilities was becoming ever clearer as the baby boom generation of students continued to swell enrollments.

But if a site were *not* chosen before the

November 1960 elections, the bond issue might again be defeated and the coalition might become unglued. The construction of the campus had to begin soon if it were to be ready for the tide of students expected by the early 1960s; otherwise the university might have to turn to other alternatives which would jeopardize the establishment of a Chicago campus.

During the next eighteen months the city, under steadily increasing pressures from the university, considered various sites. The mayor not only had to find a site that would be acceptable and available to the university within the time limits, but also had to come up with the city's share of the purchase price.

Of the three city sites recommended by the Real Estate Research Corporation, the city quickly eliminated Meigs Field, which the university preferred. Ira Bach, the head of the City Plan Commission, reported to the mayor that there would be time-consuming administrative problems in acquiring the land, and that transportation to the island would be difficult. In addition, the city newspapers and leading Loop business firms opposed surrendering the airport, and the mayor was unwilling to go against these powerful constituents.

The mayor's choice was the railroad terminal land. That site had been recommended by the City Plan Commission in its Central Area Plan of 1958, and the mayor hoped that the railroads would either give the land to the city or sell it for a nominal price in exchange for a new consolidated terminal of the type proposed in the 1909 Burnham Plan. Yet the transaction would have to be a voluntary transfer to which most of the railroads would have to agree, since the city could not use its right of eminent domain to acquire the land. While one railroad was supposedly willing to donate 30 acres for the site, others were unwilling to surrender their old terminals, or sell the land at a price the city considered reasonable. In spite of strong support for this site from other businesses, the newspapers, and the public, the differences between the city and the railroads remained so large that the negotiations collapsed before the mayor himself ever got to the bargaining table.

Since Wayne Johnston was participating in those negotiations the university was aware of the difficulties, and in May 1959 the Board of Trustees voted in favor of Garfield Park. While the Garfield Park community, including Sears, Roebuck and Company, favored location of the university campus there, the proposed site belonged to the Park District, and much of its land had been given to the Park District specifically for park use. The Park District Board was reluctant to transfer the land to the university, and there were legal difficulties which would seriously delay the transaction. Indeed, the mayor might well have been reluctant to go against the wishes of the independent Park District Board and its most powerful member, Jacob Arvey, who had preceded Daley as leader of the Democratic party in Chicago.

The Loop and Near West Side business communities continued to lobby for a location closer to downtown, forming the Joint Action Committee of Civic Organizations (including leading Loop and West Side business firms, trade unions, and the NAACP) to fight for the rail terminal location and oppose Garfield Park. This committee promised to fight the transfer of Garfield Park in the courts as long as it could. Various civic figures also spoke out against converting a large city park in a crowded area of the city to other uses. The mayor himself never favored Garfield Park; in his public statements it was always presented as an alternative to another site, and in practice he was always prepared to choose some other site in preference to it. While the mayor and the Park District acceded to the university's request to support legislation that would permit transfer of Garfield Park to the university, and to begin a test case of the legal status of such a transfer, all these negotiations and required steps dragged on. The Park District itself never stated it would sell the required land in the park, and it was obvious that the city administration had no enthusiasm for that location.

In the face of the clear difficulty with the terminal site, and the slow progress on Garfield Park, President Henry feared the loss of momentum and its consequences. In a memo of May 1959 he foresaw "the chance of losing the opportunity for action. At this point, all parties are committed to move. . . . A year from now any one of them may be an obstacle to unified action."

"I have the feeling, too pessimistic perhaps, that if we do not settle now on Garfield Park, we shall not have a site in Chicago for another ten years, if ever." Worse yet: "If we miss now, others may fill the vacuum. . . ."

But still there was no solution in sight. It was now evident that the university could not meet its target date of 1963 for the opening of the new campus, and the administration began to think seriously of other alternatives, such as enlarging the Urbana campus to meet the expected influx of students.

By the end of 1959 the city administration had just about given up on the rail-terminal site — but was secretly considering still another one. Early that year Phil Doyle, the executive director of the Land Clearance Commission, had informally mentioned the 55-acre Harrison-Halsted clearance area to the mayor as a possible site. Nothing happened then, but by December the mayor had directed his advisors to begin exploring the possibilities of this West Side location. The site had some obvious advantages. Much of the land in the 55-acre area was already owned by the city for a residential development project; more land could be acquired in the surrounding area to meet the university's total space needs; and, as a very important additional element, the city could get substantial federal funding for that project under federal urban renewal legislation. These federal funds would make it possible for the mayor to meet his commitment that the city would share the land purchase price of a city site with the university at a minimal cost to the city.

The major disadvantage of the Harrison-Halsted site, however, was that it had been committed to residential use. That commitment arose from a major effort by the residents of the area who, with the support of Hull-House, had joined together after World War II to democratically plan for the rehabilitation of the community. These citizens had set up the Near West Side Planning Board to develop those plans and to implement them. Their efforts had met with many ups and downs, but the 55-acre Harrison-Halsted clearance area, and the rebuilding that had already been started there in 1959, gave evidence of progress. Yet the progress had not been as rapid as the city administrators desired, and the board had not found a developer.

While the residents, especially those involved in this effort, were optimistic about the area's future, various city officials were pessimistic, fearing that the momentum of urban renewal to prevent the deterioration that was taking place south of Roosevelt Road had been lost. The city officials felt that placing the campus in the Harrison-Halsted site would provide both an anchor for redevelopment of the Near West Side area east of the Medical Center as well as a good site for the university. Perhaps most important, however, was the fact that the location was readily available and that it offered excellent opportunities for federal subsidy.

Internal studies of the feasibility of the

Harrison-Halsted site were started within the city administration. Unofficially, the Hull-House Board of Trustees was informed by its chairman, James Downs, president of the Real Estate Research Corporation and one of Mayor Daley's chief urban advisors, of the possibility that Hull-House would be condemned for the new campus. Leaks began to appear in the newspapers, and the university was informed that another site was being considered, although the location was not officially identified.

At the same time the discussions and legal actions concerning the terminal site and Garfield Park continued to grind on. Since the university heard nothing on another specific location, the Board of Trustees continued to favor Garfield Park, which was still deeply involved in litigation. By August, however, the university was informally aware of the new site, and Charles Havens wrote an internal memo expressing this awareness. He pointed out the political fact of life that if the university accepted the site, "the University and the site would receive the backing of the Mayor, the Council, the City Planning Commission, and many other authorities. On the other hand, should the University decide to decline . . . it would probably find all the groups against it. In other words, the Garfield Park site probably will represent an uphill battle all the way as opposed to more or less cooperation should [the university] agree to accept the Harrison-Halsted site."

On September 27, 1959, the mayor formally presented the 55-acre Harrison-Halsted

The Hull-House complex, c. 1940. It still looked much like this before its demolition in 1963. Only two of the structures — the original Charles Hull mansion (with balcony) and the residents' dining hall — were chosen to be saved.

(CHS, ICHi-14392)

clearance area and 90 surrounding acres to the university Board of Trustees as an excellent alternative, and the Board agreed to consider it. Havens, in a preparatory memo to the Board, had reported that the main disadvantage of the site was the surrounding area, which he called "probably the most depressed area in the City." He felt that this would make the development of a suitable campus more difficult, and would "probably result in a completely different type of campus" from that possible in Garfield Park or Riverside Golf Club. Following the presentation the Chicago Plan Commission formally changed the Central Area Plan for the city to move the location of the campus from the terminal site to the Harrison-Halsted area.

Thus, after almost twenty years, an actual campus appeared possible. As time had passed, with one alternative after the other being eliminated, the pressure on the mayor had become intense. The site Daley offered had been on nobody's list of preferences; it had been considered unavailable since it was an urban clearance site destined for other uses; and it was offered in the face of commitments made to the neighborhood residents because nothing else was available within the organizational constraints under which the city government functioned, and within the time limitations and space requirements set by the university.

The next problem was the vote on the bond issue in the November 1960 presidential elections. It was expected that it would be harder to get the needed majority in 1960 than in 1958 because more people would be voting in the presidential election year. The University of Illinois and the other public universities mounted a strong campaign to win votes. But more important, Mayor Daley's offer of a definite site led the Democratic party organization in Chicago to put its weight behind the measure, and directions were given to the city precinct workers to get out the vote on that issue. The bond issue won overwhelmingly in Cook County, making up for any downstate deficit in the needed special majority. 1960 also saw the election of a Democratic governor in Springfield, Otto Kerner, and a Democratic president, John F. Kennedy, both of whom were close associates of Mayor Daley. It was therefore unlikely that there would be any intergovernmental disagreements over the campus site, which required both state and federal approvals for the conversion of the urban renewal area from residential to university use.

Surprisingly enough, there had still been no objections from the community living in the Harrison-Halsted site over the plans to build the university. Before offering the site the mayor had apparently consulted with Alderman John D'Arco, the ward committeeman from the 1st district, where Harrison-Halsted is located. Supposedly the mayor informed the alderman that this change would have to be carried out, and while he would understand the alderman's vote against the conversion, it would be a party issue when it came up in the City Council. The alderman accepted this as a fact of life. While the Hull-House Board of Directors and staff knew of the location possibility, since they had been warned of it by James Downs, it had always been treated as a matter of confidence and as a possibility rather than a certainty. Perhaps most important, the Italian inhabitants of the district, who dominated its politics, were either certain that they had sufficient influence with City Hall to prevent such action (hadn't the mayor attended opening ceremonies at the new Holy Guardian Angel parish building that was part of the residential redevelopment of the Harrison-Halsted clearance project?) — or felt they could never buck City Hall.

After the formal offer of the site and the bond issue victory the university considered the site seriously. There was some modification of the site boundaries, to exclude some blocks south of Roosevelt Road and to move it further west. In addition, there was the physical difficulty of a network of underground utility lines at the site which could not be moved except at a heavy cost. (The architectural firm of Skidmore, Owings and Merrill later developed a plan to build around these facilities.) The city also agreed to take steps to improve the neighborhood environment. The Park Board gave no replies to questions on the availability of Garfield Park. Therefore, in February 1961, President Henry recommended acceptance of the Harrison-Halsted site offer, and the Board of Trustees voted to accept it.

But in February 1961 the inhabitants who would be moved from the site erupted in mass protest. The protesters were the women in the families to be moved, since many of their husbands worked for the city. They found a natural leader in Florence Scala, who was from the neighborhood, who had been closely connected with Hull-House, and who had been very active in the area's planning effort. Mrs. Scala developed excellent connections with some of the city's newspaper and TV reporters, including Georgie Anne Geyer and Jack Mabley, and organized massive public protests, including sit-ins in Mayor Daley's office. While the mayor had anticipated opposition, there was no reason in the relatively quiet year of 1961 to expect that the protest would be led by women. Thus Daley was embarrassed by the character of the protest, its apparent neighborhood strength, and its widespread city support. The protesters also began a series of legal actions to prevent the change in designation of the site use. But unfortunately for them, they were able to elicit little backing from the more influential political, economic, and social leaders of the city.

The business groups and newspapers which had urged the terminal site accepted the Harrison-Halsted decision with varying degrees of warmth, on the grounds that it was about time it was made and the area was not far from the Loop. The leaders of the Democratic liberals in the city and state, U.S. Senator Paul Douglas and former governor Adlai Stevenson among others, supported the mayor. Only a handful of Republicans, including Richard Ogilvie, supported the protesters. The Catholic Church accepted the decision, even though it meant the destruction of a church school which had only recently been rebuilt in the neighborhood.

The Hull-House Board and staff, which had done so much to initiate the entire community planning effort and which had, under Jane Addams, been so involved with the history of the neighborhood, might have led a fight against the decision since its buildings were also condemned. But the Board was split in its position on the matter. Once the university agreed in mid-1961 to preserve and reconstruct the original building and a dining hall as a memorial to Jane Addams (thereby cutting short a national protest backed by Eleanor Roosevelt and Mrs. Sidney Hillman, widow of the leader of the powerful Amalgamated Clothing Workers of America), Hull-House played no further organizational role in the controversy, though individual staff members and residents did support the protesters.

In the end the issue split the neighborhood. Residents who would be moved opposed the campus, but those living west of Racine Avenue were far more ambivalent. Some hoped that construction of the university would stimulate growth and prosperity in the neighborhood; most regretted the forced departure of family members, neighbors, and friends but felt there was nothing they could do to oppose it. Italian leaders outside the immediate area, like Alderman Vito Marzullo, opposed the character of the protests and supported the mayor. In any event the protesters lost in the courts. On February 22, 1965, the highly modern campus of the University of Illinois at Chicago Circle was ready for students.

What light does this history throw on the process of urban decision-making? Although economic factors were always significant, economic thinking in the form of cost-benefit analysis of alternatives could have played only a small part in the selection process. It is true that the population born after 1945 was the basis of the demand for the campus, and that the university sought to minimize costs in choosing a location. But one of the university's major goals was to protect its leading position in the state's public higher education systems against potential future competitors. While it initially selected from many alternative sites, the defeat of the proposal for the Miller Meadows site reflected the political and bureaucratic strength of the Forest Preserve District. Thereafter the university was no longer the decision maker. Once the city of Chicago actively entered the decision-making process the goals changed from those of the university to the planning aims of the city government and community groups: essentially to protect and strengthen the central city area, the Loop.

In the end, the choice of the site reflected the pressures of an ever compressing time framework and the inability of either the city or the university to select any preferable site in situations where the mayor was constrained by private or government organizations he did not control. But the city *could* control the Harrison-Halsted site, and could get federal money to meet the mayor's funding commitment to the university if the city changed the use of that site to a university campus. There were no alternatives to Harrison-Halsted at the end of the process, and there was no room for a careful cost-benefit analysis examining the many possible alternative sites. If the mayor was to meet the desires of the Loop business community to protect the Loop and satisfy his own sense of the importance of that goal given the constraints within which he operated, Harrison-Halsted was the only possible choice. That meant he had to sacrifice the interests of the neighborhood, which he did.

What has been the effect of that decision upon the city? While the Harrison-Halsted site is much further from the Loop than the railroad terminal site which was the mayor's first choice, the construction of the campus has created a predominantly white island between the University of Illinois Medical Center and the University of Illinois Chicago Circle campus. In that island land values have risen, occupations and incomes have changed, and further high-income development is taking place. In addition, that island may serve as an anchor for future Near West Side redevelopment in the area north of the Eisenhower Expressway.

But while the results of the decision have on the whole been desirable, they were not welcomed by the residents who were forced to move nor by community members who saw the planning efforts that had been underway in the area for some time go by the board. For these Chicagoans the costs of building the campus were by no means small.

Staging the Avant-Garde

Stuart J. Hecht

In the 1960s art, like politics, became self-consciously radical. Searching for greater freedom from traditional social and artistic conventions, artists spawned a counterculture that trumpeted spontaneity, experimentation, and freedom from inhibition as hallmarks of creativity. Centered in New York City, avant-garde theater groups brought these new ideals to the stage. The unstructured, anarchic performances by the most radical groups, such as the Living Theater, were meant to erase the distinction between art and life. Dedicated to changing American society, the avant-garde sought the transformation of theater into a powerful political force.

Although greatly influenced by the counterculture, the rise of avant-garde theater in Chicago in the 1960s was also rooted in Jane Addams's philosophy about art and social change. She believed that artistic creation would help form a healthy individual and, in turn, foster a healthy society. At the turn of the century, she began practicing this idea at Hull House, emphasizing it through her theater work. Some sixty years later, it was embraced by a new generation of Hull House workers. Struggling to ease strained black-white relations, offer young people viable substitutes for drugs and gangs, and improve conditions of the poor, social workers resurrected the Hull House theater program to meet the challenges of the sixties. Yet by the end of the decade Hull House called the program a failure and closed its theaters after narrowly avoiding economic collapse. Although Hull House theater had evolved into a vast, successful amateur organization and had won much critical acclaim for its highly original productions and daring experimental work, the settlement house's board eventually decided that this cultural program was in conflict with its larger social mission. The arts, though widely heralded throughout the 1960s as a savior for a crumbling society, proved less effective than some had hoped.

The reemergence of theater at Hull House took place at a time when the settlement was undergoing tremendous change. In 1962, amidst great controversy, Mayor Richard Daley ordered much of Hull House and its surrounding neighborhood torn down to make way for the University of Illinois's Chicago campus. Only two of the settlement's twelve buildings were left standing as monuments to Jane Addams's work. This change caused much turmoil, but it also forced Hull House to reevaluate its purpose and methods, a process that ultimately improved its effectiveness.

The Hull House Association board of trustees selected Paul Jans as its executive director in early 1962 and assigned him the task of overseeing the settlement's reorganization. Hull House faced several new challenges. Whereas Jane Addams emphasized the problems of immigrant communities, Jans's work concentrated more on black-white relations. Addams placed the original settlement directly amidst the poor tenement neighborhoods it served, but by the 1960s poor communities were so scattered throughout Chicago that Hull House needed new strategies to reach the downtrodden. Under Jans, Hull House decentralized, operating out of a number of smaller centers located throughout Chicago so that the agency might address each neighborhood's specific needs more effectively. Jans began by overseeing Hull House's relocation from Halsted Street to an old church on Broadway just north of Belmont Avenue. It was renamed the Jane Addams Center.

Jans had come to Chicago after heading settlements in St. Louis and Philadelphia. As director of Philadelphia's Lighthouse Settlement, Jans made the arts an intrinsic part of that agency's social programming. Jans's experience convinced him that black and white families could "come together through the arts better than by means of any other vehicle." He also thought a decentralized Hull House needed to devise active methods to reach the less fortunate. Jans argued that the arts in general and the theater in particular could achieve this as well as provide a positive substitute for youth involvement in "gangs and drugs."

Jans's views were in keeping with the original goals of Jane Addams. One way Hull House might come to terms with the changes imposed by Daley was to look back to Addams and attempt to apply her goals to the settlement's new conditions and situation. Hired to make this transition, Jans often referred to Addams when introducing programs or policies, such as his decision to revitalize Hull House arts.

The arts had flourished at Hull House under Addams. The settlement's original resident staff included gifted teachers in art, music, dance, and theater. By 1900 the Hull House complex featured extensive studio art space, music and rehearsal rooms, and a state-of-the-art theater. Of all the arts, theater was most closely tied to Addams's social goals. With her support and advocacy, many dramatic groups emerged at the settlement, most led by Hull House's resident staff. Various groups favored traditional ethnic dramas, light Shakespearean comedies, or popular fluff. Theatricals also allowed children to get involved at the settlement. In *Twenty Years at Hull-House*, Jane Addams recalled that

> . . . long before the five-cent theater was even heard of, we had accumulated much testimony as to the power of the drama, and we would have been dull indeed if we had not availed ourselves of the use of the play at Hull-House, not only as an agent of recreation and education, but as a vehicle of self-expression for the teeming young life all about us.

At its peak during the mid-1920s, participants in Hull House dramatics numbered several hundred children and adults.

Of the many Hull House dramatics groups, the resident-directed Hull House Players earned special local and national attention for their early productions of works by Ibsen, Galsworthy, and Shaw. Here were immigrant tenement dwellers performing works then considered avant-garde that depicted their own harsh living conditions. Addams fostered such theater because it was proof of the conditions Hull House sought to combat and, as demonstrated by their onstage accomplishments, the immigrants' potential contribution to America.

By 1940 Addams and most of her original resident staff had passed away, replaced by more professionally trained social workers who emphasized treatment rather than the arts. As a result, by the late 1950s Hull House's theater activities had all but disappeared. However, coincidental to Hull House's reorganization, the 1960s also saw a stronger federal commitment to both urban renewal and to the arts. Paul Jans took advantage of this by rekindling Hull House theater in order to recapture the social benefits Jane Addams achieved through the dramatic arts.

Jans's first step in rebuilding Hull House's theater was to hire his former colleague Robert Sickinger as its artistic director. Sickinger had operated an experimental studio theater at Philadelphia's Lighthouse Settlement, then directed by Jans. His background included the founding of several Philadelphia theaters, working with prominent New York directors Jose Quintero and Alan Schneider, and serving as casting director for the film *David and Lisa*. Accompanied by his wife Selma, a former ballet student of Anthony Tudor, Sickinger came to Chicago to administer Hull House's theater program.

Although Sickinger had extensive background in the arts, he had little social work experience beyond his association with the Lighthouse Settlement. Sickinger did study Jane Addams's theories on the relationship between art and community, as his early statements about the Hull House theater's objectives indicate. But he erroneously credited Addams with the concept "that the intellectual and cultural life of the nation should be centered in the neighborhoods." In fact Addams did promote the introduction of cultural activities in helping to improve the quality of life in poor neighborhoods, but Sickinger twisted her belief to rationalize his own theory that the arts would inherently benefit any community where they were placed. Addams actively tailored a theater that responded to a specific neighborhood's interests and needs; Sickinger did not. At the time this seemed a subtle distinction, but it would later have serious repercussions. Addams's goals were ultimately social; Sickinger's artistic.

Sickinger wanted the theater to draw other artists to Hull House and establish a cultural center for the city. He saw it as a place of experimentation and artistic innovation where individual creativity could be nurtured and developed. He paralleled this to Addams's encouragement of individual expression, overlooking her use of arts to help the underprivileged rather than to support artists. Sickinger also interpreted Addams's "neighborhood" to mean all of Chicago and hoped to build a theater on a grassroots basis, with each community center theater contributing to a centralized and coordinated citywide program.

As early as June 1962, Jans and Sickinger privately outlined a bold plan for the growth of Hull House theater. They proposed the construction of four theaters, located in settlement house centers throughout the city, "working to integrate educational, sociological, and cultural advancement with neighborhood people of varied races, nationalities and financial backgrounds." The two also discussed a possible summer arts camp sponsored by Hull House.

Sickinger began his work by building a theater program at Hull House and organizing community support for it. He enlisted an advisory board made up of local patrons of the arts, cultural figures, and nationally recognized theater practitioners. Though Hull House rarely consulted this board, it gave Sickinger's work both attention and legitimacy. In the spring of 1963 Selma

The Hull House Sheridan Playhouse was one of several neighborhood theaters located throughout the city. The Blood Knot, part of Hull House theater's inaugural season, employed professional actors, a change effected by Robert Sickinger. *(CHS)*

Sickinger recruited a volunteer staff of Chicago theater practitioners who began teaching drama classes. Around the same time, a workshop designed to help fledgling playwrights opened at Hull House. Most significantly, Sickinger started the Hull House Chamber Theater, which presented staged readings of major experimental works in private homes throughout Chicago, often to audiences of paying guests. This served several functions; it helped raise funds for Hull House theater; it allied Sickinger's work with Chicago's innovative and elite arts world, making Hull House theater fashionable; and perhaps most importantly, it built an affluent audience for experimental theater in Chicago. Such activities attracted attention to Hull House dramatics even as the Jane Addams Center was building its 110-seat theater. Reinforcing the Hull House theater tradition, the new theater was designed by William Deknatel, a former Hull House Player. Formally named the Hattie Callner Theater at its leading contributor's request, the space was usually called the Jane Addams Theater.

Sickinger's Chicago directorial debut came in November 1963, with a production of Frank Gilroy's *Who'll Save the Plowboy?* Still trying to tie the revitalized Hull House theater program to that of the past, Sickinger cast Wilfred Cleary and Dorothy Mittleman Sigel, who had both performed earlier at Hull House. But the casting effort went unnoticed, because theater critics concentrated on Sickinger's directorial work, which they praised. Richard Christiansen, then drama critic for the *Chicago Daily News,* judged the production "the most exciting, significant and promising Chicago theatrical event in years," enthusiastically claiming that "this theater is a towering tribute to the traditions and high standards of service identified with Hull House through the years." The *Chicago Sun-Times*'s Glenna Syse was more moderate in her praise, acknowledging Sickinger's blatant salesmanship while conceding that such "practical" methods bore results. In both cases, critical attention was focused more on the man than on his production.

Though the theater was amateur, its work was assessed according to professional standards. The strong critical acclaim awarded to the Gilroy play and subsequent productions is all the more remarkable given their nonprofessional casts and designers. That critics from Chicago's major newspapers attended and reviewed the play's opening indicates that from the start Sickinger wanted the theater and its work to be regarded as much more than social activities addressing the needs of poor neighbors. Sickinger intended Hull House theater to demonstrate his own considerable artistry. Yet the attention and respect he earned enabled Hull House to expand its theater programming, thereby allowing an extraordinary number of artists to develop.

The enthusiasm for Hull House theater was sparked not only by its high-quality productions, but also by Chicago's lack of serious local theater. Most of the city's major houses, including the Blackstone, Shubert, and Studebaker, presented only commercial fare that usually meant substandard tours of Broadway shows. The Drury Lane Theatre presented celebrities in popular hits, and the Goodman featured them in otherwise student-acted classics. Community groups such as the Lincoln Park Players and the Last Stage flourished, but their work was infrequent and uneven in quality. Second City's improvisational comedy was just beginning to gain notice. But outside of the universities, no one was presenting serious, up-to-date drama in a challenging and creative manner. Hull House hoped to fill this theatrical void.

As Sickinger became the centerpiece of Hull House theater, his artistic success formed a base upon which Hull House could construct an elaborate theater program. The highlight of the theater's inaugural season was its January 1964 production of Jack Gelber's *The Connection,* which portrayed a group of heroin addicts anxiously waiting for a friend to bring their "fix." Successfully produced in New York in 1957, this was the play's Chicago premiere. It also marked the Hull House debuts of Bill Terry and Mike Nussbaum, two actors who later performed regularly in Sickinger productions. All cast members were amateurs. Sickinger hired "a reformed junkie" as production consultant, prompting critic Richard Christiansen to comment on the play's faithful re-creation of addiction "in horrible detail." Christiansen also praised the director's approach, which enabled one actor, Richard Lucas, almost to eliminate "the line between acting and being." Despite the play's rough subject matter and harshly realistic presentation, the production proved an enormous commercial success. Audiences flocked to see it. Critic Glenna Syse left the play at intermission because the crowding prevented her from seeing the stage. Yet Syse acknowledged that such audience enthusiasm for theater was both special and rare, and that she "never left a theater more pleased."

Though ticket demand for the show remained high, Hull House closed *The Connection* to make way for its next scheduled pro-

Jack Gelber's *The Connection,* which portrayed a group of heroin addicts waiting for a fix, was the highlight of the 1963-64 season. *(CHS)*

duction. But Hull House rented a remodeled movie house located at 717 West Sheridan Road and in April moved *The Connection* there, naming the space the Hull House Sheridan Playhouse. Next came a revival of *Who'll Save the Plowboy?* and, later, Athol Fugard's *The Blood Knit.* This play differed from the two previous productions in that it used professional actors, a change made by the Sickingers. Bob Sickinger argued that the opening of the Sheridan facility benefited Chicago by providing a much-needed professional theater and was therefore consistent with Hull House's stated social goals. However, the not-for-profit Kate Maremont Foundation, an important benefactor to Hull House theater, disagreed and withdrew its key subsidy. This loss, coupled with insufficient audience support, forced Sickinger to close the theater by year's end.

Nonetheless, Hull House started to expand its theater programming beyond Sickinger's work at the Jane Addams Center. In 1963 Hull House opened a theater in the Henry Booth House basement, part of the Chicago Housing Authority's Harold Ickes Homes. John McFadden, a Philadelphia associate of Sickinger's, managed the theater. Though Hull House Henry Booth Theater was located in a black community, the most notable play of its first season was William Saroyan's *Slaughter of the Innocents.* By the fall of 1963 the Hull House Playwrights' Workshop was also in full swing, helping develop Chicago playwrights. The Hull House Chamber Theater continued to present readings in private homes, and in the summer of 1964 Paul Jans opened an art and music camp in Wisconsin, which he named the Bowen Country Club after an earlier camp operated by Hull House under Jane Addams.

Hull House theater's 1964-65 season built upon the previous season's success. Unlike the first season, Sickinger did not direct every production, but his work continued to draw the greatest attention. Sickinger's Hull House theater was introducing Chicago audiences to new works by the latest avant-garde playwrights. Robert Benedetti of the University of Chicago directed and performed the role of Hamm in Samuel Beckett's *Endgame.* Chicago newspaperman Leo Lerner's reaction to the production is telling:

> . . . "Endgame" seemed to us too long. I had the feeling that the principal actor and director, Bob Benedetti, took himself too seriously and spoke too loudly as if he had a "message" he wanted to deliver. We went home disenchanted with "Endgame" and swore off plays belonging to the theater of the absurd. . . . Something must have happened during the night. In the morning I had a sober second thought about "Endgame." I thought that it is a great play and should not be missed. It emphasizes the absurdity of the human condition, although Mr. Benedetti ought to get his voice down, not act as if he were delivering an oration.

Lerner's testimony shows how Chicago audiences learned to appreciate such works. Bob Sickinger directed all other productions that season except a one-act play directed by his wife Selma. He produced works by Bertolt Brecht, Harold Pinter, and Lanford Wilson. His production of Kenneth Brown's *The Brig,* in which future playwright David Mamet was an understudy, drew praise, and his production of the LeRoi Jones play *Dutchmen* earned much acclaim. Sickinger cast veteran Hull House actor Robert Curry as a young, well-mannered black man who is first seduced and then knifed by a provocative white woman. Curry's performance in this shocking, powerful work was noteworthy. Audience demand was such that Hull House extended the play's run (along with its two accompanying one-act plays) through the summer of 1965.

In 1965 the theater also earned national recognition. Producer David Susskind invited Sickinger to present a Hull House play for his television series, the Esso Repertory Theater. Hull House was the only nonprofessional company asked to participate. Sickinger directed Harold Pinter's *The Dumb Waiter,* a production that *Time* magazine pronounced "so stunningly effective as to be worth the series' syndication price alone."

Hull House theater was booming. Not only did the Playwrights' Workshop begin producing its own plays, but it also began issuing a Hull House theater and arts magazine entitled Intermission. Encouraged by the Henry Booth Theater's success, Hull House opened another theater at the Parkway Community Center in 1964 under the direction of Elaine Goldman. The members of this black company called themselves "The Skyloft Players" after Langston Hughes's company that had performed during the 1940s on the very same site. The growth of Selma Sickinger's Hull House Children's Theater began that same season with its highly successful *Captain Marbles Squad* series. Conceived and written by playwright John Stasey with music by Ricky (Rocco) Jans, Paul Jans's teenaged son, its format resembled that of the *commedia dell' arte.* Adult actors improvised a series of fantastic tales depicting the adventures of Captain Marbles and his friends, including characters such as Big Astronaut and Lovely Ballerina. The company performed a new play for children every other week in the Jane Addams Theater, using whatever set happened to be on the stage. When Stasey was killed in an automobile accident in 1967, Jay Jans, Ricky's brother, took over writing the scripts.

In an interview at the end of 1964, critic Peter Jacobi asked Bob Sickinger to sum up the social aspects of his work at Hull House. Sickinger admitted that "we don't attract many from the neighborhood with our far-out plays," but argued that by charging "sizeable prices" for a kind of theater unavailable elsewhere to Chicago's intellectual elite, Hull House was raising monies that would eventually underwrite other Hull House theater programs serving the less fortunate. Paul Jans shared Sickinger's views. He wrote that the Henry Booth Theater, located in low-income public housing, "although highly successful in terms of participation, brings in almost no income and is completely subsidized by the profitable programs of our [Jane Addams] theater," which grossed an average of $40,000 a year.

The high point of the Jane Addams Theater's 1965-66 season was Sickinger's production of Edward Albee's *Tiny Alice.* Chicago critics all praised the production, most noting that it was particularly successful given the play's difficulty. Glenna Syse stated that *Tiny Alice* proved that Hull House theater had "come of age," and that from then on its productions should be "judged by only the highest standards." Meanwhile, most of the Hull House theater program continued to prosper. In March of 1966 Hull House began a midwestern touring theater, which presented productions of works ranging from Martin Duberman's *In White America* to a John Stasey adaptation of *Mary Poppins.* The Henry Booth Theater continued to falter, despite Jans's assertions to the contrary, but the Parkway Theater began to show signs of life. Hull House appointed twenty-five-year-old Mike Miller its permanent director. Miller directed a series of plays that included LeRoi Jones's *The Slave* and James Baldwin's *The Amen Corner.* Many featured the acting of Felton Perry and were designed to appeal more to black audiences. Second City cofounder Paul Sills also directed a Hull House Playwrights' Workshop production that year. Sills's mother, Viola Spolin, had developed most of her famous improvisational concepts from her work with Neva Boyd at Hull House during the late 1930s.

Bob Sickinger, at the center of this vast theatrical network, attracted much public attention for himself and the theater. Mayor Richard Daley proclaimed the week of October 15, 1965, "Hull House Theater Week in Chicago." Impressed with the Hull House example, Daley proposed the construction of a permanent professional resident theater for the city, but the plan never materialized. In April 1966 Sickinger was one of the Chicago Junior Chamber of Commerce and Industry's ten nominees for "Chicagoan of the Year." Though Sickinger lost, he was the only candidate drawn from the city's arts community. In terms of attention and respect, as well as in terms of growth, Hull House theater had reached its zenith.

The next season brought further triumphs, but it also brought the first sign of the events that would topple the entire Hull House theater program. In September 1966 Hull House presented the Chicago premiere of Harold Pinter's *The Birthday Party*, directed by Sickinger and featuring Hull House regulars Mike Nussbaum, Beatrice Fredman, Robert Kidder, and Wilfred Cleary. Reviewer Dan Zeff called it "a very neat wedding of an intriguing play and a totally successful production." However, some critics began expressing dissatisfaction with Hull House's play selection, claiming that Sickinger's productions too often outstripped the quality of the plays themselves. That season the complaint was leveled against both Venable Herndon's *When the Monkey Comes* and John Whiting's *The Devils*. Some felt that Sickinger should direct a classic; others commended Hull House for attempting productions of new and largely untried works. The effect of these comments on Sickinger is unclear, but that season the Jane Addams Theater offered four rather than the customary five productions, the last a revival. Sickinger also announced plans to film the Herndon work, showing interests beyond the management of the Hull House theater program.

The rest of the program began to experience similar ups and downs. The Hull House Touring Theater featured eight companies that presented more than 3,000 performances in schools, churches, and civic clubs throughout the Midwest. After making Mike Miller his assistant, Sickinger named Dick Gaffield the Parkway Theater's new director, and the Parkway continued to offer its fare of black theater throughout the year. Attempting to revitalize the Henry Booth Theater, Hull House renamed it the "Hull House Underground Theater" and placed black director and playwright Gerald Wallace in charge. Wallace largely produced his own plays, including *Libertyville* and *If I Had a Hammer*. The Hull House theater program won a matching grant of $30,000 from the National Council on the Arts, the first Chicago theater so honored. In accepting the funds Sickinger again spoke in social rather than in artistic terms. He claimed that the grant demonstrated the government's "interest in the cultural climate of the community" and pointed to the Henry Booth Theater as a model that others planning theaters in "underprivileged neighborhoods" might follow.

However, by early 1967 Hull House Touring Theater folded. Furthermore, the city's growing racial tension began to affect Hull House theater. Mike Miller complained, "We're getting bottles in the head on our way in and out [of the Henry Booth Theater]." Similarly, the provocative militancy of the Parkway Theater's play selection caused representatives of the black community to protest to Hull House's board of trustees in March. Black community leaders were concerned because the plays performed there usually portrayed blacks as either the passive victims of white America or as those who could gain strength and power through a solidarity based upon violence, thereby provoking civil unrest in their neighborhoods. The board cautiously noted in its minutes that the "times were very controversial," and Jans apparently chose to placate the concerned neighbors rather than temper the Parkway's work.

Still, Hull House theater seemed healthy enough financially. The program boasted some 4,500 subscribers, representing 80 percent of capacity. Its goal was 6,000 members by the following year. Two-thirds of the theater's $150,000 operating costs came from box office receipts, while the rest came from grants and donations. The Hull House Association also quietly covered a percentage of the theater's expense.

If Hull House had overextended itself, this was not apparent in the fall of 1967. Amidst much hoopla Hull House opened the Uptown Center at 4520 N. Beacon Street. It housed the 144-seat Leo A. Lerner Theater, and Hull House sold more than 500 subscription tickets before the theater even opened. Hull House's intention to stage only musicals there probably explains this advance interest. In a *Chicago Daily News* interview with Norman Mark, Sickinger rationalized:

> "Why musicals here? Musicals combine all the talents in Hull House. There's lots of undeveloped musical talent in this city, you know. All Hull Houses have music and dance instruction. This will give the students motivation. Let them aim at performing. Our theaters are becoming more specialized. Jane Addams has current drama, Parkway focuses on Negro life. Why not musicals in Uptown?"

Sickinger never paused to consider whether a social work agency such as Hull House ought to be underwriting such a venture.

Sickinger alternated productions evenly between the Jane Addams Theater and the new Uptown theater for the 1967-68 season. *Fortune and Men's Eyes* opened at the Jane Addams Theater in November, and the Uptown debuted in December with the musical *Take Me Along,* featuring Hull House regular Pat Terry and newcomer Jim Jacobs, who later coauthored the musical *Grease.* Sickinger directed every show that season and seemed to be gaining new life. He answered earlier criticisms by directing a highly successful production of a classic, Sophocles' *Electra,* which he elegantly set in a nineteenth-century funeral home. The critics proved lyric in their praise. Richard Christiansen wrote of the "stunning tableaux in which the drape of a costume and the grouping of figures is used to ravishing effect." Glenna Syse favored the production's "earnest intimacy." Unlike the usually grand production of Greek plays, she found Sickinger's "perhaps even more compelling, its passion more personal, its anguish more touching."

As Sickinger's artistry improved, the Hull House program deteriorated. The Underground Theater closed its doors in April 1968; the Parkway closed in July. Hull House blamed the closings on the changing climate in the black neighborhoods caused by Martin Luther King's assassination. Sickinger claimed that the Parkway closed because white audiences would no longer come to the black neighborhood, and he chastised them for not mailing in donations. He said the Parkway had been losing about $25,000 a year as a result. Sickinger made no mention of why the black community failed to support the Parkway. However, the *Daily Defender,* a black Chicago newspaper, lamented the closing of both Hull House theaters, blaming lack of local audience support. The newspaper voiced bitter regret at the loss of "an opportunity to learn the craft of the stage, without regard to the economic basis of the actor or actress, playwright or set designer. Not enough interest."

Hull House theater's most difficult problems lay just ahead. A 1968-69 season began at both the Jane Addams and Uptown theaters, but the program showed signs of collapse. In November 1968 Hull House sent its theatergoers a written plea signed by Bob Sickinger and Hull House Association board president Muriel Smith, stating that its theater program needed immediate and substantial financial assistance. The letter blamed a series of unforeseen events for causing the crisis: a big snowstorm in late 1967 which cost the theater $5,000, followed by "spring riots and two assassinations" (Martin Luther King and Robert Kennedy) which also discouraged attendance. The plea hoped to draw $50,000 over the next two years. Not only did this letter reveal the theater's instability; it also signaled trouble within the Hull House Association.

Hull House itself was in danger of financial ruin, and blame for the social agency's economic troubles fell squarely upon Jans and Sickinger. The extraordinary expansion of the Hull House theater program during the 1960s could only have happened with subsidies from Hull House itself. Box office profits failed to support annual operating expenses, let alone accommodate such rapid growth. During the early 1960s Hull House had received much federal funding as part of President Lyndon Johnson's War on Poverty campaign, which had enabled the social work agency to expand greatly. But by 1968 Hull House was trying to account for its loss of funding. Rumors spread that monies intended specifically for social work were being rechanneled to cover the theater's losses, reflecting a growing resentment within Hull House. Because so much money and media attention went to cultural programming, especially the theater, more conventional professional social work projects and programs were neglected. When some suggested that Hull House had no business operating a theater, Jans immediately jumped to its defense:

> The Hull House theaters do creative artistic and highly qualitative work. The plays deliver a message pertinent to our day, reacting to today's society in the framework of Hull House's goals and history. It was Jane Addams who said that we must bring together the extremes of society and one of the best vehicles for this is the theater.

But was Hull House theater really serving neighborhood needs? Jans's argument again echoed Addams: the theater often did portray issues "pertinent to our day," specifically depicting the downtrodden and their alienation from society. Jans's opponents charged that Hull House theater failed to address the needs of the immediate neighborhoods, and that Sickinger did not produce works that might attract neighborhood audiences. Jans argued that in essence the money earned from affluent audiences attending the Jane Addams and Uptown theaters helped pay for arts programs for the poor. This enabled Hull House to operate both the Henry Booth and Parkway theaters at a loss. Furthermore, a substantial number of those working for Hull House theater did in fact come from poor Chicago neighborhoods.

Paul Jans believed the arts essential to social improvement, but most of those working at Hull House did not. Jans also still thought that Hull House needed to continue to expand in order to serve Chicago properly. This disregard for the agency's economic plight lost Jans the support of the board of trustees, and he resigned in April 1969. The Hull House Association had to cut $200,000 from its 1969 budget or face bankruptcy. The board decided that, with Hull House's survival at stake, arts programs were expendable. Hull House cut

The success that Hull House theater achieved in the mid-1960s made the Parkway Community Center and *Intermission* magazine *(opposite page)* possible. *(CHS)*

THE SKYLOFT PLAYERS OF THE HULL HOUSE
PARKWAY THEATER
500 EAST 67th STREET
"BLUES FOR MISTER CHARLIE" by JAMES BALDWIN
Directed by Dick Gaffield
FOR INFORMATION - 324- 3880
Curtain - Fri. & Sat. 8:30 p. m. - Sun. 7:30

back some of its social work services and eliminated most of its arts programming. However, the board planned to continue the theater program, probably because of its popularity and success. In order to keep a close watch on future spending, the association placed control of the theater program in the hands of a theater board.

In early May 1969 the theater board announced that Bob Sickinger was "working out his withdrawal" from Hull House and that a search had begun for his successor. At month's end Hull House announced Sickinger's formal resignation and named Robert Benedetti to replace him. Controversy erupted. Angry that his wife Selma was not

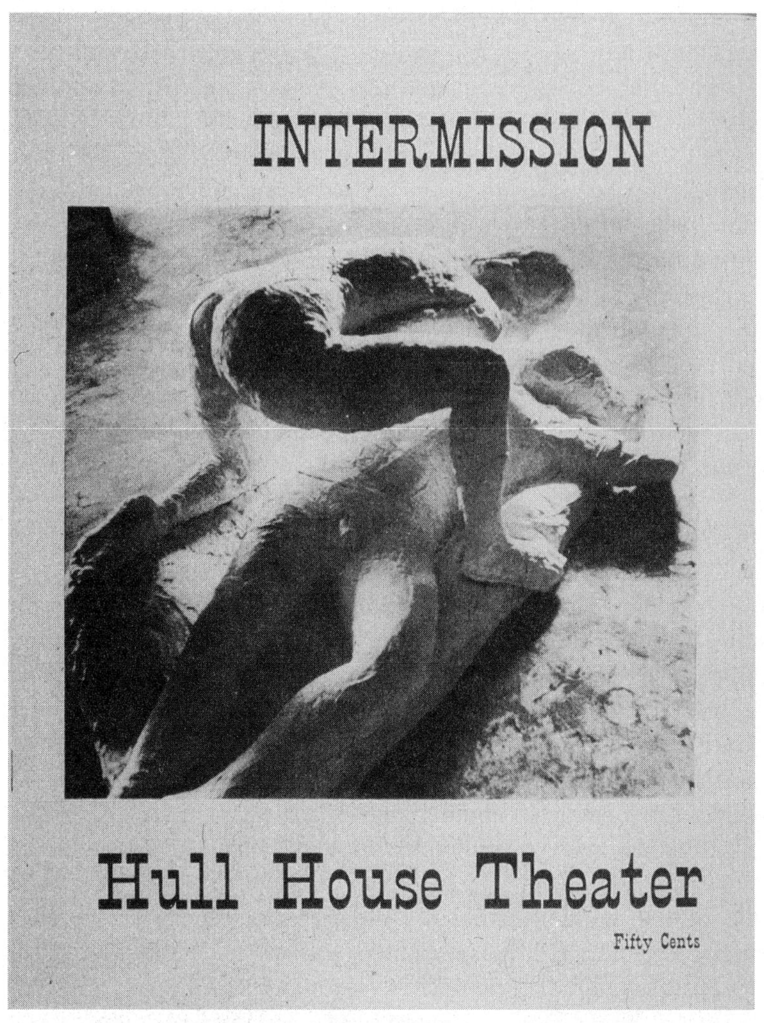

named his successor, Sickinger held a press conference, charging that the theater board had "illegally maneuvered" him out of a job and threatening legal action. Hull House countered that Sickinger had abandoned the program to make movies, even though he was "paid the highest salary in Hull House." Neither party mentioned the social value of theater. The Hull House Association seemed concerned only with cost, and Sickinger only with job security. In June Hull House awarded Sickinger an "undisclosed settlement."

Paul Jans favored an interdependent theater network because it enabled Hull House to maintain a far-reaching program. However, the system proved too costly for Hull House. Instead of building new theaters only after existing ones proved financially sound, as originally promised by Sickinger and Jans, the Hull House theater program expanded regardless of cost. Furthermore, because of centralization, the individual theaters existed only as part of Sickinger's total artistically coordinated theater program. Neighborhoods served by Hull House community centers complained that the theater program neglected community needs. Their complaints reached receptive ears. Community center social workers had increasingly resented the Hull House Association's devotion of funds and facilities to what they considered only an activity, one that failed to address more basic social needs.

When the Hull House Association board of trustees met in late May 1969, it considered a resolution proposed by the Uptown's Center's director. This resolution stated that the center's "primary function" was as a "neighborhood center," and therefore asked approval to withdraw from Hull House's "central theater program." They wanted all artistic decisions to be made by the Uptown Center's directors and staff. By the end of the meeting, the board granted the same autonomous artistic control to each of its centers. When Robert Benedetti arrived in Chicago to assume leadership of the Hull House theater program, he found that he could only work at the discretion of and under conditions imposed by each center's director. Without the permanent theater facility promised in his contract, Benedetti resigned after reaching a settlement with Hull House.

By 1970 little remained of the multifaceted Hull House theater program that had peaked three years earlier. Of all its programs only the Old Town-based Playwrights' Workshop continued to operate, though as a separate organization. Hull House had successfully withdrawn from its theatrical commitments. However, individual centers soon discovered that without formal theater programming their facilities went unused. Within a few years Hull House began renting out its spaces to professional theater companies. Among the Jane Addams Theater's tenants was the Steppenwolf Theater Company (1979-82), and one of the Uptown Center's tenants was the Organic Theater Company (1973-77). None of the professional companies provided any significant social services to the neighboring communities or even professed such a commitment. However, in recent years Hull House has encouraged and supported some community theater activities through its centers. The Parkway Center's theater in particular has regularly housed a number of black theater groups, and the Uptown Center has sponsored some children's theater programming. But these activities were not considered integral to the agency's primary concern of providing professional social work services.

Although theater fell from favor as a valid tool for social workers after Bob Sickinger resigned, the artistic program he created was rich. In addition to providing Chicago artists with several heavily used theater spaces, Hull House built the foundation for the Chicago theater renaissance of the 1970s that continues to this day. Hull House theater provided a testing ground for young actors, designers, and directors who later helped contribute much to the city's theatrical growth. Mike Nussbaum, in addition to becoming one of Chicago's most successful professional actors, helped found the North Light Theater in Evanston in 1975. David Mamet, who became Chicago's foremost playwright, also helped found the now-defunct St. Nicholas Theater.

Beyond individual achievement, Hull House theater also introduced Chicago audiences to new works by the era's most important playwrights, including Samuel Beckett, Harold Pinter, and Edward Albee. In addition, Sickinger directed in a highly emotional and grittily realistic manner, blending strong theatricalism with an almost cinematic intensity. This style later became Chicago's theatrical trademark, practiced with great effect by directors like Robert Falls and companies such as Steppenwolf.

Finally, and perhaps most importantly, Hull House theater developed an audience in Chicago for experimental theater. Before Sickinger arrived at Hull House, Chicago offered little serious theater of any quality. By the time Sickinger left Chicago in 1969, Paul Sills and two others were ready to establish the Body Politic Theater, followed shortly by the founding of the Organic Theater Company. Hull House theater spearheaded this transition. It proved that Chicago would and could support challenging provocative plays if creative and well done. This audience enabled Chicago theater to blossom in the years after Sickinger left and Hull House closed its theaters' doors.

Index

Boldface page numbers refer to illustrations.